B40 =00

MELLINKOFF'S DICTIONARY OF AMERICAN LEGAL USAGE

By

David Mellinkoff
Professor of Law Emeritus
University of California, Los Angeles

WEST PUBLISHING CO.
ST. PAUL, MINN., 1992

Library of Congress Cataloging-in-Publication Data

Mellinkoff, David.
    Mellinkoff's Dictionary of American legal usage / by David Mellinkoff.
        p.   cm.
    Includes index.
    ISBN 0–314–00068–2
    1. Law—United States—Terms and phrases. 2. Law—United States—
Language. 3. English language—Usage. I. Title.
    KF156.M45   1992
    349.73'014—dc20
    [347.30014]   92–281
                                                                       CIP

ISBN 0–314–00068–2

        Mellinkoff, Dictionary
        1st Reprint—1993

Acknowledgements

This traditional word of appreciation is a puny thanksgiving to all of those who over the years have helped me to write this dictionary. I am indebted to so many, too many to list by name, for contribution of comment, suggestion, education, intelligibility, legibility, encouragement. The list here is unranked, alphabetical—symptomatic only of dictionary style. Those listed by name are but a token of the many who have helped me in this work, for which I bear the awesome responsibility.

Benjamin Aaron

Norman Abrams

Adrienne Adan

Reginald H. Alleyne, Jr.

Michael R. Asimow

John A. Bauman

Daniel Brenner

Jesse Dukeminier

Susan F. French

the late Paul A. Freund

Carole Goldberg-Ambrose

Jan Goldsmith

Nicholas Goodhue

Kenneth W. Graham, Jr.

George Hathaway

Harold W. Horowitz

Robert L. Jordan

Kenneth L. Karst

William A. Klein

Richard A. Lanham

Philip Levine

Christine A. Littleton

Frank Lopez

Daniel H. Lowenstein

Linda Maisner

William M. McGovern

Ruth Mellinkoff

Stephen R. Munzer

the late Melville B. Nimmer

Roger F. Noreen

Marc J. Poster

Susan Westerberg Prager

Arthur I. Rosett

Myra Saunders

Maria Schroeter

Gary T. Schwartz

Murray L. Schwartz

Frederick Smith

Phillip R. Trimble

Jonathan D. Varat

William D. Warren

John S. Wiley

John Wilson

Richard C. Wydick

Kenneth H. York

Eric M. Zolt

*

Contents

*

v

Preface

This is a dictionary of the language of the law as used in America today. Most of this dictionary is written in ordinary English.

The dictionary follows a path cut through the underbrush of dead and deadly words by *The Language of the Law* (1963), *Legal Writing: Sense and Nonsense* (1982), and "The Myth of Precision and the Law Dictionary" (31 *UCLA Law Review* 483, 1983). It follows the dictate of simplicity "that the language used by lawyers [should] agree with the common speech, unless there are reasons for a difference" (Lang. of the Law, vii). Words with an old affinity for the law but no longer used or useful have been omitted. Working survivors of ancient languages and usages are translated and explained.

Most of the words that lawyers use in writing and talking about the law are the ordinary words that fill the dictionaries of the English language. They have a place in this dictionary when the law gives them a specialized sense; or to emphasize that there is none. Too often an apparent change of sense results not from the law but from bad grammar or redundancy; or from an unsorted host of possible meanings jumbled together and left to the vagaries of interpretation. At the other extreme, individual cases, each walled in by its own distinctive facts and law, may give an immaculately narrowed sense, but neither generalized definition nor standards for the gradation of sense that is the essence of clear usage.

A small number of citations to cases of special relevance to word usage are included in this dictionary. The citation count does not measure the indebtedness of this dictionary to old and current sources of American legal usage.

The definitions and examples of usage in this dictionary have roots in the law reports of thousands of litigated cases; in law writings formal and informal, profound and trivial; in the talk of lawyers and judges in court and out—the formal and the informal—colloquial and slangy, talk that is precise and talk that is mush; in a long line of dictionaries past and present—law dictionaries, and dictionaries of English and its usage. Drawing from all those sources, the definitions and examples are shaped by more than a half-century of personal immersion in the oral and written language of the law, as law student, practicing lawyer, professor, and writer. And something has been added.

This dictionary is designed to sort out the words used in the law, and to identify the different senses in which each is used, and can be used. With cross-reference, it tells how words are related to each other, and separated from each other, so that discrimination and choice of usage are possible. Words are grouped together as identical, similar, disparate, departing from or paralleling the usages of ordinary English. Where usage is not uniform, the dictionary comments on what is better, best, and worst.

In comparing and contrasting ordinary and legal usage, the dictionary carries forward the demonstration that only in comforting myth is legal usage peculiar so that it may be precise. Some technical terms, here preserved and explained, are precise. More often, the swarming imprecisions of the law give only an illusion of precision, usually curable by careful English. The dictionary offers guides to the cure.

The dictionary concentrates on general legal usage for a profession practicing in the American common law tradition. That includes Louisiana, but not its nuances blended from the civil law. The dictionary does not detail the multitude of other jurisdictional variations, but calls attention to the fact of variation. Although the distinction is often difficult to make, this is a word dictionary, not a short legal encyclopedia. Technicalities in general legal usage are included; but not the intricacies of learning in specialized fields of the law.

There is no standard legal pronunciation. Pronunciation is included here when it is unusual, exotic, controversial, or needed to prevent confusion. Pronunciation is rendered in simplified phonetics.

* * *

American law dictionaries go back to 1839. This one is new and different.

DAVID MELLINKOFF

Los Angeles
1992

How to Use This Dictionary

Index of Entries   If a word or expression is in the dictionary, it is listed alphabetically in the green sheets.

Entries   An entry is not capitalized unless it is a word or expression customarily capitalized. Some entries are single words or expressions. Some list several words or expressions together. Most entries have cross-references to an entry that discusses a word or expression together with others—that mean the same thing, that explain what this one means, that are similar to this one, or that must be distinguished from this one.

Cross-references   A specific cross-reference is identified by "□see." An auxiliary cross-reference is identified by "□see also."

Etymology   When it helps in understanding legal usage, foreign words are followed by a parenthetical notation of origin and a free translation. Etymologies of most words in this dictionary can be found in dictionaries of the English language and are not included here.

Pronunciation   In simplified phonetics; accented syllables are in solid capitals. Hyphens separate syllables. For example:

> **amicus curiae** (L., uh-MEEK-us CURE-ee-eye: friend of the court).

Examples of Usage   Examples of usage are interspersed in the text of the dictionary. Many of them are enclosed in angle brackets. For example:

> **actionable** (adj.): forming the basis of a right to sue. < Invasion of privacy is actionable. >

Special Use of the Colon (:)   In addition to their ordinary use, colons are used in the dictionary to indicate that what follows the colon is a translation or a definition. For example:

> **alibi** (L., AL-uh-buy, as in *lullaby*: elsewhere): the excuse of being at some other place.

Abbreviations   If context makes the sense of abbreviations clear, abbreviations are not listed here. For abbreviations of some reports of cases, see the entry *law reports*.

adj.	adjective
Amend.	amendment to the U.S. Constitution
amend.	amended
Ann.	annotated (as part of a title)
Art.	article of the U.S. Constitution

HOW TO USE THIS DICTIONARY

art.	article (of other writings)
ch.	chapter
cl.	clause
Const.	the U.S. Constitution
F.	French
IRC	Internal Revenue Code
L.	Latin
MBCA	Model Business Corporation Act
n.	noun (in text)
n.	footnote (in a citation)
O.E.	Old English
O.F.	Old French
reh. den.	rehearing denied
s.	section
§	section
Stat.	the Statutes at Large
U.C.C.	Uniform Commercial Code
USCA	United States Code Annotated
v.	verb (in text)
v.	versus (in citation of cases)

INDEX OF ENTRIES

[1]

Index of Entries

[2]

Index of Entries

[4]

Index of Entries

Index of Entries

Index of Entries

charged with notice □ see have notice, under notice

charge to the jury □ see jury instructions

charging lien □ see lien

charitable • nonprofit

charitable deduction □ see charitable; □ see tax

charitable trust □ see trust

charter □ see license; □ see articles of incorporation, under articles; □ see charter party

charter party

chattel

chattel mortgage □ see chattel

chattel paper □ see chattel

chattel real □ see chattel

check □ see commercial paper

check kiting □ see kiting

checks and balances □ see separation of powers

Chief □ see judge

chief judge □ see judge

chief justice □ see judge

Chief Justice of the United States □ see judge

child • infant • minor

child custody □ see custody

child labor law □ see child

children's court □ see juvenile

child support □ see alimony

child trespasser □ see child

chilling a sale □ see chilling effect

chilling effect

chilling the bidding □ see chilling effect

Chinese wall □ see vicarious disqualification

choate • inchoate

choate lien □ see choate; □ see also, lien

choateness □ see choate

choice of law □ see conflict of laws

chose in action • thing in action

chose in possession □ see chose in action

C.I.F.

circuit courts □ see United States Courts of Appeals

circuit judge □ see judge

circuit justice □ see judge

citation • cite

cite □ see citation

citizen by naturalization □ see naturalization

Citizenship Clause

city attorney □ see lawyer

civil • civil law

civil arrest □ see bail

civil contempt □ see contempt

civil death □ see civil

civil liberties □ see civil

civil rights □ see civil

civil suit □ see civil

Index of Entries

[12]

Index of Entries

Index of Entries

Index of Entries

[18]

Index of Entries

declaratory statute □ see declaratory, under declaration

declare □ see declaration

declare a default □ see default

decree □ see judgment

dedication

deed

deed of gift □ see deed

deed of trust □ see deed

deed poll □ see deed

deem and consider

deep pocket

de facto • de jure

de facto corporation □ see de facto

de facto government □ see de facto

de facto merger □ see de facto

de facto officer □ see de facto

de facto segregation □ see de facto

de facto taking □ see eminent domain

defamation

defamation of title □ see disparagement

defamation per quod □ see actionable per se, under action

defamation per se □ see actionable per se, under action

defamatory □ see defamation

defamatory per quod □ see actionable per se, under action

defamatory per se □ see actionable per se, under action

defame □ see defamation

default

default judgment □ see default

defeasance □ see defeasible

defeasible

defeasible fee □ see fee simple

defendant

defense □ see excuse, under justification; □ see immunity; □ see infancy defense, under child; □ see insanity; □ see justification; □ see privilege, under immunity

deficiency judgment □ see judgment

definite failure of issue □ see issue

defraud □ see fraud

degrees of negligence □ see negligence

degrees of proof □ see burden of persuasion, under proof

de jure □ see de facto

de jure corporation □ see de facto

de jure government □ see de facto

de jure merger □ see de facto

de jure segregation □ see de facto

delay

delegated powers

delegation of power

deliberate speed □ see with all deliberate speed

delinquency □ see contributing to the delinquency of a minor, under child

Index of Entries

Doctor of Jurisprudence □ see J.D.; □ see also, jurisprudence

Doctor of Law □ see J.D.

doctor-patient privilege □ see physician-patient privilege

doctrinaire argument □ see clichés

doctrine □ see rule

doctrine of renvoi □ see renvoi

doctrine of worthier title □ see worthier title

document

documentary □ see document

document of title

Doe □ see John Doe

do equity □ see equity

does violence to □ see clichés

doing business □ see minimum contacts

doing business as □ see alias

domicile

dominant estate □ see easement

dominant tenement □ see easement

donatio causa mortis □ see gift causa mortis, under gift

donatio mortis causa □ see gift causa mortis, under gift

donee □ see gift

donor • donee □ see gift

double jeopardy

doubt □ see beyond a reasonable doubt

dower • curtesy

draft □ see commercial paper

drawee □ see commercial paper

drawer □ see commercial paper

drunk □ see legally drunk

dry trust □ see trust

due

due and payable □ see due

due care □ see due

due notice □ see due

due process □ see due

Due Process Clauses

due process of law □ see due

duly □ see due

dummy director □ see director

duplicitous • duplicity

duplicity □ see duplicitous

durable power of attorney

duress • coercion • undue influence

Durham rule

Durham test □ see Durham rule

duty □ see obligation

duty to mitigate damages □ see damage

dying declaration □ see declaration

dynamite charge □ see jury instructions

E

each and all

each and every □ see each and all

Index of Entries

Index of Entries

Index of Entries

[29]

Index of Entries

Index of Entries

Index of Entries

Index of Entries

Index of Entries

hybrid representation □ see right to counsel

I

ICC

idem sonans

if the court please □ see court

I know it when I see it

illegal • unlawful

illegal consideration □ see illegal; □ see also, contract

illegal contract □ see illegal; □ see also, contract

illegitimate □ see legitimate; □ see also, illegal

illegitimate child □ see filiation proceeding

illicit □ see illegal

illusory contract

illusory promise □ see illusory contract

immaterial (evidence)

immunity • privilege

immunity from prosecution □ see grant of immunity from prosecution, under immunity

immunize □ see immunity

impanel □ see jury panel

impeach

impeach a verdict □ see impeach

impeach a witness □ see impeach

impeachment (of officials) □ see impeach

impeachment of waste □ see waste

implead □ see third party practice, under party

impleader □ see third party practice, under party

implied □ see imply

implied actual notice □ see notice

implied authority □ see agency

implied bias □ see bias

implied contract □ see quasi contract

implied covenant □ see covenant

implied easement □ see easement

implied equitable servitude □ see easement

implied-in-fact □ see quasi contract

implied-in-law □ see quasi contract

implied knowledge □ see knowledge

implied malice □ see malice

implied notice □ see notice

implied powers □ see enumerated powers

implied promise □ see quasi contract

implied warranty □ see warranty

imply • infer

Import–Export Clause

impossibility

impossibility of performance □ see impossibility

impossible □ see impossibility

Index of Entries

Index of Entries

Index of Entries

[42]

Index of Entries

Index of Entries

[46]

Index of Entries

Index of Entries

Index of Entries

Index of Entries

Index of Entries

nonprofit corporation □ see charitable

nonrecourse

nonremovable □ see removal (of a
case)

nonresident

nonresponsive

nonsane □ see insanity

nonstock corporation

nonsuit □ see judgment

nonsupport

nonuser

nonvoting shares □ see stock

nonvoting stock □ see stock

no par shares □ see stock

no par stock □ see stock

no priors

no recourse □ see nonrecourse

noscitur a sociis

notarize □ see notary public

notary □ see notary public

notary public

note □ see commercial paper

not-for-profit corporation □ see
charitable

not found □ see indictment

not guilty □ see guilty

notice

notice of appeal □ see notice

notice of appearance □ see appear

notice of lis pendens □ see lis

notice of motion □ see notice; □ see
also, motion

notice to creditors □ see notice

notice to pay rent or quit □ see
notice

notice to quit □ see notice

not inconsistent with this opinion

notorious □ see open and notorious,
under open

no true bill □ see indictment

not satisfied

not to be performed within one
year □ see statute of frauds

not unfair to say □ see clichés

notwithstanding

notwithstanding the verdict □ see
judgment n.o.v., under judgment

n.o.v. □ see judgment n.o.v., under
judgment

novation

novel □ see new; □ see copyright

novelty

NOW account □ see bank

nuclear hazard □ see nuclear incident

nuclear incident

nudum pactum

nuisance

nuisance at law □ see nuisance

nuisance in fact □ see nuisance

Index of Entries

Index of Entries

Index of Entries

Index of Entries

Index of Entries

Index of Entries

Index of Entries

punishment □ see penal; □ see sentence; □ see also, bill of attainder; □ see also, capital punishment, under execute; □ see also, crime; □ see also, cruel and unusual punishment; □ see also, punitive damages, under damage

punitive damages □ see, under damage

pur autre vie □ see estate

purchase • purchaser □ see buy; □ see bona fide purchaser; □ see purchaser for value; □ see vendor and purchaser, under sell; □ see words of purchase

purchase money mortgage □ see buy

purchase price □ see buy

purchaser □ see buy; □ see bona fide purchaser; □ see purchaser for value; □ see vendor and purchaser, under sell; □ see words of purchase

purchaser for value

pure comparative negligence □ see contributory negligence

purge of contempt □ see contempt

purpose □ see legislative purpose, under intent

purpresture

put □ see option

putative

putative marriage □ see cohabit

putative spouse □ see cohabit

put in an appearance □ see enter; □ see appear

put off □ see delay

put on notice □ see have notice, under notice

put up collateral □ see collateral

Q

quaere

qualified fee □ see fee simple

qualified immunity □ see immunity; □ see absolutes

qualified privilege □ see privilege, under immunity; □ see absolutes

quantum meruit

quantum valebant

quantum valebat □ see quantum valebant

quash

quasi

quasi-community property □ see community property

quasi contract

quasi-easement □ see easement

quasi in rem □ see in rem

quasi-judicial immunity □ see judicial immunity, under immunity

question of fact □ see mixed question of law and fact

question of law □ see mixed question of law and fact

quia timet

quick-take □ see condemnation, under eminent domain

quid pro quo □ see contract

quiet enjoyment □ see covenant; □ see also, let or hindrance

quiet title □ see in rem; □ see also, cloud on title; □ see also, quia timet

qui facit per alium facit per se □ see agency; □ see also, maxims

quit □ see notice to pay rent or quit, under notice; □ see notice to quit, under notice; □ see quitclaim

qui tam

quitclaim

quitclaim deed □ see quitclaim

quorum

quotient verdict

quo warranto

R

®

racket □ see racketeering

racketeer □ see racketeering

racketeering

raider □ see takeover

rainmaker

raise

R.A.P.

rape

rap sheet

ratification

ratify □ see ratification

rational basis □ see standards of review

re □ see in re

ready, willing, and able □ see tender; □ see procuring cause

real covenant □ see covenant running with the land, under covenant

real estate □ see land; □ see also, real property, under property

real evidence ● demonstrative evidence

real party in interest □ see party

real property □ see property; □ see also, land

realty □ see land

reargument

reasonable

reasonable and probable cause

reasonable care □ see due care, under due; □ see also, negligence

reasonable cause □ see probable cause

reasonable certainty

reasonable doubt □ see beyond a reasonable doubt

reasonable fee □ see fee (attorney's fee)

reasonable force

reasonable grounds

reasonable man

reasonable person □ see reasonable man

reasonable time □ see time

Index of Entries

Index of Entries

residuary bequest □ see residue

residuary clause □ see residue

residuary devise □ see residue

residuary estate □ see residue

residuary legacy □ see residue

residue

res ipsa loquitur

res judicata

respondeat superior □ see agency; □ see also, maxims

respondent

rest □ see formalisms; □ see residue

Restatement

restitution

restrain □ see enjoin

restraining order □ see enjoin

restraint of marriage

restraint of trade □ see rule of reason; □ see antitrust law; □ see also, fair trade agreement; □ see also, tying arrangement

restraint on alienation

rest, residue, and remainder □ see residue

restriction

restrictive covenant □ see covenant

resulting trust □ see trust

retained counsel □ see lawyer

retainer □ see fee (attorney's fee)

retaining lien □ see lien

retaliatory discharge □ see wrongful discharge

retaliatory eviction □ see evict

retraxit

retreat □ see retreat to the wall

retreat to the wall

retrial □ see trial

retroactive legislation

retrospective legislation □ see retroactive legislation

return □ see indictment

return of execution □ see execute; □ see also, not satisfied

return of service □ see service of process

revenue bond □ see full faith and credit

reversal

reverse □ see reversal

reverse condemnation □ see eminent domain

reverse discrimination

reverse stock split □ see stock

reversible error

reversion □ see future interest

review □ see judicial review; □ see writ of review, under certiorari

revocable trust □ see trust

revoke a will □ see will

revolving door

Richard Roe □ see John Doe

Index of Entries

Index of Entries

Index of Entries

[80]

Index of Entries

Index of Entries

Index of Entries

Index of Entries

trap □ see entrap

trap for the unwary

travel bare □ see bare

treason • sedition

treasury shares □ see stock

treasury stock □ see stock

treaty

Treaty Clause

treble damages □ see damage

trespass

trespass ab initio □ see ab initio; □ see trespass

trespasser □ see trespass

trespasser ab initio □ see ab initio; □ see trespass

trial

trial brief □ see brief

trial by jury □ see trial jury, under jury

trial court □ see trial judge, under judge

trial de novo □ see de novo

trial judge □ see judge

trial judge advocate □ see lawyer

trial jury □ see jury

trial lawyer □ see lawyer

trial on the merits □ see merit

tried to the court □ see try

trier of fact □ see try; □ see mixed question of law and fact

trifles with justice □ see clichés

trivializes the law □ see clichés

-trix □ see sex

TRO

trover □ see conversion

trover and conversion □ see conversion

true and correct □ see facts

true bill □ see indictment

true facts □ see facts

trust

trust deed □ see deed; □ see secure

trustee □ see trust

trustee by operation of law □ see constructive trust, under trust; □ see by operation of law

trustee de son tort □ see constructive trust, under trust; □ see de son tort

trustee ex malificio □ see constructive trust, under trust

trustee in bankruptcy

trustee in invitum □ see constructive trust, under trust

trust indenture □ see trust

trust instrument □ see trust

trustor □ see trust

trust res □ see trust; □ see res

truth and veracity

truth, the whole truth, and nothing but the truth □ see formalisms; □ see absolutes

try

turntable doctrine

Index of Entries

Index of Entries

[92]

Index of Entries

Index of Entries

MELLINKOFF'S
DICTIONARY OF AMERICAN LEGAL USAGE

A

abandon: to voluntarily give up a right or interest or an obligation, with no intention of ever reclaiming the right or interest or performing the obligation. This general sense of *abandon,* and its related forms *abandoned* and *abandonment,* widely used in the law, is evidenced by a course of conduct, as distinguished from agreement. The course of conduct required to prove *abandonment,* in abundant and varied detail, is governed by substantive and procedural law. Here is a sampling of labels:

abandoned child—For example: Five years ago, Mary was born in a motel and taken to a hospital by the fire department. She has been continuously in foster homes ever since, with no attempt by her parents to maintain any sort of relationship. For other examples, refer to the law of adoption, family law, guardianship, social welfare.

abandoned client—For example: She closed her law office and moved out of town, without advising the client or returning the client's files. She kept the client's funds, without filing suit as agreed, and made herself generally unavailable. For other examples, refer to the law of attorney and client, malpractice, professional discipline.

abandoned property—For example: Driving at eighty miles per hour, he fired one shot at the pursuing patrol car and threw the pistol into the adjacent river. For other examples, refer to the law of adverse possession, copyright, easements, insurance, patent, trademark, trade name.

abandoned spouse—For example: After ten years of uneventful married life, he left the house, shouting at his protesting wife, "So long. I never want to see you again." He disappeared without a trace, providing no support for the last five years. □see **desertion**. For other examples, refer to the law of divorce, family law.

abandoned child □see **abandon**.

abandoned client □see **abandon**.

1

abandoned property □see **abandon**.

abandoned spouse □see **abandon**.

abandonment □see **abandon**.

abate: to end something, as to *abate* a **nuisance** (□see), or **abatement of nuisance**. Like other **absolutes** (□see), *abate* and *abatement* cannot always be taken literally. They may refer to ending something in its particular form, e.g., of pleading an action (□see **plea in abatement**), without the finality sometimes attached to **abatement of an action**. They may also refer to ending something in its particular amount:

abatement of legacies: reduction of legacies to enable an estate to pay debts.

abatement of taxes: reduction of tax to correct an error in the taxing process, e.g., an assessment.

abatement of an action □see **abate**.

abatement of legacies □see **abate**.

abatement of nuisance □see **abate**; □see **nuisance**.

abatement of taxes □see **abate**.

abet □see **aid and abet**.

ab initio (L., ab INISH-ee-o, as in *initial:* from the beginning): the start of a status, good or bad. <This dictionary is readable *ab initio.*> Most common in the redundancy *void ab initio;* □see **null and void**. Well aged in *trespass ab initio:* later events change an innocent entry into a trespass from the beginning. <He came in as a guest, stole from his host, and is now considered a trespasser *ab initio.*> The Latin has no magic. Prefer the translation *from the beginning* or English adapted to the facts. <A trespasser from the time he came in. . . .>

able argument with variations, *able brief* and *able counsel:* a judge's compliment to the lawyer for the losing side. Massage for lawyer and

2

client; law, not the lawyer, did you in. <Despite the able argument/able brief of Ms. Smith, we are constrained to hold. . . .> Often, in an opinion, a warning of bad news; a judicial "Dear John" letter. <Able counsel for appellant urges us. . . . However. . . .> □see **clichés**.

abortion   □see **person**.

absolute divorce   □see **divorce**.

absolute immunity   □see **immunity**; □see **absolutes**.

absolute liability   □see **strict liability**.

absolute nuisance   □see **nuisance**.

absolute presumption   □see **presumption**.

absolute privilege   □see **immunity**; □see **absolutes**.

absolutes   rarely are. Their pompous finality affronts a common law pride in the nice distinction. With lawyers, as with the laity <"Never. Hardly ever." *H.M.S. Pinafore*>, an absolute challenges the creative imagination. *Void* is interpreted down to *voidable*. The lesson unlearned, others diagnose *void* as only weakly absolute; better make it *totally void*. And as that vision fades, tautology is heaped up endlessly. □see **null and void**.

The deceptive lure of the absolute is its promise of quick precision. Fascinated, the profession keeps the absolute words and, under its breath, translates them away:

eo instante (L., a-oh INSTAN-tee: at the very instant): as soon as reasonably possible.

forthwith: as soon as reasonably possible.

instanter (L., in-STAN-tur: instantly): as soon as reasonably possible.

the truth, the whole truth, and nothing but the truth: what is believed to be true. □see **formalisms**.

time is of the essence: time is important.

absolutes

When too much hangs on a word, absoluteness crumbles by degree. <"A thing may be necessary, very necessary, absolutely or indispensably necessary." *McCulloch v. Maryland,* 17 U.S. 316, 414 (1819).> Even *death* has lost its definitive sting; *brain death* may be dead enough. Unless the whole design of a writing bespeaks the absolute, the absoluteness of apparent absolutes is an illusion.

Though hedged with qualification, some legalisms traditionally use the very word *absolute.* If one can remember that they only look absolute, they serve the convenience of comparison:

absolute immunity: more immune than *qualified immunity.* □see **immunity**.

absolute liability □see **strict liability**.

absolute privilege: more privileged than *conditional* or *qualified privilege.* □see **privilege**, under **immunity**.

fee simple absolute and **absolute divorce** are special cases. □see, respectively, **fee simple** and **divorce**.

□see also, **abate**; □see also, **absolute presumption**, under **presumption**; □see also, **best evidence**; □see also, **conclusive presumption**, under **presumption**; □see also, **irreparable damage**; □see also, **per se**; □see also, **ultimate facts**.

abstention □see **overbreadth**.

absurdity: a label of disapproval of the language of a contract or statute. It is related to the logician's *reductio ad absurdum:* prove a proposition by the nonsense of its opposite; disprove a proposition by the nonsense that would logically follow from it. Absurdity is so plentiful, and so personal, that it is an unreliable guide to interpretation. When a lawyer says that the words of a statute cannot be taken literally because the legislature would not intend an absurd result, the short response is "Often they do." If the judge decides it is more likely that legislators were sloppy than silly, the words are rejected as "absurd." <No bonds may be issued after July 1, 1992, other than bonds issued prior to that date.> With an aura of classic respectability, *absurdity* lacks the offensive bluntness of "damn nonsense" and strikes no fatal blow. It is the start, not the end, of a search for meaning. □see **clichés**.

abused child □see **child**.

4

abuse of discretion: a flexible limit to the exercise of discretion. The area of discretionary decision lies between the poles of fixed rule and personal whim that the law calls *capricious*. Over that vast no-man's-land, the law hovers with tolerant watchfulness. The judge denying a stay, the administrator devising regulations to bring a statute to life, the trustee investing money, has a discretion to decide this way or that, within deliberately ill-defined limits of the accustomed ways of doing things. Discretion, if it is to survive, cannot be tightly controlled, only watched. As the exercise of discretion moves in the direction of personal whim, the law becomes more watchful. Suddenly, the limit has been reached and passed. That almost unpredictable event is called *abuse of discretion*. Progress toward the pit is so gradual that an exercise of discretion must be unexpected and extreme to arouse interest. The jolt factor is typically expressed in hyperbole. <The sentence is such as to shock the conscience, arbitrary and capricious, a gross abuse of discretion./The investments were not merely imprudent but utterly capricious, an abuse of discretion.> Since jolt factors tend to be personal, there can be abuse of *abuse of discretion,* sometimes a convenient rebuff to an innovative lower court decision. That risk is a flexible price of a flexible limit to a flexible rule of decision.

abuse of process   □see **malicious abuse of process.**

accelerated disclosure   □see **reciprocal discovery,** under **discovery.**

accept   □see **offer and acceptance;** □see also, **honor;** □see also, **dishonor.**

acceptance   □see **offer and acceptance;** □see also, **honor;** □see also, **dishonor.**

access   □see **right of access;** □see **nonaccess;** □see also, **plagiarism.**

accessory   □see **parties to crime.**

accessory after the fact   □see **parties to crime.**

accessory before the fact   □see **parties to crime.**

accident • accidental   are two of the best documented and least precise words in the legal vocabulary. With more and more people

accident

living and dying by the machine, *accident*'s old suggestions of "surprise" and "chance" have shriveled. A collision of automobiles is an *accident,* though everyone saw it coming. In law, as in the common speech, *accident* is vague, giving no certain information that what happened was the result of neglect, intentional ramming, or natural catastrophe. <They were in an accident.> *Accident* still has the popular and often the legal flavor of unscheduled "misfortune." Life is too full of misfortunes; few people schedule them. Even insurance underwriters aren't quite certain what exactly it is they are insuring against. Your "accident policy" may call it an "occurrence." What's that? Some place here it is defined as an "accident." *Accidental* struggles to hang on to a shred of the "unintended" that *accident* long ago lost. <The drunk driver died in a one-car accident. Neither the drinking nor the driving was accidental; perhaps the death was.>

accidental   □see **accident.**

accommodation director   □see **director.**

accomplice   □see **parties to crime.**

accord and satisfaction   □see **satisfaction.**

accretion: a general term for a gradual, natural increase in the quantity or area of land at water's edge. *Accretion* may occur by a gradual deposit of grains of soil. Or it may occur by a gradual receding (*recession*) of a usual watercourse or the usual reach of tides, thus exposing additional land: this process and the exposed land is also called *reliction* or *dereliction.* Whether by deposit of soil or by recession, the increase of land belongs to the owner of the original land at the old water's edge. *Accretion* is contrasted with *avulsion.*

avulsion: a general term for a sudden, substantial change by natural causes in the apparent ownership or boundaries of lands at water's edge. *Avulsion* may occur (e.g., by flooding) by the natural washing away of substantial soil from one owner's land at water's edge and natural redeposit, joining it to another owner's land at water's edge; ownership of the redeposited land remains with the original owner. Or *avulsion* may occur by a sudden, natural change of a usual watercourse or the usual reach of tides; the boundary between the original owners of the land at the old water's edge remains unchanged.

Definition and consequences of both *accretion* and *avulsion* vary by jurisdiction. Especially affected by rules in other areas of property law, largely beyond the scope of this dictionary, e.g., riparian rights (□see **law of capture**); e.g., **mining law** (□see).

accusation □see **accuse**.

accusatorial system • inquisitorial system □see **adversary proceeding**.

accuse • charge: synonyms for making formal claim of criminal wrongdoing. In less technical contexts, either verb may be used. <The grand jury accused Smith of securities fraud./The grand jury charged Smith with securities fraud.> While *charge* is used loosely to claim civil wrongdoing (□see **allege**), in criminal law *charge* is the choice for technical precision. <The indictment charges Smith with five counts of grand theft. /You are charged with murder in the first degree. How do you wish to plead?> Similarly, the specific technical noun is *charge,* rather than the more general *accusation.* <The charge is murder in the first degree./". . . the right . . . to be informed of the nature and cause of the accusation. . . ." U.S. Const.Amend. VI> In civilian criminal trials, the person *charged* is the *defendant;* in more general context, the *accused.* <"In all criminal prosecutions, the accused shall enjoy the right to a speedy and public trial. . . ." U.S. Const. Amend. VI> In military courts-martial, *charges* are preferred against the *accused,* who keeps that name through the trial. □see also, **accusatorial system**, under **adversary proceeding**.

In ordinary English, neither *accuse* nor *charge* has much regard for legal technicality. <He accused me of lying./I charge the incumbent with violating the public trust.> A police *charge sheet* is not limited to formal claims of wrongdoing. The loose newspaper usage *accused murderer* damns the innocent, though intended as nothing more than shorthand for someone not convicted. It carries the implicit croak of doom, "not yet." <"Accused Chino Hills killer Kevin Cooper [was] ordered to stand trial on four charges of murder."> For a related horror, □see **suspected murderer**, under **suspect**.

For another use of *charge,* □see **jury instructions**.

accused □see **accuse**.

accused murderer □see **accuse**; □see also, **suspect**.

acknowledge □see **acknowledge and confess**.

acknowledge and confess not emphatic, just repetitious: "Yes, that's so; yes, that's so." □see **coupled synonyms.** Separately, each of the synonyms has distinctive uses.

acknowledge: as in ordinary English, to admit that something is so, e.g., an indebtedness, a signature, whether by use of the word *acknowledge* or others. <I acknowledge/admit/agree that I owe them $500.> Usually without the suggestion of personal fault implicit in **confess** (□see). <I confess that I owe them $500.> In some contexts, *acknowledge* and *confess* may overlap. <He acknowledged/confessed paternity.>

acknowledgement

1. the ordinary English noun for the act of acknowledging.

2. a short written statement following the signature of a writing, in which the signer of the statement says that he signed the writing. The statement is signed in the presence of a notary public. <The notary took the acknowledgement.>

3. the notary's certification that the signer acknowledged signing the writing (sense 2). <The recorder refused to record the writing without a notary's acknowledgment.>

confess

1. to admit the commission of a crime. The noun is *confession,* as distinguished from an *admission* generally that something short of a crime has happened or is so. <He admitted that he is sometimes known as Joe Smith and confessed to having robbed the bank.>

2. as in ordinary English, to admit that something is so, usually with the suggestion of personal fault. □see **acknowledge.**

   a. **confess error,** usually in the noun form confession of error: an admission by the prevailing party that the court below made a mistake. <On appeal, the attorney general confessed error, and the judgment was reversed. /Appellee's failure to file a brief was treated as a confession of error.>

   b. **confession and avoidance** □see **avoid.**

3. **confess judgment:** to agree that judgment may be entered against one. <She confessed judgment for $1,000.>

   confession of judgment: the act of confessing judgment or the writing embodying the agreement. Also, but now less frequently, called a *cognovit* (L.: he has acknowledged). Sometimes takes the form of a *cognovit note:* one in which the maker agrees

8

that if it is not paid, judgment may be entered against the maker.

acknowledgement □see **acknowledge and confess.**

acquittal in a criminal case, a *verdict* of *not guilty* or a judge's determination of *not guilty*, called a judgment of acquittal (□see, under **judgment**).

act and deed as coupled, both words have the ordinary English meaning: something done. The repetition invites the misinterpretation that *act* refers to something done and *deed* refers to a document. For a special usage, □see **estoppel in pais**, under **estoppel.** □see also, **coupled synonyms.**

action • actionable

action

1. a lawsuit. In this sense, *action* is interchangeable with *case, lawsuit,* and *suit* and has no more technicality than any of them. <It was an action/a case/a lawsuit/a suit tried in the U.S. District Court.> As the mood strikes them, lawyers use all four, *action* unconsciously favored as an in-word picked up in law school. For most nonlawyers, this sense of *action* is a nonword, and the lawyer who wants to get through to a client doesn't use it. <We filed your suit today.> Dropping this sense of *action* from the legal vocabulary would also be a step in the direction of precision, limiting *action* to sense 2, which has no one-word equivalent in ordinary English. □see also, **case and controversy**, under **controversy.** □see also, **local action.**

2. a right to sue. In this sense, *action* is also called a **cause of action** (□see). <Upon failure of the seller to convey Blackacre, the buyer may have an action/a cause of action for damages or an action/a cause of action for specific performance.>

actionable (adj.): forming the basis of a right to sue. <Invasion of privacy is actionable.>

actionable per se: in the law of **defamation** (□see), said of words that *per se* (L.: by themselves) form the basis of a right to sue. The expression does not explain the substantive law of defamation but announces a conclusion arrived at by varying formulas. Those formulas vary from state to state, with distinctions between libel and slander, between different kinds of slander, and between different kinds of libel, and are now vastly changed by constitutional decisions on the relationship between defamation and free speech. <That may have been actionable *per se* at common law, but not now, not in this state.>

Apart from the varying formulas, *actionable per se* suffers the confusions of two separate usages, often muddled together.

1. the cause of action without proof of damage usage: the person defamed by the words may recover without proving damage. This is the primary usage of *actionable per se*. This sense is also expressed by *defamatory per se* (n., *defamation per se*) and—in separate categories of defamation—*libelous per se* (n., *libel per se*) and *slanderous per se* (n., *slander per se*). If recovery is conditioned on proof of some damage, the most direct statement is the simple negative *not actionable per se, not defamatory per se,* etc. That negative is sometimes expressed as *actionable per quod* (L.: because of this), and the other *nots* are frequently expressed as *defamatory per quod* (n., *defamation per quod*), etc. <This was actionable only because it caused damage; it was actionable *per quod.*>

2. the meaning of the words usage: the words are obviously defamatory, defamatory *on their face,* needing no explanation of the way in which they were used. <No one can misunderstand, "He is a bank robber"; the words are actionable *per se.*> This usage of *actionable per se* is more often conveyed by *defamatory per se, libel per se,* and *slander per se.* If the words are not obviously defamatory but need explanation to spell out a defamatory sense, they are sometimes said to be *actionable per quod,* more often *defamatory per quod, libel per quod,* or *slander per quod.* □see **innuendo**, under **colloquium.**

actionable □see **action.**

actionable per quod □see **actionable per se**, under **action.**

actionable per se □see **action.**

active trust □see **trust.**

act of God • force majeure • vis major: an *irresistible force,* imprecise whether expressed in English, French (force muh–ZHURE), Latin (vees MAY-jer), or all three together. As synonyms, all convey the sense of a *force beyond control* of the immediate parties. *Act of God* and *vis major* are usually limited to unusual natural force; *force majeure* may refer as well to unpredictable man-made calamities, e.g., war, government controls, strikes. In preliminary negotiation, and as an identifying label, lawyers use *force majeure* in preference to the more limiting *act of God* and *vis major.* <Of course the completion date would be subject to force majeure./Does the force majeure clause mention that?/Performance should be excused by reason of force majeure.> Standing alone, neither *force majeure, vis major, act of God, irresistible force,* nor *force beyond control* answers the critical questions. What is included? (Is a strike really beyond control? How strong must the force be?) When does it apply? (How long out of control? Could it have been anticipated?) How does it affect the obligation? (Does it end or extend a contract?) *Force majeure* is a convenient, quick reference to a controversial bundle. That's all it is good for.

actual in ordinary English, is a good luck charm to ward off disbelief. Most often it means not *real* but *really.* <I mean, actually.> Lawyers conform easily to old habit and scatter *actual* with indiscriminate generosity. Without adding any distinctive sense, *actual* is prefixed to *cost, fair value, loss, market value, residence, use, value, violence.* <The actual cost/the cost was $10,000.> This redundant use of *actual* not only depreciates the residual precision of *cost, fair value,* and the rest, but also befogs the difference between redundant *actual* and useful *actual.*

In the continuous search for ways to verbalize legal distinctions, lawyers find *actual* a convenient device to remake one word into two or more related words. It is a fine-slicer, e.g., remaking *damages* into *actual* and *punitive damages.* <In addition to damages for the injury, the actual damages, plaintiff is entitled to damages by way of punishing the defendant, punitive or exemplary damages.> □see **damages,** under **damage.** □see also, **actual authority,** under **agency;** □see also, **actual bias,** under **bias;** □see also, **actual controversy,** under **controversy.** Of all its word-making roles, the most creative is the duet of *actual* with *constructive.*

actual/constructive: a distinctively legal word play slicing a word into the real thing (*actual*) and something else (*constructive*), sometimes close enough to the real thing to be treated as if it were. <The money was theirs for the asking, but they deliberately refrained from asking; that was *constructive receipt of income,* taxed as if actually received.> The device is useful if there is a distinction to be made; if not, *actual* reverts to redundancy. Receipt of income is receipt of income. For other useful applications of the *actual/constructive* distinction, □see **desertion;** □see **eviction,** under **evict;** □see **knowledge;** □see **malice;** □see **notice;** □see **possession.** For the special usage *constructive trust,* □see **trust.**

actual adverse possession □see **possession.**

actual agent □see **agency.**

actual authority □see **agency.**

actual bias □see **bias.**

actual controversy □see **controversy.**

actual damages □see **damages,** under **damage.**

actual eviction □see **eviction.**

actual knowledge □see **knowledge.**

actual malice □see **malice.**

actual notice □see **notice.**

actual reduction to practice □see **patent.**

ad damnum (L.: to the damage): the statement of damages in a pleading <The ad damnum lists actual and punitive damages.>. Make it English. <The complaint lists actual and punitive damages.>

additur □see **remittitur.**

address icebergs One of the most versatile words in the English language, *address* speaks with some precision about writing on an envelope, talking to an audience, or getting ready to hit a golf ball, and then disappears into the mists *addressing* issues. You know what's going to happen to the envelope and the audience and the golf ball, but no one knows what *address* will do to an issue: point to it, sniff at it, poke it up a little, "shed light on it," indorse, condemn, or offer solutions. This capacity for vacuity recommends *address* to legal writers eager for an all-purpose nothingness. It works alone <Addressing the complex problem of products liability. . . .> and in the congenial company of a mixed metaphor. <But that is only addressing the tip of the iceberg.> *Turn to* issues, if you must, but don't *address* icebergs, especially not the tips. □see **clichés.**

12

adeem • ademption: to eliminate a gift listed in a will (a legacy or a devise) because it no longer exists (e.g., the horse died), or because the conduct of the testator after making the will is interpreted as an intent to revoke the gift or to satisfy it now. E.g., the testator gives the subject of the gift (Blackacre) to someone else. E.g., the testator gives the named beneficiary an equivalent or substituted gift. *Adeem* is the verb; *ademption* the noun. □see also, **advancement**, under **hotchpot.**

ademption □see **adeem.**

adhesion contract • adhesive contract □see **contract of adhesion.**

adjective law □see **procedural law.**

adjourn □see **stand adjourned;** □see also, **delay.**

adjudicated form: a form of such dubious merit that someone found it worth taking to court. < This book contains only adjudicated forms. > *Adjudicated* here is creative usage. It does not mean that a court decided that the form was good, only that the case was decided and that at least something in the form escaped disapproval.

ad litem □see **lis.**

administrative agency □see **administrative law.**

administrative law

1. the law of the *administrative agency* (see below), its powers, procedures and actions, and the judicial review of its actions. In short, the law of "the machinery of government." It consists of constitutional, legislative, judge-made law, and law made by the agencies themselves. (See Kenneth C. Davis, 1 Administrative Law Treatise, 2d ed., pp. 1–3, 1984).

2. the law made by the *administrative agency,* as in sense 1. In some usage, sense 2 is limited to the procedural law made by the agency, excluding the mass of agency-made substantive law in distinctive areas of the law, e.g., antitrust, tax, environment, labor, welfare, zoning. Some usage also refers to aspects of those substantive areas as *administrative law.*

administrative agency: a separate governmental individual or body that takes the abstract law made by constitutions, legislatures, judges, and executives, and puts it to work, directly affecting the lives of people and their enterprises. The acts of administrative agencies constitute a vast miscellany. In keeping with its particular authority, an agency makes rules, regulates, investigates, informs, negotiates, prosecutes, holds hearings, adjudicates, fines, disciplines, renders a wide range of services, e.g., pays entitlements, provides medical care, provides postal services, makes government contracts, etc.

In the moment of creation, each *administrative agency* is given a label. One agency is called a *commission,* e.g., the Interstate Commerce Commission (ICC), the Federal Trade Commission (FTC); □see **commission.** Another is a *board,* e.g., the National Labor Relations Board (NLRB), while another is an *administration,* e.g., the Veterans Administration (VA), the Social Security Administration (SSA). Still another is an *authority,* e.g., the Tennessee Valley Authority (TVA); sometimes even an *agency,* or *executive agency,* e.g., Environmental Protection Agency (EPA); etc. Similarly, the people who administer, as a class *administrators* (less reverently, *bureaucrats*), also go by various names—*chairman, commissioner, member,* etc.

Some administrative agencies that have relatively broad regulatory powers over a particular activity are called *regulatory agencies.* Especially noteworthy is the *independent commission,* independent of executive control and arbitrary removal, e.g., the ICC, the FTC, the Securities and Exchange Commission (SEC). Regulatory agency is not a term of art; powers and modes of operation differ substantially agency to agency: Some make rules, some don't; some adjudicate, some don't.

administrative law judge □see **judge;** □see **administrative law.**

administrator □see **executor;** □see **administrative law.**

administratrix □see **sex.**

Admiralty Clause: the part of the U.S. Constitution reading: "The judicial power shall extend . . . to all cases of admiralty and maritime jurisdiction. . . ." (Art. III, § 2, cl. 1). □see also, **constitutional clauses.**

admiralty law   □see maritime law.

admiralty lawyer   □see lawyer.

admissibility   □see admit.

admissible   □see admit.

admission   □see admit.

admit   a short verb, amply offset by grammatical and legal variations: *admissibility, admissible, admission,* and *admitted.*

1. (evidence): to permit something to be received in evidence <Admitted!>. This refers to a judge's ruling on *admissibility* (n.) under the rules of evidence. It is a ruling that something is *admissible* (adj.), as distinguished from **inadmissible** (□see); entitled to *admission* (n.), as distinguished from *exclusion.*   □see **evidence**.

2. (acknowledge): a synonym. Compare and contrast *admit* with *confess.* Similarly, compare and contrast *admission* with *confession.* □see **acknowledge and confess**. Usage often joins sense 1 and sense 2; e.g., in argument of counsel over whether or not an *admission* (sense 2) is *admissible* (sense 1).

vicarious admission: an admission attributed to one person because of the statements of another, e.g., a statement made by an agent authorized to speak for the principal attributed to the principal. Also called a *representative admission.*

3. (lawyers) □see **admitted to practice**; □see **admitted to the bar**, under **bar**.

4. (bail) □see **bail**.

admitted   □see admit.

admitted to bail   □see bail.

admitted to practice   □see **admitted to the bar**, under **bar**; □see also, **pro hac vice**.

admitted to the bar   □see bar.

15

admonition □see **reprimand**.

adopted child □see **child**.

adoptive parent □see **parent**.

ADR abbreviation of *alternative dispute resolution:* alternatives to litigation, or to full-scale litigation, e.g., arbitration, mediation, shortened trials, etc. The abbreviation appears without periods and sometimes without specific reference to what it abbreviates.

adult □see **child**.

advancement □see **hotchpot**.

advance sheets □see **law reports**.

adversary proceeding • adversary system In these combinations, *adversary* is no ordinary word. There are *adversary proceedings* without a fight, and the *adversary system* includes proceedings with no fight, no adversaries, only adversity.

adversary proceeding

1. a procedure started by allegations of wrongdoing, with an opportunity to defend against the allegations before official action is taken. Contrasted with *ex parte proceedings.* (□see **ex parte**). In this basic sense, an ordinary suit for damages is an *adversary proceeding,* even if it is *uncontested* and ends with a *default judgment.* (□see **default**).

2. a procedure in which allegations of wrongdoing are contested. Contrasted with an *uncontested proceeding.* □see **default**. □see **plea**. <Nothing went by default; it was an adversary proceeding from start to finish.>

adversary system: a very general label for the system of justice, civil and criminal, in the United States and other common law jurisdictions. Typically, opposing parties, private or government, contend with each other, in person or through lawyers, in *adversary proceedings* regulated by the rules of the system. But the label is broad enough to include *ex parte* proceedings, *uncontested* proceedings (□see **plea**), and proceedings which in theory are not ad-

16

versarial. <No one is supposed to be against children; *juvenile court proceedings* are not adversarial, though they are within the adversary system.>

accusatorial system: the criminal side of the *adversary system.* Typically, the government alleges wrongdoing, and the defendant has an opportunity to defend, as in other *adversary proceedings.* Two restrictions on the adversary nature of the system are peculiar to criminal cases: the defendant cannot be brought to trial without **probable cause** (□see), and the prosecutor must disclose evidence favorable to the defendant. Contrasted with **inquisitorial system**, typical of legal systems not following the common law: the government is to make a detailed investigation, questioning everyone, including the prospective defendant; the case is then dropped or brought to a trial heavily weighted against the defendant.

adverse party   □see **hostile witness.**

adverse possession   □see **possession.**

adverse witness   □see **hostile witness.**

advice and consent   □see **treaty;** □see **Treaty Clause.**

advisory jury   □see **jury.**

advisory opinion   □see **controversy.**

affected with a public interest   □see **public interest.**

affiant • deponent

The worthwhile connections of *affiant* to *affidavit* and *deponent* to *deposition* are easily lost in the basic similarity of *affiant* and *deponent:* both swear (in legal form) outside of court. Varied, overlapping usage of words related to *deponent* adds to the confusion. (If conscience or religion forbids swearing, *affirm* substitutes for *swear, affirmation* for *oath.*)

affiant signs an *affidavit:* a written statement under oath. The words may be someone else's. By swearing, before a person authorized to administer oaths, that the words are true, and signing at the bottom of the statement, the swearer-signer becomes an *affi-*

17

affiant

ant; before that, nothing. <She made an affidavit of ownership./Both affiants claimed title.> Traditional language at the beginning of the affidavit starts the confusion of roles. <John Smith, being first duly sworn, *deposes and says.*> It is a redundant complication, readily, and often, simplified <John Smith, *under oath, says.*>. Even better, eliminate the cumbersome third person. Make it: I, John Smith, *swear.* Traditional redundant language at the end of the affidavit continues the confusion <Further *deponent* saith not.>.

deponent, in current, useful usage, is a *witness,* outside of court, questioned under oath before a person authorized to administer oaths, usually in the presence of lawyers for both sides. Usually, question and response are oral. The questioning lawyer (as distinct from a cross-examiner) is *taking the deposition* or *deposes the witness.* The *witness (deponent)* refuses to answer or answers <The witness *deposed* that./Plaintiff gave his deposition from 3 to 5 P.M.>. That is enough; the *deponent* is a *deponent,* whether or not *deponent* ever signs the *deposition:* transcribed testimony of the *witness* and incidental comments intended for later use in court. □see also, **perpetuate testimony**.

affidavit □see **affiant**.

affinity □see **heirs**.

affirm □see **affiant**.

affirmation □see **affiant**; □see **perjury**.

affirmative action: governmental or private programs relating to jobs, business, and education designed to eliminate discrimination and to overcome the continuing effects of past discrimination. The targeted discrimination, e.g., on the basis of race, color, nationality, sex, religion, age, varies with program, legislation, and regulation. The goals are often broadly described as seeking to promote equality of opportunity for women and minorities, especially racial minorities. The boundary between permitted *affirmative action* and prohibited **reverse discrimination** (□see) remains unsettled, leaving both expressions imprecise.

affirmative covenant □see **covenant**.

affirmative defense　□see **burden of persuasion**, under **proof**.

affirmative easement　□see **easement**.

affirmative equitable servitude　□see **easement**.

affirmative pregnant • negative pregnant:　old forms of legal argot, both stigmatizing denials as inadequate pleadings because they imply an admission that the charge has substance.　The more common is the *negative pregnant:* short for "negative pregnant with a fatal affirmative."　It is a denial in the very words of the charge.　To the charge that "$100 is owing," "I deny that $100 is owing" is a *negative pregnant* with the admission that more or less than $100 is owing. Similarly, the *affirmative pregnant:* short for "affirmative pregnant with a fatal negative."　It is an ambiguous affirmative statement that does not respond to the substance of the charge.　To the charge that "$100 is owing," "I paid $50" is an *affirmative pregnant* with an admission that half of the debt has not been paid or that none of this particular debt has been paid.

afore-:　an archaic prefix that sometimes means *before*.　In *aforesaid* and *aforementioned,* it means *before,* but with no precise sense of "when"; *afore-* lends an aura of antiquity, but the words are worthless.　*Aforethought* is a special case.　The law has changed the meaning of *aforethought* but has not been able to shake itself loose of the word itself.　□see **malice aforethought**.　□see **murder**.

aforethought　□see **afore-**; □see **malice aforethought**; □see also, **murder**.

a fortiori　(L., a FOR–she–or–I: from stronger): all the more so.　<If there is no breach, *a fortiori* there is no right to damages.>　A term of logic, long ago drafted into legal service to bolster the obvious.　It was at its best when professors thundered at first-year law students, but that fervor and awe have waned.　All the more so in writing.　Let it die.

against public policy　□see **public policy**.

age　□see **lawful age**; □see also, **age of consent**.

agency: a relationship in which the *principal* authorizes the *agent* to act for the principal, and the principal is liable for the acts of the agent in furthering the interests of the principal. Agency is sometimes still expressed in the old maxim *qui facit per alium facit per se* (L., key FAKE-it purr al-ee-um FAKE-it purr say: who acts through another acts himself); the maxim oversimplifies the relationship and the liability, and is better left to legal history. Another maxim of agency, *respondeat superior* (L., re-SPOND-ee-at superior: let the superior answer), unreliable as an imperative, frequently serves as a shorthand reference to the substantive law, and limits, of the principal's liability for the acts of an agent.

actual authority

1. in loosest usage, no more than a redundancy for the agent's authority. < He had the authority/actual authority. >

2. sometimes, loosely, a synonym for *express authority.*

3. at its distinctive best, *actual authority,* while in substance a synonym for *authority,* is also a signal to the profession that the basis of the agent's *authority* is in question, and that it may rest on *express authority, implied authority,* or *apparent authority.*

express authority: the principal gives the agent authority by using the word *authorize,* or other ordinary words of like effect. < I authorize you to/I employ you to/You are my agent to/You are to act for me, etc. >

implied authority: from the circumstances of the job, the law decides that an unspoken authority existed. < The vice-president always hired a manager. We think that the job carried implied authority to hire, which, though not express, will be treated as actual authority. > □see **imply.**

apparent authority: the principal's manner of running the enterprise creates an appearance of authority in the agent, and a stranger reasonably relies on the appearance of things to believe that authority exists; it does, as a matter of law. < The sign on the booth said "Pay here," and Jones was inside the booth. Customers would reasonably believe that Jones was authorized to accept payment. That apparent authority will be treated as actual authority; the bill was paid. > *Apparent authority* is also called **ostensible authority.**

apparent agency: As with *apparent authority,* appearances may establish the agency itself. The principal may thus acquire an *apparent agent* who will be treated as if an *actual agent.* Also called **ostensible agency** and *ostensible agent.*

☐see also, **administrative agency**, under **administrative law**; ☐see also, **regulatory agency**, under **administrative law**.

agency coupled with an interest ☐see **power coupled with an interest**.

agency jurisdiction ☐see **jurisdiction**.

agent ☐see **agency**; ☐see also, **independent contractor**.

age of consent: the age at which a person may marry without parental consent, and the age at which a person (usually said of a female) may consent to sexual intercourse. The age in each instance is fixed by statute. ☐see also, **lawful age**.

age of majority ☐see **lawful age**.

aggravated assault ☐see **assault and battery**.

aggravating circumstances ☐see **mitigating circumstances**.

agree ☐see **contract**.

agreement ☐see **contract**.

agreement to agree: a vague, sometimes fraudulent, provision of a contract, indefinitely putting off some unpleasantness. <We agree to agree on the shade of white for the living room.> Best forgotten. ☐see also, **subject to change by mutual consent**, under **subject to**.

aid and abet: old synonyms for unspecific helping to do something bad, usually criminal (☐see **parties to crime**). The tug of old rhythm usually keeps *aid and abet* together, so that the uncertainties of separate shades of meaning are not uniformly resolved. It is sometimes said that *aid* relates to the physical but does not describe the mental state (☐see **mens rea**) implicit in *abet*. In criminal law usage, *aid and abet* sometimes stands alone as a description of helping in the commission of a crime; sometimes, the expression is explained in one or more characterizations of such help, e.g., advise, command, counsel, encourage, induce, instigate, plan, procure; sometimes, it is

21

aid and abet

joined in redundancy with one of those characterizations, e.g., "aids, abets, counsels, commands, induces, or procures." The helper is sometimes called an *aider and abettor*. □see **coupled synonyms**.

aid and comfort: old synonyms for unspecific helping, now treated as one word in constitutional law, as part of the crime of treason. <"Treason against the United States shall consist only in levying war against them, or, in adhering to their enemies, giving them aid and comfort." U.S. Const., Art. III, § 3, cl. 1.> □see **coupled synonyms**.

aider and abettor □see **aid and abet.**

airspace

1. (generally): in ordinary usage, the space in the air above the planet Earth, sometimes contrasted with **outer space** (□see). Both expressions are imprecise; the boundary between the two is not fixed.

2. (sovereignty): in international treaty usage, the undefined space, called *airspace,* above a nation's territory, over which it has "complete and exclusive sovereignty." (Paris Convention of 1919, "relating to the regulation of aerial navigation," 11 L.N.T.S. [League of Nations Treaty Series] [1922], No. 297, p. 173 at p. 190, Art. I; Chicago Convention on International Civil Aviation of 1944, 15 U.N.T.S. [United Nations Treaty Series] [1948], No. 102, p. 295 at p. 296, Art. I.) For the contrast on sovereignty, □see **outer space.**

3. (jurisdiction)

a. The space in the air above the land and inland waters of the United States and above "those portions of the adjacent marginal high seas, bays, and lakes, over which by international law or treaty or convention the United States exercises national jurisdiction" (refer to 49 USCA § 1508(a)).

b. The space in the air above the territorial limits of a political subdivision within the United States.

4. (ownership): That part of the space in the air above an owner's land that is owned by the landowner. The extent of that space is not limitless, as once it was according to the Latin maxim *cujus est solum ejus est usque ad coelum* (loosely, who owns the land, owns it up to the heavens). Nor is it a measurable constant. It extends high enough for what is considered at the time and place a reasonable use of the property, e.g., growing crops, forests, skyscrapers, condominiums. That space can be encroached upon for some purposes (e.g., by aircraft), but depending on the extent of its interference with the landowner's reasonable use, the encroachment may be considered an inverse condemnation or a tort.

5. navigable airspace: ". . . airspace above the minimum altitude of flight prescribed by regulations . . . includ[ing] airspace needed to insure safety in take-off and landing of aircraft" (49 USCA § 1301(29)).

a.k.a. □see **alias**.

Alford plea □see **guilty**.

alias • a.k.a. • d.b.a.

> **alias** is short for the phrase *alias dictus* (L., A-lee-us DICK-tus: otherwise called) and doubles as a noun: another name by which one is known. <John Smith, alias Jack Smith/His alias was Jack Smith.>

> **a.k.a.** (often *a/k/a*) is the standard abbreviation for *also known as,* itself a rough English translation of *alias dictus.* It introduces an *alias* (n.) and is used interchangeably with *alias* (phrase) <John Smith, a.k.a. Jack Smith/John Smith, alias Jack Smith>.

> *a.k.a.* and *alias,* (phrase and noun), without pejorative implication, make identification precise <Her passport was in the name of Beverly Smith, a.k.a. Bee Smith./The license was in the name of Mrs. John Smith, alias Beverly Martin.>. Multiplying the *aliases* <The defendant is John Smith, *a.k.a.* Roger Jones, *a.k.a.* Pete Harrah.> inevitably suggests name change to elude police or creditors, at the least a hint of the underworld. Fiction writers have helped to give *alias* a bad name <Alias Jimmy Valentine/Alias the Deacon>, and legitimate usage suffers by association.

> **d.b.a.** (sometimes *d/b/a*) is the standard abbreviation for *doing business as,* a business relative of *a.k.a.,* trying to disclaim kinship with nasty *alias.* It too introduces another name by which one is known, a **fictitious firm name**: another name, often registered, under which an individual or an organization conducts business. A variation in bilingual coupled synonyms is **name and style** <John Smith and Mary Adams, d.b.a. Speedy Atomic Company/Northpole Products, Incorporated, doing business under the name and style of Northpole>. To readers of legal advertising (the fine-print kind), *d.b.a.* is a familiar, needing no amplification.

alias dictus □see **alias**.

alias process: new **process** (□see) issued when the old one has not been effective. E.g., an *alias subpoena, alias summons, alias writ.*

alias subpoena □see **alias process;** □see **subpoena.**

alias summons □see **alias process;** □see **service of process.**

alias writ □see **alias process;** □see **writ.**

alibi (L., AL-uh-buy, as in *lullaby*: elsewhere): the excuse of being at some other place. It is a term of art. The law keeps the true faith and does not accept the colloquial meaning: any excuse. <The defense gave notice that they would rely on an alibi./The sole alibi witness placed defendant in New York at the time of the shooting in Los Angeles.>

alien • alienability • alienation As a verb, *alien* is an archaic law French synonym for *transfer* of real property. It flaunts its alien origin and is little used. It could be dropped without regret, were it not the key to understanding the related noun forms, still of technical importance: *alienability of future interests* (□see **future interest**) and **restraint on alienation** (□see). These usages tie the law to its history; but for purposes of general explanation, *alienability* is *transferability,* and *alienation* is *transfer.* The related tort usage, *alienation of affections* (transfer of a spouse's affections) is dying by abolition of the tort action itself. □see **transfer.**

alienability of future interests □see **future interest.**

alienation • alienation of affections □see **alien.**

alimony • maintenance • support: periodic payments from one spouse to the other to cover living expenses, ordered by court incident to separation or divorce. *Support* may refer to payments for a spouse or a child; *alimony* is restricted to payments for a spouse. *Maintenance* is a more general, less frequently used term for payments for a spouse or a child, becoming *the* word in an action for *separate maintenance.* □see **divorce.** <Before and during the trial, she received *alimony pendente lite (temporary alimony),* but the decree did not include permanent support./The court awarded support for the wife for one year and child support until majority./It was agreed that the wife would provide some maintenance for the husband and the two children.>

Temporary alimony, whether *pendente lite* or for some other limited period, is distinguished from the apparent foreverness of **permanent alimony**: an imprecise term, sometimes applied to lifetime payments to a spouse, payments during the joint lives of the former spouses, payments until death or remarriage, payments for an indefinite period subject to change of circumstances. □see **absolutes.**

alimony pendente lite □see **alimony;** □see **lis.**

all □see **each and all.**

all deliberate speed □see **with all deliberate speed.**

allege • alleged • allegation: standard references to the claims made in civil or criminal pleadings. < Plaintiff alleges that defendant drove recklessly./It is alleged that defendant acted with malice./The allegations of the complaint are sufficient to state a cause of action for malpractice. > In general discussion of legal pleadings, lawyers and judges may substitute *charge.* < The complaint charges breach of contract. > But if the focus is on precisely what the parties have said in their pleadings, the words are *allege, alleged, allegation.* These words have largely supplanted their older synonyms *aver, averred, averment.*

Properly used, the various forms of *allege* are neutral description. They lack the snide derogation in the popular use of *alleged* to hint that someone is lying, exaggerating, or at least saying something that can't be proved. < The candidate's alleged qualification for the office of mayor is one month's service as acting chairman of a committee to rename Main Street. > This pejorative sense is sometimes exploited in argument to a jury, with a tremolo stress on *alleged.* < The alleged damage amounts to this. > Instructions to a jury would do better to avoid *allege,* substituting *claims, says, has asked for,* etc. < Plaintiff's alleged injuries . . . ./Plaintiff says she was injured./Plaintiff claims these injuries. >

Allen charge □see **jury instructions.**

all faults □see **as is.**

allocution (L., al-low-CUE-shun: to speak to): the name of the words spoken just before sentencing. Beyond that, usage wavers, leaving *allocution* as an ambiguous stage direction. < By way of allocution, the judge said: "Do you know any reason why this court should not pass sentence upon you?"/By way of allocution, the convicted defendant said: "I didn't do it."> Who speaks to whom? The Latin origin is equivocal. History of the word and practice favors the voice of authority. The judge is to warn of impending judgment and give the defendant an opportunity to point out error or ask for clemency. <In response to allocution, the defendant said. . . .> So restricted, *allocution* is a quick statement that the judge has done his job. Permitted to wander loose between judge and defendant, *allocution* had best be dropped.

also known as   □see **alias**.

alter ego (L.: other self): a corporation in form, but not run as a corporation, and used by its owners for a fraudulent purpose. *Alter ego* is the name given a conclusion, not a formula for arriving at the conclusion. Nor is it a specification of the consequences, one of which (the commonest) may be that the owners are personally liable for what would otherwise be only a corporate obligation. It is the corporation that is labeled *alter ego,* not—as sometimes stated—the owners. Treating the sham corporation as the other self of the owners is also called **piercing the corporate veil** and **disregarding the corporate entity**. <Charming, Inc. never had any assets and was never intended to have any. It was the alter ego of its only shareholders, John Doe and Mary Roe.>

alternate juror □see **jury**.

alternative dispute resolution □see **ADR**.

alternative ground of decision □see **dictum**.

alternative writ of mandamus □see **mandamus**.

ambiguity is double meaning or general uncertainty (□see **vagueness**), the same in law as in ordinary English; the consequences are different. In ordinary English, "He is my oldest friend" is ambiguous but harmless; a bequest of $10,000 to "my oldest friend" is a prelude to litigation. For the law, *ambiguity* is neither joke nor semantic abstraction; it becomes a license for a more than ordinary scope of interpretation of language. <It is "poetic justice" to construe ambiguity in favor of the borrower against the bank that created it.> Most ambiguity is inadvertent, as with words that may be clear in writing but ambiguous orally. <The slogan for Law Day was "Sharing in justice."> One species of ambiguity, peculiar to the law, is not inadvertent, the

calculated ambiguity: deliberate use of obviously unclear language in the belief of both parties that any agreement is better than none. <With all else resolved, and desperate for some agreement to avert imminent collapse of negotiations, they hit upon a calculated ambiguity, "subject to the market."> □see **latent ambiguity**.

ambulance chaser   □see **lawyer**; □see also, **barratry**.

ambulatory: ineffective until the happening of a specific event. Usually said of a will, ambulatory until the death of the testator. <During the life of the testator, the will may be revoked or changed many times; it is ambulatory.>

a mensa et thoro   □see **divorce**.

American Indian law   □see **Indian law**.

amicus brief   □see **amicus curiae**.

amicus curiae   (L., uh-MEEK-us CURE-ee-eye: friend of the court). pl. *amici curiae:* someone not a party to the litigation, but usually favoring one of the parties, and permitted to make an argument to the court, i.e., to the judge, not to a jury. Shortened to *amicus* and *amici.* The argument is usually in writing, an **amicus brief**. <The American Bar Association and the American Civil Liberties Union filed *amicus* briefs. The Court praised the briefs of the *amici.*> The Latin plural *amici curiae* is only occasionally spoken, and as a result, pronunciation of *amici* is not uniform. Variants are uh-MY-sigh, uh-MEE-chee, uh-MEE-kee, and uh-MEE-kai. The problem disappears with *friends of the court.* □see also, **brief**.

ancillary jurisdiction   □see **federal jurisdiction**, under **jurisdiction**.

and   the ordinary English word, constantly used in the law, with the same lack of precision. Sometimes it joins additional items; sometimes it doesn't. Sometimes it means *or;* sometimes it doesn't. *And* is inevitable and, like *or,* unreliable. □see **and/or**; □see **or**.

and its progeny: a cliché of reference to the many cases that have followed the lead of another case, especially one decided by the Supreme Court of the United States. <*Brown v. Board of Education* and its

and its progeny

progeny have not settled the issue.>   A learnedly indiscriminate word, applicable to animals, plants, abstractions, and rarely to friends, *progeny* is often used with the pejorative suggestion of "too much" and "I didn't like it in the first place." <The progeny spawned by that decision. . . ./We are overwhelmed by *Miranda* and its progeny.>   □see **clichés.**

and/or: an old merger of *and* with *or,* having no fixed meaning after more than a century of litigation. The allure of brevity and the phony appearance of mathematical precision convince the lazy, the ignorant, and the harried that at one stroke *and/or* covers all the possibilities of both conjunctions. If the facts are simple, that can be true <They asked damages from those who were stockholders and/or directors.>; though it still leaves it to the reader to figure out the possibilities, which may be simply stated in ordinary English <They asked damages from those who were stockholders, directors, or both.>. With the least complication, *and/or* invites controversy. "I give Blackacre to A and/or B" is pleasant enough if A and B are. If not, the simple formula tempts the avaricious—"It's all mine." The *and/or* habit, relieving the writer of decision, degenerates into a joining of impossibles <They said it was a partnership and/or limited partnership./He might be discharged and/or paroled at any time.>   and nonsense <We want an attorney with experience in taxes and/or corporate and/or SEC practice.>. Where precision is called for, *and/or* is a disaster. At best, it means counting on your fingers.

annul   □see **null and void.**

annul and set aside   □see **null and void.**

annulment   □see **divorce.**

anomalous result   □see **clichés.**

answer   □see **pleadings.**

antedate   □see **backdate,** under **nunc pro tunc.**

antenuptial agreement   □see **marital agreement.**

anticipate   □see **patent.**

anticipatory breach   □see **repudiation**.

anticipatory repudiation   □see **repudiation**.

anti-lapse statute   □see **lapse**.

antitrust law   law that prohibits or regulates some business practices that are designed to eliminate or drastically curtail competition, or to control the availability and price of goods and services. To be distinguished from the law of trusts (□see **trust**).

Basic antitrust language studiously avoids precise definition, e.g., of *restraint of trade, monopolize* or *attempt to monopolize* (Sherman Act, 26 Stat. 209, 1890, 15 USCA §§ 1–7); *discriminate in price, substantially to lessen competition* (Clayton Act, 38 Stat. 730, 1914, 15 USCA §§ 12–27; see also, Robinson–Patman Anti–Discrimination Act, 49 Stat. 1526, 1936, 15 USCA §§ 13–13b, 21a); *unfair methods of competition, unfair* or *deceptive acts* or *practices* (Federal Trade Commission Act, 38 Stat. 717, 1914, 15 USCA § 41 et seq.) (see amendments to cited statutes in 1988 edition of USCA).

A vast literature of substantive and procedural law—statute, regulation, decision, treatise—interprets these basics in widely varying contexts, federal and state. Antitrust law, as a special field of economics, is the subject of substantial, and substantially differing, treatises and articles.

For other entries referring to antitrust law:

□see **fair trade agreement**, under **fair**;

□see **fair trade law**, under **fair**;

□see **monopoly**;

□see **rule of reason**;

□see **tying arrangement**;

□see **unfair competition**.

apartment   □see **condominium**.

apparent agency   □see **agency**.

apparent authority   □see **agency**.

appeal (n., v.)

1. the procedure (the noun *appeal*) to request (the verb *appeal*) a higher court to review the judgment of a lower court. <They took an appeal from the judgment of the trial court./They appealed the judgment of the trial court.> The side *appealing* is the *appellant;* the side opposing the appeal is the *appellee* or **respondent** (□see). The court to which an appeal may be taken is an *appellate court,* one with *appellate jurisdiction* (□see **jurisdiction**) in this kind of case.

□see **appellate brief,** under **brief;** □see **notice of appeal;** □see also, **certiorari;** □see also, **judicial review;** □see also, **writ of error,** under **writ;** □see also, **writ of review,** under **certiorari.**

2. Varying by jurisdiction and statute, usage of *appeal* similar to sense 1 may apply to a court's review of an administrative ruling or to administrative review at different stages within an administrative process.

appear • appearance: acknowledging to a court that it has jurisdiction over one as a litigant in a case (*general appearance*) or in a proceeding to question the court's jurisdiction in the case (*special appearance*). The acknowledgment is made by physical participation in the courtroom procedure or by filing a pleading or a *notice of appearance.* Physical participation or filing is usually the act of a lawyer, who *appears* for the party and is said to have *entered* or *put in an appearance.* <He appeared by a local attorney./The firm of Smith & Jones entered an appearance for defendant Rogers.> Legal *appearance* is so far removed from the usage of ordinary English that special nomenclature remarks on the fact that a person can act without a lawyer: appearing **pro se** (L., PRO say: for oneself); or, appearing **in propria persona** (L., in PRO-pree-ah purr-SOWN-ah: in one's own proper person), shortened to **in pro per,** or **pro per.** The *pro per* litigant is often referred to as a *pro per.* *Pro per* is usually not italicized and risks typographical misunderstanding <It was a proper appearance.>. The choice between *pro se* and *in propria persona* (or *in pro per*) is not standardized and is sometimes dictated by symmetry of the Latin construction. <John Smith appeared for the plaintiff, the defendant pro se./In small claims courts, appearances are all in propria persona.> □see also, **pro hac vice.** □see also, **it appears that,** under **clichés.** For the ordinary sense of *appear,* □see **personally appeared,** under **jurat.**

appellant □see **appeal.**

appellate brief □see **brief.**

appellate court □see **appeal.**

appellate jurisdiction □see **jurisdiction;** □see **appeal.**

appellee □see **appeal;** □see **respondent.**

applicant the word of the ordinary language, someone who applies for something—credit, a job, etc. If the applicant applies for something legal, e.g., an injunction, *applicant* doesn't change its meaning but loses the common touch. It becomes a formal label, described as someone making or filing an *application.* Usage varies by jurisdiction. □see **petitioner;** □see also, **motion.**

application □see **motion;** □see **pleadings;** □see **applicant.**

appoint: a loose synonym for *designate* in ordinary English, with two discrete, technical applications in the law.

1. the operative term to designate the person (the *appointee*) and the property transferred to the appointee under a *power of appointment.* The action of appointing is called *exercising* the power of appointment. <Exercising the power given me in the will of J.D., I appoint the remainder of Blackacre in fee to B.>

power of appointment, often shortened to *power:* an authorization given by the *donor* of the power, an owner of property, usually real property, permitting another person (the *donee* of the power) to transfer the donor's property to the donee's appointee. The authorization specifies the property that may be transferred, how the appointment is to be made, and who may be the appointee. *Powers of appointment* are variously, and not uniformly, classified by treatise and statute, especially tax statutes. A major classification rests on the degree to which the donee's power approaches ownership of the property—the closer called a **general power;** the more remote, a **nongeneral power,** a **special power,** or a **limited power.** For example: if the appointee may be the donee, the donee's creditors, or a deceased donee's estate or its creditors, it is a *general power;* all others are *nongeneral powers* (see Restatement (Second) of Property, § 11.4).

2. the operative term to place someone in a position of public trust or of private trust under public supervision. <The governor appointed J.D. judge of the Superior Court./I appoint J.D. executor of my will.> This

appoint

sense of *appoint* is distinguished from *nominate:* to designate subject
to someone else's approval. <The President nominated J.D. to be an
associate justice of the U.S. Supreme Court, the Senate confirmed, and the
President appointed J.D. an associate justice. See U.S. Const., Art. II, § 2, cl.
2./No executor having been named in the will, the widow nominated J.D. to be
administrator, and the court appointed J.D. administrator.>

appointed counsel □see **lawyer.**

appointee □see **appoint.**

Appointments Clause: the part of the U.S. Constitution reading:
". . . and he [the President] shall nominate, and, by and with the
advice and consent of the Senate, shall appoint ambassadors, other
public ministers and consuls, judges of the Supreme Court and all
other officers of the United States, whose appointments are not herein otherwise provided for, and which shall be established by law; but
the Congress may by law vest the appointment of such inferior officers, as they think proper, in the President alone, in the courts of
law, or in the heads of departments." (Art. II, § 2). □see also,
constitutional clauses.

approach the bench: a judge's oral order to a lawyer to come closer
for conversation more informal than ordinary in the courtroom. The
conversation is usually outside the hearing of jury or witness and is
often **off the record** (□see). The form is old ritual. <Counsel, approach
the bench.> □see **formalisms;** □see also, **bench.**

approved instructions □see **jury instructions.**

approximate □see **oral.**

appurtenant □see **easement.**

appurtenant easement □see **easement.**

appurtenant equitable servitude □see **easement.**

appurtenant servitude □see **easement.**

arbiter: a little used synonym for *arbitrator*. □see **arbitration**.

arbitrary and capricious □see **abuse of discretion**.

arbitrate □see **arbitration**.

arbitration: resolving a dispute by a procedure less formal, less rule-bound than a lawsuit, and usually faster and less expensive. The arbitration is conducted and the dispute decided, not usually by a judge but by one or more *arbitrators* chosen by the parties to the dispute. *Arbitration* may refer generally to this type of dispute resolution (*arbitrating*) or to the procedure itself. <They have agreed to arbitrate their dispute/to settle their dispute by arbitration./The arbitration is to begin at 10 A.M.> *Arbitrate* may refer to what the arbitrator does or to what the parties are doing. <They have submitted their dispute to arbitration./They have agreed to arbitrate their dispute./They chose M.J. to arbitrate their dispute.>

binding arbitration In private arbitration, the parties agree in advance to the rules governing the arbitration and to be bound by the arbitrator's decision; *binding arbitration* is a recurrent redundancy. Under some statutes, a decision of the arbitrator is not final until the time for possible review or litigation has expired and is then properly referred to as *binding arbitration*.

□see also, **mediation**.

arbitrator □see **arbitration**.

arguendo (L., argue-END-o: in the course of argument): the equivalent of ordinary English *for the sake of argument,* though not conceding the point. Used in reference to something said by a lawyer or judge in courtroom discussion or by the judge in an opinion. <Assuming arguendo that defendant owned the gun, it does not follow. . . ./It was not an admission but merely something said arguendo.> English avoids the literal interpretation of *arguendo;* it is not just anything said "in the course of argument." <Assuming for the sake of argument. . . ./. . . merely something said for the sake of argument.> Prefer the English. □see **argument**.

argue with the witness □see **argument**.

argument   in the law shares the flavor of its best and worst senses in ordinary English. <Her argument was a masterpiece./The lawyers got into a violent, name-calling argument.>   Technically, *argument* is an oral or written statement in court aimed at persuading judge or jury to decide in one's favor. Within limits of honesty as to fact and law and limits of judgment and decorum as to emotional appeal, argument in an adversary system is expected to be slanted. The effort to persuade, which is the heart of argument, becomes improper, **argumentative,** when it is switched to more or less neutral areas of trial. An *argumentative question* is not merely a hostile question <Are you being paid to testify?>   but a slanted one, *arguing with the witness,* the brawling argument. <Since we all know you are being paid for this testimony, is it not the fact that . . .?>   An *argumentative instruction* to a jury goes beyond the inevitable unpleasantness of litigation   <If you find that the defendant drove down Main Street in a reckless manner. . . .> to overstress some aspect of fact or law in favor of one side. <If you find that the drunken defendant went careening down Main Street in a wild and reckless manner. . . .>

argumentative   □see **argument.**

arm's length   □see **at arm's length.**

arraignment: the formal appearance in trial court when the defendant is informed of the charge—complaint, indictment, or information—and is asked to plead to the charge—"guilty," "not guilty," or "nolo contendere." □see **guilty.**

array   □see **jury panel;** □see also, **challenge.**

arrest   □see **lawful arrest;** □see **civil arrest,** under **bail;** □see also, **false arrest,** under **imprisonment.**

arrestee: a person who has been arrested. □see **prisoner.**

arrest warrant   □see **warrant.**

article   □see **articles.**

Article I courts   □see **federal courts.**

articles

1. a generalized label for a formal instrument of more than one *article* (provision), collectively making up a contract, a statement of principle or accusation, or, especially, the basic organization of a group that will be governed by the *articles*. E.g., *articles of incorporation* (□see **corporate**); e.g., *articles of partnership* (□see **partnership**); e.g., *articles of impeachment* (□see **impeach**).

articles of incorporation are variously called *articles of organization, articles of agreement, articles of association, certificate of incorporation,* and *corporate charter.*

2. a formal instrument (as in sense 1) dependent for its effectiveness on some official action by the sovereign. E.g., the filing (□see **file**) by a secretary of state of the incorporators' *articles of incorporation.* In this sense, the expression *corporate charter* is especially appropriate (□see **Magna Carta**). This sense 2 is to be distinguished from use of *articles* in sense 1 not dependent upon action by the sovereign, e.g., *articles of partnership* or a miscellany of *articles of agreement.*

3. a collective reference to the individual provisions *article* by *article* of a formal instrument, as in a constitution, a contract, a statute, a treaty. E.g., the articles of the United States Constitution. □see **Article I courts**, under **federal courts**; □see **Article III courts**, under **federal courts**.

articles of impeachment □see **articles**; □see **impeach**.

articles of incorporation □see **articles**; □see **corporate**.

articles of partnership □see **articles**; □see **partnership**.

Article III courts □ **federal courts**; □see **constitutional**.

artificial insemination □see **parent**.

artificial person □see **person**.

as a matter of law □see **by operation of law**.

as applied □see **overbreadth**.

as if □see **actual**.

as is • with all faults: ordinary English, commonly used in sales, especially of second-hand or bargain-priced personal property, to limit the buyer's expectations and the seller's liability. Among those familiar with the expressions, they can eliminate implied but not express warranties (UCC 2316(3)(a)). <"For sale, one horse 'as is.'" The horse may be lame and not a Derby winner, but it must be a horse.>

as of course □see **of course**.

as of right □see **of course**.

as provided by law □see **by operation of law**.

assault and battery: an old combination in tort and criminal law, sometimes loosely considered as the single operation of inflicting unlawful injury. The two words are sometimes treated as synonyms. They are distinguishable, though not always distinguished by local statutes, describing the nature of the intent and the result of the act.

assault: intentionally and unlawfully putting someone in reasonable apprehension of an offensive physical contact, whether or not contact results. As a criminal offense, assault ranges from misdemeanor to felony, often described as **aggravated assault**.

battery: an intentional and unlawful physical contact, usually, but not necessarily, accompanied by an assault, e.g., striking a sleeping person—battery without assault. The criminal offense varies from misdemeanor to felony. Sometimes included in the classification of **aggravated assault**. □see also, **mayhem**.

assign • assignee • assignor • assignment

1. **assign** (v.)

   a. The verb is one of the most widely used technical terms for the transfer of rights in any sort of personal property. It is both a general word of description and an operative word. <A assigned the note to B./A assigned the account to B for collection./I assign to X: half of my half interest in the racehorse "Dandy Lion."> □see **transfer**.

   b. The verb is the technical term, descriptive and operative, for transferring rights in leases. (The lease itself is personal property, even when it is a lease of real property. □see **chattel real**, under chattel.) With a lease of real property, *assign* carries the whole leasehold interest, distinguishing it from *sublet:* transferring a portion (physical or in time) of the leasehold interest. <A leased the building to B; B assigned to C, who sublet the second floor to D.> ☐see **lease.**

c. Though not the usual word to transfer real property, the verb is sometimes loosely used to cover all property, including real property. <He assigned all of his assets to L.B. for the benefit of creditors.> Also, uncritical reliance on old forms often results in *assign* being fastened on to apter words for the transfer of real property— *give; grant; sell.* <I grant, sell, and assign Blackacre to B.> It is a worthless appendage, adding nothing but bulk.

d. In a completely different context, the verb *assign* is a synonym for *designate.* <He *assigned error* in the judge's sixth instruction to the jury.> Similarly, *assigned counsel;* ☐see **lawyer.**

2. assign (n.). The person assigning is an *assignor,* who assigns (v.) to an *assignee.* The singular noun *assign* to describe an *assignee,* recorded in general language dictionaries, is not general legal usage. But the legal plural of *assignee* is either *assignees* or *assigns.* Standing alone, the preferred plural is *assignees.* <The assignees of the lease were in default.> As an addendum to a detailed specification of persons, the preferred plural is *assigns.* <Their heirs, executors, representatives, successors, and assigns>.

3. assignment: the act of assigning, as well as the piece of paper. <They made an assignment for the benefit of creditors./The assignment of literary rights was ten pages long.>

assigned counsel   ☐see **lawyer.**

assigned error   ☐see **assign.**

assignee   ☐see **assign.**

assignment   ☐see **assign.**

assignor   ☐see **assign.**

associate   ☐see **lawyer.**

associate judge   ☐see **judge.**

associate justice □see **judge**.

association: an imprecise term for an organized group of persons with a common purpose; often distinguished from a corporation.

assumpsit (L.: he undertook): a common law form of action for recovery of damages on an express or implied contract. Generally superseded by current forms of action. Some of the uses of *assumpsit,* usually without the name, survive in the *common counts* (□see **count**), **quasi contract** (□see), and **restitution** (□see).

assumption of risk: generally, in an action based on defendant's negligence, a defense that plaintiff knew and understood the risk of injury and voluntarily assumed it. Nuances of use and disuse or abolition of the expression and the defense vary by jurisdiction, statute, decision, and rules on contributory and comparative negligence. □see also, **volenti non fit injuria**; □see also, **burden of persuasion**, under **proof**.

at arm's length • long arm statute: the *arm* metaphor of ordinary English adapted to specialized legal use.

> **at arm's length** (prep. phr.) and *arm's length* (adj., adv.): dealing with someone on the same terms applicable to everyone else under the general law of the marketplace; no special favors; no special restraints. <The fiduciary duty of good faith prohibits a trustee from dealing with his beneficiary at arm's length./She bought the stock on the basis of inside information; it was not an arm's length transaction.>

> **long arm statute:** first cousin to the colloquial *long arm of the law.* An extension of a state's personal jurisdiction to reach nonresidents, based on their acts in the state or acts outside the state affecting people or property in the state. <Though not a resident, the corporation had agents taking and filling orders here, sufficient contacts with the state to bring the corporation within the long arm statute.>

at bar • at bench □see **bar**.

at first blush • prima facie • case of first impression: a group of first impressions, in order of increasing durability.

> **at first blush:** a cliché, unchanged from the ordinary English that lawyers grow up with. It is not the blush of modesty or shock but remotely that of temporary innocence, at first glance, a first im-

pression, soon to change. <At first blush, the complaint seemed to speak of fraud, but, on analysis, the allegations negate the intent to defraud that is essential to the action.> □ see **clichés**.

prima facie (L., PRIME-a FAY-she: at first view): based on first impression, this seems to be the fact, and we will assume it is until something else changes our minds. <Plaintiff's evidence made out a *prima facie* case, sufficient to put the defendant to his proof.> □see also, **prima facie case,** under **proof.**

case of first impression: a case with some unique element never before presented for decision in this jurisdiction. A *case of first impression* remains a *case of first impression.* <Neither side has found a precedent even close; neither have I. I face the mixed joy of deciding a case of first impression.>

at law • in equity □see **law;** □see also, **equity.**

atomic energy: "[A]ll forms of energy released in the course of nuclear fission or nuclear transformation" (Atomic Energy Act of 1954, 42 USCA § 2014(c)). □see **nuclear incident.**

attach □see **attachment.**

attachment • garnishment: procedures, usually instituted by a plaintiff claiming money, to put defendant debtor's property under court control, as security for satisfaction of an eventual judgment. The procedures, when they may be invoked, and the safeguards to the defendant are regulated by statute and decision. *Attachment* is the more general term; in some usage, it includes *garnishment.*

attachment (v., *attach*): usually directed against debtor's property in the debtor's possession, with court control established by lien or through physical seizure by an officer. *Attachment* is sometimes also called a *writ of attachment* (□see **writ**).

garnishment (v., *garnish*): directed against debtor's assets in the hands of a third party (e.g., a bank, an employer), with court control usually established by threat of personal liability against the third party who releases the assets without a court order. The creditor is called the **garnisher;** the third party is the **garnishee.**

attainder □see **bill of attainder.**

attempt: generally, the crime of intentionally taking a substantial step toward committing a particular crime, with the intent to commit it, but falling short of its commission. Definitions of *attempt* vary by jurisdiction, statute, decision, and definer.

attest: to bear witness to; as, e.g., a *subscribing* or *attesting witness*. An old formalism describing what someone else has said or done. □see **subscribe;** □see also, **declaration.**

at that point in time: a cliché for "at that time," "at that moment," etc., a weary extension of the Latin *punctum temporis* (point of time), fastened to lawyers in pompous Watergate testimony. □see **clichés.**

attorney □see **lawyer.**

attorney at law □see **lawyer.**

attorney-client privilege: a person who consults a lawyer for legal advice has the right to refuse to disclose, and to prevent the lawyer from disclosing, confidential communications between them during the course of the relationship. □see also, **work product privilege.**

attorney general □see **lawyer.**

attorney in fact: an agent with specified authority; appointment as attorney in fact and details of the authority are usually in a writing called a **power of attorney.** An *attorney in fact* may, but need not be, an *attorney at law* and has no professional or licensed status or right to appear in court by virtue of holding a power of attorney. <I appointed him my attorney in fact to sign the contract for me./I gave her a general power of attorney, making her my attorney in fact for a variety of specified acts.> □see **durable power of attorney;** □see also, **durable power of attorney,** under **right to die.**

attorney of record □see **lawyer.**

attorney's fee □see **fee (attorney's fee).**

attorney's lien □see **lien.**

attractive nuisance □see child.

at will □see wrongful discharge.

authority • authorize □see agency.

authorize and empower: synonyms; choose one. The ponderous *empower* is less generally used than the all-purpose *authorize*. □see coupled synonyms.

aver □see allege.

a vinculo matrimonii □see divorce.

avoid • evade

There are old and respectably legal meanings of *avoid:* cancel, make void, show legal reason why this rule does not apply. The act of doing those things is called *avoidance,* as in a *plea in confession and avoidance:* rule and facts admitted, the application of rule to facts denied. Even more active is *avoidable consequences;* □see **duty to mitigate damages,** under **damage.**

In ordinary English, both *avoid* and *evade* have sinister connotations. <He's avoiding me./an evasive answer.> They join to cast dark shadows over tax law.

In tax law, at its clearest best, *avoidance* labels reasonable measures taken in a good faith belief that they are not taxable; *evasion* labels measures so unreasonable as to smack of bad faith or so clearly criminal as to leave no room for honest doubt. But in a labyrinth of possible arrangements of property and business, few words are at their best. With demarcation often in doubt, the force of *avoidance* has been diluted by the frequency of its assertion and the frequency of its rejection, equated with *evasion.* The linkage of *avoid/evade* creates the unwholesome suspicion that they often are (as the popular speech would have it) synonyms. <He avoided taxes, all right, by the simple device of not paying them; that's tax evasion.> In tax law, *avoidance* is not a serviceable word and is best avoided. □see also, **shun and avoid.**

avoidable consequences □see **duty to mitigate damages,** under **damage.**

41

avoidance

avoidance □see avoid.

avulsion □see accretion.

award

1. as in ordinary English, the giving of something, especially an *award of damages* as part of a **judgment** (□see).

2. the determination of a controversy by an arbitrator or an administrative agency. <The arbitration ended with an award that Local No. 55 be recognized as the bargaining representative.> □see **decision**.

a word is not a crystal Justice Oliver Wendell Holmes, Jr. made these words sparkle in *Towne v. Eisner,* 245 U.S. 418, 425 (1918): "A word is not a crystal, transparent and unchanged, it is the skin of a living thought and may vary greatly in color and content according to the circumstances and the time in which it is used." Overuse dulls the sparkle of these words. Even the aura of Holmes will not raise the level of otherwise pedestrian writing. Use with care. □see **clichés**.

B

backdate □see **nunc pro tunc**.

bad faith: a form of dishonesty, especially dishonesty designed to benefit oneself at the expense of another to whom one owes a duty. *Bad faith* is frequently contrasted with *good faith* (from the Latin *mala fide,* as opposed to **bona fide** (□see)), describing, e.g., a breach of a *covenant of good faith and fair dealing* (□see **covenant**). *Bad faith* is also sometimes equated with **fraud** (□see). Without precise definition, *bad faith* lends a flavor of double-dealing in a dozen corners of the procedural and substantive law. *Bad faith* helps, e.g., to fine lawyers for abusing **discovery** (□see) procedures; e.g., to impose liability on insurance companies for a refusal to settle; e.g., in determining whether or not to award *punitive damages* (□see **damage**); e.g., in fixing liability for a *bad faith discharge* (□see **wrongful discharge**).

bail Its many, often disparate, senses are segregated here according to usage in criminal law, civil arrest, and bailments.

bail (criminal)

1. (n.) (the security)

    a. the security deposited in court to obtain a prisoner's release from jail. If the prisoner comes to court at the time fixed, the security is returned; otherwise, it is forfeited. This is the primary sense and pattern. <"Excessive bail shall not be required. . . ." U.S. Const.Amend. VIII./The writ fixed/set bail at $10,000 and directed the sheriff to release the prisoner on posting cash or *bond./* The prisoner was admitted to bail.> □see also, **undertaking**.

    post bail: to deposit bail in court; colloquially, *put up bail, make bail.* <She posted bail and was released./They put up bail./ He made bail.>

    bail exonerated: order releasing the bail when it is no longer needed. <The charge is dismissed. Bail exonerated./The prisoner having come to court, bail was exonerated.> Similarly, when the surety (see sense 2) *surrenders* the prisoner in court, bail is exonerated.

    bail forfeited: order forfeiting bail when the prisoner fails to come to court at the time fixed, an event called colloquially *jumping bail.* <The prisoner is not here. Bail forfeited./In street

43

terms, the prisoner has jumped bail. Bail will be forfeited; warrant to issue. >

bailable (adj.): characterization of an offense subject to bail or a person who may be *bailed* (see senses 3 and 4).

b. same as the primary sense a., except that the security is deposited to prevent the jailing of one charged with a violation of the criminal law.

c. an offshoot of a. and b., the security deposited in court as part of a system of collection of fines for petty offenses (e.g., minor traffic tickets). A standardized fine is paid by the forfeiture of bail, with no expectation that the person charged will come to court. □see **citation**.

2. (n.). the person (surety) who posts bail (sense 1). <The bail bondsman did not himself *go bail for* the prisoner but obtained Fidelity Trust as corporate bail; Fidelity posted a $10,000 bond. >

3. (v.). to obtain the release of a prisoner on bail (sense 1). <His lawyer got a writ of habeas corpus and bailed him out of Central Jail. > Not to be confused with **bailout** (□see).

4. (v.). to release a prisoner on bail (sense 1). Contrasted with **release on one's own recognizance**: release from jail on prisoner's personal agreement to come to court (abbreviated **O.R.**). <The judge refused to release her O.R. but ordered her bailed/released on bail/admitted to bail./She is *out on bail.*/He is free O.R. >

bail (civil arrest): the various senses of *bail* (criminal) applied to civil cases, in jurisdictions permitting **civil arrest** to secure court appearance. □see also, **ne exeat**.

bail (bailments)

1. (v.). to deliver personal property under a contract of bailment (□see). <The corn was sacked, not baled, and was bailed at the XYZ Warehouse. >

2. *bailment* (n.). a contract under which the **bailor** delivers personal property to the **bailee** to hold for redelivery or as directed by the bailor. Absent contractual details, the law of *bailments* fixes rights and duties that go with the relationship of bailor-bailee. A bailee who charges for holding the property is a **bailee for hire** (e.g., a warehouseman); otherwise, a **gratuitous bailee**, with lesser duties of care (e.g., a friend storing furniture for the summer).

bailable □see **bail**.

Bail Clause: the part of the U.S. Constitution reading: "Excessive bail shall not be required . . ." (Amend. VIII). □see also, **bail;** □see also, **constitutional clauses.**

bailee • bailor □see bail.

bail exonerated □see bail.

bail forfeited □see bail.

bailment □see bail.

bailor □see bail.

bailout: in tax argot, an arrangement of the affairs of a business, especially a corporation, to transfer money or property to the owners without tax or at a reduced tax. <It was not a distribution of earnings but a transfer of assets—a bailout.> Not to be confused with **bail** (□see).

balancing: a common metaphor of the common speech, related etymologically to the *scales of justice* and basic to the system of law, the inevitable *weighing* of one thing against another. Lawyers are accustomed to speaking of the *weight of the evidence* as though it were something palpable. < . . . such evidence as, when weighed with that opposed to it, has more convincing force and the greater probability of truth.> They balance *equities, conveniences, inconveniences, hardships, policies,* and *interests, state interests, private interests,* even parts of the Constitution. <On balance, we are inclined to believe that plaintiff's First Amendment rights here outweigh the countervailing argument for equal protection.> Interests may be *weighty,* of *greater weight, outweigh* other interests. We imagine something *tipping the balance* or *the scales* in favor of this position or this person. Sooner or later, an opposing sense of *balancing* comes to mind, not *outweighing* but of *equal weight.* Sometimes, a sense of stability. <If the evidence is evenly balanced. . . .> *Balancing tests* for unevenness or equality neither settle anything for very long, nor do they give precise guidance to decision. A further metaphor of the common speech is as apt as the others—the *balancing act:* the tightrope walker, high above the tumult, desperately trying to maintain a *balance* that will get him from here to there.

balancing equities ☐see **balancing**.

balancing interests ☐see **balancing**.

banc ☐see **bench**.

bank

1. A financial enterprise whose primary business is lending money. Incidental to that, the enterprise may borrow, exchange, and collect money; buy, sell, and issue commercial paper and securities; act as intermediary between other lenders and borrowers; and generally engage in almost limitless varieties of financial business. One of the most conspicuous of that variety is the borrowing of money by receiving deposits from customers (who thus lend money to the bank), the bank in return offering checking and savings accounts, interest at varying rates on various types of accounts, and miscellaneous services, e.g., safeguarding money and valuables. Statutes must be consulted for special or local definitions of *bank* or special kinds of bank.

2. A financial enterprise (sense 1), but not called a *bank* unless it "*both* (i) accepts demand deposits or deposits that the depositor may withdraw by check or similar means for payment to third persons or others; *and* (ii) is engaged in the business of making commercial loans" (Bank Holding Co. Act, 12 USCA § 1841(c)(1)(B), as amended 1987; italics added).

nonbank bank: a financial enterprise (sense 1), but not called a *bank* (sense 2), because it does not perform *both* of the specified functions.

demand deposit: a deposit that the depositor can withdraw as a matter of right, as distinguished from a *time deposit*.

time deposit: a deposit on which notice of a specified time may be required before withdrawal of any money.

NOW account, also called *N.O.W. account:* the generally used name for one kind of time deposit account, with funds withdrawable by a **negotiable order of withdrawal** (acronym **NOW**): an instrument payable to anyone, like a check, except that the bank or other financial enterprise may, but does not usually, require prior notice of withdrawal. A *NOW account* is a common type of time account referred to in *bank* (sense 2) as "deposits that the depositor may withdraw by check or similar means . . . .," as opposed to demand deposits.

banking day □see **time.**

bankrupt a waning epithet and name for the debtor in **bankruptcy** (□see).

bankruptcy

1. the condition of a debtor subject to the bankruptcy laws, whether by *voluntary* or *involuntary* proceedings. <They were in bankruptcy.> For specifics of all senses of *bankruptcy,* one must turn to the bankruptcy laws of the United States, as authorized by the U.S. Constitution (Art. I, § 8, cl. 4; see Title 11, USCA). □see also, **insolvent.**

2. **voluntary bankruptcy:** proceedings under the bankruptcy laws to obtain permanent or temporary relief from the burden of debt as rehabilitation of the debtor, coupled with equitable protection of creditors.

3. **involuntary bankruptcy:** proceedings forcing a debtor to become subject to the bankruptcy laws, as a collection device to facilitate an equitable marshalling and division of debtor's property.

bankruptcy court □see **bankruptcy judge,** under **judge.**

bankruptcy judge □see **judge.**

bar

1. collectively, all the lawyers, or all the lawyers of a particular jurisdiction or organization. <*Bench and bar* have a joint responsibility./ The bar took no stand on that ballot proposition./The federal bar is governed by local rules in each district./The American Bar Association is the largest organization of lawyers.> Distinguished from usage in England, where *bar* refers to *barristers,* as opposed to *solicitors.*

integrated bar: collectively, all the lawyers of a jurisdiction that requires membership in a state bar organization as a condition of practicing law. <California has an integrated bar; to practice, you must be a member of the State Bar of California.>

2. in specialized phrases of uncertain etymology, the equivalent of **practice of law** (□see **lawyer**), flavored with the sense of joining the community of lawyers (sense 1) and acquiring the right to be inside the courtroom railing (sense 4).

47

admitted to the bar: licensed to practice law; synonymous with *admitted to practice.* When the context is clear, often shortened to *admitted.* <She graduated law school in 1980 and was admitted in New York the same year.> □see **lawyer.**

bar examination: an examination, with passing (*pass the bar*) a prerequisite to being *admitted to the bar.*

disbar: to take away a lawyer's license to practice law generally or before particular courts. <He has been disbarred in Maryland, and disbarment proceedings are pending in two other states./He was disbarred from practice before the U.S. Supreme Court./He was disbarred from state practice in Ohio but not from practice in the federal courts sitting in Ohio.>

3. a court in session, with a judge on the bench, as in ordinary English *at the bar of justice.* <*Prisoner at the bar,* do you know of any reason why this court should not pass sentence upon you?/It has been said at bar that a fair trial is impossible in this city.>

case at bar: this case, now being heard by this court. A newer expression, **case at bench,** is sometimes said to apply only to a case before an appellate court or to a case heard by a judge without a jury, but in practice is used indiscriminately as synonymous with *case at bar.* <In the case at bar/at bench, the facts are undisputed.> Both versions are circumlocutions, in argument and in opinions, to distinguish *this* case from others. <In *Smith v. Jones,* plaintiff asked damages only; in the case at bar, plaintiff wants specific performance.> The expressions have no technical significance. Prefer ordinary language. <In this case/Here, plaintiff wants specific performance.>

sidebar: a conference between lawyers and the judge at the bench but outside the hearing of others in court, often **off the record** (□see); also, something said at such a conference. <The jurors strained to hear what was being said at sidebar./That was only sidebar, Your Honor.>

4. the courtroom railing separating spectators from participants, especially the lawyers, in court proceedings. <Step inside the bar and take the stand.>

5. In a completely different sense, *bar* and *barred* refer to a legal obstacle, especially one that defeats a claim. E.g., *barred* by judgment (□see **res judicata**); *barred by the statute* (□see **statute of limitations**). □see also, **plea in bar,** under **plea.**

bare: not covered by malpractice insurance. The word is used by professionals generally, especially doctors and lawyers. <The rates were so high, he decided to *travel bare.*/Whether you are bare or insured, take a look at this new policy.>

bar examination □see **bar.**

bargain □see **contract.**

barratry • champerty • maintenance: related common law offenses designed to discourage litigation. Grounded on ancient, medieval, and religious views of litigation as an intrinsic evil and as a disquieting threat to the secular status quo. The offenses survive in limited forms, severely restricted by less categorical condemnation of litigation and by decisions invoking the U.S. Constitution (Amends. VI, I, & XIV) on right to counsel, on access to the court system, and protecting some forms of solicitation and advertising by lawyers. These decisions have been followed by relaxed professional regulation.

barratry: habitually stirring up litigation. Surviving statutes rarely enforced. Indirect survival: (1) suits for **malicious abuse of process** (□see) and **malicious prosecution** (□see); (2) fining the **vexatious litigant:** one who repeatedly files groundless lawsuits and repeatedly loses; (3) increasingly rigorous court-imposed penalties against lawyers for bringing **frivolous** (groundless) legal proceedings; and (4) prohibitions against crasser types of personal solicitation of employment for lawyers, by their agents (called **cappers** and **runners**), and by lawyers themselves. □see **ambulance chaser,** under **lawyer.**

champerty: investing in someone else's lawsuit for a share of the recovery. Generally alive and illegal, but some important contracts, once *champertous* (and illegal), no longer are: (1) lawyer's **contingency fee:** services for a percentage of the recovery; (2) **collection agency:** a business that receives an assignment of a cause of action for money damages (usually smaller, routine cases), undertaking to collect the money by threat or suit in exchange for a percentage of the recovery.

maintenance: financing someone else's lawsuit, with or without a share of the recovery. Without an agreement for a share of the recovery, *maintenance* is dead. With a share, it is assimilated to *champerty.*

barred by the statute □see **statute of limitations.**

barrister □see **bar.**

base fee □see **fee simple.**

49

Basket Clause: another name for the **Necessary and Proper Clause** (□see).

battered child □see child.

battery □see assault and battery.

bearer paper □see commercial paper.

bearing date □see formalisms.

bed and board □see divorce.

before me □see formalisms.

being first duly sworn deposes and says □see formalisms.

be it remembered □see formalisms.

bench (O.E., *benc;* O.F., *banc;* L., *bancus:* a bench): personification of a *bench* to mean *judge,* in varied usage often reflecting the etymology.

1. collectively, all the judges, or all the judges of a particular court. <*Bench and bar* have a joint responsibility./With uncommon unanimity, the Ninth Circuit bench indorsed the change.>

2. the office of judge. <He's been *on the bench* for ten years./The federal bench is a lifetime appointment.>

3. a judge, or group of judges, presiding over a case in court. <Counsel, *approach the bench.*/The defendant wanted a **bench trial,** but the prosecutor refused to *waive a jury.*/The judge issued a **bench warrant** for the immediate arrest of the missing witness./The bench was obviously interested in the argument.> □see also, **court;** □see also, **warrant.**

4. the place in court where the judge usually sits, on a chair behind a sort of desk, which is usually on a dais at the front of the courtroom. <Counsel, *approach the bench.*/The judge is *in chambers;* she will *take the bench* at 3 P.M./Without leaving the bench, the judge stood up and moved closer to the whispering witness.>

5. en banc (O.F., UHN bank: on the bench): usually the entire group, or nearly all, of the judges of a court sitting together to hear a case, usually on appeal. *En banc* is contrasted with **panel** (□see). In the U.S. Court of Appeals for the Ninth Circuit, *en banc* can mean a group of eleven out of the twenty-eight judges of the court. <The three-judge panel split, and a rehearing was ordered for consideration by the three and their colleagues *en banc*.> *En banc* sometimes appears in the translated form *In Bank*.

enbancworthy: meriting consideration *en banc;* slang on the model of *certworthy*. □see **certiorari**.

6. **case at bench** □see **case at bar**, under **bar**.

bench and bar □see **bench**; □see **bar**.

bench trial □see **bench**.

bench warrant □see **bench**; □see **warrant**.

beneficial owner □see **beneficiary**.

beneficiary • beneficial owner All *beneficial owners* are *beneficiaries,* but not all *beneficiaries* are *beneficial owners*.

beneficiary: one who benefits, or may hope to benefit, from a legal arrangement. The title *beneficiary* applies before and after benefit is received and even if no benefit is received. <She was the sole beneficiary under J.D.'s air travel insurance policy. The flight was completed without incident./The two children were the beneficiaries named in the will, but they received nothing; by the date of death, the property had long since been sold.>

beneficiary of a trust □see **beneficial owner**, below.

beneficiary under a will □see **gift**.

third party beneficiary: a *beneficiary* under a contract to which the *beneficiary* is not a party. <A contracted with B to provide life care for C; a side effect was that D was relieved of an obligation to support C. C was an **express third party beneficiary,** D an **incidental beneficiary.**>

beneficial owner: a *beneficiary* plus. One who does not have the legal title to property but has the right to have the property used for his benefit. A synonym for **equitable owner**. □see **equity**.

beneficiary of a trust: the *beneficial owner* of property held in trust. Legal title to the property is in a *trustee*. <Under the will, Blackacre was given to X Bank in trust for A and B, beneficiaries of the trust.

beneficiary

Tax bills went to the trustee X, not to the beneficial owners A and B. > The expression *beneficiary of a trust* has the same meaning and is just as legal, easier to spell, and easier to pronounce than the older, still often used, **cestui que trust** (law F., SET-uh kuh trust: he for whom is the trust). The latter expression is affectionately known by older lawyers as the *cetty*. Prefer the legal slang, *benny*.

benefit of the bargain □see out of pocket.

benefit of the bargain rule □see out of pocket.

benevolent □see charitable.

bequeath • bequest □see give, under gift.

bequest □see gift.

Berne Convention □see copyright.

best evidence: the best evidence available, a relative not a fixed standard. **best evidence rule:** in deciding on admissibility of evidence, prefer the best evidence available; no absolute criteria. < The best evidence of the writing is the original, if available; if not, a copy may be best, better than a recollection. > Usage varies by jurisdiction. The *best evidence rule* is sometimes called the *original document rule* or the *original writing rule*. □see **secondary evidence**; □see **absolutes**.

best evidence rule □see best evidence.

bestiality □see crime against nature.

beyond a reasonable doubt means *beyond a reasonable doubt*. Tortured explanations are worthless. A juror wrestles with conscience to decide whether the civilized decency of the *presumption of innocence* saves the accused or has been stretched too thin for the saving. The system asks too much when it instructs a juror to dissect out of *beyond a reasonable doubt* some nuance of precise meaning where generations of lawyers have found none. The only precision here is the awesome invocation of the **presumption of innocence:** innocent until proved guilty *beyond a reasonable doubt*. That is a sufficient reason to hang on to the phrase—and to leave it alone. □see **proof**; □see **presumption**.

beyond control   □see **act of God**.

b.f.p.   □see **bona fide purchaser**.

bias   of a witness, a judge, or a prospective juror is too important to be left to ordinary English. It needs help and gets it. The law makes three words grow where one grew before.

bias: ordinary, old-fashioned English *bias*, a predisposed way of looking at something; used in general discussion about the prejudices of witnesses, parties, judges, and jurors. <On cross-examination, it became apparent that the witness's credibility suffered from a longstanding bias against the plaintiff./Is it possible for them to overcome their freely expressed racial prejudice and become unbiased jurors or judges?>

actual bias: ordinary old-fashioned English *bias* used in reference to disqualification of a judge or prospective juror and to distinguish *implied bias*. <Before being assigned to the case, the judge told reporters that the defendant was a killer. Counsel *moved to recuse* the judge for actual bias. □see **recuse**, under **disqualify**./The third prospective juror admitted on *voir dire* that he tended to identify the defendant actress with the disgusting roles she played on the screen. Challenge for actual bias.> Properly used, *actual bias* serves a purpose; sloppily used, it is redundant. <I mean he was actually biased.> □see **actual**.

implied bias: special grounds for disqualification, such as relationship with one of the lawyers, whether or not the judge or prospective juror is affected by *actual bias*. <She may be fair minded, but I couldn't risk the possible influence of her relationship to the other lawyer; I filed a challenge on the ground of implied bias.> Sometimes also called *presumed bias*. □see also, **imply**.

bilateral contract   □see **contract**.

bill   □see **pleadings**; □see also, **cross-bill**, under **cross-**; □see also, **indictment**.

bill in the nature of interpleader   □see **interpleader**.

bill of attainder: a legislative act that inflicts punishment on named persons or a group of persons without a judicial trial. Historically,

bill of attainder

an English *bill of attainder* applied to capital offenses, and a *bill of pains and penalties* applied the same legislative treatment to lesser offenses; *bill of attainder* now covers both and is prohibited by the U.S. Constitution. □see **Bill of Attainder Clauses**.

Bill of Attainder Clauses: the parts of the U.S. Constitution reading: "No bill of attainder . . . shall be passed." (Art. I, § 9); and "No state shall . . . pass any . . . bill of attainder. . . ." (Art. I, § 10). When the context is clearly to Article I, § 9 or to Article I, § 10, the reference is simply to *the* Bill of Attainder Clause. □see also, **constitutional clauses**.

bill of exchange □see **commercial paper**.

bill of lading □see **document of title**.

bill of pains and penalties □see **bill of attainder**; □see **pains and penalties**.

bill of particulars: the formal name for **discovery** (□see) by the defendant in a criminal case to obtain details of the alleged crime. Also, the older name for discovery of details by either side in a civil case, the name *bill of particulars* often superseded by *motion* or other discovery procedures.

Bill of Rights

1. the first ten amendments to the U.S. Constitution.

2. state constitutional provisions similar to those in sense 1.

3. the substance of the constitutional provisions (senses 1 and 2), often spelled *bill of rights*.

bill quia timet □see **quia timet**.

binding agreement □see **contract**.

binding arbitration □see **arbitration**.

binding contract □see **contract**.

54

bindover □see **preliminary hearing**.

Blackacre: a fictitious piece of real estate, useful in legal literature and teaching as a setting for hypothetical questions. <Suppose A, intending to build on Blackacre, builds partly on Blackacre and partly on adjacent Whiteacre.> The property is centuries old, with uncounted thousands of owners, renters, and trespassers. The law has never set limits to the imaginable location, shape, size, contours, or price of *Blackacre*. Only the name remains fixed. That is traditional, without substantial competition from the secondary acreage *Whiteacre* or *Greenacre*. Yet for all its ubiquity and utility, despite speculation and learned research, the origin and reason, if any, for the name *Blackacre* remains one of the mysteries of common law.

black letter law: succinct statement of basic rules of law; also called **hornbook law.** <Negligence is the absence of due care. That's black letter law, hornbook law; don't forget it.> Sometimes, a pejorative. <All he writes is black letter law; if you want the wrinkles, look elsewhere.>

blackmail □see **extortion**.

blank indorsement □see **indorsement**.

blasphemy: the offense of using language intentionally abusive of God, religion, or the elements or symbols of religious doctrine. The offense is of dubious constitutionality. Prosecution is a rarity. □see **profanity**.

blind □see **legally blind**.

blind trust □see **trust**.

blue laws: Sunday closing laws, or other laws thought to reflect puritanical morals. <The dance halls are closed on Sunday; part of their blue laws.>

blue ribbon jury □see **jury**.

blue sky laws: laws regulating public sale of securities; a lingering reference from an earlier day of unregulated freedom to peddle worthless stock. <They were selling the blue sky; enter the blue sky laws.> The expression has lost ground to *corporate securities laws.*

board   □see **director.**

board of directors   □see **director.**

boilerplate: stereotyped language—words, phrases, paragraphs, pages, whole contracts—printed, numbered, indexed, filed, computerized, waiting to be used. *Boilerplate* is cheap, easy, plentiful, time-saving, brainsaving, treacherous. Too easy to discover too late that what was plated needed more boiling.   <The boilerplate introduction reads: "Now therefore, in consideration of the agreements hereinafter made and entered into, the aforesaid parties hereto agree." It means: "We agree.">

bona fide (adj., adv., L., BONE-a FIED; in good faith); **bona fides** (n., L., BONE-a FIED-ease: good faith).

1. good faith. In a general way, distinguishes the honest, if mistaken, action or person from the dishonest. The dishonest is expressed in the less used Latin *mala fide* (in bad faith) and *mala fides* (bad faith). Although *bona fide* and *bona fides* (the less ubiquitous noun) have been around for centuries in both civil and criminal law, they have no more legal precision than the ordinary English that has adopted them. Sometimes they are interpreted as only "honesty in fact," sometimes as honesty plus.   <If we follow the notion of "the pure heart and the empty head," they acted bona fide; but the more rigorous standard of good faith for the merchant means "honesty in fact and the observance of reasonable commercial standards of fair dealing in the trade" (UCC 2–103(1)(b)).> Ordinary English and the law use *bona fide* and *good faith* indiscriminately. Some prefer *bona fide* for a touch of class or to indulge a phantasy of Latinate precision.   <They made repeated bona fide/good faith efforts to comply./Though clearly misinformed, his bona fides/good faith is unquestioned.> Used without other law words, *good faith* should be the choice over *bona fide* and over the awkward, always singular *bona fides.* The combination **bona fide purchaser** (□see) is a different story. □see also, **covenant of good faith and fair dealing,** under **covenant;** □see also, **bad faith.**

2. (adj.): genuine. A subsidiary and even less precise usage.   <It was a bona fide Leonardo.>

bona fide purchaser   is the way the expression usually appears in print, but orally, and in student examinations, in student's and lawyer's notes, it is never called anything but **b.f.p.** <The judge said the buyer was a bee-eff-pee.>

1. good faith purchaser for value. That is the usual, quick, and uninformative definition. It is no more than the general understanding of the profession, rarely made explicit, that *b.f.p.* is not merely short for *bona fide purchaser* but that both abbreviation and expression are short for *good faith purchaser for value.* The addition of *for value,* itself not precise (☐see **value**), at least rules out the recipient of a gift as a *b.f.p.* Without that qualification, the possibility is there. ☐see **words of purchase**.

2. good faith purchaser. The literal translation is a frequent substitute for the words *bona fide purchaser.* While caution is dictated to make certain that something else is not intended, one is left to infer that the words *good faith purchaser* (like *b.f.p.* and *bona fide purchaser*) are also short for *good faith purchaser for value.* With that caveat, sense 2 is a verbal, not a substantive, variation of sense 1, and the abbreviation of *good faith purchaser* is *b.f.p.*, not *g.f.p.f.v.*

3. a label for a decision that as between two honest people who both stand to suffer from another's dishonesty, this is the one who should win the toss. <By a fraudulent trick, B acquires A's personal property and sells it to C, who is ignorant of B's fraud. C is a bona fide purchaser, and can keep the property free of a claim by A.> The criteria for affixing the label *bona fide purchaser* are (1) good faith, (2) the giving of value, and (3) lack of notice of wrongdoing; but the content of each of these criteria varies with decision and statute.

☐see also, **purchaser for value**.

bond

1. in a general sense, a formal writing evidencing a promise to pay money in accordance with the detailed provisions of the writing. *Bond* refers to the piece of paper as well as the obligation. <They posted bond.> It is an old form of unilateral contract (☐see **contract**), supplanted by the promissory note (☐see **commercial paper**) for routine money matters, and now used for specialized purposes, e.g.:

☐see **bail bond**, under **bail**;

☐see **bond to keep the peace**, under **peace bond**;

☐see **completion bond**, under **performance bond**;

☐see **general obligation bond**, under **full faith and credit**;

☐see **peace bond**;

☐see **penal bond**, under **penal**;

bond

□see **performance bond;**

□see **revenue bond,** under **full faith and credit.**

For use of the bond in corporate finance, see paragraph 2 of this entry below.

2. a corporate writing, evidencing a promise to pay money, with interest, issued in series, typically issued for long-term corporate borrowing. Like stock, the *bond* is a *corporate security* but represents *debt* (borrowed money) as distinct from *equity* ownership (stock). Every corporate bond is its own contract, and though it is a corporate security, security by way of mortgage or other lien on corporate assets is not a uniform characteristic.

debenture, also called *debenture bond:* a less common name for a corporate *bond.* The distinction, often made, that *bonds* are "secured" and *debentures* "unsecured" cannot be relied on. Usage is not precise.

bondsman   □see **bail.**

bond to keep the peace   □see **peace bond.**

boycott: organized refusal to have dealings with someone as a means of exerting pressure to attain an objective, usually political or economic. The target of a boycott may be an individual, a group, or a country but is usually a business.

primary boycott: a *boycott* directed against the target of a demand. < The farm workers' union urged the public not to buy Salinas Valley grapes until the growers of those grapes recognized the union. >

secondary boycott: a *boycott* directed against someone who has dealings with the target of a demand. < The farm workers' union urged the public not to buy *anything* from stores that bought Salinas Valley grapes until the growers of those grapes recognized the union. >

brain death   □see **absolutes.**

Brandeis brief: an appellate brief of the type introduced by lawyer Louis D. Brandeis in successful support of the constitutionality of a law fixing maximum hours of work for women (*Muller v. Oregon,* 208 U.S. 412, 419–421, 1908). A *Brandeis brief* goes outside the trial record, calling the court's attention to public facts (legislation, statis-

tics, sociological and economic studies, opinions of investigators, etc.) as relevant background to the controversy. □see also, **judicial notice**.

breach • break: old synonyms of ordinary English for the fact and action of *breaking,* as the use of force to damage or intrude, and the figurative extension into *violation.* Long use has hardened some habitual legal usages and blurred others. With some exceptions, *breach* tends to be the more technical. The more violent is *break,* which has expanded to include a special sense of *destroying* an intangible.

breach

1. (n.). the fact of violation of an agreement. The common phrases are *breach of contract, breach of promise* (i.e., of marriage), *breach of trust, breach of warranty.* The gerund *breaching* is stiff, rarely used; *breaking the contract* (promise, trust, warranty) is informal and intelligible but to the legal eye and ear lacks the definitive, technical charge of *breach.* <Selling outside the allotted territory constituted breaking the contract/a breach of contract.> Prefer *breach.* □see **anticipatory breach,** under **repudiation.**

2. (v.). action of violating an agreement. Usage varies with agreement, audience, and purpose.

  a. For *contracts* generally, including warranty, both *breach* and *break* are used. The most intelligible to the widest audience is *break;* the technical edge is with *breach.* <They broke the contract/breached the contract.> Addressing a jury, use *break.* Addressing a judge on a nuance of contract law, use *breach.* <They breached the implied covenant of fair dealing.> To express any level of dudgeon, by all means *break.* <*They* broke the contract!>

  b. For *promises* of any sort, whether or not promise of marriage, the only word is the ordinary, untechnical English verb *break,* correlative of *keep.*

  c. For a formal *trust, breach* is used, but more often in reference to the obligations of the trust (or trustee). <The trustee breached the trust agreement by. . . ./The trustee breached the obligations imposed by the trust.> On a detailed specification, supplant *breach* with *violate.* <They violated Article 2 of the trust agreement.> *Break* should not be used at all. □see **break,** under **breach.**

3. **breach of the peace** (n.), also called *disturbance of the peace* (n.) and referred to by the verb forms *disturbing the peace* and *to disturb the peace:* a catchall for causing a public disturbance.

breach

Specific criminal violations are usually spelled out. <It was a breach of the peace all right, but whether riot or unlawful assembly remains to be decided.> □see also, **riot;** □see also, **fighting words.**

break

1. (v.). action of violating an agreement. Less technical, more emphatic than *breach.* □see **breach.**

2. (v.). to have an agreement declared invalid. Argot; not a term of art. <I can break that contract./They sued to break the will./They broke the trust, and the assets have been distributed./They broke up the combination as monopolistic.>

3. (v.). to *violate* the law: *break the law;* not a technical usage.

4. miscellaneous acts of criminal violence (*violations* of law), ranging from the untechnical *break in* and *jailbreak* to the common law definition of **burglary:** *breaking and entering* a dwelling at night with intent to commit a felony, also called *housebreaking.* For current definitions of *burglary,* consult local statutes. □see also, **knock and announce.**

breaking bulk: unauthorized opening of bailed packages or a sealed freight car and taking the contents.

breach of contract □see **breach;** □see **contract.**

breach of promise □see **breach;** □see **contract.**

breach of the peace □see **breach.**

breach of trust □see **breach;** □see **trust.**

breach of warranty □see **breach;** □see **warranty.**

break □see **breach.**

breaking and entering □see **break, under breach.**

breaking bulk □see **break, under breach.**

Brethren • Sistern   Until September 25, 1981, *Brethren* was a customary reference to fellow justices in opinions of the U.S. Supreme Court; favored especially in dissenting opinions of the older justices.   *Brethren* was an antique alternating with *Brother.*   <As I have noted so often, on this issue, my Brethren persist in the path of error./"My Brother Harlan's opinion. . . ."> When the first woman took her seat on the Court, *Brethren* dropped from mere antique to indiscretion, except at the option of Justice Sandra Day O'Connor; *Brethren and Sister* was pointedly awkward; *Sister* indelicate.   It now seems likely that these quaint expressions of a formal collegiality have disappeared for good, beyond possible resurrection as *Brethren and Sistern.*   Amen.   □see also, **sex**; □see also, **formalisms**.

bribe   □see **bribery**.

briber   □see **bribery**.

bribery: a felony or misdemeanor in a multitude of state and federal statutes.   The statutes are not uniform.   They forbid a variety of acts, as set out generally in paragraphs 1 and 2 of this entry, with a sampling of potential defendants in paragraph 3.

1.   the crime committed by the *briber:* offering, giving, or agreeing to give a person something of value (the *bribe*) intended to persuade that person to betray a trust, especially a public trust, or in exchange for that person's betraying or agreeing to betray that trust.   *Bribery* in this sense may be committed independently of *bribery* (sense 2), e.g., bribery, though the offered bribe is rejected or ignored.

2.   the crime committed by someone other than the briber: a person who asks for or voluntarily receives or agrees to receive something of value (the *bribe*) in exchange for that person's betraying or agreeing to betray a trust, especially a public trust.   *Bribery* in this sense may be committed independently of *bribery* (sense 1); e.g., bribery, though the bribe asked for is refused or ignored.   *Bribery* (sense 2) is sometimes equated with **extortion** (□see).

3.   the betrayal of trust that is the essence of bribery traditionally has referred to the trust imposed in the honesty of public officials, e.g., a judge, an executive, an administrator.   It has been extended to include others with a legal duty to perform honestly, e.g., a juror, a witness, a voter (not to sell the vote nor to take pay for not voting).   It has also been extended to **commercial bribery**: a faithless employee, a corrupting competitor (□see **unfair competition**).

61

brief: a written statement of facts and law supporting one side of a case and presented to a court, especially an appellate court (*appellate brief*).   Prepared by lawyers, typically in outline form, briefs are more or less "brief," with limits often imposed by court rules.   In complex cases, a brief may also be prepared for a trial court, instead of a more usual *memorandum of points and authorities:* a short outline of the issues and supporting law.   □see also, **amicus brief,** under **amicus curiae.**

Brief, as described here, is to be distinguished from a *trial brief:* an indexed compilation of issues, facts, law, exhibits, witnesses, expected testimony, etc., prepared for use by trial lawyers, sometimes with copies to a trial judge.

bright line: a sharp distinction between related cases or between related legal principles, the *bright line* is customarily referred to by its absence.   A sad cliché with a sadder companion.   A *bright line* is what you don't get when you *paint with a broad brush:* writing an opinion too generalized to be instructive.   <No bright line here; they painted with a broad brush, leaving the labor of distinguishing close cases to a befuddled posterity.>   □see **clichés.**

broad brush   □see **bright line.**

buggery   □see **crime against nature.**

burden of going forward with the evidence   □see **proof.**

burden of persuasion   □see **proof.**

burden of producing evidence   □see **proof.**

burden of proof   □see **proof.**

burglarize: an untechnical verb to describe *burglary* (□see **breach**).   The variant *burgle* is a joke.

burglary   □see **breach;**   □see also, **burglarize.**

burgle   □see **burglarize.**

business corporation   □see **corporate.**

business day   □see **time.**

business judgment rule: a court will not interfere with the running of a corporation by its directors, officers, or controlling stockholders when they act reasonably and in good faith within their corporate authority. <The dissenters do not claim that management acted unreasonably or from ulterior motives, only that they could have negotiated a more profitable deal. The business judgment rule prevents us from second guessing a reasonable, if imperfect, call.>

business trust   □see **trust.**

business visitor   □see **invitee.**

buy • purchase

　buy   (v., O.E.): acquiring property by paying for it. This is ordinary English used in the law; in this sense, O.F. *purchase* is a synonym. <I'll buy/purchase the candy./We bought/purchased the house.>   It is a sales pitch and not the law that insists on *buying* a pig and *purchasing* a diamond. The use of *buy* (and *buyer*) is closer to life, avoids unnecessary confusion with the special senses of *purchase* (and *purchaser*), and is preferred in the law as the ordinary correlative of **sell** (□see).   <I agree to sell and you agree to buy./Buyer and seller agree.>

　buy/sell agreement: agreement between co-owners that either may buy the other out at a stated price or by a stated formula. Argot, not a term of art; sometimes applied to an ordinary agreement of sale.

　buying (n.): the general fact of acquiring property and paying for it. This too is ordinary English used in the law; in this sense, O.F. *purchasing* is a synonym.   <Buying/purchasing is a business.> Again, *buying* is preferred.

　purchase   (n., adj., O.F.): the completed act of *buying* and what is *bought*. This is ordinary English used in the law. The ordinary English sense of *buy* (n.), as a *bargain* <It was a real buy.>, has no special place in the law, but by historical accident, the simple noun to complement the O.E. verb *buy* is the O.F. *purchase*.   <The buyer said it was a purchase on credit./It was the largest purchase in the history of the business.>   Working from this base (there but for the grace of

God goes *buy*), O.F. *purchase* has carved out several niches in legal usage.

purchase money mortgage: a mortgage that secures the unpaid balance of the purchase price.

purchase price: the total agreed price of any purchase.

□see also, **bona fide purchaser.** □see also, **vendor and purchaser, under sell.** □see also, **words of purchase.**

buy/sell agreement □see buy.

by and with: common old synonyms, worthless as a pair and to be shunned, *except* as the now fixed unit of reference to the role of the Senate in the constitutional treaty-making and appointing powers of the President. <"He shall have power, by and with the advice and consent of the Senate to make treaties . . . and by and with the advice and consent of the Senate, shall appoint. . . ." U.S. Const. Art. II, § 2, cl. 2.> □see **coupled synonyms;** □see **formalisms.**

by operation of law: a shorthand way of saying that on these facts, the law creates a particular status, without formal legal action by the parties affected. <Having been in adverse possession for the statutory period, he acquired *title by operation of law.*/The proceeds of A's property belong to A. Though in B's hands, the proceeds are held by B as *trustee by operation of law.*>

Something *by operation of law* is also so *as a matter of law* and *as provided by law.* Each expression emphasizes a different aspect of a common theme, the dictate of law.

as a matter of law: general reference to a conclusion that on these facts, the law requires this result. <He had been in adverse possession for the statutory period. As a matter of law, the title was his./As a matter of law, B holds the proceeds of A's property as trustee for A.>

as provided by law: reference to specific parts of the law, often statutory. <As provided by law, adverse possession for the statutory period gives the adverse possessor title./As provided by law, who owns the cow owns the calf. B must deliver the calf to A.>

bystanders □see products liability.

by virtue of □see formalisms; □see also, virtue; □see also, force and effect.

C

©: "the letter C in a circle," the symbol that is an alternative to "Copyright" or "Copr." in the notice of copyright of "visually perceptible" works. Generally understood to mean that the work is *copyrighted.* (See 17 USCA § 401(a), (b); see also, the Universal Copyright Convention, Art. III(1).) For "phonorecords of sound recordings," the notice of copyright requires the symbol ℗, "the letter P in a circle." (See 17 USCA § 402(a), (b).) □see **copyright.**

C.A.F. □see **C. & F.**

calculated ambiguity □see **ambiguity.**

calendar month □see **time.**

calendar year □see **time.**

call □see **option.**

callable □see **redeemable bonds,** under **redeem.**

cancel • terminate: to end.

1. Ordinary English synonyms, imprecise, and disgustingly interchangeable, except for these special uses of *terminate:*

    a. To emphasize *expiration* of a period, *terminate* or *expire,* but not *cancel,* usually supplants *end.* <Under Article I, the policy terminated/expired/ended at midnight, January 10.>

    b. The euphemism for *fire.* <She was terminated without cause.>

    c. The slang euphemism for *kill.* <There was a contract out on Pogo; Pogo, Jr. had already been terminated.>

2. If no one is interested in why there was an *end,* who did it, or whether anything survives the *end,* both *cancel* and *terminate,* together or separately, are usually needless complications. The word is *end.* <They canceled/terminated/ended the agreement and went about their business.>

3. If anyone is interested in the genesis or consequences of *ending,* neither *cancel* nor *terminate,* separately or together, is much help.

65

cancel

<I have canceled our agreement./Our agreement is terminated./By this letter, we cancel and terminate our agreement.> The basic questions remain: (1) Was the *cancellation* or *termination* a breach? (2) Because of a breach? (3) Is everything wiped out—past, present, future? A statutory definition may essay answers (see UCC 2–106(3), (4)). But *cancel* and *terminate* bounce in a constant turbulence of equating, differentiating, equivocating. They are uncertain companions in a pinch. If precision is the goal, don't depend on them. Spell out the consequences of *ending*.

4. Both words are to be distinguished from *rescind,* which is not to *end* but to *undo.*

C. & F. • **C.A.F.** • **C.F.:** standard abbreviations for *cost and freight.* Any of these groups of letters following a price means that the price includes the cost of the goods and freight to the destination but not the cost of insurance. The American *C.A.F.* is occasionally confused with the French use of the same letters, where the *A.* means "assurance" (insurance), not "and." □see **C.I.F.**

canon law □see **common law.**

canons of ethics □see **legal ethics.**

capital □see **stated capital.**

capital punishment □see **execute.**

capitation tax □see **poll tax.**

capper □see **barratry.**

capricious □see **abuse of discretion.**

capture □see **law of capture.**

carnal knowledge: euphemism for sexual intercourse.

carrier's lien □see **lien.**

case □see action; □see also, controversy.

case and controversy □see controversy.

case at bar □see bar.

case at bench □see bar.

case law: law as made or interpreted by decisions, case by case.

case of first impression □see at first blush.

case or controversy □see controversy.

case submitted □see submission.

cash bail □see bail.

cash collateral □see collateral.

cash dividend □see dividend.

causa mortis □see gift causa mortis, under gift.

cause
□see **cause of action;**
□see **challenge for cause;**
□see **good cause;**
□see **justifiable cause,** under **justification;**
□see **lawful cause;**
□see **legal cause;**
□see **order to show cause;**
□see **probable cause;**
□see **procuring cause;**

☐see **producing cause;**

☐see **proximate cause;**

☐see **show cause order,** under **order to show cause;**

☐see **superseding cause;**

☐see **supervening cause,** under **superseding cause.**

cause of action is an imprecise and variable expression, most commonly used by practitioners in senses 1 and 2.

1. a right to sue to redress a particular category of grievance. In this sense, *cause of action* is often shortened to **action** (☐see). <It was a cause of action for fraud./ . . . an action for fraud.>

2. the part of a civil pleading outlining the details of the plaintiff's right to sue. In this sense, *count* is a synonym. <The complaint consists of two counts, the first a cause of action based on breach of contract, the second a cause of action asking damages for trespass to real estate.>

3. the facts that give rise to a right to legal redress. <They have sufficiently pleaded the facts constituting a cause of action for interference with a contractual relationship.>

4. the rules of law that give rise to a right to legal redress. <In some jurisdictions, a series of cases state the legal rules constituting a cause of action for intentional infliction of mental suffering.> Sometimes also called a *right of action.*

caveat emptor (L.: let the buyer beware): an old and worthless maxim reflecting an ancient view of the perils of a free and fraud-ridden marketplace. ☐see **maxims.**

caveat venditor (L.: let the seller beware): a civil law maxim, the reverse of **caveat emptor** (☐see), now an embittered protest of the tangled law designed to protect the mass-market consumer. <Whether or not these laws help the consumer, they sure add the merchant to the bewildered classes. *Caveat venditor!*>

cease and desist: two French-based English words joined in saying *stop, stop.* Redundant, except as the generally understood brand identifying an order of an administrative agency, a *cease and desist order.* What might have been a simple alternative, a *stop order,* has been preempted by the stockbrokers. ☐see **coupled synonyms.**

censorship: governmental restriction or suppression of freedom of expression. Variously defined by decision and statute. Usually defined in terms of **prior restraint** (☐see).

cert • certworthy ☐see **certiorari**.

certain has been around the law courts so long that no one really believes it is anything but uncertain, more or less certain, certainly not even in the class of **absolutes** (☐see). <Move to make the pleading more certain.> Yet the sound of certainty is so compelling that *certain* attached to almost anything still manages to inspire a false sense of precision. <That certain piece and parcel of land = the land./A certain Jones = Jones./A certain hog = a hog.> *Certain* is a wasted word and pretentious to boot. Kin to the pejorative **one** (☐see). This generally loose usage is to be contrasted with **sum certain** (☐see).

certificate of convenience and necessity ☐see **convenience and necessity**.

certificate of incorporation ☐see **articles**.

certificate of rehabilitation ☐see **rehabilitate**.

certified specialist ☐see **lawyer**.

certiorari (L., sir-sher-uh-RARE-e: to be informed): short for **writ of certiorari**: order directing a lower court to send the papers in a case for review by the court issuing the writ. <The Court today granted/ denied certiorari in *Smith v. Jones*.> Further abbreviated as *cert* (without a period), a bit of working slang that has spawned *certworthy:* the court ought to grant *cert* (a usage that takes note of the discretionary nature of *certiorari*). The *writ of certiorari* and *certiorari* are terms of art, used especially in U.S. Supreme Court practice; in some other courts, *writ of review* serves the same function. When procedural rules call for a *petition for a writ of certiorari,* no other words will do. But the decision to grant or deny the writ is sufficiently translated for most lay needs as *agreed to hear the appeal* or *denied a hearing on the appeal.*

certworthy ☐see **certiorari**.

cessante ratione legis cessat et ipse lex (L., sess-SAHN-tee rash-e-O-knee LEG-iss SESS-at et IP-see lex: the reason for the law ceasing, the law itself ceases): if the reason for a rule ceases, the rule *should* cease. Without the roaring Latin (better belted out to cringing listeners), and without the false guarantee of an end of nonsense, the residue of common sense in the old maxim is an argument for a rational basis of law. No more than that. □see **maxims**.

cestui que trust • cetty □see **beneficiary**.

C.F. □see C. & F.

CFR abbreviation of the **Code of Federal Regulations** (□see, under **regulate**).

chain of title □see **title**.

challenge (n., v.)

1. in general terms, as in ordinary English, an objection to qualification (e.g., for office, for voting) or authenticity (e.g., of a signature). Often a *challenge* is simply called by the generic **objection** (□see), e.g., to admissibility of expert testimony from a witness who is not an expert. Some challenges are raised by *motion,* e.g., a *motion to disqualify* or a *motion to recuse* a biased judge (□see **disqualify**). The most common specialized use of *challenge* is in connection with selection of a jury (see sense 2).

2. a formal objection to the qualification of prospective jurors:

challenge for cause: that a prospective juror does not meet the jurisdiction's general statutory requirements (e.g., is underage) or is personally unfit for jury service in this case, e.g., **bias** (□see). □see **trial jury**, under **jury**.

peremptory challenge: an unadorned objection to a prospective juror; no reason for the objection stated. Peremptory challenges (in legal argot, *peremptories*) are usually limited to criminal cases, with the number of peremptories per side limited by statute. The *peremptory challenge* is itself subject to constitutional challenge if discriminatory, e.g., designed to prevent any member of a minority from serving on this jury.

challenge to the array: that the entire **jury panel** (□see) is disqualified as a group from which a trial jury may be selected. The challenge may be based on lack of compliance with statutory requirements, or on constitutional grounds, especially racial discrimination.

challenge for cause   □see **challenge.**

challenge to the array   □see **challenge;** □see also, **jury panel.**

chambers   □see **in camera.**

champerty   □see **barratry.**

chancery   □see **equity.**

chance verdict   □see **verdict.**

change of venue   □see **venue.**

charge   □see **accuse;** □see also, **lien.**

charged with notice   □see **have notice, under notice.**

charge to the jury   □see **jury instructions.**

charging lien   □see **lien.**

charitable • nonprofit

charitable in the law is *charitable* in ordinary English: doing something for the public good, as distinguished from doing something for personal gain. <It was a charitable corporation, organized exclusively for charitable purposes./They contributed to the United Way, a charitable deduction recognized by the Internal Revenue Service.> Varying fashions of the moment call *charitable* by other names—*benevolent, eleemosynary, philanthropic.*

nonprofit, in ordinary speech, is a facet of something *charitable.* No one is getting anything out of the enterprise; also, colloquially, a loser. <It was strictly charitable, nonprofit; we all contributed our services./It wasn't planned that way, but I can tell you it was a nonprofit deal.> The law distinguishes balance sheet profits from personal gain and

charitable

separates both by a very broad swath from *charitable*. A nonprofit corporation (also called a *not-for-profit corporation*) is one not organized to make balance sheet profits, whether or not organized for a *charitable* purpose, and whether or not the participants reap other rewards, such as salaries, recreation opportunities, etc. <The Excelsior Country Club was a nonprofit corporation. Memberships cost $50,000. The general manager was paid $100,000 per year. It was not a charitable corporation./It was a nonprofit corporation organized for charitable purposes, to provide university scholarships for needy children.> A corporation organized to make profits may be a consistent loser, but not—in the law—a *nonprofit corporation*. □see also, **nonstock corporation.**

charitable deduction □see **charitable;** □see **tax.**

charitable trust □see **trust.**

charter □see **license;** □see **articles of incorporation,** under **articles;** □see **charter party.**

charter party: the lease of a ship, or of the use of part of a ship, for particular voyages or periods. Also called a *charter.*

chattel: a synonym for tangible *personal property,* preserved for years in *goods and chattels,* an O.E./O.F. tautology. *Chattel* is still alive in other combinations.

chattel mortgage: an interest in personal property securing performance of an obligation; also the writing that evidences that interest. <The $500 note was secured by a chattel mortgage on the debtor's car.> In form only, the chattel mortgage is a transfer of title. It has been largely superseded by the more candid and broader **security interest** (□see).

chattel paper: in a general way, a writing (more often, writings) evidencing an obligation to pay money, together with a security interest in specific goods or a lease of those goods. *Chattel paper* is a unique twentieth-century coinage of uncertain technicality. Refer to the source: UCC § 9–105(1)(b); § 9–308.

chattel real: an interest in real property less than ownership of the real property itself. <They don't own Blackacre; they have a ten-year lease, a chattel real.> It is a *chattel* because it does not represent ownership of real property and is not firmly attached to the real property as is a **fixture** (□see). But unlike other chattels (e.g., a horse, a baseball, or an airplane), a *chattel real* has an intimate connection with real property. The French word order, otherwise a worthless antique, reminds lawyers of that connection.

chattel mortgage   □see chattel.

chattel paper   □see chattel.

chattel real   □see chattel.

check   □see commercial paper.

check kiting   □see kiting.

checks and balances   □see separation of powers.

Chief   □see judge.

chief judge   □see judge.

chief justice   □see judge.

Chief Justice of the United States   □see judge.

child • infant • minor

The haphazards of a multilingual past have left the law with three vague ways of saying that a person is *not an adult*, without saying by how far he misses the mark. That status may also be described as *minority, nonage, not having attained majority, not of legal age,* and *underage.* The precise age for the status (twenty or less) varies by jurisdiction, decision, and statute. In the generalized sense of being underage, *child* (O.E.), *infant* (F.), and *minor* (L.) are interchangeable. < In the eyes of the law, he was a child/an infant/a minor. >   In that generalized sense, they form a group apart from a further bilingual complication, *juvenile* (L.) and *youth* (O.E.); those two are also synonyms for a person who is not an adult, but usually in specialized contexts of age or association (□see **juvenile**).   Too late now to abolish the synonymous roles of *child, infant, minor;* not too late to end the confusion that results from using more than one of the three when there is no difference of meaning.   < Since she was a child party to the contract, she had the infant's option of disaffirming it as having been signed by a minor./When she signed the contract, she was a child/an infant/a minor and so had the option of disaffirming it.> Beyond their synonymous usage, *child, infant,* and *minor* each has specialized associations.

child is the word of the three, the only one, to express family relationship.

1. The prime sense is a son or daughter, irrespective of age. That covers the very old. <The only child of A and B, she inherited the family home on her seventy-fifth birthday.> And also those of no age at all— **en ventre sa mère** (law F., ahn VAHN-tra suh MARE: in its mother's womb): a child unborn but considered born for purposes of inheritance. <One of the beneficiaries was a child **en ventre sa mère.**> □see **in being;** □see also, **parent.**

2. As an extension of the prime sense, *child* includes *adopted child, stepchild,* and *illegitimate child,* but unless those usages are made explicit by statute or controlling decision, they are best not left to interpretation. <In this will, *child* includes an adopted child and a stepchild but not an illegitimate child.> (On disuse of *illegitimate child,* □see **filiation proceeding**.) Inept use of *child* in a will may also be interpreted to include *grandchild* and even *issue* (□see **descendant**); conversely, inept use of *issue* has been interpreted to mean only children; these are horrors to be avoided.

3. In specialized contexts, *child* conveys the sense of relationship *and* underage: *child support* (□see **alimony**), *dependent child, neglected child, abandoned child* (□see **abandon**). In those instances, a person (e.g., a guardian) having a duty of support or care may substitute for the primary sense of parental relationship. Further extensions, *abused child* and *battered child,* have roots in the psychological problems of family relationship, but the offender may be a live-in friend, sometimes a complete stranger. For *delinquent child,* □see **juvenile.**

4. Where the primary relationship *and* underage are to be expressed without other specialized context, *child* is forced to rely on its synonyms *infant* or *minor* to recapture the underage distinction. <She was the infant child/the minor child/of A and B.>

5. **child labor law**: laws governing the working hours and conditions of those underage abandon the relationship aspect of *child;* customary usage requires *child,* not *infant,* not *minor.*

infant Dealing with ordinary events, lawyers may revert to ordinary English in describing an infant as *very young* ("Mewling and puking in the nurse's arms"); not precise legal usage. **Infanticide**: killing of the newborn, has all but vanished into definitions of homicide. But for the sense of underage, which it normally shares with *child* and *minor, infant* also has its own turf.

the infancy defense, sometimes, confusingly, *the defense of infancy* or *the defense of minority.*

> **1.** in criminal law, the defense that the culprit is too young to be responsible for conduct otherwise criminal. <The infancy defense, Your Honor; he is not responsible.> The defendant may be said to be so young as to be *not* **sui juris** (L.: of one's own right): not amenable to any criminal punishment (□see **sui juris**). In other instances, the defendant may be said to be incapable of having a required criminal intent. □see also, **juvenile.** □see also, **evidence.**

> **2.** in the law of contracts, the defense that the contract is void because made by one underage or voidable and so subject to disaffirmance. □see **disaffirm.**

attractive nuisance: a condition of property so attractive and dangerous to those underage as to make the property owner liable for injury to an *infant trespasser,* also called a *child trespasser,* not a *minor trespasser.* <It could have been anticipated that the building under construction, unfenced, and close to a school, would entice infant trespassers; it is an attractive nuisance.> *Attractive nuisance* is also sometimes called the *turntable doctrine.*

minor In discussion of the *period* of being underage, the preferred term is **minority,** frequently contrasted with **majority,** sometimes *full age.* <During her minority, her maternal uncle was her guardian. On attaining majority, she petitioned the court to end the guardianship.> It is the period of *minority,* not childhood or infancy, that is customarily fixed by statute, the period varying with the object served—voting, liquor laws, etc. □see **age of consent.** For constitutional right to vote, □see **lawful age.**

contributing to the delinquency of a minor: by act or neglect, tending to cause unlawful conduct by a person underage. In the full expression, *child* is sometimes substituted for *minor.* Separately referred to, the delinquent is also sometimes a *delinquent child* but, incongruously, not a *delinquent minor,* usually a **juvenile delinquent.** <He was arrested, charged with selling a controlled substance and with contributing to the delinquency of a minor, Jane M. The juvenile delinquent was also taken into custody.> □see **juvenile.**

emancipated minor: a minor who is no longer subject to parental authority. Conditions that result in **emancipation,** e.g., marriage, active military service, consent, court order, etc.; the consequences of emancipation, e.g., right to own earnings, duty of parental support, etc.; as well as the use of the expression itself, vary by state.

child custody □see custody.

child labor law □see child.

children's court □see juvenile.

child support □see alimony.

child trespasser □see child.

chilling a sale □see chilling effect.

chilling effect Unless applied to a dry, white wine, *chill* is a pejorative, with some chills worse than others. Only one is definitive, the fatal underworld usage. <"He put the chill on Sunny Moe."> Other chills are unpleasant but inconclusive. Many chills are only discouraging. The law has had a taste for those—*chilling the bidding, chilling a sale:* improperly keeping out the competition. The *chilling effect* has found a metaphorical home in constitutional law: deterring, though not directly prohibiting, the exercise of First Amendment or other constitutional rights. <"The chilling effect upon the exercise of First Amendment rights may derive from the fact of the prosecution, unaffected by the prospects of its success or failure."> The attractive vagueness of the *chilling effect* has given it an increasing currency in the last two decades. Inevitably, it is qualified—needlessly, excessively, impermissibly *chilling;* managing to achieve not instructive refinement but status only as a loose pejorative label. It spreads from the supremest to the lower courts to the bureaucracy. <"He thought the proposed freedom-of-information law would have a 'chilling effect' on cooperation and exchange of information between the FBI and the LAPD."/ "If it [AIDS] has difficulty spreading from women to men, that will have some chilling effect on the spread of the disease."> Chill it. □see **clichés.**

chilling the bidding □see chilling effect.

Chinese wall □see **vicarious disqualification.**

choate • inchoate   For centuries, the law got along without *choate*. Enough that *inchoate* could describe something just begun or incomplete—*inchoate crimes, inchoate dower,* etc.   No need to swallow the ordinary English variations on the theme: *inchoacy, inchoant, inchoate* (as a verb), *inchoated, inchoately, inchoation, inchoative, inchoatively;* even *inchoateness* was neglected.   The law's contentment was inchoate.   An unsung demon, with a head for logic, if not Latin, concluded that everything *inchoate* was incomplete, *not* complete, even though in this instance, the *in-* prefix was not a Latin negative. It had the look and sound of a negative; if *inchoate* was incomplete, that was because it wasn't *choate:* complete.   The made-up *choate,* sometimes listed as "erroneous" or "rare" in ordinary English, has found a secure nest in American law.   And to prevent *choate* from being inchoate, American law has also adopted *choateness:* a condition that cannot be described as *inchoateness.*   For lawyers struggling with ordering the priority of liens, **choate lien** became the short label for a lien "specific and perfected," a quick contrast to an unpreferred **inchoate lien.**   But after almost half a century of use, *choate lien* has not commanded uniform agreement on how "specific," how far "perfected."   Some lawyers take the worthless cure for insecurity—addition.   <The lien was specific, perfected, and choate.>   In tax practice, *choate lien* becomes a label, as a final blessing, for a lien the court determines so far specific and perfected that it takes priority over a federal lien; it has the quality of *choateness.*

choate lien   □see **choate;** □see also, **lien.**

choateness   □see **choate.**

choice of law   □see **conflict of laws.**

chose in action • thing in action

chose in action   (law F., SHOWS in action: a thing realizable in suit.)

1.   intangible personal property whose value lies in the right it gives to sue for money or personal property.   <A borrowed $100 from B and didn't repay it.   B's right to sue A to recover the money is a chose in action./A stole B's bicycle worth $50.   B's right to recover the bicycle or the $50 is a chose in action.>

2.   a writing, e.g., a note, that embodies the right to sue for money or personal property.   <A borrowed $100 from B, giving B a promissory note for the $100.   The note is a chose in action.>

3. a technical classification of *choses* (law F.: things), distinguishing *chose in action* (sense 1) from *chose in possession:* any sort of tangible personal property that is in possession—a horse, an auto, etc. The historical reasons for even talking about *chose in posession* have faded away, and it now performs no useful function in the practice.

thing in action: chose in action.

Misleading to look at, easy to mispronounce, law French *chose in action* challenges patriotic translation. The challenge is imperfectly met with the usual American rendition *thing in action,* a literal translation of *chose* and no translation at all of the equally French *action.* The utter vagueness of thingness, a poor thing, a thingamajig, ought to disqualify *thing* for legal discourse. The *in action* part of *thing in action* is about as bad, sounding either like a very mobile sort of thing or a choice of inaction.

Instead of one bad expression, we now have two, not improved by domestication.   <A chose in action is a thing in action./A thing in action is a chose in action.>   As long as the law has any use for this classification of property, we do as well with old *chose in action.*

chose in possession □see **chose in action.**

C.I.F.: a standard abbreviation for cost, insurance, and freight. These letters following a price mean that the price includes the cost of the goods, insurance, and freight to the destination. The same as the French, but not the American, use of C.A.F. □see **C. & F.**

circuit courts □see **U.S. Courts of Appeals.**

circuit judge □see **judge.**

circuit justice □see **judge.**

citation • cite

1. (citation to appear): *citation* (n.); *cite* (v.).

a. a court order directing someone to appear in court at a stated time for a stated purpose.   <The citation was dated January 10./He was cited to appear./She was cited for contempt.>

b. a written notice to appear in court to respond to a charge of a minor traffic violation. The notice is issued by a police officer and signed by the person charged, agreeing to appear. In colloquial usage, this citation is a **ticket** or *traffic ticket*. □see **bail**.

2. (citation of authority): *citation* (n.); *cite* (v., n.).

a. written or oral presentation of legal and other materials supporting a lawyer's argument to a court. The noun is *citation* <Their citation of authority was impressive.>. The verb is *cite* <They cited authorities from twenty states.>.

b. the formalized legal reference to an authority and the place where it can be found, as, e.g., a case, *United States v. Owens*, 484 U.S. 554 (1988). After the first formal citation, citation of the same authority is frequently shortened, i.e., "in *Owens*." The noun is *citation;* also, informally, *cite.* <Do you have any other citation/cite for that case?>

parallel citation: a citation of more than one reference to the same authority, usually case citations, e.g., *United States v. Owens*, 484 U.S. 554, 108 S.Ct. 838 (1988).

cite □see **citation**.

citizen by naturalization □see **naturalization**.

Citizenship Clause: the part of the U.S. Constitution reading: "All persons born or naturalized in the United States and subject to the jurisdiction thereof, are citizens of the United States and of the state wherein they reside." (Amend. XIV, § 1, cl. 1). □see also, **constitutional clauses**.

city attorney □see **lawyer**.

civil • civil law

civil (from L., *civilis:* pertaining to citizens; from L., *civis:* a citizen): adjective of general reference to the status, the rights, the obligations of an individual in an organized state. The most widespread use of *civil* has no necessary connection with individuals; it is *civil*, as distinguished from *criminal;* **civil law** (□see), as distinguished from *criminal law.* The etymology of *civil* is still the key to some usage.

79

civil death: an antique common law metaphor for the loss of *civil rights* by monks, nuns, and felons. It is now so twisted by statute and interpretation as to merit extinction, along with its unnatural and now meaningless antithesis *natural life.* <He was imprisoned for the term of his natural life, and is now civilly dead./He was sentenced to life imprisonment, and can no longer vote.>

civil liberties: an imprecise description of the individual's rights within a state, often used interchangeably with *civil rights* but with a special emphasis on freedom from an overwhelming power of the state. <It was a typical case brought by the American Civil Liberties Union, insisting that advocates of an unpopular doctrine be permitted to speak from a public platform.>

civil rights: an imprecise description of the rights of a person within a state, whether rights sometimes called *political* (e.g., the right to vote), strictly personal (e.g., a right of privacy), or based explicitly on statutory or constitutional guarantees (e.g., due process of law, right to counsel, free speech). <"Plaintiff alleges that he was denied promotion on account of his sex, in violation of Title VII of the Civil Rights Act of 1964, 42 USC § 2000e et seq."> The expression is sometimes differentiated from, sometimes used interchangeably with, *civil liberties.*

civil law

1. the system of law adapted from the Roman law and the French Code civil, as distinguished from the system of **common law** (□see).

2. in the *common law* system, the law of *remedies* (i.e., *civil remedies*), as distinguished from *criminal law*: the law of state imposed punishment for crime. *Punishment* as the touchstone distinguishing *criminal* from *civil* loses some of its luster with *civil contempt* (□see **contempt**) and *punitive damages* (□see **damages**).

civil remedies: the procedural devices to enforce rights, declare rights, prevent their violation, redress their violation. The traditional *civil remedies—suits* for damages, injunctions, orders, etc.— are *civil,* whether available (by decision and statute) to an individual, a corporation, or government itself. <*Jones v. Smith,* a suit for damages for breach of contract./*State v. Smith,* a suit for damages for breach of contract.> □see also, **provisional remedy.**

civil suit is a frequently used redundancy. <They filed a civil suit/a suit/for libel.> A *suit,* often called a *lawsuit* (□see **action**), is a civil remedy; *suit* alone is sufficient to identify the basic dichotomy with another redundancy *criminal prosecution. Prosecution* is usually sufficient to identify legal action brought by the state to punish for crime.   <Rogers rear-ended a dump truck owned by the state of California. The state sued Rogers for damages to the truck and prosecuted him for reckless driving.>   Occasionally, the otherwise redundant *criminal prosecution* distinguishes it from *prosecution* in the sense of carrying on a suit.   <Acquittal in the criminal prosecution did not end prosecution of the suit for damages.>   □see also, **malicious prosecution.**

civil arrest   □see **bail.**

civil contempt   □see **contempt.**

civil death   □see **civil.**

civil liberties   □see **civil.**

civil rights   □see **civil.**

civil suit   □see **civil.**

civil wrong   □see **wrong.**

claim: an assertion of a legal right to something, often in the form of a **demand** (□see) or **pleadings** (□see), in an almost infinite variety of legal contexts. E.g., a claim for compensation for an injury; claim for payment of a debt; a claim against an estate.

□see **claim and delivery,** under **replevin;**

□see **claimant;**

□see **claim preclusion,** under **res judicata;**

□see **counterclaim,** under **cross-;**

□see **cross-claim,** under **cross-;**

□see **disclaim;**

□see **interpleader;**

□see **mining claim;**

□see **patent;**

□see **proof of claim,** under **proof.**

claim and delivery   □see **replevin**.

claimant

1.   in general reference, someone making or filing a **claim** (□see).

2.   in some jurisdictions, the formal title of someone filing a claim in a legal proceeding.   □see also, **applicant**.

claim preclusion   □see **res judicata**.

class   □see **class action**.

class action: generally, a suit by (sometimes against) a representative of a *class*: a large number of people "similarly situated" as to a claim that affects them all. The size of the class is so large that it would be impracticable to bring them all into court. Hence, the class is represented by a member of the class who can fairly represent them all. All members of the class who do not "opt out" are bound by the outcome. Details vary by state and federal statutes. (See Federal Rules of Civil Procedure, Rule 23, as amended 1966, and to 1987; see Uniform Law Commissioners' Model Act: Class Actions, 12 Uniform Laws Annotated (Supp.), 1976, amended 1987.)

A *class action* is also called a *class suit, representative action,* and *representative suit*. The class action is a widespread form of litigation, e.g., complaints against a common employer; mass victims of a fraud; pollution of a common water supply. In the corporate world, the typical form of *class action* is the:

stockholder's representative action: usually a suit brought by a representative of a large number of stockholders with a common grievance against the corporation, e.g., failure to pay dividends. A different form of stockholder's action brought *for* the corporation, the **derivative suit** (□see), is included in some class action statutes, excluded by others.

class suit   □see **class action**.

Clayton Act   □see **antitrust law**.

clean hands • unclean hands: a biblical metaphor for moral purity, invoked to deny equitable relief to a litigant who has the effrontery to ask a court for help in the very matter in which he is a wrongdoer (unclean). Enshrined in the maxim "He who comes into equity must come with clean hands." <"Misconduct in the abstract, unrelated to the claim to which it is asserted as a defense, does not constitute unclean hands.">

clean slate: metaphor for a point without precedent. Used as part of a cliché of rejection, an affectation of regret that the result is dictated by precedent: "We do not write upon a clean slate." Often rendered more pompously as **tabula rasa** (L.: a scraped tablet): "We do not write upon a *tabula rasa*." □see **clichés.**

clear • clearly Clearly, this adjective and adverb lack clarity. <"I want to make that perfectly clear."> In a Micawberish hope that something clearer will turn up, the law often teams them with other criteria, e.g., *clear and concise, clear and conspicuous, clearly and manifestly.* Yet lack of clarity, once recognized, need not be fatal. Where flexibility is called for, *clear* and *clearly* have a legal role. (□see and compare **clear days**).

1. easily understood or perceived (by some). *Clear* nudges in the direction of clarity, as do its substitutes *intelligible, plain, simple, understandable.* <"Written in a clear and coherent manner using words with common and everyday meanings." N.Y. "plain language" law.> The essential in clarifying *clear* and *clearly,* as well as their lack of independent clarity, is the question "Clear to whom?" <This instruction may have been clear to the lawyers, but it certainly wasn't clear to the jury.>

2. having a high degree of certainty (but not too high).

   a. related to evidence and proof—*clear and compelling, clear and convincing*: weightier than the ordinary **preponderance** (□see), though not necessarily persuasive **beyond a reasonable doubt** (□see). □see also, **proof.**

   b. legal conclusions—a clear abuse of **discretion** (□see), *clearly erroneous, clearly excessive.* <On appeal, we resolve our doubts in favor of upholding the trial court's judgment, unless it is so lacking in support as to be clearly erroneous, a clear abuse of discretion, or a clearly excessive award of damages.>

   c. justification for limiting free speech—**clear and present danger.** <"The question in every case is whether the words used are used in such circumstances and are of such a nature as to create a clear and present danger that they will bring about the substantive evils that Congress has a right to prevent. It is a question of proximity and degree." *Schenck v. United States,* 249 U.S. 47, 52 (1919).> See also, *Brandenburg v. Ohio,* 395 U.S. 444, 447 (1969). □see also, **sedition,** under **treason.**

d. methods of accounting—that *clearly reflect the income.*

e. tort liability—**last clear chance:** a rule sometimes applied to permit a negligent plaintiff to recover if the defendant had an opportunity to recognize plaintiff's peril and to avoid the injury. Here, the contribution of *clear* is partly some certainty of the opportunity to avoid injury and partly the sense of usage 1, an easily perceived sense of plaintiff's peril. <"Plaintiff contended that the railroad crew had the last clear chance to avoid the accident.">

f. pompous derogation. <The argument is clearly without merit./It was a "clearly unwarranted invasion of personal privacy."> □see **clichés.**

3. without restriction or encumbrance (for the most part). The classic is the bilingual (O.E., F.) tautology *free and clear.* <The mortgage having been paid off, the property was free and clear.> Tautology breeds contempt. <Free and clear of weeds and rubbish.> *Free* is often omitted. <The property was clear./They had a clear title.> The verb *clear* is used in this same sense. <Clear the title.> *Clear title* is variously interpreted, and may or may not be the same as **marketable title** (□see).

clear days: the days between the first and last day of a period, i.e., not counting either the first or the last day. It is a little used way of computing time in the law (□see **time**). The role of *clear* here is exceptional in its precision. <They were to have at least ten days' notice before the ruling. We interpret that to mean ten clear days, i.e., excluding the day of notice and the day the ruling was made.>

clear and convincing   □see **clear;** □see also, **proof.**

clear and present danger   □see **clear.**

clear days   □see **clear.**

clear title   □see **clear.**

clergyman-penitent privilege   □see **priest-penitent privilege.**

clergyman's privilege   □see **priest-penitent privilege.**

clergy-penitent privilege   □see **priest-penitent privilege.**

clichés In good English circles, *cliché* is a pejorative: stereotyped, trite, hackneyed, commonplace. The strong suggestion that here is something fixed (stuck) in place is almost enough to transform the pejorative into a legal term of endearment.

Most of the law's clichés are recognizable English; some are clichés of ordinary English too willingly called into legal service. □see **at first blush; at that point in time.** The clichés mentioned here do not include the law's archaic *Old* and *Middle English,* its *coupled synonyms,* old *formalisms, law Latin,* and *law French.* That vast collection of traditional malfunction is separately entered; the weight of legal history and legal forms helps explain its appeal to lawyers. The bulk of the other clichés owes its currency chiefly to opinion-writing judges (and their opinion-writing clerks), harassed to produce something right now and reaching too quickly into memory's storehouse.

As with ordinary clichés, repetition of legal clichés bores the reader. If once they sparkled ("the state of a man's mind is as much a fact as the state of his digestion," □see also, **and its progeny,** □see also, **chilling effect;** □see also, **a word is not a crystal**), the flame has dimmed. Insufficient cause to end an old love affair; the real trouble is that legal clichés have also lost their bite. Worse than boring, they befuddle lawyer and lay reader. If once they approached precision, what remains is a tuft of confusion, with no consensus on exact meaning.

We must address that issue. What exactly will you do to it when you *address* it? (□see **addressing icebergs.**) *Meaningful disclosure,* a *meaningful relationship between attorney and client.* How much meaning? □see **meaningful.**

The one-legged subjunctives are impressive until you examine them. *It would seem; it may well be; it may very well be.* If the other shoe ever drops, we may learn that what seemed to be wasn't, and that what may very well be, may very well not be. That is *perhaps* the definitive word on the subject, but I haven't said so. I want to take credit for the discovery of a work of genius; but if it bombs, I can back off. I said *perhaps.* Even worse, *it appears that,* no one can tell whether *appears* has been corrupted to *is* or whether the appearance belies an unstated reality.

Hobson's choice was once no choice at all: you take the horse nearest the door; it may now be that or a choice of two bad bargains, but no one can be certain. Poor old Hobson; shun him. Let him spin in *Webster's Third.*

Legal clichés tend to add pomp without circumstance. Any old scrap of supporting authority is *seminal, indeed* it is, with not just a link or connection but a *nexus.* A case does not have a stage or a state but a *posture.* A touch of pseudoscience is appealing: the *interfaces,* the *parameters,* and the fraction-like fraud **and/or** (□see). Legal clichés slop over easily into redundancy: facts and circumstances (□see **facts**); surrounding circumstances (□see **facts**); true facts (□see **facts**), and **surviving widow** (□see).

Most prolific are the *clichés of rejection,* the irresistible opportunity to club the opposition into submission to the *obvious,* to what is **clear** (□see), to the **rule of law** (□see). They fall into categories:

1. *The inevitable:* that's the way the law is, and nothing you or we can say will change it.

bright line (□see)

Founding Fathers (□see)

I know it when I see it (□see)

If the legislature had meant that, it would have said so. □see **plain meaning**.

If this were a tabula rasa, the result might be different. □see **clean slate**.

In the final analysis

It is well settled that

long-standing authority

need not detain us

no citation of authority is needed

no longer open to question

Our power begins and ends with determining whether any evidence supports the finding.

plain meaning (□see)

The legislature has spoken. □see **plain meaning**.

The law looks with favor upon (children, marriage, keeping agreements, upholding statutes, etc.).

To state the question is to answer it.

We are constrained to hold

We do not write upon a clean slate. □see **clean slate**.

We put those cases to one side.

2. *The inevitable* (horror division): if we decided that way, I hate to think what would happen to the law.

All commerce would grind to a halt.

anomalous result

does violence to

flies in the face of

open Pandora's box

open the floodgates to endless litigation

ride roughshod over

shocks the conscience □see **conscience**.

slippery slope (□see)

stands the rule on its head

trap for the unwary (□see)

Where will we stop?

3. *Arrogant dismissal:* only an idiot would make an argument like that.

mere (□see)

trifles with justice

trivializes the law

without merit (□see **merit**)

4. *Reluctant or thoughtful rejection:* you have a point, but it's no good.

cuts both ways

fair to say

falls between two stools

not unfair to say

two-way street

What I find disturbing about that argument

What troubles me about that argument

5. *The gentle put-down:* with due respect, you're wrong.

able argument (□see)

able brief □see **able argument**

87

cliches

> *able counsel* □see **able argument**
>
> **learned trial judge** (□see)
>
> **6.** *Time for a change:* the clichéd rejection of the inevitability of deciding the way it has been decided before.
>
> *A literal interpretation leads to an absurdity.* □see **absurdity**.
>
> *broad brush* □see **bright line**
>
> **chilling effect** (□see)
>
> *doctrinaire argument*
>
> *exalts form over substance*
>
> *slavish adherence to the rule*

Clifford trust   □see **trust**.

close   The legal noun and adjective *close* (pronounced as ordinary English *close:* near) refer to something *closed,* i.e., closed to the public.

1.   land in one's ownership or possession (archaic).

2.   close corporation: a corporation in which the stock is closely held and that is run by the small group of stockholders.   <They transferred the assets of the family business from a partnership to a close corporation.>   Also called a *closely held corporation,* sometimes a *closed corporation,* as distinguished from a *public corporation.*   □see **corporate**.   □see also, **personal holding company**.

close corporation   □see **close**.

closed court   □see **open court**, under **open**.

closed shop: an enterprise in which one must be a union member as a condition of being hired.   Compared with **union shop**, in which one must become a union member within a fixed time as a condition of remaining employed.   Both contrasted with **open shop**, in which neither hiring nor remaining employed is conditioned on union membership.

closely held corporation   □see **close**.

cloud on title: a defect, real or apparent, in the title to property. The metaphorical cloud (a stray deed recorded by someone with no genuine claim to the property, a possible interest of a divorced spouse, etc.) casts a shadow over the ownership sufficient to discourage sale or to affect the price. <The cloud on title was removed by a suit to quiet title.> □see **quiet title.**

C.O.D., also written *c.o.d.,* and in the rush of business *COD,* abbreviating *collect on delivery,* often interpreted untechnically as *cash on delivery:* the goods will not be turned over to the buyer unless the buyer pays at the time the goods are presented for delivery. <This is a C.O.D./The furniture was sold C.O.D.>

codicil □see will.

Coefficient Clause: another name for the **Necessary and Proper Clause** (□see).

coercion □see **duress.**

cognovit □see **confession of judgment,** under **acknowledge and confess.**

cognovit note □see **confession of judgment** , under **acknowledge and confess.**

cohabit (late L.: to dwell together). Three discrete definitions of *cohabit* compete for favor. It may be a nice word or a bad word; you can't tell at a glance. A reflection of enduring or changing social and sexual mores and prejudices, usage differs state to state, almost court to court, with widely varying interpretation of statutes (e.g., immigration, naturalization, alimony, etc.).

1. to live together as husband and wife. This basic offshoot of the Latin etymology (dwell together) calls for a living together, more durable than casual, more open than furtive. It implies, without specification, the usual incidents of the husband-wife relationship, including but "not necessarily dependent on sexual relations"; the "usual incidents" are sometimes referred to as *conjugal rights* or *matrimonial rights.* Here, **cohabitation** is the usual condition of *marriage;* the definition comes close to requiring marriage, without saying so. It is not "husband and wife living together," but—ambigu-

cohabit

ously—living together *as* husband and wife. <They were not divorced, but they stopped cohabiting ten years ago.> □see also, **consortium**.

common law marriage: In some jurisdictions, a man and woman who agree that they are husband and wife and *cohabit* openly, holding themselves out *as* husband and wife, are married.

putative marriage: In some states, a man and woman who *cohabit* after an ineffective marriage ceremony, which at least one of the parties believed in good faith to be effective, are married. <They cohabited, without knowing that the minister had no license. She believed in good faith that she was married. She is. It was a putative marriage, and she is a *putative spouse.*>

2. to live together as husband and wife but not married. This is the relationship described in 1. but with no suggestion or pretense of marriage, legal or illegal, even if without any intention of ever marrying. The couple nonetheless live together *as* husband and wife, i.e., in the manner of husband and wife: they are **unmarried cohabitants** (also, *nonmarried cohabitants*). With some stretching of the traditional essence of the phrase "*as* husband and wife," this sense of *cohabit* can also include a dwelling together by homosexuals, in a relationship similarly more durable than casual, more open than furtive. Under some local laws, homosexuals may *marry,* a status not generally recognized as a matter of interpretation of statutes applying to people who are *married;* married or not, they *cohabit.*

3. to have illegal sexual intercourse; in some states, a synonym for **fornicate.** This is an old and increasingly rarer use of *cohabit.* <They were charged with cohabiting on the night of January 1, a single act of cohabitation but sufficient under the incest statute.>

cohabitant □see **cohabit**.

cohabitation □see **cohabit**.

collapsible corporation: a corporation designed or used by shareholders to eliminate or minimize income taxes. The changing intricacies of the expression, including the relevance of the word *collapsible,* are involved in the ongoing battle over taxes: impose versus minimize if they must be paid. Of special interest to tax lawyers. See, e.g., the definition in 26 USCA (Internal Revenue Code) § 341(b)(1) (amended to 1988).

collateral • collateralize The many ordinary and legal uses of *collateral* (adj.: by the side of, helping) give basic sense to the ordinary and untechnical use of *collateral* (n.) as a broad synonym for *security* of any sort in real or personal property. <They want collateral, or it's no loan./The lot was inadequate collateral for a loan of that size.> Increasingly, *collateral* refers to security in personal property, the type of security often specified, e.g., *cash collateral,* of which one form is *cash bail.* □see **bail.** The almost uniform requirement of lenders that borrowers *put up collateral* was once expressed by the verb *to collateral.* That solution of convenience has been abandoned, but the *-ize* craze has produced *collateralize.* <Are you in a position to collateralize your note?/ The loan was collateralized by a pledge of T-bills and a mortgage on an office building.> Frequently used, *collateral security* is a redundancy.

cross-collateral: security for one debt made to serve also as security for another debt. The inevitable verb is *cross-collateralize* and the process *cross-collateralization.* <John's Chrysler was collateral for the bank's first loan. When John borrowed again, he offered the bank his Ford as collateral. The bank insisted that the loans be cross-collateralized; both loans would be secured by the Chrysler and the Ford.>

collateral descendant □see **descendant.**

collateral estoppel □see **res judicata.**

collateral heir □see **heirs.**

collateralize □see **collateral.**

collateral security □see **collateral.**

collateral source doctrine □see **collateral source rule.**

collateral source rule: damages recoverable from a wrongdoer are not to be reduced by what the injured person receives from a source that is wholly independent of the wrongdoer; e.g., under the injured person's insurance policy. Also called the *collateral source doctrine.* The rule is generally one of damages in tort law and varies by jurisdiction.

collection agency □see **barratry.**

collect on delivery □see **C.O.D.**

colloquium • innuendo • inducement These are relics of common law pleading of a cause of action for defamation (libel or slander). When it is not otherwise obvious that the words complained of are understood to be defamatory and to refer to the plaintiff, those elements must be specifically pleaded. *Colloquium, innuendo,* and *inducement* describe the parts of the complaint supplying the missing ingredients. Usage is not uniform. *Colloquium* and *inducement* are sometimes used as synonyms; *inducement* has been used to include *colloquium* and *innuendo;* the roles of *innuendo* and *inducement* are sometimes reversed. Here are some working definitions, not definitive.

colloquium: the part of the complaint that identifies the plaintiff as the person defamed. <The defamatory words were, "The president of the Glitz National Bank robbed his own bank on the night of January 1." It was also alleged (colloquium) that on that date, the plaintiff was the president of Glitz National Bank./The defamatory words were spoken of the plaintiff; under some statutes, that is sufficient colloquium.> The word *colloquium* may be deleted without affecting the substance of what is said.

innuendo: the part of the complaint that explains the defamatory sense in which the words were used and understood. <The complaint alleged that the *News* published the words "J.X. Doe is another Ponzi." Those words are not obviously defamatory, and the allegation would have been insufficient but for the additional allegations (innuendo) that Ponzi was a notorious crook who paid investors large dividends out of their own invested capital and stole the rest of the money; that the *News* intended "Ponzi" to refer to the crook Ponzi and that it was so understood by readers.> The word *innuendo* may be deleted without affecting the substance of what is said. □see **actionable per se**, under **action**.

inducement: the part of the complaint stating the circumstances in which the words were used, showing them capable of being understood in a defamatory sense. (When this version of *inducement* is adopted, *innuendo* is confined to a pleading that the words were understood in a defamatory sense.) <These were the allegedly defamatory words: "She owns all the houses in the 400 block on Drumpf Street." It was also alleged (inducement) that all of the houses in the 400 block of Drumpf Street are illegal whorehouses.> The word *inducement* may be deleted without affecting the substance of what is said.

At best, *colloquium, innuendo,* and *inducement* are words of reference to what are sometimes essential elements of a cause of action for defamation. Nothing of technical significance hinges on the words themselves being used. They are confusing and unneeded and should be used with caution. □see **defamation**.

collusive joinder   □see **joinder.**

color • colorable: an appearance giving the impression of genuineness. Beyond that, usage varies. Often, but not uniformly, *color* refers to an appearance that is contrary to reality. The adjective form, *colorable*, especially refers to the contrast with reality. The state of mind that accompanies the words varies with context, from good faith to fraud.

color of law: the appearance of being official by the use of the symbols of authority, e.g., a statute, a badge, a uniform, an arrest warrant. A person using those symbols—sometimes as authorized, sometimes not—is said to *act under color of law*. Often, especially in civil rights cases, equated with **state action** (□see). *Color of office* (below) is a variety of *color of law.*

color of office: the appearance of being authorized by the use of an official position, e.g., of a police officer. A person using the official position—sometimes as authorized, sometimes not—is said to *act under color of office.*

color of title: the appearance of being an authentic evidence of title, especially a title document (a deed, a conveyance), and believed to be authentic by its holder but for some reason defective. □see **adverse possession,** under **possession.**

colorable claim: an assertion of right with the appearance of conformity to law but lacking substance. When made by someone who knows the claim is *colorable* and nothing else, e.g., a phony claim in bankruptcy, *colorable claim* refers to fraud. A *colorable claim,* e.g., in a pleading, may be made without fraudulent intent: good faith and bad judgment.

colorable imitation: looks or sounds like the real thing but is not. □see **unfair competition.**

colorable   □see **color.**

colorable claim   □see **color.**

colorable imitation   □see **color;** □see **unfair competition.**

color of law   □see **color;** □see **state action.**

color of office   □see **color.**

color of title □see color.

comes now the plaintiff □see formalisms.

Comity Clause: the part of the U.S. Constitution reading: "The citizens of each state shall be entitled to all privileges and immunities of citizens in the several states." (Art. IV, § 2, cl. 1). Also called one of the **Privileges and Immunities Clauses** (□see). □see also, **constitutional clauses**.

Commander in Chief Clause: the part of the U.S. Constitution reading: "The President shall be Commander in Chief of the Army and Navy of the United States, and of the militia of the several states, when called into the actual service of the United States. . . ." (Art. II, § 2, cl. 1). □see also, **constitutional clauses**.

Commerce Clause: the part of the U.S. Constitution reading: "The Congress shall have the power . . . to regulate commerce with foreign nations, and among the several states, and with the Indian tribes. . . ." (Art. I, § 8, cl. 3). □see also, **constitutional clauses**.

commerce power □see **Commerce Clause**.

commercial bribery □see bribery.

commercial domicile □see domicile.

commercial name □see trade name.

commercial paper

1. In its most general sense: pieces of paper in a prescribed **negotiable** (□see) form that embody an obligation to pay money to the order of a designated person (**order paper**) or to an indefinite succession of persons (**bearer paper**).

The various forms of commercial paper are also known as **negotiable instruments**.

   negotiable: the piece of paper, the obligation to pay money, and the right to receive it are all freely transferable, either by **indorse-**

94

ment (□see) and delivery (**order paper**) or by delivery alone (**bearer paper**).

The commonest forms of commercial paper are the **promissory note**, usually called a **note**, and the **check**, which is a form of *draft*.

note: signed by the **maker**, who gives an unconditional promise to pay a definite sum of money at a definite time or on demand. □see **sum certain**.

draft, also called a **bill of exchange**: signed by the **drawer**, who gives an unconditional order to the **drawee** to pay a definite sum of money at a definite time or on demand. If the order is to pay on demand and the drawee is a bank, the *draft* is called a *check*.

For the varieties and details of commercial paper, the special use of the word *negotiate*, and usage of *negotiable* for other than commercial paper, refer to the Uniform Commercial Code. □see also, **NOW account**, under **bank**; □see also, **settle**; see also, Mellinkoff, "The Language of the Uniform Commercial Code," 77 *Yale Law Journal* 185 (1967).

2.   In a restricted sense, popular in the world of business and finance: promissory notes issued by a corporation for short-term financing.

commercial speech: advertising and other communication in the course of business activity; so labeled in determining the extent of First Amendment protection. Neither the boundaries of *commercial speech* nor the extent of protection is precisely fixed.

commingle • commingling   Generally, *commingle* is the same in law as elsewhere: mixing things together so that they lose their separate identity.   <Separate and community property were commingled in one joint account.>   In a pejorative sense, *commingling* is the special vice of fiduciaries (trustee, agents, lawyers, etc.) in failing to keep a beneficiary's money separate from the fiduciary's own money.   <Contrary to professional rules, money received for the client was commingled by a deposit in the lawyer's general business account./Her lawyer was disciplined for commingling. >

commingling   □see **commingle**.

commission • committee: a group charged with performance of some special duty. Beyond that, the words separate, merging occasionally for the sake of appearances.

commission: usually, an administrative unit of government, usually with some semblance of longevity, independence, and relatively broad purpose. <Interstate Commerce Commission, Civil Service Commission, etc.> Less frequently, the governmental unit is special purpose and of lesser duration, still independent. <National Commission on Law Observance and Enforcement: Wickersham Commission; Commission on Organization of the Executive Branch of Government: Hoover Commission; Warren Commission; etc.>

commissioner: a member of a *commission*. The title is also used for a lesser government official charged with a *commission* (authority to perform a duty), with or without a *commission* (group). <County Road Commissioner, Probate Commissioner, Commissioner of Patents, etc.>

committee: a subordinate unit of an organization; also, an amorphous group, governmental or private, sometimes powerful, but with a delegated authority that often can be snatched away; ordinarily, either of lesser duration than a commission or with a more transient membership and often with a very narrow purpose. <House Ways and Means Committee, County Central Committee, membership committee, creditors' committee, standing committee on rules, an *ad hoc* committee, etc.> Sometimes a committee's purpose is so narrow, or its status so in need of puffery, that it is called not a *committee* but a *task force.*

In the hierarchy of group names (board, council, etc.), *commission* carries more prestige than *committee*. *Commission* is resonant of governmental authority. *Committees* proliferate by resolution, whim, and Xerox. <Committee to Save the Green Thisbe, Committee to Elect, etc.> In the United States, every *committee* can dream of becoming a *commission,* even without the government connection. No law forbids it. <The Commission on Insurance Terminology, Commission to Study the Organization of Peace, Commission on Freedom of the Press, etc.> The American Bar Association Special Committee on Evaluation of Ethical Standards (1964), which produced the *Model Code of Professional Responsibility,* metamorphosed (1977) into the Commission on Evaluation of Professional Standards, which produced the *Model Rules of Professional Conduct.* For the ultimate degradation of *committee,* □see **commitee,** under **-ee.**

commissioner □see **commission.**

commitee □see **-ee.**

committee □see **commission.**

common carrier

1. generally, a regulated business that holds itself out as being available to the general public for transportation of passengers, property, or messages at regulated prices or rates. Usually considered a type of **public utility** (□see). *Common carrier* is distinguished from:

contract carrier: generally, a business engaged in transportation (passengers, property, messages) under individually negotiated contracts (with prices or rates) made with the person requesting the particular services. *Contract carriers* are frequently subject to license or permit but not to the detailed regulation nor to the same obligations and liabilities of the *common carrier*. A *contract carrier* is sometimes called a *private carrier*. When the two are distinguished:

private carrier: a transportation service (passengers, property, messages) privately provided for its own purposes by a business primarily otherwise engaged. E.g., a **private utility** (□see, under **public utility**), a grocer's delivery service for the grocer's own groceries. A *private carrier,* in this sense, is not subject to the regulation characteristic to either *common* or *contract carriers.*

2. A host of statutes, state and federal, give a host of definitions of *common carrier,* varying from each other and from the general definition in sense 1. Some of these statutes, adapted to special contexts, also give varying definitions of *contract carrier* and *private carrier.* E.g., see 49 USCA § 10102(2), (4), (6), (14), (15), (16); amended to 1986.

common count □see **count.**

common law

1. the *common law* of England: a body of procedural and substantive English law (practice, rule, principle), said to be based on ancient custom, as interpreted by English royal judges, whose decisions, in turn, become part of the body of law they are interpreting.

    a. called *common law,* because over the centuries after the Norman Conquest, it came to be of general application in England. In this sense, contrasted with other law in England: local law, feudal law, the law of the Chancellor's courts (equity), and *canon law* (church law). In this sense, also, contrasted with the law of the Continent, *civil law.* □see **civil.**

b. called *unwritten law,* as contrasted with the law of statutes and other writings. So labeled, even though the decisions are usually recorded. Not related to *the* **unwritten law** (□see).

c. called *judge-made law,* as contrasted with law made by legislatures, and because the *common law* changes, decision by decision, in litigated cases. So labeled, though judges disavow lawmaking, as distinguished from expounding existing law. <The judges are not "oracles"; they have been making law since the earliest days of the common law.>

2. the *common law* system:

a. law resulting from the decisions of judges, case by case, in the tradition of the *common law* of England, as distinguished from law fixed by statute, regulations, or other writing. In this sense, *common law* refers to law with both continuity and the capacity for change: a continuous growth of **precedent** (□see) in similar cases, with high court decisions often controlling; with changed facts, precedent is distinguished, yielding new law, usually a little at a time, occasionally dramatically. <"Sovereign immunity" is a common law doctrine made by the judges, and they can unmake it.>

b. law resulting from the decisions of judges, case by case, whether the decisions interpret earlier decisions or interpret written law. <The common law gloss on that statute tells you more about the law than the statute itself.>

3. the *common law* in America:

a. *common law* in the colonies: a flexible usage, referring to the *common law* of England, to the extent applied in the American colonies before the American Revolution. In this sense, varying from colony to colony as to what part of *common law* is applicable, date of its "reception," and whether *common law* includes written English law enacted before colonial settlement. <Blackstone to the contrary, many colonials insisted that "we brought over as our birthright the common law of England.">

b. *common law* in the United States: a flexible usage, referring to the *common law* of England, except as changed by the U.S. Constitution and statutes and except as varied from state to state by local decisions and legislation before statehood, by state constitutions and statutes, and by decisions under a state's own *common law* system. <Though we have abolished the common law forms of action, we still refer to them in deciding the adequacy of a cause of action under our code./This is a common law jurisdiction, the American Common Law.>

c. *federal common law:* decisions in the United States court system on distinctly federal law, in the tradition of the *common law*

system.   <Federal common law fills the interstices of the federal statutes.>

common law copyright   □see **copyright**.

common law lien   □see **lien**.

common law marriage   □see **cohabit**.

common law trust   □see **trust**.

common sense   should have no place in a law dictionary, except as a
caution that, despite constant legal use, it is no closer to sense in the
law than in ordinary English.   "[A] convenient term . . . [b]ut . . .
practically devoid of content."   (Mosk, J., dissenting, in *Commercial
Life Ins. Co. v. Superior Court,* 47 Cal.3d 473, 485, 486, 1988).

common stock   □see **stock**.

Commonwealth   □see **people**.

community   □see **community property**; □see also, **contemporary community standards**.

community property   A species of property ownership derived from
the *civil law,* based on the concept of a *community,* consisting of
husband and wife as equal owners.   Among the states that have
adopted the system, rules governing community property and its
division on dissolution of the community vary by statute and decision.
The definition itself is not uniform.   For general reference—

community property: property acquired during marriage, other than
that acquired by the husband or wife by gift, inheritance, or as the
proceeds of property owned before the marriage.   <They had no family
business, but husband and wife both worked; all of their individual earnings were
community property.>   Contrasted with **separate property** (□see).

quasi-community property   In determining what constitutes *community property* for its own residents, some community property
states push the reach of their system into states that do not recognize
community property.   This is accomplished with the label *quasi-*

99

community property. Rules and definition vary by statute and decision. For general reference—

quasi-community property: property acquired by husband or wife while domiciled outside this state that would have been community property if acquired while domiciled here. <They married in New York and years later moved to California. Their New York house, bought with the husband's earnings after the marriage, was quasi-community property and will be treated as community property in California.>

commutation: an act, usually of executive clemency, reducing the severity of a punishment imposed by a sentence; and the order setting forth the reduction. <The governor granted a commutation./The commutation changes the punishment from death to life imprisonment.> The companion verb is **commute**. <The governor commuted the sentence of death to life imprisonment.>

Without use of the words *commute* or *commutation,* the constitutional provision of the President's "power to grant reprieves and pardons" (Art. II, § 2, cl. 1) includes the power to *commute.* (*Schick v. Reed,* 419 U.S. 256, 260, 1974).

□see also, **pardon**; □see also, **reprieve**.

commute   □see commutation.

compact: another name for *contract,* used especially for contracts between states of the United States. □see **Compact Clause**.

Compact Clause: the part of the U.S. Constitution reading: "No state shall, without the consent of Congress . . . enter into any agreement or compact with another state, or with a foreign power. . . ." (Art. I, § 10). □see also, **constitutional clauses**.

company: an untechnical designation of a business association, applied indiscriminately to partnerships, corporations, and less formal associations, sometimes even to a business owned by an individual. Whatever its legal structure, the standard abbreviation is **Co.** <For years, Roger & Co. was a partnership; when it incorporated, the name was unchanged./As chief executive officer of the Baker Corporation, he claimed that whenever he traveled, he was on company business.> A *company* may also be referred to as a *firm.* □see also, **personal holding company**.

comparative equitable indemnity   □see equitable indemnity.

comparative indemnity □see **equitable indemnity**.

comparative negligence □see **contributory negligence**.

Compensation Clause: the part of the U.S. Constitution reading: "The judges, both of the supreme and inferior courts . . . shall, at stated times, receive for their services, a compensation, which shall not be diminished during their continuance in office." (Art. III, § 1, cl. 2). □see also, **constitutional clauses**.

compensatory damages □see **damage**.

competence □see **incompetent**.

competency □see **incompetent**.

competent □see **incompetent**.

complaint □see **pleadings**; for cross-complaint, □see **cross-**.

completion bond □see **performance bond**.

compromise verdict □see **verdict**.

compulsory counterclaim □see **joinder**.

compulsory joinder □see **joinder**.

Compulsory Process Clause: the part of the U.S. Constitution reading: "In all criminal prosecutions, the accused shall enjoy the right . . . to have compulsory process for obtaining witnesses in his favor. . . ." (Amend. VI). □see also, **constitutional clauses**.

computation of time □see **time**.

computer law: law relating to computers and their use. The expression is widely used in legal writing without consensus on definition, usually without attempt at definition. This state of legal usage reflects the burgeoning development of the *computer* (itself without uniform definition) and its involvement in every field of law, its language, and ways of thinking about, analyzing, studying, and practicing law. The generalized definition given here crosses all boundaries of traditional law. It leaves the lawyer, for better or worse, with a mind open to consider the yet unpredictable benefits and horrors of the computer.

conclusion □see **finding**.

conclusion of law □see **finding**.

conclusive presumption □see **presumption**.

conclusory (adj.): assuming a conclusion not supported by the facts or the law. <Your argument is that Jones was acting in good faith. But that's conclusory, counsel. What evidence supports that conclusion?/You don't make her the defendant's agent simply by saying so; that's conclusory. Neither the evidence nor the law makes out a principal-agent relationship.>

concurrence □see **opinion**.

concurrent sentences □see **sentence**.

concurring opinion □see **opinion**.

condemnation □see **eminent domain**.

condemnee □see **eminent domain**.

condemner □see **eminent domain**.

condition □see **covenant**.

conditional fee: sometimes another name for fee simple subject to condition subsequent (□see, under **fee simple**).

conditional privilege □see **immunity**.

condition precedent • condition subsequent The word order in these expressions gives immediate notice of usage different from ordinary English: In the French pattern, the adjective follows the noun.

condition precedent (pronounced pre-SEED-ent): something that must happen *before* something else can happen. E.g., in contracts: a payment of one-third of the contract price as a condition precedent to the painting of a house, i.e., *before* the house will be painted. E.g., in property law: the marriage of Betty and John as a condition precedent to Betty's getting a present interest in Blackacre, i.e., *before* Betty can have a present interest in the property. □see **contingent remainder**, under **future interest**.

condition subsequent: something that may happen that can put an *end* to something else. E.g., in a lease for ten years: a provision (condition subsequent) giving the lessor the right to cancel (*end*) the lease if the lessor later decides to sell the property. E.g., in property law: a fee simple subject to a **condition subsequent** (□see, under **fee simple**). □see also, **subsequent**.

condition subsequent □see **condition precedent**.

condo □see **condominium**.

condominium • cooperative apartment

condominium (L., *con:* together + *dominium:* ownership), abbreviated, **condo**. Usage is unsettled, varying by state, as old concepts of shared political sovereignty and civil law co-ownership are adapted to residential and commercial co-ownership of fixed or indefinite duration. For general reference—

1. a species of ownership of real property in which the individual owners of separate portions of a building (or building space) together own the underlying land and common areas. <"The creation of a condominium requires a commitment of the property to that type of ownership.">

2. a building owned as described in sense 1. <They built a thirty-story condominium on the property.>

3. an indivdual portion of a building owned as described in sense 1; sometimes loosely called an *apartment* (in a residential condominium), or—without limitation to residential or commercial use— a *unit*. <They bought a 2,500 square foot condominium on the tenth floor of The Shakespeare.>

cooperative apartment

1. an apartment house in which the lessees of individual apartments must have ownership interests in the lessor entity. The lessee is a part owner of the lessor but not of the apartment house.

2. an individual apartment in an apartment house as described in sense 1.

3. a loose designation of a building held in some form of co-ownership by the occupants, broad enough to include **condominium** (□see).

confess   □see **acknowledge and confess.**

confess error   □see **acknowledge and confess.**

confession   □see **acknowledge and confess.**

confession and avoidance   □see **avoid.**

confession of judgment   □see **acknowledge and confess.**

confess judgment   □see **acknowledge and confess.**

confidential communications privilege: a category of privilege based on a communication in confidence, which the law protects over the opposing value of the search for truth. The extent of the privilege varies in particular application and by jurisdiction. In general, the holder of the privilege has the right to refuse to disclose the confidential communication, sometimes with the additional right of preventing its disclosure by others. For particular *confidential communications privileges*: □see **attorney-client privilege**; □see **government secrets privilege, under immunity**; □see **husband-wife privilege**; □see **newsmen's privilege**; □see **physician-patient privilege**; □see **priest-penitent privilege.**

confidential relationship   □ see **fiduciary.**

conflict of interest: a collision between irreconcilable duties or between duty and self-interest. *Conflict of interest* is a recurrent problem of the **fiduciary** (□see), especially of trustees (□see **trust**), lawyers (□see **vicarious disqualification**), and public officials (□see **blind trust,**

under **trust**). Rules and regulations governing lawyers (e.g., the *Model Code of Professional Responsibility* and the *Model Rules of Professional Conduct*), state and federal statutes affecting the conduct of public officials in office and after leaving office, and abundant decisions are for the most part imprecise guides to the infinite factual variations of *conflict of interest*. □see also, **revolving door**.

conflict of laws • conflicts

conflict of laws: the field of law that deals with the special problems arising when the law of more than one state or nation may be of consequence. <The contract was made by an exchange of letters between A in New York and B in West Berlin, and was to be performed partly in Germany and partly in the United States, a classic problem in conflict of laws.> The rules of conflict of laws determine **what law governs**. <The contract was made in California; the loss occurred in Florida. What law governs, the law of California or the law of Florida?> The resolution of that problem is called **choice of law**, an expression often substituted for *conflict of laws*. <It was a conflict of laws/choice of law problem.>

conflicts is the shorthand reference to *conflict of laws*. <It was a conflicts problem./She taught a course in conflicts.> Habitual professional use of the plural *conflicts* often results in distorting the original *conflict of laws,* with a switch of plurals, to *conflicts of law,* understood but not genuine. <*Restatement of the Law of Conflict of Laws* is cited as Restatement, Conflict of Laws, or shortened to Restatement, Conflicts but miscited as Restatement, Conflicts of Law.>

□see also, **renvoi**; □see also, **private international law**, under **international law**.

Confrontation Clause: the part of the U.S. Constitution reading: "In all criminal prosecutions, the accused shall enjoy the right . . . to be confronted with the witnesses against him. . . ." (Amend. VI). □see also, **constitutional clauses**.

conjugal rights □see **cohabit**.

con law □see **constitutional**.

connect it up oral courtroom slang.

1. counsel's reply to the objection that evidence is irrelevant, often joined with a cliché of the moment. <I will connect it up when all of my witnesses have testified. Rome wasn't built in a day.>

2. part of a conditional ruling on objection that evidence is irrelevant. <I will admit it now, counsel, subject to its being connected up or stricken.>

consanguinity □see **heirs.**

conscience • unconscionable The gnawing moral sense we call *conscience* (negatively, *unconscionable*), no more precise in law than elsewhere, has several distinctively legal uses.

shocks the conscience: a judicial cliché of disapproval of conduct, contract, statute, ruling. Consciences are rarely unanimous. <After a beating, the prisoner confessed. The conduct of the police shocks the conscience.> □see also, **abuse of discretion.**

unconscionable: as a predicate for judgment, a standardized conclusion on unstandardized criteria that something does not conform to the dictates of conscience.

1. a traditional description of a grossly inequitable contract, as a basis for refusing a decree of specific performance. <The price was so disproportionate to the value of the property as to be unconscionable. Specific performance denied.>

2. an epithet of expanding range, directed especially at consumer contracts, as a basis for reformation, rescission, or damages. Applied variously to a contract grossly unfair in whole or in part, as well as to fraudulent, sneaky, or revolting conduct inducing someone to make a contract. <Plaintiff took advantage of defendant's "ignorance, illiteracy, and inability to understand the language of the agreement." Plaintiff's conduct was unconscionable, and so is the contract. Judgment for the defendant.>

consecutive sentences □see **sentence.**

consequential damages □see **damage.**

conservatee □see **conservatorship.**

conservator □see **conservatorship.**

conservatorship: a relationship similar to *guardianship,* (□see **guardian**) created by court order to take care of the person, property, or both, of one unable to do so by reason of age or disability. For the traditional guardianship requirements of minority or incompetence, *conservatorship* substitutes broader, less harsh, and more flexible terminology: *unable properly to provide, unable to resist fraud* or *undue influence,* etc. The euphemistic titles *conservator* and *conservatee* replace the cramping stigma of *guardian* and *ward.*

consideration □see **contract.**

consign • consignment Both words include usage peculiar to shipping and usage peculiar to sales.

consign

1. to designate the person to whom goods are to be delivered. <The shipment was consigned to the May Co.>

consignee: the person to whom goods are to be delivered.

consignor: the person who has delivered goods to a carrier for shipment to the consignee.

2. description of goods held on **consignment** (□see). <The store was selling consigned furniture.>

consignment

1. a shipment of goods. <The consignment was by air.>

2. the goods shipped. <The consignment was sent by air.>

3. **on consignment:** a sale made with the agreement that if the buyer does not resell the goods, they may be returned to the seller. Also known as a transaction of *sale or return.* <The store bought the books from the publisher on consignment, with the right to return unsold books within thirty days.>

consignee □see **consign.**

consignment □see **consign.**

consignor □see **consign.**

consortium

consortium • loss of consortium

consortium (L., con-SOR-shum: fellowship, participation, society, partnership).

1. the usual incidents of marital companionship (love, society, sexual relations, services, etc.); broader than, and so not a euphemism for, sex.

2. the right of each spouse to the usual incidents of marital companionship. □see also, **cohabit**.

3. In both senses 1 and 2, *consortium* has for so long been associated with its loss that *consortium* alone is frequently and confusingly used as the equivalent of loss of **consortium** (□see). <One element of consortium is loss of support./Consortium consists of many things, but its predominant element is loss of sexual relationship.>

4. an association of business enterprises under separate ownership joined together to own and operate a special, usually expensive, project. Unconnected with senses 1, 2, and 3, except by Latin origin; follows the political usage for an association of sovereigns. <"The oil companies constituting the consortium owning Alyeska submitted an application to the Department of the Interior for rights-of-way for [the Alaskan] pipeline.">

In its marital senses (1, 2, and 3), *consortium* is a collective singular. A plural is conceivable but not used. <All consortiums are not alike.> In its business enterprise sense (4), the Latin plural is *consortia;* prefer *consortiums.* <Three consortiums were competing for the franchise.>

loss of consortium

1. deprivation of the usual incidents of marital companionship by the act of a stranger. <In addition to damages for broken bones, pain and suffering, loss of employment, etc., damages may be awarded for loss of consortium.> The same deprivation by a spouse is described by other circumlocution. <"Consortium necessarily implies that each spouse has a legal right to be with the other spouse, which relationship neither can unilaterally terminate.">

2. a cause of action against a stranger for depriving one spouse (at common law, only the husband) of some or all of the usual incidents of marital companionship with the other spouse. <In addition to the husband's cause of action against the defendant for negligent injury to the husband, his wife had a cause of action for loss of consortium.>

conspiracy

1. (criminal) □see **conspirator**, under **parties to crime**.

2. (civil): What is sometimes called *civil conspiracy* is an expression without precise or uniform definition. Sometimes identified as an independent *tort:* an agreement by at least two persons (the *conspirators*) to join in achieving an unlawful end, or in achieving an otherwise proper end by unlawful means, that results in damage to another. More often identified as that sort of agreement incidental to some other tort (e.g., fraud), and so imposes joint and several liability on everyone joining in the agreement whether or not committing any overt wrongful act that damages another (□see **vicarious liability**). *Civil conspiracy* is also referred to as a *combination*.

conspirator   □see **conspiracy**; □see **parties to crime**.

constitution   □see **constitutional**.

constitutional • unconstitutional   Working with the U.S. Constitution for two centuries, American lawyers and judges have treated *constitutional* and its kin (*constitutionally, unconstitutional*) with the unmeasured intimacy of old affection. Usage is innovative and carefree. At law, as distinct from ordinary speech, you can do everything with *constitutional* except take one. Our earliest creations were *constitutionality* and *unconstitutionality;* the most recent, the verb *constitutionalize,* not in the ordinary sense of organizing a government along constitutional lines but a slangy pejorative: to subject something to the burden of passing constitutional muster. <"The judgment today unnecessarily constitutionalizes another element of American life.">

constitutional   needs sorting out.

1. refers to the U.S. Constitution (in context, other constitutions), or its provisions, as an instrument of government. This is the world of political science, from which some legal usage is derived, a *constitutional court* (also called an *Article III court*), *constitutional* office, scheme, separation of powers, etc.

2. refers to the general legal effect of *constitutional law:* the law of the U.S. Constitution (in context, other constitutions) as interpreted by the courts. <I know that's what the statute says, but is it constitutional?> Without immediately expressing an opinion, a judge may write of *constitutional* —analysis, attention, command, dimensions, freedoms,

guarantees, guidelines, immunities, implications, inquiry, muster, necessity, protection, questions, rights, standards, etc.

constitutional law brings with it the experts, the *constitutional lawyer,* professor, scholar, as well as law school courses in *constitutional law,* abbreviated **con law.**

3. refers to something approved by *constitutional law* —a *constitutional* statute, search, right; *constitutionally* protected, permissible, valid. <On balance, we hold the statute constitutional./They had a constitutionally protected right to demonstrate.>

4. refers to something disapproved by *constitutional law.* The most straightforward usage is the simple negative *unconstitutional.* But an opinion is not always ready for such bluntness. Nuance creeps into the discussion of reasons. Loose usage of *constitutional* teams with loose usage of negatives, *constitutional error,* for example. Is that sense 2, 3, or 4? Is it error of constitutional dimensions, error too slight for the brand "unconstitutional," or is it error disapproved and fatal? The same with *constitutional* invalidity, violation, deprivation; and *constitutionally* invalid, defective, and unfair. *Constitutionally obnoxious* is too emphatic to mislead anyone. With less violent combinations, doubled and redoubled in the same writing, you arrive at the point of lawsick chaos where positive and negative are indistinguishable:

constitutional deprivation is *unconstitutional deprivation;*

constitutional invalidity is *unconstitutional invalidity;*

constitutionally vague is *unconstitutionally vague;*

constitutional violation is *unconstitutional violation.*

The possibilities are almost limitless.

constitutional clauses Some parts of the U.S. Constitution, whether or not grammatically "clauses," are familiarly known to students, scholars, lawyers, and judges as special "clauses," with pet names. The names usually pick up words of the Constitution. They are often, not invariably, capitalized. They are labels of convenience for quick reference: usage is not uniform; some usage is loose, if not sloppy. The clauses listed here (not a complete list) are separate entries in the dictionary.

Admiralty Clause	Citizenship Clause
Appointments Clause	Coefficient Clause
Basket Clause	Comity Clause
Bill of Attainder Clauses	Commander in Chief Clause

Commerce Clause
Compact Clause
Compensation Clause
Compulsory Process Clause
Confrontation Clause
Contract Clause
Direct Tax Clauses
Disposing Clause
Due Process Clauses
Elastic Clause
Emolument Clause
Equal Protection Clause
Establishment Clause
Excessive Fines Clause
Ex Post Facto Clauses
Extradition Clause
Faithfully Executed Clause
Freedom of Press Clause
Freedom of Speech Clause
Free Exercise Clause
Full Faith and Credit Clause
General Welfare Clause
Grand Jury Clause
Guarantee Clause
Import–Export Clause
Incompatability Clause
Ineligibility Clause
Militia Clauses
Natural Born Citizen Clause
Naturalization Clause
Necessary and Proper Clause
Oath or Affirmation Clause
Obligation of Contracts Clause
Patent and Copyright Clause
Privileges and Immunities
    Clauses
Religion Clauses
Religious Test Clause
Self-incrimination Clause
Speech or Debate Clause
Statement and Account Clause
Supremacy Clause
Sweeping Clause
Takings Clause
Three-fifths Clause
Treaty Clause
Uniformity Clause
Warrant Clause

constitutional court □see **federal courts.**

constitutional deprivation □see constitutional.

constitutional error □see constitutional.

constitutional invalidity □see constitutional.

constitutionalize □see constitutional.

constitutional law □see constitutional.

constitutionally obnoxious □see constitutional.

constitutionally vague □see constitutional.

constitutional violation □see constitutional.

constrained to hold   □see clichés.

construction • interpretation   After centuries of continuing use in the law and out, these words remain synonyms. Sporadic attempts have failed to establish a breadth for *construction* (to include things outside the writing) said to be lacking in *interpretation* (of the writing itself). Usage remains restless, repetitive, lacking in uniformity. In the same breath, judges *construe* and *interpret.* <We construe the statutory language in the light of the legislative intent. The interpretation we adopt is a construction with ample precedent.>   In some phrases, there is a tendency for one word to be preferred: the *interpretation clause* of a statute or contract; **rules of interpretation** (□see); *strict construction,* which one boasts of, only to be denounced as a *strict constructionist,* favoring a *narrow* or *literal interpretation* over a *liberal construction* or a *rational interpretation.* What one word does, the other can do. Uniform usage would help to remove some of the muddle in legal expression. General use of *interpretation* could yield a special benefit: avoiding the confusion of *construction* with the completely different *constructive* (□see **actual**).

constructive   □see actual.

constructive adverse possession   □see possession.

constructive condemnation   □see eminent domain.

constructive contempt   □see contempt.

constructive contract   □see quasi contract.

constructive desertion   □see desertion.

constructive eviction   □see eviction.

constructive knowledge   □see knowledge.

constructive malice   □see malice.

constructive notice   □see notice.

constructive possession   □see possession.

constructive receipt of income   □see actual; □see tax.

constructive reduction to practice   □see patent.

constructive service   □see service of process.

constructive trust   □see trust.

construe   □see construction.

consumer   The economic model of a *consumer of goods* as contrasted with a *producer of goods* still holds, and there is always the off chance that *consumer* really means a *consumer of goods*.   <This manufacturer was a consumer within the meaning of the tax statute.>   Yet the law's *consumer* today is not usually any old *consumer*, not wholesale buyers or buyers of jumbo jets.   The law has turned its attention to *consumer* as short for **mass-market consumer**: the individual who typically buys and borrows for personal, family, or household purposes and is least able to understand or fight the market or the law.   The statutes must be consulted for varying and specialized definitions of the growing menagerie of *consumer* compounds: *consumer contracts,—credit,—goods,—lease,—loan,—product,—safety,—sale,—transaction*, etc.

consumer products   □see warranty; □see also, **consumer**.

contemplation of death   □see gift in contemplation of death, under gift; □see transfer in contemplation of death, under transfer.

contemporary community standards: the background against which to test whether or not something is obscene in a constitutional sense.   *Community,* once held to be a national community, is currently held to be the local (i.e., state) community of average adults.   □see obscenity.

contempt   (L., *contemnere:* despise, defy; *contemptus:* scorn)

Lay and legal *contempt* are confusingly promiscuous.   In both worlds, a judge or a lawyer may be *contemptible* (deserving of scorn).   As long as he is not *contemptuous* (expressing scorn or contempt), a lawyer may safely *hold* a judge *in contempt* (despise him). But when a judge *holds* a lawyer *in contempt,* the judge has a firmer, legal grasp. In the law, *contempt* is both cause and effect, the conduct and its result.

1. conduct constituting *contempt*—

   a. deliberate disobedience of a lawful court order (**contempt of court**), sometimes even of an order later held improper. Disobedience of the legislature may also be a *contempt,* e.g., contempt of Congress. <He had the money to pay the court-ordered child support but did not pay. That was contempt./The witness having made a valid claim of Fifth Amendment privilege, it was not a contempt to refuse to answer.>

   Contempt through disobedience is **contumacy**: stubborn resistance to authority. Loosely described as *contemptuous,* the precise adjective is **contumacious** <a contumacious witness>. Except through etymological byways, *contumacy* and *contumacious* are not related to the old pair from the law of defamation— *contumely* (humiliating scorn) and *contumelious.*

   b. displaying disrespect for a court in a way that interferes with the administration of justice (**contempt of court**); less frequently, interference with the legislative process.

   This form of *contempt* is not contumacious conduct, just plain **contemptuous:** expressing contempt for authority. <The contempt was clear, a series of comments on the judge's ruling: "You have violated every principle of fair play. . . . I am outraged to be in this court before you . . . I am saying it now, and then I want you to put me in jail if you want to." *In re Dellinger,* 370 F.Supp. 1304, 1337 (Appendix), N.D.Ill., 1973.>

   c. contemptuous conduct in a. and b. is further classified by the power of the offended authority to respond. □see **contempt power.**

2. **contempt power:** the power to use *contempt proceedings:* summary or shortened hearings by a judge to coerce obedience or to punish a **contemnor** (also, *er*): one guilty of contempt. The judge *holds* the contemnor *in contempt, cites* him *for contempt,* finds him *guilty of contempt;* in each case, *contempt* is a shortening of *contempt of court.* Exercise of the power varies with the nature of the contempt.

direct contempt: contempt in the presence of the court, or close by. <Sit down, counsel. No one calls this court an ass. That's a direct contempt. Fifty dollars or five days. Right now!> An ironic twist: Not showing up when ordered to is a direct contempt; absence is "in the presence of the court."

constructive contempt (also called *indirect contempt*): contempt outside the presence of the court. <They were cited for constructive contempt for violating the terms of the injunction and given notice of a hearing.>

civil contempt may refer to conduct or a procedure.

    a. disobedience of an order, especially an order designed to benefit someone else. <They were held in contempt for failure to comply with an order to tear down the encroachment on the plaintiff's land. It was an indirect civil contempt.>

    b. a procedure to coerce obedience to a court order, whether or not for the benefit of someone else. <Under pressure of a civil contempt order jailing him until he complied with the child support order, the defendant resumed the monthly payments./I have directed you to answer that question, and you have refused. I hold you in civil contempt, and order you jailed until you are ready to answer.>

criminal contempt may refer to conduct or a procedure.

    a. an interference with the administration of justice. <An outburst of shouting and chair throwing during the testimony of two witnesses was a direct criminal contempt.>

    b. a procedure to punish for an interference with the administration of justice. <Criminal contempt is the appropriate answer to disruptive conduct. You are fined fifty dollars.>

Criminal and *civil contempt* may overlap. The same conduct, e.g., refusal to answer, may be classified either way, as a court decides after the fact that (1) the conduct did or did not interfere with the administration of justice or (2) the measures taken in response were designed more as punishment or as coercion.

purge of contempt: to clear oneself of contempt by complying with an order the contemnor has refused to obey. <When you decide to answer the question, you may purge yourself of this contempt. Until then, you stay in jail. In the legal cliché, you *carry the key of your own prison in your own pocket.*>

contempt of court   □see **contempt.**

contempt power   □see **contempt.**

contempt proceedings   □see **contempt.**

contemptuous   □see **contempt.**

contingency fee □see **barratry.**

contingent remainder □see **future interest.**

continue □see **delay.**

continuing trespass □see **trespass.**

contra bonos mores (L., CON-tra BONE-oce MORE-aze: contrary to good morals): a faded Latinism, the loose equivalent of the loose generalization *against public policy.* Occasionally dropped into an opinion to lend a classical tone of moral uplift to a holding that a contract is void or illegal. <The contract was *contra bonos mores* and void./Was illegal because *contra bonos mores.*> □see **public policy.**

contract • agreement

1. a working generalization—

    Rough utility and desperation give general recognition to various forms of this definition of *contract* (n.): "a promise, or a set of promises, for breach of which the law gives a remedy, or the performance of which the law in some way recognizes as a duty." (Restatement (Second) of Contracts, § 1).

    Taken literally, the definition is misleading. Anyone can nibble it to death. Take away the key words (promise, remedy, duty), and you still end up using the name *contract:* no promise, an *implied contract* (□see **quasi contract**) or *contract by estoppel* (□see **estoppel**); no remedy, an *unenforceable contract;* no duty, an *illegal contract* or a *void contract.*

    Efforts to stiffen the word succeed only in adding redundancy to vagueness: *binding contract, enforceable contract.*

    The definition hangs on as a working hypothesis that points lawyers in a familiar direction. It starts them thinking about a law school course in *contracts* and the *law of contract,* dead or alive. It calls up ordinary English words—*agree, promise, bargain, exchange, understanding, obligation.* It brings forth the picturesque metaphor a *meeting of the minds.* It brings back a whiff of the Latin **quid pro quo**: something for something, and a latter-day something for something called **consideration**: a benefit to the promisor or a detriment to the promisee—replete with learned qualifications. □see also, **valuable consideration.**

116

In the end, no one is bothered too much by the defects of the definition. A word is needed, precise or not. Whatever the fate of the *law of contract* (see Gilmore, *The Death of Contract*), the word lives on in lower case; *contract* exists. □see also, **nudum pactum.**

2. *contract* or *agreement* —

a. a general noun—For general reference, *agreement* and *contract* (n.) are synonyms, with definitions chasing each other into oblivion. <An agreement is a contract./A contract is an agreement.> Statutes sometimes call out a distinction between *agreement:* the bargain in fact; and *contract:* the total legal obligation; the distinction is unreliable, not uniformly applied. In least technical contexts, the words are interchangeable. <They made an agreement./They made a contract.> As technicality increases, *contract* is preferred. E.g., the details of making <The contract was formed by a mailed *offer* and an *acceptance* by return mail.>. E.g., the kind of contract: a distinction, not uniformly recognized, between a *bilateral contract:* a promise for a promise; and a *unilateral contract:* most commonly, a promise in exchange for an act. E.g., procedure <The action was *in contract.*>. □see also, **letter agreement.**

b. the piece of paper, the whole package—is either *the agreement* or *the contract.* <Let me see the agreement./The contract was fifty pages of fine print.> The same with an oral package. <The oral agreement provided. . . ./The oral contract was complete in every detail.> As the title of a document, either word does the job <Building Contract/Agreement to Build a House>. *Agreement* is "friendlier," less intimidating to the laity.

c. part of the contract—Either word will do. <Par. 7 of the contract provided. . . ./Par. 7 of agreement provided. . . .> But if the stress is on the element of promise, the word is *agreement.* <Par. 7 is an agreement to obtain copyright.>

d. the verbs—

(1) concur: *agree,* not *contract,* expresses concurrence (giving assent), whether loosely <He agreed that a five-year option would be reasonable.> or as an operative word in a *letter agreement* <Dear Jones: If you are willing, we will buy Blackacre for $10,000. (signed) Smith. Agreed (signed) Jones.>.

(2) promise: *agree* expresses the ordinary English sense of promise and is the usual operative word in any *contract* (n.); *contract* (v.) is a clumsy substitute. The promise can come from one side (**unilateral contract**). <If you deliver the car today, I agree to pay the $8,000 sticker price.> Or the two sides (**bilateral contract**) can promise each other. <Buyer and Seller agree: (1),

(2), (3)./not: Buyer and Seller contract.> As a word of promise, *agree* is often overworked. <Buyer and Seller agree: (1) Seller agrees to deliver the car; (2) Buyer agrees to pay the $8,000.> The first *agree* is enough; delete the others. □see also, **undertake**.

(3) *referring to the making of a whole contract* —When not used as an operative word of concurrence or promise, *agree* has too many loose associations from ordinary English to yield a precise reference to the making of a whole *contract* or *agreement*. <They agreed to repair the house./They contracted to repair the house.> Prefer *contract* (v.).

3. For other specialized names: □see **articles**; □see **bond**; □see **compact**; □see **constructive contract**, under **quasi contract**; □see **contract implied-in-fact**, under **quasi contract**; □see **contract implied-in-law**, under **quasi contract**; □see **contract of adhesion**; □see **covenant**; □see **destination contract**, under **F.O.B.**; □see **implied contract**, under **quasi contract**; □see **indenture**; □see **output contract**, under **requirements contract**; □see **pact**; □see **quasi contract**; □see **requirements contract**; □see **shipment contract**, under **F.O.B.**; □see **stipulate**; □see **undertake**; □see **warranty**.

4. best forgotten—

adhesive contract □see **contract of adhesion**; □see also, **agreement to agree**; □see also, **mutually agree**; □see also, **subject to change by mutual agreement**; □see also, **verbal contract**.

contract by estoppel   □see **estoppel**.

contract carrier   □see **common carrier**.

Contract Clause: the part of the U.S. Constitution reading: "No state shall . . . pass any . . . law impairing the obligation of contracts. . . ." (Art. I, § 10, cl. 1). The *Contract Clause* is also called the *Obligation of Contracts Clause*. □see also, **constitutional clauses**.

contract of adhesion: a take-it-or-leave-it contract, with one side having all the bargaining power. A creative label based on ordinary English *adhesion* (the act of joining). Sometimes shortened to *adhesion contract*. Occasionally gummed up as *adhesive contract*.

contract under seal   □see **seal**.

contra proferentem   (L.: against the offeror; short for the Latin maxim *verba fortius accipiuntur contra proferentem:* words will be interpreted most strongly against the person offering them): the Latin label for the "rule" that ambiguity in a writing will be resolved against the one who caused the ambiguity. Also called "the preparer principle."   <Applying *contra proferentem,* we accept the insured's interpretation of the ambiguous words of the policy.>   On the worth of the "rule," □see **rules of interpretation.**

contributing to the delinquency of a minor   □see **child.**

contribution   □see **equitable indemnity;** □see also, **contributory negligence.**

contributory negligence • comparative negligence

contributory negligence

1. plaintiff's negligence that contributed to the harm of which plaintiff complains. <Plaintiff, a motorist, seeing the approaching train, tried to beat it over the crossing; that's contributory negligence.>

2. a rule of tort liability under which all recovery is barred if the plaintiff has been negligent (sense 1). <Granted that defendant was negligent; in this case, contributory negligence bars plaintiff's recovery.>

comparative negligence

1. negligence of plaintiff and defendant compared to establish the proportions in which the fault of each contributed to the harm of which plaintiff complains. <The jury found that the comparative negligence of plaintiff was 10 percent and that of defendant, 90 percent.>

2. a rule of tort liability under which plaintiff's negligence (*contributory negligence*) is compared with defendant's negligence to proportionately reduce rather than bar recovery. Thus stated, the rule is called *pure comparative negligence,* as contrasted with other versions of the rule under which all recovery may be barred if contributory negligence is sufficiently aggravated. <The jury found plaintiff's damages to be $100,000 and his fault to be 10 percent. Under the rule of comparative negligence, the award will be $90,000.>

□see **negligence;** □see also, **equitable indemnity.**

controlled substances   □see **under the influence of.**

controversy

1. a fancy name for a *dispute,* an *argument.* In that loose sense, the law on occasion joins the common speech in pinning the label *controversy* on anything from a donnybrook to a political debate. <They were all involved in the same controversy and so were properly joined as parties.> With mixed success, the law has tried to sharpen the bite.

2. a concrete, adversarial dispute that can be resolved by our legal system, through the courts, arbitration, or administrative procedures. This eliminates, in the words frequently used, the abstract, the hypothetical, the speculative, the academic. It balks at **mootness,** the **moot case:** a dispute already decided <It's moot; the strike has been settled.> or one on which a decision would have no effect. <The request for a stay is denied for mootness. Petitioner has been hanged.> Except by special statute, the law intervenes only where there are active disputants, so that what the court says will be more than an **advisory opinion:** an opinion of a court on a matter of law, without binding effect. <The legislature requested the state supreme court for an advisory opinion on the meaning of Section 2.>

3. a dispute that is **justiciable:** of the sort that under our constitutional system is traditionally resolved by courts, not reserved to the executive, the legislature, or to the individual, and with a sense of the concrete and adversarial heightened by requirements of *ripeness* and *standing.*

ripeness: the state of being **ripe:** on the facts and procedurally, the dispute is real and ready for determination by this court. <There are indications that the parties are moving toward a confrontation, but it is not ripe for judgment./When administrative remedies have been exhausted, and the state high court has ruled, perhaps the criterion of ripeness will be satisfied, but perhaps there will no longer be any dispute, ripe or otherwise.>

standing: qualification to sue or defend because of having a personal stake in the dispute that will be affected by the decision. <No doubt there is a dispute as to the constitutionality of the statute, but this plaintiff has no standing to sue; she has no interest beyond pride that will be affected by our decision.>

4. case and controversy • case or controversy: the two expressions are used interchangeably to describe the type of *case,* i.e., lawsuit, that is a *controversy* (sense 3) or the type of *controversy* that is a *case* within the judicial power (jurisdiction) of a court. Neither the *and* nor the *or* affect the sense of either expression; the heart of the matter can usually be expressed as well by *controversy* alone, sometimes by *case* alone. <Unless there was a case and controversy/a case or controversy/a controversy/the court had no jurisdiction.> The redundant combinations are compounds usually pointing in the direction of problems of jurisdiction or the propriety of declaratory relief. <It was clearly a case or controversy/a controversy/a case/for declaratory relief.>

Case (and its synonym *suit*) and *controversy* each separately, but treated as substantial equivalents (except when *case* refers to criminal law), describe the extent of the constitutional judicial power. Judicial power extends to what are called *cases* and to what are called *controversies* (Art. III, § 2), limited by specific exclusions (labeled "any *suit*" in the Eleventh Amendment). Interpretation makes it clear that in the context of judicial power, a *case* is a *controversy*, and a *controversy* is a *case*, a civil case.

5. actual controversy: a redundant reference to *controversy* (sense 3) in the federal Declaratory Judgment Act and similar statutes. The *actual* is an intensive (□see **actual**). A controversy is a controversy is a controversy.

□see also, **legal interest**; □see also, **separable controversy**.

contumacious □see **contempt**.

contumacy □see **contempt**.

contumelious □see **contempt**.

contumely □see **contempt**.

convenience and necessity: the standard used by regulatory agencies in determining that, all things considered, the public would be better served by the grant or denial of an application to operate another public utility. Both words are among the most flexible in the English language and in the legal vocabulary. *Necessity* is not an absolute (□see **absolutes**). The words are so amorphous that they occasionally run together. <"A public need without which the public is inconvenienced."> Application granted, the agency issues a **certificate of convenience and necessity**. The standard and the certificate are often phrased in terms of *public convenience and necessity*.

conversion • equitable conversion are listed together to emphasize their surface similarity and the total absence of legal relationship.

conversion

1. the civil equivalent of stealing personal property; also applied to less gross but still unlawful dominion over someone else's property. The verb is **convert**; the wrongdoer is a **converter**. <She converted the goods./She converted the goods to her own use./The converter collected interest on the stolen bonds.>

2. the name of the action for damages for conversion (sense 1). <The first count, based on theft of the stock, is framed in terms of conversion.> The action of *conversion* is sometimes indexed, though now rarely referred to, by its common law names, **trover** (O.F.: to find) or **trover and conversion**.

equitable conversion: a metaphor describing a present change in the incidents normal to ownership of one class of property (real or personal) to the incidents normal to ownership of the other class, in anticipation of an eventual change in the ownership of the property itself. Thus, e.g., under a specifically enforceable contract to sell land, the seller now has a right to the purchase money, and the buyer is the equitable (soon to be legal) owner of the land. On the death of either before consummation of the sale, the seller's estate would hold personal property (the money), the buyer's estate would hold real property (the land). <The contract worked an equitable conversion of the land.>

convert □see **conversion**.

converter □see **conversion**.

convey • conveyance • conveyancer

convey: frequently used to describe the **transfer**(□see) of real property, not usually of personal property. Not usually the operative word of transfer. <He conveyed Blackacre to Mary Smith./The words of conveyance were: "I grant Blackacre to Mary Smith.">

conveyance: the act of *conveying*, as well as the piece of paper.

conveyancer: a dying breed of specialist, not always a lawyer, expert in the art and business of conveyancing.

conveyance □see **convey**.

conveyancer □see **convey**.

convict • criminal   As the designation of a person, *convict* and *criminal* are not synonyms, though the usage is encouraged by the fact that neither has a sharp, fixed meaning.   Standing alone, *convict* is the more legalistic; *criminal* needs help to give it legal status.

> **convict**   (n.): the common denominator of the varying legal uses of *convict* is a person convicted, whose **conviction**(□see) has become final.   <The news report was in error. Smith is not a convict; he is appealing the conviction.>   Beyond that, *convict* roams through the cases, tied, often as though definitively, to one (1) not merely convicted but fined or sentenced, (2) convicted of any crime, (3) convicted of felony or serious crime, (4) serving time in prison, (5) serving a long term, or (6) who has served time in prison.   In this last sense, *ex-convict* (slang, *ex-con*) would be more accurate.   More than most words, *convict* bends with context.

> **criminal**   (n.): a term of opprobrium in and out of the law, predicated on inferences of the underworld but without a positive requirement of conviction.   It has the common touch—a *hardened criminal,* i.e., a real, bad guy; some of it with legal service—a *known criminal,* i.e., notorious for "criminal activity."   It has also achieved carefully defined legal standing with **habitual criminal**: a recidivist, under statutes specifically increasing punishment on repeated convictions.   For *criminal* (adj.), □see **crime**.

convicted felon   □see **felon**.

conviction: in a criminal case, a *verdict* of *guilty*, or a judge's finding of *guilty* after a trial without a jury or other proceedings without a jury (e.g., a plea of *guilty*).   □see **judgment**.

cooperative apartment   □see **condominium**.

co-ownership   □see **joint ownership**.

cop a plea   □see **negotiated plea**.

co-party   □see **cross-claim**, under **cross-**.

copyright

> 1.   the exclusive right to publish and reproduce, and to sell, license, or otherwise exploit a literary, artistic, or other work of the mind.

copyright

The right extends to what is original with the author, i.e., independently created—not copied—by the author, whether or not it is in fact something novel, new to the world. The right extends only to the form of expression, as distinct from the ideas. <Were it not in the public domain, "This above all: to thine own self be true" would be covered by copyright; the idea of personal integrity would not be.> The right is intangible property owned initially by the author (in the broad sense of creator) and is separate from the tangible property that embodies the form of expression. <I own this book but not its copyright; that belongs to the author.>

2. common law copyright: intangible property (sense 1) with two distinguishing features: (1) the virtue of perpetual duration if the work is not published and (2) the inherent vice, a fatal flaw, that *common law copyright* is usually lost upon publication of the work. Sometimes described as the *right of first publication*, emphasizing that the author can keep the bundle of intangible rights without time limit, and look to **statutory copyright** (□see) for protection of the work upon publication. The expression *common law copyright* is sometimes loosely applied to state statutory copyright incorporating the two distinguishing features. <California statute provides for common law copyright.> *Common law copyright* is now largely superseded by federal law. □see **Copyright Act of 1976**.

3. statutory copyright: intangible property (sense 1) of limited duration, with details of duration, rights, and mechanics of obtaining copyright, transfer, and protection fixed by statute. Until recently, the principle feature of *statutory copyright* was duration tied to date of first publication; this is now changed.

Copyright Act of 1976 (17 USCA §§ 1 et seq., as amended to 1988): the current, exclusive form of *statutory copyright*. It provides copyright for intangible property (sense 1) in works "fixed in any tangible medium of expression, now known or later developed, from which they can be perceived, reproduced, or otherwise communicated, either directly or with the aid of a machine or device." The categories of works protected are literary, musical, dramatic, pantomime, choreographic, pictorial, graphic, sculptural, motion picture, other audiovisual, and sound recording. Computer programs are included. Unlike earlier *statutory copyright,* duration is tied not to date of publication but to date of creation, i.e., the date the work is "fixed in any tangible medium of expression," whether or not published. *Common law copyright* is given temporary protection, and then eliminated as a separate basis of copyright, with two exceptions: *Common law copyright* may still exist to the extent that it is interpreted (1) to cover works not "fixed in any tangible medium," e.g., an oral story, or (2) to cover some category of work of the mind not covered by the Copyright Act of 1976.

For the two major international copyright treaties to which the United States is a signatory—the *Berne Convention* and the *Universal Copyright Convention* (abbreviated *U.C.C.*), see *Nimmer on Copyright*, 1990 ed.

□see also, ©; □see also, **infringement**; □see also, ℗, under ©; □see also, **perform**; □see also, **piracy**; □see also, **plagiarism**; □see also, **publication**; □see also, **public domain**.

Copyright Act of 1976   □see **copyright**.

coram nobis   (L.: before us): a common law writ, asking or directing the court to correct its own judgment because it was based on error of fact outside the record. With modifications, still available in some jurisdictions. Also called *writ of error coram nobis*.

coroner's inquest   □see **jury**.

coroner's jury   □see **jury**.

corporate • corporation   (L., *corporo:* to form into a body).

corporate: When pronounced COR-por-ut, it is the ubiquitous adjective of reference to anything having to do with corporations, from *corporate agents* through *corporate securities* to *corporate veils* (□see **alter ego**). The verb, pronounced COR-por-ate, is ignored by a profession that favors the verb *incorporate,* pronounced IN-cor-por-ate (L., *incorporatio,* the *in-* prefix = into: into a body). □see **incorporation**; □see also, **organize**. The adjective, pronounced IN-cor-por-ut (this time with the *in-* prefix = negative: not a body) is not used; for that role, lawyers prefer another Latin no body, *incorporeal.*   <Copyright is an incorporeal right.>

corporation: a legal abstraction that does most of the business in the United States. Almost without exception, it is a bloodless person, authorized by statute as a legal entity, with life, death, assets, and liabilities discrete from those who create it or own it. □see **artificial person**, under **person**. Apart from this unique artificiality that serves practical purposes, corporations vary greatly in form and function. Some have stock and stockholders; some don't. □see **nonstock corporation**. Some have stockholders who are themselves corporations. Some are for profit; some not (□see **charita-**

ble). Statutes give varying definitions of *corporation* to fit tax and other special contexts.

corporation sole: the "almost" exception to the corporation as a "bloodless person"; the *corporation sole* (with the adjective in that position) is now a religious corporation consisting of one person, the incumbent of a religious office recognized by statute. It may exist in perpetuity, the corporation continuing despite death or removal of the live person; so that—abstraction on abstraction— for some purposes, it is the office, rather than the person, that is the operating corporation sole. <The Roman Catholic Archbishop of San Francisco, a California corporation sole.> Though it is in fact a one-person corporation, *corporation sole* is not called that; it is to be distinguished from what lawyers know as a **one-person corporation** (□see).

municipal corporation: a political subdivision of a state, organized as an incorporated entity, and authorized by statute to exercise specified powers of governance and ownership. While an incorporated city or town is the typical municipal corporation, by statute other governmental entities, e.g., a water district with the power to tax, may be so designated. <The residents of an unincorporated area of the county took steps to form themselves into a municipal corporation to be known as the City of West Wood.>

one-person corporation (which lawyers still call a *one-man corporation*): a corporation in which the stock is owned entirely (or virtually) by a single stockholder. It is the ultimate in *close corporations* (□see **close**), as distinct from corporations with the stock widely held (□see **public corporation**). □see also, **parent corporation**; □see also **personal holding company**.

professional corporation: a corporation through which some members of a particular profession practice, e.g., law, medicine, accountancy; all of the stock must be owned by those licensed to practice that particular profession. <They formed a professional corporation to practice law.> *Professional corporation* is abbreviated **P.C.** It is a mid-twentieth century statutory creation originally designed primarily to enable professionals and their employees to qualify for tax benefits available only to corporations. A *professional corporation* may or may not be a *one-person corporation*. □see also, **professional association**.

public corporation: a loose expression, used in several different—sometimes contradictory—senses; not a term of art, except in precise reference to a particular statutory definition. The uncertainty rests solidly on a wobbly old foundation, the vagueness of the Latinate English word *public*. From time to time, *public* refers to government, to "the people," and—if enough people are interested—to things that Americans consider distinctly "private."

(1) *public corporation* sometimes means that it is a *private corporation* that has issued lots of stock (the number is not precisely fixed; hundreds of thousands is good; millions is better) owned by many stockholders; the stock is said to be *widely held*. This sort of *public corporation,* the usual large business corporation (e.g., General Motors, Ford, etc.) is also called a *publicly held corporation,* as distinguished from a *closely held corporation* (also called a *close corporation*). □see **close.** *Publicly held corporation* is not to be confused with a **publicly owned corporation**(□see).

(2) *public corporation* sometimes means that it is *not* a *private corporation* but is either a **municipal corporation** (□see) or a *publicly owned corporation,* also called a *government corporation:* a corporation like private corporations, except that the stock is owned entirely (or virtually) by the government. E.g., the Federal Deposit Insurance Corporation.

(3) *public corporation* sometimes means that it is not a *business corporation,* whether *for profit* or *not for profit* (□see **charitable**). In this sense, *public corporation* refers to a *municipal corporation* but not to a *publicly owned corporation* (government corporation) that is engaged in a business enterprise.

□see **de facto corporation,** under **de facto;** □see **foreign corporation,** under **foreign.**

corporate charter □see **articles.**

corporate merger □see **de facto merger,** under **de facto.**

corporate securities laws □see **blue sky laws.**

corporation □see **corporate.**

corporation sole □see **corporate.**

corporeal □see **corporate;** □see also, **intangible property.**

corpus (L.: body; substance): a synonym for *principal* or *capital,* as distinguished from *income,* used especially in connection with estates, trusts, and taxation. <The corpus of the trust was to be invested, and the income used for the support of Mary and John.>

invade the corpus: dipping into principal to make payments to the beneficiaries. Legal argot, without the hostile overtones of *invade* in ordinary speech. <If income proved inadequate for the support of Mary and John, the trustee was permitted to invade the corpus.>

corpus delicti (L., KOR-pus duh-LICK-tee: body or substance of the crime): the elements essential to prove that a crime has been committed. Unlike detective fiction usage <The *corpus delicti* was found hanging from a rafter.>, *corpus delicti* in the case of murder is proof that someone is dead plus proof that the death was caused by criminal means. <The *corpus delicti* of murder was proved, though the dead woman's body was never found.>

cost □see actual; □see costs.

cost and freight □see C. & F.

cost bill □see costs.

cost bond □see security for costs, under secure.

costs: the items of cost incurred in prosecuting or defending a case in court; also called **court costs**. *Costs* usually refers only to those items that by statute, court rule, or contract a court may (sometimes must) award to the successful litigant, to be recovered from the loser, e.g., filing fees, jury fees, reporter fees, etc. *Costs* does not include all of the expenses of litigation; e.g., attorneys' fees are not usually included. Procedures for claiming costs vary by jurisdiction. E.g., a motion to *tax costs,* itemizing costs in a **cost bill**; the court then determines which of the claimed costs are recoverable, i.e., *taxes costs.* For *cost bond,* □see **security for costs,** under **secure.** □see also, **in forma pauperis.**

cotenancy: a general, unspecific name for concurrent ownership of property by two or more persons, each called a *cotenant.* □see also, **estate.**

cotenant □see cotenancy.

128

counsel □see **lawyer.**

counsel fees □see **fee (attorney's fee).**

counselor • counselor at law □see **lawyer.**

counsel of choice □see **right to counsel.**

count: the part of a civil pleading, or of a criminal complaint, indictment, or information, outlining the details of the specific grievance or offense. In a civil pleading, *count* is a synonym for **cause of action** (□see). A criminal *count* outlines the details of the *charge* (□see **accuse).**

common count: a short, common law form of pleading a cause of action for a debt, by alleging the basis of the debt rather than an express promise to pay. For each of six separate bases of debt, there is a separate common count. The *common counts* are for goods sold and delivered; money due on an account stated; money lent; money paid to the use of the defendant; work done; and money *had and received* (□see **coupled synonyms).** □see also, **quantum meruit;** □see also, **quantum valebant.**

counterclaim □see **cross-complaint,** under **cross-;** □see also, **compulsory counterclaim,** under **joinder.**

county attorney □see **lawyer.**

county counsel □see **lawyer.**

coupled synonyms A long habit of coupling synonyms persists in American legal usage, e.g., *authorize and empower, null and void, true and correct.* The habit is compounded of antiquated literary style, the mixture of languages we now call English, the lawyer's gamble on venial repetition against mortal omission, and a misplaced reliance on the precision of what has endured.

The great mass of these coupled synonyms are simply redundancies, furnishing opportunity for argument that something beyond synonomy was intended. A handful have been so welded by usage as to have the effect, in proper context, of a single word, e.g., *aid and comfort, cease and desist;* these, distinguished by an asterisk, are included in

coupled synonyms

the general list here, for, except in the special context that enables them to pass as a unit, they are as redundant as the rest.

Except as otherwise noted, the coupled synonyms in this list are entered in the dictionary in alphabetical order:

acknowledge and confess

act and deed

**aid and abet*

**aid and comfort*

annul and set aside □see **null and void**

authorize and empower

**by and with*

cancel and terminate □see **cancel**

**cease and desist*

covenant and agree □see **covenant**

cover, embrace, and include

deem and consider

devise and bequeath □see **give**

each and all

each and every □see **each and all**

entirely and completely

faith and credit* □see **full faith and credit

false and untrue □see **in truth and in fact**

final and conclusive

fit and proper

fit and suitable □see **fit and proper**

fitting and proper □see **fit and proper**

for and during

force and effect

fraud and deceit □see **fraud**

free and clear* □see **clear

free and without charge

from and after

*full faith and credit

give and grant □see **give**, under **gift**

give, devise, and bequeath □see **give**, under **gift**

goods and chattels □see **chattel**

grant, bargain, and sell □see **grant**

*had and received

have and hold

heed and care

hold and keep □see **hold**

in lieu and in place of □see **in lieu of**

in my stead and place □see **in lieu and in place of**

in truth and in fact □see **facts**

just and reasonable

last will and testament □see **will**

let or hindrance

made and appointed

made and entered into

made and provided

maintenance and upkeep

meet and just □see **just and reasonable**

*metes and bounds

mind and memory

modified and changed

name and style □see **alias**

new and novel □see **new**

null and void

of and concerning

over, above, and in addition to

over and above □see, under **over, above, and in addition to**

*pain and suffering

131

coupled synonyms

pains and penalties

part and parcel □see, under **parcel**

peace and quiet

remise, release, and quitclaim □see **quitclaim**

rest, residue, and remainder □see **residue**

right, title, and interest* □see **quitclaim

save and except □see, under **save**

seised and possessed □see, under **seisin**

separate and apart

shun and avoid

situate, lying, and being in

stand, remain, and be

* *touch and concern* □see **covenant running with the land**, under **covenant**

true and correct □see **facts**

truth and veracity

understood and agreed

will and testament □see **will**

coupled with an interest   □see **power coupled with an interest.**

course of employment   □see **scope of employment.**

court

1. the institution, including its subdivisions, that administers justice. < That's a constitutional question for the courts/for the U.S. Supreme Court. >

Names for the subdivisions in the hierarchy vary by jurisdiction. A trial court, called *superior court* in one state, is called *supreme court* in another; the final appellate court in one state, the *supreme court,* is called *court of appeals* in another. Courts are also known generally by comparative, though not invidious, subordination: *highest court* (also, *high court*), *higher court, lower court, court below, inferior court.* All of these names, official and by rank, are

132

also used in sense 3. □see also, **federal courts**. □see also, **Uniform Code of Military Justice**.

2. a court (sense 1) classified by administrative characteristics, of which these are a small sampling.

court of general jurisdiction: a court without limit as to the amount in controversy before it or the nature of penalty it may adjudge, and with few or no limits as to the type of case it may consider. Distinguished from—

court of limited jurisdiction: a court limited by statute in one or more of those respects, e.g., a *juvenile court, magistrate's court, small claims court, surrogate* (probate) *court, traffic court*. The extent of general and limited jurisdiction and the titles vary from state to state.

court of record: a court that keeps an official record of its proceedings. <It was only a traffic court, not a court of record.>

3. a judge, or group of judges, of a particular court (sense 1), characterized as a unit of decision. <That's a decision of the Ninth Circuit./The court was evenly split on this issue./That court decides more cases, and is reversed more often, than any other.>

4. a judge, or group of judges, presiding over a case in court (sense 1).

a. Especially as a depersonalized reference to the judges, by officials, lawyers, and the judges themselves, emphasizing that the judge in court acts, and deserves respect, not as an individual but as representative of the institution (sense 1). □see **office of judge**, under **office**.

This honorable court is now in session: traditional phrase still used in some courts at opening of session. □see **formalisms**; □see **Honor**.

May it please the court; If the court please: traditional phrases still used as preface to a lawyer's remarks. □see **formalisms**.

The court finds: the institution speaking through the judge. <The court finds for the plaintiff./finds you in contempt.>

b. court trial: a trial by judge, as opposed to trial by jury. Interchangeable with *bench trial*. □see **bench**.

c. court witness: a witness, usually an expert, called by the judge in an attempt to resolve conflict in other testimony.

5. the courtroom, not as a physical structure but as the site of legal proceedings, e.g., *in court/out of court*. <That's what he said in court; out of court, he told a different story.> □see also, **out of court**.

court

court reporter: one qualified and licensed to record exactly what is said in court. □see **reporter's transcript**, under **transcript**.

see you in court: an end of negotiation; this case will have to be tried (legal slang). Equivalents: this one will have to *go to court;* I'll have to *take them to court.* All as opposed to: they settled *out of court.* See also sense 6.

6. the courtroom or the courthouse, as a physical structure. <The court is at First and Temple streets./That court is on the fifth floor of the courthouse.>

on the courthouse steps: a metaphor of settlement just before trial. <It was settled on the courthouse steps.>

see you in court: a place of meeting, as distinguished from the same phrase, sense 5.

□see also, **bench**.

court below　□see **court**.

court costs　□see **costs**.

court crier　□see **proclamation**; □see also, **formalisms**.

court-martial　□see **Uniform Code of Military Justice**.

court of general jurisdiction　□see **court**.

Court of International Trade　□see **U.S. Court of International Trade**.

court of limited jurisdiction　□see **court**.

Court of Military Appeals　□see **Uniform Code of Military Justice**.

Court of Military Review　□see **Uniform Code of Military Justice**.

court of record　□see **court**.

court reporter　□see **court**.

courtroom privilege   □see **immunity**.

court trial   □see **court**.

court witness   □see **court**.

covenant:

1. Once, but no longer, referred only to a *contract under seal*.   □see **seal**.

2. An old synonym for *contract* and *agreement* still used in this sense, usually as a variant of *agreement* and the verb form *agree*. The formula expression *covenant and agree* is a worthless redundancy. Standing alone, *covenant* often distinguishes an *agreement* from a *condition*, especially important in leases.   <Damages were proper for the tenant's failure to keep the premises in good repair, but that failure did not end the lease; the tenant's obligation was a covenant, not a condition of the tenancy.>

3. The word *covenant* does not usually stand alone; it is combined with modifiers and in phrases as numerous as the topics and character of agreements. The names are not uniform; the list here is not exhaustive; the alphabetical listings are catchwords of reference:

affirmative: An *affirmative covenant,* as distinguished from a *negative covenant,* is an agreement to do something, typically an agreement in a deed or lease of real property. For examples, □see **covenants of title**; □see **easements**.

against encumbrances: one of the **covenants of title** (□see).

express: An *express covenant,* as distinguished from an *implied covenant,* is one spelled out in so many words.

further assurance: one of the **covenants of title** (□see).

future: A *future covenant,* as distinguished from a *present covenant,* is an agreement to do something if the need arises. A breach, if any, occurs when someone is damaged, not at the time of delivery of a deed or lease. Typical future covenants are the title covenants of further assurance, quiet enjoyment, and warranty. □see **covenants of title**.

good faith and fair dealing: A *covenant of good faith and fair dealing* is an implied covenant that a party to a contract will do nothing to prevent the other party from receiving what is promised.

habitability: A *covenant of habitability* is a covenant, express or implied, that premises leased for occupancy are fit for that purpose. Also called *warranty of habitability.*

implied: An *implied covenant*, as distinguished from an *express covenant*, is one read into the agreement as a matter of interpretation of its language, or as a matter of law under the circumstances of the agreement. □see **covenants of title;** □see **implied easement**, under **easement.**

negative: A *negative covenant*, as distinguished from an *affirmative covenant*, is an agreement not to do something. E.g., **not to sue** (in this list), but especially **not to compete** (in this list), and a miscellany of agreements in a deed or lease of real property. □see **easements.**

not to compete: A *covenant not to compete* is an agreement, typically in a contract of employment, for the sale of a business, or in a lease of real property, not to compete with respectively, the employer, the buyer, the lessor, or adjacent lessees. Commonly referred to as a *negative covenant.* Closely restricted by substantive law. □see **antitrust law.**

not to sue: A *covenant not to sue* is an agreement not to enforce a cause of action against a particular person. Typically, it is a covenant by a plaintiff settling with less than all of the defendants in a tort case. Usually distinguished from a **release.** (□see).

personal: A *personal covenant* is one that is not a *covenant running with the land* (in this list, under *running*).

present: A *present covenant*, as distinguished from a *future covenant,* is a warranty that something is so right now. A breach, if any, occurs at the time of delivery of a deed or lease. Typical present covenants are the title covenants of the right to convey, seisin, against encumbrances, and a covenant that the grantor has not conveyed. □see **covenants of title.**

quiet enjoyment

   a. one of the **covenants of title** (□see).

   b. In a lease, a lessor's *covenant of quiet enjoyment* (sometimes *for*) is a covenant, express or implied, that neither the lessor nor anyone with a title superior to lessor's will disturb lessee's occupancy of the premises. Also called a *covenant of peaceful enjoyment.*

real: *Real covenant* is another name for a *covenant running with the land* (in this list, under *running with the land*).

restrictive

    a. *Restrictive covenant* usually refers to a covenant in a deed or lease that limits the use of the real property. In loose usage, sometimes refers especially to the now-outlawed covenants limiting the ownership or use of real property according to race.

    b. Sometimes, another name for a *covenant not to compete* (in this list, under *not to compete*).

running with the land: A *covenant running with the land,* also called a *real covenant,* is an agreement about the land that binds and benefits whoever owns it. In order to qualify, the agreement must **touch and concern** (i.e., be related to) the land; those old synonyms (□see **coupled synonyms**) have been joined for so long in the law that they are used as one word—the hallmark of a covenant running with the land. How closely a covenant must touch and concern the land in order to *run with the land* varies with local rules of real property law.

seisin: one of the **covenants of title** (□see).

title □see **covenants of title.**

warranty: one of the **covenants of title** (□see).

covenant against encumbrances   □see covenants of title.

covenant and agree   □see covenant.

covenant not to compete   □see covenant.

covenant not to sue   □see covenant.

covenant of further assurance   □see covenants of title.

covenant of general warranty   □see covenants of title.

covenant of good faith and fair dealing   □see covenant.

covenant of habitability   □see covenant.

covenant of quiet enjoyment   □see covenant; □see covenants of title.

covenant of right to convey   □see covenants of title.

covenant of seisin □see **covenants of title.**

covenant of special warranty □see **covenants of title.**

covenant of warranty □see **covenants of title.**

covenant running with the land □see **covenant.**

covenants of title, also called *warranties of title,* either express or implied, are agreements usually included in real property deeds other than a **quitclaim** (□see). The covenants and their names vary by jurisdiction. They also vary according to the type of deed, e.g., a **general warranty deed** (sometimes called a *warranty deed*), as opposed to a **special warranty deed** (sometimes called a *grant deed*). These are the common covenants of title:

against encumbrances: A *covenant against encumbrances* is the grantor's warranty that there are no encumbrances on the property, whether formal security devices (e.g., mortgage, lien) or otherwise. In a special warranty deed, the covenant is limited to encumbrances made by the grantor. □see **encumber.**

further assurance: A *covenant of further assurance* (sometimes *for;* sometimes *assurances*) is the grantor's agreement to supply any additional instruments reasonably required to give the grantee the title conveyed.

quiet enjoyment: A *covenant of quiet enjoyment* (sometimes *for*) is the grantor's warranty that the grantee's occupancy of the property will not be disturbed by anyone with a title superior to that of the grantor. In a special warranty deed, the covenant is limited to disturbance by anyone lawfully claiming title through the grantor. The covenant of quiet enjoyment is sometimes omitted as synonymous with the covenants of warranty.

right to convey: A *covenant of right to convey* is the grantor's warranty that the grantor has the right to convey the property, not, e.g., restricted by a trust prohibiting transfer. This covenant is not included in a special warranty deed.

seisin: A *covenant of seisin* is the grantor's warranty that the grantor owns the estate described in the deed. Despite current variations of its meaning in the law, **seisin** (□see) retains this distinctive usage. This covenant is not included in a special warranty deed; instead, the grantor covenants that the grantor has not conveyed the property to anyone else.

warranty: A *covenant of warranty* is a covenant of title sometimes considered synonymous with a *covenant of quiet enjoyment* (in this list). The covenant varies with the type of deed.

   a. A *covenant of general warranty* is the grantor's agreement in a general warranty deed to defend against lawful claims, and to compensate the grantee for any loss from the claim of title superior to that of grantor.

   b. A *covenant of special warranty* is the grantor's agreement in a special warranty deed to defend against lawful claims, and to compensate the grantee for any loss from the claim, by anyone claiming title through the grantor.

cover, embrace, and include: synonyms; any good thesaurus could extend the list indefinitely, without adding sense to the first word. <The leases cover/embrace/include producing horizons above the depth of four thousand feet.> □see **coupled synonyms.**

credit □see **letter of credit.**

crier □see **proclamation;** □see also, **formalisms.**

crime • criminal

crime: a violation of law punishable by the state; to be distinguished from a *civil* wrong based on the same facts for which a private person may have a right to redress. □see **tort.** <He was convicted of the crime of assault with a deadly weapon and sentenced to prison; the victim later sued for damages.> □see also, **crime against nature;** □see also, **criminal contempt,** under **contempt;** □see also, **felony;** □see also, **infraction;** □see also, **malum in se;** □see also, **malum prohibitum,** under **malum in se;** □see also, **misdemeanor;** □see also, **pander;** □see also, **prostitute;** □see also, **treason.**

criminal (adj.): a loose term of reference to *crime* and to anything or anyone connected with the law relating to crime. E.g., *criminal fraud; criminal law; criminal negligence; criminal lawyer* (□see **lawyer**); **criminal conversation** (□see). □see also, **penal.** For *criminal* (n.), □see **convict.**

crime against nature: the fading survival of an old euphemism for a variety of forbidden forms of sexual gratification, still a general rubric for variations on a theme. Also called the *infamous crime against nature.*

139

crime against nature

Taking its cue from the Bible, which doesn't say exactly what the original Sodomites were doing, the fuller euphemism has set a pattern of unspecific sin. It denounces "the abominable and detestable crime against nature, not to be named among Christians, with either mankind or beast." Statutes and decisions, naming the unnameable, have succeeded in turning *the* abomination into an embarrassed plural of abominations; a mixed bag of plain speaking and Latin fig leaves, with no uniformity of either included offenses or the specifics of the offenses themselves. *Crime against nature* may refer to all or any of the offenses in this inventory:

sodomy: the most common synonym for the *crime against nature*, is often limited to anal intercourse, also called by the Latin *per anus* (or *anum*), "contact between the penis of one and the anus of another."

bestiality: usually sex of any sort between a human and an animal.

buggery: often a synonym for *sodomy*, usually in the limited sense.

cunnilingus (L., *cunnus:* vulva + *lingere:* to lick): oral copulation, mouth to vulva or clitoris.

fellatio (fuh-LAY-she-o; L., *fellare:* to suck): oral copulation, mouth to penis.

oral copulation: copulation by mouth, also called by the Latin *per os* (mouth), including *cunnilingus* and *fellatio;* by statute, "copulating the mouth of one person with the sex organ or anus of another."

pederasty (L., *paederastia,* from the Greek for boy + lover): *sodomy,* usually in its limited sense, usually with a boy; included in special offenses against juveniles.

criminal   For *criminal* (adj.), □see **crime**; for *criminal* (n.), □see **convict.**

criminal contempt   □see **contempt.**

criminal conversation: the waning civil action for damages for adultery with plaintiff's spouse.

criminal homicide   □see **homicide.**

criminal jurisdiction   □see **jurisdiction.**

criminal law   □see **civil law, under civil.**

criminal lawyer □see **lawyer.**

criminal negligence □see **manslaughter;** □see also, **crime.**

criminal pleas □see **plea;** □see **guilty.**

criminal prosecution □see **civil suit,** under **civil.**

criminate • incriminate: synonyms, with *incriminate* the prevailing choice: to accuse one of having committed a crime, or to give evidence or information tending to prove that one has committed a crime. Most frequent use is **privilege against self-incrimination** (usually hyphenated): the privilege not to give evidence against oneself in a prosecution, nor to answer questions tending to subject oneself to prosecution. Also called the **right against self-incrimination.** Neither expression appears in the Fifth Amendment's version, "No person . . . shall be compelled in any criminal case to be a witness against himself."

Critical Legal Studies: an amorphous critique of law, its underpinning, study, and practice, with variegated suggestions that starting society and the law all over again in some undefinable way could not hurt. The adherents of Critical Legal Studies, sometimes called the *crits,* have a wobbly connection with deconstruction and with each other. *Critical Legal Studies* (abbreviated *CLS*), sometimes called a "movement," is a ferment in the law schools of the late twentieth century.

critical stage: short for *critical stage of a prosecution.*

1. in prosecutions to which the Sixth Amendment **right to counsel** (□ see) *may* apply, a *critical stage* is a stage at which it *does* apply, because (1) adversary criminal proceedings have started and (2) the presence of counsel may be critical to the outcome of a prosecution. <The preliminary hearing at which the rape victim identified the accused was a critical stage./Though after the indictment, the prosecutor's display of photographs to the victim was not a critical stage of the prosecution./Despite a certain logical appeal, commission of the crime was not a critical stage; absence of counsel was a misfortune but not a violation of constitutional right.>

2. more loosely, in prosecutions generally, a *critical stage* is one at which the defendant has a right to be personally present, not merely through counsel, because a fundamental right of Fourteenth Amendment due process is affected. <A plea of guilty is a critical stage; a stipulation to a continuance is not.>

cross □see X.

cross-

1. a prefix peculiarly apt for an adversary system, indicating that someone under attack is fighting back. It clings easily to law words, often without either technicality or uniformity. Growth is almost unlimited; only a sampling is listed here. Hyphening is not standardized; the forms here are common.

cross action: a general name for a second lawsuit filed in the original lawsuit by the original defendant against the original plaintiff, often joining other parties. Of the entries following in this list, *cross action* would include *cross-bill, cross-complaint, cross-petition,* and *cross suit,* but not *cross-claim.*

cross appeal: an appeal by the winner of a lawsuit from the same judgment from which the loser has taken an appeal; often by way of encouraging dismissal of the original appeal. <We won, but we could have done better; if there is an appeal, there will be a cross appeal.>

cross-bill: in jurisdictions using *bill* where others use *complaint, cross-bill* is the equivalent of **cross-complaint** (□see).

cross-claim: a claim (chiefly under federal procedure) filed by a party against a **co-party**: one with similar status in the lawsuit, e.g., defendant against another defendant.

cross-claimant: the party filing a **cross-claim** (□see).

cross-complaint: a second complaint filed in the original lawsuit by the original defendant against the original plaintiff, often joining other parties. Exactly what may be included in a *cross-complaint* varies by jurisdiction; often it is any cause of action against the original plaintiff. In other jurisdictions, *cross-complaint* is equated to **counterclaim**: itself a variable, in some jurisdictions a claim that would "diminish or defeat" the original claim; in others, a claim of any sort against an opposing party. □see also, **compulsory counterclaim**, under **joinder**; □see also, **offset**.

cross-defendant: defendant in a **cross-complaint** (□see). <For answer to the cross-complaint, cross-defendant realleged almost everything that he had alleged as plaintiff in the complaint.>

cross demand: a general name for opposing claims in a lawsuit.

cross-examination: usually, examination by the opposing side, as contrasted with **direct examination**, also called *examination in* *chief:* the first examination, or the examination of one's own witness. *Cross-examination* is often a reference to a scope of questioning broader than permitted on direct examination, even though there has been no direct examination. □ see **leading question.** Orally, *cross-examination* is customarily shortened to **cross,** and *direct examination,* to **direct.** <In taking plaintiff's deposition, defendant may examine him as on cross-examination./Direct and cross will be limited to fifteen minutes each.> A resumption of cross-examination after direct examination is called *recross examination,* often shortened to *recross.* A resumption of direct examination after cross-examination is called *redirect examination,* often shortened to *redirect.*

cross interrogatory: written questions requiring written answers as part of pretrial **discovery proceedings,** after opposing party has served similar questions on a party or witness.

cross motion: opposing motion, usually requesting a result opposite to original motion. <The parties have filed cross motions for judgment.>

cross-petition: where appropriate relief must be requested by *petition,* opposing relief is sometimes requested by *cross-petition.* In some jurisdictions, the equivalent of **cross-complaint** (□see).

cross-plaintiff: plaintiff in a **cross-complaint** (□see).

cross question: a general and loose name for **cross-examination** (□see), or for questioning on a **cross interrogatory** (□see).

cross suit: another name for **cross action** (□see).

2. For the prefix *cross* in other senses, □see **cross collateral,** under **collateral;** and **cross remainder,** under **remainder.**

cross action   □see **cross-.**

cross appeal   □see **cross-.**

cross-bill   □see **cross-.**

cross-claim   □see **cross-.**

cross-claimant   □see **cross-.**

cross-collateral   □see **collateral.**

cross-complaint   □see **cross-.**

cross-defendant □see **cross-**.

cross demand □see **cross-**.

cross-examination □see **cross-**.

cross interrogatory □see **cross-**.

cross motion □see **cross-**.

cross-petition □see **cross-**.

cross-plaintiff □see **cross-**.

cross question □see **cross-**.

cross remainder □see **remainder**.

cross suit □see **cross-**.

cruel and unusual punishment: the Eighth Amendment's flexible characterization of punishment so barbaric as to be forbidden.

cruelty □see **cruel and unusual punishment**; □see also, **extreme cruelty**.

c.t.a. □see **cum testamento annexo**.

cujus est solum ejus est usque ad coelum □see **airspace**; □see also, **maxims**.

cum testamento annexo (L.: with the will annexed; abbreviated c.t.a.): a phrase added to **letters of administration** (□see) or to the designation of an administrator, indicating that the person now appointed administrator deals with a will that named no executors or that executors named are not acting. No technicality is lost in translation. <The executors named in the will predeceased the testator, and John Smith was appointed administrator, with the will annexed.>

cumulative dividend □see **preferred stock,** under **stock.**

cumulative preferred □see **preferred stock,** under **stock.**

cumulative sentences □see **sentence.**

cumulative voting: a system of voting designed to increase the voting power of minority stockholders in the election of corporate directors when more than one director is to be elected. One share of stock has one vote multiplied by the number of directors to be elected, and each stockholder's total vote may be spread or bunched (cumulated) for favored directors. Depending on the number of shares held by a minority and the number of directors to be elected, a minority may be able to elect one or more directors. Contrasted with:

straight voting: one share of stock has one vote for each director to be elected, but each directorship is considered as a separate election. A majority has a majority for each directorship and always has the power to elect all the directors.

cunnilingus □see **crime against nature.**

curative statute □see **remedial statute.**

curtesy □see **dower.**

curtilage: the area around a house that includes grounds, outbuildings, and fencing intimately associated with domestic life in the house. The area has no standard limits as to square footage or size or nature of what is put on the ground. What is or is not *within the curtilage* varies with context (and decision), e.g., in considering rights of privacy, limitations on search and seizure, a burglary statute.

custodial interrogation: "questioning initiated by law enforcement officers after a person has been taken into custody or otherwise deprived of his freedom of action in any significant way." (*Miranda v. Arizona,* 384 U.S. 436, 1966). □see **Miranda rules.**

custody: the ordinary English sense of guarding, care, and temporary control of property or person, in specialized legal uses. The distinctive phrases are **to have custody,** as opposed to **in custody.**

custody

1. Of persons, *to have custody* is an expression in civil use, emphasizing personal responsibility for care, and the rights of the person having that responsibility. The most common context is *child custody,* with its companions *unfit to have custody,* and *right to custody*—short for *right to have custody.* <She was awarded custody of the minor children./They were found unfit to have custody, and custody was awarded to the Department of Social Welfare./The court found that the natural parents had forfeited their right to custody.> Civilly, though one *has custody* of another person, that person is not said to be *in custody.* That expression, criminal law usage, refers to someone under physical restraint by law enforcement officers, or under the implicit threat of physical restraint upon any attempt to walk away. <The officers stood with guns drawn and told him not to move; he was in custody./We took them into custody at the border.> □see **custodial interrogation;** □see **search and seizure.**

2. Of property, *to have custody* and *in custody* both emphasize the temporary responsibility of the *custodian,* and the terms are often interchangeable. <The bank had custody of the securities./The securities were in the bank's custody.> At the point where formal legal action is exerted over property, *in custody* takes over. Upon an officer's seizure of a debtor's goods on legal process, the goods are *in legal custody* or *in custody of the law,* English translations that have largely superseded the Latin *in custodia legis.* □see also, **possession.**

cuts both ways □see **clichés.**

cy près (law F., SEE PRAY: as near): variously described as doctrine, principle, and rule, without the fixed limits of any of those. Used as a general reference to a court's carrying out the intention (of a testator or settlor) *as near as* possible or practicable, by interpretation or reformation of a writing. Applied especially to charitable trusts when original terms cannot be carried out and to conveyances otherwise afoul of the *rule against perpetuities.* <The testator's intention was applied *cy près.*/That interpretation is *cy près* gone mad.> The usual form is *cy près,* with the hyphenated *cy-près* a poor second, and *cyprès* (F.: the cypress tree) worst of all.

D

damage

1. (v.): a synonym of *injure,* both more forceful synonyms of *harm* (v.) <The news report damaged/injured/harmed her reputation.> The common speech prefers *damage* (v.) for harming physical property and *injure* for harming a person. <They damaged the car and injured a pedestrian.> Without apology or consistency, the law blurs the distinction; and, perhaps with an eye to the plural *damages* (n.) to follow, prefers *damage* (v.), whatever the harm. <The reckless driver damaged the bus, its driver, and two passengers.> For completely abstract invasion of legal right, the preferred law verb is *injure.* <One should use his own property so as not to injure another.>

2. The legal participles *damaged* and *injured* generally follow the common distinction between harming physical property and people. <The damaged car was repaired by the insurer./The injured driver was hospitalized.> For invasion of legal right, both are used. <The suit seeks redress for a damaged/an injured reputation.> But as the sense becomes more abstract, *injured* is preferred. <He was not the injured party to the marriage.>

3. (n., singular): a synonym for both *injury* and *injuries.* <The injury was severe./The injuries were severe./The damage was severe.> The law applies *damage* (n.) to harm generally. <The policy covered damage to person and property.> But the choice is not rigid; the **personal injury** (**P.I.**) case has a special celebrity. Despite overlap, *damage* (n.) tends to focus on the harm, as distinguished from invasion of legal right, the province of *injury.* □see **damnum absque injuria.** The closest that *damage* (n.) comes to being an abstraction is in the expression **irreparable damage** (□see). For *severance damage,* □see **eminent domain.**

damages (n., plural): the money that a person may recover at law when he has been harmed. <They sued for/asked for/claimed/sought damages./They were awarded $5,000 damages./They dropped their claim for damages (□see **ad damnum**) and sued for an injunction.> The plural *damages*—often, as in this sentence, a collective singular—is a catchall of startling propensities. The label is broad enough to cover compensation for harm suffered, money awarded instead of compensation for harm suffered, and money that is not compensatory but awarded because of some connection with the harm. The harm may be of any variety from breach of contract to wounded psyche. The law has difficulty in tying down *damages*. Its sprawling, often inconsistent and redundant, vocabulary is reduced here to generally recognized essentials, under the headings **actual damages, damages that are not compensatory,** and **duty to mitigate damages.**

actual damages, also called **compensatory damages**: the law's conversion of harm into money. The expression *actual damages* serves the practical purpose of distinguishing these from damages that are not compensatory. Referring to *actual damages* as *pecuniary damages* is redundant; all damages are pecuniary. The subdivision of *actual damages* varies by jurisdiction and often varies with the type of lawsuit:

1. general damages, also called **direct damages**: the damages that usually result from the harm done. <The difference between the contract price and the market price was one measure of general damages for breach of defendant's promise to sell the land./Pain resulting from loss of an arm in the accident is an element of general damages and need not be specially pleaded.> □see **pain and suffering**.

unliquidated damages: damages that have not or cannot yet be fixed in amount. A broad term, not merely the antonym of *liquidated damages* (below, in this entry).

2. special damages: damages resulting from the harm done, but the particulars vary so from case to case as to require pleading or special proof. <Loss of earning power from physical injury is an element of special damages.> In informal usage, *special damages* are **the specials**. <The specials alone are worth more than that.> By statute and usage, *special damages* are further subdivided:

a. incidental damages: the wide variety of expectable damages incident to, but not inevitably accompanying, general damages. <The buyer's refusal to accept the goods required that the goods be warehoused until sold; the cost of warehousing was an element of incidental damages.>

b. consequential damages, also called **indirect damages**: damages not usual but arising from circumstances that could have been anticipated. This definition rules out indirect damages unless they are **foreseeable damages**. <Loss of profits while the plant was shut down for repairs was properly an item of consequential damages resulting from the delivery of defective equipment.>

damages that are not compensatory

1. exemplary damages, also called **punitive damages**: damages by way of punishment of a wrongdoer or as an example to others not to do likewise. Despite their strong element of public policy, the damages are awarded to the person suffering harm. *Exemplary damages* are said to be "in addition to actual damages," but there is little uniformity as to the degree of that relationship; often exemplary damages are large, though actual damages small. The nature of the wrongdoing that justifies exemplary damages is variable and imprecise. The usual epithets are *bad faith, fraud, malice, oppression, outrageous, violent, wanton, wicked, reckless.* <Defendant's conduct was not only fraudulent but evidenced a malice deliberately intended to oppress the plaintiff; exemplary damages were clearly justified.> □see also, **treble damages**.

2. treble damages: statutory damages, e.g., in some antitrust cases, tripling the trial award of damages. As a matter of long habit, the law keeps the usage *treble* (not *triple*) *damages.* Like *exemplary damages* in its reflection of a public policy of deterrence; different from *exemplary damages* in that the provision is specifically by statute, the increase is fixed as a multiple, and the provision is designed to encourage private enforcement of the overriding public policy behind the statute, as in the case of the *private attorney general.* □see **lawyer**.

3. nominal damages: damages awarded as an acknowledgement that some legal right has been invaded, but little harm done. The award is often a jury's way of saying that technicality favors the plaintiff, but the defendant deserves a medal. <The jury found that the plaintiff had been defamed by the defendant's words, "I was a sucker to buy that car; it was highway robbery," and awarded nominal damages—one dollar.> *Nominal damages* are sometimes contrasted with *substantial damages.*

4. prospective damages: damages that may be computed now with reasonable certainty, though based on harm not yet but likely to be incurred as a result of the wrongdoing. Claims for these damages are frequently denied as not being *prospective* but **speculative damages**, because future harm or present computation of damages is too uncertain.

5. liquidated damages: damages estimated and fixed in advance as the money to be paid on breach of contract. In a **liquidated damages clause**, the parties agree (a) in good faith, (b) that it would be difficult to assess damages precisely in the event of breach, (c) that the amount specified is a reasonable estimate of what the damages would be, and (d) that the amount fixed will be instead of other damages that might be proved and without requirement that any damages be proved. If any of the elements is lacking, the clause, though designated by the parties as a *liquidated damages clause,* is frequently disapproved as a provision for a *penalty* or *forfeiture.* □see also, **unliquidated damages**.

duty to mitigate damages: the duty of one who has been harmed to take reasonable measures to avoid **avoidable consequences** of the wrongdoing. The measures to be taken are referred to as **mitigation of damages**. <In mitigation of damages, plaintiff should have had the car repaired promptly. The cost of a substitute car will be reduced from the claimed damages for ten months' rent to the rent for one month.> Compare **collateral source rule** (□see).

For benefit of the bargain, loss of bargain, and out of pocket "rules," □see **out of pocket**; □see also, **severance damages**, under **eminent domain**.

damnum □see **ad damnum**.

damnum absque injuria (L., DAM-num ABSque in-YOUR-ee-ah: damage without violation of legal right): damage for which there is no right to legal redress. <The earthquake caused heavy damage, but it was damage *absque injuria*/without any right to legal redress./In most states, breach of promise to marry is now *damnum absque injuria.*/In most states, the cause of action for breach of promise to marry has been abolished.> The Latin has the edge in brevity and antiquity. Today, it does not carry the explicit message of the English equivalents; and *injuria,* so close to English *injury,* yet different in meaning and pronunciation, contributes an unneeded confusion. Prefer the English.

day □see **time**; □see also, **clear days**, under **clear**.

day in court: not to be taken literally and not a cliché; a metaphor for an opportunity to have one's claim or defense heard through established legal procedures before being judged. <The judge arbitrarily refused to listen to any argument; plaintiff was denied her day in court.> An element of, but not to be equated with, **due process** (□see).

d.b.a. □see **alias**.

d.b.e. □see **de bene esse**.

d.b.n. □see de bonis non.

deadlocked jury □see **hung jury**, under **hanging jury**.

dealer's talk: a seller's exaggerations, also called **puffing**, of the worth of property offered for sale, short of fraud, and within the limits of expectable haggling. It lacks precision, except as a conclusion that the talk is not actionable. <"This is the best car" may or may not be true, but it is dealer's talk that no one would rely on.> The focus should be on the individual dealer, with the apostrophe preceding the *s*. Following the *s,* the apostrophe turns idiosyncratic sin into a group libel.

death □see **absolutes**; □see also, **civil death**, under **civil**. □see also, **right to die**.

death taxes: taxes levied on the transfer of property upon the death of the owner. The usual plural softens the grim implication of *death tax*. Neither death nor the property is taxed, but rather, the transfer occasioned by death. The most common forms of death taxes are:

estate tax: on the privilege of transferring the property; and

inheritance tax, also called **succession tax:** on the privilege of receiving the property, relationship to the owner affecting the amount of the tax.

death warrant □see **warrant** (n.).

de bene esse (L., day benny essey: of being suitable): for the time being; said of something that suffices conditionally. <Testimony will be perpetuated by deposition *de bene esse* but will not be used if the witness is available at trial.> A dying Latinism, usually surplus. <Testimony will be perpetuated by deposition but will not be used if the witness is available for trial.> Abbreviated **d.b.e.**

debenture □see **bond**.

de bonis non: short for *de bonis non administratis* (L.: of the goods not administered): a phrase, or its abbreviation **d.b.n.**, sometimes added to the designation of **letters of administration** (□see) or to the designation of an administrator, indicating that the previous administrator or executor had not completed the administration of estate property. Here, the Latin version of *goods* (*bona*) translates as *property* generally, in contrast to the tautology *goods and chattels* (□see **chattel**). Use of *de bonis non* has faded, giving place to **successor administrator.**

debtee   □see -ee.

debts, defaults, and miscarriages   □see **suretyship.**

debt securities   □see **securities, under secure.**

deceased • decedent: ordinary English synonyms derived from the Roman euphemism to avoid the bluntness of *dead* (L., *decedere* = depart); on the whole, preferable to *the departed.* In and out of the law, both *deceased* and *decedent* can refer to one recently dead or simply to someone dead <the deceased's/decedent's estate>. Overexposure to the words in probate practice has led the profession into grim distortion and redundancy <She saw the decedent alive . . . then saw the decedent was dead.>, but also into practical innovation, saved from gaucherie by being instantly intelligible. The words are often shorthand for the expression: *before death, the person now dead.* <Decedent executed a typewritten will. Later, decedent executed a codicil and a few days after that drew an X through all of the writing in the codicil.>

deceit   □see **fraud.**

decision

1.   as in ordinary English, a general, untechnical term for determination of a controversy, whether by a jury, arbitrator, or administrative agency, but, most frequently, by a judge. <"John Marshall has made his decision, now let him enforce it."/A decision of the Second Circuit. . . .> In this sense, a synonym for *ruling.* <The decision/ruling will almost certainly be appealed.> □see also, **rule.** Even loosely, *decision* has limits. It should not be confused with:

   a.   opinion: a statement or discussion of the reasons for a *decision.* <In its opinion, the court cited two recent decisions of the New York Court of Appeals.> This is a generalized distinction between *decision* and *opinion.* For nuance and variety, □see **opinion.**

   b.   order: any oral or written utterance by a judge that has the force of law and directs that something be done or not done. It is more often an operative verb, rather than the noun of decision, though often loosely equated with *decision*. <The court's decision was. . . ./The court's order was. . . . > Often part of a judgment <It is ordered that Jane Doe have custody of the minor child.>, orders control the judge's routine legal business, though not part of any judgment. <Motion to strike granted; ten days to amend. So ordered.> □see **order to show cause;** □see **warrant;** □see **writ.**

    c. **holding** □see, under **hold.**

2. by statute or local usage, often equated with words more apt for a particular kind of determination of a controversy, **award** (□see), **judgment** (□see), and **verdict** (□see).

□see also, **memorandum decision.**

declarant see declaration.

declaration • declaratory

declaration (n.) and declare (v.), (L., *declarare:* to make clear): a more emphatic way of saying something, often applied to a formal statement on a special occasion, with a wide range of loose usage in and out of the law.

A good point of beginning is ordinary English, a *declarative sentence:* one that makes an assertion. But usage runs from the easygoing "Well, I do declare" to the revered *Declaration of Independence* and the solemn *declaration of war.* In-between are customs declarations, declaring meetings adjourned, and declarations at cards. Ordinary people don't do much declaring anymore, unless the occasion is very special. And, if they knew about it, most would resent being labeled legally a *declarant.*

The law has a long liaison with *declaration:* the common law name for the first pleading in a lawsuit, now usually called a *complaint.* A series of well-established labels include *declaration* to identify formal statements on special occasions and use *declare* as the operative verb: **declaration of a dividend** to be paid to shareholders <The company declared its twelfth quarterly dividend.>; **declaration of a homestead,** claiming a family residence exempt from execution <I declare that>; **declaration of trust,** giving details of the property held in trust and how it is held <I declare myself trustee.>. □see **trust.** Under some statutes, a **declaration under penalty of perjury** is accepted as a substitute for some affidavits <I declare under penalty of perjury that. . . .>. □see also, **declare a default,** under **default.**

declaration

Other *declarations*, a mixed bag, are recognized labels of convenience, but with no requisite formality nor any requirement of *declare* as an operative word:

dying declaration: something said by a person conscious of the imminence of his own death and so considered sufficiently trustworthy to be admissible in evidence, under varying rules. The occasion is special, but formality is no part of it.

declaration against interest: something said outside of court so against one's own interest as to be considered sufficiently trustworthy to be admissible, under varying rules of evidence. Neither special occasion nor formality is any part of it.

self-serving declaration: something said outside of court so obviously in one's own interest as to be considered untrustworthy and inadmissible, unless qualified for admission under other varying rules of evidence. Again, neither special occasion nor formality is any part of it. Often shortened to **self-serving.**

The routine signing of a witnessed will (□see **subscribe**) becomes the special occasion for the ultimate collapse of the legal *declaration,* in the form *declare.* "The testator must *declare* to the attesting witnesses that it is his will." Whether that be statute or rule, "declare" does not mean "use the word," simply *say* so, even "let it be known." Yet the irresistible past drives lawyers to insist that their clients' wills say, "I declare this to be my will" or redundantly worse, "I make, publish, and declare this to be my will." Few testators ever say that, and the law does not require it. "This is my will" is enough.

declaratory, despite its kinship to *declaration,* is narrowly confined:

declaratory judgment: a judgment determining a controversy as to the rights or status of the litigants, typically interpreting a contract, statute, or other writing. <They asked no damages, only a declaration of their rights under the policy; a declaratory judgment was proper.> □see **judgment;** □see also, **controversy.**

declaratory statute: one that does not change the law, but puts into statute form, or into more precise wording, what was already law. <Though in form this statute is new, plaintiff's rights date to the earlier statute; the new one is simply a declaratory statute./This is a declaratory statute, adding nothing to the law of this state; it is declaratory of the common law as it existed here before the statute.>

declaration against interest □see **declaration.**

declaration of dividend   □see declaration; □see dividend.

declaration of homestead   □see declaration; □see homestead.

declaration of trust   □see declaration; □see trust.

declaration under penalty of perjury   □see declaration; □see perjury.

declaratory judgment   □see declaratory, under declaration.

declaratory statute   □see declaratory, under declaration.

declare   □see declaration.

declare a default   □see default.

decree   □see judgment.

dedication: the giving of property, usually real property, to the public.   <They dedicated a portion of Blackacre to the city for public streets.> The transfer may be of the fee or an interest (e.g., an easement), and may be express, or implied from the devotion to a public use. As distinguished from loss of ownership through condemnation (□see **eminent domain**) or adverse possession (□see **possession**), *dedication* is said to be voluntary transfer. "Voluntary" must be taken with reservation. As a condition of granting a building permit or approving a subdivision, a city may insist on *dedication* of land for streets, sidewalks, sewers, and utilities. And *dedication* may be implied from public use insufficient to constitute adverse possession; or, in the case of copyright, by publication without compliance with requisites for copyright protection (□see **public domain**).

deed   (v., n.)

1. The verb is a common, typically American, not British, description of the transfer of real property, not usually personal property, emphasizing the use of a writing, the deed (n.). It is a word of description, not an operative word such as, e.g., **grant** (□see). <She deeded the property to the lender, described in the deed as 1st National Bank & Savings Co.>

2. The noun is the usual name for the writing transferring owner-ship of real property, but a **deed of gift** can refer to real or personal property. Deeds transferring real property vary in substance and name. □see **covenants of title**; □see **quitclaim**. A deed executed by only one party was formerly described as a *deed poll*, as distinguished from one executed by two or more parties (□see **indenture**). *Deed poll* is a rarity; a *deed* is a *deed*, whether executed by one party or many.

deed of trust, usually called **trust deed:** a writing transferring real property in trust as security for the performance of an obligation, most commonly payment of a loan. In that typical transaction, **trus-tor** (borrower-owner) conveys title to a disinterested **trustee,** which holds title in trust for the benefit of the **beneficiary** (lender) if there is a default, and reconveys to the *trustor* if the loan is paid. The *trust deed* performs the same security function as a **mortgage** of real property, where the formal transfer for security is by the **mortgagor** (borrower-owner) to the **mortgagee** (lender). □see **mortgage.**

Informally, in and out of the law, *mortgage* is equated with any borrowing on the security of real property. <What with first and second trust deeds, the house was mortgaged up to 90 percent of its market value.> In that sense, **pay off the mortgage** refers to payment of the debt, whether secured by *mortgage* or *trust deed.* <They told the beneficiary that they were ready to pay off the mortgage.>

deed of gift □see **deed.**

deed of trust □see **deed.**

deed poll □see **deed.**

deem and consider Individually or joined, these synonyms (O.E., F.) are as imprecise in the law as in ordinary English. An ancient precise legal use of *deem* (to pass judgment) has long since given way to assorted *considering* something as fact, presumed fact until some-thing better comes along, or only a matter of opinion. Lawyers can do better than *deem, consider,* or *deem and consider.* <This is not deemed, nor even deemed and considered, larceny; it *is* larceny.> □see **coupled synonyms.**

deep pocket: wealth or wealthy, an equivalent of the dated *long purse.* Informal usage in antitrust and tort law. <Control by a deep-pocket corporation may be anticompetitive./Plaintiff's injury was caused by a

very negligent pauper and a slightly negligent defendant with deep pockets; both are liable for the entire harm done. > □see also, **joint and several**.

de facto • de jure

de facto (L., day FAK-toe: in fact): as a matter of fact, contrasted with **de jure** (L., day JU-ry: in law): as a matter of law. The contrast is not as sharp as the Latin promises. Both are matters of law, *de jure* a bit more so. In the course of ordinary events, the pair is unneeded, and *de jure* is superfluous; it is a corporation, a government, not a *de jure corporation,* a *de jure government.* When something is like but not quite the same as the ordinary, *de facto* rises to the occasion as another of the law's devices for verbalizing distinctions (□see **actual**). The device is widely used; here is a sampling:

de facto corporation: an entity acting in good faith as a corporation, and that would be an ordinary corporation but for failure to comply with some technical requirement. <The articles of incorporation were not filed; it may have been a *de facto* but not a *de jure* corporation. >

de facto government: a working government in physical control of a state (as, e.g., by revolution) but not recognized by other states as being in legal control, not the *de jure government.*

de facto merger: as a practical economic matter (e.g., a purchase of assets), the joining of corporations—one surviving, one disappearing—as in an ordinary **corporate merger**, except that the statutory procedures for merger have not been followed. <A dissenting shareholder of the disappearing corporation could not be deprived of his rights on merger, though it was a *de facto,* not a *de jure,* merger. >

de facto officer: one who acts as an officer without having been elected or appointed.

de facto segregation: segregation accomplished by marketplace or neighborhood pressures without state action that would make it **de jure segregation.** □see **segregation**.

de facto taking □see **eminent domain**.

de facto corporation   □see de facto.

de facto government   □see de facto.

de facto merger   □see de facto.

de facto officer □see de facto.

de facto segregation □see de facto.

de facto taking □see eminent domain.

defamation

   1. the publication of words, or of anything having the effect of words (as, e.g., a newspaper caricature, exhibition of a statute, a mime's performance), that tend to injure another person's good reputation. *Publication* here means communication to anyone other than the person whose reputation might be injured. <The defendant told the plaintiff's wife that her husband was a blackmailer. The defamation occurred on January 10./He is accused of defaming the plaintiff on three occasions.>

   Ordinary English frequently uses *libel* and *slander* interchangeably; in some contexts, so does the law (□see **disparagement**). *Defamation* preserves a distinction:

   libel: most commonly, written defamation, but also applied to defamation in a more or less permanent form (as on a record) and occasionally to defamation that is widely disseminated (as in a radio broadcast). For *libel per se* and *per quod,* □see **actionable per se,** under **action**.

   slander: most commonly, oral defamation, but also applied to defamation more or less ephemeral (as in a mime). For *slander per se* and *per quod,* □see **actionable per se,** under **action**.

   2. the words, or anything having the effect of words (as, e.g., a caricature, a statute, gestures), that, if published (see sense 1) would tend to injure another person's good reputation. <The defamation complained of was "he is a thief."/The defamation consisted of the mime's portrayal of plaintiff robbing a bank.> For *defamation per se* and *per quod* and *defamatory per se* and *per quod,* □see **actionable per se,** under **action**.

   3. a **cause of action** (□see) based on a publication that tends to injure another person's good reputation (sense 1). <The complaint was framed in two counts, defamation and invasion of privacy.> □see also, **actionable per se,** under **action**. □see also, **colloquium, innuendo, inducement,** under **colloquium**. □see also, **privilege,** under **immunity**.

   □see also, **self-defense**.

defamation of title □see disparagement.

defamation per quod □see **actionable per se**, under **action**.

defamation per se □see **actionable per se**, under **action**.

defamatory □see **defamation**.

defamatory per quod □see **actionable per se**, under **action**.

defamatory per se □see **actionable per se**, under **action**.

defame □see **defamation**.

default

1. as a noun, failure to perform as agreed (e.g., pay the rent) or as required by law (e.g., comply with a court order). The verb, *to default.* <When the third payment was due, they defaulted.> The adjective, as in **default judgment**: a judgment after one has failed to appear or plead as required by law; also called a *judgment by default.*

2. the condition of the person who has failed to perform (sense 1) and of the obligation unperformed. Both are described as being **in default.** <They were in default./The loan was in default.>

declare a default: to give notice to a debtor, or a trustee, that an obligation is *in default* (e.g., an installment not paid), sometimes with an opportunity to *cure the default* (e.g., make a late payment plus interest and *default* or *delinquency charge*).

take a default: to file a notice in court that someone is *in default* for failure to appear or plead, as a preliminary to obtaining a **default judgment.**

3. the absence of something, as a prelude to legal consequences. <In default of issue, the property goes to A./The will provides that in default of exercise of the power of appointment, the property. . . .> This is an old usage, now strange to ordinary English and not required by technical necessity. Unlike the other *defaults,* this *in default of* is not linked to any failure to perform as agreed or required. It can be expressed as well, with less chance of confusion, in ordinary words: in the absence of issue/there being no issue/since the power of appointment was not exercised, etc.

default judgment □see **default**.

defeasance □see **defeasible**.

defeasible (adj.): liable to being undone; not ordinary English, but the law French and still the technical way of describing a title that will not, or might not, stay put, as with a *defeasible fee*. The less often used **defeasance** (n.): the undoing, describes the event of the title being ended. □see **fee simple**.

defeasible fee □see **fee simple**.

defendant (n., adj.): the person being sued or prosecuted. As an adjective, normal English word order is followed <The defendant husband. . . ./The defendant corporation. . . .>, except with *party,* where an older participial usage (the sense of *defending*) prevails and reverses the word order. <The parties defendant. . . ./She was made a party defendant.> □see also, **cross-defendant**, under **cross**.

defense □see **excuse**, under **justification**; □see **immunity**; □see **infancy defense**, under **child**; □see **insanity**; □see **justification**; □see **privilege**, under **immunity**.

deficiency judgment □see **judgment**.

definite failure of issue □see **issue**.

defraud □see **fraud**.

degrees of negligence □see **negligence**.

degrees of proof □see **burden of persuasion**, under **proof**.

de jure □see **de facto**.

de jure corporation □see **de facto**.

de jure government □see **de facto**.

de jure merger □see **de facto**.

de jure segregation   □see de facto.

delay   Often pejorative in the common speech <"The law's delay"> but almost exclusively so in legal usage.   <"To none will we sell, to none will we deny or delay, right or justice."   Magna Carta, Ch. 40./Justice delayed is justice denied./I certify that this motion is not made for purposes of delay.> For *delay* in the sense of putting off the time of something, without implicit pejorative suggestion, the law uses other words: *adjourn, continue, extend time, postpone, recess, stay,* **toll the statute** (□see). For *dilatory plea,* □see **pleadings**.

delegated powers: a reference to the Tenth Amendment of the U.S. Constitution reading: "The powers not delegated to the United States by the Constitution, nor prohibited by it to the states, are reserved to the states respectively, or to the people."   The federal government is accordingly one of *delegated powers,* but the Amendment does not presume to say *what* powers have been delegated.   For analysis of the zigzag path of Supreme Court decision on that point, refer to constitutional law.   □see **enumerated powers**.   □see also, **delegation of power**.

delegation of power: the act of the acknowledged holder of a particular aspect of the power of governing in handing over that power to someone else.   E.g., a delegation by one branch of government to another, or to an administrative agency, of powers to legislate, enforce the law, adjudicate.   The extent to which powers of governing are delegable or nondelegable is a continuing topic of constitutional decision.   □see **separation of powers**; □see also, **delegated powers**.

deliberate speed   □see with all deliberate speed.

delinquency   □see contributing to the delinquency of a minor, under child.

delinquent child   □see juvenile.

deliver: to change possession, physical or symbolic, of real or personal property.   The change is the *delivery* (n.).   These are generally understood working definitions, to be used with caution in the presence of special statutory definition and widespread and varying interpretive decisions.   Thus, e.g., *delivery* may or may not be accompanied by change of ownership.   □see **symbolic delivery**; □see **possession**; □see also, **C.O.D.**; □see also, **transfer**.

demand (n., v.): an assertion of legal right framed in terms of a request. In ordinary English, *demand* is an expression of extreme irritation erupting in a righteous imperative. Among lawyers, the rancor is usually muted, the demand often politely formal, at times informal. The operative verbs of demand are more often *request* or *pray* than the occasional, blunter *demand.* <Plaintiff demands a jury trial.>

1. the demand

a. a general statement of a litigant's claims. <The demand was for damages and an injunction.> □see also, **cross demand,** under **cross-**.

b. an itemized request for specific relief at the end of a pleading, e.g., for damages, injunction, specific performance, a declaration of rights. <Plaintiff requests judgment for compensatory damages of $15,000, costs of suit, and such other relief as is just.> Usage varies by jurisdiction; instead of *the demand,* some call it by an old usage, **the prayer.** <Plaintiff prays. . . ./Defendant prays that plaintiff take nothing, and for costs of suit.> Often it is referred to as **the relief.** <The relief requested is. . . .>

2. on demand: descriptive of a debt that is due when payment is requested; also said to be *payable on demand.* Such a debt may be embodied in an instrument called **demand paper.** □see **commercial paper.** *Demand,* in these usages, expresses a substantive legal conclusion, not a requirement that the word be used in requesting payment. Without a word spoken, you indorse a check and hand it to the teller; that's a demand for payment. For details of the types of *demand paper* and the mechanics of requesting payment, consult the Uniform Commercial Code. □see also, **honor;** □see also, **dishonor.**

3. For demand deposit, □see **bank.**

□See also, **due demand,** under **due.**

demand deposit □see **bank.**

demand paper □see **demand;** □see also, **commercial paper.**

de minimis (L., day MIN-a-miss: of the least): the law's politer version of the colloquial: "You're talking about peanuts; don't waste the court's time." *De minimis* is the active surviving remnant of the maxim **de minimis non curat lex** (L., day MIN-a-miss non CURE-at lex; freely translated: the law does not concern itself with trifles). Orally, and in writing, *de minimis* labels a claim as too insignificant to be litigated. <One rotten apple in a carload! That's de minimis.>

Orally, in court, *de minimis* often expresses impatience with a lawyer's insistence on pressing a minute side issue. <That's de minimis, counsel; let's get on to something important.>

de minimis non curat lex □see **de minimis.**

demise (n., v.) (law F., duh-MIZE): law French at its confusing worst. It means *transfer* (n., v.), *lease* (n., v.), and also *death.* <January 10 was the date of the demise./The demised property was sold by the sheriff.> Ambiguous. Best forgotten. □see **lease.**

demonstrative evidence □see **real evidence.**

demur • demurrer □see **pleadings.**

demurrer □see **pleadings.**

de novo (L., day NO-vo: anew). The common expression is

trial de novo: a completely new trial, as distinguished from a review of proceedings and decision in the first trial. <Dissatisfied with the board's ruling, they were entitled to a trial *de novo* in the superior court.>

dependent child □see **child.**

deponent □see **affiant.**

depose □see **affiant.**

deposition □see **affiant.**

depredation □see **piracy.**

dereliction □see **accretion.**

derivative action □see **derivative suit.**

derivative suit, also called *derivative action.*

1. a suit brought by a shareholder in the name of, and for, the corporation, alleging a cause of action that the corporation has but declines to assert. <The derivative suit alleged that the president of the corporation was embezzling corporate assets and, predictably, refused to let the corporation sue to recover its property.>

2. Less commonly, other forms of derivative suit are possible. E.g., suit brought by the beneficiary of a trust, on behalf of the trust, if the trustee refuses to sue.

□see also, **strike suit.**

descend • inherit

Neither these words nor their close associates—*descent, inheritance, succession*—have the fixed meanings they once had at common law. All are affected by statute and case law. Some have mingled for so long with ordinary English that their residual technicality has worn thin. Others have a revised technicality, and are to be preferred for more precise usage, but reservations are in order for all of them.

descend (of property): to pass by **descent.**

1. the word once meant the automatic (by operation of law) transfer of real property to the heir upon the death of an ancestor owner. *Descent* has suffered the same fate as **heir** (□see) in loss of a narrow and precise technicality. This sense 1 of *descent* has given way to sense 2.

2. the automatic (by operation of law) transfer of real or personal property to a relative upon the death of an ancestor without a will or without a valid will. Required relationship is determined by applicable state law on intestacy.

The property is said to *pass by descent;* and the new owner *takes by descent,* or—less technically—*takes by inheritance,* or simply **inherits** (□see). <Jones left no will; his wife left an invalid will; their children took both estates by descent.>

inherit; inheritance

Inherit is the correlative of *descend.* Property *descends;* a person *inherits.* Similarly, *inheritance* (in the sense of receiving property) is the correlative of *descent;* the property received is *the inheritance.*

1. *inherit* once meant to receive real property automatically (by operation of law) upon the death of an ancestor owner, i.e., to take as heir. Both *inherit* and *inheritance* have lost precision with the end of **heir** (□see) as a strict term of art; they have become even less precise than *descent* for having remained in common use in and out of the law. Sense 1 of *inherit* has given way to senses 2 and 3.

2. to receive real or personal property automatically (by operation of law) upon the death of an owner relative without a will or without a valid will. Required relationship is determined by applicable state law on intestacy. <She inherited the property from her mother's great-uncle.>

3. to receive real or personal property upon the death of the owner. The fortuitous receiving may result from the conditions listed in sense 2, or from having been named in the will of the owner, whether or not a relative. <He inherited a fortune, all subject to *inheritance tax.*/One of her fans willed her Blackacre and one hundred shares of General Motors stock, a substantial inheritance.>

Senses 2 and 3 together are the common usage of everyday English and increasingly the loose legal usage. Sense 1 is a rarity. Unless in conformity with special statutory language, neither *inherit* nor *inheritance* should be used with any expectation of predictable technical meaning.

succeed; succession The little used verb and the often used noun, like **inherit** (□see), once referred to taking real property as heir. They are now the equivalents of *inherit* (senses 2 and 3). Other forms are:

intestate succession: once a redundancy; now as in *inherit* (sense 2).

testamentary succession: once unthinkable; now as in *inherit* (sense 3).

□see also, **successor**; □see also, **successor in interest**.

descendant • issue

Both words are common in the law, usually synonyms. *Issue* is more durably biological, though not everlastingly so. Both are endlessly interpreted to carry out the *presumed intent* of, for example, a testator.

descendant

1. a blood relative, however remote (e.g., great-great-grandchildren, etc.), in a direct descending line of succession from a particular ancestor.

descendant

This strict definition, a synonym of *issue*, excludes from the possibility of being called "descendants" *ancestors* (e.g., a father or mother) and so-called **collateral descendants**: related to the ancestor by an ascending line (e.g., a brother or niece). It makes **lineal descendant** a redundancy. It also excludes children by adoption. The biological emphasis of this definition lends itself to the frequent inclusion of illegitimates, who might otherwise be excluded under some rules of inheritance. This strict definition is frequently rejected by statutes and interpretative decisions.

2. a relative, however remote, by blood, marriage, or adoption, in an ascending or descending line from a particular ancestor. This changes the biological meaning of *descendant* to conform to various statutory versions of the required relationship of persons who take by descent (□see **descend**).

issue

1. a blood relative, however remote (e.g., great-great-grandchildren, etc.), in a direct descending line of succession from a particular ancestor. This is a synonym for the strict definition of **descendant** (□see).

2. the biological definition (sense 1) plus the interpretative or statutory extension of **child** (□see) to include *adopted child*. □see also, **lawful issue**.

3. limited to one's children. This is an interpretative cure for careless or untechnical drafting.

die without issue: to die without having *issue*, traditionally sense 1 of **issue** (□see). The event is referred to as the **failure of issue**, defined as either *indefinite* or *definite failure of issue*.

indefinite failure of issue: there is a *failure of issue* whenever, no matter how far distant, the line of issue of the named person becomes extinct. <The will gives land "to A and his heirs, but if A dies without issue, then to B and his heirs." A dies leaving children, but the children die childless. Upon the death of A's children, there is an indefinite failure of issue, and the land goes to B.> This was the historic meaning of *failure of issue*, which has now given way to *definite failure of issue*.

definite failure of issue: *failure of issue* of the named person is to be determined by a specific event, usually the death of the named person, without further waiting on the eventualities of survival or procreation to establish extinction of the line. <The will gives land "to A and his heirs, but if A dies without issue, then to B and his heirs." A dies leaving children. Whether or not A's children have children, there was

no failure of issue at A's death, and the land stays in A's estate. B is out, even if later the line of A's issue becomes extinct.> This is the prevailing meaning of *failure of issue.*

descent □see **descend.**

desegregation □see **segregation;** □see **de facto segregation,** under **de facto;** □see also, **with all deliberate speed.**

desertion: abandoning a duty (e.g., marital or child support) without legal cause and with an intent to make the abandonment permanent; as distinguished from failing to perform that duty temporarily or by reason of misfortune or unrelated misconduct. <Failure to provide for children may be evidence of desertion but is not *per se* desertion./His imprisonment for manslaughter did not constitute desertion.>

constructive desertion: persistent gross misconduct by one spouse that compels the innocent to abandon the marital relationship.

design patent □see **patent.**

de son tort (law F., day SOWN tort): of his own wrong; as in **executor de son tort** (□see) and *trustee de son tort* (□see **constructive trust,** under **trust**).

destination contract □see **F.O.B.**

destructibility of contingent remainders □see **remainder.**

detainer □see **forcible entry and detainer.**

determinable □see **fee simple.**

determinate sentence □see **sentence.**

detriment in law is as loose as *detriment* in ordinary English, often a synonym for *harm, injury,* or **damage** (□see). <They are entitled to recover for the detriment suffered.> *Legal detriment* is not unique, though context may make it seem so. In a world with an infinite variety of *detriments,* law deals with specific instances of old fashioned *detriment:* e.g., *detrimental reliance* on someone's promise (□see promissory estoppel, under estoppel); e.g., bargained for *detriment* (doing something you were not obligated to do or not doing something you would have been free to do) that will be called *consideration* for a contract (□see).

detrimental reliance   □see **promissory estoppel**, under **estoppel**.

devise • devisee   □see **give**, under **gift**.

devise and bequeath   □see **give**, under **gift**.

devisee   □see **gift**.

devoid of merit   □see **merit**.

dicta   □see **dictum**.

dictum   (L., DIK-tum: something said), the short and usual rendering of **obiter dictum** (L., O-bit-er: by the way, DIK-tum: something said by the way): something said in an opinion that is not necessary to the decision.   <I concur in the decision; but the so-called guidelines are gratuitous, only dictum.>   *Dictum* is contrasted with **holding** (□see, under **hold**) and **decision** (□see).   Dictum is also to be distinguished from an *alternative ground of decision.*   <Section II of the opinion is not dictum but rather an alternative, independent ground of decision.>

Obiter alone, less used than *dictum,* is also short for *obiter dictum.*   <A fascinating opinion, most of it obiter.>

Dictum is typically the description not of a single word or phrase but of a number of things that a judge has said in an opinion, and is treated as a group designation, taking a singular verb.   The Latin plural *dicta* (not *dictums*) is similarly thought of as a group designation, taking a singular verb.   <The last paragraph of that opinion is dictum/is dicta.>   When the focus is on separate utterances, *dicta* takes a plural verb.   <The dicta in the two dissents were more instructive than the majority opinion.>

die without issue   □see **descendant**.

dilatory plea   □see **plea**.

diligence   □see **due**.

dilution: as in ordinary English, a weakening of strength, applied especially to stock and trademarks.

dilution of stock: a weakening of the voting power or value of outstanding stock by the issuing of new stock other than to existing stockholders in proportion to their shares.   □see **preemptive rights**.

If the new stock is voting stock, the voting power of existing stock is *diluted*.   If the new stock is issued for less than market or some fixed value, the value of existing stock is *diluted*.   *Dilution* is what happens to existing stock, as distinguished from any characterization of the new issue.   □see **watered stock**.

dilution of trademark: a weakening of the value of a trademark by unauthorized use of the trademark or the use of a closely similar mark.

diminished capacity: short of insanity, a lack of capacity to have the intent or state of mind that is an element of a crime.   <On the issue of diminished capacity, counsel argued that brain damage made the defendant incapable of premeditation or of having a specific intent to kill.>

In some jurisdictions, *diminished capacity* is a defense; in others, it may be considered in mitigation of punishment.

diminished responsibility: sometimes a synonym for *diminished capacity* in either sense; sometimes only as applied to punishment.

diminished responsibility   □see **diminished capacity**.

dimunition of record: a characterization of the incomplete state of the lower court record that has been forwarded to a higher court in connection with an appeal or other review.   The "suggestion" of *dimunition of record* is an old way of saying that the record has been improperly diminished and should now be completed.

direct   □see **cross-examination**, under **cross-**.

direct contempt   □see **contempt**.

direct damages   □see **damage**.

directed verdict □see **verdict.**

direct estoppel □see **res judicata.**

direct examination □see **cross-examination,** under **cross-.**

director: one of a group, the **board of directors** (the **board**), that has the power and duty of managing a corporation. Typically, the board manages through officers and committees it elects or appoints, collectively and informally called **management.**

> **dummy director:** a director in name only, carrying out instructions; also called a **nominal director,** or an *accommodation director.* <The initial directors were all dummy directors, the incorporators' lawyers and their secretaries.>

> **initial director:** a member of the corporation's first board, often named in the articles of incorporation, chosen by the incorporators to organize the corporation. After stock has been issued, directors are elected by the shareholders.

> **inside director:** a director who is a part of management.

> **outside director:** a director, not a part of management, chosen to obtain an independent overview of the policies of management.

directory (adj.): said of language, typically in statutes, ordinances, etc., that may be disregarded as nonessential if it conflicts with the substantial purpose of the whole writing or of other related writings. Frequently contrasted with **mandatory:** said of language that must be complied with; a *directory provision,* a *mandatory provision.* Neither *directory* nor *mandatory* is a term of art except in special context, e.g., a *mandatory sentence.* Usually, both words are applied flexibly, as a label for interpretative conclusions that by and large this provision must be, or need not be, enforced. <The requirement that objections be filed within ten days was merely directory; the time could be extended./The requirement that notice of appeal be filed within thirty days was mandatory; timely filing was jurisdictional.>

Direct Tax Clauses: the parts of the U.S. Constitution reading: ". . . [D]irect taxes shall be apportioned among the several states which may be included within this Union, according to their respective numbers. . . ." (Art. I, § 2, cl. 3); and "No capitation, or other direct, tax shall be laid, unless in proportion to the census or enumeration herein before directed to be taken." (Art. I, § 9, cl. 4). The additional provision of Article I, § 2, cl. 3 on computation of numbers is changed by Amendment XIV, § 2. The provisions of both sections are changed by the income tax amendment (Amend. XVI). □see also, **constitutional clauses.**

disaffirm: to exercise a right to repudiate what would otherwise be an obligation. Most common in referring to an infant's *disaffirmance* of a contract. □see the **infancy defense,** under **child.**

disaffirmance   □see **disaffirm.**

disbar   □see **bar.**

disclaim   (v.) and *disclaimer* (n.) say "no" in three different ways:

1. not responsible: "No, I will not be responsible for that." <They disclaimed any warranty of merchantability; the disclaimer was explicit./The insurer disclaimed malpractice coverage.>

2. not claiming any right to that: "No, I am not making any claim to that." <Three of the defendants in the quiet title suit disclaimed any interest in the property.>

disclaimer under patent law is a related usage: the giving up of a *claim* to **patent** (□see) or of the whole or part of the term of a patent. <"No, I am not making that claim.">

3. will not accept the gift: "No, I will not accept it." <She disclaimed taking anything under the will and elected to take her statutory share of the property.>

disclaimer   □see **disclaim.**

discovery,   short for **discovery proceedings:** the mechanics of learning in advance of trial an adversary's position on issues beyond what is disclosed in the pleadings, and of obtaining from an adversary or witness information, writings, or physical evidence relevant to litigation. In this broad sense, *discovery* is intended to prevent surprise and shorten litigation; it includes, e.g., *depositions* (□see **affiant),** *interrogatories* (□see **cross-interrogatory,** under **cross-),** *requests for admissions,* and **subpoena duces tecum** (□see). <We are not ready for trial; discovery will take at least another week.> □see also, **bill of particulars;** □see also, **perpetuate testimony;** □see also, **work product privilege.**

reciprocal discovery: the right of discovery by both sides in a criminal or civil case. The prosecution's right of discovery, e.g., of an alibi defense, names of defense witnesses, statements of witnesses, is limited by varying decisions and statutes to protect defendant's constitutional rights and the work product privilege. *Reciprocal discovery* is sometimes referred to as *accelerated disclosure,* i.e., earlier disclosure of something that would eventually be offered in evidence.

Adjunct to these distinctly legal usages of *discovery,* lawyers use *discovery* and *discover* as in ordinary English. <When did you discover that?>

discovery proceedings □see **discovery.**

discrete and insular minorities □see **Footnote Four;** □see **standards of review.**

discretion □see **abuse of discretion;** □see also, **ministerial.**

discretionary trust □see **trust.**

discrimination: the word of ordinary English, i.e., the making of distinctions. Usually, in the law, the making of unfair, injurious, illegal, or unconstitutional distinctions. The flexible expression runs widely through the law in constitutions, statutes, regulations, and decisions, e.g., affecting discrimination in prices, rates, tariffs, but especially concentrating on the denial of equality between human beings. □see **affirmative action;** □see **reverse discrimination;** □see **segregation;** □see **sex discrimination,** under **sex;** □see **standards of review.**

dishonor: failing to pay a negotiable instrument (□see **commercial paper**) when it is supposed to be paid, or failing to accept a draft when it is supposed to be accepted. As used here, *accept* is the drawee's signing on the instrument as a promise to pay when due. The fact of either of those failures is *the dishonor* of the instrument, which is then said to be *dishonored. Dishonor* is a term of art in the law of negotiable instruments; for the details of when an instrument is "supposed" to be paid or accepted, see the Uniform Commercial Code.

dismiss • dismissal □see **judgment of dismissal,** under **judgment;** □see **without prejudice;** □see **retraxit.**

disorderly conduct: a vague classification of minor offenses detrimental to public morals or safety, or *disturbing the peace* (□see **breach of the peace,** under **breach**). The phrase *disorderly conduct* snares the widest miscellany of undesirables, including beggars, drunks, loiterers, peeping toms, prostitutes, and squatters. Specific criminal violations are usually spelled out and frequently amended to withstand constitutional challenge. □see also, **loiter;** □see also, **vagrant.**

disparagement: the ordinary English word turned to legal use in torts for publishing false statements about the quality of property or its title. The torts reflect historical analogies to **defamation** (□see) but are distinct from it. They are not to be confused with *defamation,* though using some of the same verbiage. In particular, defamation's classic distinction between the written and the oral and its discrete usage of *libel* and *slander* are ignored.

disparagement of goods: causing pecuniary loss by publication of a false statement about the quality of property, real or personal. Often called **trade libel,** sometimes **slander of goods**. Increasingly, the phrases designate the quality-of-property subdivision of a cause of action in tort for **injurious falsehood** (□see). *Disparagement of goods* has also been called *disparagement of property.*

disparagement of property: a tort sometimes equated with **disparagement of goods** (□see), more often with **disparagement of title** (□see); sometimes includes both.

disparagement of title: causing pecuniary loss by publication of a false statement about title to property, real or personal. Often called **slander of title,** sometimes *defamation of title* or *disparagement of property.* Increasingly, the phrases designate the title-to-property subdivision of a cause of action in tort for **injurious falsehood** (□see).

disparagement of goods   □see **disparagement.**

disparagement of property   □see **disparagement.**

disparagement of title   □see **disparagement.**

Disposing Clause: the part of the U.S. Constitution reading: "The Congress shall have power to dispose of . . . . property belonging to the United States. . . . ." (Art. IV, § 3, cl. 2). □see also, **constitutional clauses.**

173

disputable presumption □see **rebuttable presumption**, under **presumption**.

disqualify • recuse

disqualify: to bar a judge from hearing, a witness from testifying, a juror from sitting, or a lawyer from appearing in a case because of legal objection to the qualifications of the particular individual. A *motion to disqualify* is the general term for wide-ranging challenge, e.g., a judge's prejudice against a litigant, a witness bound by rules of confidentiality, a juror's service in a related case, a lawyer's previous representation of the opposing litigant. *Disqualify* is also used reflexively. <The judge should disqualify himself.> □see also, **vicarious disqualification**.

recuse: to bar a judge from hearing a case because of legal objection to the qualifications of the particular judge. It is an old word of rejection or objection returning to professional favor. Unlike the multiple targets of a *motion to disqualify,* a *motion to recuse* is usually restricted to judges; it is sometimes used against a lawyer in an official position, e.g., a district attorney charged with conflict of interest, but not against lawyers generally. *Recuse* is also used reflexively. <The court should recuse itself./The court will recuse itself.>

For lawyers, the availability of both *disqualify* and *recuse* to deal with judges is a cruel if resistible temptation to double up, tending to blur the distinction between the two words. <The court hereby disqualifies and recuses itself.> □see **coupled synonyms**. Similarly, noun lovers can readily lose themselves in *disqualification (motion for disqualification)* and *recusal (motion for recusal),* again with the dismal prospect of doubling. A further possibility for confusion is that the shorter *recusal* will gradually become as all purpose as *disqualification.* The civil law's synonym for *recusal, recusation,* presents no imminent threat.

disregarding the corporate entity □see **alter ego**.

dissent □see **opinion**.

dissenting opinion □see **opinion**.

dissolution sounds like the breakup, the end. Some *dissolutions* are.

dissolution of injunction: a court-ordered ending of an injunction before expiration under its original provisions.

dissolution of marriage □see **divorce**.

Some *dissolutions* only sound like the end; there may be life after *dissolution*.

dissolution of a corporation: commonly described as "the end of legal existence" but under most statutes, only the beginning of the end. *Dissolution* marks the end of business as usual, corporate existence continuing for the limited purpose of wiping out the accumulated traces of corporate life, e.g., payment, settlement, and collection of debts, and the distribution of remaining assets, a process known as **liquidation** or **winding up**.

dissolution of a general partnership: "the change in the relation of the partners caused by any partner ceasing to be associated in the carrying on as distinguished from the winding up of the business." (Uniform Partnership Act, § 29). As with a corporation, *dissolution* is not the end; that event, known as **termination**, occurs when the *winding up* is completed. For dissolution of a limited partnership, see the Revised Uniform Limited Partnership Act of 1976, with 1985 amendments, Art. 8.

dissolve □see **dissolution**.

distribute □see **distribution**.

distribution

1. in general, the division of an aggregate of money or property and its transfer to individuals in proportion to ownership or legal claim. E.g., as in a decree of distribution that *distributes* the assets of an estate (□see **probate**; □see **per capita**; □see **judgment**).

2. a corporation's distribution (sense 1) of money or property (other than its own stock) to its stockholders or incurring debt for their benefit. A **dividend** (□see) is sometimes called a *distribution*. (See Model Business Corporation Act, 3d ed., amended to 1990, § 1.4(6).) Definition varies by jurisdiction and statute, e.g., in tax law. □see also, **dissolution of a corporation**, under **dissolution**.

district attorney □see **lawyer**.

disturbing the peace □see **breach of the peace**, under **breach**.

diversity jurisdiction □see **jurisdiction**.

diversity of citizenship □see **diversity jurisdiction,** under **jurisdiction.**

divest (v.): to take something away or get rid of something. Ordinary English, a feature of the apartheid agony in the noun form *divestiture* (and its synonym *divestment*), with traditional but discrete legal services in the law of real property and antitrust.

Real property usage focuses on the possibility of something being taken away or cut short. <They had a vested interest in Blackacre, subject to divestment.> □see **fee simple defeasible,** under **fee simple.**

Antitrust usage is "get rid of it." <The commission found that X Corp. constituted a monopoly and ordered it to divest itself of stock ownership in Y Corp. and Z Corp.>

divestiture □see **divest.**

divestment □see **divest.**

dividend, the common English word, limited, in this entry, to **corporate dividend:** usually, a payment to stockholders based on the earnings of the corporation, paid or not paid in the discretion of the board of directors, within statutory boundaries as to the financial condition of the corporation. Definitions vary by statute, some substituting for "earnings" an equivalent sense of "profits," "net earnings," or "net profits." For other variations, □see, in this entry, **liquidating dividend** and **nimble dividend.**

cash dividend: a dividend paid in cash, customarily understood by the unmodified use of the word *dividend.* Distinguished from **stock dividend:** a dividend in the form of additional stock in proportion to ownership.

cumulative dividend □see **preferred stock,** under **stock.**

declaration of dividend □see **declaration.**

extra dividend □see **regular dividend.**

liquidating dividend: a distribution to stockholders of whatever is left on the winding up of a corporation. □see **dissolution.**

nimble dividend: a dividend based on the earnings of the current fiscal year, at a time when the corporation's capital is impaired, and declared quickly, i.e., reasonably close to the end of that fiscal year. States permitting *nimble dividends* vary in precise requirements, e.g., the governing period may be the preceding fiscal year; e.g., in the safeguards that obligations will be met.

pass a dividend: omitting to declare or pay a regular **dividend** (□see) or a *preferred dividend.* <X Corp. passed its quarterly dividend./X Corp. passed its dividend on the class A preferred.>

preferred dividend □see **preferred stock,** under **stock.**

regular dividend: while still contingent on the discretion of the board, a dividend on common stock that has been paid with such periodic regularity that it is advertised and expected and its omission regarded as ominous. <This is X Corporation's eighty-fourth regular quarterly dividend.> Contrasted with a **special dividend,** also called an **extra dividend:** a dividend in addition to *regular dividends.*

special dividend □see **regular dividend.**

stock dividend □see **cash dividend.**

□see also, **distribution.**

divisible contract □see **saving clause.**

division of fees □see **fee (attorney's fee).**

divorce

1. by judgment of court, the end of a marriage. Synonyms are:

absolute divorce: a contrast with *limited divorce* (under sense 2). For general use, a redundancy.

dissolution of marriage, an old usage that has gained currency with **no-fault divorce** (□see). *Dissolution* threatens the legal, though not the popular, life of *divorce* (n.). <The court granted the petition for dissolution of marriage./They got a divorce.> It competes with *divorce* (v.) <Their marriage was dissolved./They were divorced.>, but *dissolution* is not in the race with *divorce* (adj.) <divorce lawyers/a divorce case>.

Dissolution, like *divorce,* is distinguished from **annulment:** a court order not ending the marriage but declaring that it never existed.

no-fault divorce: dissolution of a tottering marriage, variously described as being in the final stages of collapse—"irreconcilable differences," "irremediable breakdown," "irretrievably broken"—but without a washing-linen-in-public allocation of fault. The same conditions may result in *legal separation* (under sense 2).

divorce

divorce a vinculo matrimonii (L.: from the bond of marriage), often shortened to *divorce a vinculo.* In some states, never used; waning elsewhere. Understood as a contrast with *divorce a mensa et thoro* (under sense 2).

2. by judgment of court, either the end of a marriage (sense 1) or a *legal separation;* where the double usage prevails, *divorce* standing alone is ambiguous.

legal separation: by judgment of court, a new pattern of marital life not ending the marriage but ending the usual condition of cohabitation (□see **cohabit**) and regulating other aspects of the relationship, e.g., custody of children, property rights, maintenance. Synonyms are:

divorce a mensa et thoro (L.: literally, from table and bed but usually rendered *from bed and board*). The contrast with *divorce a vinculo matrimonii* (under sense 1). Old and waning usage.

divorce from bed and board: the old and rhythmic English substitute for **divorce a mensa et thoro** (□see).

limited divorce: a contrast with *absolute divorce* (under sense 1).

separate maintenance: usage is not uniform; sometimes interchangeable with *legal separation,* sometimes distinguished as being only court-ordered maintenance while spouses are living apart. (□see **alimony.**)

Doctor of Jurisprudence □see **J.D.**; □see also, **jurisprudence.**

Doctor of Law □see **J.D.**

doctor-patient privilege □see **physician-patient privilege.**

doctrinaire argument □see **clichés.**

doctrine □see **rule.**

doctrine of renvoi □see **renvoi.**

doctrine of worthier title □see **worthier title.**

document: an imprecise word of ordinary English and the law, often equated with a **writing** (□see, under **write**) or an **instrument** (□see).

178

Usually refers to something material that has on it words, symbols, or marks conveying meaning that has some significance in the law or in legal proceedings. Usually, but not always, refers to an original. Decision and statute give special sense to *document* (n., v.), especially in the law of evidence distinguishing *documentary* (adj.) from evidence in other forms. □see **best evidence**; □see **document of title**; □see **real evidence**.

documentary   □see **document**.

document of title: a document indicating that it covers identified goods, or fungible goods of an identified mass, stated to be in the possession of the bailee who issued the document or to whom it is directed. The document must be of a sort that the business and financial community regards as giving its possessor the right to deal with the document and with the bailed goods. (□see **bail**.) A numerous breed, typical documents of title are the *warehouse receipt* and the *bill of lading* (see UCC § 1201(15)). For details, refer to the Uniform Commercial Code.

Doe   □see **John Doe**.

do equity   □see **equity**.

does violence to   □see **clichés**.

doing business   □see **minimum contacts**.

doing business as   □see **alias**.

domicile,   also spelled domicil.

1. domicile of a human being: the place where a person makes his home, complete with feelings of family and fireside, intending to keep it as home, and intending to return there when living elsewhere. The word may refer to a building, an area, or a political unit. <Her domicile was the Plaza Hotel/east Texas/the United States.>

Significant in a wide range of contexts, e.g., child custody, citizenship, divorce, jurisdiction, taxation, *domicile* is a legal conclusion—"This is it"—drawn from facts, including intent, but not necessarily controlled by the honest assertion, "I live here; this is my home." Of fading force, yet a lingering usage, is the combining form **matrimonial**

domicile: the domicile (sense 1) of husband and wife living together as a family.

Despite rigorous efforts to keep *domicile* separate from **residence** <One may have many residences at the same time but only one domicile.>, *domicile* and *residence* are frequently equated. **Legal residence** and **permanent residence** are synonyms of *domicile*.

2. domicile of a corporation: the place, usually the state where a corporation was incorporated. <Delaware, its state of incorporation, is the domicile of X Corp./X Corp. is a Delaware corporation./X Corp. is domiciled in Delaware.>

As the place of incorporation, *domicile* is still widely used as the conclusion that the internal operation of a corporation is subject to the laws of that state.

Place of incorporation is sometimes called the corporation's **legal domicile**; a second domicile, its principal place of business, sometimes called the corporation's **commercial domicile,** is often equated with *residence* for varied statutory purposes.

dominant estate   □see **easement.**

dominant tenement   □see **easement.**

donatio causa mortis   □see **gift causa mortis,** under **gift.**

donatio mortis causa   □see **gift causa mortis,** under **gift.**

donee   □see **gift.**

donor • donee   □see **gift.**

double jeopardy: being "twice put in jeopardy" "for the same offense," forbidden by the U.S. Constitution, Amendment V, and state constitutions. The precise application of the quoted words is continuously litigated. *Double jeopardy* is also referred to elliptically as **former jeopardy, once in jeopardy,** and **prior jeopardy.**

in jeopardy: in danger of being convicted, generally when a person is put on trial in a criminal case. There are various exceptions; e.g., a defendant who has obtained a new trial after conviction has not been *in jeopardy;* the new trial is not *double jeopardy.*

doubt □see **beyond a reasonable doubt.**

dower • curtesy

dower: at common law, a wife's life estate in one third of certain of her husband's real property. It was *inchoate dower* (vanishing if she predeceased her husband), possessory only upon her becoming a widow.

curtesy: at common law, a widower's life estate in certain of his wife's real property, if issue of the marriage who could inherit the property were born alive.

Most American jurisdictions have abolished both *dower* and *curtesy.* Variations persist, usually without the common law distinction between the rights incident to the two estates.

draft □see **commercial paper.**

drawee □see **commercial paper.**

drawer □see **commercial paper.**

drunk □see **legally drunk.**

dry trust □see **trust.**

due: the basic sense is *owing* <The money is owing./The money is due.>. But the literal sense is expanded, figurative, and flexible in both ordinary and legal English. What is *owing* or *due* is what is usual, appropriate, required, what will satisfy. *Due* and adverb *duly* are so ordinary, so usual, that without much thought they are thrown in for good measure, without measurable change of meaning:

due demand = demand

due diligence = diligence

duly incorporated = incorporated

due notice = notice

duly organized = organized

due proof = proof

due

due regard = regard

duly sworn = sworn

Where the context is traditional, the major contribution of *due* and *duly,* when not merely redundant, is to lend flexibility. So too with the negative **undue**, as in **undue influence**—completely dependent on circumstance. ☐see **duress.**

due and payable: each word alone may mean either that money is required to be paid *right now* or is required to be paid at some *future time.* <They sued for the money due/due and payable under the note./A was designated as agent to collect rents due/due and payable under the lease.> Joined together, they are most often used in contexts carrying the sense of *now* <The debt was due and payable.> but can still point to the *future* <The rent was due and payable in installments.>. Context, preferably a specific time or specific event, is needed to make *due and payable* precise; but if that is provided, either alone will suffice, and *due and payable* is redundant. <The rent became due and payable/due/ payable on the first of the month./The note became due/payable on demand./ The rent was overdue/past due./The loan was due on sale.>

due care: the care of a reasonable man under the circumstances. For the absence of due care, ☐see **negligence.** ☐see also, **reasonable man;** ☐see also, **sex.**

due course: the ordinary or usual course of events, completely flexible, except when hogtied. ☐see **holder in due course.**

due process: the shortened and usual rendering of **due process of law:**

1. an orderly functioning of the legal system under fair rules and established general principles that limit the power of government over life, liberty, and property.

A formulation necessarily flexible; courts apply but do not rigidly define *due process.* The recurrent question "What process is due?" remains without fixed answer.

2. *due process* (sense 1) as referred to in the U.S. Constitution (☐see **Due Process Clauses**) and interpreted by the U.S. Supreme Court.

In this sense, still flexible, *due process* is subdivided into *procedural* and *substantive due process.*

procedural due process: fundamental fairness in the manner and means of government's exercise of power. For example: requirement of notice of a hearing in court or administrative tribunal that may affect one's rights; the right to be represented in court by a lawyer; the right to a fair trial. □see **day in court**.

substantive due process: reasonable exercise of power that is limited to a subject (1) within the general powers of government over life, liberty, and property, (2) included in a permitted governmental function, and (3) not barred by other constitutional provision. For example: state regulation of hours of labor; prohibition of prior censorship contrary to the First Amendment.

due and payable   □see **due**.

due care   □see **due**.

due notice   □see **due**.

due process   □see **due**.

Due Process Clauses: the parts of the U.S. Constitution reading: "No person shall . . . be deprived of life, liberty, or property, without due process of law. . . ." (Amend. V); and ". . . nor shall any state deprive any person of life, liberty, or property, without due process of law. . . ." (Amend. XIV, § 1). When the context clearly refers to Amendment V or Amendment XIV, *the Due Process Clause* suffices; otherwise, *the Due Process Clause of the Fifth Amendment,* or *Fifth Amendment due process,* etc. □see also, **constitutional clauses**.

due process of law   □see **due**.

duly   □see **due**.

dummy director   □see **director**.

duplicitous • duplicity

duplicity,   in the common sense of deceitfulness or double-dealing, may be criminal or merely loathsome. But for centuries, the law has used *duplicity,* and its less tidy version *duplicitous,* in a sense only mildly pejorative. Directed at pleadings and indictments that try to crowd too much into one count (two causes of action, two separate crimes), *duplicity* and *duplicitous* bespeak *doubleness* but

183

duplicitous

not deceit. A technical defect of pleading at common law, *duplicity* is now a waning usage. For old times' sake, some lawyers still choose *duplicity* over *double* or *multiplied;* and down that path lies *duplicitous.* <"The Congressional intent that duplicitous proceedings be avoided. . . ."> □see **multiplicitous.**

duplicity □see **duplicitous.**

durable power of attorney

1. a written power of attorney (□see **attorney in fact**) with apt words to provide that it is not to be affected by the principal's incapacity, or that it becomes effective only upon the principal's incapacity. It may also provide that it is not to be affected by lapse of time. "Incapacity" is variously described by that word or *disability* or *incompetence.* The powers given vary with the instrument, frequently dealing with management of property. See Uniform Probate Code, § 5–501, amended to 1984 (8 Uniform Laws Annotated); see Uniform Durable Power of Attorney Act, § 1, amended to 1984 (8A Uniform Laws Ann.); see Uniform Statutory Power of Attorney Act, § 1, 1988 (8A Uniform Laws Ann.).

2. For a different sort of durable power of attorney affecting issues of life and death, □see **right to die.**

duress • coercion • undue influence

Broadly defined, these are imprecise synonyms: an improper exercise of power over another person to compel action or forbearance.

Despite endless variation of impropriety, power, and what is compelled, the fact that all are headed in the same direction encourages this synonymous, loose, often redundant usage. <The contract was a product of undue influence through duress or coercion directed at a person in frail health and straitened circumstances./They interposed a defense of duress or coercion./It was economic duress or coercion./The wife claimed that the property settlement was the result of undue duress.>

Sometimes the expressions are distinguished by *degrees of force,* improper force. "Pay the rent or vacate" is unpleasantly forceful but not improper. Etymologically and historically, *duress* is the hard stuff: physical abuse, threats at gunpoint, criminality at its roughest. *Duress* may be classified as a form of *coercion,* but milder forms of *coercion* would not be *duress.* *Coercion* may or may not be illegal; *duress* usually is. And while *duress* and *coercion* are undue influences, *undue influence* is usually not physical and is the weakest in the hierarchy of force.

Ultimately, each of the expressions is an *upset label:* what a statute or court says is sufficiently illegal or gross to warrant undoing the compelled action or forbearance or excusing a criminal act. Usage is not uniform. <Persistent, prejudiced persuasion by her trusted self-interested counselor was sufficient *undue influence* to invalidate the will./The confession followed two days of harsh police interrogation of the young, uncounseled prisoner, but it was a *coerced confession* and will not be permitted in evidence./ His signature was forced by threat of imminent harm to a loved one; that was *duress,* and the contract is void or voidable.> □see also, **undue influence,** under **due.** □see also, **justification.**

Durham rule, also called the **Durham test:** a rule for determining **insanity** (□see) announced in *Durham v. U.S.,* 214 F.2d 862, 874–875 (D.C.Cir., 1954): ". . . an accused is not criminally responsible if his unlawful act was the product of mental disease or mental defect."

Durham test □see **Durham rule.**

duty □see obligation.

duty to mitigate damages □see damage.

dying declaration □see declaration.

dynamite charge □see jury instructions.

E

each and all: a worthless remnant, along with its companion *each and every,* of the old habit of doubling in ordinary English. *Each* and *every* focus on the individuals of a group; *all* on the whole group. For lawyers, one word is enough, and more precise to boot. A gift to *each and all* may be construed as a joint gift with individuals taking a share or a gift to individuals only, with a redundant *all.* ☐see **coupled synonyms.**

each and every   ☐see **each and all.**

easement • servitude

Easement (of pain) and *servitude* (as slavery) are commonplace English; in the law of real property, they are something special. As devices for the long-term, built-in control of land, *easement* and *servitude* are so overlaid with historic mumble that lawyers cannot always be certain that the device in hand is *easement, servitude,* both, or neither. Definition is not uniform, and—with an increasing use of restrictive devices in real estate development (subdivisions, condominiums, business parks, etc.)—the prognosis is for diversity, innovation, and argument, rather than uniformity.

1. **easement** and **servitude**—general definition: Broadly defined, *easement* and *servitude* are synonyms: a right to use, or restrict the use, of someone else's land (Parcel One), burdening Parcel One for the benefit of other land (Parcel Two), or for the benefit of the holder of the right, independent of ownership of land. The right to use or restrict may be given by conveyance or by law. <Blackacre was subject to an easement/a servitude for the benefit of Whiteacre.>

This generalized usage regards *easement* as the common law name for the civil law's *servitude* or for something "analogous." Each word emphasizes its own linguistic origin: *easement* as the enjoyment of a benefit; *servitude* as the burdening (enslaving) of land for the sake of that benefit. For a loose use of the word *easement,* ☐see **right of access.**

Essential auxiliary nomenclature is common to both words:

> **servient tenement,** also called **servient estate**: the land (Parcel One) that is burdened with a right of use or restriction of use.

dominant tenement, also called **dominant estate:** the land (Parcel Two) benefited by the burden on the *servient tenement* (Parcel One).

appurtenant easement or **appurtenant servitude:** an easement or servitude burdening a *servient tenement* (Parcel One) for the benefit of a *dominant tenement* (Parcel Two). Contrasted with *easement in gross* or *servitude in gross.*

easement in gross or **servitude in gross:** an easement or servitude burdening the *servient tenement* for the benefit of the holder of the right, independent of ownership of land. In this usage, there is no Parcel One and Parcel Two; there is one piece of land, a *servient tenement,* but no *dominant tenement.* <The owner of Blackacre grants John Doe a right personal to him to cross Blackacre to an adjacent stream; Doe now owns an easement in gross.>

2. **easement**—subcategories.

a. **affirmative easement,** also called a **positive easement:** a right to do something on the *servient tenement,* e.g., to walk across it (an *easement of way,* sometimes called an *easement of passage* or a *right of way*). Contrasted with *negative easement.*

b. **negative easement:** a right to prevent something being done on the *servient tenement,* e.g., obstructing air or light going to the *dominant tenement (easement of air, easement of light);* obstructing the view from the dominant tenement across the servient tenement (*easement of view*); impairing the support that the land of the servient tenement gives to the dominant tenement (*easement of support*), etc.

c. **implied easement:** an easement created by law, based on the circumstances of a conveyance that is insufficient to create an *express easement.* The *implied easement* is:

[1] *implied* from a conveyance that physically divides the land into two parcels that were constituent parts of a particular use of the land before the conveyance. <The owner's house on the rear half of Blackacre has a driveway that crosses the front half acre, connecting the house with the highway. When the owner sells the house and rear half acre, retaining the highway frontage, the grant carries with it an implied easement of way across the front half acre.>

[2] *implied* from a conveyance that does not physically divide the land, but the enjoyment of what has been conveyed is dependent on the use of the land not conveyed. <When the owner grants X Co. the right to cut timber on Blackacre, the grant carries with it an implied easement to enter Blackacre.> □see **imply.**

187

easement

Terminology incidental to *implied easements:*

[a] **quasi-easement:** a use of the original single parcel that the parties presumably intended should continue despite division, and so becomes the basis of an implied easement. <The owner's house on the rear half of Blackacre has a driveway that crosses the front half acre, connecting the house with the highway. When the owner sells the front half acre, retaining the house and the rear half acre, the owner of old Blackacre has an implied easement of way across the front half acre.>

[b] **easement of necessity,** also called an *easement by necessity:* an easement implied from the fact that the easement is necessary to the continued use of what has been retained or to the use of what has been conveyed. An *easement of necessity* is usually an *easement of way,* sometimes a *way of necessity.* <A owns Blackacre, which fronts on a public road. A sells the rear half of Blackacre to B, leaving that half acre without any access to a public road. The rear half acre sold to B now has an easement of necessity across A's frontage.>

d. **prescriptive easement,** also called an *easement by prescription:* an easement created by law when a landowner, without giving permission, does nothing to prevent strangers using the land openly and continuously as though it were a *servient tenement*; at the end of a statutory period, it is. <For twenty years, the owners of Blackacre openly and continuously use a corner of adjacent Whiteacre as a narrow but well-defined daily shortcut to the highway. The use is known to the owners of Whiteacre but occurs without their permission and without any attempted interruption until the statute of limitations has run. Too late. The shortcut is now an easement of way by prescription.> □see **adverse possession,** under **possession.**

3. **servitude**—subcategories.

a. short for **equitable servitude:** the right to enforce in a court of equity a promise made by the owner, or the owner's predecessor, as to the use or restriction of use of a parcel of land. <The recorded agreement for the sale of Blackacre requires the buyer (A) to maintain the paving on a portion of the common driveway connecting Blackacre, Whiteacre, and Greenacre. When A later sells Blackacre to B, A's agreement is an equitable servitude, enforceable against B.>

Equitable servitudes, like *easements,* may be *affirmative, negative, appurtenant, in gross,* and *implied.* Unlike *easements,* there is no prescriptive equitable servitude; prescription involves no promise. A few jurisdictions further distinguish *equitable servitudes* from *easements,* classifying *easements* as an interest in land, an *equitable servitude* only as a contract right.

b. a generic that includes in the one term *servitude* the following: *easement, equitable servitude, profit* (□see **profit à prendre**) and *real covenant* (□see **covenant**).

c. a generic that includes in the one term *servitude* the items in b., plus **license** (□see).

d. a generic that includes in the one term *servitude* the items in b., plus **restrictions** (□see).

easement in gross   □see **easement**.

easement of air   □see **easement**.

easement of light   □see **easement**.

easement of necessity   □see **easement**.

easement of passage   □see **easement**.

easement of support   □see **easement**.

easement of way   □see **easement**; □see **right of way**.

eavesdropping   □see **electronic eavesdropping**.

-ee: an old legal suffix with a well-established pedigree for recipients, e.g., *legatee* (□see **give**) and *patentee*, and especially for correlatives of agent words (*-or, -er*), e.g., *assignor/assignee* (□see **assign**), *bailor/ bailee* (□see **bail**), *mortgagor/mortgagee* (□see **mortgage**), and the indispensable *offeror/offeree* and *promisor/promisee*, etc.   The antique pairing of *debtor/debtee* has been abandoned in favor of *debtor/creditor*.

In general English, the suffix is a freewheeling participant in language invention, e.g., *debauchee, devotee, draftee, goatee, standee*, etc. Some of that creative urge has oozed into the legal vocabulary, with unfortunate results.   For example:

commitee: a juvenile who has been committed to an institution. This one *t*, sound-alike variant of *committee* is a new threat to ordinary *committee*, already fighting a losing battle for prestige with *task force* and **commission** (□see).   This confusing, apparent reversal of roles for two *t,* old-style *committee,* from taking care of things to being taken care of, is a euphemistic good deed for young law breakers but a low blow to legal English.

escapee: an escaped prisoner. Shorter, but inevitably conjures up a pseudo-correlative *escaper,* which sounds more like an escaped prisoner and is. Headline writers itch for such brevity; *an escaped prisoner* is short enough for the law, and clearer too.

For the superfluous *escrowee,* □see **escrow.**

effect □see **force and effect.**

effective counsel □see **right to counsel.**

EIR □see **environmental impact report.**

EIS □see **environmental impact report.**

ejectment □see **possessory action;** □see **evict.**

ejusdem generis (L., USE-dem generous: of the same kind): the customary Latin label of one of the so-called **rules of interpretation** (□see), this one accentuating the ordinary, that meaning depends on context: when a series of specific words is followed by a general word, the general word is usually understood to refer to the same kind of thing referred to by the specific words. <The agreement to supply cornflakes, Grapenuts, shredded wheat, and other cereals did not include fresh corn on the cob. You don't need *ejusdem generis* to tell you that.>

Elastic Clause: another name for the **Necessary and Proper Clause** (□see).

electronic eavesdropping: old-fashioned *eavesdropping* (secret listening under the eaves) expanded by twentieth-century technology into eavesdropping on a wide miscellany of communications of unconsenting people who had a reasonable expectation of privacy. The technology is usually electronic, but in some contexts, includes **wiretapping** (□see). Definitions vary with federal and state statutes that authorize, prohibit, and regulate *electronic eavesdropping* as related to espionage, enforcement of criminal law, admissibility of evidence, and invasion of privacy (□see **right of privacy**). The technology changes so fast that ordinary dictionaries cannot keep up with it, and statutes on the subject are being constantly revised. See, e.g., Title III of the Omnibus Crime Control and Safe Street Act of 1968, 18 USCA § 2510, *et seq.,* as amended 1986.

electronic funds transfer: an electronic alternative to **commercial paper** (☐see), typically in consumer transactions. As used in the federal Electronic Funds Transfer Act (15 USCA § 1693a(6), 1979), the expression, here trimmed of specific inclusions and exclusions detailed in the act, means: ". . . transfer of funds, other than a transaction originated by check, draft, or similar paper instrument, which is initiated through an electronic terminal, telephonic instrument, or computer, or magnetic tape, so as to order, instruct, or authorize a financial institution to debit or credit an account." Transactions covered by the federal Electronic Funds Transfer Act, referred to above, are not included in *funds transfers* as that expression is used in the **Uniform Commercial Code** (☐see).

electronic surveillance   ☐see **electronic eavesdropping.**

eleemosynary   ☐see **charitable.**

emancipated minor   ☐see **minor,** under **child.**

emancipation   ☐see **minor,** under **child.**

embezzle   ☐see **embezzlement.**

embezzlement: stealing property after it is lawfully in one's possession or control—the special form of *theft* (*larceny*) practiced by those to whom property is entrusted, e.g., bank clerks, messengers, trustees, lawyers.   <The $50,000 settlement money never reached the plaintiff. Defendant's lawyer, since convicted of embezzlement and disbarred, used the money to pay his own bills.>

embracer   ☐see **embracery.**

embracery: attempting to influence a juror, other than through regular courtroom procedures. A common law crime, now statutory, sometimes extended to targets other than jurors, e.g., arbitrators. The colorful names of the crime, and its practitioners—*embracers,* preserved in some jurisdictions, are more often replaced by pedestri-

embracery

an, if less misleading, terminology, e.g., "Every person who corruptly attempts to influence. . . ." In untechnical usage, the sense is conveyed by *trying to get to the jury* or *tampering with the jury.*

emergency □see **sudden emergency.**

Emergency Court of Appeals □see **Temporary Emergency Court of Appeals.**

eminent domain • condemnation —a symbiotic pair, sometimes mistaken for synonyms.

eminent domain (L., *dominium:* paramount ownership; and *eminens:* eminent).

1. the right and power of the sovereign (nation, state, municipality) to take private property for public use. <One of the indexes of sovereignty is the power of eminent domain, a right often delegated by statute to municipal agencies.>

2. Influenced by the constitutional prohibition against taking private property "for public use, without just compensation" (U.S. Const., Amend. V), usage frequently modifies sense 1 to incorporate the limitation into the basic definition: the right and power of the sovereign (nation, state, municipality) to take private property for public use upon payment of "just compensation."

3. the taking of private property for public use upon payment of "just compensation." This misuse confuses the process with the right and power. <The city acquired the parking lot by eminent domain.> □see **condemnation.**

condemnation

1. the exercise of the power of *eminent domain* upon payment of "just compensation." <The city acquired the parking lot by condemnation at a cost of $16 per square foot.> The verb is *condemn.* <The city condemned the parking lot, paying the owners $16 per square foot.>

severance damage: the injury to the portion of the land not condemned, by reason of the condemnation of less than the whole of a parcel of land.

severance damages: "just compensation" for *severance damage.*

2. the procedural steps to acquire private property for public use upon payment of "just compensation." <In the condemnation com-

plaint, the state requested immediate possession to permit road work even before the value on condemnation had been determined.>

condemner (sometimes *condemnor*): the body or authority condemning the property. <The school board is the condemner of the Fifth Street property.>

condemnee:

  a. the owner of the property condemned.

  b. the owner of the property taken by **inverse condemnation** (□see).

de facto taking: physical acts by the condemner-to-be that oust an owner from his property before condemnation proceedings have started. <Although the suit had not yet been filed, the state entered the property and deprived the owner of its use. There was a *de facto* taking.>

quick-take: statutory procedure authorizing the condemner to take possession, title, or both upon the start of condemnation proceedings.

3. inverse condemnation, sometimes called *constructive* or *reverse condemnation:*

  a. the taking of private property by a body or authority having power of eminent domain, but without condemnation proceedings and without "just compensation." <In an act of inverse condemnation, the city walled off the property owner's access to the street.>

  b. the remedy of the property owner against a body or authority having power of eminent domain that has taken the property without condemnation proceedings and without "just compensation." <Claiming that the state's storm drain was built on their property without permission and without suit, the owners started an action for inverse condemnation.>

Emolument Clause: the part of the U.S. Constitution reading: "No title of nobility shall be granted by the United States; and no person holding any office of profit or trust under them, shall, without the consent of the Congress, accept of any present, emolument, office, or title, of any kind whatever, from any king, prince, or foreign state." (Art. I, § 9, cl. 8). □see also, **constitutional clauses.**

emotional distress, also called *mental distress:* severe emotional suffering caused by another person's conduct, with or without physical contact. If the conduct is sufficiently "outrageous" and intended

emotional distress

to cause suffering, severe *emotional distress* is a tort and an element of damages, even without physical contact; e.g., a deliberately false message, "Your husband is dead." Increasingly, under similar circumstances, predictably severe emotional response to negligent conduct may be a tort and an element of damages, even without physical contact (e.g., mishandling of a corpse); sometimes even though the negligent conduct is directed at another, but closely related person; e.g., "I saw their truck crush my baby." The two torts have been called **intentional infliction of emotional distress** and **negligent infliction of emotional distress**. The topic has also been referred to as "freedom from *mental disturbance*," a designation easily confused with other classifications of mental states; □see **insanity**.

employee □see **independent contractor**.

Employee Retirement Security Act □see **ERISA**.

Employee Stock Ownership Plan □see **ESOP**, under **ERISA**.

employer • employee □see **independent contractor**.

en banc □see **bench**.

enbancworthy □see **bench**.

encroach □see **encroachment**.

encroacher □see **encroachment**.

encroachment

1. illegally occupying someone else's real property by placing or erecting something of a permanent nature on or overhanging the property, e.g., a house, a bay window, an awning, a fence, a deposit of soil. <They *encroached* on Blackacre; their encroachment started a year ago when the *encroachers* extended their house beyond the property line.>

2. the thing that illegally occupies someone else's real property (as in 1.); the house, the bay window, the awning, the fence, the deposit of soil are encroachments. <Without permission, the utility put a power line across the road; the line is an encroachment, though not an *obstruction;* it *encroaches* on public property.>

194

encumber, less often *incumber.*

1. to make property serve as security for the payment or performance of an obligation. This is a general term describing a voluntary
giving as well as obtaining security by legal process. <To get a
construction loan, they encumbered the realty with a first trust deed./Plaintiff
sued and attached, effectively encumbering defendant's property with an attachment lien until defendant posted a bond to relieve the attachment.> ☐see
lien.

encumbrance, less often *incumbrance:* the name of the legal device
that makes property serve as security, as in 1., e.g., a **deed of trust**
(☐see, under **deed**), **lien** (☐see), **mortgage** (☐see), **pledge** (☐see), **security
interest** (☐see, under **secure**), etc. <The encumbrance took the form of a
first mortgage.> Like *encumber, encumbrance* is a general term but is
sometimes limited to security in real property.

encumbrancer: the person who holds an *encumbrance* for security,
not the person who gives the encumbrance. Despite the confusion of -
ee and *-er/-or* endings, a *mortgagee,* for example, is an *encumbrancer,* a
mortgagor is not. ☐see **-ee.** *Encumbrancer* is usually limited to one
who holds security in real property.

2. to burden property with a legal obstacle or claim, whether or not
as security, that affects the ability of the apparent owner to convey a
clear title. <Blackacre was encumbered by a first mortgage that could be
paid off, but the property was so encumbered by litigation over a boundary
dispute that it was not readily salable.>

encumbrance, less often *incumbrance:* the legal obstacle or claim,
whether or not a security device, as in 1., that affects the ability of the
apparent owner to convey a clear title. <The party wall encroached on
Blackacre; the **encroachment** (☐see) was also an encumbrance.> ☐see
also, **cloud on title;** ☐see also, **lis pendens.**

encumbrance ☐see **encumber.**

encumbrancer ☐see **encumber.**

enforceable contract ☐see **contract.**

enhance, enhanced, enhancement, in ordinary English mean increase, greater, usually in a favorable direction. Civil practice shares
that usage, e.g., *enhanced value.* For criminal lawyers, the words are
unmitigated negatives. **Enhancement** is short for *enhanced punishment:* an additional penalty because of a prior conviction or because

195

of specially evil aspects of the offense, e.g., use of a deadly weapon, great bodily harm, etc. □see also, **special circumstances**.

enjoin • injunction

enjoin has fallen out of fashion in ordinary English, and good riddance. It is one of those strange "yes" and "no" words: to direct that something be done ("do it") or to forbid something being done ("don't do it"). (For a soul mate of *enjoin,* □see **sanction**.) In ordinary English, *enjoin*'s residual vitality is mostly of the "do it" variety, with a religious or moral cast. <We enjoin you to follow the Golden Rule.> In the law, *enjoin* is very much alive, but only as "don't do it." It is the principal operative word of the *prohibitory* or *preventive injunction:* an **injunction** (□see) that stops or prevents something from being done. <The defendants are enjoined from erecting a fence more than five feet high on the perimeter of Blackacre.> The qualification *prohibitory* (or *preventive*) is critical; *enjoin*'s association with *injunction* begins and ends with the negative; *injunction* has broader horizons.

injunction: the name of the order, exercising powers of a court of equity (□see **equity**), directing that something be done ("do it") or not done ("don't do it"). A "do it" *injunction,* called a **mandatory injunction,** typically uses as operative words *order* or *require,* but not *enjoin,* to which *injunction* is etymologically related. A "don't do it" *injunction* (the **prohibitory** or **preventive injunction**) typically uses as operative words *enjoin* or *restrain,* often, redundantly, *enjoin and restrain.* □see also, **cease and desist**. Mandatory and prohibitory aspects of *injunctive relief* may be combined in one *injunction.* <The defendant Jones is ordered to vacate Blackacre today, and is enjoined from entering the premises during this calendar year.>

Classification of *injunctions* according to their duration varies by jurisdiction:

permanent injunction, also called *final injunction* or *perpetual injunction:* an injunction granted as part of a judgment, after a full determination of the rights of the parties.

preliminary injunction, also called *injunction pendente lite* (□see **lis**), *interlocutory injunction, provisional injunction, temporary injunction:* an injunction granted after a hearing before a judge in advance of trial, usually after argument by opposing lawyers, to last until the granting or denial of a *permanent injunction* or some shorter fixed time.

temporary restraining order, abbreviated TRO, in many jurisdictions not classified as an *injunction:* an injunction typically granted **ex parte** (□see) on a showing of urgency, in advance of a hearing on a request for a *preliminary injunction,* or in advance of other interlocutory hearings before trial, e.g., in domestic litigation, to prevent harassment. A *temporary restraining order* is often referred to as a *restraining order.*

entail   □see **fee tail.**

entailed estate   □see **fee tail.**

enter • entry

Ordinary English senses of both words are amply represented in legal contexts, e.g., enter the United States under a quota; enter without a warrant; enter the legal profession; a bookkeeping entry. Statutes spell out special requirements and varying consequences of *entry.* Here are distinctive aspects of *enter* (v.) and its companion *entry* (n.) in frequent use. (Names of records referred to vary by state.)

1. to write something (an *entry*) in a specially designated set of official records cataloging chronologically acts, proceedings, or determinations affecting lawsuits. In this sense, *enter* is a species of clerical record making, distinct from the events recorded, from the keeping of legal papers (□see **file**), and from the *recording* of legal documents in a form and place that gives public notice of their contents. □see also, **of record.** <The deed was recorded; the complaint filed; the judgment entered.> Common examples of *enter* and *entry* are:

enter a judgment (entry of judgment): writing down the judgment, in all its detail, in a *judgment book* or similar set of records. □see **judgment.** <The time for appeal ran from the entry of judgment.>

enter an appearance (entry of appearance): writing in the court's minutes (a *minute entry*) that a named lawyer has appeared for a litigant. (□see **appear**). This clerical *entry* is distinct from *entry,* sense 2. <The clerk entered an appearance for each of the defendants.>

2. to make a legal presentation to a court that usually results in a clerical *entry* (sense 1). This is usually the work of a lawyer. Common examples:

enter an appearance (entry of appearance): to announce in court orally or in writing that a lawyer is appearing for a litigant. (□see **appear**). The lawyer's *entry* is distinct from the clerk's (sense 1). <Yes, Your Honor, we have entered an appearance for both defen-

dants, whether or not that is reflected in the court's minutes.> *Enter an appearance* is a stiffer version of the informal *put in an appearance.*

enter a plea: to announce in court, usually orally, how a defendant pleads to a criminal charge. <The defendant entered a plea of nolo contendere.> The phrase is sometimes used as a formal statement by a lawyer. <The defendant Smith wishes to enter a plea of nolo contendere.> More often, the phrase itself is omitted. <The defendant Smith pleads "not guilty."/"Not guilty."> □see **plea.**

enter an objection, shortened to *"object"* or *"objected to"*: to announce in court orally that a lawyer objects to what is happening in court; this *entry* is not usually reflected in a clerical *entry* (sense 1). <Motion denied. Objection.> It is distinct from the litany of *objections* to questions by an adversary or to the offer of evidence (□see **objection**). *Enter an objection* is often a substitute for *"let the record show."* Whether or not required by local law, the oral protest, recorded in a reporter's transcript of court proceedings, becomes an adjunct to later argument of error, sometimes a memento of events not otherwise reported. <Your Honor, we wish to enter an objection to the shackling of the defendant./Let the record show that the prosecutor/defense counsel is leaning into the jury box.> □see also, **for the record.**

3. to go onto land under a claim of right, e.g., as an element of *adverse possession* (□see **possession**) <The entry was twenty years ago.>; e.g., as part of a claim of ownership of land in the public domain. □see also, **preemption right.**

4. to go into a building with criminal intent, as an element of various crimes. <Entry with intent to commit a felony is burglary.> □see also **breaking and entering,** under **breach.**

5. enter into (an agreement): to agree. Roundabout for *made an agreement* or simply *agree.* <They entered into an agreement/made an agreement/agreed.> At worst, better than made and entered into (□see **made**).

enter a judgment   □see **enter.**

enter an appearance   □see **enter;** □see **appear.**

enter an objection   □see **enter;** □see **objection.**

enter a plea   □see **enter.**

enter into   □see **enter**; □see **made**.

entirely and completely: common English synonyms, redundant (□see **coupled synonyms**). The couplet's insidious appeal to lawyers lies in the exhilarating absoluteness of each word, tempered by an unsettling suspicion that in a tough case, no one will believe that *entirely* means *completely*. (□see **absolutes**). The time-honored hedge against that horrible possibility is repetition, as if to say "I really mean it!" The trouble is that the cure is applied so mechanically that the couplet is no more believable than each word alone. If *entirely* or *completely* is not enough, doubling won't improve the chances of success. Better try something else. Maybe even, "Completely. And I really mean it!"

entirety   □see **estate by the entirety**, under **estate**.

entitle   □see **entitlement**.

entitlement

1.   a general, flexible term for the right to have something, anything. This substantive outgrowth of the verb *entitle* is rarer in ordinary English than in the law; the verb ordinarily suffices.   <Their views are entitled to respect./The defendant is entitled to a trial by jury./Both parents are entitled to reasonable visitation.>

2.   short for *statutory entitlement* as the name of a right to some particular thing, as well as the name of the thing to which one is *entitled:*

   a.   for those made eligible by special statute, the right to receive money from the government.   <Her entitlement to Medicare benefits was not questioned.>   The money to be paid is *the* entitlement, e.g., Social Security payments, military retirement pay, government pensions.   <The legislation would provide funds to cover their accumulated social welfare entitlements.>

   b.   for those made eligible by special statute, a right that, once granted, cannot be *withdrawn* without due process, e.g., right to a license, to welfare payments, to a parole. The license, the payment, the parole are *the* entitlements.   <The right to a driver's license was an entitlement; the license could not be suspended without a hearing.>

3.   a right to a benefit in the nature of a property interest that cannot be *withheld* without due process, e.g., a right to continuity of employment. The benefit, the employment, is *the* entitlement.

entitlement

< "[T]he existence of rules and understandings promulgated and fostered by state officials, that may justify [a] legitimate claim of entitlement to continued employment. . . ." (*Perry v. Sinderman,* 408 U.S. 593, 602 (1972).)>

entity □see **legal entity,** under **person.**

entrap • entrapment

entrap: an old synonym for the common verb *trap,* with a special emphasis on using guile to get someone into your power. The verb and the common noun *entrapment* (the action or "condition of being entrapped or caught by artifice"—*Oxford English Dictionary,* 2nd ed.) have a special place in American criminal law.

entrapment

1. the creative act of government agents in planning a crime and persuading someone, who needs persuading, to commit it. The government's role in persuading the innocent, or at least the unconvinced, is distinguished from merely providing an opportunity, as in the now popular *sting.* < "To determine . . . entrapment . . . a line must be drawn between the trap for the unwary innocent and the trap for the unwary criminal." (Warren, C.J., in *Sherman v. U.S.* 369, 372 (1958). □see also, **trap for the unwary.**>

2. the measures taken to design the criminal act and persuade the person targeted for *entrapment* (sense 1). < The entrapment consisted of importuning one never engaged in smuggling to join with immigration officers in smuggling illegals across the border, importunities rejected for two years and finally successful.>

3. the name of a defense to a prosecution for the crime the defendant was *entrapped* into committing, as in 1. and 2. < They did not deny the physical acts but relied on the defense of entrapment.>

entrapment □see **entrap.**

entry □see **enter.**

entry of appearance □see **enter.**

entry of judgment □see **enter.**

enumerated powers: a label for the broad principle that the federal government is not a government of unlimited powers but rather of powers enumerated in the Constitution (□see **delegated powers**). In this constitutional sense, *enumerated powers* includes what is implied in and incidental to the enumerated. "Implied" by decisions of the U.S. Supreme Court on a variety of theories, e.g., implicit in national sovereignty at home and abroad, incidental to exercise of the enumerated powers of each branch of government, authorized by the **Necessary and Proper Clause** (□see) or the **Supremacy Clause** (□see). The expression *enumerated powers* has not been abandoned, nor its limitations forgotten, but it embraces, often controversially, *implied powers* and *incidental powers.* See *McCulloch v. Maryland,* 17 U.S. 316, 406 (1819). □see also, **inherent powers**.

en ventre sa mère   □see child.

environmental impact report (abbreviated **EIR**), also called **environmental impact statement** (abbreviated **EIS**): a writing giving detailed information about how a proposed change in the use of private or public property might significantly and adversely affect the environment, how that effect might be avoided or minimized, and why it might be tolerated. Whether or not an *EIR* or *EIS* is required for government approval of a proposed change varies by the law of the jurisdiction (national, state, and local), and especially by bundles of circumstance, e.g., types of construction or operations with a history of pollution (power plants, chemical factories, oil drilling, disposal of sewage and toxic wastes, etc.); zone changes or street construction affecting character of a neighborhood; high-rise building affecting traffic. The name of the writing, *EIR* or *EIS,* and the myriad details of the writing and its use likewise vary by jurisdiction.

environmental impact statement   □see environmental impact report.

environmental law: a growing body of law—decision, statute, regulation—evidencing increasing concern at home and abroad over the deterioration of the once natural world. And what to do about it. E.g., the Environmental Protection Agency (□see **administrative agency, under administrative law**); e.g., **environmental impact report** (□see). *Environmental law* is uncramped by precise definition.

eo instante   □see absolutes.

EPA abbreviation of Environmental Protection Agency. □see **environmental law**.

equal protection: the shortened and usual rendering of **equal protection of law** and **equal protection of the laws**:

1. the protection of laws that treat every person as the equal of every other person. *Equal protection* does not mean that every person will be treated the same—different facts beget different results—only that the law as written and as administered will maintain an unranked society, where no one is "more equal than others." (Orwell, *Animal Farm*, ch. 10, 1945).

As with **due process** (□see), a formulation necessarily flexible; courts apply but do not rigidly define *equal protection*.

2. *equal protection* (sense 1) as referred to in the U.S. Constitution (□see **Equal Protection Clause**) and interpreted by the U.S. Supreme Court.

For legislative *classification* tested against *equal protection*, □see **standards of review**.

Equal Protection Clause: the part of the U.S. Constitution reading: ". . . . nor [shall any state] deny to any person within its jurisdiction the equal protection of the laws." (Amend. XIV, § 1). □see also, **constitutional clauses**.

equal protection of law □see **equal protection**.

equal protection of the laws □see **equal protection**.

Equal Rights Amendment, abbreviated **ERA**: A proposed twenty-seventh amendment to the U.S. Constitution, the key provision (s. 1) reading: "Equality of rights under the law shall not be denied or abridged by the United States or by any state on account of sex." Passed by Congress on March 22, 1972, and submitted to the state legislatures. Not ratified by the required three-fourths of the legislatures by the extended deadline, June 30, 1982.

equal time rule □see **fairness doctrine**, under **fair**.

equitable □see **equity**.

equitable conversion □see **conversion.**

equitable estate □see **equity.**

equitable estoppel □see **estoppel.**

equitable indemnity

1. as a general expression: a court's use of the procedure of indemnity and the equitable principle of fairness to prevent or allocate loss. (□see **equity;** □see **hold harmless,** under **hold**). Variously interpreted by decision and statute. The border between allocation of loss under the name of *contribution* among tortfeasors (proportionately) and allocation by *indemnity* (often limited to a complete shifting of loss) is in violent flux.

2. the equitable principle of fairness applied to require a person unjustly enriched to indemnify the other when two persons are liable in tort or contract for the same harm to a third person and only one of them discharges the liability of both (□see **restitution**).

3. the right of one against whom a claim is asserted in tort or contract to have potential liability among wrongdoers apportioned or shifted.

   a. Indemnity by apportionment varies with theories of tort liability. This aspect of equitable indemnity is also referred to as *comparative indemnity* and *comparative equitable indemnity* (□see **comparative negligence,** under **contributory negligence**).

   b. Complete shifting of liability under equitable indemnity varies with the substantive law of the jurisdiction. For example, liability imposed on the basis of relationship, as in **vicarious liability** (□see).

equitable interest □see **equity.**

equitable jurisdiction □see **equity;** □see **jurisdiction.**

equitable lien □see **lien.**

equitable owner □see **beneficiary.**

equitable ownership □see **equity.**

equitable redemption   □see **equity**.

equitable relief   □see **equity**.

equitable remedy   □see **equity**.

equitable servitude   □see **easement**.

equitable servitude in gross   □see **easement**.

equitable title   □see **equity**.

equity • equitable

In the law and in ordinary English, both words are related to the Latin *aequitas:* equality, justice, fairness.

equity

1. law derived from the English courts of chancery and other courts outside the system of **common law** (□see), consisting of a distinctive bundle of: *powers* (e.g., over divorce, probate, trusts); *procedures* (e.g., trial by judge with no right to a jury, discovery); and *remedies* (e.g., injunction, specific performance, declaratory relief, constructive trusts).

The courts of chancery were headed by the Lord Chancellor, "keeper of the King's conscience," originally a cleric, who administered a species of justice at one time less rigid and less technical than could be had in the courts of common law; also, it was justice suffused with moral principles of fairness expressed in a multitude of **maxims** (□see). For *equity acts in personam,* see below in this entry. □see also, **clean hands**. Over the years, the principles have yielded to their more specific expression in powers, procedures, and remedies defined by decision and statute.

In the United States, the tradition of separate courts of law and *courts of equity* (also called *courts of chancery*) has given way to single courts for all law, including *equity* as a special way of dealing with particular legal problems. <There are no legal issues here. All you want is an injunction; that's equity, not law; and you are not entitled to a jury.>

equity acts in personam: a misleading English version of the equally misleading Latin maxim *aequitas agit in personam;* misleading, for equity also acts *in rem*. ☐see **in personam**. At its best, describes a traditional procedural device of equity to enforce a court order by compulsion directed literally at the person, as distinguished from property, e.g., by holding a defendant in contempt, in prison if necessary, until compliance with a court order, as distinct from relying only on seizing property or awarding damages. ☐see also, **maxims**.

equity jurisdiction: power to use **equitable remedies** (see below in this entry). <The municipal court cannot grant an injunction; it has no equity jurisdiction.> Also called *equitable jurisdiction.*

2. a right enforceable by a court using *equity* (sense 1).

equity of redemption: the right of a debtor in default (e.g., under a mortgage or trust deed) to redeem property from forfeiture by making specified payments to the secured creditor.

3. fairness, as a condition of invoking, exercising, or denying the exercise of the distinctive powers, procedures, and remedies of *equity* (sense 1).

do equity: e.g., "If they want specific performance of the agreement to convey Blackacre, they must first do equity by tendering the purchase price."

in equity and good conscience: a traditional, repetitive phrase, adding nothing but background music to a decision to grant or deny a decree. <In equity and good conscience, I must/I cannot/give judgment for the plaintiff.> Orally, it risks misinterpretation as *inequity.*

want of equity: e.g., "Having defaulted in their own obligations, plaintiffs' request for specific performance must be denied for want of equity." ☐see also, **clean hands**.

☐see also, **equitable indemnity**.

4. equity of the statute: the spirit or policy of a statute, used as a matter of interpretation to include things that are not expressly covered. <While this precise situation is not mentioned, the equity of the statute provides a reasonable basis for our conclusion that the statute governs here as well.>

5. an untechnical usage shared with ordinary English: net ownership interest, or ownership as opposed to debt. <After deduction of two mortgages, their equity in the property was $10,000./The corporation raised money by *equity financing* (sale of stock), rather than incurring further debt by borrowing and issuing bonds.>

equitable

1. relating to *equity* (sense 1). <The law of trusts is equitable, not legal.>

equitable jurisdiction: synonym for *equity jurisdiction* (□see **equity**).

2. **equitable interest:** an interest in property based on an *equity* (sense 2), e.g., an *equitable servitude*. □see **easement**.

equitable owner: the **beneficial owner** (□see, under **beneficiary**) of property.

equitable ownership, also called *equitable title* and *equitable estate:* ownership enforceable in equity, but with the legal title in someone else, e.g., a *trustee,* or a *trustee de son tort.* □see **trust**. □see also, **beneficial owner,** under **beneficiary**.

3. the adjective of *equity* as fairness (*equity,* sense 3). <The equitable thing to do would be. . . .> □see also, **equitable indemnity**.

4. **equitable relief:**

   a. synonym for **equitable remedy** (□see).

   b. redress available applying *equity* (sense 1), especially emphasizing inadequacy of common law remedies. <The complaint asked for damages, equitable relief by way of injunction, and a declaration of rights under the contract.>

5. **equitable remedy:** remedy not available at common law, but available applying *equity* (sense 1). The availability of any *equitable remedy* (e.g., specific performance) is subject to the rule of fairness (*equity,* sense 3), its special crystalization known as **clean hands** (□see), and to the equitable discretionary substitute for statutes of limitations known as **laches** (□see). □see also, **enjoin**.

inadequacy of the remedy at law: The need for an *equitable remedy* or for *equitable relief* (see above) is often expressed in terms of the *inadequacy of the remedy at law* or there being an *inadequate remedy at law.* The words *inadequacy* and *inadequate* here are euphemisms for *unavailable.*

6. **equitable title:** □see **equitable ownership,** above, in this entry.

equity acts in personam □see **equity**.

equity financing □see **equity**.

equity jurisdiction □see **equity.**

equity of redemption □see **equity.**

equity of the statute □see **equity.**

equity securities □see **securities,** under **secure.**

ERA □see **Equal Rights Amendment.**

ERISA: abbreviation of Employee Retirement Income Security Act of 1974, amended to 1989 (29 USCA §§ 1001(a) *et seq.*): a federal law regulating "establishment, operation, and administration" of private employee benefit plans, providing, among other things, "minimum standards . . . assuring the equitable character of such plans and their financial soundness." Subject to qualifying conditions, one type of plan that may be included under ERISA is an **ESOP:** Employee Stock Ownership Plan, covering investment for employees in securities issued by the employer (see 29 USCA § 1107(d)(6)). □see also, **prudent man rule,** under **prudence.**

error □see **confess error,** under **acknowledge and confess;** □see **fatal error,** under **fatal;** □see **harmless error,** under **fatal;** □see **invited error;** □see **plain error;** □see **reversible error;** □see **prejudicial error;** □see **writ of error,** under **writ;** □see **writ of error coram nobis,** under **coram nobis.**

errors and omissions □see **malpractice.**

escapee □see **-ee.**

escheat

1. the passing to the state of title to real or personal property when the owner dies leaving no one entitled to take, or when the property is abandoned or unclaimed. <The state took by escheat.>

Escheat is regulated by statute, and occurs by operation of law or by court order. The other senses of the word all refer to *escheat*, sense 1.

2. the right of the state to title by *escheat*. <The state filed suit, claiming escheat of Blackacre, stock, and money.>

3. (v.) to pass, or cause to pass, by *escheat.* <The property escheated./ At the suit of the attorney general, the court escheated the property.>

4. (n.) the property that passes by *escheat.* <The escheat consisted of Blackacre and five hundred shares of stock.>

escrow

1. a mechanism for the transfer of ownership or possession from A to B by deposit of the necessary writings, property, or money with a disinterested third party for delivery to A and B in accordance with their instructions. <Buyer and Seller of the stock opened escrow at the First National Bank./Under the *escrow instructions,* escrow for the sale of Blackacre was to close when the bank recorded the deed and delivered the purchase money to the seller.>

in escrow: the state of a transaction, or of the writings, property, or money that are part of a transaction, being handled through an *escrow.* <That deal is in escrow./The deed is in escrow, but they are waiting for the money.>

2. (v.): to place something in **escrow** (□see). <They decided to escrow the transfer of title./The two title deeds were escrowed.>

3. the writings, property, or money to be delivered through an escrow (sense 1). <The escrow—a ten-year lease—was to be delivered when the lessor received the deposit of the first year's rent.> This, an older usage, is now less common than a participial description. <Counterparts of the *escrowed lease* were to be delivered to lessee and lessor.>

4. *escrow holder:* the disinterested third party who is the intermediary in the *escrow* (sense 1). This is the perfect description when *escrow* is used in sense 3 and is often used in any event. Other equivalents are:

escrow agent —a frequent current use; the disinterested third party is the agent of both the other parties to the escrow.

escrowee has a modest appeal on the theory that the escrow holder is a sort of trustee rather than agent. The ending of *escrowee* inevitably suggests the complications of the correlative (□see **-ee**). *Escrowee* is short, but unneeded, and there is something shorter.

escrow alone is sometimes used as shorthand for both the *escrow agent* and the place where the *escrow* (sense 1) is being held. <First National Bank, Main Street, is the escrow.>

escrow agent   □see **escrow.**

escrowee   □see **escrow**.

escrow holder   □see **escrow**.

escrow instructions   □see **escrow**.

ESOP   □see **ERISA**.

Esq.   □see **Esquire**.

Esquire: a flattering if archaic addition to a lawyer's name, more often as abbreviated, *Esq.* Waning, but still live, its strength (not virility) has been somewhat increased by the controversy over sexism. Historic maleness forgotten or ignored, *Esquire* or *Esq.* is added to the written names of male and female lawyers, ducking the choices of *Mr., Mrs., Miss,* or *Ms.* <John Smith, Esq./Mary Smith, Esquire>. □see also, **sex**. □see also, **formalisms**.

Establishment Clause: the part of the U.S. Constitution reading: "Congress shall make no law respecting an establishment of religion, [or prohibiting the free exercise thereof]. . . ." (Amend. I). The *Establishment Clause* and the bracketed *Free Exercise Clause* are also referred to as the *Religion Clauses,* sometimes as the *religious clauses.* □see also, **Religious Test Clause**; □see also, **constitutional clauses**.

estate • tenancy

Ordinary English may connect *estate* and *tenancy* (or *tenant*), but does not confuse them; the distinction is clear between the property and holding it. <They had a five-year tenancy, the first tenants ever, of the five-acre estate at Point Blackacre.> (The distinction breaks down with that other kin of *tenancy,* the American *tenement house.*) In their least technical senses, *estate* and *tenancy* (and *tenant*) are clearly distinguishable in the law; in the entries below, the overlap begins with *estate* (sense 4) and *tenancy* (sense 2).

estate

1.   a piece of land, especially a big one, especially with a house and trees. <The estate was on a hilltop overlooking the city.> This is but one instance of *real estate,* in and out of the law, land of whatever size, with or without building or trees. <He was in the business of

buying and selling real estate.> For technical usage, □see **real property**, under **property**; □see **land**.

2. all of the property, real and personal, under a particular ownership, especially an ownership suddenly changed by some unique event, e.g., death (the *deceased's estate*), divorce (□see **marital estate**), bankruptcy (the *bankruptcy estate* or the *bankrupt's estate*). <Including the house, stock, and money in the bank, the estate was worth $100,000.> For *estate tax,* □see **death taxes**.

3. a statutory label of reference to the administration of some kinds of *estates* (sense 2) and to those designated to do the administering. Best known is the *Estate of* ________ in probate proceedings and litigation, with a capitalized title and an **executor** (□see) or *administrator* appointed to take charge of the property of someone who has died. <The court appointed J.S. as executor of the Estate of Smith./*In re Estate of Smith.*> □see **legal entity**, under **person**.

4. an interest in property, usually in real property, described in terms of distinctive features of origin, extent, ownership, right to possession, or duration. In this generalized sense, *estate* and *tenancy* are synonyms, tied together from antiquity. With uniformity the exception, the law sometimes prefers *estate* or *tenancy* as the label for a particular interest or for a category of interests, but often the labels are interchangeable. Forms of an *estate,* or a general kind of *estate* with that word in the label, are listed here in alphabetical order. For an *estate,* or a general kind of estate, more commonly known as a *tenancy* or by some other expression, there is a cross–reference. □see also, **timeshare**.

entailed estate □see **fee tail**.

equitable estate □see **equity**.

estate at sufferance □see **tenancy at sufferance**.

estate at will □see **tenancy at will**.

estate by the entirety, also called *estate by the entireties* and, interchangeably, *tenancy by the entirety* and *tenancy by the entireties:* by whichever label, the estate is one jointly held by husband and wife as owners of the undivided whole (the entirety), with all the characteristics of a **joint tenancy** (□see), including survivorship, except that neither husband nor wife, acting alone, can sever joint ownership of the whole. Varies by decision and statute. The bastard plural *entireties,* relict of antique spelling, possibly influenced by rhythmic association with its antithesis *moieties* (plural of *moiety*) ought to be discarded in favor of the logical singular *entirety*.

estate for life: a less common name for a **life estate** (see, below, in this entry).

estate for years □see **tenancy for years**, below, in this entry.

estate in common: an uncommon name for estates in concurrent ownership. □see **estate by the entirety**, above, in this entry; □see below, in this entry, **joint tenancy**; □see **tenancy in common**, below, in this entry.

estate in expectancy □see **expectancy**, under **future interest**.

estate in fee □see **fee simple**.

estate in fee simple □see **fee simple**.

estate in fee tail □see **fee tail**.

estate in futuro —a tottering Latin remnant: estate in the future. □see **future interest**.

estate in possession, also called *possessory estate*, also called a *present estate:* a reference to the estate of someone who has a right to its possession now, as contrasted with a **future interest** (□see).

estate in remainder □see **remainder**, under **future interest**.

estate in reversion □see **reversion**, under **future interest**.

estate in severalty: a general term for sole ownership.

estate of freehold □see **freehold**.

estate pur autre vie □see **life estate**, below, in this entry.

estate tail □see **fee tail**.

freehold estate □see **freehold**.

leasehold estate □see **leasehold**, under **lease**.

legal estate □see **equity**.

life estate: an estate that lasts a lifetime and no more. The lifetime is usually the life of the owner of the *life estate.* <A owns Blackacre in fee and conveys Blackacre to B for life; B has a life estate in Blackacre.> There is a subspecies:

> **estate pur autre vie** (law F., poor O-tra vee: for another's life): like a *life estate*, except that the lifetime is the life of someone who is not the owner of the *estate pur autre vie.* <A owns Blackacre in fee and conveys Blackacre to B for the life of C; B has an estate *pur autre vie*, measured by C's life./A owns Blackacre in fee and conveys to B for life; B, having a life estate, conveys Blackacre to C; C has an estate *pur autre vie*, measured by B's life.>

nonpossessory estate □see **future interest**.

periodic estate □see **periodic tenancy**, below, in this entry.

5. land benefited or burdened by easements and servitudes. For this sense of *estate,* and in particular *dominant estate,* also called *dominant tenement,* and *servient estate,* also called *servient tenement,* □see **easement**.

6. for the relationship between owners of *estates* or *tenancies,* known as *privity of estate,* □see **privity**.

tenancy

1. the relationship of **landlord and tenant** (□see), as distinct from the specification of a particular property interest (sense 2). In this sense 1, common in and out of the law, *tenancy* may refer to the relationship as a unit of property use and management. <The new rent control law will not affect their present tenancy.> It may also refer to the period of the relationship. <Throughout the tenancy, I paid rent to the landlord's agent.>

2. an interest in property, usually in real property, described in terms of distinctive features of origin, extent, ownership, right to possession, or duration. Synonym for sense 4 of **estate** (□see). Forms of a *tenancy,* or a general kind of *tenancy* with that word in the label, are listed here in alphabetical order. For a *tenancy,* or a general kind of *tenancy,* more commonly known as an *estate* or by some other expression, there is a cross-reference.

joint tenancy: a medieval creature of such intellectual ingenuity and practical utility that it has not only survived in the modern world of real property but has expanded into every sort of personalty, including popular joint tenancy bank accounts. *Joint tenancy* is a tenancy of two or more persons whose interests are equal in every respect. Each simultaneously owns all of the undivided whole; each has a nonexclusive right to possess that undivided whole; each has the *right of survivorship:* the estate of a deceased joint tenant takes nothing; the whole property continues to be owned by whoever survives.

At common law (in some states still), creation of a joint tenancy required the **four unities**: not only of interest and possession, as described above, but also of time and title, i.e., all joint tenants had to acquire their interests at the same time from the same owner.

A *joint tenancy* can be severed (broken up) by the conveyance or legal seizure of the interest of one or more of the joint tenants; as to that interest, this results in a **tenancy in common** (□see).

life tenancy: less common name for *life estate* (□see), but in either case, the owner is called the *life tenant.*

periodic tenancy, less commonly called a *periodic estate:* a tenancy that continues for successive periods of the same duration as the original period until terminated by notice from either party to the other. Timing and length of the notice is fixed by decision, statute, or agreement. The most common periodic tenancy is a *month-to-month tenancy.* <He had been a tenant from month to month for ten years.> A *year-to-year tenancy* is a periodic tenancy; not to be confused with the much different **tenancy for years** (□see).

tenancy at sufferance: more an embarrassment than a tenancy. The traditional name for the status of someone invited in as a tenant who stays on without consent or right when the legitimate tenancy ends. Not a trespasser; the *tenant at sufferance* is called that, rather than something worse.

tenancy at will: a tenancy by consent, but without fixed duration, and so terminable at the will of either party. Regulated by statute.

tenancy by the entirety, also called *tenancy by the entireties,* and, interchangeably, *estate by the entirety* and *estate by the entireties.* □see **estate by the entirety,** under **estate.**

tenancy for years, also called *estate for years,* also called *term of years:* a tenancy for a fixed period whose beginning and ending dates are specified or can be figured out in advance with the aid of a calendar. The names are misleading; despite the use of *years,* a *tenancy for years* may be for one day, two weeks, five months. The expressions include a tenancy for a specified number of years, as contrasted with a *year-to-year tenancy* (□see **periodic tenancy**).

tenancy in common: a tenancy of two or more persons, each owning a separate but undivided interest in the whole. Unlike a **joint tenancy** (□see), the interests need not be equal, but like a *joint tenant,* each *tenant in common* has a nonexclusive right to possession of the undivided whole. Unlike joint tenants, tenants in common have no right of survivorship. Transfer of the interest of one tenant in common makes the transferee tenant in common with the other tenants in common. □see also, **cotenancy.**

tenancy in fee, more commonly called a *fee,* or *estate in fee;* whatever the name, the owner is the *tenant in fee.* □see **fee simple.**

estate

tenancy in fee tail, also called *tenancy in tail, fee tail, estate tail,* and *entailed estate;* whatever the name, the owner is the *tenant in tail.* □see fee tail.

tenancy in tail □see fee tail.

estate at sufferance □see tenancy at sufferance, under estate.

estate at will □see tenancy at will, under estate.

estate by the entirety □see estate.

estate for life □see life estate, under estate.

estate in common □see estate.

estate in expectancy □see expectancy, under future interest.

estate in fee □see fee simple.

estate in fee simple □see fee simple.

estate in fee tail □see fee tail.

estate in futuro □see estate; □see future interest.

estate in possession □see estate.

estate in remainder □see remainder, under future interest.

estate in reversion □see reversion, under future interest.

estate in severalty □see estate.

estate of freehold □see freehold.

estate pur autre vie □see life estate, under estate.

estate tail   □see **fee tail.**

estate tax   □see **death taxes;** □see **marital deduction.**

estop   □see **estoppel.**

estoppel   (law F., ess-TOP-ul): the law won't let you, stops you, you are *estopped* from saying this is a fact, when saying so is contrary to what you said before, did before, or were a party to before. <Having repeatedly insisted that they were principals, they are now estopped to assert that they were acting only as agents. Estoppel bars that assertion, even if true.>

The anathema *estoppel* is invoked to prevent damage from reasonable reliance on an earlier representation:

In writings—**estoppel by contract, estoppel by deed, estoppel by record** of proceedings that one was a party to, as *estoppel by judgment, estoppel by verdict,* and *judicial estoppel* (applied loosely to pleadings, other writings in judicial proceedings, sworn statements).

By conduct—**equitable estoppel,** barring the inequitable disappointment of reasonable expectations based on what had been said or done. Often used interchangeably with **estoppel in pais** (law F., pay: country), originally an estoppel to assert facts contrary to facts of such notoriety that jurors (once referred to as "the country") would probably know them. *Equitable estoppel* has a wide-ranging offspring called **promissory estoppel:** a bar to going back on a promise that could be expected to induce reliance and did; the resulting enforcement of the promise is sometimes called *contract by estoppel.*

For **collateral estoppel** and **direct estoppel,** □see **res judicata.**

estoppel by contract   □see **estoppel.**

estoppel by deed   □see **estoppel.**

estoppel by judgment   □see **estoppel.**

estoppel by record   □see **estoppel.**

estoppel by verdict   □see **estoppel.**

estoppel in pais □see **estoppel**.

et al., sometimes *et al:* as a reference to people, abbreviates the Latin masculine or feminine singulars (*alius, alia*)—*and another,* or the respective plurals (*alii, aliae*)—*and others.* When the cast is known, or instant detail is not required, the versatile *et al.* serves for one male, one female, a group of each, or a mixed assortment. Almost an ideal legal abbreviation. □see **sex**.

Euclidean □see **zoning**.

euphemism: softening the harsh blows of language with something softer, sometimes more elegant, often amorphous. The law has welcomed ways of ducking reality. For example:

> **carnal knowledge** (□see);
>
> **conservatorship** (□see);
>
> **crime against nature** (□see);
>
> **criminal conversation** (□see);
>
> **deceased** (□see);
>
> **demise** (□see);
>
> **errors and omissions** (□see, under **malpractice**);
>
> **gender** (□see, under **sex**).

For the lawyer just cited for **contempt** (□see), *Your Honor* is a euphemism. □see **formalisms**; □see **Honor**; □see **office of judge**, under **office**.

euthanasia □see **right to die**.

evade □see **avoid**.

evasion □see **avoid**.

even date □see **of even date**.

evict, and the companion noun *eviction*—as applied to real property, especially in the relationship of **landlord and tenant** (□see).

216

1. to put someone out of possession of real property, whether the putting out, the *eviction,* is proper or wrongful. <A evicted B from Blackacre./The eviction was under a claim of right, but was found to be wrongful.> Sometimes the words are limited to obtaining possession by legal process or by assertion of **paramount title** (□see, below, in this entry); generally these are considered varieties of means to an end—*evict, eviction.*

actual eviction: physical removal of the person in possession. This end result is the *eviction,* as distinguished from what accomplishes that result, e.g., illegal seizure; **self-help** (□see); action of *ejectment; unlawful detainer,* or other summary actions; or assertion of *paramount title.* Except by way of explanation, or in contrast with **constructive eviction** (□see), the expression *actual eviction* is usually shortened to *eviction.* □see **forcible entry and detainer.**

constructive eviction, eviction by paramount title, wrongful eviction, and *retaliatory eviction,* primarily part of the vocabulary of the person evicted, are entered here under *evict,* sense 2.

2. to be put out of possession of real property, the receiving end of sense 1. <B was evicted from Blackacre.> Only the grammatical voice is passive.

actual eviction —as in sense 1, with tenants the usual butt, e.g., the *holdover tenant:* one who remains in possession after the lease has ended.

eviction by paramount title: vacating in response to the assertion of the unanswerable, a title to the property superior to that under which the possessor claims. This is sometimes described in terms of sense 1; the lessor did it by letting it happen, or the new title holder did it; they *evicted* the tenant. More often, the plight of the tenant without an alternative is described by personifying the thing that did the job, *paramount title.* <She was evicted by paramount title.>

wrongful eviction: a catchall, and the name of an action, for being illegally put out of possession; sometimes referred to as *ouster* (verb, *oust*), currently a loose, amorphous usage. A *wrongful eviction* may be one properly motivated (tenant doesn't pay rent) but rendered wrongful by excessive force. It may be improperly motivated, as in the case of **retaliatory eviction:** a landlord getting even with a complainer (against the landlord's delinquencies).

constructive eviction: short of an *actual eviction,* the landlord, in violation of duty to the tenant, substantially interfered with the tenant's possession or quiet enjoyment of the premises. That state of affairs itself is often called *constructive eviction,* justifying a tenant's leaving the premises. Without consistent pattern, other usage reserves *constructive eviction* for the state of affairs plus the tenant's giving up possession.

eviction   □see **evict**.

eviction by paramount title   □see **evict**.

evidence

1. the basic meaning is the ordinary meaning, things presented to the senses that tend to establish a fact. Though legal definition may spell out what those things are—e.g., testimony, writings, material objects, "other things," the basic meaning remains, often used by lawyers and often difficult to distinguish from more technical senses. <Is there any evidence of that?>   □see **real evidence**.

2. the general body of the law of evidence and instruction in that branch of the law. <That's covered in evidence./Evidence is a required course.> It is this sense of *evidence* that makes the big difference between the ordinary (sense 1) and the *evidence* that lawyers live with. It is this sense that includes the **rules of evidence**:

> rules that attempt to detail the exact nature of the things that the law will consider in determining facts, how it will consider them, and their effect. The details of this sense of *evidence,* and the *rules of evidence,* are covered in the lawbooks, statutes (e.g., Federal Rules of Evidence, 28 USCA), decisions—a mountain of legal writing studied by law students and lawyers, beyond the scope of this dictionary, except by incidental reference.

3. what tends to establish a fact in a particular kind of legal proceeding. This sense connects senses 1 and 2 with the substance of other branches of the law—torts, contracts, criminal law, etc. <Perhaps evidence of negligence, counsel, but not evidence of fraud./The telephone conversations between them provided evidence of the conspiracy.>

evidence of indebtedness: loosely used in sense 3 <His acknowledgement in the letter was certainly evidence of indebtedness.> More precisely, a general name for a writing that embodies an obligation to pay money, e.g., **commercial paper** (□see).

4. **the evidence:** collectively, the mass of things presented in court (the testimony, writings, etc.) that have been held *admissible* over objection or have been presented without objection. <The evidence in this case shows. . . ./The evidence does not support a finding of assault with intent to kill.>

in evidence: a conclusion that something has been accepted as a part of the collective mass (sense 4); distinguished from *in the record,* which encompasses whatever goes on in court, e.g., argument to the jury, whether or not *in evidence.* In courtroom argot, the expression is shortened to *in.* <That may go in./That's already in./That's not yet in./I'll let it in, with the understanding that it will be connected up later.> The judge's pronouncement *received* is an ellipsis for *received in evidence.* Similarly, the pronouncement *admitted* is an ellipsis for *admitted in evidence.*

□see also, **narrative evidence;** □see also, **newly discovered evidence;** □see also, **opinion evidence;** □see also, **spoliation of evidence.**

evidence of indebtedness   □see evidence.

exalt form over substance   □see clichés.

examination in chief   □see cross-examination, under cross-.

except   □see reservation; □see also, **save.**

exception   □see reservation; □see also, **zoning;** □see also, **objection.**

excessive bail   □see Bail Clause.

Excessive Fines Clause: the part of the U.S. Constitution reading: ". . . nor excessive fines imposed. . . ." (Amend. VIII). □see also, **Bail Clause;** □see also, **constitutional clauses.**

excessive force   □see reasonable force.

exchange   □see contract.

exclusionary rule: a judge-made rule that evidence obtained in violation of a person's constitutional rights (e.g., unreasonable search and seizure, Amend. IV) is inadmissible in a prosecution of the person whose rights have been violated.

ex-convict   □see convict.

excusable homicide   □see justification; □see homicide.

excusable neglect   □see justification.

excuse   □see justification.

execute • executed • execution

1. capital punishment. This is not the prime use of *execute* in the law, but an old one, listed here first because it is the only one regularly in the morning news. In ordinary English, *stay of execution* means only one thing: they didn't kill him. *Execute* and *executed* evoke the varieties of capital punishment—hanging, gas chamber, electric chair, poison, the firing squad, as well as expert gangland or terrorist killing. The hangman is the *executioner*.

2. a sharp contrast with the popular understanding (sense 1), one of the law's most active *execute*'s is to do what is required to bring an instrument to life, the formalities varying according to the instrument and local law, e.g., signing, signing and delivery, acknowledgement, witnessing, etc. The fact of doing those things is the *execution*, and in this sense, the contract, the will, the trust have been *executed*. When you get down to the infighting over the details of whether or not a contract has been *executed*, the terminology of *execute* is useful. <The contract was signed but never delivered; it was never executed.> *Make, made, making* are usually ready substitutes, sometimes much better. Because of another meaning of *execute* (see sense 3), the simple statement "the contract was executed," standing alone, is ambiguous; "the contract was made" is clear.

3. to perform what is required to be performed by the provisions of an instrument (contract, trust, etc.). <It was an oral contract to build a house; the house having been built, the contract has been executed and is no longer objectionable for want of a writing./Payment having been made, the consideration is executed.> Thus, a contract may have been *executed* (sense 2) but not *executed* in this sense, and so still *executory*; context usually explains it. Long habit, reinforced by the redundancy *fully executed*, perpetuates *execute* (sense 3). *Perform* is a good substitute, even with a competitive redundancy *fully performed*. □see **perform**.

4. to perform what is required to be performed to carry out the duties of an office or task. <". . . I will faithfully execute the office of President of the United States. . . ." (U.S. Const., Art. II).>

5. to enforce the law, a duty of the *executive branch* of government. <". . . he shall take care that the laws be faithfully executed. . . ." (U.S. Const., Art. II, § 3).> A specialized instance of this is sense 6 (see).

6. to enforce court orders and judgments, especially a *writ of execution.* This *execute* is part of the duty of an officer (see sense 4), who, armed with the writ, *levies execution:* attempts to seize property in satisfaction of court judgments, reporting success or failure with a *return of execution.* In practice, the creditor's lawyer personalizes the whole process of *execution.* <We're going to levy on that./We're going to execute on that.> As with the condemned (see sense 1), *stay of execution* at least temporarily halts the process. □see also, **not satisfied.**

executed   □see **execute.**

execution   □see **execute.**

executive agreement   □see **treaty.**

executive branch   □see **execute.**

executive immunity   □see **immunity.**

executive privilege   □see **immunity.**

executor • administrator

An *executor* is the person named in a will who upon the death of the *testator* is to carry out the provisions of the will and administer the estate. Distinguished from an *administrator,* who has similar functions but is appointed by a court when there is no will or no executor. *Executors* and *administrators* are also referred to as *legal representatives, personal representatives,* or *representatives*—terms of varying application under local usage. For the still-used female versions *testatrix, executrix,* and *administratrix,* □see **sex.**

executor de son tort   (law F., day SOWN tort: of his own wrong): a person who without being either **executor** (□see) or *administrator* presumes to act as if he were, and thus becomes responsible for estate property that he meddles with. □see also, **trustee de son tort,** under trust.

executory

executory ☐see execute.

executory interest ☐see future interest.

executrix ☐see sex.

exemplary damages ☐see damage.

exercise an option ☐see option.

exercise a power ☐see appoint.

ex gratia ☐see of grace.

exhaust (n., *exhaustion*)—the ordinary English words with a twist: try something else first, in phrases telling you what to try first and with the law telling you what comes next.

exhaustion of administrative remedies: as a condition of resort to the courts when administrative remedies are still available.

exhaustion of state remedies: as a condition of resort to the federal courts, e.g., for habeas corpus, when remedies under state law are still available.

exhaust the security: as a condition of getting a personal judgment against a debtor when the creditor has the debtor's as yet untapped security.

exhaustion of administrative remedies ☐see exhaust.

exhaustion of state remedies ☐see exhaust.

exhaust the security ☐see exhaust.

existing person ☐see person.

ex officio (L., ex o-FISH-ee-o: according to office): because of the office. <Under association rules, she didn't have to be elected to the board; as immediate past president, she was a member *ex officio.* >

exonerate bail □see **bail.**

ex parte (L., ex PAR-ty: on one side): at the instance of one side only, without representation of any other side and without advance notice to any other side. <On *ex parte* application to Judge Smith, they obtained a temporary restraining order.> *Ex parte* proceedings are contrasted with **adversary proceedings** (□see). In the title of a reported case, *Ex parte* is followed by the name of the person applying for action by the court. E.g., petition for a writ of habeas corpus, *Ex parte Milligan,* 71 U.S. 2 (1866).

expectancy □see **future interest.**

expert witness □see **witness.**

ex post facto (L.: from what is done afterwards): though the entry here does not conform precisely to the Latin spelling or sense, *ex post facto* is the accepted spelling, freely translated *after the fact.*

ex post facto law: one making criminal what was innocent when done, or retroactively changing the punishment or manner of proof of a criminal act to the detriment of the accused.

Ex Post Facto Clauses: the parts of the U.S. Constitution reading: "No . . . ex post facto law shall be passed" (Art. I, § 9); and "No state shall . . . pass any . . . ex post facto law. . . ." (Art. I, § 10). When the context is clearly Article I, § 9, or Article I, § 10, the reference is simply to the *Ex Post Facto Clause.* □see also, **constitutional clauses.**

Ex Post Facto Clauses □see **ex post facto.**

ex post facto law □see **ex post facto.**

express authority □see **actual authority,** under **agency.**

express covenant □see **covenant.**

express easement □see **easement.**

express malice □see **malice.**

express notice □see notice.

express third party beneficiary □see beneficiary.

express trust □see trust.

express warranty □see warranty.

expressio unius est exclusio alterius (L.: expression of the one is exclusion of the other), also rendered *inclusio unius est exclusio alterius* (L.: inclusion of the one is exclusion of the other): when something but not everything of the same category has been expressed, one may infer that omissions are deliberate. Opinions and other legal writings still use the Latin, often shortened to **expressio unius** or **inclusio unius**. It is an old legal maxim, loosely described as a rule or principle of interpretation of writings. □see **rules of interpretation**.

expunction □see expunge the record.

expungement □see expunge the record.

expunge the record: to physically wipe out the official record of something, e.g., a minor's conviction; as distinguished from sealing a record or making a notation in the record. Pleasant participles reduce the need for the nouns *expunction* and *expungement*. <The court ordered the record expunged./She obtained an order expunging the conviction.>

ex rel., the abbreviation and usual substitute for *ex relatione* (L., ex re-LAY-she-o-knee: on the relation (i.e., information) of): at the instance of the *relator:* a person or a lesser public entity with special information or interest at whose instance a case of sufficient public concern is prosecuted by the state, e.g., questioning the functioning of a charity. In the title of a reported case, *ex rel.* is followed by the name of the relator, e.g., *People ex rel. Jones v. The Why Corp.* The abbreviation *ex rel.* can refer to a *relator* of either sex, the female sometimes called a *relatrix* (□see **sex**).

ex relatione □see ex rel.

extend time □see **delay**.

extortion: a form of theft characterized by the victim's capitulation to an illegal demand for money or property, the demand coupled with the threat of some dire alternative. Under widely varying statutes and decisions, the threats range a wide spectrum, including to accuse of crime, to expose defamatory secrets, to testify or withhold testimony, to strike or boycott, etc. for the benefit of the threatener rather than the union, to take or withhold official action, etc. Threat of bodily harm is generally included, resulting in local rules equating *extortion* with **robbery** (□see) or making some distinction of *robbery,* as, e.g., on the basis of the immediacy and seriousness of its threatened harm. *Blackmail,* the popular and literary equivalent of *extortion,* is, in some jurisdictions, also a legal synonym. □see also, **bribery**.

extradite □see **extradition**.

extradition: the surrender of a person by one government to another that requests the surrender, charging the person with having committed a crime over which it has jurisdiction. *Extradition,* sometimes called *rendition* (□see **render**), may be between nations under international law or treaty or between states or territories of the United States. The companion verb is *extradite,* which describes the surrender (and, in this sense, sometimes called *render*) or obtaining the surrender. <California extradited/rendered John Doe to Maryland./California extradited John Doe from New York.>

interstate rendition: frequently used to refer to extradition between states or territories of the United States. Also called *interstate extradition. Interstate rendition* or *extradition* is prescribed in the **Extradition Clause** (□see) of the U.S. Constitution, without using either expression. The practice is also detailed in state compacts and various statutes, especially the Uniform Criminal Extradition Act, adopted by most states.

Extradition Clause: the part of the U.S. Constitution reading: "A person charged in any state with treason, felony, or other crime, who shall flee from justice, and be found in another state, shall on demand of the executive authority of the state from which he fled, be delivered up, to be removed to the state having jurisdiction of the crime." (Art. IV, § 2, cl. 2). □see also, **constitutional clauses**.

extra dividend □see dividend.

extrajudicial

1. out of court. In frequent phrases referring to events occurring out of court, *extrajudicial admission, —bias, —confession, —identification, —oath, —sale.*

2. beyond a judge's authority as a judge. <That comment on current politics was strictly extrajudicial.>

extrajudicial admission □see extrajudicial.

extrajudicial bias □see extrajudicial.

extrajudicial confession □see extrajudicial.

extrajudicial identification □see extrajudicial.

extrajudicial oath □see extrajudicial.

extrajudicial sale □see extrajudicial.

extraordinary is a very ordinary word. It is here because, like **actual** (□see) and **special** (□see), *extraordinary* is part of the law's effort to express distinctions. An inherently flabby word, *extraordinary* has a small measure of precision as a warning, prompting the question: Compared to what? When the object of comparison is itself flabby, e.g., *ordinary care, extraordinary care* remains flab, and sets the lawyers to collecting myriads of circumstantial detail. When the object of comparison has more or less defined limits, e.g., *statutory services* described by statute and decision, then *extraordinary services* (of a lawyer or executor) firms up; the services may be quite commonplace, but they are still *extraordinary* because not *statutory.* As long as one recognizes that *extraordinary* in the law lives only for the sake of comparison, it serves a useful purpose, changing its content by the season.

For **extraordinary remedies**, also called *extraordinary writs,* also called *prerogative writs,* and now not so *extraordinary,* □see **habeas corpus;** □see **mandamus;** □see **ne exeat;** □see **prohibition;** □see **quo warranto.**

extraordinary care □see **extraordinary**.

extraordinary remedies □see **extraordinary**.

extraordinary services □see **extraordinary**.

extraordinary writs □see **extraordinary**.

extreme cruelty: a flexible characterization of one spouse's conduct, causing the other physical or mental suffering that need not be tolerated, and so may constitute ground for divorce.

mental cruelty: subdivision of *extreme cruelty* focusing on mental suffering.

extrinsic fraud □see **fraud**.

F

face With that word or another, the law faces the common meanings of *face*.

1. to confront or be confronted with someone or something, *face to face*. <"In all criminal prosecutions, the accused shall enjoy the right . . . to be confronted with the witnesses against him. . . ." (U.S. Const.Amend. VI)./ "Detached reflection cannot be demanded in the presence of an uplifted knife." (Holmes, J., in *Brown v. U.S.,* 256 U.S. 335, 343 (1921)).> This sense includes the metaphorical *flies in the face of* (everything we know). □see **clichés**.

2. the obverse side of a writing—*face of the instrument,* as distinguished from the back or reverse side. <The face of the form contract had all the essentials; hidden on the back were a dozen special conditions in fine print.>

3. the very words and numbers in a writing (e.g., in an instrument, a statute, record, judgment, will), as distinguished from what can be discovered by other evidence. <*Face value* of the bond was $100, but with accumulated interest, it was worth $110./On the face of the will, she is the sole beneficiary./The ordinance plainly prohibited free speech; it was *unconstitutional on its face.*/The statute was not unconstitutional on its face, but as applied in this instance, it violated plaintiff's First Amendment rights.> □see **facial,** under sense 5.

4. the general appearance of a writing—*fair on its face* (e.g., no obvious forgery), as distinguished from what may be discovered by other evidence. □see also, **regular on its face**.

5. the human *face,* and especially the variation *facial*. An active ingredient in a grim horde of medical terms, *facial* also has a mass following in the beauty industry. As *facial disfigurement,* it was once a minor theme in the legal vocabulary. Whether under the pressure of this sense 5 or as a shortcut to *on its face* (senses 3 and 4), lawyers are now obsessed with *facial*. Statutes are *facially invalid, facially unconstitutional, facially vague,* subject to *facial challenge*. □see also, **overbreadth;** □see also, **vagueness**. Even a concept is said to be "*facially inconsistent* with the evidence," suggesting not sense 3 but something akin to sense 4, possibly related to **prima facie** (□see, under at **first blush**). For the moment, *facials* are in.

face of the instrument □see **face**.

face value □see **face**.

facial □see face.

facial challenge □see face.

facially inconsistent, —invalid, —unconstitutional, —vague
□see face.

facile: pejorative *easy* in ordinary English. Its legal kin are suspect.
Whatever it touches wobbles; too easy.

facilitation: making it easier for someone to commit a crime; how
easy is not certain.

facility: a something sort of building, when the drafter doesn't know
or doesn't care. E.g., a *penal facility,* which may or may not be a
prison; a *major emitting facility,* a bad polluting thing. How bad?
As bad as it is facile.

facilitation □see facile.

facility □see facile.

facts These bits of reality are no different in the law than anywhere
else. That fact of life can be obscured by redundant legal expression:

facts and circumstances = *facts*

in truth and in fact = *facts*

surrounding circumstances = *facts*

true and correct = *facts*

true facts = *facts*

Redundancy eliminated, what remains are context labels for the facts
that swarm into every legal cranny. Here are some of them:

attorney in fact □see;

finding of fact □see **finding;**

implied-in-fact □see **quasi contract;**

mistake of fact □see **mistake;**

mixed question of law and fact □see;

special facts □see **special circumstances;**

facts

trier of fact □see try; □see mixed question of law and fact;

ultimate facts □see.

facts and circumstances □see facts. □see also, clichés.

fail (n., *failure*), one of the most popular negatives in a law full of them.

1. not doing something you are expected to do. <They failed to pay the rent.> It is the disappointment that gives *fail* its special flavor, as distinguished from simply not doing. <They failed to bid./They did not bid.> If you are not interested in calling attention to disappointment, the uncritical bookkeeper's simple negative says it more directly than *fail*. <They did not pay the interest./They failed to pay the interest.>

Carefully used, *fail* (sense 1) does not go beyond disappointed expectations; it does not pass judgment on the character of the *failure* — careless, intentional, or stubborn. Accordingly, *fail* (sense 1) should not be encrusted with excess that is either redundant or ambiguous, as *failed and neglected, failed and refused,* or *failed, neglected, and refused.* These combinations, as unplanned equivalents of *fail* (sense 1), invite interpretive argument and water down the force of *neglect* or *refusal* when either is wanted. <Despite repeated demand, they refused to pay the note; it was no neglect; they knew what they were doing.>

2. not meeting a standard, with a suggestion of legal guilt or personal fault. <He failed to stop at the red light./She failed the sobriety test.> The *failure* might be explained away, but unlike sense 1, in usual context, *fail* (sense 2) passes at least preliminary judgment on the character of the not doing.

3. neglect of fiduciary duty. <The trustee failed to render an accounting./They failed to preserve the attorney-client confidences./Asked to give a misleading legal opinion, the lawyers failed to refuse the request.>

4. not meeting all of the requirements to achieve a particular legal result.

failed gift: one that does not take effect, e.g., because not delivered. On *failed gifts by will,* □see lapse.

failed trust; failed will: one that does not take effect because not in compliance with local law as to content or execution.

fail to state a cause of action: a defect in pleading: the allegations, even if proved, do not make out a case for legal redress. <Plaintiff's complaint failed to state a cause of action for breach of contract.>

failure of proof: a defect in proving a case or a defense: even though well-pleaded, what has been proved is inadequate to establish the case or defense. <The charge of fraud hinged on proof of defendant's knowing of the falsity, and on that critical element, there was a failure of proof.>

5. special varieties of *failure:*

bankrupt □see **insolvent.**

failure of consideration: the promised consideration for a **contract** (□see) is not delivered.

failure of issue □see **issue,** under **descendant.**

failure of title: absence of sufficient evidence that the seller owns the property. <The escrow was canceled for failure of title.>

failure to perform □see **perform.**

insolvent □see.

failed and neglected   □see **fail.**

failed and refused   □see **fail.**

failed gift   □see **fail.**

failed, neglected, and refused   □see **fail.**

failed trust   □see **fail.**

failed will   □see **fail.**

fail to state a cause of action   □see **fail.**

failure of consideration   □see **fail.**

failure of issue   □see **issue,** under **descendant.**

failure of proof   □see **fail.**

failure of title   □see **fail.**

failure to perform □see **perform**.

fair (adv., *fairly;* n., *fairness*) readily accommodates such incongruities as *mediocre* and the usual legal synonym **equitable** (□see); it evokes subjective judgments of degree. What is *fair to say* (□see **clichés**) or *not unfair to say* (or even *unfair to say*) is anybody's guess. *Fair* is a political word—*fair* credit reporting, *fair* employment practices, *fair* housing, *fair* labor standards, **fair trade agreement** (□see). *Fair* gives no clue to substance, except that it is supposed to be something good, or good for you, whether you like it or not. Lawyers-to-be absorb so much of flexible *fair, fairly,* and *fairness* from infancy on that casual word drop has become habitual. When in doubt, be *fair*. Add a touch of class to an incomprehensible blob like **preponderance of the evidence** (□see). Restated as a fair preponderance of the evidence, only the lilt has improved; a blob remains a blob.

With the strong reservation that *fair* is flexible in the extreme, it is still possible to identify a number of labels that incorporate *fair* and yet carry some special legal sense.

fair and equitable: the character of protection to be given the priorities of creditors, between themselves and as opposed to stockholders, in a reorganization in receivership or bankruptcy. Often said to be a term of art; apt for convenience of reference but not as a description of a specific degree of protection. In other usage, *fair and equitable* is a redundant form of *equitable*.

fair comment: defense to an action of **defamation** (□see) that the words spoken or written were not statements of fact but honest expression of personal opinion about someone or something of public concern, and without **malice** (□see). In some courts, *fair comment* negates defamation; in others, it is a **qualified privilege** (□see, under **absolutes**). With expanded First Amendment protection of free speech, fair or otherwise, the defense of *fair comment* has a waning tenure. □see **freedom of speech**.

fair consideration: something proportionate in value to what it is given for; sometimes rendered as a *fair equivalent*. Critical in determination of whether or not a transfer is in fraud of creditors. (See Uniform Fraudulent Conveyances Act, § 3.)

fair equivalent □see **fair consideration**.

fair hearing: an administrative procedure that, like a *fair trial,* complies with **due process** (□see).

fair market value: the price that would be paid by a willing buyer to a willing seller, neither under compulsion and both reasonably informed. Full of flexible words, but with a general sense of direction; whatever worth it has is weakened by claims of the same meaning for similar expressions—*actual cash value, fair cash value, reasonable market value,* etc.

fairness doctrine, sometimes *Fairness Doctrine:* a general requirement that broadcasters adequately cover issues of public importance and give fair coverage to varying views. The *fairness doctrine* was a Federal Communications Commission doctrine, now repealed. It was related to, broader than, and often confused with a more specific provision of the Federal Communications Act generally, and inaccurately, called the

> **equal time rule:** if a licensee permits a "legally qualified candidate" for public office to broadcast, it must "afford equal opportunities" to all other candidates for that office. (See 47 USCA § 315(a).)

fair on its face □see **face.**

fair to say □see **fair.**

fair trade agreement: one in which the manufacturer, distributor, or wholesaler fixes the resale price of its name-brand article. The agreement is between those in a vertical commercial relationship (e.g., between manufacturer and retailer), as opposed to those in a horizontal commercial relationship (e.g., between manufacturers; between retailers). An article covered by such an agreement is said to have been *fair-traded.*

fair trade law: one permitting **fair trade agreements** (□see). The *fair* part is variously described as preventing *unfair* price cutting, avoiding the social evils of price wars, reducing the consumption of alcohol, etc.

fair trial □see **day in court;** □see **due process.**

fair use: a limited use of a copyrighted work permitted by law, without need of permission from the copyright owner. The purposes of *fair use* are "such as criticism, comment, news reporting, teaching (including multiple copies for classroom use), scholarship or research." Some of the factors to be considered in determining *fair use* (e.g., character and substantiality of use, effect on potential market) are detailed in the Copyright Act, § 107.

fair and equitable □see **fair.**

fair comment □see **fair.**

fair consideration □see fair.

fair dealing □see covenant of good faith and fair dealing, under covenant.

fair equivalent □see fair.

fair hearing □see fair.

fair market value □see fair.

fairness doctrine □see fair.

fair on its face □see face.

fair to say □see fair.

fair trade agreement □see fair.

fair trade law □see fair.

fair trial □see day in court; □see due process.

fair use □see fair.

faith and credit □see full faith and credit.

Faithfully Executed Clause: the part of the U.S. Constitution reading: ". . . he [the President] shall take care that the laws be faithfully executed. . . ." (Art. II, § 3). □see also, **constitutional clauses.**

falls between two stools □see clichés.

false □see false and untrue.

false and untrue: not true; □see **coupled synonyms**. Separated, the two words can usually be distinguished. Usually, *untrue* is uncomplicated, simply not true, no matter why. <The report of the verdict was untrue.> *False* can mean that too. <The false report of the verdict.> More often, *false* means deliberate untruth. <They falsified the books.> Coupling *false* and *untrue* brings out the worst uncertainties of both words; they become misleading and redundant, not emphatic. Absent clarification, the charitable interpretation is redundancy. *False and untrue* has antonymous couplets— **true and correct** (□see) and *in truth and in fact* (□see **fact**).

false arrest: another name for false imprisonment (□see **imprisonment**).

false imprisonment   □see **imprisonment**.

false light   □see **right of privacy**.

false pretenses   □see **fraud**.

false representation   □see **fraud**.

false swearing   □see **perjury**.

family law: a current rubric for the organization and teaching of the miscellany of law that deals with the family relationship—beginnings, endings, and everything in-between, e.g., annulment, children, cohabitation, community property, custody, division of property, divorce, marital duties, marriage, support of children and spouses. The boundaries of the topic are not now fixed.

F.A.S., also *FAS*, also *f.a.s.*: the abbreviated and usual rendering of the commercial delivery term *free alongside ship*, also expressed *free alongside vessel*. The term obligates the shipper at its expense and risk to "deliver the goods alongside the vessel in the manner usual in that port or on a dock designated and provided by the buyer; and . . . . obtain and tender [to the buyer] a receipt for the goods. . . ." (UCC § 2319(2)(a) and (b)). The term is usually part of the quotation of a price for the goods. <Our price is ten dollars per ton, FAS, San Francisco.>

fatal: figuratively, used to describe a deviation from the law resulting in a substantial adverse effect that cannot be readily cured. As opposed to what is *harmless.*

fatal error, also called *fatal defect*: a deviation in a determination (e.g., verdict of guilty) or a proceeding (e.g., a trial) that must be killed to be corrected, i.e., reversed, set aside, or disregarded, in order to right the wrong. <Two of the jurors swore they were not related to the victim; they lied; there was fatal error. Conviction reversed./The tax was levied without approval of the board; it was a fatal error, and the tax must be held invalid.>

fatal variance: a gap between the allegations of a pleading and what is proved so wide as to be a **failure of proof** (□see, under **fail**). Liberal laws permitting amendment of pleading to conform to proof turn much of what would once have been *fatal variance* into **harmless error** (□see).

fatal defect □see **fatal.**

fatal error □see **fatal.**

fatal variance □see **fatal.**

Fathers □see **Founding Fathers.**

federal common law □see **common law.**

federal courts: courts established by federal law, as distinguished from *state courts.* Defined that broadly, *federal courts* could, but in ordinary usage does not, include courts in the armed services. □see **Uniform Code of Military Justice.** Though the distinction is not always clearly drawn, a *federal court* is further classified as either an *Article III court* or a *legislative court.*

Article III courts, also called **constitutional courts**: federal courts that are (1) "one supreme court, and . . . inferior courts . . ." established by Congress under the authority of Article III, § 1 of the U.S. Constitution; (2) to exercise the judicial power of the United States described in Article III, § 2; (3) through judges who have tenure "during good behavior"; and (4) whose compensation "shall not be diminished during their continuance in office." For particular *Article III courts,* □see **Supreme Court of the United States;** □see **U.S. Courts of Appeals;** □see **U.S. District Courts;** □see also, **U.S. Court of**

International Trade; □see also, **Temporary Emergency Court of Appeals**.

legislative courts, also called **Article I courts,** also called **non-Article III tribunals:** federal courts that are (1) established by Congress under the authority of various provisions of the U.S. Constitution, especially Article I, § 8 and in particular the **Necessary and Proper Clause** (□see), (2) to exercise powers falling within or outside of the judicial power of the United States described in Article III, § 2, frequently as an administrative agency with judicial functions, and (3) through judges who do not have the Article III assurance of judicial independence in the form of tenure during good behavior and no salary cuts. For particular *legislative courts,* □see **bankruptcy judge,** under **judge;** □see **U.S. Claims Court;** □see **U.S. Tax Court.** For a new and unique variety of legislative court, □see **United States Court of Veterans Appeals.**

federal jurisdiction   □see **jurisdiction.**

federal question: a question "arising" under the U.S. Constitution, United States law, or the treaties of the United States, as distinguished from one arising under state law.

substantial federal question: a *federal question* that a federal appellate court considers of sufficient importance to warrant exercise of its **federal question jurisdiction** (□see).   <The petition for a writ of certiorari is denied for want of a substantial federal question; see *Smith v. Jones.*>

federal question jurisdiction:

1.   the judicial power of the United States extending ". . . to all cases, in law and equity, arising under this Constitution, the laws of the United States, and treaties . . ." (U.S. Const., Art. III, § 2), but not extending to suits ". . . against one of the United States by citizens of another state, or by citizens or subjects of any foreign state." (U.S. Const., Amend. XI).

2.   the power of federal courts under Article III, § 2 of the U.S. Constitution, as limited by Amendment XI (sense 1), and as limited by acts of the Congress.

3.   the power of state courts to decide *federal questions,* subject to the exercise of *federal question jurisdiction* by the federal courts (sense 2).

federal question jurisdiction   □see **federal question.**

federal rules □see **evidence**; □see **rule**.

fee (attorney's fee): compensation for the services of a **lawyer** (□see). Usually referred to as an *attorney's fee*, often *attorneys' fees*, without fine concern about placement of the apostrophe, whether compensation is for one or more lawyers, or whether *fee* or *fees* is the word. Less commonly called *attorney fee*, a locution more likely to be used when the word is *fees—attorney fees*. Variations are *counsel fees, fee for legal services, lawyer's fee, legal fees*.

contingency fee, or contingent fee □see **barratry**.

fee splitting: sharing of an *attorney's fee*, especially with a nonlaw-yer, suggestive of unprofessional practice. It is a harsh expression, common in oral usage, less frequent in professional writing, where the favored, more generalized expression is *division of fees*. Professional rules generally forbid *fee splitting* or *division of fees* with a nonlawyer, except with the estate of a lawyer who had some claim to a fee or in office retirement plans. Professional rules also generally restrict *fee splitting* or *division of fees* with a lawyer outside the office to sharing of fees based on rendering of services or shared responsibility.

forwarding fee: sharing of an *attorney's fee* by payment to another lawyer for referring a case. Usually permissible only if within professional rules for *division of fees*. □see **fee splitting**.

lodestar: legal argot for the base (guiding) element in the computation of attorney's fees under statutes providing for a court award to the prevailing party; e.g., civil rights, class actions, private attorney general. The lodestar figure is usually the ordinary reasonable hourly rate multiplied by the number of hours reasonably spent. The lodestar figure is then adjusted up or down by other factors, e.g., risk, novelty, importance of results obtained.

reasonable fee: an *attorney's fee*, which, when scrutinized by a court or a professional disciplinary group, is found to be reasonable. The criteria of reasonableness, never definitively fixed, have been discussed in cases and professional literature for centuries; some are incorporated in professional rules, e.g., time, skill, difficulty, amount, results, relationship of lawyer and client, fee fixed or contingent, what is customary.

retainer:

1. an agreement between lawyer and client specifying services, fees, time of payment, etc.

2. a specific sum agreed to be paid by client to lawyer in an agreement (sense 1) for specific services, whether as a single payment or in periodic payments of the same sum. Often, the retainer is a payment in advance, as a portion of fees at an agreed rate or a total for all services. Also called a *retaining fee.*

fee (property law) □see **fee simple.**

fee for legal services □see **fee (attorney's fee).**

fee simple: an estate unlimited in time and with an indefinite succession of owners, each in turn able to transfer the estate by deed or will, or to permit it to pass under the laws of inheritance. It is as absolute as ownership can be. Usually applied only to real estate. Short for *estate in fee simple,* and itself usually shortened to *fee.* <It was owned in fee./She owned the fee.>

fee simple absolute: an apparent redundancy, saying exactly what is said by *fee simple* (L., simplex: absolute) or by *fee* alone. <He had a fee/a fee simple/a fee simple absolute.> Superfluous as a superlative, it has utility as a comparative, to emphasize the difference between a *fee simple* and a **fee simple defeasible** (□see). <Their estate was not a defeasible fee; it was a fee simple absolute.> □see also, **absolutes.**

fee simple defeasible, also called a *defeasible fee:* a *fee simple* but for the fact that in the word derived from Old French, it is *defeasible*—capable of being *undone, defeated.* More explicitly, it is an estate that would be a *fee simple* but for a shadow over its future—the possibility, no more than that, of coming to an end. The nature of that possibility, though not the odds, is spelled out in three varieties of *fees simple defeasible:*

fee simple determinable: a *fee simple* but for the fact that in the word derived from Old French, it is *determinable* —capable of becoming *finite.* More explicitly, upon the happening of an event specified or implied in the grant, an event that may or may not occur, the estate automatically ends. So that the *fee simple determinable* carries with it a potentially deadly appendage, a *future interest,* usually in the grantor and therefore called a *possibility of reverter:* upon the collapse of the *fee simple determinable,* without a word being spoken, the estate *reverts* (goes back) to the original owner. <A owns Blackacre in fee. A conveys Blackacre to B as long as Blackacre is used as a golf course. B has a fee simple determinable in Blackacre. If Blackacre is no longer used as a golf course, it reverts to A.> The *fee simple determinable* is also known by other names: sometimes, a *base fee;* a *qualified fee* (not unqualified like a *fee simple* *absolute*); a *fee simple on a special limitation* (as long as, for as long as, during, during that time and no longer, etc.).

fee simple subject to executory limitation: upon the happening of an event specified or implied in the grant, an event that may or may not occur, the estate automatically ends, as in a *fee simple determinable*—with this important distinction: the estate does not revert to the grantor; instead, the original grantee's estate is supplanted (*divested,* cut short) by an estate in a second grantee specified in the grant. So from the start, the second grantee has a *future interest* called an *executory interest.*   <A owns Blackacre in fee. A conveys Blackacre to B. The deed to B further specifies that if ever Blackacre is not used as a golf course, A gives Blackacre to C. B has a fee simple subject to an executory interest. C has an executory interest in fee.>

fee simple subject to condition subsequent: upon the happening of an event specified or implied in the grant, an event that may or may not occur, the estate does not automatically end, but the grantor has the right to end it. That right, a *future interest,* goes by a number of names—*right of entry, right of reentry, right of entry for condition broken,* and *power of termination.* Properly speaking, the *fee simple subject to condition subsequent* is subject to two conditions, i.e., the specified event plus the election of the grantor to exercise the *right of entry.*   <A owns Blackacre in fee. A conveys Blackacre to B, the deed specifying that if Blackacre is not used as a golf course, A has a right to reenter Blackacre, ending B's estate. B has a fee simple subject to condition subsequent.> The *fee simple subject to condition subsequent* is also sometimes called a *conditional fee;* that has the virtue of brevity, but two vices: (1) all *fees simple defeasible* fit the description *conditional;* and (2) possible confusion with the no longer viable common law estate known as a *fee simple conditional.* (□see **fee tail**).

The language curiosities of *fees simple defeasible* are antique and still litigated. They are often the subject of radical statutory surgery; more is needed.

fee simple absolute □see **fee simple.**

fee simple conditional □see **fee tail.**

fee simple defeasible □see **fee simple.**

fee simple determinable □see **fee simple.**

fee simple on a special limitation   □see **fee simple.**

fee simple subject to condition subsequent   □see **fee simple.**

fee simple subject to executory limitation   □see **fee simple.**

fee splitting   □see **fee (attorney's fee).**

fee tail: an estate that lasts as long as there are blood relatives in a direct descending line of succession from the first *tenant in tail*, and can be inherited only by those in that line, so-called *lineal descendants* (□see **descendant**).   <A has a fee in Blackacre and conveys Blackacre to B and the heirs of his body. B has a fee tail and is a tenant in tail.>   If the line runs out, the estate reverts to the original owner. A *fee tail* also goes by other names: *estate tail, entailed estate, tenancy in tail.* □see **estate.**   The *fee tail* was a medieval successor to the medieval *fee simple conditional*, both abolished in most states, barely extant in others, regulated by statute, and shrinking fast.

fellatio   □see **crime against nature.**

felon: a person who has *committed* a **felony** (□see), or one who has been *convicted* of a felony. Short of a conviction, the commission of a felony is beset with uncertainty. The ambiguity is sometimes directly resolved by *convicted felon*, sometimes by context, e.g., a felon's loss of the right to vote, unthinkable except upon conviction. □see **civil death.**   *Felon* is not indispensable; its ambiguity encourages a short explanation as a substitute.   <He had committed a felony/had been convicted of a felony.>

felonious   □see **felony.**

felony: the category of crimes that includes the most serious, e.g., murder, manslaughter, robbery, rape, etc., may include **treason** (□see), which nonetheless has its own unique place. *Felony* is generally described in terms of possible punishment: a crime *punishable* by death (a *capital offense*), by imprisonment for more than one year (sometimes even for one year), or by imprisonment in a penitentiary (state prison). Definitions vary by jurisdiction. Under some statutes, a particular offense, e.g., one involving drugs, is classified as *felony* or *misdemeanor* dependent on the *punishment* at sentencing.

felony

felonious (adj.) and **feloniously** (adv.) seem descriptive of *felony,* once were, and—loosely—still are. But they have been overworked and undernourished, used to duplicate or substitute for *criminal intent, fraudulent, intent to steal, malicious, unlawful, wicked, wilful,* and much more. They have been fastened onto misdemeanors, without turning them into felonies, and have been regularly omitted in charges of felony, without serious effect. They lack precision and should not be used without the insurance of a definitive statute or decision.

felony murder, also **felony-murder:** an unlawful killing in the course of committing a felony is **murder** (□see), even though the killing was unintended. The definition is tentative. The scope and boundaries of *felony murder* are in controversy. Some states reject it completely; some limit it to killing resulting from reckless indifference; some limit it to killing in the course of dangerous felonies; etc. In some circles, it is referred to simply as *felony murder;* in some, as the *felony murder rule;* in others, as the *felony murder doctrine.* The profession cannot even agree on a hyphen, probably a declining commodity.

felony murder   □see **felony.**

feme covert   (law F., fem KUV-ert): a married woman. The law French is a little-used relic, better unused, except as history. □see **cohabit;** □see **wedlock.**

feme sole   (law F.): a single woman. The law French is a little-used, imprecise relic, better unused, except as history. The English is also imprecise. It can refer to: a woman who has never been married, one who is now without a husband (dead or divorced), or one who is separated from her husband. If it matters, spell out the precise status. □see **unmarried.**

feminist jurisprudence: the law in theory and practice, as it has been, is, and might be, when viewed by women as women. With roots in the struggles for equality with men (□see **Equal Rights Amendment**), and honed in resistance to discrimination and harassment (□see **sex**), *feminist jurisprudence* is a late twentieth-century attempt to carve out a distinctive approach to law within or without traditional categories. The definition here is a working definition. Principle, program, and definition are without consensus. (See "Feminism in the Law: Theory, Practice and Criticism," 1989 *University of Chicago Legal Forum* 1.)

fence   ☐see **receiving stolen property.**

ferae naturae   (L., FAIR-rye nuh-TOO-rye: of the wild part of nature; from L. *ferus:* a wild animal): substantively, freely translated as *wild animals;* as a modifier, describes animals of a wild nature, *animals ferae naturae,* as distinguished from domestic animals. The translation *wild animals* must be handled with care: *wild* refers to the usual state; *animal* is the broad sense, as in "animal, vegetable, mineral"; bees are *ferae naturae.* The Latinism *ferae naturae* still has vitality, especially in property law—how to acquire ownership of wild animals, and—by analogy—how to acquire ownership of migrant gas and oil, *minerals ferae naturae.* ☐see **law of capture.**

fiction   ☐see **legal fiction.**

fictitious defendant: a person named as a defendant in a complaint, but under an obviously fictitious name, usually when the plaintiff or prosecutor is uncertain about the identity of a possible defendant. < *Smith v. Jones, Doe I, Doe II, and Doe III.* > ☐see also, **John Doe.**

fictitious firm name   ☐see **alias.**

fiduciary: an individual or corporation bound to act with the *utmost good faith* in the management of property or affairs for the benefit of another person, the beneficiary of the *fiduciary relationship.* That obligation to act in a *fiduciary capacity* may be incurred by agreement or imposed by law; it is predicated on the specific or implied trust reposed by the beneficiary in the competence and faithfulness of the fiduciary. Statute and decision describe many special fiduciary relationships; most typical is *trustee and beneficiary* (☐see **beneficiary**); most demanding is *lawyer and client.*

Fiduciary relationship is sometimes referred to as a *confidential relationship* or a *relationship of confidence.* This *confidence* is the sense of *having confidence in,* or *reposing confidence in,* the *fiduciary,* as distinguished from *confidential communications,* typical of the lawyer-client relationship. ☐see **attorney-client privilege,** under **privilege.**

Utmost good faith, though not a term with precise limits, has the sound and practice of greater rigor than ordinary *good faith* (☐see **bona fide**). Among other duties, *utmost good faith* requires the fiduciary to disclose anything that might interfere with duty to the beneficiary, forbids the fiduciary to profit at the beneficiary's expense

fiduciary

(*self-dealing*), and forbids **commingling** (□see) of money of beneficiary and fiduciary. *Utmost good faith* is sometimes referred to in writing by its Latin name *uberrima fides,* a locution almost never indulged in orally.

fiduciary capacity   □see fiduciary.

fiduciary relationship   □see fiduciary.

fighting words

1. words likely to start a fight with the person addressed. Ordinary English does not rest on its own naked definition. American usage has long recognized that words *per se,* even the worst—*son of a bitch* —are not *fighting words* unless used in a context of anger or provocation that makes the fight almost inevitable. "Smile when you say that" recognizes the danger inherent in some words as well as the fact that context may be a sufficient antidote to render them harmless. <Bill, you old son of a bitch.>

2. a label of constitutional law for *fighting words* (sense 1) removed from First Amendment protection of free speech because publicly uttered in a context of anger or provocation that makes a fighting response almost inevitable. <"Fuck the Draft" on defendant's jacket was not "directed to the person of the hearers"; it involved no "direct personal insult"; in context, they were not fighting words. (See *Cohen v. California,* 403 U.S. 15, 20 (1971).)>

file

1. the bundle of legal papers relating to a case or other official proceeding. <I want the file in *Smith v. Jones,* # 45689.>

2. to deposit a legal paper with the proper official to become part of a *file* (sense 1). <They filed the complaint on the last day./They filed for bankruptcy.>

3. to officially receive a legal paper and make it part of a *file* (sense 1). <The clerk filed the complaint in *Smith v. Jones,* # 45689.>

filiation proceeding: a general term for civil proceedings to establish paternity and obligation to support an *illegitimate child.* Once called *bastardy proceedings, filiation proceeding* is falling into disuse, along with the expression *illegitimate child.* Under the Uniform Parentage Act, the proceeding is called an "Action to determine existence or nonexistence of father and child relationship," with a parallel "Action to determine existence or nonexistence of mother and child relationship."

final and conclusive: synonyms joined together to no effect except the hollow echo of finality. Sometimes *final and conclusive* is <This judgment is final and conclusive; there can be no appeal.>, and sometimes it isn't. <This judgment is final and conclusive, so there may now be an appeal.> *Final* is not more *final, conclusive* not more *conclusive,* by being hitched (□see **absolutes**). Separately, they have specialized uses, e.g., a *final decree* (□see **judgment**), a *final injunction* (□see **enjoin**), a **conclusive presumption** (□see). They function better unhitched. □see **coupled synonyms.**

final decree □see **judgment.**

final injunction □see **enjoin.**

finding • conclusion English synonyms with legal functions, mostly discrete.

finding of fact: a determination by the jury, or by a judge in a case tried without a jury, that the evidence proves that something is fact. Often shortened to *finding.* <On disputed evidence, the jury made a finding of fact/finding/that plaintiff was exceeding the speed limit.>

findings of fact: the group of separate determinations of what the evidence has proved, usually embodied in a writing. Often shortened to *the findings.* <There were fifteen findings of fact./The findings were incomplete./They waived findings.> Sometimes, confusingly, called *conclusions of fact.*

special finding: a *finding of fact* on a particular point of evidence, used to identify a finding made in response to a special request, or to identify a finding as to an **ultimate fact** (□see). <The judge instructed the jury to find specially as to the pilot's experience with the type of plane in suit. They made a special finding that the pilot has never before flown a 747.> □see **general finding,** at the end of this entry.

conclusion of law

1. a determination by the judge of the legal result that follows from the evidence. <The jury found that the letter was mailed January 10. The judge's conclusion of law was that the offer had been accepted.>

conclusions of law: the group of separate determinations of the legal results that follow from the evidence, especially as based on *findings of fact.* Usually embodied in a writing. <The

245

finding

record on appeal included twenty pages of Findings of Fact and Conclusions of Law.> Sometimes, confusingly, called *findings of law.*

2. a legal result pleaded, as opposed to a pleading of the fact on which the result is based. <Plaintiff pleaded that "defendant fraudulently promised." That was a conclusion of law, an inadequate substitute for pleading the facts constituting the alleged fraud.>

3. loosely, a statement of a legal result, as opposed to a statement of facts. Also called a *legal conclusion.* Often shortened to *conclusion.* <The witness: "He blackmailed me." Lawyer: "Move to strike that as a conclusion of the witness."> □see also, **conclusory**.

general finding: a loose reference to a **decision** (□see) by a judge or a **verdict** (□see) by a jury in favor of one side. The expression is broad enough to encompass *findings of fact* and *conclusions of law.* <The judge made a general finding in favor of the defendant. What he actually said was, "We find for the defendant. Case dismissed.">

finding of fact □see **finding**.

fines □see **Excessive Fines Clause**.

fireman's rule: negligence in starting a fire does not make one liable to a professional firefighter injured fighting the fire. The rule has been extended to police injured in the line of their hazardous duties. Whether the rule applies to conduct beyond negligence, or survives within limits or at all, varies with local statute and decision.

firm

1. as a business enterprise, a synonym for **company** (□see). □see also, **fictitious firm name**, under **alias**.

2. as a professional enterprise, a loose, untechnical designation applied indiscriminately to partnerships, corporations, and less formal associations, but not usually to a *sole practitioner.*

law firm: usually refers to a group of lawyers practicing law together, whether as partners, a professional legal corporation, a partnership including one or more professional legal corporations, or in some other form of association in apparently shared responsibility. For purposes of rules of professional responsibility and bar discipline, special definitions apply.

246

first appearance: the first time a person arrested appears in court (□see **appear**), to be informed by the judge (magistrate) of the charge and of his rights (including the substance of Miranda warnings) and for the setting or denial of bail or release without bail (□see **bail**).   If an indigent is entitled to appointed counsel, sometimes counsel will be appointed at the first appearance.   If the charge is felony, a date may be fixed for a **preliminary hearing** (□see).   If the charge is a misdemeanor, the first appearance serves as an **arraignment** (□see).

first blush   □see **at first blush.**

first-degree murder   □see **murder.**

first impression   □see **at first blush.**

first option   □see **right of first refusal.**

first party • second party   □see **party.**

first publication   □see **copyright.**

first refusal   □see **right of first refusal.**

fiscal year   □see **time.**

fishing expedition: slang characterization of meandering cross-examination or of interrogatories beyond the scope of proper *discovery.*

fit and proper: a worthless redundancy, usually used to describe a person's suitability for a particular function, e.g., to have the custody of a child.   Equally worthless substitute redundancies are *fit and suitable* and *fitting and proper.   Fit* alone or *proper* alone is adequate. When it becomes necessary to discriminate between ordinary suitability and legal competence, the distinction ought to be explicit and not blurred by a false sense of achievement with *fit and proper.*   □see **coupled synonyms.**

fit and suitable   □see **fit and proper.**

fitness for a particular purpose □see **warranty**.

fitting and proper □see **fit and proper**.

fix bail □see **bail**.

fixture: a hybrid form of property that starts out in life as personal property (□see **chattel**) and becomes so firmly attached to real estate and so used as part of it as to be considered part of it—real property.

Labeling the hybrid *fixture* simply says that in the present incarnation, the former *chattel,* e.g., a chandelier, wall mirror, heater, is real property. On another day, removed from the real estate, the former *fixture* may be reincarnated as a *chattel;* some say that it was always a chattel and never achieved fixturehood.

A vast body of law struggles over the problems of when to call particular property in a particular context *fixture.* Who paid for the property? What did the installer intend? Was there common or diverse ownership of real estate and chattel? How seriously would removal damage the real estate? What is customary? Are we talking about *fixture* in the law of landlord and tenant, taxation, condemnation, security interests, etc., etc.? The unresolved problems are epitomized in the definition by the late Professor "Bull" Warren of the Harvard Law School, that a *fixture* is "realty with a chattel past and fear of a chattel future."

trade fixture: personal property, e.g., pumps, freezers, shelving, firmly attached to real estate for the purpose of carrying on an enterprise on the real estate and generally understood to be removable when the purpose has ceased. The name *trade fixture* can be misleading and is sometimes classified as an exception to the definition of *fixture.* When to call particular property in particular contexts *trade fixture* raises problems of the same nature as with **fixture** (□see).

flee to the wall □see **retreat to the wall**.

flies in the face of □see **clichés**.

floating charge, also called a **floating lien:** a general term for a continuing security interest not limited to the indebtedness or the collateral as it was at the time of the agreement. A *floating charge* typically covers future advances and after-acquired property and—within limits—permits the debtor to dispose of the collateral.

floating lien   □see **floating charge**.

floodgates   □see **open the floodgates**, under **clichés**.

F.O.B.,   also FOB, also f.o.b.: the abbreviated and usual rendering of the commercial delivery term *free on board*. The term is usually part of the quotation of a price for goods, either *F.O.B.* place of shipment—a *shipment contract,* or *F.O.B.* place of destination—a *destination contract.* To the commercial community, those labels carry these meanings:

A **shipment contract** requires the shipper: (1) at its expense and risk, to put the goods in the carrier's possession; (2) to contract with the carrier for shipment of the goods; (3) to notify the buyer of the shipment; and (4) to deliver or tender to the buyer the documents the buyer needs to get possession of the goods. (UCC § 2319(1)(a) and § 2504).

A **destination contract** requires the shipper (1) at its expense and risk, to transport the goods to their destination and (2) at that place, to tender delivery to the buyer. (UCC § 2319(1)(b)).

FOIA: abbreviation of the Freedom of Information Act (5 USCA § 552, amended to 1986). The act requires a wide range of federal authorities to tell the public what they have done and are doing, by publishing specified information and making unpublished information as to their internal operations available on proper request. The authorities affected (not Congress or the courts) include, e.g., administrative agencies generally, government corporations, the executive and military departments. Certain information is exempt from disclosure. E.g., secrets affecting national defense, foreign policy, foreign intelligence, international terrorism, and, generally, disclosure that would interfere with law enforcement, fair trial, or be an "unwarranted invasion of personal privacy."

Footnote Four: constitutional law shorthand for footnote 4 in *U.S. v. Carolene Products Co.,* 304 U.S. 144, 152n (1938), a footnote more famous than the opinion. The opinion upholds a ban on interstate shipment of "filled milk" (coconut oil substitute for milkfat): a statute regulating business presumed to be constitutional if supported by a rational basis. The footnote, thirty-three lines of dictum, suggests

Footnote Four

that a "more exacting judicial scrutiny" may be called for on other constitutional issues, e.g., involving the Bill of Rights, political processes, and protection of "discrete and insular minorities." □see **standards of review**. *Footnote Four* has had a pervasive influence on constitutional decision and discussion. On the darker side, this celebrity of a mere footnote is a documented, if unneeded, encouragement to legal writers to reach for glory below the line.

for and during: synonyms, not improved by doubling. Choose one, and save two words. <For and during/For/During the first option period, the rent is. . . .> □see **coupled synonyms**.

for and in consideration of: *for* and *in* are sometimes interchangeable; here they don't quite make it. The phrase starts out to say "for a consideration of" and switches to "in consideration of." Torn by indecision, it drops grammatical nicety in a shower of words. Omit *for and. In consideration of* is enough if you like the word *consideration;* more than enough for plain speaking. <A promises . . .; B promises. . . ./This costs $5,000.> □see **coupled synonyms**.

forbear □see **forbearance**.

forbearance (v. *forbear*)

1. refraining from doing something that you have a right to do, e.g., not insisting on payment of a debt when it is due.

2. *forbearance* (sense 1) as agreed. The added ingredient of agreement, i.e., *forbearing* as part of a contract, or later agreeing to a request for *forbearance,* is the common legal use of *forbearance.* When the binding quality of forbearance is called into question, this *forbearance* (sense 2) is often called *agreed forbearance,* emphasizing the distinction from sense 1. <True, he did not enforce the note when due, but that was not an agreed forbearance and does not constitute consideration.>

forbearance of money: agreement giving further time for a payment due. <The original interest plus that charged for the forbearance of money exceeded the limits of the usury law.>

force and effect: ordinarily a force produces an effect; here the effect is redundancy. Usually *force* and *effect* are interchangeable; either suffices. <The order then in force and effect/in force/in effect. . . .> Nuance may favor one or the other <the force of the law/ the effect of the law>. *Force and effect* is a waste of time. □see **coupled synonyms**. The expression is not improved as *full force and*

250

effect nor changed for the better as *full force and virtue.* The negative version is even worse; *no force and effect* is confusing, ungrammatical, at best only redundant. □see **null and void.**

force and virtue   □see **force and effect.**

force beyond control   □see **act of God.**

force majeure   □see **act of God.**

forcible detainer   □see **forcible entry and detainer.**

forcible entry and detainer: a summary civil action by a landlord to regain possession of premises from a tenant who disputes the landlord's right to possession. Also called *forcible detainer* and *unlawful detainer.* Despite the ancient sound of violence, the usual basis of the action is neither wrongful entry nor any force other than a stubborn refusal to get out, i.e., *detainer.*

foreclose   □see **foreclosure.**

foreclosure   (v. *foreclose*): proceedings on behalf of a secured creditor to obtain payment, either from the debtor under pressure of being required to make payment in full without the right to cure a default, a *strict foreclosure* (□see **equity of redemption,** under **equity**), or through sale of the property that is the security. □see also, **deed of trust,** under **deed;** □see also, **default;** □see also, **mortgage.**

foreign: connected with a nation, state, or similar political entity other than *this* one. *Foreign country* and *foreign nation,* like *foreigner,* look beyond the United States. Other usage of *foreign,* determined by a host of statutes and decisions, varies with the activity called *foreign,* e.g., taxation, incorporation, service of process.

foreign corporation: a corporation incorporated under the laws of a foreign country or under the laws of a state or similar political entity other than *this* one. < Though it does business here in Los Angeles, XYZ Co. was incorporated in Delaware, and under California law, it is a foreign corporation. >

foreign jurisdiction □see **jurisdiction.**

251

foreign

foreign law: the law of a foreign country, the law of a state other than *this* one, and—except for federal law—the law of a political entity other than *this* one.

foreign will: an imprecise expression referring to wills with some connection to a foreign country or to a state or similar political entity other than *this* one. The connection is not uniform, e.g., not executed here, not executed here and affecting property here, executed in accordance with foreign law, executed by someone not domiciled here.

foreign corporation □see foreign.

foreign country □see foreign.

foreigner □see foreign.

foreign jurisdiction □see jurisdiction.

foreign law □see foreign.

foreign nation □see foreign.

foreign will □see foreign.

foreman (of a jury): the juror, elected by the jury, to preside over their meetings and to represent them in speaking to the court. Some writers, considering *foreman* sexist, have run *foreperson* up the flagpole; few have saluted. □see sex.

foreperson □see foreman.

foreseeable damages □see damage.

forfeiture □see liquidated damages, under damage.

form □see adjudicated form.

formalisms To the uninitiated, all of the special usages of the language of the law are formalisms. *Formalisms* listed here are formal even to casehardened professionals, who do not wince at archaic Old

252

and Middle English, law Latin, or law French. The listings are samplings; some are separate entries in the dictionary.

Oral formalisms are largely ceremonial, a kind of old etiquette, ritual, working little harm, sometimes impressive.

approach the bench (□see).

Hear ye, hear ye, hear ye: the call of the bailiff or court clerk to announce the opening of a court session. It is the translation of *Oyez, oyez, oyez* (law F., O-yes), still used in some courts. In making the announcement, the bailiff or clerk is acting as a *crier,* also called a *court crier.* □see **proclamation.**

honorable, also *Honorable:* the traditional epithet of respect used by the bailiff or court clerk at the opening of a court session to describe the court <This *honorable court* is now in session.> and the judge. <The *Honorable* Mary Smith, judge presiding.> □see also, **court.**

May it please the court: the opening of a lawyer's argument to a court. □see also, **court;** □see also, **Honor.**

Oyez see **Hear ye** (above in this list).

rest (*plaintiff rests; defendant rests*): we have nothing further to offer in argument or in evidence. Short for: we *rest our case.* <Judge: You rest? Lawyer: Plaintiff rests.> □see also, **submit,** under **submission.** After resting, a party is usually permitted to offer a rebuttal and, for special cause, to **reopen a case** (□see). For *rest,* in the sense of what is left, □see **residue.**

solemnly swear: part of the administration or taking of an oath. <You do solemnly swear./I solemnly swear.>

the truth, the whole truth, and nothing but the truth: part of the rhythmic swearing of the witness. Were it not required ritual, redundant. □see also, **absolutes.**

Your Honor: the lawyer's form of address to a judge on the bench.

Written formalisms are flourishes of a style long dead, an encumbrance; those listed here should be liquidated—not replaced, liquidated.

Be it remembered

Brethren (□see)

Brother (□see **Brethren**)

By virtue of the authority vested in me

Comes now (the plaintiff; the defendant)

formalisms

Esquire (□see)

Further affiant sayeth not □see **affiant**

Further deponent saith not □see **affiant**

In Witness Whereof

Know All Men By These Presents

ss (□see)

To All To Whom These Presents Come, Greetings

Whereas

Wherefore

WITNESSETH

forma pauperis   □see **in forma pauperis.**

former jeopardy   □see **double jeopardy.**

form instructions   □see **jury instructions.**

form over substance   □see **exalts form over substance,** under **clichés.**

formula instruction   □see **jury instructions.**

fornicate   □see **cohabit.**

for the record: reference to a statement that a judge or lawyer makes with special emphasis, for use in later proceedings or for its force when spoken.   <For the record, counsel, you should know that about fifteen years before I became a judge, I once represented the son of the plaintiff in this case./I want to state for the record that despite my repeated objection, His Honor persists in referring to my client as "the accused drunk.">   Similar to *let the record show.*   □see **enter an objection,** under **enter.**

forthwith   □see **absolutes.**

forum (L.: court of law), a Latin word, sometimes naturalized in English, e.g., *law of the forum,* sometimes unnaturalized Latin, e.g., *forum non conveniens.* The law uses *forum* in three senses, often fused. Those senses are listed, then illustrated.

254

1. a court of law. This is ordinary English, also used in the law, especially with reference to a particular court, as distinguished from courts generally.

2. the geographical location of a court.

3. a jurisdiction, considered as a court system with its own distinctive law. □see also, **jurisdiction.**

law of the forum (senses 2 and 3), the English translation of the still-used Latin *lex fori* (FOUR-ee): the law of the place where a suit is filed or is being tried.

forum shopping (sense 3): hunting for a jurisdiction with law most or more favorable to one's case; includes taking steps to remove a case from the *forum* (senses 1, 2, and 3) where a suit was filed or is being tried. Often a pejorative. In its best light, *forum shopping* is described as a search for a *proper forum* (sense 3) in the best interests of a client. At worst, it is the search for a *forum* (sense 1) with a sympathetic judge, the practice denounced as *judge shopping.*

forum non conveniens (L.: an unsuitable court) (sense 1, 2, or 3): an inconvenient court for the trial of a particular case. The determination can be made if there is more than one *proper forum* (sense 1, 2, or 3) and rests in the discretion of the court where the suit is pending, when it has the power to try the case. The decision that *forum non conveniens* dictates a transfer may hinge on a variety of considerations; e.g., the present *forum* (sense 1) is overcrowded; the convenience of litigants or witnesses (sense 2); a court of another state, or a federal court, is better able to handle the litigation (sense 3).

□see also, **public forum.**

forum non conveniens   □see **forum.**

forum shopping   □see **forum.**

For value received,   also *for value received:* a traditional vague recital of consideration in promissory notes, deeds, and other instruments designed to be executed by only one party to a transaction.

forwarding fee   □see **fee (attorney's fee).**

Founders   □see **Founding Fathers.**

Founding Fathers

Founding Fathers • Framers

Founding Fathers (also called *Founders,* also *Fathers*) and *Framers* are all usually preceded by *the.* Often the words produce a mood, rather than a meaning, and slip easily into the category of **clichés** (□see). They are invoked so often, on so little provocation, and with such assurance, as to suggest that everyone, especially lawyers, must know these people and their habits of mind. <In their wisdom, the Founding Fathers did not say/never intended/must have intended. . . .> Casual word dropping in context with the U.S. Constitution, the Constitutional Convention of 1787, and the American heritage makes synonyms of *Founding Fathers* and *Framers.* Distinctions can be made.

Framers: the fifty-five delegates who attended one or more sessions of the Constitutional Convention of 1787, which drafted the U.S. Constitution and had it signed and submitted to the Continental Congress on September 17, 1787. The fifty-five are considered *Framers* whether or not continuously at the Convention, whether or not they took pen in hand, and whether their contributions at the Convention were major or insignificant. This distinguishes them from the sixty-five (including the fifty-five) who were appointed delegates, the forty-two who were present at the signing, and the thirty-nine who signed. *Framers* is also rendered *framers.*

Founding Fathers: those who made significant contributions to the founding of the United States of America, whether or not they attended the Constitutional Convention of 1787. A *Founding Father* might or might not have been a *Framer;* Thomas Jefferson, for example, in France during the Constitutional Convention, was not a *Framer* but clearly a *Founder.* Unlike *Framers,* there is no consensus on the number of *Founders.* Whether status as a *Framer* (despite an insignificant contribution at the Convention) automatically qualifies a *Framer* as a *Founder* is debatable. *Founding Fathers, Founders,* and *Fathers* are also rendered *founding fathers, founders,* and *fathers.*

four corners □see **four corners of the instrument.**

four corners of the instrument, often shortened to **four corners:** a metaphor for the contents of a writing. <Judging the contract by its four corners, it is clear that. . . .> A loose term of reference, dignified but not made precise as the *four corners rule:* the meaning and intent of a writing is to be gathered from what is written there, all of it. Like other **rules of interpretation** (□see), undependable.

four corners rule □see **four corners of the instrument.**

four unities □see **joint tenancy,** under **estate.**

Framers □see **Founding Fathers.**

franchise □see **license.**

fraud is rampant in the language of the law, with definitions by statute and decision as varied as the specific applications in criminal law, contracts, torts, equity, bankruptcy, securities regulations, tax, etc. The old rubric *fraud and deceit,* sometimes still used, couples synonyms in a loose reference to a vast spectrum of odious conduct. *Fraud* (n.) [*defraud* (v.), *fraudulent* (adj.)] has two principal senses:

1. damaging someone by a representation, knowing it to be false, and intending that it be relied on. This is the most common legal sense. The precise nature of representation, intent, and knowledge (Latin *scienter,* sigh-EN-ter) or what may substitute for knowledge, varies with the application of the charge of fraud. These are some expressions based on *fraud* (sense 1):

actual fraud: sense 1 *fraud,* as distinguished from what is sometimes called constructive fraud (see sense 2). □see also, **actual.**

deceit, also called *intentional misrepresentation:* the tort action for fraud.

fraudulent representation: another name for *fraud,* sense 1.

intent to defraud: often an element of a specific crime, e.g., obtaining money by *false pretenses.*

2. gaining an advantage by deceiving someone. This is a general sense, in law as in ordinary English. Sense 2 concentrates on the effect on the victim, rather than a fine focus on the mental state of the wrongdoer. < The investors were defrauded./It was a fraudulent scheme from start to finish. > This is the sense used more often in determining the basis of *equitable relief* or defenses in **equity** (□see). The sin of inactivity by one under a duty to act, especially fiduciaries, falls under this head. These are some expressions based on *fraud* (sense 2):

constructive fraud: as distinguished from *actual fraud* (see sense 1); sometimes used to describe conduct condemned on equitable principles, though not *fraud* in sense 1.

worked a fraud: describing the result of conduct, irrespective of the intent that produced the result. <The advertisement worked a fraud on the consuming public.>

3. These are some expressions that may refer to *fraud*, sense 1, sense 2, or both:

extrinsic fraud: fraud that prevents a critical court appearance (e.g., of a witness or heir) or prevents one from fully presenting a case, e.g., fraudulent concealment of property in a division between partners or spouses. <The judgment was set aside on the ground that it was obtained by extrinsic fraud.> Contrasted with *intrinsic fraud,* e.g., perjury.

fraud in the factum: fraud as to the nature of the writing that one signs, *factum* (L.: the act); also called *fraud in the making.* <She was told it was a petition, but she signed a deed to Blackacre: fraud in the *factum.*>

fraud in the inducement: fraud, other than *fraud in the factum,* that induced one to make an agreement, e.g., a false representation as to the reason for the agreement.

fraudulent conveyance: a transfer of property in fraud of creditors, i.e., that has that effect, e.g., because lacking in adequate consideration. □see also, **transfer in fraud of creditors,** under **transfer.**

intrinsic fraud see **extrinsic fraud,** above, in this entry.

4. statute of frauds (□see) has only an historical connection with *fraud.*

fraud and deceit □see **fraud.**

fraud in the factum □see **fraud.**

fraud in the inducement □see **fraud.**

fraud in the making □see **fraud.**

fraudulent conveyance □see **fraud.**

fraudulent representation □see **fraud.**

free alongside ship □see **F.A.S.**

free alongside vessel □see **F.A.S.**

free and clear □see **clear**; □see also, **coupled synonyms.**

free and without charge: free. A relic; **coupled synonyms** (□see).

freedom of assembly □see **right of assembly.**

freedom of association: a fundamental constitutional right that is not mentioned in the Constitution, either as a freedom or a right. Despite this verbal neglect, *freedom of association* is fixed in the Constitution by Supreme Court interpretation; implied from a variety of clauses. E.g., rights of assembly, petition, free press, free speech, exercise of religion, due process, privileges and immunities of citizenship. The breadth of its sources leaves *freedom of association* with no single, constricted sense. It represents what is repeatedly called a "spectrum" of associational freedoms, from the most tightly knit and restricted groupings (e.g., marriage) to the most public (e.g., political parties), from sexual intimacy to membership in Kiwanis and Rotary. The extent of permissible governmental limitations on freedom of association, varying with the degree of size and closeness of association, is in continuous litigation. One creative and controversial sorting out takes a special name:

freedom of intimate association: the freedom to choose a closely intimate personal relationship, such as exists within a family, or otherwise so much a part of one's identity as an individual as to be similarly secure against unjustified intrusion. (See Karst, "Freedom of Intimate Association," 89 *Yale Law Journal* 624, 629, 1980; see *Roberts v. United States Jaycees,* 468 U.S. 609, 618, 1984.) This freedom has roots in the **right of privacy** (□see), with a potential for protection without regard to social acceptability. It also represents a more formidable obstacle to government intervention than less intimate forms of association. Its boundaries are as yet unfixed.

□see **liberty interest.**

Freedom of Information Act □see **FOIA.**

freedom of intimate association □see **freedom of association.**

freedom of petition □see **right of petition**, under **right of assembly.**

Freedom of Press Clause: the part of the U.S. Constitution reading: "Congress shall make no law . . . abridging the freedom [of speech, or] of the press. . . ." (Amend. I). Here, the *Freedom of Press Clause* is reproduced with the bracketed *Freedom of Speech Clause*. □see also, **constitutional clauses**.

Freedom of Speech Clause: the part of the U.S. Constitution reading: "Congress shall make no law . . . abridging the freedom of speech. . . ." (Amend. I). □see also, **constitutional clauses**.

Free Exercise Clause: the part of the U.S. Constitution reading: "Congress shall make no law [respecting an establishment of religion, or] prohibiting the free exercise thereof. . . ." (Amend. I). The *Free Exercise Clause* and the bracketed *Establishment Clause* are also referred to as the *Religion Clauses,* sometimes as the *Religious Clauses.* □See also, **Religious Test Clause;** □see also, **constitutional clauses.**

freehold: an *estate in fee* (□see **fee simple**), an *estate in fee tail* (□see **fee tail**), or a *life estate* (□see **estate**). Also called an *estate of freehold* and *freehold estate.*

freehold estate □see **freehold.**

free on board □see **F.O.B.**

French □see **law French.**

fresh pursuit, also called **hot pursuit:** the timely pursuit of a person suspected of crime to arrest the person or seize property. The *pursuit* is *fresh* or *hot* when started promptly after the crime and carried on continuously. The expressions, not precisely defined, are used frequently to justify what would otherwise be an illegal arrest, search, or seizure, e.g., because without a warrant, beyond an officer's territorial limits, or because the owner used excessive force to recover stolen goods.

friendly witness □see **hostile witness.**

friend of the court □see **amicus curiae.**

frisk (v., n.) was once, perhaps still is, underworld slang for searching through a person's clothing or picking pockets, at best a suspect, furtive pursuit. Over the years, *frisk* has moved upward on the social scale and is now generally understood as some sort of quick search of clothing, especially for weapons, especially by the police. In the twentieth century, *frisk* has achieved special status as an aspect of the constitutional law of *search and seizure* (Amend. IV). But a background in the shadows has left *frisk* an ill-defined law word. Along the way, it has bred, or bred with, variant usage, usually regarded as synonyms: *frisk search, pat down* (often *pat-down* or *patdown*), *pat down search, pat frisk, pat search,* etc., all merging under the banner *stop and frisk. Frisk* is still too frequently litigated to be hogtied. This entry attempts only to rescue *frisk* from "blurdom," to separate the physical facts of a *frisk* from *frisk* with legal overtones.

1. *frisk,* the basic physical description: a police officer's quick, on-the-spot patting and feeling of outer clothing to find out if a person is armed. The vivid synonym *pat down* conveys the reality of head-to-toe search.

Some usage extends the *frisk* to include: (a) tactile search of pockets in outer clothing; (b) visual search (e.g., seeing a protruding gun); (c) search for objects other than weapons; (d) seizure of weapons or other objects discovered; and (e) a similar quick, on-the-spot superficial inspection of packages, luggage, and vehicles.

2. *frisk,* the physical elements dissected: a *pat down* (as in sense 1), plus the *stop* that precedes and accompanies it: a temporary restraint on the person's freedom to walk away. □see **stop and frisk** (sense 3).

Physically, the *frisk* (1. and 2.) is contrasted with more detailed and prolonged searches, e.g., the *strip search, full-blown search,* etc.

3. *frisk,* with legal overtones: the legalism **stop and frisk**. The best indication that you deal here with a legalism is the indifference to grammatical nicety that permits lawyers to regard *stop and frisk* as a synonym of *frisk* (sense 2), which itself includes a *stop.* < It was a frisk/a stop and frisk. > Though not spelled out, in the context of *stop and frisk,* the *frisk* part is not the whole bundle; it concentrates on the physical *pat down* (as in sense 1) as contrasted with the *stop* (as in sense 2). So regarded, *stop and frisk* is more amenable to scrutiny as a *search and seizure,* with the word order reversed: the *stop* is a *seizure* (the restraint on personal freedom), whether or not legal, and the *frisk* is a *search.* The constitutional ramifications of permissible *stop and frisk* are beyond the scope of this dictionary. □see also, **Terry stop,** under **search and seizure.**

frisk search □see **frisk**.

frivolous: groundless. The ordinary English sense applied in the law to claims, defenses, appeals, etc., as a reason for dismissal, assessment of penalties against lawyers, award or denial of attorney fees, etc. Usually an objective standard; sometimes equated with bad faith. The law takes a dim view of the *frivolous;* it has none of the colloquial English sense of gaiety. *Frivolity* is ignored.

from and after: a traditional redundancy (□see **coupled synonyms**). Even worse, as a means of fixing a time of beginning, the prepositions coupled or uncoupled are undependable. □see **time**.

fruit of the poisonous tree: a metaphor in which a violation of a person's constitutional rights is *the poisonous tree* and evidence directly or indirectly obtained through that violation is the *fruit of the poisonous tree.*

fruit of the poisonous tree doctrine: a metaphorical extension of the **exclusionary rule** (□see): the *fruit of the poisonous tree* is inadmissible in a prosecution of the person whose constitutional rights have been violated. The recurrent question of whether particular evidence is a *fruit,* or too remote from *the poisonous tree* to be so classified, is not answered by the metaphor. The *doctrine* has also been called *the fruits doctrine,* the *tainted fruit doctrine,* and *primary taint doctrine.*

fruits doctrine □see **fruit of the poisonous tree**.

FTC: abbreviation of Federal Trade Commission. □see **administrative agency,** under **administrative law.**

full age □see **lawful age**; □see also, **child**.

full-blown search □see **frisk**.

full faith and credit

1. (constitutional law): old synonyms for belief and giving credence to, emphatically redundant with *full,* become a single catchword of federal union in court interpretation of the *Full Faith and Credit Clause:* the part of the U.S. Constitution reading: "Full faith and credit shall be given in each state to the public acts, records, and judicial proceedings of every other state. And the Congress may by general laws prescribe the manner in which such acts, records and proceedings shall be proved, and the effect thereof." (Art. IV, § 1). The *Full Faith and Credit Clause* is also called the *Comity Clause.* □see also, **constitutional clauses;** □see also, **coupled synonyms.**

2. (public finance): *faith* (keeping promises) and *credit* (money-raising capacity) joined in the pledge of a governmental unit to faithfully repay borrowed money. That undertaking distinguishes a *general obligation bond* < . . . and the full faith and credit of the state are pledged for the punctual payment of . . .> from, e.g., a *revenue bond* obligating only what comes in from a special source.

Full faith and credit (sense 2) is often abbreviated *faith and credit.*

Full Faith and Credit Clause   □see **full faith and credit.**

full performance   □see **perform.**

funds transfer   □see **Uniform Commercial Code;** □see **electronic funds transfer.**

fungible   (n., adj.): property "of which any unit is . . . the equivalent of any other like unit"; said especially of goods (e.g., grain) and securities. (See UCC § 1201(17).)

future covenant   □see **covenant.**

future goods: goods that "are not both existing and identified." (UCC § 2105(2)).

future interest: an existing property interest that for the time being lacks the quintessential attributes of the *present interest,* the right to possession and use of the property. The *future interest* awaits the moment (sometimes only deferred, sometimes chancy) when its career as a *future interest* ends and a new life as a *present interest* begins. A *future interest* is sometimes referred to as a *nonpossessory estate.* □see also, **possessory interest.**

A *future interest* is usually distinguished from an *expectancy* (also called an *estate in expectancy):* an imprecise term for the hope of receiving property, e.g., the *expectancy* of an inheritance by an only child. Some *expectancies* may have better odds of amounting to something than some *future interests.* The *expectancy* is still not usually regarded as a *future interest,* more often referred to not even as an *expectancy* but as a *bare* or *mere expectancy.* One man's *property* is another man's *expectancy,* but it lacks the traditional clout of the named *future interests.* These are:

executory interest, also called *executory limitation:* a *future interest* in someone other than the present property owner that has the possibility of becoming a *present interest* only by *divesting* (cutting short) another property interest. *Executory interests* are subdivided into *shifting executory interests* and *springing executory interests:*

> **shifting executory interest:** an executory interest in which the property interest cut short is that of another transferee. <A owns Blackacre in fee. A conveys Blackacre to B. The deed to B further specifies that if ever Blackacre is not used as a golf course, A gives Blackacre to C. C has a shifting executory interest in fee.>

> **springing executory interest:** an executory interest in which the property interest cut short is that of the transferor. <A owns Blackacre in fee. A conveys Blackacre to A's daughter B, to take effect when B marries. B has a springing executory interest in fee, which will divest A and become a present interest when B marries.>

possibility of reverter: the interest retained by the owner in fee who transfers a **fee simple determinable.** (□see, under **fee simple**).

remainder: a *future interest* in someone other than the present property owner that has the possibility of becoming a *present interest* upon the natural expiration (not cutting short) of the other property interests created at the same time. <A owns Blackacre in fee and conveys Blackacre to B for life and to C in fee. C has a remainder in fee that becomes a present interest upon the death of B.> *Remainders* are subdivided into two principal categories, *contingent remainders* and *vested remainders,* the latter with subcategories studied in the law of property:

> **contingent remainder:**

> **1.** a *remainder* to a person not ascertained at the time the interest is created; or

> **2.** whether or not the person is ascertained, a *remainder* whose possibility of becoming a *present interest* is subject not only to the basic requirement of natural expiration of the preceding property interests but also to a special condition precedent.

> <A owns Blackacre in fee. While B and C are alive, A conveys Blackacre to B for life, remainder to the heirs of C. The heirs of C are not yet ascertained; they have a contingent remainder in fee./A owns Blackacre in fee and conveys Blackacre to B for life and then to C if C marries D. C has a

contingent remainder in fee, conditioned on the death of B and marriage to D.>

vested remainder: a *remainder* to an ascertained person, with the certainty or possibility of becoming a *present interest* subject only to the basic requirement of natural expiration of the preceding property interests. <A owns Blackacre in fee and conveys Blackacre to B for life and then to C. C has a vested remainder in fee.>

remainderman: the person, male or female, who has a *remainder*, vested or contingent. For centuries, this has been the accepted label. Experiments are now under way for the substitution of *remainderperson, remainderer, remainderor,* or *remainor.* □see **sex**.

reversion: the *future interest* remaining in the owner who transfers out of his property one or more of these interests and no others: (a) interests lower in the hierarchy of interests than what he has, (b) *contingent remainders* of whatever level in the hierarchy. The hierarchy, in descending order, is *fee simple* (all varieties), *fee tail, life estate, tenancy for years.* <A owns Blackacre in fee and conveys Blackacre to B for life. B has a life estate, and A now has a reversion in fee./A owns Blackacre in fee and conveys Blackacre to B for life and then to C if C marries D. C has a contingent remainder in fee, and A now has a reversion in fee.> Unlike other future interests, the *reversion* is not *created;* it is simply there as a matter of law without any special words.

right of entry: the interest retained by the owner in fee who transfers a *fee simple subject to a condition subsequent* (□see, under **fee simple**). *Right of entry* is also called *right of reentry, right of entry for condition broken,* and *power of termination.* This *right of entry,* a *future interest,* is to be distinguished from the landlord's *right of entry* in the relationship of landlord and tenant.

G

gag order: a colloquial name for a restraining order designed to stop out-of-court comment or information that could seriously interfere with the selection of a jury or a fair trial. The order is usually directed at the media and at those connected with an impending or actual trial, especially lawyers. Rights of free speech and press upset many gag orders. Lawyers' professional rules often inhibit comment not otherwise restrained. The expression *gag order* is usually used in the metaphorical sense, as distinguished from the physical gagging of an unruly defendant or prisoner.

garnish □see attachment.

garnishee □see attachment.

garnisher □see attachment.

garnishment □see attachment.

gender □see sex.

general appearance □see appear.

general bequest □see gift by will, under gift.

general counsel □see lawyer.

general damages □see damage.

general devise □see gift by will, under gift.

general finding □see finding.

general intent □see intent.

general jurisdiction □see court of general jurisdiction, under court.

general legacy □see **gift by will, under gift.**

general lien □see **lien.**

general obligation bond □see **full faith and credit.**

general partner □see **partnership.**

general partnership □see **partnership.**

general power □see **power of appointment,** under **appoint.**

general power of appointment □see **power of appointment,** under **appoint.**

general verdict □see **verdict.**

general warranty deed □see **covenants of title.**

General Welfare Clause: the part of the U.S. Constitution reading: "The Congress shall have power to lay and collect taxes, duties, imposts and excises, to pay the debts and provide for the common defence and general welfare of the United States. . . ." (Art. I, § 8, cl. 1). □see also, **constitutional clauses.**

get to the jury □see **embracery.**

gift • give To *give a gift* is not necessarily redundant. Despite a strong relationship, each word lives a life of its own.

  gift: In law as in ordinary English, the usual sense of *gift* is property transferred from the *giver* without cost to the *recipient.* With no qualifying label or other context, *gift* refers to both real and personal property.

  The English synonym *donation,* derived from Latin, is usually a *charitable gift,* rather than a general substitute for *gift.* For the people connected with a *gift,* lawyers prefer the traditional Latinate labels *donor* (giver) and *donee* (recipient), though these depend on context to make clear that they are givers and receivers of a *gift.* <Both donor and donee are required to file a gift tax return.> For other usage of *donor* and *donee,* □see **power of appointment,** under **appoint.**

gift by will usually goes by the label *legacy* or *bequest* for personal property and a *devise* for real property. But for centuries, the usage has been, and remains, loose; those labels cannot be counted on to identify the type of property. If the gift is of specific property or an identified fund, it is a *specific legacy, specific bequest,* or *specific devise;* as distinguished from a *general legacy, —bequest,* or *—devise:* described in general terms, as, e.g., by quantity, and payable out of the general assets of the estate. □see **give, devise, and bequeath,** under **give.** For the recipients of a *gift by will, legatee* is used with either *legacy* or *bequest; devisee* with *devise.*

> *vested bequest, legacy,* or *devise:* one fixed as to the right to receive it, either now or at a later time.

gift causa mortis (L., COW-sah MOR-tis: loosely, because of death), also called *donatio causa mortis* (L., dohn-NAH-tea-o: gift) and *donatio mortis causa:* whether partly or all Latin, a conditional *gift* of personal property, delivered to the recipient by the giver, who believes death is imminent, and it is a *gift* only if that belief is confirmed. Variously defined and regulated by statute, the *gift causa mortis* (with its limited reliance on Latin) still serves a purpose in identifying death gifts. It is to be distinguished from a **gift in contemplation of death** (□see) and a **gift inter vivos** (□see).

gift in contemplation of death sounds like an all-English *gift causa mortis* but isn't. It is a *gift* of real or personal property made before death but subject to death taxes as property of the *giver.* It is so classified if the gift was made within a statutory period of death or if it is considered nothing but a device to reduce taxes—a contemplation of the almost inevitability of taxes, as opposed to the normal human contemplation of eventual death. □see also, **transfer in contemplation of death,** under **transfer.**

gift inter vivos (L.: between the living): a gift of real or personal property (sometimes limited to personal property), unconditionally completed during the lifetime of giver and recipient. □see also, **inter vivos trust,** under **trust.**

gift over: a property interest that follows a preceding property interest. Not a term of art, not an operative term of transfer, and not confined to property that is a *gift.* Rather, it is loose usage to describe the state of a title. <To A for life, with gift over to B in fee.>

take by gift: a description of a transfer of property that is a gift. This is special usage in the law of real property. □see **purchase,** under **buy.**

give: an operative word to transfer real or personal property without cost to the recipient, but sufficient for this purpose only if the context makes clear that a *gift* is intended. <The will read, "I give Blackacre to Mary."/She gave him a car for his birthday.> The usual sense of *gift* is gratuity, but *give* (in law as in ordinary English) has a wide range of meaning without any suggestion of gratuity, e.g., *offer, deliver* <How much will you give for an option?/He gave the deed to the bank for safekeeping.>.

give and grant: a frequent combination, both unnecessary and confusing. In a will, where *gift* is clearly intended, *give* is sufficient. Where there is no *gift*, the operative word **grant** (□see) is more precise standing alone, eliminating speculation as to whether or not *give* suggests that a *gift* was intended.

give, devise, and bequeath: an old rhythmic accumulation of synonyms for making a *gift by will*. In this and variant forms (*give and bequeath; give and devise; give, bequeath, and devise;* etc.) it persists, although *give* alone is adequate and more precise. *Bequeath* is not rigidly limited to *bequests* of personal property, nor *devise* rigidly limited to a *devise* of realty (□see **gift**). *Give*, by itself, disposes of either or both.

gift by will □see **gift**.

gift causa mortis □see **gift**.

gift in contemplation of death □see **gift**.

gift inter vivos □see **gift**.

gift over □see **gift**.

gift tax □see **marital deduction**; □see **tax**.

give □see **gift**.

give and bequeath □see **give**, under **gift**.

give and devise □see **give**, under **gift**.

give and grant □see **give**, under **gift**.

give, bequeath, and devise □see **give**, under **gift**.

give, devise, and bequeath □see **give**, under **gift**.

give notice □see **notice**.

giver □see **gift**.

go bail □see **bail**.

going and coming rule: an employee with fixed hours and place of work is not within the scope of employment while going to and coming from the premises where the work is performed. Any succinct statement of the rule omits exceptions and exceptions to exceptions. If the rule applies, one consequence is that the employee is not entitled to **workers' compensation** (□see) benefits for injuries going and coming; another is that the employer is not liable for the employee's going and coming torts.

going private • going public

Nontechnical terms for changing the character of ownership of a business organization.

going private: the change of a corporation from being a *publicly held corporation* (□see **corporate**) to becoming a *closely held corporation*. Also referred to as *privatizing*.

going public:

1. the change of a corporation from being a *closely held corporation* to becoming a *publicly held corporation*. In this sense, the reverse of *going private*.

2. the change from being an unincorporated business to becoming a *publicly held corporation*. <The partners decided that their best bet for added capital was to *go public.* >

going public □see **going private**.

golden parachute   ▢see **tender offer**.

good   ▢see **goods**.

good behavior: a flexible expression in and out of the law.

1. as in "*during good behavior*": the constitutional limit on the tenure of federal judges of Article III courts (▢see, under **federal courts**).

2. in the criminal law, e.g., as a condition of a suspended sentence; and in the penal system, e.g., to reduce the period of imprisonment, also called *good time credits*.

good cause   If you speak of *a good cause,* you are speaking English, not law; law is *good cause,* without the *a.* If you speak of *good causes,* again you are speaking English, not law; the law's *good cause* has no plural. It is the statement of a condition of affairs. In the law's *good cause,* the *cause* is the *reason why.* The *good* thrown in makes it clear that this is law, not philosophy. If the good is not expressed, as in *show cause* (▢see **order to show cause**), it is there anyhow; the law puts it in. The law is not moved by any old reason; it's got to be *good cause.* If you can't show *good cause,* you are close to the put-down of colloquial English, "You've got no reason to complain," i.e., no good reason. There is *good cause* for firing, for quitting, for filing late, for vacating a roadway, etc. The *cause* or *good cause* that will excuse, justify, require, or permit something is such cause as the law approves or finds legal, sufficient, just, reasonable, or some other such amorphous epithet—that has in the past excused, justified, required, or permitted something, or something nearly like this—or that in its discretion this court thinks ought to excuse, justify, require, or permit. In short, *good cause* is *good cause.*

good faith   ▢see **bona fide**.

good faith and fair dealing   ▢see **covenant**.

good faith purchaser   ▢see **bona fide**.

good faith purchaser for value   ▢see **bona fide**.

goods: a catchall for tangible personal property. Statutes using the word customarily give *goods* special definition and should be con-

271

sulted. In many general language dictionaries, *goods* is listed as a special plural under the singular noun *good*. The logical conclusion that a single item of *goods* is a *good* is unpalatable in commercial law usage, more common in legal usage with economic overtones. Generally, in legal usage, *goods* refers to one or many items, each with a plural verb. < Sale of goods is governed by the Uniform Commercial Code./ They had one TV set left; the goods were sold at a discount. >

Good Samaritan, or **good Samaritan,**   gets a mixed reception in the law. Often referred to as the *Good Samaritan doctrine* or *Good Samaritan rule,* yet the only sure guidance is that despite the parable of the good Samaritan (Luke 10:30–37), there is no legal duty to be one. Some leaning to the moral side of the road comes in a typically perverse setting—suit against the good Samaritan by the victim he was trying to help. The doctrine or rule, in various forms, frees the good Samaritan of civil liability unless his negligence or recklessness has hurt, not helped, or that harm has been suffered by reliance on the Samaritan's efforts. So-called *Good Samaritan statutes* give varying degrees of immunity from liability to those who render voluntary, uncompensated medical aid at the scene of an accident.

Good Samaritan doctrine   □see Good Samaritan.

Good Samaritan rule   □see Good Samaritan.

Good Samaritan statutes   □see Good Samaritan.

goods and chattels   □see chattel.

goods sold and delivered   □see common count, under count.

good time credits   □see good behavior.

go over   □see adjourn.

go public   □see going private.

go to court   □see court.

governmental immunity   □see sovereign immunity, under immunity.

government lawyers □see **lawyer.**

government secrets privilege □see **immunity.**

grandchild □see **child.**

grandfather □see **grandfather clause.**

grandfather clause: exemption or special treatment of those engaged in an activity before enactment of a statute or regulation
prohibiting or controlling the activity. The practice is called
grandfathering, the verb, *grandfather.* <Those licensed before the new,
stricter regulation were grandfathered in.> A *grandfather clause* is a type
of **saving clause** (□see).

grandfathering □see **grandfather clause.**

grand jury □see **jury;** □see **indictment.**

Grand Jury Clause: the part of the U.S. Constitution reading: "No
person shall be held to answer for a capital, or otherwise infamous
crime, unless on a presentment or indictment of a grand jury, except
in cases arising in the land or naval forces, or in the militia, when in
actual service in time of war or public danger. . . ." (Amend. V).
□see also, **constitutional clauses.**

grant (n., v.)

1. (procedure)

   a. to approve a motion, as opposed to *deny.* <Motion granted.>
   □see **overrule.**

   b. to give immunity, or the act of giving immunity. □see **grant of
   immunity from prosecution,** under **immunity.**

2. (property)

   a. the verb is a traditional operative, sometimes descriptive, word
   of *transfer,* usually of real estate. <A grants Blackacre to B./A granted
   B a life estate in Blackacre.>

   b. the noun has several meanings:

      [1] the act of granting. <The grant has been carefully planned.>

grant

[2] the property covered. <The grant stretched into two counties.>

[3] the piece of paper. <The grant had been hidden in an oak tree.> In technical usage, the usual word is **deed** (□see).

c. The person *granting* is the *grantor;* the person receiving the *grant* is the *grantee.*

d. **grant, bargain, and sell**: an archaic form, awaiting only interment. *Grant* is sufficient. □see also, **give and grant**.

grant, bargain, and sell   □see **grant**.

grant deed   □see **covenants of title**.

grantee   □see **grant**.

grant of immunity from prosecution   □see **immunity**.

grantor   □see **grant**.

grantor trust   □see **trust**.

gratuitous bailee   □see **bail**.

Greenacre   □see **Blackacre**.

greenmail   □see **tender offer**.

Greetings   □see **formalisms**.

grievable   □see **grievance**.

grievance (labor law)

1. the bundle of facts and law that leads a worker, a union, sometimes even an employer, to feel that it is being denied legal rights in the employer-employee relationship and is, accordingly, *aggrieved,* in the ordinary sense of that word.

2. a *grievance* (sense 1) that is *grievable:* one that is properly the basis for initiating procedures (e.g., arbitration) within the employer-employee relationship for settlement of a dispute without resort to the courts. What is *grievable* and procedures for settlement vary by statute, decision, and provisions of collective bargaining agreements. Typically, *grievance* (sense 2) is a violation of a collective bargaining agreement (e.g., wrongful discharge, withholding of wages, improper discipline, etc.), as distinguished from need for a new collective bargaining agreement. <The supervisor's conduct amounted to an annoyance, rather than a grievance; not grievable.>

3. the filing of a complaint, or the complaint itself, formal or informal, initiating settlement of a *grievance* (sense 2). <Smith was fired on Monday and filed a grievance with the union on Tuesday.>

grievant: the one who filed the *grievance* (sense 3).

grieve: to file the *grievance,* i.e., the verb for the noun *grievance* (sense 3). <Despite the grievance, the contract required them to work now and grieve later./It could have been grieved but wasn't.>

grievant   □see **grievance.**

grieve   □see **grievance.**

grind to a halt   □see **clichés.**

gross negligence   □see **negligence.**

ground lease   □see **lease.**

ground rent   □see **lease.**

ground water   □see **law of capture.**

group legal services   □see **prepaid legal services.**

guarantee • guaranty: now, alternative spellings of the same word, *guarantee* usually the verb, *guaranty* usually the noun.

guarantee

1. guaranty (n.)

a. as in ordinary English, an assurance that something will be done or not done. <You have my guaranty that housing will be available./ The constitutional guaranties of personal freedom have a long history.>

b. an agreement giving assurance of quality. In this sense, often used loosely as a substitute for, or as a reference to, the more technical **warranty** (□see). <The new car carried a five-year guaranty covering specified parts of the motor./The guaranties took the form of a limited warranty.>

c. an agreement to be responsible for another's obligations. <The bank refused to lend to the corporation without the personal guaranty of the principal stockholder.>

> **guarantor:** the person who makes the agreement to be responsible for another's obligations. Under some statutes and decisions, *guarantor* and *surety* are synonyms, both looking to the debtor if obliged to pay his debt. But distinction is traditional: the *guarantor's* agreement is a separate, collateral obligation, i.e., if the debt is not paid, the *guarantor* will pay it; the *surety,* together with the surety's *principal,* undertakes directly that the obligation shall be met. In the money market, the usual term is *guarantor.* For a variety of bonding activities, e.g., a bail bond, the usual term is *surety.* □see also, **suretyship.**

2. guarantee (v.): to give a *guaranty* in any of its senses. <I will guarantee any loans up to $10,000./Guaranteed 99 percent pure.> □see **Guarantee Clause.**

guarantor, as one who *guarantees,* in legal usage, usually refers to one who guarantees another's obligations (sense 1.c).

Guarantee Clause: the part of the U.S. Constitution reading: "The United States shall guarantee to every state in this Union a republican form of government. . . ." (Art. IV, § 4). □see also, **constitutional clauses.**

guarantor □see **guarantee.**

guaranty □see **guarantee.**

guardhouse lawyer □see **lawyer.**

guardian

1. a person appointed by court order to take care of the person, property, or both of one unable to do so by reason of minority or incompetence.

ward: the one whose person, property, or both are taken care of by the *guardian*.

guardianship: the relationship of *guardian* and *ward*. □see also, **conservatorship**.

2. a person entitled to court appointment as *guardian* (sense 1) of a minor or to exercise the powers and have the responsibilities of *guardian* of a minor, though not appointed by court. E.g., *testamentary guardian:* one named by will; *natural guardian:* the parent of a minor.

3. guardian ad litem (L., ad LIGHT-em: for the lawsuit): a person appointed by a court (or permitted by a court) to sue, or defend a lawsuit, for someone who is under legal disability. <The plaintiff is Mary Smith, guardian *ad litem* for Joe Smith, a minor.>

next friend: often a synonym for *guardian ad litem*. Sometimes distinguished on the ground that *guardian ad litem* is a party to the suit, *next friend* is not. <Joe Smith, plaintiff, appearing by his next friend, Mary Smith.>

guardian ad litem □see **guardian**.

guardianship □see **guardian**; □see also, **conservatorship**.

guest □see **licensee**, under **license**; □see **passenger**; □see also, **invitee**.

guest passenger □see **passenger**.

guidelines: more or less brief statements of policy about things trivial (e.g., office procedure) or important (e.g., sentencing criteria), presumed to be for general guidance, as distinguished from detailed compliance. Not a term of art. Frequent references to what guidelines "require" have turned a useful bit of vagueness into a first-class weasel.

guilt: the common Old English noun, the antonym of *innocence*.

guilty

1. the *plea* of a criminal defendant admitting commission of the offense charged. To be distinguished from:

nolo contendere (L., NO-lo con-TEN-duh-ree: I do not wish to contend), in legal slang, *nolo;* in colloquial English, *no contest:* the plea of a criminal defendant, neither admitting nor denying commission of the offense charged. In the prosecution in which the plea is *nolo contendere,* the legal consequences are the same as with a plea of *guilty.* In other proceedings, e.g., a civil action based on the same facts, the charges, uncontested in the criminal proceedings, may be denied.

not guilty: the plea of a criminal defendant that requires the prosecution to prove the commission of a criminal offense. The plea may echo righteous indignation or something less. Whatever the facts known to the defendant, whatever the indignation or moral accountability, the plea of *not guilty* is no more than a technical denial of the commission of the offense charged. "They pleaded *innocent*" is colloquial, not legal.

2. Alford plea: a special version of a plea of *guilty.* The defendant rejects "admitting commission of the offense" (sense 1) or the neutral indifference of *nolo contendere.* The defendant insists that he has not committed the criminal acts charged; but faced with strong evidence of guilt and the threat of a severe penalty, defendant enters an informed, counseled plea of *guilty,* in a bargain for a lesser penalty. E.g., in the case that gives the plea its name (*North Carolina v. Alford,* 400 U.S. 25, 1970), a negotiated plea of *guilty* to second degree murder (maximum thirty years) under threat of conviction of first degree murder (death). The Supreme Court rejected contentions that the plea was involuntary and the sentence unconstitutional. Jurisdictions vary on validity of an *Alford plea.*

3. the *general finding* (□see, under **finding**) of the trier of fact in a criminal prosecution that the defendant has committed an offense charged.

not guilty: the general finding that the prosecution has not proved commission of an offense charged. "They found the defendant *innocent*" is colloquial, not legal. □see also, **nullification**.

4. an adjective sometimes used to describe a state of mind with knowledge of something criminal or wrong, an imprecise usage. □see **mens rea**.

H

habeas: short for **habeas corpus** (□see). <The court denied habeas relief./The habeas petitioner asks . . .>

habeas corpus (L.: loosely, have the body): a writ (order) directing a jailer, a warden, or someone else who has a person in custody to bring the person before a court to inquire into the legality of the restraint, i.e., show that restraint is proper or release the prisoner. The writ of *habeas corpus* is the common means of obtaining release on **bail** (□see) <"Get me a writ.">or of challenging the constitutionality of a conviction.

habitability □see **covenant.**

habitual criminal □see **criminal,** under **convict.**

had and received: separately, *had* and *received* are synonyms. Joined, the redundancy is ignored in the traditional name of the common count for *money had and received.* □see **common count,** under **count.** □see also, **coupled synonyms.**

hand down • hand up: in legal argot, a judge *hands down* a **decision** (□see); a grand jury *hands up* an **indictment** (□see).

hand up □see **hand down.**

hanging judge: legal slang and colloquial English for a criminal judge regarded as being predisposed to convict and to sentence to death.

hanging jury • hung jury

    hanging jury: legal slang for a criminal jury regarded as being predisposed to convict and to vote for the death penalty. Especially, a jury from which prospective jurors who have expressed themselves as opposed to capital punishment have been systematically eliminated.

    hung jury: legal argot for a civil or criminal jury that cannot agree on a verdict. <They were hung 7 to 5 in our favor.> The *hung jury* is

hanging jury

the terminal stage of a **deadlocked jury**: one that has not been able to agree on a verdict. Sometimes a "hopelessly deadlocked" jury reaches a verdict after additional deliberation, with or without additional instruction (□see **Allen charge**, under **jury instructions**). If the deadlock is not broken, the jury is *hung*.

hang out a shingle   □see **shingle**.

harassment   □see **sex**.

hard-core pornography

1. In the ill-defined and constantly changing vocabulary of ordinary and legal English that classifies words, pictures, and other representations with sexual connotation, *hard-core pornography* is the imprecise catchphrase for what is regarded at the moment as the worst, the easiest to brand *illegal*. Starting with the mildest of epithets, a vague hierarchy includes stigmas that may or may not have sexual connotation: *vulgar* (unrefined); *offensive* (to right-thinking people); *indecent* (e.g., unzipped; too much cleavage); *obscene* (immoral one way or another, especially with regard to sex and excrement); *lewd* (intended to arouse sexually); *pornographic* (intended to arouse sexually). The crowning offensiveness is *hard-core pornography*: typically, the mechanics of sexual activity portrayed not as a matter of education or aesthetics but to sexually excite the beholder. It is *pornography* and nothing else. □see also, **pandering**.

2. the particular variety of *pornography* (sense 1) that clearly is not entitled to First Amendment protection. With sometimes annual and certainly geographical defining and redefining of *obscenity* that is denied First Amendment protection, *hard-core pornography,* still not a term of art, is beyond the pale. Even if not precise, at least negatively it serves to keep First Amendment protection for what is not *hard-core pornography*. The recurrent standard is Justice Stewart's disclaimer of definition, "But I know it when I see it. . . ." (*Jacobellis v. Ohio*, 378 U.S. 184, 197 (1964)). □see also, **I know it when I see it**.

harmless error: an error or defect in proceedings in or out of court, in pleadings, in other legal papers, that does not affect substantial rights and can be readily cured or disregarded. As distinguished from **fatal error** (□see, under **fatal**), **plain error** (□see), **prejudicial error** (□see), and **reversible error** (□see).

have and hold: joined together, an old and worthless redundancy. □see **coupled synonyms.** For special legal usage, □see **hold.**

have custody □see **custody.**

have notice □see **notice.**

head tax □see **poll tax.**

hearing: at the top of the hearing ladder, a court session for presentation and consideration of argument on an appeal. On down, a general designation for an almost infinite variety of legal proceedings of lesser scope and formality than a trial, for examination of facts and law by a judge, a specially designated official who is not a judge, an administrative or legislative committee, or a board. Some hearings result in definitive decisions: e.g., extradition, parole, zoning variance; some are investigative: e.g., on violence, drug abuse, corruption. Some hearings are independent of trial: e.g., prison discipline; **workers' compensation** (□see); cutting relief payments. Many hearings are adjunct to a trial: e.g., order to show cause why *temporary alimony* (□see **alimony**) should not be granted; citation for **contempt** (□see); application for *preliminary injunction* (□see **enjoin**); *preliminary hearing* to determine whether or not defendant should be tried for a criminal offense (□see **probable cause**). □see also, **fair hearing,** under **fair;** □see also, **rehearing;** □see also, **trial.**

hearing de novo □see **rehearing.**

hearsay: a statement (oral, written, body language, etc.), other than one made by the witness now testifying, that is offered to prove the truth of the statement. <The witness testifies, "I heard A say he was married." If A's statement is offered to prove that A was married, it is hearsay.>

hearsay objection: an objection made in court that evidence offered is inadmissible because it violates the *hearsay rule.*

hearsay rule: a rule of evidence that makes *hearsay* inadmissible in evidence, unless it comes within one of the many exceptions to the *hearsay rule.* The exceptions are explained in abundant detail in treatises and in law school courses on the law of evidence.

hearsay objection □see **hearsay.**

hearsay rule   □see **hearsay**.

hear ye   □see **formalisms**.

heat of passion: a state of such emotional intensity as to replace deliberate judgment by rash, unpremeditated response, provoked by circumstances that might similarly arouse a normally reasonable person. The expression *heat of passion* is used in the criminal law to describe an emotional state that might reduce a charge of murder to manslaughter. Sometimes, in slang, called *hot blood*.

heed and care   One or the other, not both together. *Heed* the warning; take *care*. □see **coupled synonyms**.

heir   □see **heirs**.

heirs • next of kin: those entitled by statute to have a dead relative's property that is not disposed of by a valid will. *Relative* refers to relationship by blood (consanguinity), marriage (affinity), and, with increasing frequency, to relationship by adoption. *Property* refers to real or personal property, or both. □see **intestate**; □see also, **inherit**, under **descend**.

In that common, generalized sense, *heirs* and *next of kin* are now synonyms. Synonyms, despite a long history of radical distinction that, e.g., reserved *heirs* for inheritance of real property, *next of kin* (nearest relatives) for inheritance of personal property, and restricted both expressions to blood relatives. Some of the old distinctions are perpetuated in enough statutes and decisions to give lawyers pause in determining the sense of conveyances and inheritance state by state. Except where changed by statute or decision, usage still separates the expressions in particular contexts:

collateral heir: one related by blood to a common ancestor but not in a direct line, e.g., a brother or a cousin. As opposed to a *lineal heir:* one related by blood in a direct line, e.g., a child, grandchild, grandparent. □see **descendant**.

laughing heirs: slang, for heirs so distantly related as to have no sense of bereavement.

lineal heir □see **collateral heir**, above, in this entry.

pretermitted heir: one who would inherit property if there had been no valid will and who has been unintentionally omitted (*pretermitted*) from a valid will. A parallel usage refers to a *pretermitted spouse,* a *pretermitted child.*

henceforth: from now on. □see **hereafter,** under **here–.**

here– These are the common *here*-compounds of Old and Middle English, unfit for anything other than a touch of nostalgia.

hereafter: after this. Uncertain as to when and where. Also uncertain as to duration, a vice it shares with **henceforth** (□see). Correlative of the equally worthless **heretofore** (□see).

hereby: by means of this (as in a writing). The whole or only part of the writing? Right now, or only after other things have been done? If detail is needed, supply it. *Hereby* is superfluous. <I hereby agree./ I agree.> For a companion in excess, □see **herewith.**

herein: in this. Where? This sentence, this paragraph, this contract, this statute? <As provided herein. . . .> *Herein* is the start of a treasure hunt rather than a helpful reference. The traditional additives are equally vague:

hereinabove: above this. How far?

hereinbefore: before this. How much before?

hereinafter: after this. Where? When?

hereof: of this; concerning this. *Hereof* what? <The other provisions hereof. . . .>

hereto: to this. < . . . attached hereto/ . . . attached.>

heretofore: before this. Uncertain as to when and where. Correlative of the equally worthless **hereafter** (□see). □see also, **hitherto.**

hereunder: under this. *Hereunder* what? <As authorized hereunder./ As authorized by par. 10/this contract/this statute.>

herewith: with this or by means of this (as in a writing). <I enclose herewith. . . ./I enclose. . . .> Like **hereby** (□see), *herewith* is superfluous.

hereafter □see **here–.**

hereby □see **here–.**

herein □see **here–.**

hereinabove □see **here-**.

hereinafter □see **here-**.

hereinbefore □see **here-**.

hereof □see **here-**.

heretofore □see **here-**.

hereunder □see **here-**.

herewith □see **here-**.

high court □see **court**.

highjacking □see **hijacking**.

high seas: "[A]ll parts of the sea that are not included in the territorial sea or in the internal waters of a State." (Geneva Convention on the High Seas, April 29, 1958, 13 U.S.T. (U.S. Treaties and Other International Agreements) pt. 2 at pp. 2313, 2314, Art. 1; in force, Sept. 30, 1962). For a complex statement of *high seas*, refer to Part VII, Articles 86–116, pp. 85–116 in the United Nations Convention on the Law of the Sea, Dec. 10, 1982, cited in **law of the sea** (□see). And refer to Restatement (Third) Foreign Relations Law of the United States, vol. 2, pt. V, ch. 3, 1986. □see also, **airspace**; □see also, **maritime law**; □see also, **piracy**.

hijacker □see **hijacking**.

hijacking: illegal seizure of a moving vehicle or aircraft, directed at robbery of cargo (especially illegal cargo), kidnapping, or other crime. Now often associated with seizure and redirection of aircraft, also called *skyjacking*. □see **aircraft piracy**, under **piracy**. *Hijacking* is more often a popular than a legal term; not a term of art. Also spelled *highjacking*. One who *hijacks* is a *hijacker*.

hire (a person)   For *hire* (property), □see **lease**.

1.   to initiate a relationship of employer and employee, usually with employees who are to be paid wages (e.g., hourly, daily), as distinguished from a salary (e.g., monthly, more permanent, or compensation for higher paid employees).   Often used to indicate a *hiring at will,* i.e., duration as determined by the employer.   (□see also, **wrongful discharge**).   *Hire* is not a term of art, except as defined by particular statutes or in special contexts.

hiring hall: a job placement center, usually union-run, especially in industries characterized by irregular and short-time employment (e.g., maritime, longshoring, construction).

2.   to have an employer-employee relationship of the sort initiated in sense 1.   <They had a hired work force of five hundred men and women.>

3.   the relationship initiated in sense 1.   <It was a contract of hire.>

4.   hire a lawyer: the client's usual expression for *employing* or *retaining* a lawyer or *engaging* the services of a lawyer.   <We hired the law firm of Smith and Jones.>   Lawyers might prefer *retain* (□see **retained counsel**, under **lawyer**).   But any of these words can establish the unique relationship of attorney and client, different from the employee-employer relationship ordinarily created by *hire* (sense 1). *Hired gun* is much different (□see, under **lawyer**).

hire (property)   □see **lease**.

hire a lawyer   □see **hire (a person)**.

hire at will   □see **hire (a person)**.

hired gun   □see **lawyer**.

hiring hall   □see **hire (a person)**.

hit-and-run,   or *hit and run:* characterizing a statutory criminal offense in which a driver involved in an accident flees the scene without identifying himself or giving aid.   *Hit-and-run* (accident, auto, driver, insurance coverage, statute) is old baseball slang freely adapted to legal usage.

hitherto: until now. Another compound of Old and Middle English best discarded for uncertainty of reference to time. Is *now* included or excluded? □see also, **heretofore.**

Hobson's choice □see clichés.

hold

1. to have, i.e., own, property, especially real property. <She holds Blackacre in fee.> Variations are the relic *to have and to hold,* for long years a redundancy, along with to *hold and keep.* □see **coupled synonyms.** The person who *holds* the property is the *holder.* <She is the holder of the freehold.> For a more technical sense of *holder,* □see **holder (commercial law).**

2. to announce the precise issue or principle being decided by a court. <We now hold that. . . .> The precise issue or principle decided is the *holding,* as contrasted with **dictum** (□see). Sometimes *holding* is equated with **decision** (□see); to determine the value of a case as a precedent, the *holding* is more informative than the *decision.* <I know that the decision was for the plaintiff, but what did they decide? What was the holding in that case?>

3. **hold harmless**: to assume liability that another may incur. <Manufacturer agrees to hold Retailer harmless of liability to buyers for manufacturing defects./Lessee agrees to hold Lessor harmless of any liability for Lessee's failure to keep the premises in a safe condition.> Instead of *hold harmless,* lawyers sometimes use the synonymous expression *save harmless.*

> *hold harmless* is understood to protect another against the risk of loss as well as actual loss. Whether or not *hold harmless* includes defense of lawsuits is sufficiently uncertain to warrant detailed provision.

> *indemnify (indemnity)*

>> **a.** sometimes used as a synonym of *hold harmless.* The identity is made clearer in the expression *indemnify against liability.*

>> **b.** when distinguished from *hold harmless, indemnify:* to reimburse for any damage. This sense is spelled out as *indemnify against loss.*

> *indemnify and hold harmless:* a lawyer's hedge against the imprecision of both expressions, by including assumption of loss and liability. Defense of lawsuits still best spelled out.

> □see also, **equitable indemnity.**

4. hold in contempt □see **contempt.**

5. hold over □see **holdover tenant,** under **evict.**

6. holdover tenant, also spelled *hold-over tenant,* also spelled *hold over tenant.* □see **evict.**

hold and keep □see **hold.**

holder □see **hold.**

holder (commercial law) For *holder* (property law), □see **hold.**

1. a person as defined in UCC § 1–201(20). The section specifies both the form and the kind of legal paper that must be held to make one a holder. This is more an alarm than a definition; just enough to warn anyone not an expert to consult one.

2. The term-of-art "definition" of *holder* in the Uniform Commercial Code reads:

" 'Holder' means a person who is in possession of a document of title or an instrument or a certificated investment security drawn, issued, or indorsed to him or his order or to bearer or in blank." (UCC § 1–201(20)).

That is not much of a definition either. □see **holder in due course.** □see also, **commercial paper.**

holder in due course

1. in the law of *negotiable instruments* (□see **commercial paper**), a variety of **bona fide purchaser** (□see) who takes the instrument free of many defenses that would otherwise affect the instrument. That is as much as anyone but an expert in negotiable instruments need know, and as much or more than most lawyers in other fields know, or want to know.

2. The term-of-art "definition" of *holder in due course* in the Uniform Commercial Code reads:

"A holder in due course is a holder who takes the instrument (a) for value; and (b) in good faith; and (c) without notice that it is overdue or has been dishonored or of any defense against or claim to it on the part of any person." (UCC § 3–302(1)).

That "definition" is unintelligible without detailed study of statute and case law on *holder, value, good faith, notice, overdue, dishonored, defenses,* and *claims.* Thus, it is not a definition but an index to selected portions of the law of negotiable instruments, beyond the scope of this dictionary. □see **commercial paper**; □see **due**.

hold harmless   □see **hold**.

hold in contempt   □see **contempt**.

holding   □see **hold**; □see also, **personal holding company**.

hold over   □see **holdover tenant**, under **evict**.

holdover tenant   also spelled *hold-over tenant,* also spelled *hold over tenant.* □see **evict**.

holographic will: a witnessed or unwitnessed will signed and hand-written by the person whose will it is. Under some statutes, "hand-written" applies to the whole will; under others, only to "material portions."

homestead: a family residence (land and buildings) with statutory exemptions from execution. □see also, **declaration**. □see also, **pre-emption right**.

homicide: the generic term for the killing of one person by another. Popular usage, influenced by detective fiction (e.g., *homicide squad, homicidal*), tends to consider *homicide* at least criminal if not identical with murder. For the law, *homicide* has no precise technicality and may be a lawful or unlawful killing. For the sense of *homicide* that is unlawful, refer to specific crimes, e.g., **murder** (□see), **man-slaughter** (□see). For *excusable homicide* and *justifiable homicide,* □see **justification**. Insurance policy mention of unadorned *homicide* is a recurrent source of litigation.

Hon.:   abbreviation of *Honorable,* □see **Honor**.

honor   (v.)

1. Upon formal request, a person, usually a bank, pays or agrees to pay out money in accordance with the provisions of a *negotiable instrument* (□see **commercial paper**) or of a *credit,* better known as **letter of credit** (□see). This is a rough rendering of a very technical term of art, complicated by the fact that the apparent negative *dishonor* is not a precise reciprocal. See sense 2.

2. The term-of-art "definition" of *honor* in the Uniform Commercial Code reads:

> "To 'honor' is to pay or to accept and pay, or where a credit so engages to purchase or discount a draft complying with the terms of the credit." (UCC § 1–201(21)).

That "definition," like the definition of **holder in due course** (□see), is unintelligible without detailed study of the statute and case law of *negotiable instruments* (in this case, especially the intricacies of *presentment, acceptance,* and *payment*), plus an examination of the unsettled law of *letters of credit.* The search for definition of *honor* is even less satisfactory if one looks for an antonym: "They *did not honor*" is not the same as "They *dishonored.*" □see **dishonor**.

In short, for *honor,* look for an expert, not a dictionary.

Honor (n.): a formal term of oral address or reference to a judge. <Your Honor, our position is. . . ./His Honor, Joseph Smith, judge presiding./Her Honor, Jane Smith, judge presiding.> □see also, **formalisms**.

Honorable (adj.); also *honorable:* like *Honor,* an oral reference to a judge <The Honorable . . .> □see **formalisms**; □see also, **courts**. *Honorable,* usually in the abbreviated form *Hon.,* is also a common written prefix to a judge's name in an address, a listing, etc. <Hon. Mary Jones, Judge of the Superior Court.>

Honorable □see **Honor**.

horizontal privity □see **privity**.

hornbook law □see **black letter law**.

horse case □see **on all fours**.

hostile □see **adverse possession**, under **possession**.

hostile witness: a loose characterization of a witness whose attitude is at least unfriendly, if not outright antagonistic, toward the lawyer asking the questions or toward the party who has called the witness to testify. The expression distinguishes *hostile witness* from the even looser *friendly witness,* and sometimes alternates synonymously with *unfriendly witness, unwilling witness,* or **adverse witness** (□see). The label *hostile witness,* requested by the examining lawyer, if approved by the judge, permits greater freedom in examining the witness, a liberality stated variously as in the nature of *cross-examination* (□see, under **cross-**), permission to ask **leading questions** (□see), and permission to **impeach** (□see) one's own witness where not otherwise permitted under local rules.

adverse witness: a witness whose testimony is, or may be expected to be, opposed to the position of the party calling or examining the witness. Sometimes a synonym for **hostile witness** (□see). Increasingly, more specifically identified not as *adverse witness* but as "an *adverse party,* or . . . *identified with an adverse party,*" permitting (as with a *hostile witness*) the use of leading questions. (See Federal Rules of Evidence, Rule 611(c).)

hot blood □see **heat of passion.**

hot cargo: a union anathema on products produced or services rendered under circumstances the union considers inimical to its interests, e.g., produced by nonunion employers. Use of the anathema (blacklisting) is a continuing topic of collective bargaining and restrictive legislation.

hotchpot: an ancient description become a metaphor for mixing things into a common pot or ownership. In the law, the old metaphor is now most commonly applied to a distribution of intestate property in shares that take into account **advancements.**

advancement: a gift (typically parent to child) by a live donor who intends that if the donor dies intestate, the lifetime gift will reduce the donee's share of the estate.

Applying *hotchpot:* A mother dies intestate leaving $100,000 and only two heirs, her children A and B. During her lifetime, the mother made an advancement to A of $50,000. If A chooses to share in the estate, A's advancement is *put into hotchpot,* a hypothetical $150,000, consisting of the $50,000 A has already received plus the $100,000 left in the estate. Of the $100,000 in the estate, A's share is $25,000 and B's share is $75,000.

hot pursuit □see **fresh pursuit.**

housebreaking □see **breach.**

house counsel □see lawyer.

hung jury □see **hanging jury**.

husband-wife privilege: a label for two distinct privileges, neither generally available over the objection of a husband or wife harmed by the other:

1. also known as the **marital communications privilege**: the right of husband or wife to refuse to disclose, and to prevent the other from disclosing, confidential communications between them during the course of the marriage.

2. the right of husband or wife not to be a witness against the other on trial for crime, and the right of the one on trial to prevent the other from being an adverse witness.

hybrid representation □see **right to counsel**.

I

ICC: abbreviation of Interstate Commerce Commission. □see **administrative agency,** under **administrative law**.

idem sonans (L., EYE-dem SO-nans: sounding the same)

1. names, or a reference to names, that as spelled (correctly or incorrectly) sound substantially the same. <Louis is *idem sonans* with Lewis./Yougn and Young have been held to be *idem sonans*.>

2. a rule or doctrine: if instead of an intended correct name one uses an incorrect name that is *idem sonans* (sense 1), the variance alone is not material. Applied to writings (e.g., indictment, pleading, contract), proceedings (e.g., rendering a verdict), or activity (e.g., engaging in a business or profession). <Under the rule of *idem sonans,* the indictment was valid despite the misspelling of the defendant's name.>

if the court please □see **court**.

I know it when I see it: rapidly becoming a **cliché** (□see) as a too confident assertion that this is just what the law is talking about, whether the facts of pornography or something else. So used, and overused, it distorts both the sense and words of a most literate justice. Declining to delimit **hard-core pornography** (□see), diffident about being able to, Justice Potter Stewart wrote, "But I know it when I see it, and the motion picture involved in this case is not that." (*Jacobellis v. Ohio,* 378 U.S. 184, 197 (1964)).

illegal • unlawful

In the general sense of what is *contrary to law,* these words are synonyms. **Illegal** and **unlawful** stand together, separated by long tradition from lesser, specialized forms of contrariness:

illegitimate, usually in the combination *illegitimate child.* □see **filiation proceeding**.

illicit: either illegal (unlawful) because not licensed (*illicit drugs, illicit beverages*), or viewed at least with raised eyebrows if not subject to prosecution (*illicit sex*). □see also, **cohabitation**.

As with many other law words, interchangeable use of *illegal* and *unlawful* stems from the old mixture of Latin and French (*legal*) into the mainstream of English (*law;* □see **lawful**). And it's too late to outlaw either of them.

Uniform choice of one word over the other is a rarity. **Unlawful assembly** (□see) is one; *unlawful detainer* is another. □see **forcible entry and detainer.** Lawyers favor *illegal consideration* and *illegal contract* over a sometime usage of *unlawful* in both instances.

Attempts at generalized distinction between what is contrary to specific prohibition (*illegal*) and what is grandly or morally contrary to law (*unlawful*) fall apart against an unrationalized choice of one word or another in statutes and legal writing generally. The widest range of activities are condemned by both words: accumulations, arrests, combinations in restraint of trade, gambling, picketing, practice of law, search and seizure, sentencing, etc. There is no organized lobby for consistency; the best one can hope for is consistency within the same writing.

illegal consideration   □see **illegal;** □see also, **contract.**

illegal contract   □see **illegal;** □see also, **contract.**

illegitimate   □see **legitimate;** □see also, **illegal.**

illegitimate child   □see **filiation proceeding.**

illicit   □see **illegal.**

illusory contract: something that looks or sounds like a **contract** (□see) but isn't, because it contains an **illusory promise:** an apparent promise that promises nothing. E.g., "I promise to give you a house if I want to."

illusory promise   □see **illusory contract.**

immaterial (evidence)

1. a fading description of evidence of no substantial significance to the outcome of a lawsuit, the opposite of **material,** and now swallowed up by **irrelevant.** □see **relevant.**

2. part of a once popular general objection to the admissibility of evidence. □see **incompetent, irrelevant, immaterial,** under **incompetent.**

immunity • privilege   In ordinary English and in ordinary legal usage, both of these words speak of a freedom, right, or exemption not enjoyed by others.   **Immunity**: a *freedom from* what burdens others, is separated by a hair from **privilege**: a *right not to do* what others must and separated by two hairs from **privilege**: a *right to do* what others may not.   □see also, **license**.   Close to synonymity, *immunity* and *privilege* frequently trade places, and readily satisfy the law's craving for redundancy, as in "the immunity privilege" (Corwin, *The Constitution,* 1973 ed., 24).   □see **Privileges and Immunities Clauses**.

For the generalized role of **privilege** as an expression of social values that might free one from tort liability, consult the substantive law of torts.   For special property law definitions, *Restatement of Property,* § 2 (*privilege*) and § 4 (*immunity*); better yet, the Hohfeldian analysis in 23 *Yale Law Journal* 16–59 (1913) and 26 *Yale Law Journal* 710–770 (1917).   This entry deals with the sometime preference of one word or the other in specific usage, choices more a matter of habit than reason.

immunity

absolute immunity: a general and imprecise label for freedom from liability for acts in the course of official conduct.   The expression must be taken with the skepticism due **absolutes** (□see); some *absolute immunities* are more absolute than others.   *Absolute immunity* usually refers to immunity from liability for civil damages, sometimes from both civil and criminal liability.   *Absolute immunity* takes on intelligible sense only when spelled out in reference to particular officials and particular conduct (see below) and to federal or state law.   *Absolute immunity* is not always, but usually, set apart from areas of immunity covered by **absolute privilege** (□see).   Frequently, *absolute immunity* is simply an expression of contrast with *qualified immunity*.

qualified immunity: as contrasted with the greater immunity of *absolute immunity,* a limited freedom from civil damages for acts in the course of official conduct.   Dependent not only on the variables that beset *absolute immunity* but additionally (and variously stated) on the acts being reasonable, in good faith, without malice, and not clearly in violation of statutory or constitutional rights.

executive immunity:

1.   a *qualified immunity* from liability for acts in the course of official conduct by officers of the executive branch of government, other than the President of the United States (see sense 2).   *Executive immunity* is distinguished from **judicial immunity**

(□see, below, in this entry) and **legislative immunity** (□see, below, in this entry). The expression is applied not only to chief executives (e.g., governor of a state) but by statute or decision to other executives and officers, federal, state, and local. Sometimes limited to conduct that involves *discretionary* (e.g., when to call out the National Guard), as opposed to *ministerial* (e.g., routine issue of a license) functions.

2. the *absolute immunity* of the President of the United States from liability for civil damages for acts in the course of the conduct of that office. (Whether the immunity would survive imposition of liability by Congress is uncertain. See *Nixon v. Fitzgerald,* 457 U.S. 731 (1982).) *Executive immunity,* as applied to the President, is also sometimes called **presidential immunity**, as contrasted with **presidential privilege**, usually referred to as **executive privilege** (□see, below, in this entry).

governmental immunity □see **sovereign immunity**, below, in this entry.

grant of immunity from prosecution: a device, and its use, to compel the testimony of a witness who could otherwise refuse to testify under a claim of the **privilege against self-incrimination** (□see, under **criminate**). The *grant of immunity* is of two sorts:

transactional immunity: a *grant of immunity from prosecution* for a crime to which the testimony relates.

use immunity: a *grant of immunity from a prosecution* that directly or indirectly uses the compelled testimony or information derived from that testimony. Unlike *transactional immunity, use immunity* does not bar a prosecution for a crime to which the testimony relates, if the prosecution is based on evidence obtained independently of the compelled testimony.

immunity from prosecution □see **grant of immunity from prosecution**, above, in this entry.

immunize (v., adj.): to *grant immunity from prosecution.* <The witness was immunized and proceeded to testify./ . . . the immunized testimony.>

intergovernmental immunity: the freedom of the federal and state governments from interference by the other, as determined by the Constitution and decisions of the U.S. Supreme Court. The expression is used especially with reference to the taxing power. □see also, **sovereign immunity**, below, in this entry.

interspousal immunity: a shrinking prohibition of tort actions between husband and wife.

judicial immunity: the *absolute immunity* of a judge from liability for civil damages for decisions and other "judicial acts," right or wrong, malicious or not, while acting as a judge. "Judicial acts," also called "adjudicative functions," not precisely defined. Have been distinguished from "administrative, legislative, or executive functions" of a judge, to which the immunity does not extend. E.g., damages for sex discrimination in violation of federal civil rights statute, in state judge's discharge of a probation officer. (*Forrester v. White*, 484 U.S. 219, 1988).

quasi-judicial immunity: an *absolute immunity* of officials from liability for civil damages for acts similar to the discretionary judicial acts of judges judging: e.g., administrators while adjudicating claims or deciding whether or not to start administrative proceedings against someone. □see also, **prosecutorial immunity**, below, in this entry.

legislative immunity: the *absolute immunity* of legislators and their assistants from civil or criminal liability for legislation, and for the debate, voting, reports, and incidental acts in legislative sessions. For the federal government, the substance of the immunity, but not the expression, is derived from the U.S. Constitution, Article I, § 6, the **Speech or Debate Clause** (□see); for state or local governments, from common law roots and local laws. Federal *legislative immunity* is sometimes used interchangeably, and confusingly, with **legislative privilege** (□see, below, in this entry).

official immunity: a generalized reference to the different sorts of immunity of various public officers.

presidential immunity □see **executive immunity**, above, in this entry; □see also, **executive privilege**, below, in this entry.

prosecutorial immunity, also referred to as the **quasi-judicial immunity** (□see **judicial immunity**, above, in this entry) of the prosecutor: the prosecutor's *absolute immunity* from liability for civil damages for acts connected with the decision to prosecute and with presenting the prosecution case, whether or not accompanied by illegality or malice. <In participating in a police raid, the district attorney did not enjoy prosecutorial immunity, at most a qualified immunity.>

qualified immunity □see **absolute immunity**, above, in this entry.

quasi-judicial immunity □see **judicial immunity**, above, in this entry.

sovereign immunity: an ill-defined freedom of the sovereign from suit without its consent. It is a changing matter of common law and constitutional interpretation (especially of Article III, Eleventh Amendment, and Fourteenth Amendment), numerous statutes consenting to suit, and local law in the states, some denying the existence of the immunity.

governmental immunity: sometimes equated with *sovereign immunity,* more often a *qualified immunity* of government and governmental agencies from suit for tort claims, except as permitted by statute or decision.

privilege

Usage of *privilege* included in this entry directly overlaps *immunity* in sense or form. Other usage of the word *privilege* is cataloged at the end of this entry but is entered alphabetically in the dictionary.

absolute privilege

1. sometimes used interchangeably with *absolute immunity.*

2. freedom from liability for defamation in the course of judicial, legislative, and executive proceedings and communications. It is a defense to an action for defamation, available generally to those officially involved in the proceedings. Under some statutes and decisions, the absolute quality is watered down by other requirements, e.g., that the words be relevant to the business at hand.

3. a right not to disclose something.

conditional privilege, also called **qualified privilege,** as contrasted with the greater freedom of *absolute privilege:*

1. sometimes used interchangeably with *qualified immunity.*

2. freedom from liability for defamation, dependent on conditions that vary with statute and decision, commonly: (a) good faith and lack of malice in a communication to someone having a common interest; (b) a fair report, especially in the media, of public proceedings. (Note: the separate question of lack of liability for defamation as dependent on constitutional protection of free speech, sometimes referred to as *qualified privilege,* sometimes as a *constitutional privilege,* is in flux and beyond the scope of this dictionary.)

courtroom privilege □see **judicial proceedings privilege,** below, in this entry.

executive privilege, sometimes called **presidential privilege:** a *qualified (conditional) privilege,* the right of the President of the United States to withhold documents under his control, despite demand or order from Congress or the courts. Limits of the privilege not precisely defined, but matter relevant to a criminal prosecution not privileged. (*U.S. v. Nixon*, 418 U.S. 683 (1974)). □see **government secrets privilege**, below, in this entry.

government secrets privilege: the government's right to refuse to disclose or deliver information and documents whose secrecy is essential to an important government function, sometimes with the additional right to prevent disclosure or delivery by others. This is an amorphous, much interpreted category of privileges, some common law, some statutory, federal and state. Included are military and diplomatic secrets of state, agency policy deliberations, law enforcement investigation, and identity of an informer. The *government secrets privilege* is generally a *qualified privilege;* and even where said to be *absolute* (e.g., military and diplomatic secrets), circumscribed by judicial discretion for protection of constitutional rights of those on trial.

judicial proceedings privilege

1. as distinguished from judicial immunity, this is specifically a freedom from liability for defamation for what goes on in the courtroom. Applies generally to those involved in judicial proceedings—judge, lawyers, witnesses, jurors, etc. Generally described as an *absolute privilege,* but statutes vary, some imposing a condition of relevancy. Sometimes also called the **courtroom privilege**.

2. as an extension of sense 1, also applied to words written or oral directly related to proceedings in the courtroom (e.g., pleadings) or in anticipation of the courtroom (e.g., a lawyer's demand letter).

legislative privilege

1. sometimes used interchangeably with *legislative immunity.* To the extent that *debate* is free of civil liability, including defamation, an *absolute privilege.*

2. the very restricted freedom from arrest of United States senators and representatives. "They shall in all cases, except treason, felony and breach of peace, be privileged from arrest during their attendance at the session of their respective houses, and in going to and returning from the same. . . ." (U.S. Const., Art. I, § 6). Leaves the privilege applicable only to arrest in civil suits.

presidential privilege □see **executive privilege**, above, in this entry.

qualified privilege □see **conditional privilege**, above, in this entry.

For other usage of *privilege,* not an exhaustive list:

◻see **attorney-client privilege;**

◻see **clergyman-penitent privilege,** under **priest-penitent privilege;**

◻see **clergyman's privilege,** under **priest-penitent privilege;**

◻see **clergy-penitent privilege,** under **priest-penitent privilege;**

◻see **confidential communications privilege;**

◻see **doctor-patient privilege,** under **physician-patient privilege;**

◻see **husband-wife privilege;**

◻see **journalist's privilege,** under **newsmen's privilege;**

◻see **marital communications privilege,** under **husband-wife privilege;**

◻see **newsmen's privilege;**

◻see **patient-physician privilege,** under **physician-patient privilege;**

◻see **physician-patient privilege;**

◻see **priest-penitent privilege;**

◻see **privilege against self-incrimination,** under **criminate;**

◻see **privileged communication;**

◻see **privilege of self-defense,** under **self-defense;**

◻see **reporter-source privilege,** under **newsmen's privilege;**

◻see **testimonial privilege;**

◻see **work product privilege.**

immunity from prosecution   ◻see **grant of immunity from prosecution,** under **immunity.**

immunize   ◻see **immunity.**

impanel   ◻see **jury panel.**

impeach   (v.) and impeachment (n.) are entered here in their common legal contexts. For the real property usage, *impeachment of waste,* ◻see **waste.**

impeach

1. impeach a verdict: to discredit a verdict by evidence that it was improperly arrived at. □see **chance verdict**, under **verdict;** □see **compromise verdict**, under **verdict;** □see **quotient verdict.**

2. impeach a witness: to discredit a witness's testimony, by examination of the witness or by other evidence tending to show that the witness is not to be believed. <The *impeachment* of the witness proceeded first by cross-examination and then by *impeaching evidence* of a recent conviction of perjury./The witness left the stand, thoroughly *impeached.*>

3. impeachment (of officials): a formal accusation by a designated public body charging high public officials or judges with misconduct in office. Under the U.S. Constitution, the House of Representatives has the "*power of impeachment*" (Art. I, § 2, cl. 5), the Senate the power to "*try all impeachments*" (Art. I, § 3, cl. 6). Thus, one may be *impeached*, i.e., charged with "treason, bribery, or other high crimes and misdemeanors" (Art. II, § 4), but not *convicted.*

impeach a verdict □see **impeach.**

impeach a witness □see **impeach.**

impeachment (of officials) □see **impeach.**

impeachment of waste □see **waste.**

implead □see **third party practice**, under **party.**

impleader □see **third party practice**, under **party.**

implied □see **imply.**

implied actual notice □see **notice.**

implied authority □see **agency.**

implied bias □see **bias.**

implied contract □see **quasi contract.**

implied covenant □see **covenant.**

implied easement □see easement.

implied equitable servitude □see easement.

implied-in-fact □see quasi contract.

implied-in-law □see quasi contract.

implied knowledge □see knowledge.

implied malice □see malice.

implied notice □see notice.

implied powers □see enumerated powers.

implied promise □see quasi contract.

implied warranty □see warranty.

imply • infer

Grammarians have insisted for years that speakers and writers *imply*, i.e., say something by indirection, and that from what they say, hearers and readers *infer*, i.e., deduce or figure out some logical sense. <He didn't come right out and say it, but he implied that I was a thief./From what he said and didn't say, I inferred that he was calling me a thief.> Despite that insistence, the words are often used interchangeably, but the good English people wince when this occurs. Lawyers frequently use the two words in ways that satisfy the most fastidious. <That provision was not express, but it was certainly *implied* by the language used./The only *inference* we can draw from that is . . .> □see **presume**; □see **presumption**.

The language of the law also has distinctive uses for *imply*, especially in the form *implied*, that go beyond standard or nonstandard usage of ordinary English. The legal *imply* is a marvelous word for filling in gaps in the law and in the written creatures of the law. There is no stock remedy for that? *Imply* one, i.e., *create* one. Something missing in this contract to carry out its intent or what the law considers fair? *Imply* it, i.e., *read into it* what is missing. Without a unifying statement of principle that ties together all of the distinctive legal usage of

301

imply, lawyers have a working vocabulary of specific *implieds,* some of them controversial. Some of the *implieds* are solid matters of express law that distinguish an *implied* something from something else; some are creatures of circumstance and particular judges. Potential uses are almost infinite; here is a representative sampling:

implied actual notice □see **notice**;

implied authority □see **agency**;

implied bias □see **bias**;

implied contract □see **quasi contract**;

implied covenant □see **covenant**;

implied easement □see **easement**;

implied equitable servitude □see **easement**;

implied-in-fact □see **quasi contract**;

implied-in-law □see **quasi contract**;

implied knowledge □see **knowledge**;

implied malice □see **malice**;

implied notice □see **notice**;

implied powers □see **enumerated powers**;

implied promise □see **quasi contract**;

implied warranty □see **warranty**.

Import–Export Clause: the part of the U.S. Constitution reading: "No state shall, without the consent of the Congress, lay any imposts or duties on imports or exports, except what may be absolutely necessary for executing its inspection laws. . . ." (Art. I, § 10, cl. 2). □see also, **constitutional clauses**.

impossibility deserves notice here to disabuse any who are tempted to believe that legal usage approaches the precision of the physical sciences. Rather, like other **absolutes** (□see), *impossibility* and *impossible* in the law have the flexibility of common English usage. <As a practical matter, it was impossible.> Recurrent use of *impossibility,* as in the phrase *impossibility of performance,* does not point to refined term of art but to the frequency of the law's encounter with reality.

impossibility of performance □see **impossibility**.

impossible □see **impossibility**.

impression, case of first □see at **first blush**.

imprisonment: old, persistent, and misleading usage, echoing the sound of *prison*, but referring to a wide range of involuntary restraint, rather than the place of restraint, unless that is specified. Broad enough to include arrest without jailing, confinement in a local jail or in a state penitentiary, etc.

> **false imprisonment**, also called **false arrest:** an intentional, unlawful restraint of a person, without consent and for an appreciable time; the tort, and the action for redress of that grievance.

imputed disqualification □see **vicarious disqualification**.

imputed knowledge □see **knowledge**.

imputed negligence □see **negligence**.

imputed notice □see **notice**.

inadequacy of remedy at law □see **equitable remedy**, under **equity**.

inadequate remedy at law □see **equitable remedy**, under **equity**.

inadmissible: not admissible over objection. □see **evidence**.

in bank: a little used substitute for the traditional *en banc*. □see **bench**.

in being, a common English rendering of the Latin *in esse:* existing.

> 1. (of humans): referring to someone alive; or to an unborn child later born alive (□see **en ventre sa mère**, under **child**). Enshrined in the enduring phrases of property law, **life in being** and **lives in being**, keystone of the **rule against perpetuities** (□see). Despite historic preeminence in property law, perhaps because of that antique aroma, *in being* and *in esse* are little used in other references to the born or unborn, in tort law, or in what might be considered a natural habitat—the continuing controversy over abortion.

2. **not in being; not in esse**: occasionally refer to what will be a corporation, but is not yet, or to personal property not yet *existing goods.* <Incorporation was not complete; the corporation was still not in being./The toys were not then *in esse.*>

in blank   □see **indorse.**

in camera • in chambers

> **in camera**   (L.: literally, in chamber) is customarily translated **in chambers**, both expressions referring to a judge's private quarters off the courtroom.   Both expressions suggest the contrast between that privacy and the openness of the courtroom.   Sometimes used interchangeably, *in chambers* more often refers to the physical fact of the judge being *in chambers,* not *on the bench* (□see **bench**). What goes on in those chambers is more often referred to as being *in camera: in camera proceedings,* inspection of documents *in camera, in camera* interrogation of jurors, an *in camera hearing;* all of these stress the fact that the proceedings are not in open court, not in the presence of a jury, sometimes not in the presence of counsel.

in camera hearing   □see **in camera.**

in camera proceedings   □see **in camera.**

incest: the crime of marriage or sexual intercourse between those so closely related that marriage between them is prohibited.   Definition varies by jurisdiction.

in chambers   □see **in camera.**

in chief   □see **cross-examination, under cross-.**

inchoate   □see **choate.**

inchoate lien   □see **choate;** □see also, **lien.**

incidental beneficiary   □see **beneficiary.**

incidental damages   □see **damage.**

incidental powers □see **enumerated powers.**

included offense: an offense that is necessarily committed when one commits another offense. *Included offense* also goes by longer names: **lesser included offense** and **necessarily included offense;** they mean the same thing. E.g., robbery is an included offense in **armed robbery.**

inclusio unius est exclusio alterius □see **expressio unius est exclusio alterius.**

income □see **tax.**

incompatability: a flexible characterization of a severe inability of husband and wife to get along together, and so a ground for divorce, especially *no-fault divorce.* □see **divorce.**

Incompatability Clause: the part of the U.S. Constitution reading: ". . . no person holding any office under the United States, shall be a member of either house during his continuance in office." (Art. I, § 6, par. 2, cl. 2). □see also, **constitutional clauses.**

incompetence □see **incompetent.**

incompetency □see **incompetent.**

incompetent (adj.): the condition of not being **competent.** A person who is not *competent* is an **incompetent** (n.). The general noun for the condition of not being competent is **incompetency.** *Incompetency* and *incompetence* are sometimes regarded as synonyms, sometimes as alternate spellings. In legal usage, *incompetency* is most common in all senses, *incompetence* preferred by some in reference to lack of mental qualification. The positive forms are *competency, competence,* and *competent* (only as an adj.). The major entry is *incompetent,* rather than *competent,* because specifically legal usage most often revolves around questions of the negative state.

1. the common English sense of lacking in qualification, ordinary or special, physical, mental, or technical, is also the basic legal sense. <A hearing was held to determine competency to conduct the ordinary affairs of life./She was found to be an incompetent, and a guardian was appointed./An incompetent lawyer. . . .>

305

incompetent

2. special applications of sense 1 in the law of evidence:

incompetency (of a witness): characterization of the varying common law or statutory technical disqualifications of a person from testifying; e.g., a juror cannot sit as a juror and testify as a witness in the same case.

incompetent (evidence): inadmissible under the **rules of evidence** (□see).

incompetent, irrelevant, immaterial: a joining of the general objection of inadmissibility (*incompetent*) in a jumble of disparate notions of what is **immaterial** (□see) and what is *irrelevant* (□see **relevant**). Once popular, still heard, not technical.

in contemplation of death □see **gift in contemplation of death, under gift.**

in contempt □see **contempt.**

in contempt of court □see **contempt.**

incontestability clause □see **incontestable clause.**

incontestable clause: typically, in a policy of life or disability insurance. A provision that after a specified time, the insurer cannot cancel the policy because of various misstatements made by the insured in applying for the policy. Not all misstatements are incontestable; for details, consult insurance law. An *incontestable clause* is also called an *incontestability clause* and a *noncontestable clause.* None of those is to be confused with a *no contest clause;* □see **in terrorem.**

incorporate □see **corporate.**

incorporated □see **due.**

incorporation: forming a corporation. □see **corporate;** □see also, **organization.**

incorporation by reference: referring to a group of words (e.g., a contract, a paragraph, a recorded document) not otherwise part of this piece of writing, and stating in writing that that group of words is

306

now part of this writing. <The A & B agreement of 1–5–87 contained this sentence: "Our Building Agreement of 12–5–86 is attached as Exhibit 'A' and made part of this agreement." That was a sufficient incorporation by reference./ All of the allegations of paragraphs 1, 2, and 3 of plaintiff's first cause of action are incorporated here by reference.>

incorporeal □see **corporate;** □see also, **intangible property**.

incorporeal hereditament: in a loose, general way, intangible property that can be inherited as real property. Pronounced, if at all, incor-POR-e-al hair-uh-DIT-uh-ment.

Incorporeal hereditament is a remnant of medieval property law reeking of primogeniture and exotic property rights now largely of historical interest, e.g., an advowson (a right to nominate a parson to a particular church), a common of turbary (a right to cut turf), a common of estovers (a right to cut timber), etc. Shorn of medieval significance and utility, the name *incorporeal hereditament* is a needless and confusing survivor. Sometimes applied, without uniform usage, to property rights that have other names, e.g., **easements** (□see) and **profits** (□see **profit à prendre**).

in court □see **court**.

incriminate □see **criminate**.

incumber □see **encumber**.

incumbrance □see **encumbrance**.

in custodia legis □see **custody**.

in custody □see **custody**.

in custody of the law □see **custody**.

in default □see **default**.

indefinite failure of issue □see **issue,** under **descendant**.

indemnify □see **hold harmless**, under **hold**.

indemnity □see **hold harmless**, under **hold**.

indenture: an old name for an *agreement* (the piece of paper) or a **deed** (□see) signed by more than one party. Still used to describe various forms of financing documents, e.g., a corporate indenture, a trust indenture.

independent commission □see **administrative agency**, under **administrative law**.

independent contractor: a person who is engaged to accomplish a specified result and who controls and has the responsibility for the means to that end. E.g., a lawyer, doctor, builder. Contrasted with those whose conduct in doing a job is subject to the direction and control of another, e.g., *servant, employee,* and, usually, *agent.* □see **agency.** Local rules on tort liability, workers' compensation, etc., can affect the determination of status, *independent contractor* or something else. □see also, **master and servant.**

independent counsel □see **lawyer**.

indeterminate sentence □see **sentence**.

Indian law: a collective of convenience for a vast, undefined body of law relating to those called "Indians" in the laws and treaties of the United States and in the laws of the several states.

Varying definitions of *Indian* is but one of the complications in the lack of uniform definition of *Indian law*. Who is an *Indian* varies by treaty, statute, decision, and usage—according to origin as aboriginals, blood lines, tribal membership, residence on reservations, land ownership, etc. *Indian law,* often called *American Indian law,* may refer to federal law specifically labeled "Indians" (see Title 25 USCA), to treaties between the United States and other states and with Indian nations, to tribal law, to problems of conflicting jurisdiction and sovereignty, to general law in the United States as it affects Indians, etc. Lack of precise definition may be a virtue.

indict □see **indictment**.

indictment • presentment • information: mechanisms for commencing a criminal prosecution for serious crimes, varying by jurisdiction.

> **indictment:** a formal written statement in which a *grand jury* charges a named person with commission of a specific crime. <The grand jury *returned/handed up* an indictment of A for the murder of B./ The grand jury *indicted* A for the murder of B.> The statement is prepared by the prosecutor for approval or rejection by the grand jury; when approved, it is the *indictment,* the charge made by the grand jury. The approval is sometimes still indicated by the grand jury's indorsement of the prosecutor's draft as *a true bill,* rejected by the indorsement *no bill, not a true bill, not found,* or *no true bill.*

> **presentment:** a near obsolete formal written statement in which a *grand jury* charges a named person with commission of a specific crime; unlike an *indictment* in that the statement is prepared by the grand jury without the intervention of a prosecutor. Where it still exists, the mechanism of the *presentment* is ignored or equated with an indictment (□see **Grand Jury Clause**) or becomes a direction to the prosecutor to prepare an indictment.

> **information:** a formal written statement in which a prosecutor charges a named person with commission of a specific crime. The *information* is the charge made by the prosecutor, without the intervention of a grand jury.

indigent: in law as in ordinary English, an imprecise reference to a person who is poor. "How poor" is a matter of substantive law for specific benefits, e.g., public welfare; **right to counsel** (□see); assistance of a *public defender* (□see **lawyer**); right to litigate **in forma pauperis** (□see).

indirect contempt □see **contempt.**

indirect damages □see **damage.**

indispensable party □see **necessary party,** under **party.**

individual □see **person.**

individual proprietorship □see **sole proprietorship.**

indorse

indorse □see **indorsement**.

indorsee □see **indorsement**. □see also, **-ee**.

indorsement

1. In its most general sense, *indorsement* is a signature added to the instrument by, or for, the *holder* of the instrument, as distinguished from a signature by someone who signs in some other capacity, e.g., as the drawer of a check. By *indorsing*, the holder becomes an *indorser*, secondarily liable for payment, e.g., if the indorsed check is *dishonored* (bounces). □see **commercial paper**; □see **holder**; □see **dishonor**.

Indorsements are divided into two basic categories, *indorsement in blank* (sense 2) and *special indorsement* (sense 3):

2. indorsement in blank, also called a **blank indorsement**: typically, consists of only a signature (sense 1), but is more generally described as an indorsement that does not name a particular person to whom the instrument is indorsed, i.e., no *indorsee;* and so the instrument is payable to **bearer.** The words "Pay to cash" or "Pay to bearer" followed by the signature (sense 1) are examples of indorsement in blank. □see **commercial paper**.

3. special indorsement: in addition to the signature (sense 1), the indorsement names a particular person, a **special indorsee**, "to whom or to whose order" the instrument is now payable. (UCC § 3–204(1)). The words "Pay A.B." or "Pay to the order of A.B." followed by the signature (sense 1) are examples of special indorsement.

For the effect of further language added to the two basic forms of indorsement, □see **without recourse**, under **nonrecourse**; for other language, refer to the Uniform Commercial Code.

indorsement in blank □see **indorsement**.

indorser □see **indorsement**.

inducement □see **colloquium**.

in due course □see **due**; □see also, **holder in due course**.

in effect □see **force and effect**.

Ineligibility Clause: the part of the U.S. Constitution reading: "No senator or representative shall, during the time for which he was elected, be appointed to any civil office under the authority of the United States, which shall have been created, or the emoluments whereof have been increased during such time. . . ." (Art. I, § 6). □see also, **constitutional clauses.**

in equity □see equity.

in equity and good conscience □see equity.

in esse □see in being.

in evidence □see evidence.

in extremis □see nuncupative will.

in fact □see facts.

infamous crime: the imprecise vestige of common law crimes that permanently marked the culprit with the stain of infamy. The name survives in some laws designating crimes affecting credibility or punishable by death or long imprisonment. E.g., the U.S. Constitution requirement of indictment for "a capital or otherwise infamous crime." (Amend. V). □see **Grand Jury Clause.** □see also, **indictment.**

infamous crime against nature □see crime against nature.

infancy defense □see child.

infant □see child.

infanticide □see child.

infant trespasser □see child.

infer □see imply; □see also, **presume;** □see also, **presumption.**

inference   □see **imply**; □see **presume**; □see **presumption**.

inferior court   □see **court**.

influence   □see **undue influence, under due**; □see **under the influence of**.

in forma pauperis   (L., in FOR–muh PAW–per–iss: loosely, as a poor person), in the expressions to appear, litigate, or proceed *in forma pauperis:* to litigate without usual liability for court costs and fees, sometimes with procedures simplified for economy, sometimes with a lawyer serving without fee or at public expense.   <Motion for leave to proceed *in forma pauperis* is granted.>

information   □see **indictment**.

information and belief: characterization of statements, especially in pleadings, that are not based on personal knowledge.   Commonly referred to as allegations on information and belief, or denials for lack of information or belief.

infraction: In addition to the ordinary English sense of violation, *infraction* is a species of minor offense not punishable by imprisonment, e.g., parking violations.

infringe   □see **infringement**.

infringer   □see **infringement**.

infringement: In addition to the ordinary English sense of violation of any rights, *infringement* especially refers to violations of **copyright** (□see), **patent** (□see), and **trademark** (□see).   The violator of these rights is distinguished as an **infringer**: one who *infringes*.   □see also, **piracy**; □see also, **plagiarism**.

in gross   □see **easement**.

in haec verba   (L., in HIKE verb-uh: in these words): verbatim.   <He pleaded the note *in haec verba*/verbatim.>

inherent powers: powers not dependent on specific grant, but possessed by an entity by its very nature because the powers are essential to the carrying out of required functions. E.g., the power of a court to manage the working of the judicial process, preserve order in the court, compel obedience to its orders, etc. *Inherent powers* is sometimes equated with *implied powers* (e.g., of a corporation, of an agent). The boundaries of *inherent powers* are not uniformly defined. Often controversial, especially as related to government and the courts, as in the assertion of *inherent powers* that might encroach upon or be restricted by specific powers, e.g., in constitutions, statutes, rules of court (*Chambers v. Nasco, Inc.*, 111 S.Ct. 2123, 1991). □see **enumerated powers.**

inherit □see **descend.**

inheritance □see **descend.**

inheritance tax □see **death taxes.**

in-house counsel □see **lawyer.**

initial director □see **director.**

in invitum (L.: against one's will): a fading bit of Latin, sometimes still used to describe proceedings (e.g., taxation) taken *without consent* of those affected; also occasionally in the expression a *trust in invitum;* □see **constructive trust,** under **trust.**

in jeopardy □see **double jeopardy.**

injunction □see **enjoin.**

injunction pendente lite □see **enjoin;** □see also, **lis.**

injunctive relief □see **enjoin;** □see also, **equity.**

injure □see **damage.**

injurious falsehood: the tort of publishing a false statement, knowing or reckless of its falsity, and causing pecuniary loss (not including damage to reputation) that was intended or should have been recognized as likely. Damage to reputation is the province of **defamation** (□see); otherwise, the losses here can affect the widest variety of business or other interests. As a newer designation of a tort, *injurious falsehood* includes the traditional torts for *disparagement of goods* and *disparagement of title* (for both, □see **disparagement**).

injury   □see **damage**.

in kind

1. in property, as distinguished from money.   <Short of cash but long on pigs, he repaid the loan in kind.>

2. in property or money of the same sort as received.   <The loan was made in U.S. dollars and was to be repaid in kind.>

in legal custody   □see **custody**.

in lieu   □see **in lieu of**.

in lieu and in place of   □see **in lieu of**.

in lieu of: instead of. That basic sense of *lieu* (F., through L., *locus:* place) the language of the law shares with ordinary usage; the older and more common English *instead of* works just as well.   <Payment by note in lieu of/instead of cash. . . ./A license fee in lieu of/instead of the statutory tax . . . .>   Long use of *lieu* in the law has perpetuated some variations and encouraged others that make ordinary English seem unimaginative:

in lieu (drop the *of*): as an *in lieu tax:* a tax instead of other taxes. Better yet—

lieu (drop both *in* and *of*) and get the same thing: as a *lieu tax:* a tax instead of other taxes. In the same pattern, *lieu lands:* lands instead of other lands.

Long and free use has also nurtured worthless repetition:

in lieu and in place of, with the elaborate variation—

in lieu, in place, instead, and in substitution of. By comparison—

in my stead and place is refreshing. Almost as good as *instead of me*. □see **coupled synonyms**.

in limine (L., in–LIM–in–e: at the threshold): a characterization of something done as a preliminary and not necessarily decisive of an issue.

motion in limine: typically, a pretrial motion made outside the presence of a jury to bar the opposition from offering or alluding to evidence said to be both inadmissible and prejudicial, e.g., a prior conviction. A *motion in limine* may also be made during the course of a trial; and may be designed to clear the decks of anticipated matters regarded as irrelevant. The order granting or denying a *motion in limine* is itself *in limine* (an *order in limine,* an *in limine ruling*); the motion may be renewed and the order changed after further proceedings.

in loco parentis (L.: in the place of a parent): the relationship to another's child of an adult who, without adoption of the child, voluntarily assumes obligations incident to the natural parental relationship. <She did not stand *in loco parentis* merely because of the stepparent-stepchild relationship./The long history of their living together as a family was evidence of an *in loco parentis* relationship.> □see **surrogate parent**, under **parent**.

in my stead and place □see **in lieu of.**

innocence □see **guilt**; □see also, **beyond a reasonable doubt.**

innocent □see **guilty**; □see also, **beyond a reasonable doubt.**

innuendo □see **colloquium.**

in open court □see **open court,** under **open.**

in pais □see **estoppel.**

in pari delicto (L., in parry DUH-lick-toe: in equal fault): descriptive of those whose wrongdoing is joint, or of equal or closely similar degree, so that one may not recover from the other. <From the beginning, both knew the business was illegal. Being *in pari delicto,* neither can recover losses from the other.>

in pari materia (L., in parry MUH-tear-ee-uh: on a like topic): loose-ly, on the same topic. Shorthand for the proposition that when context of topic is similar, the meaning of words should ordinarily be uniformly interpreted. Applied especially to interpretation of stat-utes. <The two statutes, enacted only two months apart, were *in pari materia,* and it is reasonable to assume that "in the absence of fraud" in statute 2 means what it has been held to mean in statute 1.>

in personam (L.: against the person)

1. (of a lawsuit): to make someone personally liable, a suit *in per-sonam,* as distinguished from one against property. □see **in rem.** <They were suing for damages only, a suit *in personam.*>

2. (of a court) having *jurisdiction in personam,* also called **personal jurisdiction**: the power of a court to make someone personally liable (sense 1), as by a *judgment in personam.* The power is predicated on the person's having some contact with the place where the court is, e.g., physical presence, doing business there, doing something else-where that has an effect there. □see **long arm statute,** under **arm's length.** □see also, **quasi in rem,** under **in rem.**

3. (of a court's procedure) acting *in personam:* compulsion directed at the person, as distinguished from property. <The judge said, "Sit down!" That's *in personam.*> □see **equity acts in personam,** under **equity.**

in plain view □see **plain view.**

in point: a reference to a case or other authority that is pertinent to the present case or argument. <A case in point, Your Honor, is *U.S. v. Gladstone,* in the Fifth Circuit.> A case may be *in point* if it bears on the present case, though not a controlling precedent or not close enough to be right *on point.*

in pro per □see **appear.**

in propria persona □see **appear.**

inquisitorial system □see **adversary proceeding.**

in re (L., in ray: about the thing): in regard to; in this sense, usually abbreviated *re.* In the title of a reported case, use of *In re* is not uniform; often used to designate a proceeding **in rem** (□see).

in recess   □see **delay**.

in rem   (L.: against the thing)

1. (of a lawsuit): to directly affect a specific property, a suit *in rem,* as distinguished from the personal liability of the owner of the property. □see **in personam**. E.g., a suit to **quiet title**: to establish the plaintiff's title to property against all conflicting claims.

2. (of a court) having **jurisdiction in rem**: the power of a court where the property is located to make orders or give judgment affecting the property, a *judgment in rem,* whether or not it has jurisdiction over the owner of the property. □see **in personam**.

3. (of a court's procedure) acting *in rem:* directly affecting property whether in carrying out a *judgment in rem* (e.g., dividing property) or a *judgment in personam* (e.g., seizing the property). □see **writ of execution**, under **execute**.

4. **quasi in rem** (L., KWAYS-eye in rem: as if against the thing): an amorphous creature with no uniformly accepted meaning. These are two common classifications:

  a. a suit *as if* against property but actually against the person. The suit *quasi in rem* seeks control of property, e.g., by **attachment** (□see), not to adjudicate claims to the property, but as a device to assert jurisdiction to render a personal judgment against someone not otherwise subject to *jurisdiction in personam*. □see **in personam**.

  b. a suit to adjudicate rights of specific persons in specific property, e.g., to *partition* (divide up) property between joint owners, as opposed to a "true" *in rem* suit framed to adjudicate claims against "everyone," e.g., as in a suit to *quiet title.*

insane   □see **insanity**.

insanity: a word without precise generalized definition in or out of the law. When used in the law (many find the word worthless or abhorrent), it labels a condition of the mind so far removed from what is considered "normal" as to call forth special rules centered on a lack of "normal" responsibility for conduct.

Insanity is loose shorthand for that special condition of mind. Other expressions compete in statute and decision for definition of the condition or its elements, e.g., *mental defect, mental disease, mental disorder, mental illness, mental incompetence, non compos mentis,*

insanity

nonsane, unsound mind. Rules for what constitutes insanity, and what to do about it, vary sharply by jurisdiction and by the purpose for which the word is used, e.g., tort liability of the *insane;* invalidity of a will or contract signed by an insane person; commitment to an institution; criminal responsibility and punishment, the *insanity defense:* "Not guilty by reason of insanity," or "Guilty but insane." On tests for insanity in the criminal law, □see **Durham rule;** □see **M'Naghten rule.** □see also, **diminished capacity.**

insanity defense □see **insanity.**

in session □see **session;** □see **open court,** under **open.**

inside director □see **director.**

inside information □see **insider trading.**

insider □see **insider trading.**

insider trading

1. buying or selling stock on the basis of confidential information obtained directly or indirectly by or from those inside the corporation and not generally available to the public. The practice has spawned its own special argot:

> **inside information:** the information that is the basis of *insider trading.*

> **insider:** a person who obtains *inside information* by reason of a special relationship to the corporation, e.g., officer, director, substantial shareholder, employee, auditor.

> **outsider:** a person who sells stock, buys stock, or simply holds on to stock in ignorance of the *inside information.*

> **tipper:** a person who reveals *inside information* to someone outside the circle of *insiders.*

> **tippee:** a person who receives *inside information* from a *tipper.*

2. the practice (sense 1) as prohibited or regulated by statute and decision.

insolvency □see **insolvent.**

insolvent: having more debts than property (including money), or unable to pay debts as they become due, or no longer paying debts in the ordinary course of business. That general definition of *insolvent* (adj.) describes the condition called *insolvency* (n.) of a business, a legal entity, or an ordinary person. One in that condition is the *insolvent* (n.), not the same as a **bankrupt** (□see). The definition of *insolvent* varies by statute and decision. □see also, **bankruptcy**.

instant: this. <The instant case./This case.> Constantly used, but without special legal meaning. Prefer the intelligible *this*.

instanter □see absolutes.

instructions □see jury instructions.

instrument: a writing intended to have some legal effect. Context readily distinguishes this imprecise word from violins and forceps. The swarming **instruments in writing** and **written instruments** are expensive redundancies. For *negotiable instruments*, □see **commercial paper**.

instrument in writing □see instrument.

insurance: a contract, the **insurance policy**, one of a number made under an insurer's plan of risk distribution, in which the **insured** pays the **insurer** money, the **premium**, as a hedge against uncertainty. The insurer agrees that if ("God forbid," as the old policies used to say) a named contingency becomes a reality, the insured will incur no liability arising from that happening, or the insurer will reimburse the insured for any resulting loss, or will pay a sum of money as specified in the policy.

The nuances of the meaning of *insurance* vary with the almost infinite variety of insurance policies; those of common experience—life, fire, and auto insurance—are the barest sampling. In addition, the underlying sense of reaching for security against the unknown is manifest in some contracts labeled "insurance" that are contracts to provide professional services, e.g., medical, dental, legal; manifest also in social institutions bearing the name "insurance" with little relationship to the lawyer's ordinary usage, e.g., *deposit insurance, unemployment insurance*. The general definition here is no substitute for recourse to the vast substance and vocabulary of insurance

319

insurance

law. □see also, **no-fault insurance**; □see also, **incontestable clause**; □see also, **indemnity**, compared with *hold harmless,* under **hold**.

insurance policy □see **insurance**.

insured □see **insurance**.

insurer □see **insurance**.

intangible □see **intangible property**.

Intangible property • tangible property: frequently described as contrasting types of property, those without physical substance— **intangible** or **incorporeal**, as opposed to those with physical substance—**tangible** or **corporeal**. These are classifications of apparent difference, e.g., between the intangible **copyright** (□see) and the tangible book that contains copyrighted writing; between an **easement** (□see) and the land that is subject to the easement. Even the apparent difference is often ignored; a right to sue for $100 is intangible property, and often the tangible note that represents that right is also called an intangible. □see **chose in action**. The same property changes classification as it wanders through the labyrinth of varying tax statutes—sales, income, and property taxes, with something like a home in accounting classification, if not treatment, of *intangible assets,* e.g., goodwill, patents, copyright, trademarks. The *intangible/ tangible* classification has no generalized consistency, sidesteps the abstract nuances of **property** (□see), and serves only a rough convenience.

Integrated bar □see **bar**.

Integrated contract □see **parol evidence rule**.

Integration □see **segregation**; □see also, **parol evidence rule**.

Intellectual property: a catchall label for property that is recognized in works of the mind, without general acceptance of any definitive listing of what is covered by the expression. At a minimum, it includes what is included in **copyright** (□see) and **patent** (□see), with miscellaneous references to **trademark** (□see), **trade name** (□see), and **service mark** (□see), and the potential for unlimited expansion.

intend □see intent.

intent

1. as a word of general utility, *intent* means what it means in ordinary English, the design or purpose one has in mind for doing or not doing something. So too with the related *intend, intended, intentional, intentionally.* In this general sense, *intent* and its relatives are flexible words, inoffensive in loose usage but fractious abstractions when confined. In a role fitter for philosophers or alchemists, lawyers have been unable to make the flexible precise; the resulting makeshifts are used often but without consensus. □see also, **letter of intent**.

2. (meaning of a writing): what the writer meant by the words used; and, by personified extension, what the writing means. For example, the *testator's intent,* also expressed as the *intent of the will,* both distinguished from *testamentary intent* (in par. 5 of this entry).

legislative intent: what the legislators meant by the words used in the statute; and, by extension, what the statute means, **statutory intent**, or the *intent of the statute. Legislative intent* is sometimes equated with the immediate **legislative purpose**, itself sometimes reserved for an underlying objective.

original intent: a speculative conjecture as to what the Framers (□see **Founding Fathers**) and their contemporaries meant by the words of the U.S. Constitution; and, by gossamer extension, what the Constitution means today.

3. (criminal law): the state of mind (sense 1) that accompanies a prohibited act, *intent* and act together constituting a particular crime. That state of mind, of varying definition, traditionally has been subdivided into:

general intent: an intent to do what is prohibited, the joining of that state of mind with the prohibited act often expressed as *wilfully and unlawfully* (□see **willful**). For some crimes, e.g., assault, bigamy, unlicensed driving, *general intent* suffices; neither knowledge that the act is prohibited nor elaboration of mental process is required.

specific intent: a particular set of mind that accompanies a general intent and a prohibited act. As in common law larceny, charging the defendant with taking and carrying away another's personal property *with intent to steal.* Other notorious specific intents are *intent to kill* (□see **murder**) and *intent to defraud* (□see **fraud**).

intent

The classifications *general intent* and *specific intent,* much criticized, perhaps headed for extinction, still live in case law. For detailed dissection of the state of the criminal mind, focusing on *purposely, knowingly, recklessly, negligently,* enter the domain of the Model Penal Code, statutes in its pattern, and treatises on criminal law.

□see also, **malice;** □see also, **mens rea;** □see also, **motive;** □see also, **presumed intent.**

4. (torts): a confined version of *intent* (sense 1), a desire to cause the consequences of one's act, or a belief that they are substantially certain to result from the act. This common tort usage of *intent* (*Restatement (Second) of Torts,* § 8A) contrasts the intentional with **negligence** (□see) and **recklessness** (□see). The definition is not precise, not uniformly followed, and is often conflated with **motive** (□see).

intentional infliction of emotional distress □see **emotional distress.**

intentional interference: an *intent to interfere,* the usual predicate of liability in tort for causing damage by injecting oneself into the relationships of others, e.g., *interference with contractual relations, interference with prospective advantage.*

intentional misrepresentation □see **fraud.**

5. (miscellany)

donative intent: intent to make a gift. (□see **gift,** under **give.**)

testamentary intent: intent to make a will. (□see **will.**)

transferred intent: when a blow or a bullet, etc., goes off course and hits an unintended victim, the intent to harm the intended victim is treated as an intent to harm the actual victim. Applied in some jurisdictions in criminal law and torts.

intentional □see **intent.**

intentional infliction of emotional distress □see **emotional distress.**

intentional interference □see **intent.**

intentional misrepresentation □see **fraud.**

intent to defraud □see **fraud.**

intent to interfere □see **intent.**

intent to kill □see **murder.**

inter alia (L., IN-tur AL-e-uh: among other things): among other things. The Latin has no special virtue, except to stimulate argument over its pronunciation. Use the English.

interest is a useful word of the common vocabulary. Legal contexts for the common meanings hold no exotic terrors. Special legal combinations are entered in alphabetical order, e.g., *declaration against interest* (□see **declaration**); **future interest** (□see); **legal interest** (□see); **present interest** (□see, under **future interest**); **liberty interest** (□see).

intergovernmental immunity □see **immunity.**

interlocutory injunction □see **enjoin.**

intermeddler: a person who interferes (*intermeddles*) in another person's affairs, without request, requirement, or the need to protect his own interests. A more legal sounding synonymn for a *meddler,* often made to sound more emphatic in the synonymous expression **officious intermeddler.** Also described as a **volunteer**, sometimes as a **stranger.** To brand someone as an *intermeddler* is the usual prelude to denying recovery of funds expended, e.g., in needlessly paying off someone else's debt.

Internal Revenue Code □see **tax.**

international law: the principles, customs, and rules that are generally accepted by nations as governing the relations between them, and as governing the relations between one nation and persons of another nation. The definition is neither precise nor standardized. *International law* is embodied in a variety of concrete forms, such as institutions (e.g., the United Nations); organizations (e.g., the International Court of Justice); treaties—e.g., affecting **airspace** (□see); the **high seas** (□see); **piracy** (□see); e.g., Convention on International Bills of Exchange and International Promissory Notes; □see also, **maritime law;** □see also, **law of the sea.**

International law is still sometimes called by its older name—the *law of nations* (see U.S. Const., Art. I, § 8, cl. 10). It is also called *public*

international law

international law, as distinguished from *private international law:* another name for **conflict of laws** (□see), when the law of more than one nation is involved in private controversy.

interplead   □see **interpleader.**

interpleader

1. an equitable remedy by which the man in the middle of more than one claim to the same property, money, or obligation sues all of the claimants, i.e., *interpleads* them.   The suit requires the *interpleaded* claimants to *interplead,* i.e., assert their claims in court, for a decision as to whom, if anyone, the man in the middle owes anything. <Faced with conflicting claims by buyer and seller, the escrow holder filed an action of interpleader against them, deposited the escrowed funds in court, and left them to battle it out.>

2. in the nature of interpleader, also called **bill in the nature of interpleader**: like interpleader (sense 1), except that the person filing the action (not necessarily the man in the middle) may assert a claim to the property, money, or obligation claimed by the others.

interpret   □see **construction.**

interpretation   □see **construction.**

interrogatories   □see **discovery;** □see also, **cross interrogatory,** under **cross-.**

in terrorem   (L., in tuh-ROAR-em: as a warning): a threat of dire consequences intended to inhibit unwanted conduct.   <"Bailiff, arrest the next member of the audience who interrupts me." The judge's words operated *in terrorem.*>

in terrorem clause: a provision of a will threatening the loss of a gift by will if the intended beneficiary does something objectionable to the testator. Typically, an *in terrorem* clause is a **no contest clause**: one forfeiting a gift, or giving a token gift instead of a more substantial though disappointing gift, if the unhappy beneficiary contests the validity of the will or its provisions.   □see **will contest.**

in terrorem clause   □see **in terrorem.**

324

interspousal: one of the law's most disagreeable sounds, an increasingly used substitute for *between spouses* or, for the even plainer English, the mildly sexist *between husband and wife*. A trifle more precise than *spousal*, but hardly worth the grating harshness of *interspousal torts, interspousal disability,* and *interspousal immunity* (□see immunity). As this is written, it has not yet displaced the *marital communications privilege* nor the **husband-wife privilege** (□see).

interspousal disability □see **husband-wife privilege.**

interspousal immunity □see **immunity.**

interspousal torts □see **interspousal immunity,** under **immunity.**

interstate commerce

1. in a narrow sense, commerce between the states, as opposed to commerce within a state, *intrastate commerce.*

2. an expression used by the U.S. Supreme Court in long, changing, and continuing interpretation of the **Commerce Clause** (□see), which does not use the expression but speaks of "power . . . to regulate commerce . . . among the several states." In the Court's usage, *interstate commerce* refers to the greatest variety of tangible and intangible things, of activities commercial or otherwise, that can affect more than one state or the intercourse between them, whether a particular thing or activity itself moves across state lines or is *intrastate.* The Court's spelling out of the scope of *interstate commerce,* and what affects it or relates to it, is more concerned with the federal government's *power* over interstate commerce, pragmatically blurring the distinction between that power and *interstate commerce* itself.

interstate extradition □see **extradition.**

interstate rendition □see **render;** □see **extradition.**

intervene □see **third party intervention,** under **party.**

intervening cause □see **superseding cause.**

intervenor □see **third party intervention,** under **party.**

intervention □see **third party intervention**, under **party**.

inter vivos □see **gift inter vivos**, under **gift**; □see also, **inter vivos trust**, under **trust**.

inter vivos trust □see **trust**.

intestacy (L., intestatus: that has made no will): the condition that exists when someone dies without having made a will or whose will is invalid.

partial intestacy: the condition that exists when a will does not dispose of all of the testator's property.

□see **intestate**.

intestate

1. referring to **intestacy** (□see). <He died intestate.> For *intestate succession,* □see **inherit**, under **descend**.

2. referring to partial **intestacy** (□see). <He died intestate as to Blackacre.>

3. the person who died intestate (senses 1 and 2). <The intestate was a resident of California.>

4. referring to the property left by the intestate (sense 3). <The intestate property went to the heirs.>

intestate succession □see **inherit**, under **descend**.

in the final analysis □see **clichés**.

in the nature of interpleader □see **interpleader**.

in the record □see **in evidence**, under **evidence**.

intimate association □see **freedom of intimate association**, under **freedom of association**.

intoxicated □see **legally drunk**.

326

intrastate commerce   □see **interstate commerce**.

intra vires   □see **ultra vires**.

in trial   □see **trial**.

intrinsic fraud   □see **fraud**.

in trust   □see **trust**.

in truth and in fact   □see **facts**.

invade the corpus   □see **corpus**.

invasion of privacy   □see **right of privacy**.

invention   □see **patent**.

inverse condemnation   □see **eminent domain**.

invited error: a legal error that is not a cause for complaint because the error occurred through the fault of the party now complaining. E.g., an erroneous instruction given at the request of the complainer; a prosecutor arguing facts outside the record in response to defendant's argument of facts outside the record.

invitee: a mark of distinction, decisive or a factor, in determining the standards of liability of an occupier of land to those who are injured on the property.

Invitation readily separates *invitee* from the unloved *trespasser* (□see **trespass**). From that point on, the standards spawn, multiplying and dividing beyond the limits of this dictionary. One standard equates *invitee* with *business visitor:* invited in connection with the occupier's business (e.g., a customer), as distinguished from a *licensee*'s own purposes (e.g., a solicitor for a charity). □see **license**. By another standard, *invitee* is a business visitor or a *public invitee:* invited along with all members of the public (e.g., a visitor to a public park). Neither of those standards of *invitee* includes a social visitor (a guest), still called a *licensee*. By yet another standard, that of ordinary

invitee

English, *invitee* means one who is invited, a simple solution that ignores too many volumes of law.

The effect of the labeling process, very little in some states, is even more varied than the criteria of labeling. Considerations of liability often blur definition of the person. Consult the law of torts of the jurisdiction of immediate concern.

involuntary bankruptcy □see **bankruptcy**.

involuntary manslaughter □see **manslaughter**.

In Witness Whereof □see **formalisms**.

IOLTA: acronym for "Interest on Lawyer Trust Account" Program. Under that and similar plans, a lawyer deposits in a special bank account client trust funds so small or short-term as to be impractical for an individual interest-bearing account. Funds in the special account are pooled with similar accounts of other lawyers; interest from the pooled account is used to provide legal services for indigents.

IRC: abbreviation (also, I.R.C.) of Internal Revenue Code. □see **tax**.

irrebuttable presumption □see **conclusive presumption**, under **presumption**.

irreconcilable differences □see **divorce**.

irrelevant □see **relevant**.

irreparable damage: Like most **absolutes** (□see), *irreparable damage,* also called *irreparable injury,* is not to be taken literally. Most lawyers don't. They are long accustomed to degrees of irreparable damage and to explanations of why not all *irreparable damage* is really irreparable. Still wiggling, though long and firmly embedded in the law, *irreparable damage* is understood as a species of shorthand: a special way of saying that this is a proper case for an *equitable remedy* (□see **equity**). What makes it special, and the case proper, is the variety and generality of reasons it evokes; here are some of the common ones:

1. A legal remedy is inadequate to do full justice. <The stink of the nuisance will not abate with an award of damages. The neighbors suffer an

irreparable damage. The injunction will issue./An award of damages is not a substitute for plaintiff's right of free speech; denial of her First Amendment rights would be an irreparable injury.>

2. It would be too difficult to determine with any precision what award of damages would compensate for an invasion of plaintiff's rights under the contract. <Any damages that might be awarded here would be highly speculative. The damage is irreparable.>

3. By and large, these are insufferable wrongs that had better be stopped than compensated in repeated suits. <The recurrent trespasses constituted irreparable damage.>

□see also, **damage.**

irreparable injury   □see **irreparable damage.**

irresistible force   □see **act of God.**

irrevocable letter of credit   □see **letter of credit.**

irrevocable proxy   □see **power coupled with an interest.**

irrevocable trust   □see **trust.**

issue   □see **descendant;** □see also, **res judicata.**

issue preclusion   □see **res judicata.**

I take it   □see **take.**

it appears that   □see **clichés.**

item veto   □see **veto.**

it is fair to say   □see **fair;** □see also, **clichés.**

it may well be   □see **clichés.**

it would seem   □see **clichés.**

J

J.: abbreviation of the titles *Judge* and *Justice;* not a general abbreviation for those words when not used as titles. Used in a broad miscellany of legal writings; especially, within an opinion when referring to an opinion of another judge or justice, and at the end of an opinion to note a simple dissent or concurrence. < . . . Smith, J., dissenting./ . . . Jones, J., concurring./Smith, J., dissents./Jones, J., concurs. > The plural, similarly used, is *JJ.*

Also used in combinations, e.g., *P.J.* = Presiding Judge, Presiding Justice; *C.J.* = Chief Judge, Chief Justice, Circuit Judge.

The abbreviations give no clue that the reference is to a judge or justice; that distinction must be picked up from full titles elsewhere in a report or by context, e.g., the name of the court. □see **judge**.

jail: a public building for the temporary confinement of those arrested, and for term confinement of those convicted of relatively lesser offenses or serving relatively shorter sentences. The contrast is usually with the more serious offenses resulting in longer sentences served in a prison or penitentiary. No single touchstone distinguishes *jail* from *prison* or *penitentiary*. The distinction is not precise, not uniform, is sometimes spelled out in legislation. □see **imprisonment**. □see also, **convict** (n.).

jailbreak □see **breach**.

jailhouse lawyer □see **lawyer**.

Jane Doe □see **John Doe**.

J.D.

1. the basic degree awarded on graduation from law school. The initials are generally thought of as the name of the degree, rather than as an abbreviation of a name, and with some reason (sense 2). The *J.D.* supplants the traditional **LL.B.** (□see). < She received the J.D. in 1987. >

2. initial letters of the basic law degree (sense 1), considered variously the abbreviation of:

   Doctor of Jurisprudence;

   Doctor of Law, a translation of the Latin *Juris Doctor;*

   Doctor of Laws, a translation of the Latin *Jurum Doctor;*

   Juris Doctor (L., JOOR-iss Doctor: Doctor of Law);

   Jurum Doctor (L., JOOR-um Doctor: Doctor of Laws).

JJ.: abbreviation of the titles *Judges* and *Justices.* □see **J.**

jeopardy □see **double jeopardy.**

job action □see **strike.**

John Doe (pronounced *dough*): a fictitious person. Often abbreviated as *Doe,* multiplied as *Doe I, Doe II,* etc., with a sex change to *Jane
Doe* and an infant version *Baby Girl Doe,* etc. Doe's principal rhym-
ing companion is *Richard Roe,* with endless variations, such as *Poe*
and *Soe,* or plain *Roe,* male or female. *John Doe,* and his variants, is
frequently used in pleadings and other legal papers to denote temporary uncertainty as to a correct name (□see **fictitious defendant**); to
avoid public identification, e.g., of a minor, e.g., of a plaintiff seeking
abortion (see *Roe v. Wade,* 410 U.S. 113, 1973; see *Doe v. Bolton,* 410
U.S. 179, 1973); to preserve secrecy while resolving disputes over
disclosure of government information (see *John Doe Agency and John
Doe Government Agency v. John Doe Corp.,* 488 U.S. 1306, 1989, reh.
den. 110 S.Ct. 884, 1990); etc. Some combining forms are the *John
Doe action, —indictment, —proceeding, —summons, —warrant.*
Framing a hypothetical problem, professors and writers resort to
John Doe for instant recognition of a traditional phony. The historical use of *Doe* and *Roe* as fictitious persons in actions that required
fiction (e.g., ejectment) has faded from the legal scene, but the names
persist, as they have for centuries. For some speculation on the
mystery of John Doe's identity, see Mellinkoff, "Who Is 'John Doe'?",
12 *UCLA Law Review* 79 (1964).

joinder: in the law, as in ordinary English, the act of joining. The
difference is that most people are content with *joining* and get along
nicely without *joinder.* Lawyers find it irresistible. The puniest
form of *joinder* is joining in signing a writing that affects property in

which you and someone else have interests. <There must be a joinder.>

Joinder attains full stature in the law of procedure: the joining together in one lawsuit or in one prosecution, whether at the pleading stage or the trial stage, of more than one party to a side or more than one claim or offense. A vast learning must be consulted for the rules, guidelines, and practices, changed and changing, varying by federal and state statute and decision, by civil litigation and by criminal prosecution, the latter in particular overlaid with constitutional requirements. Here is basic terminology:

compulsory joinder: usually, a requirement that someone must be joined as a party to civil litigation, or the litigation will be dismissed. □see **indispensable party,** under **party.** Also, indirectly, a reference to a **compulsory counterclaim,** barred if not asserted. □see also, **res judicata.**

permissive joinder: the propriety, as distinguished from a requirement, of joining someone, or some claim or offense, in a pleading or trial. □see **proper party,** under **party.**

misjoinder: joining someone in a pleading or trial who should not have been joined, or joining a claim or offense that should not have been joined.

collusive joinder: the worst kind of misjoinder: joining someone in a pleading or trial in an improper attempt to give the court jurisdiction.

nonjoinder: failing to join someone in a pleading or trial who should have been joined, or failing to join a claim or offense that should have been joined.

□see also, **sever.**

joint adventure □see **joint venture.**

joint and several liability: a liability that may be enforced by one suit against all of those liable (the *joint* part), or by separate suits against one or more of those liable (*several* here meaning *separate*). <The overdue note read, "I promise to pay to the order of A $500 on demand," and was signed individually by B and C. B and C are jointly and severally liable, A having the option of suing B and C together or either of them separately. In any case, A's recovery cannot exceed $500.> □see also, **joint tortfeasors,** under **tortfeasor.**

joint enterprise □see **joint venture.**

joint ownership: a loose, untechnical description of ownership of property by more than one person, also called *co-ownership*. It has been applied indiscriminately to characterize an assorted bag of ownership interests, e.g., by partners, by husband and wife, interests in condominiums. *Joint ownership* inevitably suggests the peculiarities of *joint tenancy* as opposed to *tenancy in common* (□see **estate**), and is especially misleading as a description of **community property** (□see). For general reference to the varieties of ownership by more than one person, *co-ownership* is a better gamble.

joint tenancy   □see **estate**.

joint tortfeasors   □see **tortfeasor**.

joint venture: a commercial enterprise organized by the participants who control it and share its profits and losses. It is governed generally by the substantive law of **partnership** (□see), differing from a partnership in that a *joint venture* is usually for a more limited purpose and of shorter duration, often devoted to a single, specific transaction. E.g., subdivision of a particular tract; launch of a space satellite; drilling an oil well. *Joint venture* also goes by other names:

joint adventure: in some jurisdictions and in some legal writing, a synonym for *joint venture*.

joint enterprise

1.   in loose usage, a synonym for *joint venture*.

2.   a transient undertaking by two or more persons of a noncommercial, personal nature, e.g., sharing a ride. This label of *joint enterprise* is sometimes applied in tort law as a predicate for attributing to the participants some responsibility for the conduct of the others. □see **imputed negligence**, under **negligence**; □see **vicarious liability**.

journalist's privilege   □see **newsmen's privilege**.

J.P.:   abbreviation of the title *Justice of the Peace*. □see **judge**.

judge • justice: the official who administers the many forms of justice in court or similar proceedings.

That is a broad definition of both words, and in some very limited contexts, the words are interchangeable. E.g., the justices of the

judge

Supreme Court of the United States are referred to in the Constitution as "judges of the Supreme Court" (Art. II, § 2, cl. 2; see also, Art. III, § 1).

But the words are not general synonyms. The generic is *judge* and includes *justice*. In general contexts, *justice* does not include *judge*. "American judges," as a general reference, includes justices. "American justices," as a general reference, does not include judges. A justice is often addressed as "Judge"; a judge is not usually addressed as "Justice."

Choice of one word or the other in particular contexts has no uniform functional rationale, e.g., trial or appeal, higher or lower in the hierarchy. Reasons for particular usage vary, most a product of long or local habit, reinforced by statute or constitution, changed by the same process. Usage listed here is illustrative of the breadth of variation in particular contexts. For more general descriptions, □see **bench**; □see **court**. For a dated term of reference, □see **Brethren**.

administrative law judge: the official who performs the function of a judge in hearings within an administrative agency; □see, under **administrative law**.

associate judge □see **chief judge**, below, in this entry.

associate justice □see **chief justice**, below, in this entry.

bankruptcy judge: a judicial officer of the U.S. District Court who hears and determines cases and related matters under the Bankruptcy Code, including so-called "core proceedings" of the bankruptcy process. The bankruptcy judges of each district constitute a unit of the U.S. District Court called the *bankruptcy court,* also called the *U.S. Bankruptcy Court.*

Chief: informal reference to a particular **chief judge** (□see, below, in this entry), or a particular **chief justice** (□see, below, in this entry). <The Chief will write the opinion in that case.>

chief judge: in courts with more than one judge, one is called the *Chief Judge* or *Presiding Judge,* the others *Associate Judge,* often simply *Judge.* In addition to judging, the chief judge or presiding judge has administrative duties and presides at sessions of all the judges. Terminology varies by court: e.g., the intermediate appellate courts in the federal system (Court of Appeals) and the highest appellate court in New York (Court of Appeals) each has a Chief Judge; in the Alabama Court of Civil Appeals, there is a Presiding Judge. □see **circuit judge**, below, in this entry.

chief justice: in courts with more than one justice, one is called *Chief Justice* or *Presiding Justice,* the others *Associate Justice,* often simply *Justice.* In addition to judging, the chief justice or presiding justice has administrative duties and presides at sessions of all the justices. Terminology varies by court: e.g., the Supreme Court of the United States has a Chief Justice; so too the New Jersey Supreme Court. Each division of the intermediate appellate court in California (Court of Appeal) has a Presiding Justice. □see **Chief Justice of the United States,** below, in this entry.

Chief Justice of the United States: the formal title of the constitutional officer who is chief justice of the **Supreme Court of the United States** (□see). Apart from general references to "judges of the Supreme Court," the only specific reference in the Constitution is to the role of the *Chief Justice* on impeachment of the President (Art. I, § 3, cl. 6). The longer title is used repeatedly in legislation (e.g., 28 USCA § 1), with *Chief Justice* the customary shortened version.

circuit judge: a judge other than a chief judge of one of the U.S. **Courts of Appeals** (□see). □see also, **circuit justice,** below, in this entry.

circuit justice: an additional role of a justice, including the Chief Justice, of the Supreme Court of the United States. Each is "allotted," i.e., assigned, to one or more of the U.S. Courts of Appeals. A circuit justice has limited administrative duties and is competent to sit as a judge of the court.

justice of the peace: the judge of a court of limited civil and criminal jurisdiction, called a *Justice's Court* or *Justice Court,* the lowest or one of the lowest in the judicial hierarchy. The title *Justice of the Peace* (abbreviated *J.P.*) is now often supplanted by *Justice* or *Judge.*

magistrate □see.

presiding judge □see **chief judge,** above, in this entry.

presiding justice □see **chief justice,** above, in this entry.

surrogate judge: a judicial office of old and scarce vintage, the judge presiding over a *surrogate's court,* with jurisdiction primarily in probate.

trial judge: the judge who presides at a **trial** (□see), also referred to as the *trial court.*

□see also, **rent-a-judge.**

judge-made law □see **common law.**

judge pro tem □see **pro tem.**

judge shopping □see **forum shopping**, under **forum**.

judgment: a judge's formal determination of a controversy, detailing outcome, how arrived at, and its consequences. Some judgments may be reduced to bare essentials, e.g., the *judgment of acquittal* in this list; e.g., some judgments of appellate courts, "Affirmed," "Reversed."

Names substituted for *judgment:*

award: may be part of a judgment, should not be equated with it. □see **award**.

decision: a more general, untechnical term. □see **decision**.

decree: primarily for a judgment in exercise of a judge's equitable powers (□see **equity**). E.g., decree of dissolution of marriage, divorce decree (□see **divorce**), decree of distribution (of a deceased's estate; □see **estate**). The verb *decree* is often included, redundantly, as part of the introduction to any judgment <It is ordered, adjudged, and decreed . . .>.

order: more precisely, an operative term, often part of a judgment. □see **decision**.

sentence: often, part of a judgment in a criminal case. □see **sentence**.

Names for special kinds of *judgment:*

declaratory judgment □see **declaration**.

default judgment □see **default**.

deficiency judgment: a personal judgment against a debtor for the portion of a debt remaining unpaid after **foreclosure** (□see) or levy of execution (□see **execute**). The so-called *deficiency judgment* is often not a separate judgment but incident to another judgment, e.g., of foreclosure. Availability restricted by statute and decision.

judgment in personam □see **in personam**.

judgment in rem □see **in rem**.

judgment non obstante □see **judgment n.o.v.**

judgment non obstante veredicto □see **judgment n.o.v.**

judgment not on the merits □see **judgment on the merits**.

judgment notwithstanding the verdict □see **judgment n.o.v.**

judgment n.o.v.: an abbreviated form of *judgment non obstante veredicto* (L., non ob-STAN-tay ver-uh-DIK-toe: notwithstanding the verdict): a judgment given in favor of the side that has lost by verdict.

Those who prefer Latin, but in smaller doses, call the same thing *judgment non obstante.* Those who insist on English, no matter how mouth-filling, call the same thing *judgment notwithstanding the verdict.* As long as you know what you are talking about, the abbreviated Latin has a strong appeal. <The jury has spoken, but the verdict is clearly contrary to the law. Motion for judgment n.o.v. granted.>

judgment of acquittal: a judgment reciting the fact of **acquittal** (□see), dismissing the charges, and discharging the defendant from custody.

judgment of conviction: a judgment reciting the fact of **conviction** (□see) and imposing **sentence** (□see) or granting **probation** (□see).

judgment of dismissal: a judgment ending a case (a) without a trial, for technical reasons, e.g., failure of prosecution, or (b) because the claims or charges have not been proved. □see **without prejudice.**

judgment on the merits: a judgment based on the substance of a controversy, as distinguished from one based on a curable procedural defect—a *judgment not on the merits.* □see **without prejudice;** □see also, **without merit;** □see also, **res judicata.**

judgment on the pleadings: a judgment considering only the pleadings, and determining that as a matter of law plaintiff has no cause for complaint, or that defendant has no defense. □see **pleadings.**

judgment on the verdict: a judgment based upon a **verdict** (□see).

nonsuit: judgment against a plaintiff who fails to go forward with a case, or whose evidence at trial is insufficient as a matter of law to require presentation of a defense. <On motion, the plaintiff was *nonsuited.*> Also called *judgment of nonsuit.*

personal judgment □see **in personam.**

summary judgment: judgment without a trial, upon the judge's determination that pleadings and affidavits show that there is not a "genuine" issue of fact to be tried. <Having looked through this heavy bundle of competing affidavits, I am convinced that there is a genuine issue of fact here. Motion for summary judgment denied.>

□see also, **offer of judgment,** under **offer to compromise;**

□see also, **open a judgment,** under **open.**

judgment book   □see **enter a judgment,** under **enter.**

judgment in personam □see in personam.

judgment in rem □see in rem.

judgment non obstante □see judgment n.o.v., under judgment.

judgment non obstante veredicto □see judgment n.o.v., under judgment.

judgment not on the merits □see judgment on the merits, under judgment.

judgment notwithstanding the verdict □see judgment n.o.v., under judgment.

judgment n.o.v. □see judgment.

judgment of acquittal □see judgment.

judgment of conviction □see judgment.

judgment of dismissal □see judgment.

judgment on the merits □see judgment.

judgment on the pleadings □see judgment.

judgment on the verdict □see judgment.

judgment-proof, or *judgment proof:* said of someone who is insolvent, or whose assets for one reason or another are beyond the reach of the law. An expression of common English, not a special law word, but used by lawyers with the same note of resignation that produces "You can't get blood out of a turnip."

judicial estoppel □see estoppel.

judicial immunity □see immunity.

judicial knowledge   □see **judicial notice.**

judicial legislation   □see **legislation;** □see also, **judge-made law,** under **common law.**

judicial notice: a judge's recognition that something is so without the necessity of its being proved by evidence in a case. Applied to a wide range of matters of common knowledge, the facts of life and science, and a broad assortment of laws. Details of what may be, and what must be, *judicially noticed* often regulated by statute. □see also, **take judicial notice,** under **notice.**

judicial knowledge: a less precise term than *judicial notice,* often equated with it. Sometimes used to distinguish common knowledge from what lies within a judge's private knowledge, and so not the subject of judicial notice. Sometimes a reminder to lawyers that a judge's knowledge may be limited, and must be broadened or refreshed by reference to dictionaries, history books, literature, learned treatises, etc., before something will be judicially noticed. □see also, **Brandeis brief.**

judicial power of the United States   □see **federal question jurisdiction,** under **federal question.**

judicial proceedings privilege   □see **immunity.**

judicial review

1. the power of courts, ultimately the Supreme Court of the United States, to determine the constitutionality of legislation and of other acts and decisions of government and its officers. □see **standards of review.**

2. the exercise of the power of judicial review (sense 1), often shortened to *review.*   <Having reviewed the scope of that statute, we have no hesitancy in declaring it an unconstitutional denial of due process.>

3. a higher court's reexamination of the proceedings and decision of a lower court to determine their conformity to law generally, whether or not involving constitutionality (sense 1).

4. an examination by a court to determine the conformity to law generally of the proceedings and decision of an administrative agency or officer, whether or not involving constitutionality (sense 1).

jump bail □see **bail**.

junior □see **subordinate**.

jurat: attached to an affidavit, a *jurat* is an authentication by an officer qualified to administer oaths, certifying that the affidavit was sworn to and signed by the person whose signature it bears. The jurat is usually a repository of old formalisms: *subscribed and sworn to* and *personally appeared before me.* □see **affiant**; □see **notary public**; □see **subscribe**.

jurisdiction

1. the geographical location of a political entity. <Five miles to the border; we'll be out of this jurisdiction by noon.> □see also, **venue**; □see also, **airspace**.

2. a political entity with a distinctive system of law. <California is a community property jurisdiction./In some jurisdictions their Supreme Court is a trial court.> □see also, **forum**.

3. a general term for the authorized power of an instrument of government. <That activity is within the *jurisdiction of the courts,* not the jurisdiction of the legislature (*legislative jurisdiction*) or of an agency (*agency jurisdiction*).>

The term is loosely used and defined as authority, as power, sometimes both. What is said to be the necessity of distinguishing *jurisdiction* from *power* is often the need of distinction between this general sense of jurisdiction and particular kinds of jurisdiction or particular grants of power. When lawyers speak of *jurisdiction,* they usually refer to *jurisdiction of courts* (sense 4) and especially to *jurisdiction of a court* (sense 5).

4. jurisdiction of courts: the authorized power of courts generally to hear and determine cases and to administer a system of justice. □see also, **venue**.

This usage has an inherited imprecision. The Latin *juris-dictio* is translated as administration of justice, jurisdiction, power, and much more. It is based on Latin *jus* + *dicere,* translated *to declare the law,* and also *to do justice,* not always the same thing. Both concepts are long imbedded in our legal system, with limits and interpretation still controversial.

5. jurisdiction of a court: the authorized power of a particular court in a particular case or a particular kind of case. <We move to

dismiss on the ground that this court has no jurisdiction.> The succeeding numbered paragraphs of this entry are particularized usages of this sense. □see also, **court of general jurisdiction**, under **court**; □see also, **court of limited jurisdiction**, under **court**.

6. federal jurisdiction: the authorized power of courts in the federal judicial system, as provided in the U.S. Constitution or in the laws and treaties of the United States. (U.S. Const., Art. III; Art. IV, § 3, cl. 2; Amend. XI). □see **federal question jurisdiction**, under **federal question**.

ancillary jurisdiction: the discretionary power of a federal court to exercise jurisdiction over a claim not otherwise within its jurisdiction but logically related to the case over which it has jurisdiction. Sometimes equated with *pendent jurisdiction* (in this list), but typically applied to new claims by a defendant or by someone not a party to the original litigation (□see **joinder**; □see **third party intervention**, under **party**). The expression *ancillary jurisdiction* is not uniformly defined. (See Judicial Improvement Act of 1990, Public Law 101–650, 104 Stat. 5089, § 1367.)

diversity jurisdiction: jurisdiction of federal courts based on the fact that the controversy is between citizens of different states, or between a citizen and a foreigner (or a foreign country). □see **foreign**.

pendent jurisdiction: the discretionary power of a federal court to exercise jurisdiction in a single trial over claims under state law that are closely related to the case in which the court has **federal question jurisdiction** (□see, under **federal question**).

7. original jurisdiction: jurisdiction to try a case, as distinguished from *appellate jurisdiction* (□see **appeal**). E.g., the original jurisdiction of the Supreme Court of the United States in cases "affecting ambassadors, other public ministers, and those in which a state shall be a party." (U.S. Const., Art. III, § 2, cl. 2).

8. subject matter jurisdiction: jurisdiction described in terms of particular kinds of cases, e.g., the dollar amount (*jurisdictional amount*); e.g., misdemeanors, felonies, etc. (*criminal jurisdiction*); e.g., request for an injunction (*equity jurisdiction*). □see **court of limited jurisdiction**, under **court**.

9. jurisdiction in personam □see **in personam**.

10. jurisdiction in rem □see **in rem**.

11. jurisdiction quasi in rem □see **in rem**.

jurisdictional amount   □see **jurisdiction**.

jurisdiction in personam　□see **in personam.**

jurisdiction in rem　□see **in rem.**

jurisdiction of a court　□see **jurisdiction.**

jurisdiction of courts　□see **jurisdiction.**

jurisdiction quasi in rem　□see **in rem.**

Juris Doctor　□see **J.D.**

jurisprudence

1. law, in its broadest aspect, considered as an organized system of principles, practice, and goals. In this sense, often described as "the science of law" or "the philosophy of law."

2. loosely, a synonym of law. E.g., *Doctor of Jurisprudence* (□see **J.D.**).

In particular usage, absent heavy doses of context, it is impossible to know for sure whether the meaning is sense 1 or sense 2, e.g., medical jurisprudence, equity jurisprudence, American jurisprudence. □see also, **feminine jurisprudence.**

juristic person　□see **person.**

juror　□see **jury.**

jury: collective name for those individually called *jurors* (male or female), brought together to make a judicial inquiry under oath. The nature of that inquiry—and with it, the role of the jury—varies sharply in the two principal types of jury, *trial jury* and *grand jury.* For the latter, □see **grand jury,** under **indictment.**

trial jury: the jury referred to in the historic phrase *trial by jury;* also called a **petit jury** (F., PET-ee, as in *petty:* little), as distinguished from the larger grand jury.

Drawn from a **jury panel** (□see), prospective members of a trial jury, civil or criminal, are examined in open court to test their qualifications (□see **voir dire**). Those who survive **challenge** (□see) are sworn as jurors or *alternate jurors:* to fill a vacancy, e.g., death, illness, removal for misconduct. The jury hears and sees the evidence as it is presented, listens to argument and to instructions on the law (□see **jury instructions**), *deliberates* in secret, and reports to the trial judge a group determination of facts based on the evidence, or a failure to agree. (□see **verdict;** □see also, **hung jury,** under **hanging jury;** □see also, **poll the jury;** □see also, **view.**)

Details of right to trial by jury, and of size of a trial jury, are matters of constitutional law (U.S. Const., Art. III, Amend. VI, Amend. VII, Amend. XIV), federal law, and state law.

Some other forms of jury:

advisory jury: like a **trial jury** (□see), but called "advisory," because its determination may be accepted or rejected by the trial court. In cases where there is no right to trial by jury, typically in **equity** (□see), the trial court, in its discretion, may have the assistance of an advisory jury.

blue ribbon jury: a trial jury of jurors specially selected for their unusual qualification to try an especially difficult case. It is governed by special statute.

coroner's jury: a group of jurors specially chosen to assist a coroner (the officer in charge) in a **coroner's inquest:** an official inquiry about a death under circumstances that might give rise to a criminal prosecution. A coroner's jury is not a trial jury, for the inquest is not a trial, not an adversary proceeding. The coroner's jury may express an opinion, called a *verdict,* e.g., that the cause of death is unknown, or that a crime has been committed by a named or unknown person. But that verdict does not bind the prosecuting authorities, and the vocabulary of a trial jury's **verdict** (□see) is inapplicable. A coroner's inquest, coroner's jury, and its verdict are governed by special statute.

jury box: the section of the courtroom where the jury sits during a trial. Typically, it is separated by a railing from the area reserved for lawyers and is adjacent to the *witness stand.* In some usage, *jury box* is the functional equivalent of the **jury wheel** (□see).

jury fixer: slang for *embracer.* □see **embracery.**

jury instructions: a series of written statements addressed to a trial jury about the law governing the case and the jury's duties in trying to reach a verdict. Usually referred to in the shortened form *instructions.* Each separate statement is an *instruction,* also called a *charge.*

jury instructions

The instructions are read aloud to the jury, typically just before it *retires* to deliberate in secret in the *jury room*. The reading aloud is called **instructing the jury**, also **charging the jury**, or the **charge to the jury**. Under some practice, written instructions are taken into the jury room.

Some instructions have special names:

Allen charge: an instruction of a type approved in *Allen v. United States*, 164 U.S. 492, 501 (1896), designed to produce (some say "blast") a verdict from a deadlocked jury. The typical Allen charge is given after the deliberating jury returns to the courtroom with a report of disagreement. The charge urges a minority to rethink its position in light of an unconvinced majority: to give "proper regard and deference" to the opinions of others, "with a disposition to be convinced," in view of their "duty to decide the case if they can conscientiously do so." Of the many variations, one tells the jury that sooner or later, this case must be decided, under circumstances no better than now. The coercive effect of an Allen charge on the independent judgment of a juror, especially a *holdout juror,* has banned it in many jurisdictions. The *Allen charge* is also called *dynamite charge, nitroglycerin charge, shotgun instruction, third-degree instruction.*

form instructions: printed instructions on the law covering a wide range of recurrent facts in civil and criminal cases. The instructions are customarily devised to be adjustable to variant facts. The force of form instructions varies by jurisdiction, some specifically approved by a court, some required, some recommended, typically annotated to cases where they have been used. Often computerized, form instructions save time of lawyers and judges. Above all, whether or not jurors have understood the instructions, the use of an approved instruction usually avoids a reversal for failure to properly instruct the jury. *Form instructions* are also known as *approved instructions, model instructions, standard instructions, uniform instructions.* A *form instruction* is to be distinguished from a **formula instruction** (□see).

formula instruction: an instruction that if the jury finds specified facts, it must return a verdict for a particular party. Also called a *mandatory instruction.*

mandatory instruction □see **formula instruction**, above, in this entry.

peremptory instruction: an instruction to return a verdict precisely as specified by the judge, e.g., for the plaintiff; for the defendant. The jury has neither choice nor discretion. Some courts equate this with a *formula instruction.* □see also, **directed verdict**, under **verdict**.

jury nullification   □see **nullification**.

jury panel: those selected, or being selected, for service on a grand or a trial jury (□see **jury**). The same expression *jury panel* thus sometimes refers to a final selection of jurors before being sworn, and sometimes refers to a group of individuals in a selection process. The different senses, representing chronological stages of forming a *jury panel,* are often compressed together in varying usage:

1. the group of individuals called to the courthouse to be available for service on a grand or trial jury. This *panel* is sometimes also called the **array** (□see **challenge**); it is sometimes also called the **venire,** from the old writ *venire facias* (L., vuh-NEE-ray FAY-shus: that you cause to come), directing a sheriff to bring in people for jury service. The individuals making up the venire are traditionally known as **veniremen** (sometimes *venirepersons* or *venire persons*). If there are not enough *veniremen,* additional persons (*talesmen*) are sometimes called at random from the courtroom or by special order to fill out the panel.

2. the group of individuals selected at random for jury service from among those who come in as part of the panel (sense 1). *Array, venire,* and *veniremen* sometimes also refer to this panel (sense 2).

3. the group of individuals ultimately chosen for service on a particular grand jury or a particular trial jury from among those in a panel (sense 2). Members of a trial jury panel (sense 3) are said to be **impaneled.**

jury trial   □see **jury**.

jury wheel: a device, sometimes still in the form of a wheel, from which the names of prospective jurors are drawn at random. □see **jury panel**.

just and reasonable: one of the law's most enduring and pervasive **coupled synonyms** (□see), and still without any precise meaning, deliberately flexible. Also rendered as *meet and just,* without improvement. In the contexts where lawyers use *just and reasonable,* either of the words will work, eliminating the redundancy, remaining vague. <The fee was just and reasonable/just/reasonable.> □see also, **equitable, under equity**; □see also, **fair**; □see also, **good cause**.

just cause   □see **good cause**.

justice □see **judge**.

justice of the peace □see **judge**.

justiciable □see **controversy**.

justifiable cause □see **justification**.

justifiable homicide □see **justification**.

justification • excuse

1. In the law generally (as opposed to criminal law), *justification* and *excuse* are freely used as synonyms: for one good legal reason or another, under the circumstances the apparent wrong or neglect is not blameworthy. *Justification* (along with *justifiable* and *justify*) is the less common, as in *justifiable cause* (e.g., a good reason for not making a support payment).

Excuse and *excusable* are more common, as in *excuse* for failure to perform a contract, *excusable neglect* for a late appearance in court, etc. The variety of good legal reasons is covered by the substantive law, e.g., contract, tort, criminal law. □see also, **immunity**. A good legal reason in one area, e.g., tort, may or may not be a good legal reason in another, e.g., criminal law (sense 3).

2. In the law of suretyship, unconnected with *excuse,* a special sense of *justify:* to show that a bond is adequate or that a surety has adequate assets.

3. In the criminal law—

justification

(1) a defense that defendant's conduct, otherwise within the definition of a specific crime, is not criminal because authorized or permitted by other provisions of law. Contrasted with **excuse** (□see, below, in this entry) for conduct that *is* criminal.

Typical justifications are *self-defense,* and various aspects of *law enforcement* by officers and those assisting them, e.g., preventing a felony, making an arrest. Criteria of justification are not uniform. Classification of some defenses as justification or excuse is in dispute, e.g., **duress** (□see), **mistake** (□see), even **self-defense** (□see). Criminal statutes must be consulted for details.

(2) a defense often equated with **excuse** (□see). Usage over the centuries has wobbled, and still varies jurisdiction to jurisdiction, e.g., on what is *justifiable homicide* or *excusable homicide.*

excuse

(1) a defense that defendant should not be held responsible for criminal conduct because of (a) the native condition of defendant's mind or (b) the stress upon it of unusual circumstances. Contrasted with **justification** (□see, above, in this entry).

Typical excuses based on the native condition of the mind are **insanity** (□see), **infancy** (□see **infant**, under **child**). Typical excuses based on stress are **duress** (□see) and **entrapment** (□see). Criteria of excuse are not uniform. Classification of some defenses, including *duress,* as justification or excuse is in dispute. □see **justification**. Criminal statutes must be consulted for details.

(2) a defense often equated with **justification** (□see, above, in this entry).

justify □see **justification**.

juvenile: like *child, infant,* and *minor* (□see **child**), a *juvenile* is a person who is not an adult, age limits not uniform. But unlike the others, *juvenile* is an aloof characterization, with none of the warmth of childhood, infancy, or even minority. Not exclusively so, but more often than with the other words, *juvenile* in the law tends to appear in contexts of criminality (*juvenile offender*) or some other species of degradation. It is an unfortunate child who is battered. An evil person contributes to the delinquency of a minor. And while some laws speak harshly of a *delinquent child,* the real opprobrium is reserved for the sort of half-adult *juvenile delinquent. Juvenile court* is for those underage, is not inevitably punitive; still no wonder that some jurisdictions prefer a *children's court.*

A *juvenile,* though sometimes referred to as a *youth,* is usually distinguished from a **youthful offender** (□see).

juvenile court □see **juvenile**.

juvenile delinquent □see **juvenile**.

juvenile offender □see **juvenile**.

K

keep □see hold; □see also, **coupled synonyms.**

key of your own prison □see **contempt.**

kidnapping: the crime consisting of an unlawful restraint sufficient to constitute **false imprisonment** (□see) plus unlawfully moving the victim farther than a trivial distance.

This definition joins a multitude, few of them in agreement. Some eliminate the old criterion of *carrying away* (moving) the victim. Many couple the basic acts with the purpose of the *kidnapper,* e.g., ransom. Consult the statutes.

kin □see **next of kin,** under **heirs.**

kind □see **in kind.**

kite □see **kiting.**

kiting

1. a fraudulent scheme to obtain money or credit by using an *overdraft* (a check drawn on insufficient funds) on a Bank I account to establish a Bank II account, and overdrafts on the Bank II account to cover overdrafts on the Bank I account. The continuing scheme, with many variations, rests on the time lag between deposit of a check and its presentment for payment. During that time, the fictitious balances can be withdrawn or used for further credit.

The scheme of *kiting,* commonly known as *check kiting* (*check-kiting*), is also called a *kite.* <The bank suspected a kite was in progress.> The overdrafts are also called *kites.* <They kited ten checks. The kites were drawn on four different banks.> The schemer is a *kiter.*

2. less commonly, obtaining credit or interest at Bank II by depositing an overdraft on Bank I, intending to deposit sufficient funds in Bank I to cover the overdraft before it is presented for payment.

3. less commonly, raising the amount of a check by forgery.

knock and announce: a generalized, shorthand description of procedure to be followed by officers before breaking into a house, as in execution of a search warrant. They must make those inside aware of their presence (knock), and announce the authority and purpose of their requested entry (e.g., "Police! Narcotics!"). Sometimes called the *knock and announce rule,* referring to judicial interpretation of constitutional and statutory limitations on search and seizure; sometimes a reference to requirements of a *knock-and-announce statute.*

know has no uniform, precise meaning in the law, any more than it does in ordinary English. That has never been an obstacle to its constant use in and out of law. It is a word of such magnificent scope as to be indispensable. It rambles at ease from barest acquaintance, through slight awareness, to profound understanding, and sexual intercourse. There is not yet an end to the exploration of the possibilities of meaning and nuance of *know* and its kin, *knowing, knowingly, knowledge, knowledgeable, known.* Only in very confining contexts does it speak plainly, sometimes confined only by the lines of a single statute or a single opinion.

For lawyers, *know* and its kin must be handled with caution. The alphabetical entries that follow illustrate the variety of usage.

Know All Men By These Presents: a worthless announcement, introducing a deed or contract; not quite dead, but should be. A long history makes *presents* a singular noun requiring a plural pronoun. *Presents* = this legal writing. □see **formalisms.**

knowing and intelligent waiver: aware of giving up a right + aware of the critical information bearing on that decision + understanding the significance of the information and the giving up. If you want to be sure of what you are saying, spell it out like that. Joined to waiver, *knowing* alone can mean all of those things; *intelligent* adds nothing to the pot, except a hint of lack of confidence and a prayer for greater understanding. The formula *knowing and intelligent* mimics the words of some cases, but is no guarantee that either word is immune to being disemboweled and analyzed in light of the facts. □see **waiver.**

knowingly is as imprecise as its parent **know** (□see), and likewise in constant use, especially in criminal law. It can mean that you are aware of what you are doing, or also aware of the probable consequences. It is commonly equated with intentionally (□see **intent**), and with **willfully** (□see **willful**) and often joined with them, *knowingly*

knowingly

and intentionally, knowingly and willfully. The joining stems from uncertainty, habit, or obedience to some required pattern, itself a creature of uncertainty or habit. *Knowingly* is a common feature of statutory definitions of particular crimes and, as a consequence, a common feature of indictments. Consult the statutes.

knowingly and intentionally □see **knowingly.**

knowingly and willfully □see **knowingly.**

know it when I see it □see **I know it when I see it.** □see also, **hardcore pornography.**

knowledge: something known. As imprecise and as widely used as **know** (□see) and **knowingly** (□see). Legal attempts to tie down *knowledge* by the use of additives and synonyms are not completely discouraging. Here are some of them:

actual knowledge

1. the same as *knowledge; actual* is superfluous. That's the easiest definition to cope with; you're back where you started.

2. something that you *are* aware of, as distinguished from **constructive knowledge**: something that from the circumstances, you *ought* to have been aware of. If you have constructive knowledge of something, you are treated as if you had actual knowledge. In some usage, *constructive knowledge* is called *implied knowledge.* For the *actual/constructive* word play, □see **actual.**

3. a synonym for **notice** (□see).

carnal knowledge □see.

constructive knowledge □see **actual knowledge, above, in this entry.**

imputed knowledge

1. something that you may not know, and may have reason to know, but are *treated* as knowing, because of a legal relationship to someone who *does* know. Substantive law determines what relationships carry such a burden of imputed knowledge, typically a relationship where one acts for another, e.g., the agent's knowledge imputed to the principal. <The landlord had imputed knowledge that the rent had been paid, because the tenant paid the agent authorized by the landlord to receive rents.> □see also, **imputed notice**, under **notice.** □see also, **vicarious disqualification.**

2. sometimes, loosely, equated with constructive or implied knowledge. □see **actual knowledge,** above, in this entry.

judicial knowledge □see **judicial notice.**

to my knowledge is an ambiguous phrase, its meanings poles apart. Relatively harmless in daily speech, it is potentially disastrous in the law. For example: "*To my knowledge,* the Ford ran the red light." That can mean (a) "I know it of my own knowledge. I saw it happen." It can also mean (b) "As far as I know; to the best of my knowledge. That's what I was told."

knowledgeably: a vogue variation of **knowingly** (□see). A space-filler in the phrase *intelligently, knowledgeably, with her eyes open,* a competitor of **knowing and intelligent waiver** (□see).

known criminal   □see **criminal,** under **convict.**

L

labor union   □see **person**; □see **closed shop**.

laches   (law F., LATCH-es: lax): an equitable defense that excessive delay in asserting a claim should result in its denial. Laches invokes a court's equitable discretion to determine the aptness of the defense, especially what delay is excessive under the circumstances. Distinguished from a fixed time bar of a **statute of limitations** (□see).   □see also, **equitable**, under **equity**.

lack of jurisdiction   □see **jurisdiction**.

land

1. (physical: basic): the more or less solid part of the Earth's surface, as distinguished from oceans and seas, but including lakes, flowing waters, and minerals in solid or liquid state. This basic sense of *land*, common English, shows up in legal expressions, e.g., *unimproved land* (on the tax rolls); *land and growing crops; land and buildings*, thus distinguishing land from buildings. In the basic physical description, *land* (sense 1) is one kind of **real property** (□see), and is usually referred to as *real estate*.   <The real estate was a piece of raw land.>

2. (physical: legal): land (sense 1) + those things natural or artificial that through deposit, growth, or construction have become an integral part of it. *Land* (sense 2) is one kind of **real property** (□see), commonly referred to as *real estate*.   <The land in dispute was ten planted acres and a farmhouse, real estate valued at $500,000.>   Within its surface boundaries, a particular piece of land is said to include the space indefinitely upwards and downwards; this is an ancient formulation subject to so much regulation that it must be taken with reserve.   □see also, **airspace**.

3. (ownership): land (senses 1 and 2), considered as the subject of ownership, is usually described by lawyers as *real property,* by brokers as *realty* or *real estate*. Lawyers frequently use the expressions *land* and *real property* interchangeably.   <Some of the land was in California, some in New York; together, the real property was appraised at $1.5 million.>   But *land* does not have the broad sweep of *real property;* they are not universal synonyms.   □see **real property**. For the variety of forms of land ownership, □see **estate**.

landlady □see landlord and tenant.

landlord □see landlord and tenant.

landlord and tenant

1. the general rubric for the body of law governing the relationship between lessors and lessees of real property.

The rubric is historic, once a feudal relationship between an English lord and the person who held the property, his *tenant* (F., from L. *tenere:* to hold). The law of the relationship changed slowly—retaining, discarding, acquiring; the law, now mountainous. A *landlord* may or may not be a lord, may be male or female (a *landlady*). Many *tenants* are no part of a landlord and tenant relationship (e.g., a life tenant). The rubric remains. In the rubric, *landlord* describes the *lessor* element in the relationship, *tenant* the *lessee* element. The law of *lessor and lessee* is not a satisfactory substitute; it refers to both real and personal property; it does not call up quickly some still live antique parts of the law of landlord and tenant. □see **lease;** □see also, **sex.**

2. the relationship between a lessor and lessee of real property. Through subleases, there may be a series of landlord and tenant relationships in the same property, but the relationship (or the first in a series) starts with the owner of the real property and the person who leases from the owner. In the basic relationship, the lessor gives the lessee the right to a temporary possession of the real property in return for payments by the lessee. Many details of the relationship are fixed by lease provisions. What is not spelled out by agreement is supplied by the law of landlord and tenant (sense 1). □see **lease.**

landlord's lien □see lien.

lands and tenements □see real property.

lands, tenements, and hereditaments □see real property.

language of the law: the customary language of lawyers that sets their speech and writing apart from the language of ordinary people.

The label for that customary language is not uniform. *Legalese* is common; so is *legal jargon.* Some of the labels are less polite, e.g., "excrementitious matter," "literary garbage." (3 Bentham, *Works*

353

language of the law

260, Bowring ed., 1843). A more recent label for the least needed and most widespread elements of the language of the law is **lawsick**:

"a peculiar, English-like language commonly used in writing about law; peculiar in habitual indifference to ordinary usage of English words, grammar, and punctuation; and in preferring the archaic, wordy, pompous, and confusing over the clear, brief, and simple; persists chiefly through a belief of its writers that these peculiarities lead to precision." (Mellinkoff, *Legal Writing: Sense and Nonsense*, xii, 1982). For a detailed description of the language of the law and how it got that way, see Mellinkoff, *The Language of the Law* (1963). □see also, **plain language**.

lapse

1. the end of a right because the requirements for its continuing have not been met. E.g., a *lapsed insurance policy:* one that has expired by its own terms, as by failure to pay premiums or by failure to renew; a *lapsed power of appointment:* one that has not been exercised within the allotted time. □see **appoint**.

2. the end of the possibility of a right coming into being because the requirements for its coming into being have not been met. E.g., a lapsed gift by will (*lapsed legacy, lapsed devise*): one that does not pass by will because of some legal incapacity of the donee, or the donee's death after the will is executed and before the death of the testator. Also called a *failed legacy, failed devise.* □see **fail**.

anti-lapse statute, sometimes called a *lapse statute:* one providing that a gift by will that would otherwise lapse shall not lapse but shall go to beneficiaries specified in the statute, e.g., issue of the donee.

lapse statute   □see **lapse**.

larceny: a name derived from French for the common law crime of taking and carrying away personal property with the intent to deprive the owner of the property. That **intent** (□see) is described as *intent to steal*, the common English word. The same crime is also known by the English name *theft*. The present crime of *larceny* or *theft*, taking its basic cue from the common law, has innumerable statutory definitions that must be consulted for the greatest variety of *stealing*, misdemeanors and felonies. Some *larceny* or *theft* is *grand*, some *petty* (also *petit*), depending on value. Some jurisdictions include in the crime what others exclude, e.g., **embezzlement** (□see), **extortion** (□see). Newly defined crimes of the genre crop up to meet every new ascent and descent of the creative mind, e.g., in areas of credit cards, computers, software.

last clear chance □see **clear**.

last will □see **will**.

last will and testament □see **will**.

latent ambiguity: a hidden uncertainty in the meaning of a writing. It is "hidden" in the sense that uncertainty is not apparent (patent) from the words alone, but arises when one tries to apply the words to what they apparently refer to. E.g., "My oldest friend" is a *patent ambiguity.* "My niece Mary," apparently clear, turns out to be a latent ambiguity when you learn that I have two nieces named Mary. □see **ambiguity**.

latent defect: a defect, e.g., in an item of manufacture, not revealed by reasonable inspection, as distinguished from one that is: *patent defect.*

lateral support

1. support of land in its natural state by the land adjoining it on all sides; as distinguished from **subjacent support**, support by the land underneath.

2. **the right of lateral support**: the right of the owner of land to lateral support (sense 1), as distinguished from the right of subjacent support.

Latin □see **law Latin**.

laughing heirs □see **heirs**.

laundering

1. the common English word for washing clothes, imaginatively transformed into common English for washing away the taint of crime by disguising the proceeds of illegality and so making them usable. The process has become big business and itself a separate crime (sense 2). Typically, illegally obtained cash is moved in one or more transfers to apparently legitimate banks or businesses, in ex-

change for other forms of money, property, or interest in a business, blurring or wiping out the track to the original proceeds of crime. *Laundering* is short for *laundering of money* or *money laundering.* An individual participant is a *launderer;* a bank or other business engaged in laundering is, in slang usage, a *laundry.*

2. money laundering, as a crime, is described, with varying details, in state and federal statutes. E.g., the Money Laundering Control Act of 1986, especially 18 USCA § 1956: using the proceeds of crime to carry on a crime, to disguise the illegal origin of the proceeds, or to avoid a reporting requirement of a bank or similar enterprise. Whether or not the dealing is in cash or cash substitutes (e.g., freely transferable bearer paper), the crime is referred to as *money laundering.*

law

1. (*the* law): the entire body of principles, precedents, rules, and procedures intended to assure order and justice in a civilized society. It includes constitutions, legislation, decisions—federal, state, and local, civil and criminal. It includes the **common law** (□see) and constitutional law (□see **constitutional**). This is the law in *the law of the land* and *as provided by law.* □see also, **jurisprudence**.

2. (*a* law): a particular rule, statute, or decision. <Look it up in the Civil Code; there is a law covering that./That's the law as decided in *Smith v. Jones.*/The red light means "stop"; that's the law, mister.>

3. (a branch of law): a grouping by category of law (sense 1) that embodies distinctive rules, statutes, and decisions (sense 2), classified by special names, e.g., criminal law, contract law, international law, the law of torts, the law of negligence.

4. (law of a jurisdiction): collectively, the distinctive law (senses 1 and 2) of a particular **jurisdiction** (□see). This is the law of "*What law governs?*" □see **conflict of laws**.

5. (law, not equity): practices and remedies included in law (senses 1 and 2), as distinguished from **equity** (□see). <This action is at law, and they are entitled to a jury trial.>

6. (the academic discipline): the formal study of law (sense 1) or some aspect of it, including the particulars (sense 2). <She switched from philosophy to law./They are enrolled at the law school.>

7. (the profession): the practice of law. <The law is one of the learned professions.> □see **lawyer**. □see also, **lawful**; □see also, **illegal**.

law clerk: a lawyer, usually a recent graduate, who performs miscellaneous tasks (*clerks*) for a judge: e.g., researches, drafts memorandums of law, analyzes argument and briefs, drafts or ghostwrites opinions for which a judge takes credit and responsibility. <He was a law clerk for two years after graduation./She clerked for Justice White.> Also sometimes applied to a student who has not yet passed the bar, doing similar work for a judge or a lawyer.

law firm □see **firm**.

law French: words of French origin used in the law, as distinguished from ordinary French. Law French words and phrases identified in this dictionary are survivors of a variety of French some have called "barbarous" or "bastard French," once the spoken language of the English courtroom and the written language of English lawyers and judges. *Law French* is not a term of art. Content has changed over the centuries, leaving in its wake argument over provenance and pronunciation, and a mixed bag of expressions, still regarded as exotic, yet almost unshakable. The legacy ranges from the precise (e.g., □see **voir dire**) to the confusing (e.g., □see **demise**), with intermediate dispensable stops, e.g., *cestui que trust* (□see **beneficiary**); e.g., *en ventre sa mère* (□see **child**). The expression is usually written *law French*, sometimes *Law French*, both forms sometimes hyphenated.

lawful • legal

The historic mixture of language streams gives us two words where one would otherwise suffice (□see **illegal**). Unlike the negatives *unlawful* and *illegal*, which are usually interchangeable, *lawful* and *legal* more often lead independent lives, even to the extent of separate expression for the same bit of substance. Some overlap continues in the two principle senses:

1. in conformity with the law. *Lawful* and *legal* are often used as synonyms. E.g., a lawful (or legal) business; a lawful (or legal) order. □see also, **legitimate**.

2. pertaining to the law. An occasional overlap, e.g., *lawful age* or *legal age*. But *legal* is the clear favorite, often to the point of redundancy, e.g., *in legal custody = in custody*. □see **custody**. In most usage in this sense (sense 2), *lawful* would be plain wrong, no substitute for *legal;* e.g., *legal fees, legal conclusions, legally blind*.

Combinations using one word or the other are alphabetical entries of the general index.

357

lawful age: the age at which for various legal purposes one becomes an adult.   Also called *legal age, full age, of age, age of majority, majority.*   As with the opposite, *minority* (□see **child**), precise age varies by jurisdiction, decision, and statute.   Right to vote for those eighteen or older is guaranteed by the U.S. Constitution, Amendment XXVI.   □see also, **age of consent**.

lawful arrest: taking a person into **custody** (□see) in conformity with the requirements of law, especially constitutional requirements.   Also called *legal arrest.*

Lawful arrest and *legal arrest* are often used interchangeably, sometimes in the same writing.   There can be distinctive usage:

   1.   To an accusation or claim that an arrest is unlawful or illegal, a quick, especially oral, response is likely to be "It's legal," or "It's a legal arrest."   A more considered response, oral or written, as in courtroom argument, in a brief, in an opinion, is more likely to be "It was a lawful arrest."

   2.   To emphasize to someone being arrested that the arrest is not haphazard or unauthorized, an oral explanation is more likely to be "This is a *legal* arrest," i.e., not merely in conformity with law but pertaining to law.   □see **law**; □see also, **knock and announce**.

lawful cause: an equivalent of **good cause** (□see).   Also called *legal cause,* a usage unconnected with the causation sense of **legal cause** (□see).

lawful discharge (of employee):   a generalized, untechnical label for the conclusion that a discharge did not violate an employee's rights, as contrasted with **wrongful discharge** (□see).   □see also, **bad faith**.

lawful interest   □see **legal interest**.

lawful issue: often understood, and in frequent use, to mean *legitimate issue.*   □see **legitimate**; □see **issue**, under **descendant**.   It is an unreliable usage, subject to more than ordinary interpretation in the light of presumed intent and of statutes and decisions affecting the legitimacy of children (□see **filiation proceedings**), the forms of marriage (□see **cohabitation**), and the changing rules of intestate succession.   If a testator or trustor is insistent on old-fashioned legitimacy as a prerequisite to inheritance, that intent had best be spelled out. *Lawful issue* is sometimes, not usually, called *legal issue.*

lawful money: an older, fading expression of the medium of exchange sense of **legal tender** (□see).

lawful wedded wife   □see **wedlock.**

law Latin: Latin words and phrases used in ways peculiar to the law, as distinguished from the Latin of classical scholarship and from Latin used outside of the law.   Some of the Latin in law Latin has become common English, e.g., *bona fide, quorum, versus,* needing only an occasional reminder that legal and common usage may diverge sharply, as with **alibi** (□see).   Latin in the law is an inheritance from the earliest days of the profession in England.   A small part of it has produced terms of art and useful professional shorthand, glued to the profession, at least for the rest of this century.   Even more law Latin is worthless affectation, imprecise, often misused, and ripe for discard.   Entries of law Latin in this dictionary suggest English substitutes when they better serve the purpose.

Pronunciation of law Latin is not classical, tending more to the slurring of a live language, as in *sir-sher-uh-RARE-e* (□see **certiorari**). Nor is pronunciation of law Latin uniform, because neither taught as a language nor spoken enough to develop a standard.   Variations are hotly defended as the one true sound, on the basis of indoctrination by a favorite professor, now dead: *res* is most certainly RACE, unless it is REECE.   □see **res.**

law list: a commercial publication listing lawyers by area, sometimes with advertisements of specialization, sometimes with ratings of integrity and competence based on the opinions of other lawyers in the community.

law looks with favor upon   □see **clichés.**

law merchant: an old translation of the Latin *lex mercatoria:* an old international law of merchants and mariners growing out of their customary practices.   It was a law practiced and enforced by businessmen and shipowners in their own courts, without professional judges or lawyers.   Some of the law merchant, especially the law of commercial paper, became a part of the common law of England and, in turn, a major influence on common and statutory commercial law in the United States.

law of capture, also called **rule of capture**: a general label for law relating to acquiring ownership where no ownership by anyone existed before. The law of capture has been applied to:

1. *wild animals:* ownership of wild animals (□see **ferae naturae**) is obtained by capturing them. Short of the hunter obtaining physical possession of the animal, "capture" hinges on the activity of the hunter and the condition of the hunted.

2. *migratory minerals,* specifically, underground oil and gas, sometimes called *minerals ferae naturae* (□see **ferae naturae**): subject to government and private regulation, oil and gas produced from wells drilled on an owner's land become the property of the landowner, even though the minerals migrated there from other land. Some decisions limit this law of capture out of concern for injury to adjacent owners.

3. *water*

a. groundwater, also called **percolating waters**, i.e., underground water that is not within a definite channel and saturates the rocky subsoil of an owner's land: in some jurisdictions, this freely moving water, like other migratory minerals (sense 2), no matter where it came from, may be used or diverted by the landowner. Other jurisdictions limit capture by the landowner.

b. flowing surface streams:

(1) Under rules of **prior appropriation**, a flowing surface stream not otherwise owned may be diverted from its natural channel and become the property of those who thus first appropriate it. This application of the law of capture is variously applied, modified, regulated, and rejected.

(2) In contrast to the law of capture, under rules of **riparian rights**, the waters of a flowing surface stream belong in varying proportions to the *riparian owners,* those who own the land bordering on the water, whether or not they use the water.

Details of the rules of prior appropriation and riparian rights, varying by jurisdiction, are beyond the scope of this dictionary.

law of nations: an older term for what is now generally called **international law** (□see). (See U.S. Const., Art. I, § 8, cl. 10.)

law of the case: the points of law that have been decided (not merely dicta) by an appellate court in a particular case and now govern all later proceedings in the same case between the same parties. The *law of the case* is to be followed, not relitigated, in a retrial or another appeal. The *law of the case* can be nibbled away: a substantial change of evidence, a changed statute, a controlling new interpretation of law by a higher court will undercut it. Local practice establishes degrees of rigidity or flexibility, sometimes limiting it to law decided by a court of last resort, sometimes relaxing its application to prevent injustice.

law of the forum □see **forum**.

law of the land: a general expression of **law** (□see) as the governing element in a state, an imprecise yet enduring inheritance from **Magna Carta** (□see).

law of the place □see **lex loci**.

law of the sea: in general, the aspect of **international law** (□see) that deals with the rights and limitations of nations in, over, under, and connected with the sea. The scope of those rights and limitations is subject to international agreement and disagreement. The most wide-ranging international agreement is the United Nations Convention on the Law of the Sea, Dec. 10, 1982 (United Nations Document A/CONF 62/122, Oct. 7, Nov. 23, and Nov. 26, 1982, in American Society of International Law's *International Legal Materials,* vol. 21, 1982, pp. 1261–1354). The United States has rejected the Convention, chiefly because of its provisions on deep seabed mining. (See *Restatement (Third) Foreign Relations Law of the United States,* vol. 2, pt. V, ch. 3, § 523, 1986.) Law of the sea is to be distinguished from admiralty and **maritime law** (□see).

law reports: collectively, the volumes of printed opinions, decisions, and some orders, of state and federal courts, commonly referred to as *the reports* or *the reporters* (books, not people). The reports are to be distinguished from a case-by-case publication in **slip opinions** (□see). The reports first appear in print as paperback *advance sheets;* many reports are computerized.

The reports have names given by their official or unofficial (private) publishers. The names, hundreds of them, vary by jurisdiction, by courts, by geographical area, by specialized editions for particular courts and particular legal topics. For a readily available listing (massive, though not exhaustive) of named reports and abbreviations, refer to *A Uniform System of Citation*, 14th ed., 1986 (Harvard Law Review Association), generally called the *Bluebook*. For a small sampling, here, in alphabetical order, are report names and latest edition abbreviations used in this dictionary:

California Appellate Reports	Cal.App.3d
California Reports	Cal.3d
English Reports	Eng.Rep.
Federal Reporter	F.2d
Federal Supplement	F.Supp.
New York Reports	N.Y.
Southern Reporter	So.2d
Supreme Court Reporter	S.Ct.
United States Reports	U.S.

□see also, **citation**.

law review: a scholarly periodical devoted to articles, comments, and notes about the law as it is and as it ought to be. Ordinarily published by law schools, with professional and student contributions, the American law review is distinctive for being run by honors students. With minimal guidance, and despite some pressures, they generally select and edit what is published and write some of it. Law review content ranges from the trivial to the brilliantly innovative; style is characterized by massive, interlocking, argumentative footnotes, overlaid by lawsick (□see **language of the law**).

Law School Admission Test □see **LSAT**.

lawsick □see **language of the law**.

lawsuit □see **action**.

lawyer

1. the most general term for someone licensed as competent to follow the occupation of both representing others in court and guiding them in legal matters in court and out.

The occupation is called the **practice of law**, but, itself having no uniform definition, that description does not help in defining *lawyer*. It lends itself to the circular platitude: a lawyer is one who practices law, which is what is done by a lawyer. Since most lawyers call themselves by more stylish synonyms, some prefer the terse *lawyer* as a subtle suggestion of quality. □see also, **officer of the court,** under **office.**

a. *General synonyms*

attorney (pl. *attorneys*) is the most common. Short for **attorney at law;** both distinct from **attorney in fact** (□see). *Attorney* is the standard usage in the **attorney-client privilege** (□see). □see also, **attorney's lien,** under **lien.**

counsel may be singular <She was counsel on the appeal.>, unspecifically singular or plural <The accused has a right to counsel.>, or plural <Both counsel were competent.>. The plural with *s* is occasionally used. <The two counsels conferred.>

counselor and **counselor at law,** in the practice of some jurisdictions.

member of the bar □see **bar.**

b. *Government lawyers*

Attorney General (pl. *attorneys general*): chief law officer of the United States or of a state.

Solicitor General: the principal lawyer representing the United States in the courts, especially the Supreme Court.

district attorney: prosecuting officer of a county or similar unit; also called *county attorney, county prosecutor, prosecuting attorney, public prosecutor, state's attorney.* Also, the *United States attorney* for a federal judicial district.

county counsel, sometimes *solicitor:* handles civil matters for a county or similar unit.

city attorney: handles civil and criminal matters for a city.

legislative counsel: has miscellaneous duties in connection with legislation, especially advising legislators on preparation of proposals for new laws.

public defender (federal, state, or local): defends indigents charged with crime; sometimes provides limited civil representation to indigents; distinct from occasional services in either capacity by any lawyer as **appointed counsel** (□see, below, in this entry).

trial judge advocate: prosecuting officer, usually but not necessarily a lawyer, in a *court martial.*

United States attorney □see **district attorney.**

c. *Private lawyers*

general counsel: chief lawyer or firm of lawyers for a business.

house counsel, or **in-house counsel:** regular employee of a business, usually working at the business premises; distinct from **outside counsel,** hired for a special job.

of counsel: designation of a lawyer with a continuing relationship with another lawyer or lawyers, but neither as *associate* (usually a newer, younger lawyer employed by a firm) nor *partner.* <The firm's letterhead listed John Smith under the heading "Of Counsel.">□ see also, **of counsel on the brief,** below, under **trial lawyer,** in this entry.

public interest lawyer: regularly employed in a *public interest law firm* (sometimes abbreviated *PILF*), serving clients at reduced or no fee **pro bono,** short for *pro bono publico* (L.: for the public good); distinct from occasional *pro bono* work by any lawyer. □see also, **legal aid.**

d. *Expertise or specialization*

criminal lawyer, divorce lawyer, tax lawyer, etc. Under some state rules, certified specialist in designated fields.

An **admiralty lawyer** specializes in maritime law, but any lawyer handling a maritime matter is acting as a **proctor in admiralty.**

litigator is a spreading designation for lawyers specializing in litigation, as distinct from their clients. The name is used by those in a *litigation department* of a law firm, as well as by those who go to court.

e. *Role of the moment*

attorney (or **counsel**) **of record:** the lawyer whose name is on the papers in court as appearing for a particular client. □see **appear.**

trial lawyer, *defense counsel, plaintiff's counsel; of counsel on the brief:* lawyer hired to work with others on the brief in this case.

retained counsel: hired—as distinct from being **assigned** or **appointed counsel:** a lawyer who is "assigned" or "appointed," i.e., ordered or "requested" by a judge to represent someone. □see **fee (attorney's fee);** □see **right to counsel.**

prosecutor or **prosecuting attorney:** lawyer conducting a criminal investigation or prosecution, whether or not regularly

so employed; also sometimes called an **independent counsel.**
<To avoid a conflict of interest in the Attorney General's office, they appointed a special prosecutor/an independent counsel.> □see also, **prosecuting witness.**

private attorney general: lawyer suing to right a public wrong and claiming fees for benefiting the public.

f. *Uncomplimentary synonyms,* acquired from the laity, but refined by lawyers to apply to other lawyers.

ambulance chaser: uses questionable means to get business.

shyster: uses questionable means to take care of business.

pettifogger: dealer in small and sharp practice.

Philadelphia lawyer: high-priced trickster skilled in finding loopholes.

legal eagle, also **legal beagle:** less high-priced trickster skilled in finding loopholes.

hired gun: unscrupulous lawyer, anything for a fee.

lip, also **mouthpiece:** unscrupulous criminal lawyer, anything for a fee, with a hint of underworld connection.

Wall Street lawyer: located on that street and acting only for big business and high finance.

g. *Complimentary additions*

Esquire, abbreviated Esq. □see **Esquire.**

distinguished member of the bar: a form introduction for almost any lawyer.

successful attorney: part of the eulogy for a dead lawyer.

2. one representing himself in court, whether or not licensed as a lawyer. Phrases are *acting as his own* lawyer; appearing *pro se,* or appearing *in propria persona.* □see **appear.**

3. one not licensed as a lawyer who performs some of the services of a lawyer (sense 1), or tries to.

a. a common feature of problems of unlicensed practice of law.
<He represented himself to be a lawyer./She was acting as a lawyer, though not admitted to practice.>

b. In administrative proceedings (and in the U.S. Tax Court) where a lawyer (sense 1) is not required, a representative may be said to be *acting as a lawyer* or to be a *lay lawyer.* Before the U.S.

Patent Office, **patent agents** act as lawyers without using the word.

  c. *Uncomplimentary synonyms*

    In prisons: **jailhouse lawyer** or **writ writer.**

    In the military: **guardhouse lawyer.**

4. as a verb, lawyer and lawyering: to act as a lawyer. <She lawyered in every court in the land./He was lawyering all over the state.> *Lawyering* is also used as a noun. <That professor really taught lawyering.>

lawyering □see **lawyer.**

lawyer's fee □see **fee (attorney's fee).**

lay

1. in special contexts, to allege, e.g., damages, venue. <Plaintiff amended the complaint to lay the damages at $10,000./They laid the venue in Wyoming.> □see also, **lie.**

2. lay a foundation: presenting preliminary evidence to establish the admissibility of other evidence, e.g., qualification of a witness to give expert testimony. □see **voir dire.**

lay a foundation □see **lay.**

leading □see **leading question.**

leading case: a case repeatedly cited by the profession for a decision that is an important precedent, or for an opinion that clarifies difficult issues in a particular area of law. Usually, not always, the case is one on appeal. E.g., in tort law (negligence), the *Palsgraf Case* (*Palsgraf v. Long Island Railroad Co.,* 248 N.Y. 339; reargument denied, 249 N.Y. 511 (1928)); in libel law (First Amendment), *New York Times v. Sullivan,* 376 U.S. 255 (1964).

leading question

1. a question so framed as to suggest to the witness an answer desired by the examining lawyer and to guide (lead) the witness into giving that answer. <You really didn't see any gun at all; you were just guessing; isn't that right?>

This is the principle sense of *leading question,* the sense that has resulted in rules of evidence limiting the occasions when leading questions are permissible. □see **cross-examination,** under **cross-;** □see also, **hostile witness.** The judge's broad discretion in determining what is permissible is invoked by the elliptic objections "*Leading!*"; "*Leading and suggestive!*"; "You're *leading the witness!*"

2. a question directing the witness's attention to a particular set-ting—date, time, place, events, etc.—as a prelude to another question. <On December 25 of this year, at about 4 p.m., were you at the southwest corner of Main and Tulsa, in front of the Smith & Company store?> At its worst, this type of question may partake of the same vice as sense 1, tending to "create," rather than "refresh," a recollection. At its best, it may be a time-saver over protracted detailed questioning.

learned in the law: an old and loose expression, applied without fine discrimination to refer to lawyers and judges. Sometimes refers to anyone who has been admitted to the bar; sometimes restricted to lawyers who have not been disbarred; sometimes applies to anyone who serves as a judge, whether or not ever admitted to the bar.

learned profession: law, medicine, and theology have been for cen-turies described as "the three learned professions."

learned trial judge: a customary reference to the trial judge whose decision is reversed on appeal. <With due respect to the learned trial judge, we hold. . . .> In the same category with *able argument.* □see **clichés.**

lease • rent • hire (property)

lease

1. An agreement in which a *lessor* gives a *lessee* temporary posses-sion of property, and the lessee in turn agrees to pay **rent** (□see, below, in this entry). A lease may be of real or personal property; and, except as provided by special laws, e.g., a **statute of frauds** (□see), a lease may be oral or written. If written, the writing embodying the agreement is also called the *lease.* <Plaintiff at-tached a copy of the lease to the complaint.>

leasehold, also called *leasehold estate:* the estate created by a lease of real property. The expression is not applied to a lease of personal property. Lessor and lessee of a leasehold are also described as **landlord and tenant** (□see); lessor and lessee of personal property are not. For the variety of leasehold estates, □see **estate**. □see also, **chattel real**.

sublease, also called *sublet* (n., v.): a lease by the original lessee to someone else, covering the whole or part of the property and the balance or part of the term of the original lease (the *master lease*). The original lessee is the *sublessor* of the sublease, having sublet to a *sublessee*. Typically, subleases are of real property, in which case the sublessee may be referred to as a *subtenant*. Unless forbidden by law or agreement, a succession of subleases is possible, each called a *sublease*, or *sub sublease*, etc.

ground lease, also *groundlease* (n., v.): a lease of unimproved real estate. Not related to *ground rent* (□see **rent**, below, in this entry).

leaseback: a lease that is part of a transaction for the sale of property (typically real property), designed with an eye to taxes. The purchaser of the property, as lessor, leases (leases back) the property to the seller, as lessee.

mining lease (□see).

2. To *give* or *obtain* the use of property under a lease (sense 1).

Without some reference to lessor or lessee, or other informing context, the verb *lease* is ambiguous. <They leased the property.> It leaves in doubt who is giving (leasing to, leasing out) and who is obtaining the use (leasing from).

let: to *give* the use of property under a lease. <They let the premises.> *Let* avoids ambiguity but is no longer a popular American substitute for the verbs *lease, rent,* or *hire,* except in the curt sign "Apt. *to let*" and in the form *sublet* (□see **sublease**).

demise (n., v.): this law French horror is frequently used as a synonym for *lease* in opinions and other writings. <The leased premises. . . ./The demised premises. . . .> Avoid it. □see **demise**.

□see **rent**, below, in this entry; □see **hire (property)**, below, in this entry; □see also, **hire (a person)**.

rent

1. As a verb, *rent* is a synonym of *lease* (sense 2). There are some nuances of choice:

a. For both real and personal property, *lease* is more characteristically the lawyer's word, *rent* the lay term. *To lease* suggests more formality, especially the preparation of leases, as opposed to a *rental agreement,* which may be the same thing. <I'll rent it, but I won't sign a lease.> Personal property is increasingly "leased" or "rented." In the language of computer people, *renting* is user-friendly.

b. Lawyers as well as ordinary people tend to regard *leasing* real property as implying a longer term than *renting* it, though no legal barrier stands in the way of synonymous usage. <The owner is willing to rent the property, but she won't give a lease.>

2. As a verb, *rent* (not lease) has crossed the barrier between people and property. It is now possible to **rent-a-judge** (□see).

3. As a noun, *rent* is payment by a lessee (sometimes called a *renter*) to a lessor for the temporary right to possession of property under a **lease** (□see). Also called *rental. Rent,* especially of real property, is usually paid periodically.

ground rent: a periodic payment by the purchaser of land to the owner of the fee, or by the lessee to the lessor for renewal of a very long-term lease. A medieval survival in some jurisdictions. Not related to *ground lease* (□see **lease**, above, in this entry).

hire (property)

1. As a verb, *hire* (property) is, in a general sense, a synonym of *lease* (sense 2). It is less popular than to lease or to rent, and, as a matter of customary usage, *hire* carries distinguishing restrictions:

a. *Hire* most often refers to personal rather than real property, e.g., a horse, autos, trucks, boats, mechanical tools. *Lease* and *rent* are frequently used in the same sense, but are also the verbs of choice for a wider range of personal property, e.g., a fleet of autos; massive manufacturing equipment; not merely a computer but a computerized system for a firm or corporation.

b. *Hiring* real property usually refers to possession of only a small portion of a building, e.g., rooms rather than an apartment; a banquet hall; an auditorium. *Lease* or *rent* may be used in the same sense, but *hire* does not share the unrestricted scope of either of those words.

c. *Hiring* real or personal property is more often for a short-term use, e.g., a day, a trip, a celebration, a political event. *Lease* or *rent* may be used in the same sense; but *hiring* is not usually for the long term, as *lease* or *rent* often are for personal property, and as *lease* especially frequently is for real property.

□see also, **hire (a person)**.

2. As a noun, *hire* (property):

a. An agreement, called a *hire* or a *hiring,* for the temporary use of property, similar to a lease (sense 1). The noun carries the same usage restrictions applicable to verb *hire* (sense 1). The person obtaining the use of the property is sometimes called the *hirer.*

b. The price to be paid by the *hirer.* Often a lump-sum payment, as distinguished from periodic rent.

leaseback □see **lease.**

leasehold □see **lease.**

leasehold estate □see **leasehold,** under **lease.**

leave of court: an exercise of a court's discretion to change a usual practice or procedure. *Leave of court* is given or denied by court order; accordingly, recital of the words *leave of court* or *by leave of court* is usually a redundancy. <By leave of court/plaintiff obtained an order shortening defendant's time to plead to the second amended complaint.>

legacy □see **gift.**

legal

1. For the overlap of *legal* and *lawful,* □see **lawful;** □see also, **illegal.** Expressions using *legal* as an adjective are separate alphabetical entries.

2. the legal (argot): the usual professional substitute for *legal description:* the official description of a piece of real estate. That description varies by historical patterns of settlement and the subdivision habits of particular areas of the United States. It is usually expressed in surveyor's language (□see **metes and bounds**) or in the details of a recorded map, e.g., Tract 20, Block 1, Lot 1, as recorded in Book 5752, page 2 of Records, Official Records of Mushwah County, California. <Please send me the legal on your client's acreage./The legal you asked for is. . . .>

□see also, **legals.**

legal age □see **lawful age;** □see also, **child.**

legal aid

1. general name for an organization or office that provides legal services without fee or at reduced fees to those otherwise unable to hire a lawyer. Legal aid is funded by private and public contributions. □see also, **public interest lawyer**, under **lawyer**. ·

2. the legal services provided by a legal aid organization or office (sense 1). The services are usually in civil matters, including litigation, not generally provided by a public defender (□see **lawyer**) and not generally covered by **right to counsel** (□see).

legal arrest   □see **lawful arrest**.

legal beagle   □see **lawyer**.

legal capacity: the basic qualification that the law requires an individual to have in order to perform or be accountable for certain acts, e.g., to sue, to contract, to be subject to criminal punishment. *Legal capacity* is a general term of reference, often expressed in the negatives for lack of legal capacity—**legal incapacity**, also called **legal disability**. The expressions take on a measure of precision in specific applications of capacity or incapacity, e.g., □see **lawful age**; □see **infancy defense**, under **child**; □see **sui juris**, under **child**; □see **guardian**; □see **conservatorship**.

legal capacity to sue   □see **legal capacity**.

legal capital   □see **stated capital**.

legal cause

1. another name for **proximate cause** (□see).

2. another name for **lawful cause** (□see), a sense unconnected with sense 1.

legal conclusion   □see **conclusion of law**, under **finding**.

legal custody   □see **custody**.

legal description   □see **the legal**, under **legal**.

legal detriment □see detriment.

legal disability □see legal capacity.

legal domicile □see domicile.

legal eagle □see lawyer.

legal entity □see person.

legal estate □ see equity.

legal ethics Casting aside the cynic's view that *legal ethics* is an oxymoron, the profession still searches for consensus. Most law school courses once labeled "Legal Ethics" have been relabeled "Professional Responsibility." As a general term, **professional responsibility** has been described as "the obligation to perform properly as a lawyer"; it is commonly referred to as *professional ethics*. Here are two working definitions of *legal ethics:*

1. general moral principles as adapted to the unique role of the lawyer in our society.

Adaptation and specific applications of moral principle to lawyers, the profession of law, and the practice of law leave room for sharp disagreement. Aspects of legal ethics regarded by some as essential to the role of lawyer, others regard as abandonment of moral principle. E.g., defense of the guilty; confidentiality between lawyer and client.

2. that part of legal ethics (sense 1) set forth in statutes, decisions, canons, codes, and rules. E.g., the *Model Code of Professional Responsibility* and the *Model Rules of Professional Conduct,* both prepared by the American Bar Association; one or the other is followed in whole or in part by statutes and rules in most jurisdictions. <They follow legal ethics by the book; if it's not there, they're on their own.>

legal excuse □see justification.

legal fees □see fee (attorney's fee).

legal fiction

1. in pleadings and other legal writings, a standardized false statement that is not permitted to be exposed, and so serves as a mechanical device to make the law apply where otherwise it would not. E.g., the historic allegation that an event in Spain took place in London, thus giving an English court jurisdiction. E.g., that a corporation is a person, though no one can see it, a legal fiction so standardized that it is often regarded not as a fiction but as a redefinition of *person*. E.g., that A has a book in her possession, when everyone can see that B is holding it, a fiction obscured by speaking of *actual* and *constructive* **possession** (□see).

2. law expressed as a metaphor. E.g., when a tenant of Blackacre acquires the fee, the tenant's lease ends, a legal effect described as a *merger* of the lesser in the greater estate. □see also, **merger**, under **parol evidence rule**. □see **equitable conversion**, under **conversion**.

3. a standardized rationalization for a judicial conclusion. E.g., the conclusion that regulation is justified because a business is *affected with a public interest*.

legal incapacity: for some legal reason lacking the power to act. E.g., not of **lawful age** (□see). □see also, **child**.

legal instrument   □see **instrument**.

legal insurance   □see **prepaid legal services**.

legal interest

1. (on money)

    a. the maximum rate of interest permitted by law for the use or forbearance of money (□see, under **forbearance**). Also sometimes called *lawful interest*. Interest in excess of legal or lawful interest is **usury**, also called *usurious interest, unlawful* or *illegal interest*. <The state usury statute fixed legal interest at different rates, varying with the type of loan and the business of the lender.> *Legal interest* and *lawful interest* in this sense a. are to be sharply distinguished from the same expressions in sense b.

    b. the rate of interest fixed by law for overdue money obligations and for interest-bearing obligations that do not specify the rate of interest, e.g., "payable with interest." Also called *lawful interest*.

legal interest

Legal interest or lawful interest in this sense b. is usually less than the maximum under sense a.

2. (in property): a general, unspecific expression of some ownership or right of property recognized at law, as distinguished from an **equitable interest** (□see, under **equity**). <She conveyed to him whatever legal interest she had in the property.>

3. (in a lawsuit): a property interest (sense 2) or other interest recognized by law (e.g., freedom from defamation) that gives one a right to participate in a lawsuit. □see **standing**, under **controversy**.

legal investments: investments of money or property that may be made or held by fiduciaries and some regulated funds and businesses. Commonly called **legals**. Statutes, local and federal, detail forms of permitted investment (e.g., types of securities, bank accounts) and who is subject to regulation (e.g., pension funds, banks, insurance companies).

legally binding agreement □see **contract**; □see also, **arbitration**.

legally blind: characterization of one who is not totally blind, but whose sense of sight is sufficiently impaired to meet the standards of statute or regulation designed to help those so affected.

legally drunk, also called *legally intoxicated:* the condition of one whose physical or mental functions are impaired by alcohol or drugs, and who flunks a drunk test. These tests (e.g., percentage of alcohol in the blood) are designed to fix the otherwise flexible meaning, in law as in the common speech, of the ordinary words *drunk, intoxicated, inebriated.*

legally intoxicated □see **legally drunk**.

legal malice □see **malice**.

legal malpractice □see **malpractice**.

legal newspaper

1. a general designation of a newspaper that qualifies under particular laws to publish legal notices (□see **notice**). Under some statutes and ordinances, to the same effect are *newspaper of general circulation* and plain *newspaper*.

2. looser than sense 1, a newspaper that concentrates on news and other writing of particular interest to lawyers.

legal notice   □see **notice.**

legal obligation: an obligation imposed by law or undertaken by contract.   □see **obligation;** □see also, **contract.**

legal owner: one having the **legal title** to property, as distinguished from the *equitable owner.*   □see **beneficial owner,** under **beneficiary.** □see also, **equitable ownership,** under **equity.**   In looser usage, *legal owner* is a mildly emphatic redundancy.   <He was an intruder; she was the legal owner of the property./ . . . she was the owner of the property.>

legal representative   □see **executor.**

legal residence   □see **domicile.**

legals   □see **legal investments.**

legal separation   □see **divorce.**

Legal Services Corporation: a private, nonprofit corporation established in 1974 "for the purpose of providing financial support for legal assistance in noncriminal proceedings or matters to persons financially unable to afford legal assistance." (42 USCA § 2996b(a)).   The corporation's financial support to local groups is funded by the Congress; its board is appointed by the President of the United States with the advice and consent of the Senate.

legal tender

1. (medium of exchange): the kind of money, prescribed by law, that a creditor cannot refuse in discharge of a money obligation that does not specify other form of payment.   E.g., "United States coins and currency (including Federal reserve notes and circulating notes of Federal reserve banks and national banks) are legal tender for all debts, public charges, taxes, and dues. . . ." (31 USCA § 5103, as amended 1983).   Sometimes called **lawful money** (□see).

2. (of performance): sometimes used loosely to describe a **tender** (□see) that meets all legal requirements.

legal title □see **legal owner.**

legatee □see **gift.**

legislation

1. the act of making a law by an official body authorized to make laws (a legislature). E.g., the Congress, a state legislature, a city council. Contrasted with the pejorative *judicial legislation;* □see **judge-made law,** under **common law.**

2. the laws made as in sense 1. Legislation goes by a variety of names, not uniform or precise; the two most commonly differentiated are generally understood to refer to the source of the legislation:

statute: a law enacted by the highest legislature in the nation or state.

ordinance: a law enacted by a municipal legislature.

legislative counsel □see **lawyer.**

legislative courts □see **federal courts.**

legislative drafting: writing a law.

legislative history: the events, large and small, that show step-by-step how this law became a law. E.g., proposal, drafts, redrafts, changes of language, committee reports, legislative debate. The scope of legislative history is sharply debated. Disagreement goes beyond specific detail to the class of detail: whether limited to what may be gleaned from official records of this law's enactment.

legislative immunity □see **immunity.**

legislative intent □see **intent.**

legislative jurisdiction □see **jurisdiction.**

legislative privilege   □see immunity.

legislative purpose   □see intent.

legislature   □see legislation.

legislature has spoken   □see clichés; □see also, **plain meaning rule**.

legitimacy   □see legitimate.

legitimate

1.   The oldest usages of *legitimate* and *illegitimate* refer to children. Those usages, relating to children born in and out of **wedlock** (□see), still survive against the pressures of changing mores that affect the very use of words of *legitimacy*.   No one can now rely on a fixed, precise sense of the words.   For further details: □see **lawful issue**; □see **filiation proceedings**; □see **descendant**; □see **child**; □see **cohabit**; □see also, **conclusive presumption**, under **presumption**.

> **legitimate** (v.): to cause an otherwise illegitimate child to be treated by the law as a *legitimate* (n.).   The steps that result in the child becoming a **legitimated child** vary by state law, e.g., intermarriage of the parents after birth of the child; e.g., formal recognition of a child as offspring.

2.   As a general adjective (exclusive of reference to children as in sense 1), *legitimate* is a weak synonym of *lawful* and *legal* (□see **lawful**).   Not as generally used as either of those words, partly as a matter of habit, partly because *legitimate* also retains in the law usages of the common speech, *reasonable* and *genuine*.   The same comments apply to the negatives.   □see **illegal**.

legitimated child   □see legitimate.

lessee   □see lease; □see also, **landlord and tenant**.

lesser included offense   □see included offense.

lessor   □see lease; □see also, **landlord and tenant**.

let   □see lease; □see also, **let or hindrance**.

let or hindrance: coupled synonyms (□see), using the old sense of *let:* hindrance, hinder. Sometimes still used in the phrase *without let or hindrance* in expressing a lessee's right of **quiet enjoyment** (□see **covenant**) of leased premises. Apart from redundancy, this use of *let* clashes confusingly with its current and common senses—allow, permit, award. <They let them use it./They let the contract to the low bidder.>

letter agreement: lawyer's argot for a contract in the form of a letter. <"Dear Mr. Doe: You and I agree. . . . Very truly yours, Richard Roe. Agreed: John Doe.">

letter of credit: a writing (letter, cable, etc.) usually from a bank to enable one of its customers to get money or credit. In the letter of credit, the bank says that within stated limits it will **honor** (□see), or is authorized to honor, drafts and other commercial paper drawn on the bank by the person for whom the letter of credit is issued. Also called a *credit.* For details, refer to the Uniform Commercial Code.

letter of intent: a letter summarizing the key features of a contract that the parties intend to make. The letter of intent may tentatively resolve sticky points in a massive contract to be, may guide lawyers in writing a contract, may help in obtaining financing, and may discourage competitors; but it is not a contract.

letters: a shortened label for various types of official documents, each with a special name, listed here as separate entries, e.g., **letters of administration** (□see). When context makes the sense clear using *letters* alone, the special names are frequently dropped <Petition for appointment of administrator granted; letters to issue.>. Whether alone or in a combination form, *letters* is a singular, customarily used with a plural verb. <The letters/letters of administration/bear the court seal.>

letters of administration

1. an official document from a court appointing, or evidencing appointment of, an *administrator* to administer the estate of someone who has died. □see **executor.** For letters of administration, with the will annexed, □see **cum testamento annexo.** For letters of administration when an estate has not been completely administered, □see **de bonis non.**

2. In some jurisdictions, in addition to sense 1, the expression *letters of administration* includes **letters testamentary** (□see).

letters of administration, c.t.a. ☐see **cum testamento annexo**.

letters of administration, d.b.n. ☐see **de bonis non**.

letters of guardianship: an official document from a court appointing, or evidencing appointment of, a **guardian** (☐see).

letters patent (L., *litterae patentes:* open letters): an older, generic term for a grant by the government of some right or property. It describes the grant as well as the document containing the grant. Whether referring to grant or document, and whether referring to land, an invention, or something else, *letters patent* is largely superseded by **patent** (☐see).

letters rogatory (L., *rogatio; rogatorius:* request): a formal written request from a court here to a court in a foreign country for assistance in obtaining evidence. The request is usually to take the deposition (☐see **affiant**) of a witness to obtain answers to written interrogatories attached to the letters.

letters testamentary: an official document from a court confirming, or evidencing confirmation of, the authority of the **executor** (☐see) to administer the estate. <The petition for admission of the will to probate is granted; letters to issue.> In some jurisdictions, called **letters of administration** (☐see).

let the record show ☐see **enter an objection**, under **enter**. ☐see also, **for the record**.

levy (v., n.)

1. to seize property by legal process, as on **execution** (☐see) or **attachment** (☐see): **levy, levy execution, levy an attachment**; and the act of seizure: **the levy, the levy of execution, the levy of attachment**.

2. to impose taxes, and the act of imposing a tax. Details of usage vary by statute.

levy execution ☐see **execute**.

lewd ☐see **hard-core pornography**.

lex actus   □see lex loci actus.

lex contractus   □see lex loci contractus.

lex delicti   □see lex loci delicti.

lex fori   □see forum.

lex loci   (L., lex LOW-sigh: law of the place): still frequently used instead of the English translation, as a shorthand reference to the *law of the place,* where something is done or where something is located; those details are spelled out in more Latin phrases and English translations. *Lex loci* and its variations are fading reminders of what were once attempts at condensed statement of rules of **conflict of laws** (□see). Neither in Latin or English translation can they be relied on as guides to *what law governs.* The varieties of *lex loci* appear in entries immediately following.

lex loci actus: the law of the place of the act. Sometimes shortened to *lex actus.* □see lex loci.

lex loci contractus: the law of the place of the contract. Sometimes roughly translated as the law of the place of contracting, of the place where the contract was made, of the place where the contract is to be performed. Sometimes shortened to *lex contractus.* □see lex loci.

lex loci delicti,   also called *lex loci delictus:* the law of the place of the wrong (tort or crime). Sometimes roughly translated as the law of the place where the wrong was committed. Sometimes shortened to *lex delicti.* □see lex loci.

lex loci rei sitae   (L., lex LOW-sigh RAY-eye SIGH-tee: law of the place where the thing is located): the usual reference is to the law of the place of the real estate. Sometimes shortened to *lex situs.* □see lex loci.

lex mercatoria   □see law merchant.

lex situs   □see lex loci rei sitae.

liability without fault □see strict liability.

liability without negligence □see strict liability.

libel

1. a type of **defamation** (□see). This is the principal sense of *libel*.

2. the first pleading in a case in admiralty (maritime law). *Libel* is older usage, still in the statutes (including current amendments), but in the practice, largely ousted by the word *complaint* (□see **pleadings**).

libelant

1. in some general language dictionaries: a person who defames another by publishing a libel. □see **libel** (sense 1); □see **defamation**. *Libelant* is not general legal usage for a person sometimes called a *libeler,* more often referred to descriptively: the publisher of a libel, one who has libeled or is accused of libeling, ultimately—the *defendant.*

2. the plaintiff in a case in admiralty. *Libelant* is older usage, still in the statutes (including current amendments), but in the practice, largely ousted by the word *plaintiff.*

libelee: the defendant in a case in admiralty. *Libelee* is an older admiralty usage, along with *respondent.* In the practice, both are superseded by the word *defendant.*

libeler □see libelant.

libel per quod □see **actionable per se**, under **action**; □see **defamation**.

libel per se □see **actionable per se**, under **action**; □see **defamation**.

liberties □see civil liberties, under civil.

liberty □see liberty interest; □see also, civil liberties, under civil.

liberty interest: a general term of reference to any one of the many specific personal rights or freedoms included within the unspecific term *liberty* used in the **Due Process Clauses** (□see) of the U.S. Constitution. For example: a person has a *liberty interest* in freedom from physical restraint, in a right to marry, in a right to bear and rear children, which cannot be taken away without due process. See *Meyer v. Nebraska*, 262 U.S. 390 (1923). Neither the list of specific *liberty interests* nor the criteria of definition are matters of consensus. The list and the criteria (topics of constitutional law) expand, shrink, and wobble with majority, plurality, concurring, and dissenting opinions, and especially with the next decision of the U.S. Supreme Court. See *Michael H. v. Gerald D.*, 491 U.S. 110 (1989). □see also, **freedom of association**.

license (n., v.)

1. a permission to do something. This is the broad sense of *license* that is the unifying element in a wide range of disparate senses, varying by particular application, and often by jurisdiction. Whether the license is express or implied, and whether or not a matter of contract, the permission is said to be given by a *licensor* to a *licensee;* these designations are a convenience of legal classification, no matter how startling to the parties. When the permission is given in writing, the writing is also called a *license,* sometimes a *permit.* In some senses, a license is called a *franchise.*

2. permission to enter real property. This category of license has its chief utility in determining standards of liability for injury as fixed by the law of torts; it does not represent an interest in property.

   a. the status of this licensee is usually said to be characterized by an entry for the licensee's own purposes, e.g., to prospect for gold. It is distinguished from the status of **invitee** (□see). The permission is frequently implied, rather than express, and the entry is often characterized as "tolerated," "condoned," "suffered." <The doorbell rings. "I'm getting signatures to put initiative X on the ballot." That's a licensee at the door.>

   b. a **social visitor** (a guest) is placed in this category. Invited or not, a guest is not an **invitee** (□see).

3. permission from government:

   a. to conduct a business or practice a profession, e.g., a license to practice law; a license to sell liquor; a licensed building contractor. □see also, **prior restraint**.

   b. to do any of the various things that make life livable yet fall within the regulatory powers of government, e.g., a driver's license; a fishing license; a building permit.

c. to use public property as an exclusive privilege. This category of license is usually called a **franchise**, e.g., a franchise to operate a street railway. □see **privilege**, under **immunity**.

d. to exist as a corporation. This category of license is sometimes called a *franchise,* more often a *charter.*

4. permission from the owner of personal property:

a. to make limited use of **intellectual property** (□see): e.g., licenses under patent or copyright.

b. to conduct a private business at a specific location as the licensee (*franchisee*) of the licensor (*franchiser*), using the franchiser's products, techniques, secrets, and names, under provisions of a detailed contract. The license here, though limited and private, is an exclusive privilege in its own area and is usually called a *franchise.*

licensee □see **license.**

licensor □see **license.**

lie • sound: The usages described here are distinctly legal and closely related.

lie: to conclude that an action or remedy or legal position can be maintained. <An action in tort will lie./On the same facts, an action in contract will lie./No appeal lies from that judgment.>

sound: to characterize the basis of an action or remedy or legal position that is being or can be maintained. <This action sounds in tort./As now pleaded, your action sounds in contract./Specific performance has not been requested; the complaint sounds in damages.>

lien (v., n.)

1. to make property serve as security for the payment or performance of an obligation; and the legal device that makes the property serve as security. As verb and noun, in this sense, *lien* is a synonym of **encumber** (□see) and *encumbrance,* a general reference to the widest range of security devices, e.g., **mortgage** (□see), **pledge** (□see), *deed of trust* (□see **deed**), **security interest** (□see). Lien is also sometimes described as a *charge,* a loose term without precise meaning except as it is explained in terms of being a lien or encumbrance. One who has a lien is a *lienor* or *lienholder;* one whose property has been liened is a *lienee.* In the law, *lien* is pronounced as two syllables (LEE-en) or one (lean); take your choice.

2. as distinguished from being a word of general reference (sense 1), *lien* in combination with other words describes particular applications of property as security, a multitude of special instances, varying by jurisdiction. Liens are now usually provided for by local and federal statutes, and are sometimes called *statutory liens,* but that term itself is differently defined by different statutes; the statutes describe the means of establishing a lien. Here is a representative sampling of *lien* words:

attorney's lien: a lawyer's lien on a client's property as security for payment of fees and other charges. The two general types of attorney's lien are:

retaining lien: a general, possessory lien on a client's money and property, usually personal property, that has come into the lawyer's possession in the course of the attorney-client relationship.

charging lien: a special lien, which need not be possessory, on a client's money or property that has been recovered through the lawyer's services. The lien may affect a judgment, money in court or in the possession of other lawyers.

carrier's lien □see **special lien.**

charging lien □see **attorney's lien.**

choate lien and **inchoate lien** refer to battles for priority between a number of lienors. □see **choate.**

common law lien: an historical designation of liens, usually possessory, usually on personal property.

equitable lien: usually a special lien, enforceable in equity, that need not be a possessory lien; e.g., a **vendor's lien** against realty sold to lienee, the lien security for the unpaid purchase price.

general lien: lienee's property as security for what lienee owes lienor on a general account, whether or not the obligation secured is connected with the property. Contrasted with a special lien. □see **attorney's lien.**

landlord's lien □see **special lien.**

mechanic's lien: a special lien, which need not be possessory, to secure payment to those supplying work, labor, and materials to improve the lienee's property. The property is usually, not always, real property. The mechanic's lien is provided for in statutes of great variety and detail. As a lien of common lay experience, it has developed a subsidiary argot. <We'll lien the job./ . . . plaster the house with liens.>

possessory lien: security dependent on lienor's having and keeping possession of lienee's property. Lienor has the right to keep possession until the obligation is discharged. □see **attorney's lien.**

retaining lien □see **attorney's lien.**

special lien: lienee's property as security for what lienee owes lienor in connection with that property, e.g., a *carrier's lien* on cargo; a *landlord's lien* on tenant's goods in rented premises. Contrasted with a general lien.

vendor's lien □see **equitable lien.**

lienee   □see **lien.**

lienholder   □see **lien.**

lienor   □see **lien.**

lieu   □see **in lieu of.**

lieu tax   □see **in lieu of.**

life   Despite continuous involvement in the law and legal decisions, *life* is *life,* not a legal term of art. For *natural life,* □see **civil death.** □see also, **wrongful life.**

life estate   □see **estate.**

life in being   □see **in being;** □see also, **rule against perpetuities.**

life tenancy   □see **life estate, under estate.**

life tenant   □see **life estate, under estate;** □see also, **life tenancy, under estate.**

limitation (conveyancing)

1. the duration of an estate, e.g., life, fee, etc., as in the expression **words of limitation.** For details, □see **words of purchase,** under **buy.**

2. all of the language that creates an estate, including physical description, **words of limitation,** and **words of purchase;** □see, under **buy.** <Under the will, there was a limitation of Blackacre to A for life, *limitation over* to B in fee.> This is a broader, looser use of the word *limitation,* not to be confused with the technicality of sense 1.

limitations □see **statute of limitations.**

limited jurisdiction □see **court of limited jurisdiction,** under **court.**

limited partner □see **partnership.**

limited partnership □see **partnership.**

limited power of appointment □see **appoint.**

limited publication □see **publication.**

lineal descendant □see **descendant.**

lineal heirs □see **heirs.**

lip □see **lawyer.**

liquidated damages □see **damage.**

liquidating dividend □see **dividend.**

liquidation □see **dissolution.**

lis (L., leece: lawsuit). Various phrases using Latin forms of the noun are generally recognized technical shorthand:

ad litem (ad LIGHT-em: for the lawsuit), as in the title **guardian ad litem**. □see **guardian**.

lis pendens (leece PEN-dens: lawsuit pending)

    1. sometimes used literally to refer to a pending lawsuit.

    2. a paper filed or recorded that gives notice of a lawsuit, usually one affecting real estate; regulated by statute. The Latin has the virtue of brevity and widespread use among lawyers. It is sometimes spelled out as a *notice of lis pendens,* less often as a *notice of the pendency of an action.* <They filed a *lis pendens,* so anyone buying the property knew he was buying a lawsuit./They filed a notice of the pendency of an action.>

pendente lite (pen-DEN-tee light: as long as the lawsuit lasts). <The judge granted an injunction *pendente lite.* > □see **alimony;** □see **injunction, under enjoin.**

lis pendens   □see **lis.**

literary property   □see **copyright;** □see also, **intellectual property.**

litigator   □see **lawyer.**

lives in being   □see **in being;** □see also, **rule against perpetuities.**

living trust   □see **trust.**

living will   □see **right to die.**

LL.B.: the standard abbreviation of the Latin *Legum Baccalaureus:* Bachelor of Laws. For years the basic law degree awarded on graduation from law school; now generally supplanted by the **J.D.** (□see).

local action: a lawsuit that must be filed in the particular jurisdiction with which it has a specific connection; e.g., a suit over title in the jurisdiction where the real estate is located. Contrasted with:

transitory action: a lawsuit with no specific connection with a particular jurisdiction, and so may be filed wherever there is jurisdiction over the defendant; e.g., suit on a debt.

□see also, **venue.**

location □see **mining claim**.

lockout

1. the action of an employer in withholding employment from a group of employees as pressure to accept employer's terms of employment. The verb is usually *lock out*.

2. sense 1, as interpreted under statutes denying unemployment benefits to striking employees but not to those locked out: Employees' refusal to work because employer unreasonably refuses to continue employment under expired contract while a new one is being negotiated is a *lockout*, not a **strike** (□see).

loco parentis □see **in loco parentis**.

locus contractus □see **lex loci contractus**.

locus delicti □see **lex loci delicti**.

locus poenitentiae (L., locus PEN-uh-TEN-shuh-ee: place of repentance): an opportunity to change your mind before it is too late, e.g., about committing a crime.

locus sigilli □see **L.S.**

lodestar □see **fee (attorney's fee)**.

loiter has come up in the world. To linger or wander about aimlessly, to dawdle, no longer packs the distinctive burden of criminality it once did. Time was when the brand of *loiterer* could be a literal brand. Under heavy constitutional attack for vagueness, loiter has lost some of its forthright nastiness, at the same time losing ground in legal precision. The criminal law still clings to loiter, but it is now only special kinds of *loitering* that amount to anything legally, e.g., loitering around public toilets for lewd purposes. Best check the latest statutes and constitutional decisions to see how loiter is faring. It is not alone. □see **vagrancy**.

loiterer □see **loiter**.

long arm statute □see **at arm's length.**

long-standing authority □see **clichés.**

loss of bargain □see **benefit of the bargain,** under **out of pocket.**

loss of consortium □see **consortium.**

lower court □see **court.**

L.S.: the standard abbreviation of the Latin *locus sigilli:* the place of the seal. This is an abbreviation good everywhere: to indicate where a seal should be placed if required, to substitute for a seal where permitted, or to satisfy a yearning for old form where nothing is required. □see **seal.**

LSAT: the trademark and general name of reference of the Law School Admission Test. The result of that standardized examination is used as one of the criteria for admission to law school.

M

made is common, common English, long suffering in the law from the careless abandon of historic intimacy. The law does not respect *made*. It is thrown in where not needed, e.g., *made and appointed; made and provided.* And where *made* can achieve a simple clarity, e.g., *We made a contract* (an agreement), it is put down in redundancy as *We made and entered into a contract.* The bloated formula also introduces the *contract made and entered into*. . . . As useful as *made* can be, it is not indispensable. It never would be missed; no tears for *entered into* either (□see **enter**). □see **coupled synonyms**; □see also, **execute**.

For the trials of the present tense *make,* □see **make, publish, and declare**; □see **declaration**.

made and appointed □see **made**.

made and entered into □see **made**; □see also, **enter**.

made and provided □see **made**.

magistrate is loosely defined in general English as a civil official with assigned powers. That definition, broad enough to include the President of the United States (a "first magistrate") or a court clerk, is of no help at all in the law. Legal usage concentrates on the functions of a magistrate. Whoever performs those functions is, for the time at least, a magistrate. The entries here cannot be considered uniform; usage varies by jurisdiction, statute, and current decision.

1. the judge who presides over one or more of the preliminary steps in the criminal process that lead to dismissal of charges or prosecution for misdemeanor or felony. Those preliminary steps generally include: issuing or refusing to issue search warrants and arrest warrants; informing the person arrested of the charge and his rights (□see **first appearance**); setting or denying bail; **preliminary hearing** (□see) in felonies; transfer to a trial court.

2. the judge who sits in a *magistrate's court*, tries low penalty misdemeanors, and also performs the functions of a magistrate (sense 1).

magistrate's court: a court of limited jurisdiction (□see **court**), sometimes called by that very name. Often a reference to other

390

courts of limited jurisdiction, e.g., traffic court, police court, recorder's court, where the judge functions as a magistrate (sense 1).

3. United States Magistrate: a judge, but not a U.S. District Court judge, who performs the functions of a magistrate (sense 1) in the U.S. District Courts. In addition, the U.S. Magistrate tries all federal misdemeanors (subject to statutory options in the defendant), and may conduct other pretrial procedures as requested by the District Court. A U.S. Magistrate is appointed for a term of years by the U.S. District Court judges of a particular district.

4. a court clerk who is authorized to issue or refuse to issue search warrants and arrest warrants, i.e., one of the functions of a magistrate (sense 1).

magistrate's court □see **magistrate**.

Magna Carta (L.: Great Charter): the English charter of rights and liberties (1215). A strong and enduring influence on American lawyers as a symbol of limited constitutional government, its "law of the land" frequently equated with due process of law (□see **due**).

maim □see **mayhem**.

maintenance □see **alimony**; □see also, **barratry**.

maintenance and upkeep: a worthless pair of bilingual (French and English) synonyms, too long associated with the obligation of tenants. One of the pair suffices; neither is precise. When a choice is made, the mouth-filling French usually gets the call. □see **coupled synonyms**.

majority □see **lawful age**; □see also, **child**.

majority opinion □see **opinion**.

make, publish, and declare: part of a redundant ritual, *to make, publish, and declare a will.* A poor substitute for "This is my will." □see **declaration**.

maker: the signer of a promissory note. □see **commercial paper**.

make whole: to give the injured party what the injured party has been deprived of by reason of the wrong. E.g., reinstatement with seniority status for an employee wrongfully discharged; e.g., wages employee would have received but for the employer's wrongful refusal to bargain. The ordinary expression *make whole*, also rendered *make-whole* and *makewhole*, is in frequent use in labor law and in civil rights cases. The verb form has been creatively converted into a noun <The board ordered *makewhole./*In these circumstances, *makewhole* is inappropriate.>, and into an adjective <a *makewhole remedy, make-whole relief*, a *make whole purpose*>.

mala fide   □see **bad faith**; □see **bona fide**.

mala in se   □see **malum in se**.

mala prohibita   □see **malum in se**.

malfeasance • misfeasance • nonfeasance

Three kinds of trouble, related by the law French *feasance:* doing, best known to lawyers in the form **tortfeasor** (□see), law French for wrongdoer.

These words are also types of wrongdoing. What wrong? *Malfeasance* is said to be doing something plainly bad (*mal-*); *misfeasance*, doing badly (*mis-*) what might have been done if done properly; and *nonfeasance*, not doing (*non*) what you should have done. That oversimplifies a complicated etymology but gives a clue to similarities, differences, and a general imprecision.

malfeasance   is the worst of the trio, with an aroma of criminality; to be used with caution. It often gives way to special words for something bad, as in **malpractice** (□see), various kinds of **malice** (□see), and assorted names of specific crimes and intentional torts. *Malfeasance* most frequently describes the acts of those who violate a trust, e.g., trustees, agents, and the faithless public official. A corrupt official ought to be prosecuted, but ought also to be removed and barred from office holding for what is often called *malfeasance in office*. Since the line between the corrupt and the grossly inept is not always sharp, *malfeasance* and *misfeasance* are frequently equated.

misfeasance   when not equated with *malfeasance*, is the key villain in the law of negligence. Sometimes characterized as a *neglect*

392

of duty, its chief role in tort law is active misconduct, as opposed to the passive inaction of *nonfeasance.*

nonfeasance is the least culpable of the trio. In tort law, nonfeasance, like malfeasance, represents a neglect of some duty found owing from defendant to plaintiff. The role of passive misconduct assigned to nonfeasance often blends imperceptibly with the active role of *misfeasance.*

When making charges, as opposed to analyzing shades of wrongdoing, the lawyer's instinct to repeat rather than omit swells the charge to the full litany: the wrongdoer—especially the public official—is guilty of *malfeasance, misfeasance, and nonfeasance.* What ultimately sticks, if at all, and ousts the official, is *malfeasance.*

malfeasance in office □see **malfeasance.**

malice: an inexcusable intent to injure. That is a generalized definition of a word that has no precise definition. Despite centuries of legal usage, *malice* remains vague. It draws from the courts' stunningly indefinite vituperation—"evil design, the dictate of a wicked, depraved, and malignant heart"; bad faith; personal hostility; intent to oppress, vex, and annoy; deliberate intent, as if a special species of **intent** (□see).

As a word, *malice* is so rooted in the language of the law that rather than abandon it, the law has stretched it in order to live with it. Vague as it is, *malice,* as defined in this entry, is sometimes called **actual malice, express malice,** or **malice in fact.** Those expressions, not uniformly applied, distinguish *malice* from the even vaguer **constructive malice, implied malice, legal malice,** or **presumed malice:** expressions that find the wickedness that is *malice* in something short of proof of the real thing, e.g., a disregard of foreseeable consequences so reckless as to be treated as if it were *malice.*

Under varying criteria, *malice* becomes a special ingredient of the right to *exemplary damages* (□see **damage**); damages for defamation of a **public official** (□see) or a **public figure** (□see); and, negatively, *qualified privilege* (□see **immunity**). Expressions linking *malice* or *malicious* with other law words are separate entries.

malice aforethought: At one time, this was the English translation of **malice prepense,** the latter word Old French for premeditation. Thus, *malice aforethought* packed together the evil in **malice** (□see) with the vileness of advance planning. In that form, it became an

malice aforethought

indispensable element of the crime of **murder** (□see). Some still regard *malice aforethought* as a statement of premeditated evil, a view not generally accepted. *Malice aforethought* is regarded as a single word, an essential, though vague, verbal ingredient of criminal wickedness, especially, not exclusively, murder. What exactly does it mean? No one is quite sure. As discussed in the cases, it usually sounds like *malice;* that's bad enough. □see also, **afore-**.

malice in fact   □see **malice**.

malice prepense   □see **malice aforethought**.

malicious abuse of process: using legal process for an ulterior personal purpose that the process was not created to serve; and the civil action to redress that grievance. The process (e.g., attachment, subpoena, arrest) may be supported by probable cause and yet abused. E.g., a subpoena obtained not to get testimony that might be useful but intended as harassment, e.g., to reinforce a demand that an undesired tenant move out. The *malicious* element is satisfied by the same ulterior purpose that constitutes the *abuse;* □see **malice**. Some jurisdictions dispense with *malicious*, and call the same thing *abuse of process*. By whatever name, local law varies, with general agreement that *abuse* or *malicious abuse of process* is different from **malicious prosecution** (□see).

malicious mischief: a crime against property, characterized by the inexcusable intent to injure that is malice, or the recklessness that is equated with **malice** (□see). It is a catchall classification of a miscellany of offenses, e.g., stripping an auto; spray painting a wall with graffiti. It may, but need not, include personal ill will, as in defacing a cemetery or a place of worship, or poisoning a neighbor's dog. *Malicious mischief* has no precise boundaries and, like malice, has inspired some classic hyperbole: what is done "either out of a spirit of wanton cruelty, or black and diabolical revenge." (4 Blackstone, *Commentaries* *244; Jones ed. 1916). Sometimes includes, sometimes a synonym of, **vandalism**.

malicious prosecution

1. initiating or carrying on a prosecution or suit without probable cause and for an ulterior personal purpose, the prosecution or suit ending in favor (indicating innocence) of the defendant. The malicious element, still vague as in **malice** (□see), often inferred from the still separate element—lack of probable cause. □see also, **malicious abuse of process.**

2. the civil action for redress of malicious prosecution (sense 1). Defendant in this civil action is not a public prosecutor. □see **prosecutorial immunity**, under **immunity.**

malpractice

1. failure of a professional to render professional services up to the standards of the ordinary reputable members of the profession in similar circumstances and localities. The standards, which vary by profession, statute, and regulations, include learning, skill, care, diligence, judgment, and ethics.

2. the civil action (tort or contract) of a person harmed to whom the professional owed a duty violated by malpractice (sense 1).

3. **legal malpractice**: malpractice (sense 1) pertaining to the practice of law.

4. **malpractice insurance** is known by euphemisms, e.g., policies covering *professional liability, errors and omissions.* For no insurance, □see **bare.**

malpractice insurance   □see **malpractice.**

malum in se   (L.: an evil in itself): an act intrinsically wrong (e.g., murder); as opposed to **malum prohibitum** (L.: a prohibited evil): an act wrong *only* because prohibited (e.g., overparking). Plurals: *mala in se; mala prohibita.*

An old classification of crime, making a distinction not always clearly marked. Still called upon in criminal law, e.g., on question of required intent; called upon in other areas of the law as to the effect of different kinds of criminal conduct on, e.g., contract, bar discipline, immigration, impeachment of a witness. □see also, **moral turpitude.**

malum prohibitum   □see **malum in se.**

management   □see **director.**

mandamus   (L., man–DAY–mus: we command): short for **writ of mandamus**: an order to a lower court, or to an individual, a corporation, or a unit of government, directing performance of a public duty. Issued when no other remedy is available, or when the time for an

mandamus

appeal or an ordinary lawsuit would defeat the end sought. In some jurisdictions, called **writ of mandate** or **mandate**. Mandamus is one of a group called *prerogative* or *extraordinary* writs; □see **extraordinary**. Varying with local procedure, *mandamus* is sometimes divided between a *peremptory writ of mandamus* (do it!) and an *alternative writ of mandamus* (do it, or show cause why not), often supplanted by the **order to show cause** (□see).

mandamus (v.)

1. to get something done by a writ of mandamus. <If you are entitled to the default right now, mandamus the trial court that refused it.>

2. to exert pressure by a writ of mandamus (lawyer's argot). <We mandamused the hell out of them.>

mandate

1. another name for **mandamus** (□see).

2. the communication of a decision or instruction to a lower court. <The mandate came down yesterday.> □see also, **remittitur**.

mandatory   □see **directory**.

mandatory injunction   □see **enjoin**.

mandatory instruction   □see **jury instructions**.

mandatory presumption   □see **presumption**.

mandatory sentence   □see **sentence**.

manifest   (adj.) means in the law what it means in ordinary English, evident to the senses, obvious. It is one of the profession's favorite flexible words, tacked on to error, hardship, injury, injustice, necessity, and much more. Manifest describes none of those words. It describes a feeling of the writer that the reader is expected to share, like it or not. Same for *manifestly* (adv.).

manslaughter: an unlawful, unjustified killing short of **murder** (□see). How far short of murder varies with widely varying definitions of manslaughter. The offense is sometimes divided into degrees of seriousness, as an alternative to the more usual, not uniform, classifications of voluntary and involuntary manslaughter:

voluntary manslaughter: an intentional killing, not justified, but under extenuating circumstances, especially a killing in the **heat of passion** (□see).

involuntary manslaughter: an unintentional, unjustified killing, often described as a killing through **criminal negligence**. The expression is deliberately chilling and indefinite. What constitutes that neglect varies by jurisdiction; e.g., conduct involving a high risk of death or serious bodily injury, especially if the defendant is aware of the risk; e.g., equated with recklessness; e.g., can include neglect of duty when omission creates the risk (e.g., care of a sick child).

Involuntary manslaughter is itself sometimes subdivided into killing through *criminal negligence* and killing in the commission of an *unlawful act*. What constitutes that act also varies by jurisdiction, e.g., an act that is not a felony; one not involving risk of serious bodily harm; e.g., *malum in se,* as opposed to *malum prohibitum* (□see **malum in se**).

mariner's will　□see **sailor's will**.

marital agreement:　a loose catchall describing an agreement made between those contemplating marriage (**antenuptial agreement** or **prenuptial agreement**) or between husband and wife (**postnuptial agreement**). Typically, the agreement deals with property and business affairs before, during, and after marriage; but it may deal with the greatest variety of topics included in **family law** (□see).

marriage settlement

1.　loosely, another name for a marital agreement.

2.　an antenuptial agreement in which property is transferred; and the transfer itself.　<They executed a marriage settlement settling the Los Angeles home on the bride-to-be.>

3.　an agreement by a third person, usually a relative, to transfer property to one or both of those contemplating marriage; and the transfer itself.

marital communications privilege　□see **husband-wife privilege**.

marital deduction:　generally, a deduction permitted when a married person dies or makes a gift to the other spouse. Shorn of the qualifying intricacies fit only for the mind and expertise of a specialist, this is the essence of marital deduction for the respective federal tax laws:

1. Estate tax: the property that is included in a spouse's gross estate and "passes or has passed" from spouse to the surviving spouse is deductible from the taxable estate. (IRC § 2056).

2. Gift tax: a gift from one spouse to the other is deductible from the donor's taxable gifts for that calendar year. (IRC § 2531).

marital domicile □see **matrimonial domicile.**

marital estate: the whole of the property of husband and wife in which they have interests as a result of the marriage; also called **marital property.** Both are loose, collective expressions that adapt to the local law, whether in community property or common law states. They are terms of convenient reference in a variety of contexts, e.g., divorce, inheritance, insurance, separation, support.

marital property □see **marital estate.**

maritime law • admiralty law: the law of the high seas and navigable waters and whatever is connected with either, e.g., ships, ship channels, commerce, contracts, torts, offenses, and wartime seizure of enemy shipping (**prizes**). The roots are ancient in the English courts of admiralty, with continuing influence from the international **law of the sea** (□see). As applied here, the law is American. The judicial power of the United States extends "to all cases in admiralty and maritime jurisdiction." (Art. III, § 12, cl. 1.; refer 28 USCA § 1333). The expressions are generally interchangeable, with a tendency to discuss the whole body of substantive law as *maritime*, and procedural matters as *admiralty*. □see **admiralty lawyer, under lawyer;** □see **libel;** □see **libelant;** □see **libelee;** □see **perils of the sea;** □see also, **high seas.**

mark □see **X.**

marketable title: a title in such a state that the property is readily salable. Stated negatively, it is a title without restriction, encumbrance, or other circumstance peculiar to the property that prevents its being readily salable. Some call it *clear title* (□see **clear**), but that can miss the mark. <The title was clear; even so, unless the required sewer bonds were posted, nothing could be built on the property. It was not a marketable title.> Marketable title usually refers to real property; in that sense, **merchantable title** is a synonym. This latter usage is not to be confused with *merchantable* in the personal property sense, as used in **warranty of merchantability** (□see **warranty**). If title is not *marketable,* it is an *unmarketable title.*

market value   □see **fair market value,** under **fair;** □see also, **actual.**

marriage   □see **cohabit;** □see **wedlock;** □see also, **legitimate.** For *common law marriage* and *putative marriage,* □see **cohabit.**

marriage settlement   □see **marital agreement.**

married   □see **cohabit;** □see **wedlock;** □see **feme covert.**

marry   □see **cohabit.**

marshaling: an equitable device to assure that as many claims as possible may be satisfied out of a debtor's limited assets. A creditor with realizable recourse to a debtor's assets (e.g., by lien) not available to other creditors may be required by marshaling to satisfy claims first from those assets, before sharing in assets available to all the creditors. In various forms, referred to as *marshaling assets, —liens, —remedies, —security.*

marshaling assets   □see **marshaling.**

marshaling liens   □see **marshaling.**

marshaling remedies   □see **marshaling.**

marshaling security   □see **marshaling.**

martial law • military law

   martial law: a temporary law of military necessity superseding civil authority in time of invasion, threatened invasion, or the inability of civil government to preserve order. Subject to constitutional restraint but otherwise without precise boundaries of authority, martial law is administered under a government's military power, applicable alike to civilians and to those in the military. Martial law may be made applicable as part of military government in enemy territory occupied by the military. *Martial law* is not to be confused with the law of *courts-martial;* □see **military law**, below, in this entry.

military law: the special law governing those in the military service. The military trial courts that administer military law are called **courts-martial,** not to be confused with **martial law** (□see, above, in this entry). □see **Uniform Code of Military Justice**.

Mary Carter agreement: a type of settlement with less than all of the defendants in a tort case, but with the case proceeding against all defendants. The settling defendants appear to continue as active litigants. They guarantee a minimum payment to the plaintiff, even if the case is lost. Plaintiff agrees not to enforce any judgment against the settling defendants; and, if judgment against nonsettling defendants goes to some stated figure, the agreed payment from settling defendants to plaintiff will be proportionately reduced. The patterns vary but take their name from the agreement in *Booth v. Mary Carter Paint Co.,* 202 So.2d 8 (Fla.Dist.Ct.App., 1967). Some Mary Carter agreements are "secret," a criticized element forbidden in some jurisdictions. Also spelled *Mary Carter Agreement.*

mass market consumer □see **consumer**.

Massachusetts trust □see **trust**.

master

1. a judicial officer appointed by a judge to assist a judge in a particular case, typically one requiring detailed, often massive evidence on a technical issue, e.g., the course of a river, a state boundary, the domicile of a person of wealth whose lifetime wanderlust inspires conflicting claims to death taxes. The powers of the master, regulated by statute and the terms of the appointing order (the **reference**), may include taking testimony, hearing argument, making proposed findings of fact and conclusions of law, ultimately reporting to the judge. The report is an aid to decision, not the decision of the case. Under some statutes, **referee** and **master** are synonyms. Depending on the scope of the inquiry, a master is sometimes called a **special master**.

2. as in **master and servant** (□see).

master and servant: a traditional, not rigid, classification of an **agency** (□see) relationship stressing the immediacy of the master's right to direct and control the servant's work. The closeness of that direction and control, e.g., over physical acts, may, under varying local rules, call forth the label *master and servant*. The label, in turn, affects, or states a conclusion, as to the extent of the master's **vicarious liability** (□see) in tort.

Ugly historical connotations of *master* have driven the combination *master and servant* out of popular usage; it continues in the law as a measuring rod of vicarious liability. It serves in that role, even when other names are used for a particular agency relationship and its substantive ramifications in the law, e.g., **principal** and **agent** (□see **agency**), e.g., **employer/employee** (□see **workers' compensation;** □see also, **boycott;** □see also, **grievance;** □see also, **closed shop**). <The employer in this case so controlled the employee's every act that it is liable in tort under familiar rules of master and servant.>

master lease   □see **lease.**

material   □see **immaterial (evidence).**

material witness: an ordinary English sense of *material* (adj.), of substantial significance, but more than merely the opposite of **immaterial** (□see). A *material witness* is one whose testimony is not only admissible but might have a substantial, perhaps a decisive effect, on an important issue or on the outcome of the case itself. E.g., an eyewitness to a fatal shooting.

matrimonial domicile   □see **domicile.**

matrimonial rights   □see **cohabit.**

matter   is one of those marvelous words of ordinary English that mean pretty much what you want it to mean. Lawyers love it, hug it, and run with it. Some of the usage is routinely indispensable: a **matter of course** (□see **of course**); a **matter of record** (□see **of record**). But best of all is the all-purpose *matter,* simply something you are talking about—a case, a hearing, a problem, a nice point of law, no restraints. <A matter in federal court/a custody matter/the matter we discussed last week/too many matters on my calendar/the guts of the matter.> You don't have to be a lawyer to talk *matter,* but it helps.

maxims The law is full of them, mostly in Latin, once, no longer, regarded as sacrosanct distillations of truth. Truth and untruth and half-truth, platitude and nonsense, they still flesh out opinions fleshy enough without them. And they crop up in discussions of equity and rules of interpretation. A few maxims have acquired an independent existence, no longer significant as pithy truth but as shorthand reference to a body of substantive law. Today, most maxims are no more than formalized nostalgia, not to be relied on. A maxim for maxims: "A maxim is to law as a fortune cookie is to philosophy." (31 *UCLA Law Review* 423, 434, 1983).

A small parcel of maxims, some in abbreviated form, are entered alphabetically in this dictionary:

caveat emptor;

caveat venditor;

cessante ratione legis cessat et ipsa lex;

clean hands;

contra proferentem;

cujus est solum ejus est usque ad coelum □see **airspace;**

de minimis;

de minimis non curat lex □see **de minimis;**

equity acts in personam;

expressio unius est exclusio alterius;

inclusio unius est exclusio alterius □see **expressio unius est exclusio alterius;**

mobilia sequuntur personam;

noscitur a sociis;

qui facit per alium facit per se □see **agency;**

respondeat superior □see **agency;**

volenti non fit injuria.

may • shall

The standard grammatical use of *may* (permitted) and *shall* (required) is also a legal use, often described as the "presumed" use. But *may* and *shall* in legal writing, especially in statutes, are so frequently treated as synonyms that the grammatical standard cannot be considered the legal standard. Context and interpretation so easily overwhelm either word. $<$ . . . may consider the guidelines./ . . . shall consider the guidelines. $>$ Unless context can be made crystal clear, prefer *must* or *required* to *shall*. Reinforce *may* with *but not required*. □see **directory**. Some special legal usage, most often oral:

> **may be amended**: motion to amend granted. (*may = permitted.*)

> **may go out**: motion to strike from the record granted. E.g., a judge's ruling on an objection to a witness's volunteered comment, "That may go out." (*may = required,* i.e., shall go out.)

> **may have additional time**: motion granted for additional time, e.g., ten days, in which to file an answer. (*may = permitted.*)

> **May it please the court** □see **formalisms**.

may be amended   □see **may**.

may go out   □see **may**.

may have additional time   □see **may**.

mayhem: the crime of intentionally permanently disabling, dismembering, or disfiguring another. Sometimes called *maiming,* more often *battery* or *aggravated assault* (□see **assault and battery**). At common law, mayhem did not include disfiguring, only injuries that would deprive the king of fighting men. Nature of intent, duration of injury, and precise description of the crime vary by jurisdiction.

May it please the court   □see **formalisms**.

meaningful   Once upon a time, *meaningful* was a natural antonym for *meaningless;* it now approaches the role of synonym. At the least, *meaningful* has developed a sense of vacuity on a par with **address** (□see). Attach it to almost anything: a natural for a legal writer searching for a way of expressing unclearly what is unclear to writer and will be unclear to reader. The law has toyed with all manner of things *meaningful,* e.g., —association, —connection, —contact, —disclosure, —opportunity, "meaningful access to the judicial process" (Opinion of Black, J., in *Meltzer v. C. Buck LeCraw & Co.,* 402 U.S. 954, 959, 1971), "meaningful attorney-client relationship" (*Morris v. Slappy,* 461 U.S. 1, 13, 1983). Pause before describing anything legal as *meaningful.* Compare the law's venture into *meaningful relationship* with that entry in the latest unabridged dictionary (Random House, 2d ed., 1987): "a romantic relationship based on mutual re-

meaningful

spect and supportiveness and marked by a sense of commitment and fulfillment." □see **clichés**.

measuring lives   □see **rule against perpetuities**.

mechanic's lien   □see **lien**.

meddler   □see **intermeddler**.

mediate   □see **mediation**.

mediation: encouraging settlement of a dispute through the intervention of a disinterested third party, a *mediator*.   *Mediation* may refer generally to this type of dispute resolution or to the procedure itself. <They would not agree to arbitration but agreed to try mediation./Mediation lasted ten days.>

mediator: a disinterested third party, without an arbitrator's power to decide a dispute, functioning only to help the parties settle a dispute themselves.   Some mediators are private persons, chosen by the parties who have agreed to rules for the conduct of the mediation; some are designated by government agency, with rules prescribed for the mediation.   The parties may agree to *mediation,* but only the mediator *mediates.*   <Mediating the dispute, the mediator was unable to bring the parties together, except to get them to agree to arbitrate the key issue.> □see **arbitrate**.

mediator   □see **mediation**.

meet and just   □see **just and reasonable**.

meeting of the minds   □see **contract**.

member of the bar   □see **bar**.

memorandum decision: a brief statement, giving the bare bones of decision, typically in a case where no opinion will be written; e.g., ruling on a motion; unanimous affirmance.

memorandum of points and authorities   □see **brief**.

mensa et thoro □see **divorce**.

mens rea (L., mens RAY-uh: guilty mind): criminal intent or guilty mind, a general reference to the mental element of crime. It is the surviving remnant of the maxim *actus non facit reum, nisi mens sit rea,* loosely translated, "An act does not make one guilty unless there is a guilty mind." *Mens rea* is still used, though there is no consensus as to precisely what sort of criminal intent or guilty mind it refers to. □see **guilty**; □see **intent**.

mental cruelty □see **extreme cruelty**.

mental defect □see **insanity**.

mental disease □see **insanity**.

mental disorder □see **insanity**.

mental distress □see **emotional distress**.

mental disturbance □see **emotional distress**.

mental illness □see **insanity**.

mental incompetence □see **insanity**; □see also, **incompetent**.

merchantability □see **warranty of merchantability**.

merchantable □see **warranty of merchantability**.

merchantable title □see **marketable title**.

mercy killing □see **right to die**.

mere in law, as in English, merely that and nothing more. Too weak to put starch in something already flabby (inadvertence); redundant when attached to something that can stand on its own (license).

mere

Sometimes adds a touch of arrogance (merest nonsense). □see **clichés.**

merger □see **corporate merger**, under **de facto**; □see **de facto merger**, under **de facto**; □see **parol evidence rule**; □see also, **legal fiction**; □see also, **claim preclusion**, under **res judicata.**

merger clause □see **parol evidence rule.**

merit In a number of positive contexts, the law tries to preserve the standard meaning of *merit* and *meritorious:* something of substantive worth, deserved recognition, as distinguished from puffery or form. E.g., **on the merits, a meritorious cause of action, a meritorious defense.** □see **judgment on the merits**, under **judgment.** <The preliminaries are over; we can now have a trial on the merits.>

The weakness of *merit* as a word of precision is the subjective evaluation that brings forth the conclusion "merit." In legal writing, that vulnerability is exploited in the negatives of merit. The primary example is **without merit**; no one believes it. The phrase is in sharp competition for honors of the negative with **devoid of merit.** Each finds adverbial reinforcement: totally without merit, wholly and completely devoid of merit. The simple truths *no merit, lacks merit, nothing to it* are overwhelmed. <"While the appeal is plainly without merit, it is not clearly frivolous. . . ." *Corns v. Miller,* 181 Cal.App.3d 195, 202, 1986.> *Merit* itself is diluted. □see **clichés.**

mesne (law F., pronounced mean: in the middle): intermediate. Can refer to almost anything in-between: *mesne assignments* or *—conveyances,* e.g., in the sequence A to B to C to D, those to B and C; *—encumbrances,* e.g., a second mortgage between a first and a third mortgage; *—process,* e.g., an attachment issued during a lawsuit; **mesne profits**: rental value of land in an intermediate period, e.g., during a period of wrongful possession. *Mesne,* and its nasty law French pronunciation, are waning bits of the law's feudal inheritance, with a residual vitality for *mesne profits* in the law of real property.

mesne profits □see **mesne.**

metaphor As "a profession of words," the law and metaphor are seldom parted. Metaphor is the core of **legal fiction** (□see). Metaphor can provide lawyers with rememberable and colorful reference, e.g., at **arm's length** (□see), **clean hands** (□see), **fruit of the poisonous tree** (□see), *meeting of the minds* (□see **contract**), *piercing the corporate veil* (□see **alter ego**). For lawyers, more than for other writers, recognition of metaphor as metaphor is essential lest colorful expression be mistaken for precision (□see **Chinese wall**, under **vicarious disqualification**). For lawyers, as for other writers, mixed or muddled metaphor is an occupational hazard, e.g., "unleashing Pandora's box"; "riddled with constitutional infirmities on its face" (□see **face**); "No judge is a tabula rasa, deciding cases in a vacuum." (*Los Angeles Times,* Pt. II, p. 4, Nov. 5, 1985). □see **clean slate**.

metes and bounds (law F., *metes et boundes,* meats and bounds: boundary and boundary): a surveyor's measurement of the perimeter of a piece of land. <The land had no lot and block number; it was sold by a metes and bounds description./The legal was a metes and bounds description.> □see **legal description**, under **legal**; □see also, **coupled synonyms**.

might-have-been □see **rule against perpetuities**.

military law □see **martial law**; □see **Uniform Code of Military Justice**.

Militia Clauses: the parts of the U.S. Constitution reading: "The Congress shall have power . . . To provide for calling forth the militia to execute the laws of the Union, suppress insurrections, and repel invasions; [and] To provide for organizing, arming, and disciplining, the militia, and for governing such part of them as may be employed in the service of the United States, reserving to the states respectively, the appointment of the officers, and the authority of training the militia according to the discipline prescribed by Congress. . . ." (Art. I, § 8, cls. 15 and 16). □see also, **constitutional clauses**.

mind and memory: as two separate words, *mind* and *memory* mean in the law what they mean in the ordinary language. In another age, they were synonyms, joined together in a bilingual (Old English and Old French) redundancy, i.e., mind and mind. Today, they are too frequently part of a worthless introduction to wills, in which a testator, sane or insane, certifies himself to be of **sound and disposing mind and memory**. A valid will requires that the will maker know what he is doing, i.e., intend to dispose of his property by willing it to the beneficiaries. These are matters of proof, with the precise criteria varying state to state. The formula certification does not help. □see **declaration**; □see **coupled synonyms**.

mineral lease   □see **mining lease**.

minerals ferae naturae   □see **ferae naturae**; □see also, **law of capture**.

minimal contacts   □see **minimum contacts**.

minimum contacts: sufficient contact of a nonresident natural person or a foreign corporation with a state to give that state jurisdiction over the nonresident or corporation. *Minimum contacts,* also called *minimal contacts,* is often referred to as a theory, a principle, or a test of whether a state has **in personam** (□see) jurisdiction, jurisdiction to tax, jurisdiction to regulate, and whether its judgments are entitled to **full faith and credit** (□see). Exactly what facts constitute *minimum contacts* is in constant litigation under due process (□see **due**). E.g., a conclusion that a foreign corporation is **doing business** in a state is not enough to subject it to local process; there must be something "substantial"—one of the most durable and flexible words in the legal vocabulary. □see **domicile**; □see **foreign corporation**; □see **long arm statute**, under at arm's length.

mining claim

1. In the public mineral lands open to private prospecting, an identified portion of those lands in which valuable minerals have been discovered, and which is "claimed" (in the ordinary sense) by a miner and held for mining purposes in accordance with the law. The mining claim is the land within the physical boundaries and—of more importance—the minerals. A mining claim is sometimes called a *location.*

   location: sometimes equated with *mining claim;* more accurately, *location* is the series of acts required by law to acquire a mining claim, in particular the identification of the limits of the claim on the surface of the land and the giving of public notice of the claim. The person who *locates* or makes the *location* is called the *locator.*

2. the exclusive rights to mine and occupy the mining claim (sense 1) and to apply for title (□see **patent**), all subject to detailed provisions of mining law.

mining law: the special body of law that covers the acquiring and dealing with all manner of natural resources that are usually in the ground. These resources are usually thought of as *minerals,* mostly inorganic, such as gold, silver, uranium, but also include substances of organic origin, such as coal, oil, and gas. The field is broad enough to include geothermal steam, heat, and energy, and deep-seabed hard minerals. The law is mostly federal (refer especially to USCA, Title 30), state, and customary law as developed in mining districts by those engaged in prospecting and mining. Some international law can also be a part of mining law; refer to the United Nations Convention on the Law of the Sea, Dec. 10, 1982 (U.N. Document A/Conf. 62/ 122 of Oct. 7, 1982, as corrected to Nov. 26, 1982, reproduced in 21 *International Legal Materials* p. 1961 (1982)). Mining law has a specialized vocabulary, only a small portion of which is included in this dictionary. E.g., □see **location,** under **mining claim;** □see **minerals ferae naturae,** under **ferae naturae;** □see **mining claim;** □see **mining lease.**

mining lease, also called *mineral lease:* an agreement in which a lessor gives a lessee the right to enter on real property to explore for, extract, and remove named minerals; and the lessee agrees to pay the lessor rent, royalties, or a share of the produce. The mining lease is thus substantially different from an ordinary **lease** (□see), in that its essence is the right to take from the substance of the soil (□see **profit à prendre**), with a limited right of possession of the land incidental to that essence. The nature of the mining lease, its duration, and form of payment vary with the kind of mineral, ownership of the land (government or private), custom, government regulation, and negotiation. The best known variety of mining lease, with a law of its own, is the *oil and gas lease.*

ministerial: describing an act, duty, or function that is routine and specifically required by law, as opposed to the discretionary or judicial. E.g., a board's decision whether to award a contract may be discretionary; decision made, the signing is ministerial. □see **executive immunity,** under **immunity;** □see also, **abuse of discretion.**

minor □see **child.**

minority □see **child.**

minority stockholder □see **stock;** □see also, **cumulative voting.**

minor offense □see **petty offense.**

minute entry □see **enter.**

Miranda rules • Miranda warnings: Rules and companion warnings announced in *Miranda v. Arizona,* 384 U.S. 436 (1966), based on Fifth Amendment **Self–Incrimination Clause** (□see). Often rendered *rule* and *warning; Rule* sometimes capitalized. (Consult later decisions for interpretation and modification.)

Miranda rules: "[T]he prosecution may not use statements, whether exculpatory or inculpatory, stemming from custodial interrogation of the defendant unless it demonstrates the use of procedural safeguards effective to secure the privilege against self-incrimination." □see **custodial interrogation.**

Miranda warnings: the warnings required before custodial interrogation, absent other effective compliance with the *Miranda* rules: ". . . a right to remain silent, that any statement he does make may be used in evidence against him, and that he has a right to the presence of an attorney, either retained or appointed."

Mirandized: shorthand for "The person was given *Miranda* warnings." <"Suspect was Mirandized and said he wanted an attorney."> Legal argot on the pattern of **Shepardize** (□see).

Miranda warnings □see **Miranda rules.**

Mirandized □see **Miranda rules.**

misappropriation: a wrongful use or taking of another's money or property. Sometimes equated with **embezzlement** (□see). Not a term of art except as specially defined by statute.

miscarriage of justice: justice gone so awry in some substantial aspect of court proceedings as to require a different result. A flexible standard or conclusion expressing the probability that serious, not trivial, error has deprived a litigant of legal right.

misdemeanor: often described as a crime other than a felony, a description that omits the least of offenses, **infraction** (□see). In general, misdemeanor is a crime punishable by fine, or by imprisonment in other than a penitentiary or for one year or less, or by both fine and imprisonment. If, by statute, a felony is a crime punishable by imprisonment for even one year, misdemeanor would be one punishable by imprisonment for less than one year. The same type of offense may, by statute, be misdemeanor or felony, depending on the extent of harm (□see **larceny**) or the punishment at sentencing. □see **felony**.

misfeasance   □see **malfeasance**.

misjoinder   □see **joinder**.

misprision of felony   (law F., mis-PRIZH-un): an old and fading crime; knowing that someone else has committed a felony and failing to report it to the public authorities. The crime, where still recognized, is limited by statute or decision to failure to report plus an affirmative act to conceal the felony.

misprision of treason: in the absence of definitive court interpretation, it is presumed that *misprision of treason* follows the pattern of **misprision of felony** (□see), substituting treason for felony. Under the federal statute, *misprision of treason* can be committed only by a person "owing allegiance to the United States." (18 USCA § 2382).

misrepresentation   □see **fraud**.

mistake   means the same thing in law that it means in ordinary English. The consequences vary by context and the substantive law in different areas of the law, e.g., rescission of a contract on the ground of mistake; recovery of money paid by mistake; mistake as affecting criminal intent; malpractice. Again varying by context and substantive law, the consequences of mistake may be affected by the nature of the mistake:

mistake of fact: a misapprehension or plain ignorance of what the facts are; as distinguished from—

mistake of law: an erroneous conclusion or plain ignorance of what the law is in relation to the facts; and—

mutual mistake: the same mistake of fact or law made by both parties to a transaction.

mistake of fact   □see **mistake**.

mistake of law □see **mistake.**

mistrial: an aborted trial, terminated by the judge because of incurable error (e.g., lack of jurisdiction; drunken jurors) or because the jury cannot agree on a verdict. <The jury had been hung 11 to 1 for two days, and the judge declared a mistrial.>

mitigating circumstances: as opposed to **aggravating circumstances,** which tend to increase, *mitigating circumstances* tend to decrease the:

seriousness of crime; e.g., a killing in the **heat of passion** (□see), as opposed to a calculated killing (□see **manslaughter;** □see **murder);**

severity of punishment; e.g., no prior convictions, the defendant's troubled background, as opposed to an habitual criminal (□see **convict)** or **special circumstances** (□see);

degree of discipline; e.g., a reprimand for a single instance of professional misconduct, as opposed to disbarment for repeated misconduct;

award of damages; e.g., duty to mitigate damages, as opposed to intentional harm and punitive damages (□see **damage).**

The areas of mitigation and aggravation in this entry are instances; the dichotomy is common throughout the law.

mitigation of damages □see **duty to mitigate damages,** under **damage.**

mitigation of punishment □see **mitigating circumstances;** □see also, **diminished capacity.**

mixed nuisance □see **nuisance.**

mixed question of law and fact: a twilight zone between questions of law to be decided by the judge and questions of fact to be decided by the jury. E.g., Was the plaintiff an employee of the defendant? On a mixed question of law and fact, the division of decision remains, with frequent claims that judge or jury has invaded the other's turf. □see also, **try.**

M'Naghten rule, also called the M'Naghten test: a rule for determining **insanity** (□see) announced in *Daniel M'Naghten's Case,* 8 English

Reports 718, 722 (1843), that an accused is not criminally responsible if ". . . at the time of committing of the act, the party accused was laboring under such a defect of reason, from disease of the mind, as not to know the nature and quality of the act he was doing; or, if he did know it, that he did not know he was doing what was wrong." The M'Naghten rule is sometimes called the *right and wrong rule* or the *right and wrong test.*

M'Naghten test   □see M'Naghten rule.

mobilia rule   □see mobilia sequuntur personam.

mobilia sequuntur personam   (L., mo-BEEL-ya sah-QUUN-tur per-SOHN-am: movables follow the person): an old, unreliable maxim interpreted as saying that movable personal property is governed by the law of the owner's domicile.   Sometimes it is, and sometimes it isn't.   Some writers puff the maxim to the status of a "rule," called with undue familiarity the **mobilia rule**.   Consult the substantive law, e.g., conflicts, tax, probate, divorce.

Model Acts   □see Uniform Laws.

Model Code of Professional Responsibility   □see legal ethics.

Model Codes   □see Uniform Laws.

Model Rules of Professional Conduct   □see legal ethics.

modified and changed: an especially bad product of the habit of using two words for one.   *Changed* can, but does not necessarily, mean *modified,* itself a flexible word.   A writing can be changed in large or small doses.   The coupling raises questions of interpretation. Does this mean changed by being modified, its severity reduced, a slight change?   Or is it only pattern redundancy, intended to include all manner of change?   Make it *modified* if nothing more precise will do; make it *changed;* not both.   □see **coupled synonyms.**

modus operandi   (L., MO-dus op-uh-RAN-die: manner of working): a pattern distinctive to this defendant in committing other criminal acts, as evidence of guilt of this crime in the same pattern.   In some opinions, influenced by police and crime fiction usage, shortened to *modus* or *M.O.*

money due on an account stated □see **common count**, under count.

money had and received □see **had and received**.

money laundering □see **laundering**.

money lent □see **common count**, under **count**.

money paid to the use of the defendant □see **common count**, under count.

monopoly: control over a market for particular goods or services, either an absolute control, e.g., an exclusive government franchise to operate a street railway; or a control so substantial that price and availability may be fixed and competition excluded. □see **antitrust law**.

month □see **time**.

month-to-month tenancy □see **periodic tenancy**, under **estate**.

moot □see **controversy**.

moot case □see **controversy**.

moot court: a law school mock court in which students argue hypothetical cases.

mootness □see **controversy**.

moral turpitude: an old redundancy for *turpitude* = depravity = immorality. The double-barreled turpitude has a special hometown appeal to lawyers, but with or without the moral additive, it is as imprecise in the law as in ordinary English. The only certainty is that the characterization of an act or crime as "involving moral turpitude" means that the consequences will be more severe, e.g., degree of crime, punishment, discipline, impeachment. Serious felonies usually qualify; so do some misdemeanors. Sometimes moral turpitude describes a crime that is **malum in se** (□see). Jurisdictions and decisions vary; there is no consensus on what it takes to make moral turpitude.

mortgage (v., n.): to make real or personal property serve as security for the payment or performance of an obligation; and the writing that makes the property serve as security. <The owner (*mortgagor*) delivered the *mortgage* to the escrow, *mortgaging* the property to secure payment of the debt owed to the lender (*mortgagee*).> □see **deed of trust,** under **deed;** □see **encumber;** □see **lien.** □see also, **wraparound mortgage.**

mortgagee □see **mortgage;** □see also, -ee.

mortgagor □see **mortgage.**

mortmain statutes: laws restricting the right to make charitable gifts by will. The laws vary by jurisdiction, are usually directed at will provisions made a short time before death, to the detriment of family. Whether or not the name is used in the statute, they are referred to as *mortmain* (law F., *morte mayn:* dead hand) statutes or acts, the term inherited from old usage in England. The English laws originally prohibited gifts of land to religious corporations, then to corporations generally. The *mortmain* is variously explained as the dead hand of the Church (possibly related to **civil death,** □see, under **civil**), of a corporation avoiding feudal obligations, and later the dead hand of a testator continuing to control property.

motion: a formal request, written or oral, that a court do something. To make the request is to *move.* <The lawyer moved for a new trial and for reduction of bail. Both motions will be heard next week.> Unlike ordinary English, *move* is used only as a verb, and *motion* only as a noun. The lawyer does not "make a move" nor "motion for a new trial." In particular contexts, what would otherwise be described as a *motion* is called a *petition,* e.g., for a writ of certiorari (□see **certiorari**), or an *application,* e.g., for an injunction (□see **enjoin**). The variety of motions is limited only by a lawyer's imagination and local rules of procedure. For a sampling of what may be requested by motion: □see **disqualify;** □see **judgment** (nonsuit, notwithstanding the verdict,

motion

on the pleadings, summary); □see **motion to dismiss**, under **pleadings**; □see **strike**; □see **suppress**; □see **in limine**.

motive: an underlying reason for doing something. Often equated with **intent** (□see). When differentiation becomes critical, as in the criminal law, the immediacy of intent accompanying an act can be differentiated from the underlying motive. Intent is part of the crime; motive is not; its presence or absence may affect the logic of guilt.

mouthpiece □see **lawyer**.

movables: generally, a synonym for *personal property* (□see **property**). Sometimes limited to tangible personal property; sometimes limited to personal property that is movable right now, as distinguished, e.g., from growing crops. □see also, **mobilia sequuntur personam**.

move □see **motion**.

Ms. □see **Esquire**.

multiplicitous • multiplicity

The outrageous legal adjective *multiplicitous* describes the legal sin of *multiplicity:*

multiplicitous indictment: one charging the same offense in more than one count, the flip side of **duplicitous** (□see).

multiplicity of suits: a number of suits on the same issue against the same defendant; sometimes enjoined to prevent harassment.

multiplicitous indictment □see **multiplicitous**.

multiplicity □see **multiplicitous**.

multiplicity of suits □see **multiplicitous**.

municipal corporation □see **corporate**.

municipal court: in some states, a court of limited jurisdiction for a local political entity. □see **court**.

murder: the most extreme form of unlawful, unjustified killing, often described in traditional language, a killing with **malice aforethought** (□see). The uncertainty of that language, plus the fact that murder is traditionally a capital offense, has produced definition varying by jurisdiction. The emphasis is on intentional killing characterized by premeditation and deliberation, and a secondary emphasis on the opposite—a killing characterized by a wanton disregard for the lives of others. Statutes customarily subdivide murder for purposes of severity of penalty. For example only:

first-degree murder, also called **murder in the first degree**, and in legal argot, **murder one**: a killing characterized by advance planning, or a killing under specified abhorrent circumstances such as poisoning, torture, in the course of committing or attempting to commit specified felonies, e.g., arson, child molesting, burglary, rape, robbery (□see **felony murder**). All other murder would then be **second-degree murder**, also called **murder in the second degree**.

For other entries discussing murder: □see **felony**; □see **heat of passion**; □see **homicide**; □see **malum in se**; □see **manslaughter**.

murder in the first degree □see **murder**.

murder in the second degree □see **murder**.

murder one □see **murder**.

must □see **may**.

mutuality: in law, as in ordinary English, the quality of being reciprocal, i.e., it works both ways. In some legal writing, *mutuality* is elevated to the status of the **mutuality principle**: it must work both ways or not at all. Spelled out in catch phrases that must be tested against the substantive law:

mutuality of obligation: unless both parties are obligated, neither is. E.g., in a contract based on mutual promises, if one promise is not binding, neither is; also called **mutuality of contract**. E.g., a right to set off one debt against another must be of debts between the same parties (**mutuality of parties**), sometimes also relating to the same matter or time (**mutuality of debt**).

mutuality of remedy: a reason sometimes given for denying specific performance: unless both parties have a right to specific performance, neither has.

mutuality of contract □see mutuality.

mutuality of debt □see mutuality.

mutuality of estoppel □see collateral estoppel, under res judicata.

mutuality of obligation □see mutuality.

mutuality of parties □see mutuality.

mutuality of remedy □see mutuality.

mutuality principle □see mutuality.

mutually agree is redundant; best forgotten. <"A and B mutually agree"; make it "A and B agree.">

mutual mistake □see mistake.

mutual release □see release.

mutual wills □see will.

N

naked trust □see **trust.**

name and style □see **alias;** □see **coupled synonyms.**

narrative evidence: continuous testimony in an ordinary conversational manner, as distinguished from a series of answers to a series of specific questions. <Now, will you please tell us in your own words exactly what happened after you arrived there?> □see **evidence.**

Natural Born Citizen Clause: the part of the U.S. Constitution reading: "No person except a natural born citizen, or a citizen of the United States, at the time of the adoption of this Constitution, shall be eligible to the Office of President. . . ." (Art. II, § 1, cl. 5). □see also, **constitutional clauses.**

Natural Death Act □see **right to die.**

natural guardian □see **guardian.**

naturalization: legal procedure by which an alien becomes a citizen of the United States. The person is then referred to as a **naturalized citizen,** or a *citizen by naturalization.*

Naturalization Clause: the part of the U.S. Constitution reading: "The Congress shall have power . . . To establish an uniform rule of naturalization. . . ." (Art. I, § 8, cl. 4). □see also, **constitutional clauses.**

naturalized citizen □see **naturalization.**

natural life □see **civil death,** under **civil.**

natural person □see **person.**

navigable airspace □see **airspace.**

navigable waters: waters that are navigable or with reasonable improvement can be made navigable.

necessaries: the law's special plural made up of a multitude of items, each a **necessary**, characterizing what at the moment are considered essentials. Deliberately imprecise, bending more or less gracefully to accommodate a thousand circumstances without rewriting the substantive law. E.g., a contract for food and clothing that an infant may not disaffirm (□see **infant**, under **child**); e.g., named items, varying by jurisdiction, that are exempt from execution; e.g., items included in an obligation to support, varying according to accustomed life-style—for some, false teeth; for others, a fur coat.

necessarily included offense   □see **included offense**.

necessary   For the noun, □see **necessaries**. For the equally imprecise adjective, □see **absolutes**.

necessary and proper   For *necessary,* □see **absolutes**; for *proper,* □see **fit and proper**.

Necessary and Proper Clause: the part of the U.S. Constitution reading: "Congress shall have power . . . To make all laws which shall be necessary and proper for carrying into execution the foregoing powers, and all other powers vested by this Constitution in the government of the United States, or in any department or officer thereof." (Art. I, § 8, cl. 18). The Necessary and Proper Clause is also called the *Basket Clause,* the *Coefficient Clause,* the *Elastic Clause,* and the *Sweeping Clause.* □see also, **constitutional clauses**.

necessary party   □see **party**.

necessity   like the related *need,* means in the law what it means in ordinary English, no more precise. □see **absolutes**; □see **convenience and necessity**; □see **necessaries**; □see **self-defense**.

need   □see **necessity**.

need not detain us   □see **clichés**.

ne exeat   (L., KNEE EX-e-at: Let him not depart.), a shortening of **ne exeat republica**, the American version of the English *ne exeat regno* (L.: Let him not go out of the kingdom.): an extraordinary writ ordering the defendant in a civil case not to leave the jurisdiction, and to post bond as security for appearance in court. Fading, but still used in some states and by the United States in some tax cases. □see also, **civil arrest,** under **bail.**

ne exeat republica   □see **ne exeat.**

negative covenant   □see **covenant.**

negative easement   □see **easement.**

negative equitable servitude   □see **easement.**

negative pregnant   □see **affirmative pregnant.**

neglect   □see **excusable neglect,** under **justification;** □see **fail;** □see **malfeasance;** □see **negligence.**

neglected child   □see **child.**

negligence: failure to exercise the care of a **reasonable man** (□see) under the circumstances; shortened to failure to exercise due care (□see **due**). The failure, a neglect, can be by act or omission, ordinarily contrasted with the intentional (□see **intent**); often contrasted with **recklessness** (□see), but at that point, the waters are even muddier. The definition here, including the sex of the standard bearer (□see **sex**), is traditional. It is flexible in the extreme, spawning acres of explanations for jurors, not more enlightening than the *negligence, neglect,* or plain *carelessness* of ordinary English. The endless and costly contexts of *negligence* in the law continue to produce more printed and computerized repetitions and variations of the definition than most lawyers have time for. In combinations, *negligence* also produces:

comparative negligence □see **contributory negligence.**

contributory negligence (□see).

criminal negligence □see **manslaughter;** □see also, **crime.**

negligence

gross negligence: an expression without fixed meaning. It is an expression of some sense of aggravated negligence, a remnant of diminishing reliance on degrees of negligence—usually characterized as *slight, ordinary,* and *gross,* as opposed to what is the *due* of *due care* in a particular instance. The expressions of degree are still used in the law of bailments (□see **bail**), in discussions of comparative negligence (□see **contributory negligence**), and in special statutes.

imputed negligence: the negligence of one person imposed as a burden on another because of the relationship between them. As with *imputed knowledge* (□see **knowledge**), substantive law determines what relationships can make one responsible for someone else's negligence. E.g., negligence of the driver of an automobile imputed to the owner. *Imputed negligence* is a form of **vicarious liability** (□see).

negligence per se: conduct that is negligent as a matter of law; typically, conduct in violation of a law affecting public safety. E.g., failure to yield right of way to a fire engine.

ordinary negligence: another name for *negligence.*

negligence per se   □see **negligence.**

negligent homicide   □see **manslaughter.**

negligent infliction of emotional distress   □see **emotional distress.**

negligent misrepresentation: a false representation made through negligence (□see), damaging someone who reasonably relies on the representation, believing it to be true. A tort action based on negligent misrepresentation is distinguished from the intentional misrepresentation called *deceit.*   □see **fraud.**

negotiability   □see **negotiable,** under **commercial paper.**

negotiable   □see **commercial paper.**

negotiable instrument   □see **commercial paper.**

negotiable order of withdrawal   □see **NOW account,** under **bank.**

negotiate   □see **commercial paper.**

negotiated plea: in a criminal case, the defendant's plea arrived at by **plea bargaining** between the defendant and the prosecutor. Typically, the plea is "guilty" or "nolo contendere" to a lesser offense or to fewer offenses than charged, in return for dismissal of some charges and recommendation of lighter punishment. □see also, **Alford plea**, under **guilty**. In ordinary and legal slang, to arrive at a *negotiated plea* is to *cop a plea.*

net Not a legal term of art. It is a flexible word of ordinary English, the pride of accountants, and frequently embroiled in the law, as in *net estate, net income, net profit, net worth.* Statutes often define *net* for a special context, definitions not transferable to general legal usage.

never □see **absolutes.**

new in ordinary English is *new* in the law, sometimes repeated as *new and novel* (□see **coupled synonyms**). There is also special legal usage of *new* and synonymous variations:

new and useful □see **patent.**

novelty □see **patent;** □see also, **copyright.**

original □see **copyright;** □see **patent.**

new and novel □see **new.**

new and useful □see **patent.**

newly discovered evidence: evidence not discovered until after a decision has been made, and that would have substantially affected the outcome if presented at the hearing or trial. For details of classification as *newly discovered evidence* and usability to effect a change in outcome, refer to the rules of evidence. □see **evidence.**

newsman's privilege □see **newsmen's privilege.**

newsmen's privilege: a qualified privilege of a reporter to refuse to disclose the source of information used in a news story, or obtained in connection with news gathering. With varying qualifications, the privilege is recognized by so-called **shield laws** in a number of states. Despite rejection in *Branzburg v. Hayes,* 408 U.S. 665 (1972), the privilege continues to gain support as an aspect of First Amendment free speech.

The name of the privilege is still not fixed. It is also called *newsman's privilege, journalist's privilege, reporter-source privilege,* and *reporter's privilege. Newsmen* and *newsman* are sexist, and some prefer *newsperson's privilege* and *newsperson's shield law.* Plain-speaking *reporter* is frowned upon in pompous newspaper circles. *Journalist* gives a vague preference to some media over others, and has been used to refer to the fair reporting of public proceedings. □see **conditional privilege,** under **immunity.**

new trial   □see **trial.**

next friend   □see **guardian ad litem,** under **guardian.**

next of kin   □see **heirs.**

nexus   □see **clichés.**

nil: a Latin way of saying *nothing,* which says it better.

nimble dividend   □see **dividend.**

NLRB: abbreviation of National Labor Relations Board.   □see **administrative agency,** under **administrative law.**

no bill   □see **indictment.**

no citation of authority is needed   □see **clichés.**

no contest: colloquial English for a plea of *nolo contendere.*   □see **guilty.**

no contest clause   □see **in terrorem.**

no-fault divorce   □see **divorce.**

no-fault insurance: a type of automobile accident insurance that pays for direct expenses and loss of income from personal injury regardless of fault. The policy fixes maximum payment, and typically covers the insured, family, authorized drivers and passengers, and any pedestrian hit. Claim is typically made against the insured's carrier, rather than searching out the carrier of someone at fault. The trade-off is that those covered and the carrier are immune to usual tort liability, unless injuries are severe with damages exceeding fixed payment limits. Compulsory no-fault statutes vary by state.

nolle □see **nolle prosequi.**

nolle prosequi (L., NOL-e PROS-e-kwi: unwilling to pursue).

1. (n.) in some jurisdictions, an entry of record or an acknowledgement that the prosecutor is dismissing a criminal case. Abbreviated *nol pros* or *nol. pros.*, sometimes *nolle.*

2. (v.) in some jurisdictions, to dismiss a criminal prosecution, more often abbreviated *nol pros.* <They nol prossed the charge of murder.>

nolo □see **guilty.**

nolo contendere □see **guilty.**

no longer open to question □see **clichés.**

nol pros □see **nolle prosequi.**

nominal damages □see **damage.**

nominal director □see **director.**

nominal party □see **party.**

nominate □see **appoint.**

nonaccess

1. absence of opportunity for sexual intercourse, e.g., as a defense in a **filiation proceeding** (□see).

2. absence of opportunity for copying, as a defense in an action based on **plagiarism** (□see).

nonage □see child.

non-Article III tribunal □see federal courts.

nonbank bank □see bank.

nonclaim: failure to claim a right within a time specified by law; as in a **statute of nonclaim** fixing deadlines for presenting claims against an estate or a municipality. □see also, **statute of limitations.**

non compos mentis (L., non COM–pos MEN–tis: not having mastery of one's mind): not of sound mind. A generalized expression, sometimes still used. □see **insanity.**

nonconforming use □see zoning.

noncontestable clause □see incontestable clause.

nonfeasance □see malfeasance.

nonjoinder □see joinder.

nonmarried cohabitants □see cohabit.

non obstante veredicto □see judgment n.o.v., under judgment.

nonobviousness □see patent.

nonpayment □see payment.

nonperformance □see perform.

nonpossessory estate □see future interest.

nonprofit □see charitable.

nonprofit corporation □see charitable.

nonrecourse: no recourse, i.e., without personal liability. In a variety of references: e.g., a *nonrecourse loan:* a secured lending agreement in which the lender has agreed to look only to the security for repayment, not to the borrower personally. E.g., an indorsement of commercial paper *without recourse.*

nonremovable □see **removal (of a case)**.

nonresident (n., adj.): not a resident of a particular place or in a particular jurisdiction. □see **residence**; □see **domicile**.

nonresponsive: legal argot characterizing something said by a witness that does not answer the question asked. <Lawyer: How old are you? Witness: How old are *you?* Lawyer: Move to strike that as nonresponsive. Judge: Granted. The witness is directed to answer the question.>

nonsane □see **insanity**.

nonstock corporation: a corporation that does not issue stock; typically, a nonprofit corporation, with ownership represented by memberships. □see **corporate**; □see **charitable**.

nonsuit □see **judgment**.

nonsupport: failure to provide support, e.g., for a child, a spouse, as required by law or agreement.

nonuser: not exercising a right or privilege, e.g., a franchise, a right of way. Consequences, if any, of nonuser, e.g., abandonment, forfeiture, vary by agreement and law.

nonvoting shares □see **stock**.

nonvoting stock □see **stock**.

no par shares □see **stock**.

no par stock □see **stock**.

no priors: legal argot for *no prior convictions*.   □see **prior**.

no recourse   □see **nonrecourse**.

noscitur a sociis   (L., KNOW-sa-ter ah SOSH-e-ees: loosely, known by one's associates): an old Latin maxim, often said to be a "rule of interpretation" of language.   Some believe it lends class (read "pomp") to the commonplace that words are understood in the context of other words.   <She had a contract for life./There was a contract on her life.>

notarize   □see **notary public**.

notary   □see **notary public**.

notary public   (pl. notaries public): a person authorized by law to administer oaths, authenticate signatures and documents, and—by special authorization—to certify that acts required by law have been performed.   E.g., □see **protest**.   The standard shortening of *notary public* is **notary**; orally, almost the only usage.   <Is there a notary here?>   The notary typically *notarizes* by adding to the end of a document the notarial **jurat** (□see), certifying what has been done, signing, and sealing (where a seal is still required).

The usual function of the notary public in the United States is largely mechanical, customarily incidental to more important duties, e.g., legal secretary, deposition reporter.   The title is to be used with caution when there is the possibility of confusion with the far more significant role and status of notaries public in civil law jurisdictions.

note   □see **commercial paper**.

not-for-profit corporation   □see **charitable**.

not found   □see **indictment**.

not guilty   □see **guilty**.

notice   (n.): information.   Often a synonym of **knowledge** (□see), equally imprecise.   *Notice* is indispensable, and freely, loosely used.   Lawyers are not always clear that they are talking about the information that is *notice,* or about how it gets around and its effect. Best start with the most forthright—*a notice* notice. Then try to sort out the notice that is hooked to adjectives—*actual, constructive, implied,* and *imputed notice.* Often those combinations are the unspoken predicates that shape the overlapping usage—*give, have, put on, receive,* and *take notice.*

1. a notice: words with a message—oral, printed, painted, inscribed, photographed, computerized; usually *a notice* refers to a piece of paper. If, e.g., you *file a notice,* it is a piece of paper. Filed or not, some of the pieces of paper have special names. Here is a representative sampling:

a legal notice: a message to the public, required to be published at a particular time, in a prescribed form of advertisement, in an authorized newspaper. Usually the print is illegible; token compliance with a requirement, not communication. Some typical messages: a fictitious firm name; □see **alias**; competitive bidding on public construction; proposed settlement of a **class action** (□see). *A legal notice,* the advertisement, is not to be confused with the conclusion *legal notice,* in the sense that a notice is legal.

notice of appeal: telling a court and litigants that a party intends to **appeal** (□see).

notice of appearance □see **appear.**

notice of lis pendens □see **lis.**

notice of motion: telling a court and litigants when and where a lawyer will present a **motion** (□see).

notice to creditors: to file claims, e.g., against a bankrupt or probate estate.

notice to pay rent or quit: from landlord to tenant; regulated by statute. A prelude to an action of *unlawful detainer;* □see **forcible entry and detainer.**

notice to quit: from landlord to tenant, without the alternative of paying rent. A prelude to ending a tenancy; regulated by statute.

2. actual notice: the real thing (□see **actual**). E.g., "I told him so." The simplicity of actual notice is sometimes complicated by subdivision:

express notice, also called *direct notice:* the real thing, really. E.g., "I told him so."

implied notice: from the circumstances you ought to have been aware; your own fault if you weren't. This is sometimes called *implied actual notice,* a redundancy, except for the fact that *implied notice* also has ties to *constructive notice.*

3. constructive notice: something that the law says will be treated as if it were actual notice, even though it's not (□see **actual**). E.g., notice of transfer of title to real property by recording a deed, even though a particular person never saw it, never heard of it, and had no reason to know about it.

implied notice: sometimes a synonym for constructive notice. Not to be confused with implied notice as a type of actual notice. *Implied notice* to mean *constructive notice* concentrates on the proposition that this is a notice that the law creates, whether or not it reflects reality.

imputed notice

a. a variety of constructive notice, in that the law treats notice to someone else as notice to you; this usage is a synonym for *imputed knowledge* (□see **knowledge**).

b. sometimes used as a synonym for *implied notice,* the constructive notice variety.

4. give notice: a technical label for doing whatever it is that the law requires to be done to inform someone of a legal event that has happened or is about to. The key here is what the law requires, whether or not giving notice results in receiving notice (sense 5). Giving and receiving notice may coalesce, as in the simplest form of actual notice, "I told him so." But you can give notice by actual or constructive notice, as by doing what a statute may specifically prescribe for giving notice; e.g., advertising, filing, mailing, posting, publishing, recording, serving *a notice* (sense 1).

5. receive notice: coming into possession of information of legal significance. A statute may specify when you receive notice; e.g., it may call for actual notice by personal delivery of *a notice;* it may be satisfied by imputed notice or some other form of constructive notice. You may receive notice without having been given notice: you may learn something on your own; you may have implied actual notice.

6. have notice: the result of having been given notice, having received notice, or both. *Have notice* is the legal conclusion that precedes saddling someone with the legal burden that follows from notice. <Whether or not they ever received notice of entry of default, they were given notice by the required mailing to the proper address; accordingly, they had notice more than six months ago, and it is now too late to move to set aside the default.> To *have notice* is also called *put on notice* and *charged with notice.*

7. take notice

a. an attention-getting device, often rendered TAKE NOTICE, as an introduction to *a notice* (sense 1). Unlike many written formalisms (□see **formalisms**), this one is sometimes useful.

b. take judicial notice: the form of request, as well as the form of decision to grant or deny a request, for **judicial notice** (□see). <We ask that the court take judicial notice of the fact that sunset on the day of the alleged rape was 7 p.m., Pacific Daylight Time./The court takes judicial notice that. . . .>

□see also, **due notice, under due.**

notice of appeal □see **notice.**

notice of appearance □see **appear.**

notice of lis pendens □see **lis.**

notice of motion □see **notice;** □see also, **motion.**

notice to creditors □see **notice.**

notice to pay rent or quit □see **notice.**

notice to quit □see **notice.**

not inconsistent with this opinion: a favorite double negative of the appellate bench. When an appellate court sends a case back to the trial court for "proceedings not inconsistent with this opinion," the usual meaning is "consistent with this opinion." Once in a purple moon, a creative job of fine tailoring might discover a nuance neither consistent nor inconsistent but somewhere in-between. Few appellate judges expect that and fewer trial judges have the brass or time to try for it. Everyone assumes that *not inconsistent* means *consistent.* Why not say so? Many respected judges do.

notorious □see **open and notorious, under open.**

no true bill □see **indictment.**

431

not satisfied: a notation of lack of success, sometimes made by an officer on a *return of execution* (□see **execute**). *Not satisfied* is less specific than the older notation **nulla bona** (L., NUL-uh BONE-uh: no goods): no property found.

not to be performed within one year □see **statute of frauds**.

not unfair to say □see **clichés**.

notwithstanding: a Middle English negative roughly translating the Latin *non obstante;* a favorite of the law in spite of, perhaps because of, it can mean in spite of, nevertheless, still, yet, although, however. What is given in other parts of an agreement or statute is, or can be, deftly, ambiguously, snatched away by *notwithstanding* joined by old cohorts, as in *Anything herein to the contrary notwithstanding.* Except where it has acquired a fixed status, as in **judgment n.o.v.** (□see, under **judgment**), *notwithstanding* is a dangerous word even for lawyers. The writing lawyer is too apt to throw it in without considering all of its side effects; the careful, reading lawyer is compelled to examine its possibilities. Readers at large must inevitably regard *notwithstanding* as a warning of legal trickery.

notwithstanding the verdict □see **judgment n.o.v.**, under **judgment**.

n.o.v. □see **judgment n.o.v.**, under **judgment**.

novation

1. the substitution of a new agreement for an earlier agreement, which is extinguished by the new agreement.

2. the new agreement that is substituted for the earlier agreement (sense 1).

novel □see **new**; □see **copyright**.

novelty: a requirement of patentability; □see **patent**. Not a requirement of **copyright** (□see).

NOW account □see **bank**.

nuclear hazard □see **nuclear incident**.

nuclear incident: "[A]ny occurrence, including an extraordinary nuclear occurrence, within the United States causing, within or outside the United States, bodily injury, sickness, disease, or death, or loss of or damage to property, or loss of use of property, arising out of or resulting from the radioactive, toxic, explosive, or other hazardous properties of source, special nuclear, or byproduct material. . . ." (Atomic Energy Act of 1954, amended to 1978, 42 USCA § 2014(q)).

That much of the definition is only an alert, a provocative point of departure. A series of provisos make *nuclear incident* include specified occurrences outside of the United States. In addition, the definition is a single-sentence, assembly-line job using expressions defined elsewhere in the Act: *extraordinary nuclear occurrence, source material, special nuclear material,* and *byproduct material* (respectively, 42 USCA §§ 2014(j), (z), (aa), and (e)). The principal definition and the special definitions are changeable, facets of lawyers' dependence on scientists and policymakers foreign and domestic, e.g., for accuracy in *nuclear* or *nuclear hazard* clauses in insurance policies. □see also, **atomic energy**.

nudum pactum (L., NOO-dum PAK-tum: a bare agreement): loose, vestigial usage for an informal promise, not enforceable as **contract** (□see), usually for lack of consideration.

nuisance: a well-aged generality for an amorphous group of private and public wrongs. Standing alone, *nuisance* is vituperative, not definitive, best understood, if not conquered, by dividing it into *private nuisance* and *public nuisance.*

private nuisance: a substantial and unreasonable interference with the use and enjoyment of another person's land. The interference may be physically obvious; e.g., obstructing access from the land to the street; e.g., an overhanging tree. Or it may be one of a miscellany of pollutions affecting a neighbor's use and enjoyment of his land that go beyond trivial annoyance, beyond the tolerance of "live and let live." E.g., vibrations, stinks, vapors, howls, blasts, blasting music, loud noises, a next-door whorehouse. The interference gives the landowner or other person with an interest in the land (e.g., a tenant) a cause of action in tort, for damages, sometimes for an injunction, sometimes a right to step in and end (*abate*) the nuisance by **self-help** (□see).

433

nuisance

public nuisance: an unreasonable interference with the rights of the public, as distinguished from the rights of a particular individual. The interference is usually a minor crime. The interference may be, but is not limited to, interference with the public's use and enjoyment of public property or property in which the public has rights, e.g., streets, public beaches, parks, navigable waters (□see also, **purpresture**). It may be an interference with any right in the broad spectrum of rights that are common to people generally: interference with public health, safety, morals, peace, comfort, convenience. If the miscellany of localized pollutions that are private nuisances interfere with the rights of the community at large, they may be public nuisances. At times, *private* and *public nuisance* may overlap—a **mixed nuisance**; e.g., the next-door whorehouse that is a private nuisance to a neighbor may also be a public nuisance, interfering with public morals and illegal to boot. But the vast sweep of public nuisance encompasses all manner of interference with all manner of public rights. E.g., indecent exposure (public morals); unlicensed practice of medicine (public safety); acid rain, a malarial pond (public health).

The prime adversary of those creating a public nuisance is the state, with criminal prosecutions, direct action to end (*abate*), or civil actions to enjoin a public nuisance. With local variation, a private cause of action predicated on public nuisance must rest on the individual's special damage, not the damage shared as a member of the public. □see also, **red light abatement laws.**

Some jurisdictions make the additional, not uniform classifications:

nuisance per accidens: a nuisance because of the circumstances, e.g., a business ordinarily lawful but a nuisance because of its location or the way it is operated. Also sometimes called a *nuisance in fact*. As distinguished from—

nuisance per se: a nuisance at all times, e.g., an illegal business. Also sometimes called a *nuisance at law* or an *absolute nuisance*.

For a worse nuisance, but not the *nuisance* of this entry, □see **attractive nuisance**, under **child.**

nuisance at law □see **nuisance.**

nuisance in fact □see **nuisance.**

nuisance per accidens □see **nuisance.**

nuisance per se   □see **nuisance**.

nulla bona   □see **not satisfied**.

null and void: void and void, which is to say, *void*. That is what it should mean, that what it is attached to is a nothing, as a *void contract* or a *void marriage,* one that never was. But no one believes it. *Null and void* is one of those once fashionable **coupled synonyms** (□see) that refuses to admit that it is dead. It has developed a flair for redundancy.

Writers shower the corpse with faded blossoms: absolutely null and utterly void; null, void, and of no force and effect; null, void, and of no further force and effect; totally null and void; void *ab initio* (□see). One result of this excess is that you can never be quite sure that *null and void* speaks of what never was, what once was, or what won't be from here on. *Null and void,* as well as *void,* is frequently interpreted to mean *voidable.* The related *annul* and *annulment* still have the pristine sense of *void* in the context of marriage and **divorce** (□see); but elsewhere, *annul* doubles itself as *annul and set aside* and mingles haphazardly with *rescind* and **cancel** (□see). The time sense of *never was, once was, won't be from here on* are best explained in detail. *Null and void* is best abandoned.   □see **absolutes**.

nullification: the power of a jury to acquit, even though the verdict is contrary to the evidence and contrary to the law as given in the instructions. Also called *jury nullification.*

nunc pro tunc • backdate

nunc pro tunc   (L., nunk pro tunk: now for then)

1. the official fixing now of the date on which some official action was taken, but at the time was not officially recorded, or not correctly recorded. The effect is to make the official action speak as of the time it occurred. <Through clerical error, the judgment book shows entry of judgment on March 10, 1985; it was actually entered March 10, 1984; amend the entry *nunc pro tunc* to show the correct date.> Since the revision shows the correct date, *nunc pro tunc* carries none of the opprobrium sometimes associated with *backdating.*

2. the doing now of some ministerial act improperly omitted and permitted to be done now with retroactive effect. <Through inadvertence, the approved costs were not included in the judgment. Costs awarded *nunc pro tunc.* >

3. slang usage: taking care of something forgotten. <She took office ten months ago; you'd better congratulate her *nunc pro tunc.*>

backdate: to give a contract or other writing a date earlier than the date on which it was signed. With commercial paper, the date may be earlier than the date of issue; also called *antedate,* as distinguished from *postdate.*

1. legitimate agreed fixing of an earlier time for rights to become effective, interest to start accruing, etc. <The contract was signed today but was backdated, it having been agreed that everything was to run from the first of the month.>

2. a pejorative when done for a fraudulent purpose. <The tax return was backdated to make it appear that it had been filed on time.>

nuncupative will

1. loosely, an oral will. □see **will.**

2. a distinctive type of oral will: the spoken words of a person near death telling one or more witnesses how his property is to be disposed of at death. Not merely an informal will, the nuncupative will is oral by "necessity, not choice." It is to be distinguished from other informal wills that may be oral or written, e.g., □see **sailor's will.** Statutes that still recognize the nuncupative will usually limit it to personal property with a low dollar value, and require that the oral words be reduced to writing within a short time after the death. Statutes vary widely as to the number of witnesses to the oral disposition, and as to the physical condition of the testator at the time, described as last illness, near death, or, in the Latin version, *in extremis.*

O

oath ☐see **affiant**.

Oath or Affirmation Clause: the part of the U.S. Constitution reading: "The senators and representatives before mentioned, and the members of the several state legislatures, and all executive and judicial officers, both of the United States and of the several states, shall be bound by oath or affirmation, to support this Constitution. . . ." (Art. VI, cl. 3). ☐see also, **constitutional clauses**.

obiter ☐see **dictum**.

obiter dictum ☐see **dictum**.

object ☐see **objection**.

objection

1. a written or oral statement of reasons for legal opposition to something that can affect legal proceedings or legal rights. In limited contexts, an objection is called a **challenge** (☐see). A limitless variety of irritations can call forth an objection: e.g., a question to a witness; an offer of evidence; testimony; a proposed ruling; a ruling; conduct of judge, lawyers, jurors, courtroom audience; procedures in and out of court; a title report; requests for admissions (☐see **discovery**). The most frequent and emphatic objections are oral objections in the course of trial; for some types, ☐see **hearsay objection**; ☐see **immaterial**; ☐see **incompetent**; ☐see **irrelevant**, under **relevant**.

exception: a form of objection in some jurisdictions. E.g., to preserve a point for appeal, especially when the court has overruled an objection.

2. the lawyer's staccato rendition of an objection (sense 1), reported as "Objection!"; abbreviated further as "Object!" Details are supplied on order.

obligation

1. something that the law compels a person to do or not to do. This broad legal sense of the word includes whatever the law lends its authoritative weight to, whether imposed ("Stop at the red light!") or

obligation

voluntarily undertaken ("Perform your contract!"). This legal sense, broad as it is, narrows the ordinary English sense of the word that includes moral and religious obligations.

Some special legal terms resting on the broad legal sense of obligation:

"**obligation of contracts**": the constitutional expression in the **Contract Clause** (□see). By interpretation, it refers to the legal enforceability of a contract as an inducement to the undertaking and, accordingly, an aspect of the "obligation" that the states cannot impair.

general obligation bond □see **full faith and credit.**

2. Often obligation (sense 1) is used interchangeably, sometimes repetitively, as a synonym of **duty.** E.g., a duty/an obligation to do something—obey the law, perform a contract; fiduciary obligations/ fiduciary duties (□see **fiduciary**); a duty and obligation to pay for the support of the minor children (□see **alimony**).

3. a debt, i.e., an obligation to pay money.

4. a **bond** (□see), a special formal writing evidencing an obligation to pay money (sense 3), as distinguished from other specialized types of writings evidencing obligations to pay money, e.g., **commercial paper** (□see).

5. loosely, any writing that embodies an obligation to pay money (sense 3), e.g., *obligations of the United States,* including bonds, treasury bills, paper money.

Obligation of Contracts Clause   □see **Contract Clause;** □see **obligation.**

obligee: a person to whom another person (the *obligor*) owes an obligation.

obligor: a person who owes an obligation to another person (the *obligee*).

obnoxious   □see **constitutionally obnoxious, under constitutional.**

obscene   □see **hard-core pornography.**

obscenity   □see **hard-core pornography;** □see also, **pandering.**

obstruction □see encroachment.

obstruction of justice: illegal or improper interference with the administration of the system of justice in any of its aspects. The specifics of obstruction are limitless, e.g., preventing a police officer from making an arrest; destruction of evidence of criminality; encouraging witnesses to perjure themselves or to disappear; disruption of court proceedings. Obstruction of justice may be the basis of criminal prosecution, contempt proceedings, discipline of lawyers for unprofessional conduct. □see also, **spoliation of evidence.**

occupy: to be in physical possession of real property, legally or not. Statutes and local decision give special definitions. The usage here is in addition to frequent legal use of the ordinary English senses of *occupy.* □see **possession.**

occupy the field □see **preemption.**

of age □see **lawful age.**

of and concerning: a redundant expression frequently used in complaints alleging defamation, e.g., that the words were spoken *of and concerning* the plaintiff. *Of* is enough. □see **colloquium.** □see also, **coupled synonyms.**

of counsel □see **lawyer.**

of counsel on the brief □see **lawyer.**

of course: as a matter of right, i.e., not a matter of judicial discretion. Usually, in the form *as of course.* <Under the rules, they were entitled to amend once as of course.> The same sense is often expressed as *of right* and *as of right.*

of even date: of the same date. An old, yet current, form of reference in one dated writing to the date of another writing. <A trust deed dated November 10, 1988, securing a note of even date.> A timesaver in printed forms to avoid inserting a second date; a horror if the dates don't match.

offense: a general, untechnical name for a **crime** (□see) of whatever sort. E.g., □see **included offense.** Combined with other words, *offense* sometimes achieves definition by statute or decision. E.g., □see **petty offense;** □see **prior offense.**

offer □see **offer and acceptance (contracts).**

offer and acceptance (contracts)

offer: a proposal by one person to another (*offeror* to *offeree*) inviting an acceptance that will make a contract between them.

acceptance: a response by the offeree to the offeror expressing agreement to the proposal in a form sufficient to make a contract between them.

This is the common usage of these words in the formation of a **contract** (□see). For the details of *offer* and the sufficiency of an *acceptance,* consult the law of contracts.

offeree □see **offer and acceptance (contracts);** see also, **-ee.**

offer of compromise: a specific proposal to settle a dispute for less than demanded but without admission of liability. The consequences of no settlement vary by statute and decision: e.g., the offer is usually inadmissible at trial; e.g., if offeror gets judgment for more than he offered, extra interest; e.g., if offeree gets judgment for less than was offered him, no costs to offeree, costs to offeror. Also called *offer to compromise* and *offer of settlement.* An offer of compromise may include, or consist of, an *offer of judgment,* i.e., to have judgment entered on the compromise.

offer of judgment □see **offer of compromise.**

offer of proof: a statement of what a lawyer proposes to elicit by questioning or prove by the introduction of documents. The offer is made in response to the court's sustaining an objection to a question or inquiring as to the purpose of a line of questioning or offer of a document. □see **proof.**

offeror □see **offer and acceptance (contracts).**

office • officer • official

office

1. *a place* where business is conducted, especially business of a service or managerial sort, as distinguished from a store or shop. This is ordinary English, with legal implications whenever location is of consequence, as in jurisdiction, licensing, service of process, taxation, venue.

> **principal office** of a corporation: sometimes a synonym for *principal place of business.* □see **domicile**. Sometimes only a place designated for the service of legal papers.

2. *a position* requiring performance of a duty of trust, as distinguished from ordinary employment. The kind of position and its duties have no generalized sense. Thus, substantive constitutional law must be consulted for interpretation of *office* in the U.S. Constitution, e.g., "any civil office under the authority of the United States," "any office under the United States" (Art. I, § 6, cl. 2); "any office of profit or trust under [the United States]" (Art. I, § 9, cl. 9; Art. II, § 1, cl. 2). Except as particular positions are identified in substantive law, *office* is broad and loose, e.g., *in office, oath of office, term of office, office holder;* and its imprecision is contagious, infecting the related words **officer** and **official**. Office may be public or private, elective or appointed, exalted (the office of President of the United States) or run-of-the-mill (the office of tenth assistant vice-president of Zilch Savings & Loan). It pays to check out an *office* before taking one or accusing someone of holding one.

> **office of judge**: the institution, as distinguished from the human being. □see **court**; □see also, **contempt**. <Whatever your feelings toward me, counsel, you have a duty to respect the office of judge. I hold you in contempt.>

officer: a person who holds **office** (□see above, in this entry). Like office, it has no single generalized sense. Thus, constitutional law must be consulted for interpretation of *officer* in the U.S. Constitution, e.g., "inferior officers" (Art. II, § 2, cl. 2); "principal officers" (Amend. XXV, § 4); "officers of the United States" (Art. II, § 3). Except as particular officers are identified in substantive law, *officer,* like *office,* is broad and loose, e.g., a corporate officer, union officer, inspecting officer, a *public officer* (□see **official**, below, in this entry).

officer of the court

1. a public employee having duties in a court, e.g., a court clerk, a bailiff.

2. a lawyer. An old and badly mauled description of the role of a lawyer as a participant in the administration of justice, having duties to court as well as client. The expression is not intended to indicate that the lawyer is in any way an agent of the court (sense 1); lawyers do not usually refer to themselves as officers of the court. More often they are "reminded of it," on occasions of contempt, discipline, **sanctions** (□see), and criticism of legal ethics.

officer of the law: one of the many synonyms for *police officer*: e.g., police, policeman, policewoman, peace officer, officer of the peace. □see **knock and announce**. In some jurisdictions, officer of the law may be a magistrate or a court clerk. □see also, **sheriff**.

official (n., adj.)

1. a person who holds public office, invested with public authority, great or minuscule. Except for the qualification of *public,* the same as **officer** (□see, above, in this entry); often called a *public officer.* □see also, **public official**.

2. loosely, an officer of a private organization, especially a big one. <An official of General Motors announced today. . . .>

3. pertaining to an official—the position, status, acts; or something bearing the imprimatur of an official.

official immunity □see **immunity**.

office of judge □see office.

officer □see office.

officer of the court □see office.

officer of the law □see office.

officers of the United States □see office.

official □see office.

official immunity   □see **immunity.**

officious intermeddler   □see **intermeddler.**

offset   (n., v.): a claim, usually for damages, by one party to litigation asserted (offset) against the claim of the other; often called **setoff** (n., v.).   Under either name, usually equated with one or another version of *counterclaim*; for which, □see **cross-complaint**, under **cross-**.   The rules governing *offset* and *setoff*, and the fortuities of alternate spell-ings—*off-set* and *set-off*, vary widely by jurisdiction.

off the record: words that are not intended to be included in the reporter's transcript of a hearing or trial, even though spoken in court or in a judge's chambers; as opposed to **on the record** (□see).   <Counsel, this is off the record.   Both of you are shouting at each other.   That's enough./Counsel, off the record, how long do you estimate it will take you to finish your case?>   □see **approach the bench;** □see **sidebar**, under **bar.**

of grace: as a favor, as distinguished from as a matter of right.   □see **of course.**   *Of grace* is a rough rendering of the still used Latin **ex gratia** (ex GRAY-she-uh: out of goodwill); e.g., an *ex gratia payment* by an insurance company while still asserting "no liability."

of record

1.   a generalized reference to information that is contained in an official record, or to a document that is part of an official record.   <That's a *matter of record.*/Your objection is now of record.>   In this sense, the reference may be to any of a miscellany of official records, e.g., something filed in court or in a clerk's office (□see **file**), whether or not recorded (sense 2).   □see also, **on the record.**

2.   reference to a document, e.g., a deed, a mortgage, that has been **recorded:**   copied into an official set of records, e.g., a record of property transfers in a county.   <We have been unable to find any deed of record showing a transfer of Blackacre./In the only mortgage of record, Adam Smith is the mortgagee.>   □see also, **enter.**

3.   reference to someone whose status is evidenced by some writing that is *of record,* whether recorded (sense 2)—e.g., owner of record, mortgagee of record; or filed (sense 1)—e.g., *attorney of record* (□see **lawyer**); *party of record.*

4.   □see **court of record**, under **court.**

of right □see of course.

oil and gas lease □see mining lease.

omnibus (L.: for all): a general term of description of a writing that covers a variety of subjects or persons. E.g., *omnibus bill* in a legislature; *omnibus clause* in a contract, a will, an insurance policy.

omnibus bill □see omnibus.

omnibus clause □see omnibus.

on all fours: legal argot describing an earlier case that is just like this one on the significant facts and law, or so similar as to be persuasive in deciding this case. <Your Honor, this case is on all fours with *Smith v. Rogers,* just decided in the Second Circuit.> In oral slang, a case *on all fours* is often called a **horse case.** For quick communication lawyer to lawyer or lawyer to judge, *on all fours* is a useful metaphor.

on and after □see time.

once in jeopardy □see double jeopardy.

on consignment □see consign.

on demand □see demand.

one: a legal sneer masquerading as precision. <One Mary Smith is the legal owner./One John Jones, accused of murder. . . .> Delete *one.* □see also, certain.

one-man corporation □see one-person corporation, under corporate.

one man, one vote □see one person, one vote.

one-person corporation □see corporate.

one person, one vote: a shorthand reference to the constitutional requirement "that a state make an honest and good faith effort to construct districts, in both houses of its legislature, as nearly of equal population as is practicable." (*Reynolds v. Sims,* 377 U.S. 533, 577, 1964). Sometimes called *one man, one vote.*

on its face □see **face.**

on or about: a frequently used, deliberately flexible expression of approximate time or location. E.g., an offense committed on or about January 10, 1980; an injury incurred on or about the premises; a firearm on or about the person.

on or before □see **time.**

on point □see **in point.**

on the bench □see **bench.**

on the courthouse steps □see **court.**

on the face □see **face.**

on the merits □see **merit;** □see **judgment on the merits,** under **judgment.**

on the record

  1. words that are part of a reporter's transcript of a hearing or trial, as opposed to **off the record** (□see). <Let's get back on the record.>

  2. reference to something that is **of record** (□see).

on trial □see **trial.**

open (v., adj.): the ordinary English senses of *open,* contrasted with concealed or closed; and *open* = to start something—adapted to legal settings:

open a judgment: to reexamine a judgment to determine the merits of a claim of error or inequity, e.g., a claim that the judgment was obtained by fraud. The reexamination is by the court that gave judgment, as distinguished from an appeal. Opening, sometimes called *reopening*, a judgment can lead to denial of the claim or to a change of the judgment. Grounds, time, and procedure vary by jurisdiction. By a similar process, a ruling or order may be reexamined.

open and notorious

1. an old redundancy—in public (open) and commonly known (notorious)—descriptive of the kind of possession that can be adverse possession (□see, under **possession**).

2. a description of something not only public (open) but evil (notorious) to boot, e.g., open and notorious adultery.

open cohabitation □see **common law marriage**, under **cohabit**.

open court: to commence proceedings in court. <This court is now open; the Honorable John Doe, Judge presiding.> An opened court is then **in session**, after which proceedings or statements made are said to be *in open court*. <In open court they waived trial by jury.> Sometimes, as distinguished from a *closed court:* one not open to the public. □see **public trial**; □see also, **in session**, under **session**.

open shop □see **closed shop**, under **close**.

open the case: to begin the presentation of one side of a case <Deputy District Attorney Susan Wong opened the case for the prosecution.>; usually abbreviated to *open for*. <Richard Roe opened for the defense.> Often, especially in jury trials, the case is opened, not by the presentation of witnesses, but by an **opening statement** of lawyers outlining the nature of the case and what they expect to prove. <Opening statement waived.> □see also, **reopen the case**.

open the door: to introduce evidence that paves the way to introduction of rebutting evidence not otherwise admissible.

open the floodgates □see **slippery slope**.

open a judgment   □see **open**.

open and notorious   □see **open**.

open cohabitation   □see **common law marriage**, under **cohabit**.

open court   □see **open**.

opening statement   □see **open the case**, under **open**.

open shop   □see **closed shop**, under **close**.

open the case   □see **open**.

open the door   □see **open**.

open the floodgates   □see **slippery slope**.

operation of law   □see **by operation of law**.

opinion: a sort of legal essay written by a judge, giving the reasons why a case should be decided one way or another. *Opinion* most often speaks of a writing that names the litigants, gives the facts and legal setting of their case, their contentions, citations to decided cases and to other legal writings, and—after giving reasons—ends up with the **decision** (□see) and **judgment** (□see). Most often, too, *opinion* refers to one by an appellate court, especially as printed in the **law reports** (□see). □see also, **slip opinion**.

But all of that impossibly cramps the usage of *opinion*. Many trial judges write opinions. Opinions vary in endless ways, of substance, style, length. Some are oral opinions; some are written opinions read aloud from the bench. Some cases are decided without opinions. Some judges whose names appear in a printed opinion express themselves so curtly that their views are *opinions* only in the ordinary, nonlegal sense—that's what I think of that: "I dissent," or "Jones, J., dissenting."

> **the opinion** When lawyers speak of "the opinion in *Smith v. Jones*," they speak of what counts right now. It is the opinion of a one-judge court, a **unanimous opinion**, or a **majority opinion**, less often a **plurality opinion**: an opinion short of a majority but that has more votes for it than any other opinion, e.g., in the U.S. Supreme Court, 4–3–2. The author of the opinion, or, if it is ghostwritten (□see **law clerk**), a judge who takes authorship credit and responsibility for the opinion, is usually identified. Those who *join in* the opinion may be simply listed as among the judges participating in the case; in other courts, they may be listed by the addition of their names after the opinion, with the notation "concur" or "concurring."

> **per curiam opinion:** a short opinion, usually—not always—unanimous. An individual author is not identified. The opinion commences with the words *Per Curiam* (L.: by the court); some juris-

dictions use the English translation *By the Court*. A *per curiam opinion* is sometimes referred to as a *per curiam*.

concurring opinion: as distinguished from the notation "concur" or "concurring" at the end of *the opinion* described above, a *concurring opinion* by one or more judges gives reasons for agreeing with another judge but usually expresses reservations about language, statements of law, or points made in another opinion, or gives different reasons for arriving at the same conclusion.

Judges with greater regard for idiosyncratic independence than for the appearance of certainty in adjudication give wide range to *concurring opinions*. They may concur only in the judgment, only in the general result, only in a portion of a majority or minority opinion, or may couple a concurring opinion with a *dissenting opinion*. Strangest of all: a judge may successfully negotiate agreement among other judges on an opinion, write it, and then express unshared views in a separate opinion, concurring with himself. A *concurring opinion* is sometimes referred to as a *concurrence*.

dissenting opinion: as distinguished from a curt word of dissent without opinion, a *dissenting opinion* by one or more judges may be a blanket dissent to the whole of *the opinion* or—like a concurring opinion—dissent only in part. A **dissent**, as the opinion is referred to, looks to change in the composition of the court or, broadly, to change of the law, judicial or statutory. It may consist of reiteration of an old theme, e.g., the dissents of Justices Brennan and Marshall in any case directly or indirectly approving a death penalty, which they insisted, year in and year out, was a "cruel and unusual punishment prohibited by the Eighth and Fourteenth Amendments." More typically, the dissent argues and documents a new position, a differing view of what the law is or should be; and frequently in the course of years becomes the voice of the majority.

For *advisory opinion,* □see **controversy**.

opinion evidence: an expression of opinion, in the ordinary sense of that word. The rules of evidence determine when opinion evidence is admissible. □see **witness**.

opinion letter: a lawyer's letter, usually to a client, giving an opinion of the state of the law on a particular topic; or, of the effect of the law upon a given set of facts, real or hypothetical. Especially, an opinion of the legal consequences that may be anticipated to flow from particular action or inaction.

option: a contract, made like any other contract, but distinguished by a special provision that gives a later choice to one of the parties to the contract, *optional* in the ordinary sense of the word. By that special provision, one party (the *optionor*) agrees that the other (the *optionee*) has a right, but not an obligation, to require the optionor to do something if, within a specified time, the optionee chooses to have it done (*exercises the option*). If not so exercised, the option no longer exists (*lapses*). <They paid $1,000 today for an option to purchase Blackacre for $100,000; the last day to exercise the option is December 10, 1990./ The lessee has an option to extend the lease for another five years.> □see also, **right of first refusal.**

In the language of the stock market, some options have special names. The common ones:

call: an option to buy stock.

put: an option to sell stock.

straddle: an option to buy or sell stock; also called a *spread eagle.*

□see also, **stock option, under stock.**

optionee □see **option.**

optionor □see **option.**

O.R.: abbreviation of *own recognizance.* □see **bail.**

or The ordinary English word, constantly used in the law, with the same lack of precision. Sometimes it joins alternatives; sometimes it doesn't. Sometimes *or* means *and;* sometimes it doesn't. In short, *or* is short and unreliable. □see **and;** □see **and/or;** □see **order.**

-or □see **-ee.**

oral

1. in a general sense, something spoken. The synonym *parol* <Their understanding rests in parol.> is waning, except as used in the **parol evidence rule** (□see). *Verbal,* which refers to words spoken or written, is often used as a synonym of *oral,* in and out of the law.

2. **oral contract,** also called *oral agreement:* a special use of *oral* identifying a contract that is entirely oral, or partly oral and partly written. It is also described as an *unwritten contract* or a *contract not*

in writing, as contrasted with a *written contract* or a *contract in writing.* In loose usage, *oral contract* is often referred to as a *verbal contract* or *verbal agreement.* The definition of *oral contract* here is a matter of usage, separate from substantive rules governing the introduction of oral or written evidence relating to a contract, and separate from the writing requirements of a **statute of frauds** (□see).

3. oral will □see **nuncupative will;** □see also, **sailor's will.**

4. referring to words that are heard but not seen. Some words spoken in court, though ultimately written in a reporter's transcript, are intended for immediate effect. And the immediate effect can be to mislead or confuse jurors and others whose understanding is shaped by what they hear. *Abet* is heard as *a bet, apart* as *a part,* approximate as *a proximate,* and vice versa. For example: "A proximate cause of the accident was . . ." can be understood as "Roughly speaking, the cause of the accident was . . ." or "One of the causes of the accident was. . . ." Similarly, words designed with readers in mind may be heard but not read. For example: a lawyers' slogan of self-praise reads "Sharing In Justice" and is heard broadcast as "Sharing Injustice." The role difference of words to be heard, read, or both, calls for special attention. For the difference between oral formalisms and those written, □see **formalisms.**

oral contract   □see **oral.**

oral copulation   □see **crime against nature.**

oral will   □see **nuncupative will;** □see also, **sailor's will.**

order   In addition to ordinary English usage, *order* has special functions in the law:

1. (procedure) □see **decision;** □see **judgment;** □see **decree,** under **judgment;** □see **order to show cause.** □see **citation;** □see **warrant;** □see **writ.**

2. (commercial paper) For **order paper** and general usage, □see **commercial paper.** For the technical details of **payable to order,** as in "Pay to the *order of* Jane Doe" and "Pay to John Doe, *or order,*" refer to the Uniform Commercial Code.

order paper   □see **commercial paper.**

order to show cause: an order requiring someone to come to court and try to convince a judge *not* to take some action. Also called a *show cause order.* □see **good cause.**

ordinance □see **legislation.**

ordinary: in the law is *ordinary* in common English, the usual, the normal. It is a flexible word, adapting readily to a flow of facts, e.g., the *ordinary course of business.* It is a word of contrast, *ordinary care,* as opposed to *extraordinary care* (□see **extraordinary**), but still flexible, sometimes redundant; □see **negligence.** □see **regular course of business.**

ordinary care □see **ordinary;** □see **extraordinary.**

ordinary course of business □see **ordinary.**

ordinary negligence □see **negligence.**

organization

1. a loose word of reference to almost any group in society with some common purpose and some continuity of structure. Unless the reference to a particular group is clear <Local 138 was the organization calling for a strike.>, *organization* is mouth-filling enough to sound like a law word yet lacking in substance. <We have a nice little organization here.> It is not a legal term of art, but manages to achieve some status by ad hoc definition in some laws; typically, they define by telling what the word *includes,* e.g., a corporation, a government, a business, but don't give a clue as to what is excluded. An organization may or may not be a **legal entity** (□see **person**). The word gets into enough litigation to verify its amorphous flexibility. Though it can be done, it is difficult to misuse *organization.* That makes it attractive but not recommended. □see **person.**

2. the fact of forming an organization (sense 1). If it is clear that the word refers to a corporation, *organization* (sense 2) is a synonym of **incorporation** (□see). <The organization of AB Corp. was completed in July.>

organize: to form an **organization** (□see), whatever that may be. If it is clear that the word refers to a corporation, *organize* is a synonym of **incorporate** (□see **corporate**).

original

original □see copyright; □see patent.

original document rule □see best evidence.

original evidence □see real evidence.

original intent □see intent.

original jurisdiction □see jurisdiction.

original writing rule □see best evidence.

ostensible agency □see agency.

ostensible agent □see agency.

ostensible authority □see agency.

oust • ouster □see wrongful eviction, under evict.

ouster □see wrongful eviction, under evict.

outer space

1. (generally): in ordinary usage, the space in the known and unknown areas of the universe beyond **airspace** (□see). Both expressions are imprecise; the boundary between them and the limits of *outer space* are not fixed. Unlike the current spelling of *airspace, outer space* is still two words, except when shortened to the even less precise *space.* The special jargon, e.g., *astronaut, space suit, space vehicle,* usually refers to *outer space,* but cannot be relied on for a firm separation from *airspace.*

2. (sovereignty): in international treaty usage, the undefined space in the known and unknown areas of the universe, called *outer space,* over which there is no national sovereignty. "[E]xploration and use of outer space . . . shall be the province of all mankind" and "is not subject to national appropriation by claim of sovereignty, by means of use or occupation, or by any other means." These agreements apply to "outer space, including the moon and other celestial bodies." (Art.

I and Art. II, of the **Outer Space Treaty**, ☐see). For the contrast on sovereignty, ☐see **airspace**.

Outer Space Treaty: the short title of "Treaty on Principles Governing the Activities of States in the Exploration and Use of Outer Space, Including the Moon and Other Celestial Bodies," January 27, 1967, in force in the United States, October 10, 1967 (18 U.S.T. (U.S. Treaties and Other International Agreements), pt. 3, p. 2410). This basic United Nations treaty does not define **outer space** (☐see).

outlaw

1. (v.)

   a. to become unenforceable by reason of the time limits of a **statute of limitations** (☐see). Usually refers to a debt. <That debt was outlawed five years ago./The debt will outlaw in two years./They tried to sue on an outlawed debt.> May also refer to a cause of action. <A cause of action for slander outlaws in one year.>

   b. to make illegal or abolish. <Slavery was outlawed.> Untechnical usage.

2. (adj.) informally, descriptive of something unauthorized or illegal, e.g., an *outlaw strike*.

3. (n.) slang for a criminal on the loose.

out of court

1. literally, not *in court*, specifically the courtroom, as in an *out of court settlement*. ☐see **court**.

2. legal slang, to lose a case. <If she takes the stand, we're out of court.>

out of pocket: damages (☐see **damage**) measured by the difference between what was paid and the value of what was received. Sometimes applied in some jurisdictions in some misrepresentation cases. Also spelled *out-of-pocket*. Also called the *out of pocket rule*, as contrasted with:

benefit of the bargain, also benefit-of-the-bargain:

1. damages measured by the difference between value received and value as represented or as warranted; a more common measure applied in cases of misrepresentation or breach of warranty of

value. Also called the *benefit of the bargain rule.* Also called *loss of bargain.*

2. in a more general sense, characterization in breach of contract cases of the normal expectation that parties will get what the contract calls for.

Both *out of pocket* and *benefit of the bargain* are to be taken with caution; they are often "rules" in name only, not rigidly or exclusively applied, and subject to variation by statute, decision, and jurisdiction.

out of pocket rule □see out of pocket.

out on bail □see bail.

output contract □see, under **requirements contract.**

outside counsel □see **lawyer.**

outside director □see **director.**

outsider □see **insider trading.**

over, above, and in addition to: a traditional and worthless redundancy, a grander variation of the redundant *over and above.* Either way, it means *in addition to,* in a word—*plus.* <They are entitled to punitive damages over, above, and in addition to actual damages./They are entitled to actual plus punitive damages.> □see **coupled synonyms.**

over and above □see over, above, and in addition to.

overbreadth

1. an imprecise label for a special kind of defect in a law. The defect consists in covering more than is permissible under the Constitution: the language so wide-ranging that the law includes unconstitutional regulation or prohibition along with regulation or prohibition that is, or by itself might be, constitutional. A law with the defect of *overbreadth* (n., adj.) is said to be *overbroad* (adj.) or *overly broad* (adv.).

2. a court's characterization of the defect (sense 1) and how to deal with it. This confusing conflation of the trouble with what to do about it is sometimes simply called *overbreadth,* frequently **overbreadth doctrine**. Variants are *overbreadth technique* and *overbreadth analysis.* For the full panoply of overbreadth (sense 2) and its variations court to court, refer to constitutional law. In general, overbreadth (sense 2) categorizes the nature of different sorts of overbreadth (sense 1) and couples with that the court's response, typically these:

partial invalidity: overbreadth (sense 1) here can be separated out. The law is held unconstitutional *as applied* to the litigant on the facts of this case, i.e., invalid in part. It is sufficient that overbreadth frees the litigant of the regulation or prohibition, leaving the rest of the law untouched.

facial invalidity: overbreadth (sense 1) here strikes directly and substantially at fundamental constitutional rights (e.g., First Amendment speech and association) in language that cannot be selectively confined, e.g., a total ban on solicitation of funds. Its sweeping overbreadth reaches beyond this litigant's particular behavior, inhibiting the exercise of fundamental constitutional rights by people generally, litigant or not (□see **chilling effect**). Overbreadth renders the whole law invalid *on its face* (□see **face**), unconstitutional.

abstention: overbreadth (sense 1) here is slight or its chill speculative. This court had best leave the law alone (abstain), giving opportunity to a legislature to narrow the law or to another court to interpret away the overbreadth.

overbreadth doctrine   □see **overbreadth**.

overbroad   □see **overbreadth**.

overdraft   □see **kiting**.

overrule

1. to render a decision disapproving an earlier decision that has become final, and deciding the same or a substantially similar point of law in a way contrary to the earlier decision. The *overruling* decision may be rendered by the court whose decision is *overruled* or by one with appellate jurisdiction over that court. <*Smith v. Jones* has outlived its day. We now overrule it.> □see also, **strike down**, under **strike**. *Overrule* is to be distinguished from **reverse** (□see).

2. of a court's response to a lawyer at a trial or hearing:

a. to disapprove an **objection** (□see), as opposed to approving an objection—*sustaining* it. <Objection overruled. The witness will answer the question.>

b. in a general procedural sense: a synonym of *deny,* as opposed to *grant* = approve. <Motion overruled./Motion denied.>

overt act   □see **conspirator,** under **parties to crime.**

owing   □see **due.**

own   □see **owner.**

owner: a general, unspecific name for a person who has some right of property (□see). An *owner* is often referred to as one who *owns* property or has the *ownership* of property. Usage of the three words varies sharply with context, statute, and decision in particular areas of the law, e.g., bankruptcy, insurance, mechanic's liens, tax. Above all else, the words are part of the staple of the law of property, filled with countless subspecies of owners, haunted by the quest for identity—owners of what? In that quest, the only useful meanings of *owner* are to be found in special enclaves of the law of property. This is a sampling of places to look:

□see **beneficial owner,** under **beneficiary;**

□see **easement;**

□see **equitable owner,** under **beneficiary;**

□see **equitable ownership,** under **equity;**

□see **estate;**

□see **fee simple;**

□see **fee tail;**

□see **land;**

□see **legal owner;**

□see **owner of record,** under **of record;**

□see **possession;**

□see **property;**

□see **title.**

ownership □see owner; □see also, seisin.

own recognizance □see bail.

Oyez □see formalisms.

P

Ⓟ □see Ⓒ.

P.A.: abbreviation for **professional association** (□see).

pact: Apart from usage in ordinary English, *pact* is another name for a contract between nations, usually called a **treaty** (□see). □see also, **compact;** □see also, **nudum pactum.**

pain and suffering: synonyms coupled so long in the law as to be regarded as a single word classifying an element of general damages in tort. Omission of one word or the other plus the conjunction, a small blow for brevity. The gain would strike most lawyers as too modest to justify depriving the profession of an old friend. □see **coupled synonyms.**

pains and penalties: the *penalty* sense of *pain* joined in redundancy, but historically considered as a unit and still so regarded in reference to a *bill of pains and penalties.* □see **bill of attainder.** □see also, **coupled synonyms.**

paint with a broad brush □see **bright line.** □see also, **clichés.**

pais □see **estoppel in pais,** under **estoppel.**

palimony

1. current slang of the popular vocabulary giving the impression that unmarried cohabitants (□see **cohabit**) are entitled to support payments on separation, akin to **alimony** (□see). The impression is not part of the law; the expression has made modest headway (sense 2).

2. a label for a court's division of property or a money award, as distinct from periodic support, upon the separation of unmarried cohabitants. The label typically describes a division or award that is based on contract, trust, other equitable remedy, or *quantum meruit,* and that rejects any explicit payment for sexual services. The label is imprecise, sometimes used by writers on legal topics, rarely by judges.

palming off: a type of **unfair competition** (□see), also called *passing off.*

pander

    1. (sex offenses)

        a. (n.): a person who arranges for another person to engage in sex for pay and who shares in those earnings. Also called a *procurer* or *pimp.* Usage and detail vary by jurisdiction. The roles of *pander, procurer,* or *pimp* are sometimes segregated, as, e.g., reserving *pimp* for the sharer of the earnings of a **prostitute** (□see).

        b. (v.): to act as a pander (sense 1.a).

    2. (obscenity) □see **pandering**.

pandering: commercial advertising directed exclusively at arousing sexual desire, as bearing on the question of the obscenity of what is advertised. (See Brennan, J., in *Ginzburg v. United States,* 383 U.S. 463, 466, 1966.)

panel

    1. a **jury panel** (□see).

    2. a panel of judges: a group of substantially less than all of the judges of a particular court. One court may have several panels. A *panel* is designated to hear and determine a particular case or group of cases. *Panel* is contrasted with **en banc** (□see).

par □see **stock**.

parajudge: an informal name for a **paraprofessional** (□see) who is not a judge but is qualified to perform some of the functions of a judge, e.g., considering pretrial motions, subject to a judge's approval.

paralegal: an increasingly popular name for a **paraprofessional** (□see) who is not a lawyer but is qualified to perform some of the functions of a lawyer, e.g., drafting a complaint. Paralegals usually, not always, work in a law office, as assistants to lawyers.

parallel citation □see **citation**.

459

paramount title □see evict.

paraprofessional: a person who is not a professional but is qualified to perform some of a professional's functions, in medicine, law, etc. □see **parajudge;** □see **paralegal.**

parcel: a word of the common vocabulary, used so often by lawyers describing a *piece of land* as to give an impression of legal precision that it does not have. Even worse in the redundant *part and parcel.* □see **coupled synonyms.** *Parcel* is sometimes used to identify a numbered individual lot as part of a specified **tract** (□see).

pardon (n., v.): the freeing of an individual from punishment for a criminal offense. The power to grant a pardon rests with the President "for offenses against the United States, except in cases of impeachment" (Art. II, § 2, cl. 1), and with the governors for state offenses. □see also, **commutation;** □see also, **reprieve.**

parens patriae (L., PAY-renz PAY-tri-e: parent of the country): the sovereign state in a role with undefined powers and duties, chiefly as protector of those under some legal disability, e.g., minors, incompetents.

parent There is no single sense of the word. Decisions and statutes old and new define *parent* in particular contexts. Refer especially to the law of property governing inheritance (□see **descend**), **family law** (□see), **filiation proceedings** (□see), and **evidence.** The Uniform Parentage Act (9B Uniform Laws Annotated 295, 1973) speaks of a *parent and child relationship* (§ 1), rather than *parent.* The senses listed here are guides to interpretation.

1. a person who "begets or brings forth" a child, i.e., a natural father or mother. This ancient, ordinary, and legal sense is now subject to qualification by the expanding technologies of procreation, in particular—for the moment—*artificial insemination* (sense 5).

2. a parent (sense 1) of a child born in wedlock.

3. a parent (sense 1) of a child born in an equivalent of wedlock, e.g., a *common law marriage, putative marriage* (□see **cohabit**), *legitimated* (□see **legitimate**).

4. an **adoptive parent:** an adult who has adopted a **child** (□see).

460

5. a parent by *artificial insemination:*

a. the husband whose wife (with their mutual consent) bears a child artificially inseminated by another male's semen. The donor is not "treated in law as if he were the natural father." (Uniform Parentage Act, § 5).

b. a biological claim to be a *parent* that could be asserted by a husband or a *surrogate mother* in what is currently, commonly, but not uniformly, called a *surrogate mother* arrangement: a husband and wife agree with another woman (the **surrogate mother**) that she will be artificially inseminated with the husband's semen, bear the resulting child, and transfer to the husband and wife all rights and obligations to the child. Husband and wife agree to pay expenses and a fee to the surrogate mother and to accept the child at birth. The appropriate words for the parties to this, and other possible technologies of procreation, are not fixed.

6. surrogate parent: a loose reference to someone acting as a parent. □see **in loco parentis.**

parent corporation: a corporation that controls another corporation—a subsidiary corporation, through ownership of all, substantially all, or majority voting power of the subsidiary's stock.

pari delicto   □see **in pari delicto.**

pari materia   □see **in pari materia.**

pari passu (L., parry PAS-oo: with equal step): simultaneously and proportionately. <Every dollar of profits shall be divided according to our respective shares and paid *pari passu;* at the same time we get our seventy-five cents, you get your twenty-five cents.>

parliamentary law: a general name for the rules of procedure of legislative and deliberative bodies of every character. The rules vary, each organization fixing its own rules, e.g., the houses of Congress (U.S. Const., Art. I, § 5). For most private organizations, e.g., corporations, clubs, etc., the most commonly adopted rules are those in the current revisions of *Robert's Rules of Order* (rev., 8th ed., 1981).

parol   □see **oral;** □see also, **parol evidence rule.**

461

parole: a conditional release from imprisonment after a convict has served only part of a sentence. If the convict (now called a **parolee**) violates a condition of parole, the parole may be revoked, and the convict again imprisoned to serve out the sentence. *Parole* is distinguished from **pardon** (□see), **probation** (□see), and **suspended sentence** (□see).

parolee □see parole.

parol evidence rule: an old, still used, and misleading label for a loose bundle of rules (not *a* rule) of substantive law limiting the use of either oral (*parol*) or written evidence to change a written contract. In general, the rules prohibit contradiction of what a court blesses with the words *integration* or **integrated contract**: one that the parties intend to include everything that they have agreed to, all preliminary or contemporaneous talk or other writings *merged* in this contract. The question of integration or not may be influenced by a **merger clause**: one specifically excluding oral representations or promises (e.g., by an agent) that vary the written terms. For details of "integration," "contradiction," "intend to include," consult the law of contracts. Parol evidence rules are sometimes applied to other writings, e.g., a will, a deed.

part and parcel □see parcel.

partial intestacy □see intestacy.

partial invalidity □see overbreadth.

partial performance □see perform.

participating preferred □see stock.

particulars □see bill of particulars.

parties □see party.

parties to a contract □see party.

parties to crime: a general rubric for those sufficiently connected with the commission of a crime to be punishable for some criminal conduct. Most jurisdictions have dropped the common law classifications and consequences of parties to crime; but some of the common law nomenclature persists, even if only to say that words here and now embrace or exclude what other or similar words meant at common law. This is a general guide; there is wide local variation.

accessory

1. a short form of reference to an **accessory after the fact**: a person who obstructs justice by trying to help someone who has committed a crime escape arrest or prosecution. Not a participant in that crime, nor—properly—a party to it. Not an **accomplice** (□see, below, in this entry).

2. a short form of reference to an **accessory before the fact**: the common law expression for someone who **aids and abets** (□see) the commission of a felony without being present at the scene. Sometimes still used to identify a party to a crime, present or not, who aids and abets the commission of a crime. Now usually regarded as a **principal** (□see).

accessory after the fact □see **accessory**, above, in this entry.

accessory before the fact □see **accessory**, above, in this entry.

accomplice: a general term for a person who participates with others in the commission of a crime, whether as principal or accessory (sense 2).

conspirator: a participant in a criminal **conspiracy**: a crime that consists of an agreement between at least two persons to join in committing a crime, followed by an open act (**overt act**) by any of them directed to that end.

principal: a prime actor in the commission of a crime, felony or misdemeanor. *Principal* now usually includes what at common law was called an *accessory before the fact* (□see **accessory**, above, in this entry), as well as two named varieties of principal:

principal in the first degree: a person who commits a felony, either directly, or using as an instrument an innocent (e.g., a child) or an irresponsible (e.g., an insane person).

principal in the second degree: a person present, actually or constructively (□see **actual**), at the scene of a crime, who **aids and abets** (□see) a principal in the first degree commit a felony.

parties to litigation □see **party**.

partition: a division of a specific piece of property, usually real property, held in some form of co-ownership. Partition ends the co-ownership of the whole, and vests in each of the former co-owners a separate ownership of one part of the property. *Partition* does not refer to the dissolution of a business. Partition may be court ordered or by voluntary action of the co-owners.

partner □see **partnership.**

partnership: "[A]n association of two or more persons to carry on as co-owners a business for profit." (Uniform Partnership Act [UPA], § 6(1)). The co-owners are **partners.**

general partnership: in general terms, a partnership in which all the partners are personally liable for partnership debts, run the business, share equally the profits and losses, and are agents of the partnership. These characteristics can be varied by agreement that binds the partners. Limitations on a partner's authority as agent do not bind outsiders ignorant of a limitation. A general partnership may be formed by oral and informal agreement, formally by a written agreement sometimes called *Articles of Partnership*. For details, consult the UPA. □see also, **dissolution.**

limited partnership: a partnership formed in accordance with a limited partnership statute that requires a public filing of a certificate of formation; the agreement of limited partnership is usually in writing. A limited partnership has one or more *general partners* and one or more *limited partners*. In general terms: a general partner has the personal liability of a partner in a general partnership and runs the business; a limited partner has only a general oversight of the running of the business; keeping within that limitation, the limited partner's liability to the partnership and to outsiders is usually limited to the amount of an agreed contribution to capital. Shares of profits and losses are specified in the agreement; unless otherwise specified, the limited partner's share of losses is limited to the agreed contribution. For details, consult the Uniform Limited Partnership Act of 1916 [ULPA] and the Revised ULPA of 1976, with 1985 amendments.

part performance □see **perform;** □see also, **statute of frauds.**

party: usually, a participant contrasted with another participant with a different interest (e.g., party plaintiff, party defendant), or contrasted with outsiders: *third parties,* as in *third party beneficiary*

(□see **beneficiary**). *Party* (pl. *parties*) is blandly noncommital, for the moment not embroiled in the multiple definitions of **person** (□see). A party may participate in almost anything: an event, a transaction, most often in a contract or litigation; for a slightly different usage, □see **parties to crime**.

parties to a contract

Participants in a contract are called *party* and *parties* in all manner of legal writing, including statutes, e.g., *party to be charged,* in the **statute of frauds** (□see). In the contract itself, *party* is waning. The wordy archaisms *party of the first part* and *party of the second part* are becoming infrequent, along with *first party* and *second party.* Increasingly, the named parties are identified functionally, and proceed as "Seller and Buyer agree," "Publisher and Author agree," etc. The standoffish "The parties agree" is often eliminated in the letter form "We agree" (□see **letter agreement**).

parties to litigation

In litigation, there is a constant reference to the *parties plaintiff* and the *parties defendant.* Even so, most of the formal or technical labels for parties to different kinds of litigation, or different phases of the same litigation, do not use the word *party* as part of the label itself: □see **appellant**, under appeal; □see **appellee**, under **appeal**; □see **applicant**; □see **claimant**; □see **complainant**, under **pleadings**; □see **cross-complaint**, under **cross-**; □see **cross-defendant**, under **cross-**; □see **cross-plaintiff**, under **cross-**; □see **defendant**; □see **intervenor**; □see **libelant**; □see **libelee**; □see **petitioner**; □see **plaintiff**; □see **respondent**.

But in the language of litigation procedure, *party* is everywhere.

fictitious party □see **fictitious defendant**; □see **John Doe**.

indispensable party □see **necessary party**, below, in this entry.

necessary party

1. a person who should be made a party to a lawsuit in order to give complete relief or to prevent unfairness to that person or to the parties to the suit. Absence of the *necessary party,* in this sense, does not result in dismissal of the suit.

2. a person as in sense 1, but who must be made a party to a lawsuit, or the suit will be dismissed. This sense is sometimes called an **indispensable party**, as distinguished from a *necessary party* (sense 1); sometimes in this sense, *necessary party* and *indispensable party* are used as synonyms.

465

The circumstances of statute, procedure, fact, and judicial discretion that lead to the determination of sense 1 or sense 2 vary by jurisdiction and statute. Refer, e.g., to Federal Rules of Civil Procedure, Rule 19. □see also, **compulsory joinder**, under **joinder**; □see also, **absolutes**.

nominal party: has no interest in the suit but is required to be a party as a matter of form. E.g., assignor as plaintiff, though the suit is brought by the assignee. E.g., a court as a defendant in a petition for a writ of prohibition, though the suit will be defended by someone else. A *nominal party* is sometimes called a *pro forma party;* □see **pro forma**.

party aggrieved: has personal or property rights substantially affected by another's action, whether or not the action was directly against the party aggrieved. E.g., a grant of a zoning variance to A that affects B's property.

party of record □see **of record**.

prevailing party: is the one who wins, e.g., a judgment; e.g., entitled to costs of suit.

pro forma party □see **nominal party**.

proper party: has some relation to the suit and may be made a party at plaintiff's option. □see **permissive joinder**, under **joinder**.

real party in interest: has a substantive right to enforce the claim, whether or not enforcement will benefit someone else. E.g., a trustee suing for monies due the trust. Often shortened to *real party*.

third party claim: a claim to an interest in, right to possession or ownership of property that is in legal custody, as, e.g., on an execution or attachment initiated by someone else. Proceedings to establish a *third party claimant's* interest vary by jurisdiction; sometimes regarded as a form of **third party intervention** (□see).

third party complaint □see **third party practice**, below, in this entry.

third party defendant □see **third party practice**, below, in this entry.

third party practice, also called **impleader**: a procedure that enables a party to a suit to bring in (**implead**) a new party. The defendant in the suit files a *third party complaint* against a *third party defendant*, alleging that the new party is or may be liable for what is asked in the suit. Under some statutes, a plaintiff may implead a third party defendant who is or may be liable for what is asked in a counterclaim against the plaintiff.

third party intervention: a procedure that enables an outsider (an **intervenor**) to become a party to a suit between others without being asked in. The intervenor alleges an interest in the litigation or the property involved adverse to one or more parties to the suit. An *intervenor* (also spelled *intervener*) is sometimes called a *plaintiff in intervention*. □see also, **third party claim**, above, in this entry.

party aggrieved □see **party**.

party of record □see **of record**.

party of the first part □see **party**.

party of the second part □see **party**.

party to be charged □see **statute of frauds**.

party wall: physically, a building wall right at the boundary, or straddling the boundary, between adjoining lots that are separately owned. By agreement, statute, or prescription, the wall takes on varying "party" characteristics, usually these: If the wall is all on one lot, the adjoining landowner has an easement of support and maintenance; if the wall straddles the boundary, each landowner has such an easement in the other's part of the wall. □see **party**.

par value □see **stock**.

par value shares □see **stock**.

pass a dividend □see **dividend**.

pass by descent □see **descend**.

passenger: In addition to the ordinary English meaning, *passenger* often refers to someone who pays for riding, in an airliner, a bus, a private auto, etc., as contrasted with a rider who is a *guest*, in the ordinary sense of that word. The distinction is often spelled out with

passenger

the status *passenger for hire,* opposed to *guest* or *guest passenger.* Payment is a critical factor in a variety of contexts, e.g., liability for injury to the rider, insurance coverage.

passenger for hire □see **passenger.**

passing off □see **palming off;** □see **unfair competition.**

passive trust □see **trust.**

pass the bar □see **bar.**

past consideration: something of value in the past, e.g., a benefit already received, an obligation already incurred, that now induces someone to make a promise. It is an expression sometimes rejected out of hand, tortured by controversy as to its effect, still called into service in the law of contract in determining whether or not the promise will be enforced. □see **contract.**

past recollection recorded: a record about something once within the knowledge of a person who is now a witness; and, while memory was fresh, the person either wrote it down or adopted another's writing about the same thing, as by signing it at the time. The recollection now faded, and unable to testify at length or at all about the things recorded, the witness *is* able to identify the record and tell how it was made. That record is traditionally called *past recollection recorded,* but is also known as *past recorded recollection, recorded past recollection,* or simply *recorded recollection.* Under varying rules, the record, e.g., an appraisal, a police report signed by the witness, may be read into evidence as an exception to, or as not within, the hearsay rule; sometimes the record itself is received in evidence if offered by an adverse party.

Past recollection recorded is distinguished from what is usually called **present recollection revived** or **present recollection refreshed**: neither the record nor its contents is placed in evidence, but the record is shown to the witness, whose recall, now "jogged," testifies of the witness's own knowledge about the things recorded.

pat down □see **frisk.**

pat down search □see **frisk.**

468

patent   (n., v.)

1. (land): the government's grant (i.e., the act of conveyance), and the instrument containing the grant, of public lands or mineral rights. Sometimes called **letters patent** (□see). As a verb, to grant or obtain a grant of public lands or mineral rights.

2. (inventions): the U.S. government's grant of rights, and the instrument containing the grant, giving an inventor a monopoly on the inventor's invention for a limited period, i.e., "the right to exclude others from making, using, or selling the invention throughout the United States," usually for seventeen years. (See 35 USCA § 154.) Sometimes called **letters patent** (□see). As a verb, to obtain a patent. <She patented her invention./The government issued her a patent.>

That bare-bones definition is fleshed out in this list of some key expressions, part of the vast vocabulary of technical detail in the bowels of *patent law*:

invention

    a. The thing that is invented or discovered (see 35 USCA § 100(a)), as set out in a claim.

    claim: a formal assertion of invention and right to patent, with a detailed description of the exact limits of what it is that constitutes the invention. □see also, **disclaim**.

    b. "[T]he act of invention through original conception and reduction to practice." (Chisum, *Patents,* vol. 1, p. G1–11, 1988).

    reduction to practice: a demonstration that the invention will work. The demonstration may be by making and testing it (actual **reduction to practice**) or by a description in the patent application of sufficient detail to enable a person skilled in the art to make and test it (**constructive reduction to practice**).

    c. The technical requirement described by the grotesque negative **nonobviousness** (□see, below, in this list, under **patentability**).

patentable: the subject matter of what can be patented. "Whoever invents or discovers any *new and useful* process, machine, manufacture, or composition of matter, or any new and useful improvement thereof, may obtain a patent therefor, subject to the requirements of this title." (35 USCA § 101; italics added).

    design patent: a patent for a "new, original, and ornamental design for an article of manufacture" (35 USCA § 171), usually for fourteen years (see 35 USCA § 173).

plant patent: a patent on the asexual reproduction of some new varieties of plant. (See 35 USCA §§ 161, 163.)

patentability: the basic requirements that must be met for something *patentable* to be patented:

nonobviousness: at the time of invention the subject matter taken as a whole was sufficiently different from the prior art as not to be obvious to a person of ordinary skill in that art. (See 35 USCA § 103.)

prior art: the knowledge of a particular art (principles, instruments, products, processes, ways of using them) reasonably available to a person of ordinary skill in that art before and at the time of a claimed invention.

novelty: patent law's own version of what's *new,* mostly expressed in negatives, i.e., no one has been here before. This is not your common, garden variety of *novelty.* It is an umbrella of a word covering the details of fact and law and, especially, state of the art, that entitle something to be blessed as *new,* having *novelty,* or damned for lack of novelty (not new), *anticipated.* Novelty may be lacking, e.g., because of what was publicly "known or used by others in this country, or patented or described in a printed publication in this or a foreign country before the invention. . . ." (See 35 USCA § 102.) The spelling out of *novelty,* often said to be beyond definition, rests in the statutes, decisions, and the writings of experts in patent law.

utility: a requirement that the invention be workable, and capable of some claimed practical use that is not illegal, immoral, or contrary to public policy. This compressed edition of *utility* is patent law's version of being *useful* and promoting the "progress of [the] *useful arts.*" □see **Patent and Copyright Clause.** The *utility* requirement does not apply to design and plant patents.

patentability □see **patent.**

patentable □see **patent.**

patent agent □see **lawyer.**

patent ambiguity □see **latent ambiguity.**

Patent and Copyright Clause: the part of the U.S. Constitution reading: "The Congress shall have power . . . to promote the progress of science and useful arts, by securing for limited times to authors and inventors the exclusive right to their respective writings and discoveries." (Art. I, § 8, cl. 8). □see also, **constitutional clauses**.

patent defect □see **latent defect**.

patentee: a person to whom a patent has been issued, or that person's successor in interest. (See 35 USCA § 100(d).)

patent law □see **patent**.

paternity □see **filiation proceedings**.

pat frisk □see **frisk**.

patient-physician privilege □see **physician-patient privilege**.

pat search □see **frisk**.

pauper □see **in forma pauperis**; □see **indigent**.

pawn (n., v.): a lesser used synonym of **pledge** (□see), especially referring to chattels and their delivery, as security, to a *pawnbroker:* a person in the business of making small loans.

pawnbroker □see **pawn**.

payable on demand □see **demand**.

payable to bearer □see **commercial paper**.

payable to order □see **commercial paper**.

payee: the person designated to receive payment. □see **commercial paper**.

payment: what is to be paid, what is paid, and the act of paying. A word of little intrinsic technicality but vast utility in every branch of

payment

the law where money and its substitutes play a role; in short, ubiquitous. The obligations of payment, kinds of payment, offers of payment, consequences of payment—substantive and procedural—and, above all, the equally ubiquitous ugly twin *nonpayment* keep the law in motion.

pay off the mortgage   □see **deed of trust**, under **deed**.

payor: the person who pays, or is expected to pay, e.g., the maker of a note, or a bank on which a check is drawn. □see **commercial paper**. The spelling *payer* is not legal usage.

P.C.:   the abbreviation of **professional corporation** (□see, under **corporate**).

peace: the *peace* of ordinary English, in a variety of legal contexts. E.g., □see **breach of the peace**, under **breach**; □see **covenant of quiet enjoyment**, under **covenant**; □see **disturbing the peace**, under **breach**; □see **justice of the peace**, under **judge**; □see **peace and quiet**; □see **peace bond**; □see **officer of the law**, under **office**.

peace and quiet: a double indorsement of tranquillity, the individual words sometimes used interchangeably. □see **covenant of quiet enjoyment**, under **covenant**; □see also, **coupled synonyms**.

peace bond: a bond conditioned on the good conduct of one who has threatened to commit a breach of the peace. Also called a *bond to keep the peace.*

peace officer   □see **officer of the law**, under **office**.

pecuniary damages   □see **damages**, under **damage**.

pederasty   □see **crime against nature**.

penal • penalty   (both rooted in L. *poena:* punishment, penalty).

1. The prime meaning, a reference to punishment for crime, the state imposing a *penalty,* e.g., time in a *penal institution,* often a *penitentiary* (a word with related etymology). Sometimes *penal* is

interchangeable with **criminal** (□see), e.g., a *penal* (criminal) *code* or statute. □see also, **pains and penalties**.

2. In an extended sense, a reference to punishment or penalty that is not criminal, but the price exacted for breaking a promise or not conforming to some requirement of law.

> **penal bond**: a bond with a money penalty (*penal sum*) for failure to perform as agreed or required.

> **penalty clause**: a provision of law or contract that extra money be paid or less money be received for failure to perform as required by law or as agreed. E.g., an increased filing fee for delay in filing a notice. E.g., an increased price for delay in acceptance of delivery. E.g., a reduction in price for delay in completion of construction.

For another etymological relative, *punitive damages,* also punishment that is not criminal, □see **exemplary damages**, under **damage**.

penal bond   □see **penal**.

penal code   □see **penal**.

penal institution   □see **penal**.

penal sum   □see **penal**.

penalty   □see **penal**.

penalty clause   □see **penal**.

pendente lite   □see **lis**; □see also, **alimony**; □see also, **injunction**, under **enjoin**.

pendent jurisdiction   □see **federal jurisdiction**, under **jurisdiction**.

penetration: an element of various sex crimes: the insertion, "however slight," of the penis into the vagina, anus, or mouth. Under some statutes, the insertion of something other than the penis into the vagina or anus. □see **rape**; □see **crime against nature**.

penitentiary   □see **jail**; □see also, **imprisonment**; □see also, **penal**.

pension: a periodic payment by government, business, or other organization, based on remembrance of things past, as distinguished from compensation for current services, such as wages or salary. The criteria for pensions to an individual (or relatives) vary by statute and agreement, e.g., for past services, on retirement of an employee, office holder, or military officer; valor in combat; disability; old age.

vested pension: a pension, the conditions for payment of which have been met, and hence fixed as to right to payment, regardless of later change in status of pensioner or fund. Varies by statute and terms of pension plan.

penumbra (L., *paene:* almost + *umbra:* shadow): a disputed and muddled metaphor for an area of legal uncertainty (shadow and light), for an area of subtle extension of the law, for an area of judicial discretion. *Penumbra* started life as a technical term of early seventeenth-century astronomy, became a nineteenth-century metaphor of ordinary English for an area of partial shadow, and in the same century was introduced into American legal writing by Oliver Wendell Holmes, Jr. It has been widely used and vigorously rejected. It is a metaphor without a consensus, and without any strong claim to survival. □see **metaphor.**

people In addition to popular usage of ordinary English:

1. the ultimate sovereignty in the United States. <"one people," Declaration of Independence./"We the people of the United States . . .," Preamble, U.S. Constitution; see also Amends. IX and X.>

2. citizens of the United States. <". . . the right of the people to keep and bear arms . . .," U.S. Constitution, Amend. IV; see also the Preamble.>

3. *People,* the usual shortening of *The People* or *The People of the State of . . . .*: one of the sovereign states in its role as a named litigant in civil and criminal cases. <*People v. Jones.*/The People rest.> Varying with local usage, a synonym of *State* or *Commonwealth* in the same roles. In cases involving a *relator,* □see **ex rel.**

per anus □see **crime against nature.**

per autre vie: a misspelling of *pur autre vie.* □see **estate.**

per capita (L.: by heads): per person. Most commonly refers to distribution of property on death in equal shares per person among the survivors. As opposed to **per stirpes** (L., per STUR-pease: by the stocks): loosely, by family. Refers to distribution on death according to the share that a particular ancestor (e.g., a parent) would have taken.

For example. A takes property under a will that says "To A for life, and then to A's issue per capita" or under a will that says "and then to A's issue per stirpes." A has two children B and C, who *predecease* (die before) A. A dies, survived by all six grandchildren, B's two children and C's four children.

If distribution is to "A's issue per capita," B's two children and C's four each take a one-sixth share.

If distribution is to "A's issue per stirpes," the grandchildren take what their respective parents would have taken if they had survived A: B's two children take one half, i.e., one fourth each; and C's four children together take the other one half, i.e., one eighth each.

The pattern of distribution, *per capita, per stirpes,* or something in-between, varies by state law and should be defined when the expressions are used.

Per stirpes distribution is also called distribution by *right of representation* and, as an adjective, *stirpetal* distribution.

percolating waters   □see **law of capture.**

per curiam   □see **per curiam opinion,** under **opinion.**

per curiam opinion   □see **opinion.**

peremptory challenge   □see **challenge.**

peremptory instruction   □see **jury instructions.**

peremptory writ of mandamus   □see **mandamus.**

perform • performance

1. (contract): doing, or having done, something, especially what ought to be done. That sense of the ordinary English words is almost a monopoly of the law. Most ordinary citizens regard *perform* and *performance* as theatrical, scientific, or—legal. Lawyers revel in *performance,* especially *performance of a contract:* short for performing the obligations of a contract. The things prescribed are *performed,*

perform

often interchangeable with *executed* (□see **execute**); *performance,* as contrasted with *nonperformance.*

This relatively plain speaking is often befogged with *full performance,* a knee-jerk redundancy if all it means is *performance;* useful if deliberately contrasted with *part* or *partial* performance; or to distinguish the flexible *substantial performance,* which gives a court some leeway in overlooking the nits of *failure to perform.* Carried away by excessive exposure to *perform* and *performance,* lawyers often speak of performing, or the performance of, conditions, which are not performed but happen, or don't happen.

For an equitable remedy, the prize *performance* in contract, □see **specific performance.**

2. (copyright): technical words of copyright law (□see **copyright**), which must be consulted for detail and qualification beyond these entries:

perform: "[T]o recite, render, play, dance, or act [a work], either directly or by means of any device or process or, in the case of a motion picture or other audiovisual work, to show its images in any sequence or to make the sounds accompanying it audible." (Copyright Act of 1976, § 101).

performance right: subject to statutory limitations, a copyright owner's exclusive right to **publicly perform**, and to authorize others to publicly perform "literary, musical, dramatic, and choreographic works." (See Copyright Act of 1976, § 106(4).) Also referred to as **performing rights.**

publicly perform: to give a **public performance:**

(1) A performance at a *place* open to the public or where a substantial number of people (not counting family circle and social acquaintances) has gathered; or

(2) A performance communicated to such a *place,* or to the *public,* by "any device or process" making the performance available to members of the public capable of receiving it, whether at the same or different places and times. (See Copyright Act of 1976, § 101.)

performance   □see **perform.**

performance bond: typically, a bond posted by a contractor as security that construction will be performed as contracted. Also called a **completion bond.** Date of completion of construction is an aspect of performance sometimes contained in a separate completion bond.

performance right □see **perform**.

performing rights □see **perform**.

perhaps □see **clichés**.

perils of the sea: those extraordinary perils peculiar to the sea that do not yield to human prudence and skill. A flexible term, sometimes overlapping the irresistible force of **acts of God** (□see); not limited to the battering of natural forces, such as an especially violent storm, but also extended to include, e.g., the peril of piracy. An old expression, common in statutes on **maritime law** (□see) and in agreements connected with shipping, e.g., policies insuring against loss from perils of the sea; bills of lading and charter parties relieving a shipowner from liability for such loss.

periodic estate □see **periodic tenancy**, under **estate**.

periodic tenancy □see **estate**.

perjury: the crime of lying, in a material matter, while under oath. An **affirmation**: a solemn statement that the person regards as binding the conscience may substitute for an oath. The lie may be spoken in court or in other proceedings, or written in or out of court, as in an affidavit or deposition (□see **affiant**). Statutes vary the description of the crime and related offenses. Under some statutes, a lying *declaration under penalty of perjury,* without oath or affirmation, is also perjury; e.g., verification of a complaint. □see **declaration**.

subornation of perjury: the crime of inducing someone to commit perjury: to *suborn* perjury. With perjury understood, the expressions are sometimes shortened to *subornation* (v., *suborn*). <He suborned the witness.> But both of those words can also be applied to inducing a person to commit offenses other than perjury.

permanent alimony □see **alimony**.

permanent injunction □see **enjoin**.

permanent residence □see **domicile**.

permissive joinder □see joinder.

permissive waste □see waste.

permit □see license.

per os □see crime against nature.

perpetual injunction □see enjoin.

perpetuate testimony: to take testimony by deposition of a person who is expected to be needed as a witness but may be unavailable at time of trial. The procedure (n., *perpetuation of testimony*) is most common after suit has been filed, sometimes before filing, on a showing of the person's age, absence or anticipated absence from the jurisdiction, disability, etc. □see **affiant;** □see **discovery.**

perpetuation of testimony □see perpetuate testimony.

perpetuity □see rule against perpetuities.

per quod □see actionable per se, under action.

per se (L., per SAY: by or of itself, oneself, themselves): a way of saying that one thing, without anything more, is sufficient to produce a particular legal result, e.g., that a certain word is defamatory (*defamatory per se*). Like most **absolutes** (□see), *per se* cannot be relied upon as a firm prediction of things to come.

1. as a phrase: For the vagaries of *defamation per se, defamatory per se, libel per se,* and *slander per se,* □see **actionable per se,** under action. In some other contexts, □see **negligence per se,** under **negligence;** □see **nuisance per se,** under nuisance.

2. as an adjective: a characterization of an inevitable result that follows from a particular set of facts or legal situation, e.g., *per se contraband;* a *per se rule,* also called a *per se doctrine;* a *per se violation.*

per se rule □see per se.

478

per se violation   □see **per se.**

person   An indispensable word with varied, overlapping meanings. Often used without definition, as in the U.S. Constitution (Arts. I, II, III, IV; Amends. IV, V, XII, XIV, XXII). Defined, and redefined, in an endless succession of special purpose statutes, with no assurance to the profession that this is the *person* you thought you were talking about. The definitions here give an overview of current usage. This omits a whole list of historical horrors in the ugly shadows of slavery, racism, and sexism.

1.   a human being—without regard to sex, legitimacy, or competence. This *person* is the central figure in law, as elsewhere, characterized by personal attributes of mind, intention, feelings, weaknesses, morality common to human beings; with rights and duties under the law. This is the *person,* sometimes called an *individual,* and often referred to in the law as a **natural person**, as distinguished from an *artificial person* (sense 3).

2.   the physical, biological human being. This is the *person* who is injured or killed, the *person* of "injury to the person" and of firearms "concealed upon the person." This sense overlaps the sense of the person with rights (sense 1), e.g., "No person shall be excluded on the basis of sex." Overlaps again on the question of when one becomes a *person:*

> **existing person**: a child unborn, **en ventre sa mère** (□see), a *person* for purposes of inheritance, but not a person in the criminal law generally. As of this writing, in the abortion controversy, " 'a person' as used in the Fourteenth Amendment does not include the unborn." (*Roe v. Wade,* 410 U.S. 113, 158, 1973).

3.   an **artificial person**: an abstraction of convenience regarded by the law as a distinct being, having an existence independent of those who create or own it. The classic example of this *person* is the **corporation** (□see, under **corporate**), a being distinct from its shareholders; in its own name owning property, contracting, suing and being sued, taxed, and regulated, with rights and duties often spelled out in statutes and constitutional decision. A labor union and a business trust (□see **trust**) have also been described as *artificial persons.* The expressions **juristic person** and **legal entity** (□see, below, in this entry) are frequently used as synonyms of *artificial person.*

4.   a **legal entity**, often described as a *person,* is itself an expression without uniform meaning:

> **a.**   frequently, a synonym of **artificial person** (□see, above, in this entry).

b. most commonly, a "some kind of a" *person* other than a human being, distinguished by the fact that it can sue and be sued in its own name, i.e., be a **party** (□see) to litigation, whether or not also classified as an *artificial person*. Under this criterion, the "some kind of a" person varies widely by decision, by jurisdiction, and special definition: a *sovereign* (□see **sovereignty**) is a legal entity and a person; a **partnership** (□see), not an artificial person (the partners own the property), is usually a legal entity; a labor union, whether or not regarded as an artificial person, is usually a legal entity; an ordinary **trust** (□see) and an **estate** (□see) consisting of property under administration may or may not be legal entities; an unincorporated association is usually not.

5. a catchall *person,* avoiding repetition, clarity, and precision, according to the needs of the legal writer. E.g., " 'Person' *includes* a natural person, partnership, limited partnership (domestic or foreign), trust, estate, association or corporation . . ." (Uniform Partnership Act, Ga.Ann.Code, § 75–102(6), 1984, italics added). E.g., " 'Person' means an individual, a corporation, an organization, or other legal entity" (Uniform Probate Code, § 1201(29)), a definition that incorporates the open-ended language "Organization *includes* a corporation, government or governmental subdivision or agency, business trust, estate, trust, partnership, or association, two or more persons having a joint or common interest, or any other legal entity." (Uniform Probate Code, § 1201(27), italics added).

6. the essence of **in propria persona**. □see **appear**.

7. *person,* as a substitute for **sex** (□see).

8. *person in loco parentis* □see **in loco parentis**.

9. a *third person:* a **third party**; □see, under **party**.

personal covenant   □see **covenant**.

personal effects: tangible, personal property for personal use, especially items of clothing or adornment. Not a term of art; interpretation varies widely with context of statute and will, and with the personal habits of a particular owner.

personal holding company: a particular type of closely held corporation (□see **close**) targeted by the federal government in the unending search for ways of collecting more taxes from those who prefer to pay less. An interlock of statutory definitions, which must be read to be believed, imposes a special tax on some kinds of undistributed income. For separate definitions of *personal holding company, per-*

sonal holding company income, and *undistributed personal holding company income,* see Internal Revenue Act of 1986, 26 USCA §§ 541 et seq.

personal holding company income ☐see personal holding company.

personal injury ☐see damage.

personal judgment ☐see in personam.

personal jurisdiction ☐see in personam.

personal liability ☐see in personam; ☐see also, alter ego.

personally appeared ☐see jurat.

personal property ☐see property.

personal representative ☐see executor.

personal service ☐see service of process.

personalty: another name for personal property. ☐see property.

persona non grata (L., per-SOHN-uh non grahta: a person not acceptable): a person who is not acceptable to the host country as the head or a member of the diplomatic mission of a foreign country.

person in loco parentis ☐see in loco parentis.

per stirpes ☐see per capita.

petition ☐see pleadings; ☐see also, motion.

petitioner: one who files a petition (☐see, under pleadings).

petit jury ☐see jury.

pettifogger □see lawyer.

petty larceny □see larceny.

petty offense: usually a "less serious" misdemeanor in terms of the nature of the offense and severity of possible punishment. Limits on fine, imprisonment, or both, give one measure of what is considered "less serious," but classification is not uniform. If sufficiently petty and not punishable by more than six months' imprisonment, there is no constitutional right to trial by jury. Trial procedures are often simplified. *Minor offense* is an equally imprecise synonym.

Philadelphia lawyer □see lawyer.

philanthropic □see charitable.

physician-patient privilege, also called *doctor-patient privilege,* also called *patient-physician privilege:* a patient who consults or is examined by a medical doctor for treatment, or diagnosis in anticipation of treatment, has the right to refuse to disclose confidential communications between them and confidential information revealed during the course of that relationship. The patient also has the right to prevent the doctor from disclosing the communications and information.

The privilege, and its names, varies by statute and decision. *Doctor-patient privilege* is the common name. *Patient-physician privilege* stresses the fact that the privilege is that of the patient, not the doctor. *Physician-patient privilege,* the frequent technical name, stresses the fact that the privilege refers not to any "doctor" but to the traditional medical doctor. In some jurisdictions, the privilege has been expanded to other branches of medicine, such as psychiatry (*psychiatrist-patient privilege*), and to related fields of technical expertise.

P.I. □see damage.

picket □see picketing.

picketing: posting and maintaining a line, usually moving, of placard-carrying demonstrators (*pickets*) at or near a place (e.g., a store, factory, farm, construction site, government office) where some activity is being carried on that the pickets object to. By statute or ordinance, some picketing is regulated or explicitly made legal or illegal. Picketing is a feature of all manner of causes. It is especially connected with labor union activity, where the picketing is intended to carry a specific message to employers, employees, scabs, customers, the general public, and to anathematize those who *cross a picket line.* Labor law must be consulted for subspecies of *picketing,* e.g., *primary* and *secondary picketing,* kin to that subdivision of **boycott** (□see); *informational picketing, peaceful picketing, recognition picketing.*

piercing the corporate veil   □see **alter ego.**

PILF: short for **public interest law firm** (□see, under **lawyer**).

pimp   □see **pander.**

piracy

1. (sea and air)

    a.   Under international law: an illegal act of violence, detention, or "depredation" for private ends by the crew or passengers of a private ship or aircraft; the act must be either (i) on the **high seas** (□see), against another ship, aircraft, or the persons or property aboard either, or (ii) "[I]n a place outside the jurisdiction of any state," "[a]gainst a ship, aircraft, persons or property." Voluntary participation, incitement, facilitating such acts are also piracy. *Depredation,* not uniquely legal, is an old word for *plundering,* a good old description of piracy. Persons committing piracy are *pirates;* their ship or aircraft is a *pirate* ship or aircraft. (See Geneva Convention on the High Seas, April 29, 1958, 13 U.S.T. (U.S. Treaties and Other International Agreements), pt. 2, pp. 2313, 2317, Art. 15; in force, Sept. 30, 1962. Refer also to Art. 101, in the United Nations Convention on the Law of the Sea, Dec. 10, 1982, cited in **law of the sea** (□see). Refer also to *Restatement (Third) Foreign Relations Law of the United States,* vol. 2, pt. V, ch. 3, § 522, 1986.)

    b.   Under federal law:

    (1) For *piracy* "on the high seas," federal law adopts the international law definition, using the older term **law of nations** (□see). (18 USCA § 1651; see also 18 USCA §§ 1652, 1661, 1665; see also U.S. Constitution, Art. I, § 8, cl. 10).

(2) aircraft piracy: "[S]eizure or exercise of control" by force, violence, threat, intimidation, "with wrongful intent, of an aircraft within the special aircraft jurisdiction of the United States." (See 49 USCA § 1472(i)(2).) Sometimes referred to as **hijacking** (□see) or *skyjacking*.

2. (copyright): a loosely used synonym for **infringement** (□see) and **plagiarism** (□see), e.g., *record piracy.* An infringer or plagiarizer is sometimes called a *pirate;* the work *pirated, piratical,* or also a *pirate,* e.g., a *pirate chip.*

3. (patent): an occasional reference to a bad faith acquisition of another's invention, e.g., acquired by *piracy.*

pirate   □see **piracy**.

P.J.:   abbreviation of Presiding Judge or Presiding Justice.   □see **judge**.

place of public accommodation   □see **public accommodations**.

place of the contract   □see **lex loci contractus**.

plagiarism

1. violating another's **copyright** (□see) by unauthorized copying. *Plagiarism* is one specific type of **infringement** (□see), sometimes loosely used as a synonym for infringement. The violator (in this sense, as well as senses 2 and 3) is a *plagiarist,* an *infringer,* a *pirate* (□see **piracy**).

2. a loose term for unauthorized copying of someone else's intellectual property of the sort that is subject to copyright and passing off the work as one's own. The work, in this sense, has been plagiarized, whether or not copyrighted.

3. a loose general term for unauthorized copying of someone else's intellectual property of the sort that is subject to copyright. The work, in this sense, has been plagiarized, whether or not copyrighted and whether or not credit is given to the original author.

For a defense to a charge of plagiarism, □see **nonaccess**.

plagiarist   □see **plagiarism**.

plain English   □see **plain language**.

plain error: an error in court proceedings with such fundamental consequences that it must be corrected, even though not objected to at the time the error was made. In advance of the moment when a court decides to do something about it (e.g., grant a new trial, reverse a judgment), *plain error* is anything but plain, even when given status as a *plain error doctrine* or *plain error rule*. The label is applied case by case to prevent serious injustice to an individual or an "affront" to the system of justice itself. More likely in cases of constitutional right or the death penalty; less likely in civil than in criminal cases. A far cry from **harmless error** (□see), and not run-of-the-mill **reversible error** (□see). □see also, **fatal error**, under **fatal**.

plain error doctrine □see **plain error**.

plain error rule □see **plain error**.

plain language: an imprecise expression of hope for improvement in the **language of the law** (□see). Criteria of plainness are not standard: e.g., "plain," "clear and coherent," "common and everyday meanings," "easily readable," "understandable," understandable "without . . . the assistance of a professional"; patterns of typography; limits on syllables per word, words per sentence, and words per paragraph; and a host of specific do's and don'ts. In some jurisdictions, regulations and *plain language laws* require some sort of *plain language* in a variety of legal writings, e.g., consumer contracts, loan agreements, insurance policies, pleadings, regulations, statutes. *Plain language* is also referred to as *plain English*.

plain language laws □see **plain language**.

plain meaning rule: if the meaning of the words in a writing (statute, contract, will, etc.) is clear, other evidence is inadmissible to change the meaning. The *rule* is not a rule, but rather a rationalization of a judge's conclusion that, by and large, the sense here is clear enough to the judge. <"Objection sustained. Plain meaning rule."> If the judge finds that the words produce absurdity, ambiguity, a literalness never intended, the first casualty is the plain meaning rule. <Objection overruled. No plain meaning.> □see **rules of interpretation**.

plaintiff: the usual technical name for the person who complains about something by filing (starting) a lawsuit. Other technical names

plaintiff

for complainers, varying by the kind of suit or proceeding and by jurisdiction, are separate entries in the dictionary.

plaintiff in intervention □see **third party intervention**, under **party.**

plain view: the ordinary English words, with constitutional overtones:

1. in plain view: openly visible by the natural sense of sight of anyone who has a right to be there and cares to look, passerby or police officer. Detection of crime in this way is not a *search* under the Fourth Amendment. □see **search and seizure.**

2. plain view doctrine: Unlike the generality of sense 1, the *plain view doctrine* applies to personal property that comes into plain view "inadvertently" during the course of a permissible "intrusion" (usually a *search*) by a police officer. Then, if "immediately apparent" to the officer that the property is probably evidence of some crime, it may be seized without a search warrant describing the property. (See *Coolidge v. New Hampshire,* 403 U.S. 443, 1971.) The oft-quoted words from *Coolidge* are variously interpreted by courts and scholars, with subcategories for the doctrine as related to search of premises, vehicles, and persons. Despite controversy, this less plain view of *plain view* is still referred to as the *plain view doctrine;* sometimes as the *plain view rule;* or the *plain view exception* to the Fourth Amendment requirement of a search warrant. □see **search and seizure.**

plain view doctrine □see **plain view.**

plain view exception □see **plain view.**

plain view rule □see **plain view.**

plant patent □see **patent.**

plea: a formalized request for justice presented to a court. The word *plea,* once the keystone of common law procedure, now gives way to other procedural names, especially the varieties of **pleadings** (□see) and endless motions. The word persists.

1. The *criminal pleas,* usually oral.

a. the specific responses of a defendant to a charge of commission of a crime: a **plea of guilty, —not guilty, —nolo contendere.** □see **guilty;** □see also, **Alford plea,** under **guilty.**

b. enter a plea: the making of the responses in sense 1. □see **enter**.

c. plea bargaining, and its slang version, **cop a plea**. □see **negotiated plea**.

2. Generic categories of *plea*. These are civil or criminal, principally defensive, vary by jurisdiction, usually presented by written motion or pleading. Common among them are these:

dilatory plea: a request that will stay proceedings but not defeat an action. E.g., a motion that a nonresident file a bond to secure payment of costs.

plea in abatement: raises questions that do not go to the merits, e.g., **misjoinder** (□see **joinder**). Often characterized as a **dilatory plea** (□see, above, in this entry.). Sometimes referred to as a plea that will *abate* (end) an action or other proceedings, equating it with a **plea in bar** (□see, below, in this entry). □see also, **abate**.

plea in bar: usually takes the form of a motion to dismiss the action or proceeding because of a substantial (fatal) defect. E.g., res judicata; lack of jurisdiction; double jeopardy.

plea in confession and avoidance: defensive matter usually included in an *affirmative defense,* e.g., self-defense. □see **avoid**.

plea bargaining   □see **negotiated plea**.

plead

1. to respond to a charge of commission of a crime. <The charge has been read to you. How do you wish to plead?> □see **enter a plea**, under **plea**.

2. to set forth a cause of action, defense, or a part of either, in the form of a written pleading (□see **pleadings**). <In the first count, they plead a cause of action for breach of contract./They are pleading the statute of limitations.>

3. to argue before a court or jury. An old, fading usage.

The past tense or past participle *pleaded* of ordinary English is not the lawyers' favorite. More often they opt for the shorter *pled,* sometimes spelled *plead,* but still pronounced as the gutteral *pled.*

pleadings

1. In *civil* cases: the written statements by litigants of their claims and responses, in forms prescribed or approved for presentation to a court. Usually, the word *pleadings* is limited to those statements that fix the basic framework of a lawsuit. The forms, and their names, vary by jurisdiction, sometimes by the nature of the lawsuit. The two most generally accepted civil pleadings are the first plead-ing—the **complaint**: the plaintiff's statement of claim; and the de-fendant's response—the **answer**, sometimes called a *reply.* Some less used equivalents of *complaint:* a **declaration** (□see); in equitable ac-tions, a *bill* or *petition;* in admiralty, a **libel** (□see). In some special proceedings, the first pleading is called an *application,* a *claim,* a *petition.* For additional varieties of pleadings, □see **cross actions** and **cross-claim,** under **cross-;** □see **third party practice,** under **party.** □see also, **judgment on the pleadings,** under **judgment.**

demurrer, now usually called a **motion to dismiss,** sometimes classified as a pleading, sometimes not: a written statement for presentation to court, admitting for the sake of argument that the facts alleged in the complaint or a defense are true, but that they still do not constitute, respectively, a cause of action or a defense. Where demurrers are used, that form of demurrer is called a *general demurrer;* others, pointing out legal defects, are called *special demurrers.* To file a demurrer is to *demur.*

speaking demurrer: a demurrer that raises matters not men-tioned in the pleading to which the demurrer is addressed. Also called a *speaking exception.* Also called a *speaking motion* where *motion to dismiss* supplants demurrers.

2. In *criminal* cases—

a. The written charge of commission of a crime is the first plead-ing in a prosecution—a *complaint* (for less serious offenses), *indict-ment,* or *information.* □see **indictment.**

b. The first oral response to the charge, customarily called a *plea,* is also referred to as the defendant's *pleading.* For other varieties of defensive pleading, □see **plea.**

plea in abatement   □see **plea.**

plea in bar   □see **plea.**

plea in confession and avoidance   □see **plea;** □see **avoid.**

pled   □see **plead.**

pledge (n., v.): to give security in personal property, accompanied by delivery of the property (the *pledge*) from the *pledgor* to *pledgee*. <He pledged the ring to get a loan of $50.> □see also, **pawn**; □see also, **bailment**, under **bail**; □see also, **encumber**.

pledgee □see **pledge**.

pledgor □see **pledge**.

plurality opinion □see **opinion**.

pocket veto □see **veto**.

point □see **in point**.

point in time □see **at that point in time**.

points and authorities □see **brief**; □see also, **in point**.

poisonous tree □see **fruit of the poisonous tree**.

poison pill □see **tender offer**.

police officer □see **officer of the law**, under **office**.

police power: the inherent power of a government to act for the welfare of those within its jurisdiction. The term has never been precisely defined, is not used in the U.S. Constitution. Yet it has been repeatedly recognized and litigated; and is channeled in decisions of the Supreme Court that mark out a wobbling boundary between police power and specific provisions of the Constitution. *Police power* is usually described in terms of the general goals of the numerous regulations and statutes enforced in its name, e.g., on speed limits, working conditions, zoning, pollution, storage of atomic waste. Most common, in a miscellany of vagueness, are the "safety," "health," good "morals," "good order," and "general welfare" of the public, with frequent additions of "comfort" and "prosperity." *Police power*, a traditional province of state government, is broad enough to include a national police power.

policy   □see **insurance**; □see **public policy**.

poll tax: a tax of a fixed amount per person, not based on income or property. Also called a **capitation tax** (U.S. Const., Art. I, § 9) and a **head tax**. Payment of a poll tax as a condition of the right to vote is prohibited (U.S. Const., Amend. XXIV; *Harper v. Virginia Board of Elections,* 383 U.S. 663 (1966)).

poll the jury: to ask the individual jurors, immediately after a verdict has been read in open court, "Is that your verdict?" The jurors are polled by the trial judge or a clerk at the request of either side of a criminal or civil case or on the judge's own initiative. If the jurors (unanimously, or a lesser number required for a verdict under law of the jurisdiction) agree that the verdict is theirs, the verdict is entered, and the jury is discharged. If the required number does not agree, the jury is sent out for further deliberations or is discharged.

pollution: ordinary English, except as special legal standards and measures of redress are part of an increasing popular and political sensitivity to old and new ways of fouling the environment. *Pollution* has no all-purpose legal definition. Local, state, national, and international law must be consulted for special definitions covering every manner and place of pollution that someone may eventually think of. E.g., smoke (old style from chimneys, new style from tobacco); chemicals in the air and water; atomic radiation and waste; the noise of airports and traffic; sewage disposal; backyard barbecues and pesticides; ecosystems of Antarctica; and the Trans–Alaska Pipeline. □see **environmental impact report**.

pornography   □see **hard-core pornography**.

positive easement   □see **easement**.

posse   □see **posse comitatus**.

posse comitatus   (L., PAW-see kom-a-TAH-tus: power of the county.

1. the entire group of able-bodied adults of the county, who must, at the request of a peace officer for help on a specific occasion, join with the officer in keeping the peace, making an arrest, searching for a criminal, or executing legal process.

2. those called upon for service in sense 1.

In both senses, *posse comitatus* is frequently shortened to *posse;* in oral use, almost always.

possess   □see **possession**; □see also, **seised and possessed.**

possession: a word of ordinary English with only a modest glimmer of legal technicality.   More than most technical terms of the law, *possession* is dependent on bundles of facts and on the particulars of the diverse ends that it serves: e.g., the crime of possession of a deadly weapon; adverse possession (in this entry); or delivery (□see **deliver**) in the law of sales.

1.   The most widespread legal attempt to squeeze some sort of precise sense into *possession* relies on the dichotomy, *actual* and *constructive possession.*

actual possession: the immediate, physical control of real or personal property by one person to the exclusion of all others, whether that control is legal or illegal, and whether or not coupled with ownership. E.g., in simplest form: holding a book, a sack of cocaine, or stolen money; living in a rented apartment.   To be in *actual possession* of real property is to *occupy* it.

constructive possession: the power to have *actual possession* coupled with the intention of controlling the property but without the exercise of immediate, physical control.   E.g., in simplest form: a thief's possession of securities by having the key to a bank security box where he has placed the securities he has stolen; possession of a vacant house in Seattle, Washington, by its owner who lives in New York City.

Consult criminal law, commercial law, and property law for variations of facts and ends that blur or distinguish *actual* and *constructive possession.*

2.   *Possession,* as a loose synonym of *ownership,* is not general legal usage, except as identifying the physical items of ownership, i.e., *possessions* <All of their possessions were lost in the fire.>; and—indirectly—in the **covenant of seisin** (□see, under **covenants of title**).   □see also, **seisin.**

3. adverse possession: a special variety of *possession* of property by a stranger, who, meeting the requirements of local laws, eventually, under the banner of *adverse possession,* acquires title to the property.   The title is good against everyone, including the original owner.   <They acquired title by adverse possession.>   Under some statutes, one may acquire title to personal property by adverse possession; most often, the expression refers to real property.

possession

adverse possession (of real property): a stranger (the **adverse possessor**) who *claims* the property takes **actual possession** (□see, above, in this entry) *without* the owner's *permission*. The adverse possessor continuously uses the property *openly* in the way that owners usually do, long enough for the original owner to be legally barred from retaking the property (□see **statute of limitations**). In some states, the adverse possessor must also have paid taxes on the property during actual possession.

With considerable variation by jurisdiction, the italicized words in the preceding paragraph are typically described:

openly = **open and notorious** (□see **open**).

without permission = *adverse* or *hostile,* though no one but the original owner need be mad at anyone.

claims = *claim of right* or *claim of title.* Under widely varying statutes, the *claim* element may be ignored, must be made in good faith, or may be blatantly intended to acquire title by this means. Sometimes the *claim* is under *color of title* (e.g., a defective deed), which may affect the required period of possession, or permit a subtype of adverse possession called **constructive adverse possession**: (1) adverse possession of a larger tract of land by actual possession of only a portion or (2) adverse possession without actual possession but with payment of taxes on the property. □see also, **chose in possession**, under **chose in action**; □see also, **estate in possession**, under **estate**; □see also, **prescription**; □see also, **writ of assistance**, under **writ**.

possessory action: a suit to obtain possession of real or personal property. Of real property, e.g., the common law action of *ejectment;* e.g., the statutory action of **forcible entry and detainer** (□see). Of personal property, e.g., the action of **replevin** (□see).

possessory estate □see **estate in possession**, under **estate**.

possessory interest: ownership of property or of a lesser interest in property (e.g., a tenancy) that carries with it a present right of **possession** (□see); as contrasted, e.g., with a **future interest** (□see).

possessory lien □see **lien**.

possibility of reverter □see **fee simple**; □see **future interest**.

post bail □see bail.

postdate □see backdate, under nunc pro tunc.

postnuptial agreement □see marital agreement.

postpone □see delay.

posture □see clichés.

pourover: the characterization of a provision in an instrument, usually a will (a *pourover will*), directing that specified property or a residue be distributed or transferred to a trust (a *pourover trust*) established, or to be established, by some other instrument. Details of pourover provisions vary by jurisdiction. *Pourover* is also spelled *pour over* and *pour-over*.

pourover trust □see pourover; □see trust.

pourover will □see pourover.

power: the ordinary English word—ability, capacity, authority, right, jurisdiction (□see). No single, general sense unifies an almost infinite variety of legal referents of *power*—sources (e.g., the U.S. Constitution), exercise (e.g., tax), offices (e.g., executive), relationships (e.g., agency), instruments of government (e.g., legislative), capacities (e.g., to contract, to commit a crime), etc. Sense varies with the substantive law. A number of expressions, using the word *power* in some special legal sense, are alphabetical entries in the dictionary. Not the least of these is **power of appointment** (□see, under **appoint**); in short form, a *power*.

power coupled with an interest: a power irrevocable as long as the holder of the power continues to have an interest in the property, debt, business, or other matter affected by the exercise of the power. The power and the interest may operate as a *power given as security,* e.g., a *power of sale* in a mortgage. The best known powers coupled with an interest operate under aliases:

agency coupled with an interest: an agency in which the agent's authority to act is not, as with ordinary agents, ended by the principal's death, incapacity, or attempted revocation of agency; the agent has an interest in the agency apart from compensation as agent.

proxy coupled with an interest: a proxy irrevocable because the proxy holder has, or acts on behalf of those who have, an interest in the corporation that will be affected by how the proxy is voted. E.g., proxy given by shareholders as part of an agreement to vote their interests together. E.g., a proxy given a lender as further security for a loan to the corporation, another form of a *power given as security.* □see also, **proxy.**

power given as security □see power coupled with an interest.

power of appointment □see appoint.

power of attorney □see attorney in fact; □see also, **durable power of attorney;** □see also, **durable power of attorney,** under **right to die.**

power of sale □see power coupled with an interest.

power of termination □see fee simple.

practice of law □see lawyer.

pray □see demand.

prayer □see demand.

precatory trust □see precatory words.

precatory words: words of entreaty, rather than command; "I hope you will do it," as opposed to "Do it!" Words of this character—*hope, wish, recommend, beg, desire*—are frequently embroiled in battles over construction of a will, with unpredictable results. Where, despite their precatory flavor, the words in context are held, by and large, all things considered, to impose a duty, they are sometimes said to create a *precatory trust,* a fading expression.

precedent

1. (n.; PRESS-uh-dent): the decision of a court in one case that controls, guides, or influences the decision of a later case with similar facts and legal issues, an essential of the common law system (□see **common law**). Beyond that generalization, the limits of *precedent* are not precise. Some apply *precedent* only to those decisions that must be followed: e.g., a decision on a federal question by the U.S. Supreme Court that binds all other courts; e.g., a decision of an appellate court that binds lower courts in the same court system. Some equate *precedent* with a decision that should be followed for the sake of the continuity of law—*stare decisis* (L.: to stand by things decided). Some apply *precedent* to any case that manages to get into the printed reports, a vast assembly of precedents that point in every direction. *Precedent* is followed, distinguished, criticized, overruled, sometimes forgotten or overlooked, but seldom completely ignored. □see also, **holding**, under **hold**.

2. (adj.; pre-SEED-ent) □see **condition precedent**.

preclusion □see **res judicata**.

preempt Also spelled *pre-empt*. □see **preemption**.

preemption Also spelled *pre-emption*.

1. a doctrine based on the **Supremacy Clause** (□see) of the U.S. Constitution: a valid federal law displaces (makes invalid) a state or local law that is in the same field and is in conflict or inconsistent with the federal law. When a federal law does not make clear that state or local law is to be *preempted,* lawyers and judges labor in the fogs of **legislative intent** (□see, under **intent**). Application of *preemption* then hinges on whether or not the federal law was intended to **occupy the field,** i.e., to the exclusion of other law.

2. a doctrine of state law, parallel to *preemption* in sense 1, including intent to *occupy the field,* but not based on the Supremacy Clause: a valid state law displaces (makes invalid) local law or regulation that is in the same field and is in conflict or inconsistent with the state law. *Preemption* within the states varies with individual state constitutions, provisions for the powers of political subdivisions, and the decisions of state courts.

3. **Preemption right** (□see) and **preemptive right** (□see), both related by etymology to the word *preemption,* have completely independent legal meanings and follow as separate entries.

preemption right: the right of a person to acquire title to a portion of unappropriated public land by occupying it, doing required work, and paying a nominal fee.   The right was given by various statutes, especially the *homestead laws,* since repealed.   *Preemption right* (also spelled *pre-emption right*) is historic, except for titles so acquired. The expression *homestead laws* is not to be confused with the current use of **homestead** (□see).   □see also, **preemption.**

preemptive right: generally, the right of stockholders to buy newly issued stock, each in proportion to the stockholder's present ownership of stock in the corporation, before the new stock is offered to others.   Definition, grant, or denial of preemptive right (also spelled *pre-emptive right*) varies with articles of incorporation, statutes, and decision.   □see **dilution of stock,** under **dilution.**   □see also, **preemption.**

prefer: in general, the ordinary English sense of giving special treatment or priority.   Widely used in the law not only as *prefer* but also in the related forms *preferred, preference,* and *preferential.*   The law's contribution here is a sharp distinction between those words as pejoratives and as used with the sense of approval.   The lead word, often in both senses, is **preference** (□see).   (*Prefer,* in the expression to *prefer charges,* has no special technicality.   □see **accuse.**)

preference

1.   a payment or other transfer of property by an **insolvent** (□see) to one or more creditors not legally entitled to any special treatment. <The preference/preferential treatment/preferring A over B/treating A as a preferred creditor/was clearly improper.>

2.   a specially defined type of transfer of the property of an insolvent debtor that may be voided by a trustee in **bankruptcy** (□see).   □see **transfer in fraud of creditors,** under **transfer.**

3.   a legal right to special treatment or priority.   E.g., a statutory *preference* of a widow or widower to administer a spouse's estate. <The statute gives the surviving spouse a preference/a preferential right/the right to be preferred over strangers.>   E.g., a statutory *preference* for wage claims in probate.   <They had preferred claims./They were preferred creditors.>   E.g., a *preferred maritime lien,* a type of **priority** (□see). □see **preferred stock,** under **stock.**

preferential   □see **prefer;** □see **preference.**

preferred creditor   □see prefer; □see preference.

preferred shares   □see stock.

preferred stock   □see stock.

prejudice   □see without prejudice.

prejudicial error: an error in proceedings that substantially affects the outcome. A flexible expression, bending with facts, law, and the judge. □see reversible error.

preliminary examination   □see preliminary hearing.

preliminary hearing: one or more sessions before a judge in the capacity of a **magistrate** (□see), to determine whether or not there is **probable cause** (□see) to believe that an arrested defendant has committed a felony as charged. The prosecution presents evidence directed only to that issue; the defense has a like opportunity. The judge may then dismiss for lack of probable cause. Or, with the prosecutor's concurrence, the judge may reduce the charge to a misdemeanor and set that for trial. Or, the judge may find that there is probable cause, and **bindover** (also spelled *bind over*) the case and the defendant: holding the defendant, or releasing on bail or on the defendant's own recognizance, to await **arraignment** (□see) on an information or indictment. *Preliminary hearing* is also called *preliminary examination*.

preliminary injunction   □see enjoin.

premeditated   □see aforethought, under afore-; □see **malice aforethought**.

premium   □see insurance.

prenuptial agreement   □see marital agreement.

prepaid legal plans   □see prepaid legal services.

prepaid legal services: a general term for periodic payment to a private organization for providing the services of a lawyer as needed for specified types and duration of legal problems. The term is sometimes equated with **group legal services**: an existing organization (e.g., a labor union) supplies the services as a benefit of membership dues. *Prepaid legal services* is also sometimes equated with *legal insurance:* an insurance company provides the services for a premium. Neither *legal insurance* nor *prepaid legal services* refers to the legal services provided by a general insurer in connection with other types of insurance, e.g., auto, fire, general liability. Participation of a lawyer in plans of prepaid legal services is regulated by professional rules.

preparer principle □see **contra proferentem**; □see also, **rules of interpretation.**

preponderance □see **preponderance of the evidence.**

preponderance of the evidence: the evidence that outweighs the other evidence. In countless opinions and jury instructions, the expression is the usual measure of the **burden of proof** (□see, under **proof**) in civil cases. Yet the measure is a flexible one, with no uniform yardstick. *Preponderance of the evidence* is variously and vaguely described in terms of evidence that has more or most convincing force, is more or most satisfying, has greater probability of truth; worst of all, as the evidence that *preponderates.* Often shortened to *preponderance,* it is also frequently lengthened with adjectives that testify to the imprecision of the naked expression, e.g., a *clear* or a *fair* preponderance of the evidence. Lawyers take comfort in its function of comparison and contrast with other measures of burden of proof. There is no preponderance of the evidence that jurors know what it means.

prerogative writs □see **extraordinary.**

prescription

1. acquiring a right (called a *prescriptive right*) to use another person's land in a particular way—without the owner's permission, by open and continuous use for a specified statutory period. In general, the requirements for acquiring a prescriptive right, e.g., a **prescriptive easement** (□see, under **easement**), correspond to the requirements for acquiring title by **adverse possession** (□see, under **possession**).

Unlike adverse possession, which hinges on exclusive *possession*, the essence of prescriptive right is *use*. Use is consistent with ownership or possession of the land by others, even with use by others that does not interfere with the use that ripens into a prescriptive right. **Statutes of limitation** (□see) frequently fix different periods for adverse possession and prescription.

2. in loose usage, *prescription* sometimes refers to prescriptive right (sense 1), as well as to **adverse possession** (□see). <They acquired title to Blackacre by prescription./They acquired a right of way across Blackacre by prescription.>

prescriptive easement □see easement; □see prescription.

prescriptive right □see prescription.

present covenant □see covenant.

present estate □see estate in possession, under estate.

present interest □see future interest.

presentment

1. (of commercial paper): demand for acceptance or payment, made by or on behalf of the holder. Demand for acceptance is made upon the drawee. Demand for payment is made upon the maker, acceptor, drawee, or other payor. □see also, **dishonor.** For details, consult the Uniform Commercial Code.

2. (by a grand jury) □see **indictment.**

present recollection refreshed □see past recollection recorded.

present recollection revived □see past recollection recorded.

presents □see Know All Men By These Presents.

presidential immunity □see executive immunity, under immunity.

presidential privilege □see privilege, under immunity.

presiding judge □see **judge.**

presiding justice □see **judge.**

presume

1. a verb of common English converted by stages into a rule of law: (1) to be convinced that something (A) is a fact; and then (2) to infer from A that something else (B) is also a fact, though you are not certain that it is; and then (3) to conclude as a matter of law that, in the absence of sufficient evidence to the contrary, B is a fact. E.g., From the fact that a properly addressed letter was mailed (A), one infers (draws an *inference*) that the letter was received (B). In the absence of sufficient evidence to the contrary, one then *presumes* that the letter was received. Rules of procedure and substantive law determine what constitutes "sufficient evidence." Kin to *presume* are *presumed, presumptively,* and **presumption** (□see).

2. loosely used, as in common English, as a synonym of *assume, infer,* and *suppose.*

presumed bias: another name for **implied bias;** □see, under **bias.**

presumed intent: that a person intends the natural and probable consequences of an act. As used in criminal cases, *presumed intent* is subject to constitutional scrutiny, if not rejection, in terms of the burden of proof, and its classification as a *conclusive, mandatory,* or *permissive presumption.* □see **presumption.**

presumed malice: another name for **legal malice;** □see, under **malice.**

presumption: the ubiquitous noun of the verb **presume** (□see): the combination of an inference from A that there is a B *plus* the decision as a matter of law to consider B a fact in the absence of sufficient evidence to the contrary.

That is a general definition of a word without uniform definition in the law. Definitions vary by statute, decision, and treatise. Many jumble a general sense of *presumption* with its effects, notably how presumptions affect, or are affected by, the *burden of producing evidence* and the *burden* of *persuasion* (□see **proof**). Some partisans insist that if what lawyers and judges call a *presumption* does not have this or that origin, purpose, or effect, "it is not really a presumption": a sad truth if a case is controlled by authoritative statute or decision. Frequently nominated for oblivion, with definitions in conflict, the word *presumption* remains inextricably rooted in the law. The names and descriptions listed here (some, among hundreds) inevitably refer the reader to the law of evidence for the ramifications of causes and effects of presumptions, their durability, and desirability.

absolute presumption □see **conclusive presumption**, below, in this entry.

conclusive presumption: a rule of law (varying in definition and application) that once one fact has been proved, it inevitably follows that something else is also a fact. <A child born in wedlock is conclusively presumed legitimate.> At its rigorous and logical extreme, the rule bars evidence to contradict the presumed fact. Natural resistance to **absolutes** (□see), coupled with the urge to use habitual language, results in anomalous usage. <It is conclusively presumed unless the jury is "persuaded by a preponderance of evidence offered in rebuttal."> When interpretation does not reduce the conclusive presumption to sniveling inconclusiveness, legislation often does. <A child born in wedlock is conclusively presumed legitimate, unless the husband is impotent, or sterile, or blood tests disprove fatherhood, etc.> A *conclusive presumption* is also called an *irrebuttable presumption,* less often—an *absolute presumption.*

disputable presumption □see **rebuttable presumption**, below, in this entry.

irrebuttable presumption □see **conclusive presumption**, above, in this entry.

mandatory presumption: the finder of fact (judge or jury) *must* find that the B inferred from A (□see **presume**) is a fact, in the absence of *some* evidence to the contrary. A special concern in criminal cases raising questions of the burden of proof. □see **proof**.

permissive presumption: the finder of fact (judge or jury) *may* (is never required to) find that the B inferred from A (□see **presume**) is a fact. A frequent contrast with the *mandatory presumption.* The expression *permissive presumption* is loosely used; also called a *presumption of fact,* a *permissive inference,* or simply an *inference.*

presumption of death: presumed from prolonged, unexplained absence; a common, statutory presumption. The period of absence, and the effect of the presumption, vary by jurisdiction.

presumption of fact: a loosely used alternative for *permissive presumption, permissive inference,* or simply an *inference.* Sometimes explained as what may be logically inferred, as distinguished from the equally loose *presumption of law:* an inference required by law.

501

presumption

presumption of innocence □see **beyond a reasonable doubt.**

presumption of law □see **presumption of fact,** above, in this entry.

presumption of legitimacy □see **conclusive presumption,** above, in this entry.

presumption of negligence □see **res ipsa loquitur.**

presumption of survivorship: a rule of law fixing the sequence of death of two or more persons in a common disaster, in the absence of evidence of survival. A common statutory presumption, based on sex, age, physical condition, etc.

rebuttable presumption: the common characterization of most presumptions, in terms of what evidence is sufficient to destroy them ("burst the bubble") or limit their effect. Or in terms of how the presumption affects, or is affected by, the *burden of producing evidence,* the *burden of persuasion,* or both (□see **proof**). *Rebuttable presumption,* sometimes called a *disputable presumption,* is contrasted with the *conclusive* or *irrebuttable presumption.*

presumption of death □see **presumption.**

presumption of fact □see **presumption.**

presumption of innocence □see **beyond a reasonable doubt.**

presumption of law □see **presumption.**

presumption of legitimacy □see **conclusive presumption,** under **presumption.**

presumption of negligence □see **res ipsa loquitur.**

presumption of survivorship □see **presumption.**

pretermitted child □see **pretermitted heir,** under **heirs.**

pretermitted heir □see **heirs.**

pretermitted spouse □see **pretermitted heir,** under **heirs.**

prevailing party   □see **party**.

preventive detention: jailing of a defendant pending trial for an otherwise bailable crime, not to assure presence at trial but to prevent the defendant from committing other crimes.   Also used in connection with other legal proceedings, e.g., deportation hearing. *Preventive detention,* based on danger to society, is to be distinguished from *protective custody:* keeping a person in custody primarily for the person's own protection.   □see **custody**.

preventive injunction   □see **enjoin**.

preventive law: an approach to the practice of law stressing consultation, planning, and writing to avoid potential problems and the consequences of their neglect, e.g., litigation, alternative dispute resolution, taxes, disappointment, frustration.   *Preventive law* has been described as "the nonadversarial practice of law."   ("Lou Brown's Preventive Law Glossary, Part II," 7 Preventive Law Reporter 19, Sept., 1988).

price fixing   □see **antitrust law**; □see **monopoly**.

priest-penitent privilege: A person who seeks spiritual help from a member of the clergy then acting in the role of religious adviser has a right to refuse to disclose confidential communications between them during the course of that relationship.   The seeker also has the right to prevent the religious adviser from disclosing the confidential communications.

The traditional name *priest-penitent privilege* has the flavor of the Roman Catholic confessional, but with or without name change, the privilege has been extended to religions generally, and to confidential communication whether or not part of religious discipline.   Some jurisdictions prefer *clergyman-penitent privilege,* a still sexist note sometimes eliminated as the *clergy-penitent privilege.*   Some jurisdictions recognize a similar *clergyman's privilege:* the spiritual adviser's right to refuse to disclose the confidential communications.

prima facie   □see **at first blush**.

prima facie case   □see **proof**; □see also, **at first blush**.

503

primary boycott □see boycott.

primary liability □see secondary liability.

primary picketing □see picketing.

primary taint doctrine □see fruit of the poisonous tree.

principal □see agency; □see master and servant; □see parties to crime.

principal and surety □see suretyship; □see also, **guarantee**.

principal in the first degree □see parties to crime.

principal in the second degree □see parties to crime.

principal office □see office; □see domicile.

principal place of business □see domicile; □see office.

prior (n.) □see prior conviction.

prior appropriation □see law of capture.

prior art □see patent.

prior censorship □see prior restraint; □see also, **censorship**.

prior consistent statement: a witness's statement on another occasion usually offered to rebut an inference of recent fabrication, or as evidence of prompt complaint, e.g., of rape. □see also, **prior inconsistent statement**.

prior conviction

1. an earlier conviction of a different offense that may be used to increase the penalty for this offense. □see **enhance**.

2. a conviction that may be used to impeach a witness.

In customary usage, usually oral, *prior conviction* is shortened to *prior,* the adjective becoming a noun in the legal argot of the criminal bar. <There are two priors.> □see also, **no priors.**

prior inconsistent statement: a witness's statement on another occasion usually offered to impeach the witness. □see **impeach.** □see also, **prior consistent statement.**

priority: a right or claim that takes precedence over some other right or claim. Substantive and procedural statutes establish all manner of priorities, pecking orders adapted to particular areas of the law, e.g., bankruptcy, execution, liens, mining claims, probate, security interests. □see also, **prefer;** □see also, **preference;** □see also, **encumber.**

prior lien □see **priority.**

prior offense □see **prior conviction.**

prior restraint: restriction or suppression of freedom of expression, typically freedom of speech and press, imposed by government in advance of expression or publication, e.g., requirements of licensing, submission to a censor; injunction. With some exceptions, prior restraint is prohibited by U.S. Supreme Court interpretation of the First Amendment. □see **censorship.**

prison □see **jail;** □see **imprisonment;** □see also, **convict.**

prisoner: used loosely as a general word that can include anyone who is under some immediate legal restraint, whether or not considered in **custody** (□see). Usage varies from application to a person arrested, awaiting trial, on trial, released on bail, confined in jail or in a state prison, and to every stage in-between. Specific use or rejection of the word *prisoner* depends on various statutory definitions, and on interpretation of statutes using the word in special contexts, e.g., escape, juveniles, liability of government for torts, expenses, injury.

prisoner at the bar: an old usage, usually oral, to describe the defendant in court, in a criminal case. □see **bar.**

prisoner at the bar □see **prisoner;** □see **bar.**

privacy

privacy □see **right of privacy.**

private act □see **public law.**

private attorney general □see **lawyer.**

private bill □see **public law.**

private carrier □see **common carrier.**

private corporation □see **corporate.**

private international law □see **international law.**

private law □see **public law.**

private nuisance □see **nuisance.**

private statute □see **public law.**

private trust □see **trust.**

private utility □see **public utility.**

privatize

1. an imprecise usage in the law, as in ordinary English: to substitute private for government control, operation, or ownership. The companion word horror *privatization* has also invaded the law.

2. in the sense of changing the form of corporate ownership, □see **going private.**

privilege □see **immunity.**

privilege against self-incrimination □see **criminate.**

privileged communication: a general rubric for communication without liability (□see **immunity**) or protected against disclosure (□see **confidential-communications privilege**).

privilege of self-defense □see **self-defense**.

Privileges and Immunities Clauses: the parts of the U.S. Constitution reading: "The citizens of each state shall be entitled to all privileges and immunities of citizens in the several states." (Art. IV, § 2) (also known as the *Comity Clause*); and "No state shall make or enforce any law which shall abridge the privileges or immunities of citizens of the United States. . . . (Amend. XIV, § 1). The *Privileges and Immunities Clause* often refers to one or both of the clauses, despite the *and* (Art. IV) and the *or* (Amend. XIV) difference between the two. When distinction is made, the references are sometimes to the *Article IV privileges and immunities clause*, the *Comity Clause*, and the *Fourteenth Amendment privileges or immunities clause*. □see also, **constitutional clauses**.

privity: a relationship between persons in connection with a particular transaction, property, right, or thing, that carries with the relationship benefits, burdens, or both. The persons in the relationship are said to be *in privity* and are called *privies* (singular, *privy*).

The relationship that is *privity* may be *simultaneous* (also called *mutual*), e.g., between parties to a contract, a sale, or conveyance. Or the relationship may be *derivative* (usually called *successive*), e.g., from ownership of the same property or an interest in the same property, as grantor/grantee; party to a lawsuit/nonparty bound by *res judicata*.

Privity is a conclusion, often said to be undefinable. What is sufficient to establish *privity,* and to determine what benefits or burdens follow, varies by jurisdiction, by court, by writer, and by the law of the myriad topics (of substantive law, not for this dictionary) into which the word is injected, e.g., adverse possession, covenants running with the land, easements, estoppel, *res judicata*. In short, *privity* exists when and because there is *privity*.

The uncertainties of *privity* have been no bar to its division, subdivision, and overlap. The big names in the field are the least complex *privity of contract* and the most complex *privity of estate*.

privity of contract: the relationship of parties to a contract. Those in privity of contract may also be in privity of estate. E.g., A and B make a contract to buy and sell Blackacre. Pursuant to the contract, B conveys Blackacre to A.

privity of estate: the relationship between those who have or had rights in the same land. In one view, the rights must be identical, e.g., grantor and grantee. In another view, different rights in the same land suffice, e.g., landlord and tenant. *Privity of estate* is also called *privity of title*.

For some purposes, especially in dealing with covenants running with the land and easements, *privity of estate* is divided into *horizontal* and *vertical privity*:

horizontal privity: the relationship between the original parties to a transaction that may later involve other parties. E.g., adjacent property owners join in a covenant burdening one of the properties and benefiting the other.

vertical privity: the relationship between one or the other of the parties in horizontal privity and those whose rights or burdens stem only from that party's rights or burdens, directly or successively. E.g., A, the owner of Blackacre, covenants with B, the owner of adjacent Greenacre, restricting Greenacre for the benefit of Blackacre. A and B are in horizontal privity. If A conveys to C, A and C are in vertical privity. If B conveys to D, B and D are in vertical privity.

privity of possession: the relationship between successive adverse possessors of land sufficient to permit *tacking,* i.e., adding successive periods of possession together. *Privity of possession* is a type of *privity of estate.*

privity of contract □see **privity.**

privity of estate □see **privity.**

privity of possession □see **privity.**

privity of title □see **privity.**

privy □see **privity.**

prize □see **maritime law.**

probable cause: a reasonable, particularized basis for believing that a particular act is justified. Most commonly describes the legally proper basis for an arrest, a search, an arrest warrant or a search warrant, a criminal prosecution, a civil action. □see **search and seizure**; □see **Warrant Clause**; □see **preliminary hearing**; □see **malicious prosecution**. Also used in wide-ranging contexts to describe the legally proper basis for assorted legal moves, e.g., an appeal, a writ of habeas corpus. The language of *probable cause* is not standardized, either in constitutional opinions or others. It is sometimes described in terms of "fair probability" that something is so, of what would warrant belief by a "cautious" or "prudent" man, even of "suspicion," rather than "belief." Usually, *probable cause* is distinguished from hunch, generalized belief, suspicion, and, at the other end of the spectrum, is distinguished from **proof** (□see). □see also, **Terry stop**, under **search and seizure**.

probate

1. (n.) the gamut of procedures of judicial supervision over the administration of decedents' estates and of adjudication connected with decedents' estates, e.g., the proving and interpretation of wills, will contests, issuing of **letters of administration** (□see) and **letters testamentary** (□see), approval of claims against an estate, determination of intestate succession, approval of reports of administration and fees, and distribution of estate property. In this sense, a will is said to be *admitted to probate;* a will or an estate is said to be *in probate.* □see also, **prove the will**, under **proof**.

2. (v.) to subject a will or a decedent's estate to one or more of the procedures described in sense 1, and to other allied procedures required or permitted by local law. The will, the estate is being *probated.* <Judge Smith probated the Estate of Jones./The law firm of Kaplan & Wright is probating the Estate of Jones./ . . . is probating her will.>

For a completely different sense of the verb, □see **probation**.

3. (adj.)

    a. probate court: a court of limited jurisdiction (□see **court**) dealing with decedents' estates (sense 1), and with additional matters as provided by local law, e.g., guardianship (□see **guardian**), **conservatorship** (□see), minors, missing persons. In some jurisdictions, called a *surrogate court.*

    b. identification of law or particular procedures connected with probate (sense 1) or dealt with by a *probate court,* e.g., *probate code; —jurisdiction; —proceeding; —bond*—sometimes required of an executor, administrator, guardian, or conservator.

probation: after conviction, a release from custody without sentence, subject to the defendant's satisfying specified conditions. Typically: the release is under supervision of a probation officer; if the conditions are not satisfied, probation is revoked, and the defendant is subject to sentence of imprisonment. Some statutes and some usage include probation as a part of sentencing, rather than as an alternative to sentencing. □see **judgment of conviction,** under **judgment;** □see **sentence.** *Probation* is to be distinguished from **parole** (□see).

General usage describes a defendant as being *granted* or *given probation;* being *released on* or *placed on probation;* a *probationer.* In some jurisdictions, the appropriate usage is a form of the verb *probate:* the defendant was *probated; probating* the defendants; a *probated* offender; a *probated* sentence; not to be confused with the usage in decedents' estates (□see **probate**).

probationer □see **probation.**

probative □see **proof.**

pro bono □see **lawyer.**

pro bono publico □see **lawyer.**

procedural due process □see **due process,** under **due.**

procedural law: the law dealing with **procedure** (□see). Often shortened to *procedure.* Also called *adjective law.* In usage, distinguished from **substantive law** (□see).

procedure: the mechanisms of the law: the ways and means through which legal principles come out of the books and go to work. For pedagogy, the topic is subdivided. Broadly, *procedure* includes pleading, practice, courts, trials, evidence, remedies, and the accompanying shower of paper forms. *Procedure* is usually distinguished from *substantive* principles and rules, e.g., the details of a trial for murder, as distinguished from a law making murder a crime. The distinction is not sharp, in that for the law substance and procedure must co-exist. E.g., *procedural due process* and *substantive due process;* □see **due process,** under **due.**

proceeding: an untechnical, generalized description of some measure taken to pursue a legal end: proceedings in court (e.g., a trial);

proceedings to enforce a judgment (e.g., levy of execution); administrative proceedings (e.g., a hearing before an agency); the swearing-in proceedings (e.g., taking an oath of office); etc.

process

1. the way the legal system functions—*process of law.* □see **due process**, under **due**.

2. official pieces of paper embodying court orders concerning persons, property, or both, designed to give notice to those affected and to enforce orders and judgments, e.g., arrest warrant, subpoena, summons, writ of attachment. □see **service of process**. □see also, **alias process**.

> **malicious abuse of process** □see.

> **mesne process** □see **mesne**.

> **process server** □see **service of process**.

process server □see service of process.

proclaim □see proclamation.

proclamation

1. a special form of official announcement of some action by an executive or administrative officer of a government—federal, state, or local. E.g., a proclamation by the President of American neutrality in a war between foreign states, or that 1976 is the Bicentennial Year; a proclamation by a governor of a statewide election.

2. an official, ceremonial, oral announcement. E.g., by a *court crier* proclaiming that court is now in session. □see **formalisms**.

proctor in admiralty □see lawyer.

procurer □see pander.

procuring cause: a conclusion characterizing the acts of a broker that together are a condition of the right to a commission. Usually, the conclusion is predicated on a broker's acts in initiating a deal, tied to the continuity of events that lead to its consummation. The conclusion may also be predicated on a broker bringing a seller an offer from someone ready, willing, and able to buy on the seller's terms.

procuring cause

Procuring cause is also sometimes called **producing cause** (□see). □see also, **proximate cause**.

producing cause: a general term for the events that cause a particular result. Used especially to identify the cause of injury, as in a workers' compensation case. □see also, **procuring cause**; □see also, **proximate cause**.

products liability: liability of manufacturers and others in the marketing chain who supply "defective products." The liability— **strict liability** (□see) or based on negligence—runs to those who are damaged or injured, whether as buyers, users, or *bystanders,* i.e., hurt without buying or using. The extent of *products liability* and what constitutes "defective products" are spelled out in ever-widening areas of the law of tort and contract.

profanity: a waning and vague offense prohibiting the use of offensive language, sometimes imbedded in laws on disturbing the peace. Sometimes regarded as a synonym of **blasphemy** (□see) or related to it as offensive, general irreverence toward religion. More often *profanity* has degenerated into one of the labels for vulgar expression, and, as an offense, is frequently held unconstitutional. *Profanity* is to be distinguished from **fighting words** (□see), and from pornography (□see **hard-core pornography**).

professional association: a group of licensed professionals, e.g., lawyers, doctors, accountants, practicing together in a variety of personal arrangements, other than as a **professional corporation** (□see, under **corporate**). *Professional association* is abbreviated **P.A.**

professional corporation □see **corporate**.

professional liability □see **malpractice**.

professional responsibility □see **legal ethics**.

profit

1. an accounting term widely used in the law, without a specialized or uniform legal sense, e.g., *profit and loss, net profits, nonprofit.* □see **charitable**.

2. for real property usage, □see **mesne profits**, under **mesne**; □see **profit à prendre**.

profit à prendre (F., profit uh PRAWN-der: profit to take): a right to take from another's land something that is part of the land itself, e.g., minerals and gravel, or something produced from the land, e.g., timber. The expression is often spelled without the accent—*profit a prendre*—and is familiarly referred to as a *profit* (pl. *profits*). □see **mining lease.**

pro forma (L.: for the sake of (judicial) form): a form or procedure that is used to comply with a technical requirement without affecting substance; e.g., a *pro forma party.* □see **nominal party**, under **party**. The more frequent use of *pro forma* in the law is an accounting or commercial term, without a special legal sense; e.g., a *pro forma balance sheet. Pro forma* is also spelled *pro-forma* and *proforma.*

pro forma party □see **pro forma**; □see **nominal party**, under **party**.

progeny □see **and its progeny.**

pro hac vice (L., pro HACK vice: for this time): for this time only. Said of someone permitted to exercise particular functions for a limited period. Especially, of a lawyer's admission to practice *pro hac vice,* i.e., for this time only; as, e.g., an out-of-state lawyer permitted to represent a named client in this case, though not a member of the bar in this jurisdiction. <On motion, she was admitted *pro hac vice* to represent the defendant.>

prohibit means what it means in ordinary English but weighted with the boom of authority. One of the law's favorite negatives, whether in this verb form or as the noun **prohibition** (□see).

prohibition

1. short for **writ of prohibition**: an order directing a lower court to stop further proceedings in a case over which it has no jurisdiction. Prohibition is one of a group called *prerogative* or *extraordinary* writs. □see **extraordinary.**

2. tied forever to intoxicating liquor in two amendments to the U.S. Constitution: the *Eighteenth,* using only the verb "prohibited," but

prohibition

responsible for the capitalized noun *Prohibition;* and the *Twenty-First,* commonly referred to as *Repeal.*

prohibitory injunction □see enjoin.

promise □see **breach**; □see **contract**; □see **illusory promise**, under **illusory contract.**

promisee: the person to whom a *promisor* makes a promise. Typical usage in discussion and writing *about* contracts, not *in* contracts. □see -ee; □see **contract.**

promisor □see **promisee.**

promissory estoppel □see **estoppel.**

promissory note □see **commercial paper.**

proof: an ambiguous yet basic law word that can refer to cause (evidence, data) or effect (the resulting belief). The opposed senses are often blended, or are not distinguished. The verb, similarly afflicted, is *prove.*

1. the evidence that is intended to produce belief (sense 2), often does, or at least tends to produce belief, is *probative.* <The proof consisted of two exhibits and the testimony of one witness./Counsel, put in your proof./ . . . prove up your damages./ . . . prove the will.> □see **offer of proof**; □see **due proof**, under **due.**

2. as a result of the evidence (sense 1), a belief, or some degree of conviction, that something is so. <The evidence was overwhelming; it created proof beyond a reasonable doubt./She was proved guilty beyond a reasonable doubt.>

3. specific data that satisfies the requirements of a particular statute or agreement. E.g., *proof of financial responsibility* (often, a public liability policy); *proof of claim* (often, an affidavit with accompanying unpaid note); *proof of loss* (details as specified in an insurance policy).

4. the piece of paper that contains the required data (sense 3). <Their proof of loss was filed on time.>

5. burden of proof: the general name for a litigant's task of proving what is required by law to win a case, or even to continue presenting a case (or a particular issue) in court. The expression is frequently called *burdens of proof,* calling attention to a subdivision of burden into *burden of producing evidence* and *burden of persuasion.* Who bears the burden of proof or the burdens of proof, and the details of what must be proved, vary according to the rules of evidence, procedure, and the substantive law of a particular case.

burden of producing evidence: a litigant's task of presenting evidence that would be sufficient for a reasonable trier of fact to decide the case or a particular issue in favor of that litigant. E.g., sufficient in a jury trial to deny a motion for a directed verdict; i.e., there is a *prima facie case.* □see **prima facie**, under **at first blush**. *Burden of producing evidence* is also called *burden of going forward with the evidence.*

burden of persuasion: the task of the litigant who wants to change the status quo (e.g., prosecutor or plaintiff) to convince the trier of fact (judge or jury) that the evidence proves all the essential elements of the case. *Burden of persuasion* may also be a particular litigant's task on a particular issue, e.g., an *affirmative defense,* such as self-defense, or assumption of risk. *Burden of persuasion* is also called the *risk of nonpersuasion,* i.e., the litigant to whom the law assigns the burden of persuasion has a cause at risk: persuade or lose. How lawyers persuade judges and juries is an art, and what persuades is a mystery; but for some purposes, e.g., instructing a jury, considering whether or not a case was correctly decided, *burden of persuasion* is measured in formulaic degrees of *proof:*

beyond a reasonable doubt (□see).

clear and convincing (□see, under **clear**).

preponderance of the evidence (□see).

pro per   □see **appear**.

proper   □see **fit and proper**.

proper forum   □see **forum**.

proper party   □see **party**.

property: a special type of *thing* and a special type of *rights.* *Thing* and *rights* are blended in the all-inclusive word *property.* It has no uniform definition, still reflecting an ultimate origin in the related

515

property

Latin words *proprium:* a possession, property; *proprius:* one's own; and *proprietas:* ownership, right of possession, property.

1. a thing, tangible or intangible, that can be owned by a person, an artificial person, or a legal entity. □see **person;** □see **intangible property.** <The property in the estate consisted of Blackacre and the copyright in two novels./All of their property was seized on execution./The property on Main Street has been vacant for one hundred years.>

The notion of *property* as a *thing* is old in the law and in general English. Despite its rejection by some as "vulgar," i.e., fit for ordinary people but not for lawyers, *property* as *thing* roams through every branch of the law. That it is a thing that can be *owned* makes *property* speak of worldly things, measurable in terms of money or power, as contrasted with things of the spirit. Things identified as *property* also have an almost endless variety of special names, e.g., **land** (□see), **goods** (□see), **commercial paper** (□see), **easement** (□see), a **cause of action** (□see), a **chattel real** (□see, under **chattel**), an **estate** (□see), a **lease** (□see), a **mining lease** (□see).

2. the rights that a person, an artificial person, or a legal entity can have in relation to a thing (sense 1). This old usage, predecessor of more sophisticated usages (senses 3 and 4), still lives.

Rights, as used in this sense, is the notion of what you can do with the thing (sense 1) that you have, e.g., possess it; use it; transfer it; grant others rights in it; exclude others from deriving any benefit from it, even from stepping on it. In short, the rights that the law recognizes as aspects of ownership. The specific rights that constitute this sense of *property* vary by jurisdiction, and by the special nature of the various kinds of property, e.g., as absolute as can be, in a **fee simple** (□see); lesser rights in a **lease** (□see). <Their property in Blackacre turned out to be more valuable than the owner's fee interest; they owned the exclusive right to drill for oil.>

3. the rights between persons, artificial persons, and legal entities, or between any of them, with respect to a thing (sense 1).

Rights here are the various aspects of ownership as in sense 2, but the usage emphasizes that these rights relate not merely to a thing (sense 1) but to the whole gamut of legal relationships between owners of various interests and others; e.g., between an owner and a stranger, between a landlord and a tenant, between the owner of the fee and the owner of an easement. It is in this sense that reference is frequently made to the *bundle of rights* or the *bundle of sticks* that constitute *property.*

4. the "legal relations between persons with respect to a thing." (1 *Restatement of Property,* ch. 1, p. 3, "Introductory Note").

This definition is widely quoted to emphasize the focus of *property* on relationships between persons and others (sense 3), as opposed to the relation of a person to a thing (sense 2). Less widely followed is the *Restatement*'s imperative subdivision of "legal relations" into types involving Hohfeldian correlatives—*right* (duty), *privilege* (absence of right), *power* (liability), and *immunity* (disability). (1 *Restatement of Property*, §§ 1, 2, 3, and 4). See Wesley Newcomb Hohfeld, "Some Fundamental Legal Conceptions as Applied in Judicial Reasoning," 23 *Yale Law Journal* 16–59 (1913), and "Fundamental Legal Conceptions as Applied in Legal Reasoning," 26 *Yale Law Journal* 710–770 (1917).

5. Property is generally subdivided into *real* and *personal property*, definitions of each varying by decision and statute:

> **real property**: usually, property in land and in things more or less permanently attached to land. □see **land**; □see **fixture**. To be classified as *real property*, an estate must be a **freehold** (□see); □see also, **estate**.

> The concept of *real property* as tied to particular forms of action is historical only. The concept of *real property* as that which is inheritable, or inheritable by the heir, is historical, occasionally vestigial (□see **descend**; □see **heirs**).

> **personal property**: usually described as *movables,* tangible and intangible, often as property that is not real property. □see **chattel**; □see **movables**; □see **chose in action**.

property settlement: a division of property between spouses in connection with divorce, dissolution of marriage, or legal separation. The division is by *property settlement agreement* between the spouses and approved by court, or imposed by court in absence of agreement. Though it may provide for payment in installments, a *property settlement* is usually differentiated from **alimony** (□see) or other periodic payment. Property settlements are without standard pattern, and are not necessarily limited to marital property (□see **marital estate**). □see also, **marital agreement**.

property settlement agreement □see **property settlement**.

propria persona □see **appear**.

proprietorship □see **sole proprietorship**.

pro se □see **appear.**

prosecute: usually overshadowed by the criminal law usage <He was prosecuted for embezzlement.>, *prosecute* also refers to starting or continuing civil proceedings. □see **civil suit,** under **civil.**

prosecuting attorney □see **lawyer.**

prosecuting witness: the victim, or other person with personal knowledge of an alleged criminal offense who instigates a prosecution, as by filing a complaint. The expression is used whether or not the person testifies as a witness for the prosecution. A *prosecuting witness,* male or female, is also called a *prosecutor,* not to be confused with that word to designate a *prosecuting attorney* (□see **lawyer**). A female *prosecuting witness* is sometimes referred to by the fading usage *prosecutrix* (□see **sex**).

prosecution □see **civil suit,** under **civil.**

prosecutor □see **lawyer;** □see also, **prosecuting witness.**

prosecutorial immunity □see **immunity.**

prosecutrix □see **prosecuting witness;** □see **sex.**

prospective damages □see **damage.**

prostitute: a person, male or female, who engages in *prostitution:* sex for pay, a criminal offense. Varies by statutory definition. Sometimes limited to a person who is so engaged regularly and indiscriminately, as a business. Sometimes still limited to a female so engaged. □see also, **pander.**

prostitution □see **prostitute.**

protective custody □see **preventive detention;** □see also, **custody.**

protective order: a general name for a wide range of court orders auxiliary to some legal proceeding. The orders are designed to insure the integrity of the proceeding, and to protect those connected with it from harassment, violence, and invasion of rights of person and property. E.g., to prevent abuse of discovery proceedings by limiting their scope and volume; to prevent recurrent violence of litigating spouses by injunction requiring physical separation; to keep secret the identity of witness-informants threatened with violence in nuisance abatement proceedings.

pro tem: short for Latin *pro tempore:* for the time; temporarily. *Pro tem* is a common version, as in *judge pro tem:* a lawyer who is not a judge temporarily serving as judge, by court order pursuant to stipulation of the litigants.

pro tempore □see **pro tem**.

protest: a formal expression of dissatisfaction that something has gone wrong or is about to, usually intended to prevent some action or to preserve one's rights. *Protest,* in this sense, takes different forms in different branches of the law; one of the most technical is the limited use of a notary public's certificate of **dishonor** (□see) of a negotiable instrument (UCC § 3509(1)). Often a protest consists of a filing with an official objecting to some government action, e.g., assessments, duties on imports, election tallies, grant of liquor licenses, taxes, utility rates, zone change. Payment *under protest* is a frequent locution, sometimes required (sometimes not) as a condition of resisting an improper tax; also used loosely in objecting to a bill.

prove □see **proof**.

provided □see **proviso**.

provisional injunction □see **enjoin**.

provisional remedy: a temporary remedy in aid of a civil action to preserve the value of an ultimate judgment. The remedies vary by statute, e.g., arrest, attachment, garnishment, injunction, appointment of a receiver.

proviso: a part of a writing (e.g., of a statute, a contract) that usually qualifies what has gone before by adding a condition or an exception. It is typically introduced by the words *provided* or *provided however.* Typically also, it is a feature of the long, long sentence, with multiple

proviso

provisos often qualifying each other. It is one of the horrors of legal writing, in a class with **notwithstanding** (□see).

proximate □see **proximate cause**; □see also, **approximate**, under **oral**.

proximate cause: a vague label for a sufficient causal and legal connection between conduct and harm to impose liability for the conduct. Widely used throughout the law, especially in tort law (especially in the law of negligence) and in criminal law.

An offshoot of the Latin *proximus* (nearest), the expression in one form or another has been tied to the law for centuries, interpreted in thousands of cases, without consensus. It has been called the continuous, direct, dominant, efficient, immediate, moving, next, nearest, procuring, producing, substantial, uninterrupted cause, and much more. It is freely used as a synonym of *legal cause* (which is the *Restatement*'s rejection of *proximate cause; see Restatement (Second) of Torts,* §§ 9, 431). Statutes, judges, writers, and jury instructions give individualized explanations.

proxy

1. the authority given by one person to another to serve as a substitute in performing a specific act that is personal to the giver of the proxy. E.g., voting; e.g., a marriage vow. Most commonly used by shareholders in corporate elections. Less common, a statutory *proxy marriage,* where a substitute for an absent bride or groom participates in the ceremony.

2. the writing containing the authority (sense 1).

3. the person to whom the authority (sense 1) is given; also called the *proxy holder.*

4. the exercise of the authority (sense 1).

<A majority of the shareholders *voted by proxy.*>

proxy coupled with an interest □see **power coupled with an interest**.

proxy holder □see **proxy**.

proxy marriage □see **proxy**.

prudence: one of those marvelous virtues of ordinary English vague enough to find a natural home in the law. Depending on who describes it, *prudence* can be one or more or all of these: practical wisdom, care, circumspection, skill in management of business affairs, good judgment, discretion in working out means to ends, caution, economy, cautious use of resources with an eye to the future, a special regard for one's own interests. On and on. If that is not vague enough, *prudence* can be, and is, easily qualified as *common, ordinary,* or *reasonable prudence;* qualified by words, but indistinguishable from each other or from *prudence.*

With so much to choose from, *prudence* is almost a perfect standard by which to measure those who must be measured by imperfect judges. So many different kinds of *prudence*; and so many *prudent* (or imprudent) people: *prudent* directors, investors, lawyers, managers, pedestrians, police officers, drillers for oil, trustees, fiduciaries generally, etc.

prudent man: the law's measuring rod for *prudence*. Long before the law embraced prudence, a man or a woman was often described as having *prudence* or being *prudent.*

In creating a hypothetical creature to make quick use of the wonderful flexibility of those words, the law typically called the creature the *prudent man* (□see **reasonable man**). The creature is now also called the **prudent person** (□see **sex**), sometimes both in the same writing. Under either title, the vagueness remains.

prudent man rule: in general, a rule, also called the *prudent man test,* that in this case, this person's conduct ought to be measured against what might be expected of a *prudent man* (or *person,* or director, investor, etc., etc.) under similar circumstances. Calling this a *rule* or *test* gives an impression of some order out of vagueness. *Prudent man rules* vary by jurisdiction, statute, and area of law, e.g., trusts, corporations, negligence, malpractice, investment. Typically, they invoke the magic words (*prudence, prudent*); also typically, they rely on redundancy and some specifics, e.g.:

> "[A] fiduciary shall discharge his duties . . . (B) with the care, skill, prudence, and diligence under the circumstances then prevailing that a prudent man acting in a like capacity and familiar with such matters would use in the conduct of an enterprise of a like character and with like aims; (C) by diversifying the investments of the plan so as to minimize the risk of large losses, unless under the circumstances it is clearly prudent not to do so . . . ."
> (ERISA, 29 USCA § 1104(a)(1)). □see **ERISA**.

prudent man

prudent man □see **prudence**.

prudent man rule □see **prudence**.

prudent person □see **prudence**; □see **sex**.

psychiatrist-patient privilege □see **physician-patient privilege**.

public: in general, the ordinary English sense of things that belong to, pertain to, or are available to the community at large—whether in terms of government, or numbers of people (*the* public). In this general sense, *public* is contrasted with what is private, restricted, or secret.

In specific usage, the general sense cannot always be relied on. E.g., a **public utility** (□see) may be a privately owned utility; a *public corporation* may be a *private corporation* (□see **corporate**). In addition to general English usage, the law has special usages of *public* and of its language relatives *publication* and *publish;* many of these follow as separate entries. □see also, **going public**, under **going private**; □see also, **open and notorious**, under **open**.

public accommodations: places publicly or privately owned that are generally open to the **public** (□see) or to some form of public patronage, e.g., hotels, restaurants, theaters, railroads, businesses. Also called a *place of public accommodation*. The *public* quality lies at the heart of constitutional litigation over prohibition of discrimination in *public accommodations* on the basis of race, color, creed, or sex. *Public accommodations* is not frozen; it has sometimes been extended to include organizations with a public right of participation.

public act □see **public law**.

publication: in general, as in ordinary English, making known or available to the public, the noun of the verb *publish*. Special legal usage:

1. (copyright): "[T]he distribution of copies or phonorecords of a work to the public by sale or other transfer of ownership, or by rental, lease, or lending. The offering to distribute copies or phonorecords to a group of persons for purposes of further distribution, public performance, or public display, constitutes publication. A public performance or display of a work does not of itself constitute publication." (Copyright Act of 1976, § 101). □see **copyright**.

limited publication: communication or distribution of a work to a relatively small, selected group, for a limited purpose, and without any right to reproduce, distribute, or sell, e.g., to reviewers, to immediate friends.

For other usage of *publication* and *publish* in copyright law, see *Nimmer on Copyright*.

2. (wills): the statement or acts by which a testator makes known to witnesses at a ceremonial signing that this bundle of papers is intended to be a will. □see **declaration**.

3. □see **defamation**.

publication of summons □see **service of process**.

public convenience and necessity □see **convenience and necessity**.

public corporation □see **corporate**.

public defender □see **lawyer**.

public domain

1. (intellectual material): intellectual material that, under substantive law, is open to everyone's use. This may be something that cannot be personally owned; e.g., the multiplication tables; e.g., an abstract idea; e.g., the intellectual substance of a government publication. Or it may be something that for technical reasons was never, or is no longer, protected under **copyright** (□see) or **patent** (□see) law; e.g., those laws have not been complied with, or copyright or patent has expired. Collectively, this intellectual material constitutes the *public domain*. The individual item is said to be *in the public domain*. The expression *public domain* is in common use in copyright law; the sense, but not the expression, is in common use in patent law.

2. (public lands): land owned by the federal or a state government that is available to the public for outright purchase or for acquisition of other rights, as distinguished from land held for the government's own use. □see **patent**; □see **mining claim**. In this collective sense, *public domain* is often used synonymously with *public lands*. An individual parcel in the public domain is called *public land*.

public figure

1. (defamation): a person who, though not a public official nor a candidate for public office, has a position of substantial influence, or has sought and achieved public prominence. A characterization used in the law of defamation, as modified by constitutional rights of free speech. The effect is to restrict recovery of damages, with a requirement of *actual malice* (□see **public official**) or similarly unreasonable conduct.

2. (privacy): □see **right of privacy.**

public forum: a specific public place, or a type of public place, which by government designation or by tradition has been used at least in part as a place of assembly and free speech, e.g., streets, parks, sidewalks. "Place" is a variable, not necessarily geographical, e.g., a government guidebook.

public forum doctrine: regulation that affects a *public forum* is subject to careful scrutiny to assure that First Amendment rights of access, assembly, and free speech are neither completely denied nor controlled more than narrowly necessary to serve a significant governmental interest. The extent of regulation permitted, as well as what qualifies as a *public forum,* are subjects of continuing constitutional litigation.

public forum doctrine   □see **public forum.**

public interest

1. *the* public interest: what is good, better, or best for the **public** (□see). It is a flexible generality, often described as the *public welfare* or the *public good,* as in the Latin *pro bono publico* (□see, under **lawyer**); sometimes used synonymously with, sometimes distinguished from, **public policy** (□see). *Public interest* appears in statutes, regulations, and decisions across the board, approving (*in* the public interest) or disapproving (*not* in the public interest) the regulation of private business, the interpretation of contracts, the scope of tort law, constitutional limits, etc. It is a variable conclusion, without firm guidelines.

affected with a public interest: an old, vague, criticized, but widely used expression to describe a private enterprise or profession that is or ought to be regulated in some way by some arm of the government. The criteria for being *affected with a public interest* vary with statute and constitutional decision, are often equated with the criteria for exercise of the **police power** (□see). A typical enterprise labeled as *affected with a public interest* is a **public utility** (□see), requiring for operation a certificate of *public convenience and necessity* (□see **convenience and necessity**). The practice of law is often described as being *affected with a public interest;* □see **officer of the court**, under **office**. The state of *being affected with a public interest* is sometimes rendered with bewildering grammatical nicety as *affection.*

2. the public's attention drawn to something. For this popular sense of *public interest,* with a legal twist, □see **right of privacy**.

public interest law firm   □see **lawyer**.

public interest lawyer   □see **lawyer**.

public international law   □see **international law**.

public invitee   □see **invitee**.

public lands   □see **public domain**.

public law

1. a public law: a statute or other law of general application, also called a *public act,* as distinguished from a *private bill* or *private act,* a statute or other law affecting a particular person or entity.

2. a general, unspecific classification of law concerning the state as sovereign. Topics usually included in the classification (the listing here not definitive) are the law of the state's organization, powers, and limits (e.g., constitutional law); its machinery of government (e.g., administrative law); its relations with other states (□see **international law**); its system of criminal justice. The classification also usually includes the various relations between the state and the individuals within the state, as opposed to their relations with each other, sometimes called *private law.* The latter usage is to be distinguished from a private law, usually called a *private statute* or a *special act:* legislation that specifically affects a named person or a small group of persons.

publicly held corporation   □see **corporate**.

publicly owned corporation   □see **corporate**.

publicly perform □see **perform**.

public nuisance □see **nuisance**.

public officer □see **official**, under **office**.

public official: in the law of defamation, as modified by constitutional rights of free speech, a characterization that restricts recovery of damages. The public official (including a candidate for public office) may not recover for defamation relating to official conduct or fitness for office, unless the statement was made with *actual malice*. That expression is defined as "with knowledge that it was false or with reckless disregard of whether it was false or not." (*New York Times Co. v. Sullivan*, 376 U.S. 254, 279–280, 1964). □see **public figure**; □see also, **official**, under **office**; □see also, **malice**.

public performance □see **perform**; □see also, **publication**.

public place: a place that is **public** (□see). The expression is so shaped by statute, context, and particular usage in civil and criminal law as to make general definition worthless. Some principal senses are these:

1. property owned by the government; e.g., a government office building, a public library, a public park.

2. a place where the general public has a right to be; e.g., a public park, a highway, rooms in a government building (sense 1) that are open to the public generally, as opposed, e.g., to storage rooms.

3. private property to which the public usually has access by open invitation of the owners or lessees; e.g., during business hours, the sales or viewing rooms of most businesses—restaurants, theaters, markets, gas stations, pool halls.

4. a place, privately or publicly owned, that is open to the view of the general public, e.g., the show window of a department store in which a person indecently exposes the naked body; a privately owned telephone pole on which official notices are customarily posted.

□see also, **public forum**.

public policy

1. an unspecific way of saying that the attitude and operation of government and the law in general are dictated by principle, not ad

hockery.   <It was a small step in the right direction, in keeping with the public policy of the state.>

2.   the general course of principled action of a government gathered from its constitution, statutes, decisions, and traditions, as a guide in instances or detail not specifically covered.   <This particular restriction is vague, perhaps picayune, but clearly contrary to a longstanding public policy commitment to freedom of the press; I find the ordinance void.>

3.   the specific expression of the underpinning of a statute.   <The legislature declares that it is the public policy of this state to conserve and protect the environment.>

4.   a general synonym for **public interest** (□see).   *Public policy* is sometimes distinguished as being of more particularized application. <This contract is not only contrary to the public interest, but it is in direct conflict with our public policy as expressed in numerous laws against trafficking in drugs.>

public prosecutor   □see **lawyer.**

public purpose

1.   in a general sense: a result broadly beneficial to the **public** (□see), in the **public interest** (□see), that the government is supposed to have in mind in whatever it does. As opposed to serving some private or corrupt purpose. The expression is flexible, not uniformly inter- preted, especially variable as to exactly what constitutes a public purpose when some private advantage appears. Still flexible, the expression is given a sharper legal focus when, as often happens, *public purpose* is identified as a doctrine (sense 2).

2.   **public purpose doctrine**: a standard of public purpose (sense 1) testing the legality, especially the constitutionality, of government action, e.g., taxing, granting tax-exempt status, spending public funds, taking private property. When governmental action directly or indirectly benefits some private interest, e.g., condemning property for a private toll road; e.g., using the power of eminent domain or the power to tax in slum clearance and redevelopment projects, the *public purpose doctrine* may yet find the action constitutional because of an ultimate public benefit (sense 1).

3.   **public use**: the expression used in the **Takings Clause** (□see. □see also, **eminent domain**) is often equated with *public purpose,* often doubled as *public purpose and use.* The expression *public use* is generally said not to require "use by the public," as distinguished from something that is beneficial to the public, as in *public purpose* (senses 1 and 2). For *public use* in patent law, □see **patent.**

public service corporation   □see **public utility**.

public trial: a trial to which the public has access, as opposed to a secret trial. It is the express right of a criminal defendant (Sixth Amendment, applicable to the states under the Fourteenth Amendment); a less firmly entrenched right, access to the trial by public and press, has been recognized under the First Amendment. The rights are subject to limited court control. Under federal and state rules, a parallel right in civil cases, but with considerably more court control, is generally referred to as a right to trial in **open court**.

public use   □see **public purpose**; □see also, **patent**.

public utility: a business enterprise that supplies essential commodities or services to the public, that is required to serve the public, and that is subject to government regulation of its operation and usually its prices and rates. What is "essential" varies with time, place, invention, public demand, and tradition. E.g., commodities such as gas, electricity, water, and power; services such as transportation— rail, air, sea, pipeline, etc.; garbage collection and sewage disposal; all manner of communication—telephone, telegraph, television, fax, etc. □see also, **common carrier**.

What is designated a "public utility" may vary by statute. A *public utility* in corporate form is often referred to as a *public service corporation.*

The "public" of *public utility* refers to the **public** (□see) served, not to ownership. A public utility may be publicly or privately owned.

The "utility" of *public utility* is frequently used as a synonym of *public utility*; the plural *utilities* usually refers to a number of public utilities or their stock. But **utility** can also refer to a business enterprise supplying commodities or services of the sort supplied by public utilities but not subject to public utility regulation. In this sense, a *public utility,* whether publicly or privately owned, is to be distinguished from a **private utility**: a utility that does not serve the public but rather some special private person or group, e.g., a rail line owned and used only by a coal company in its own operations.

□see also, **affected with a public interest**, under **public interest**; □see also, **convenience and necessity**.

public welfare   □see **public interest**.

528

publish: in general, as in ordinary English, to make known or available to the public, the verb of the noun *publication*. Special legal usage:

1. (copyright) □see **publication**.

2. (wills) □see **publication**.

3. □see **defamation**.

4. (forgery and counterfeiting): to put forged papers or counterfeit money into circulation, usually described by the verb **utter**, sometimes as *utter and publish*.

puffing □see **dealer's talk**.

punishment □see **penal**; □see **sentence**; □see also, **bill of attainder**; □see also, **capital punishment**, under **execute**; □see also, **crime**; □see also, **cruel and unusual punishment**; □see also, **punitive damages**, under **damage**.

punitive damages □see, under **damage**.

pur autre vie □see **estate**.

purchase • purchaser □see **buy**; □see **bona fide purchaser**; □see **purchaser for value**; □see **vendor and purchaser**, under **sell**; □see **words of purchase**.

purchase money mortgage □see **buy**.

purchase price □see **buy**.

purchaser □see **buy**; □see **bona fide purchaser**; □see **purchaser for value**; □see **vendor and purchaser**, under **sell**; □see **words of purchase**.

purchaser for value: a person who has given **value** (□see) for property received. The expression is loosely used. Sometimes it is another way of saying **bona fide purchaser** (□see); sometimes of describing a transaction involving the giving of value, but without the required good faith. Sometimes part of a special statutory definition.

pure comparative negligence □see contributory negligence.

purge of contempt □see contempt.

purpose □see legislative purpose, under intent.

purpresture: a private enclosure of, or encroachment or obstruction on, land or waters owned or controlled by the government. E.g., front steps of a private home extending onto the public sidewalk; a dry dock on state tidal waters. <The dock was a purpresture.>

With some variation by state, a *purpresture* is usually a *purpresture* whether or not it is an unreasonable interference with the rights of the public that could also make it a **public nuisance** (□see).

put □see option.

putative

1. the ordinary English sense of *reputed;* or *supposed;* as in *putative marriage* and *putative spouse.* □see **cohabit.**

2. might become. A recent legal usage that ignores both Latin origin and ordinary English (sense 1). E.g., a *putative client,* a *putative lawyer:* not a client, not a lawyer, but might become one.

putative marriage □see cohabit.

putative spouse □see cohabit.

put in an appearance □see enter; □see appear.

put off □see delay.

put on notice □see have notice, under notice.

put up collateral □see collateral.

Q

quaere

    1. the Latin spelling of *query*: a writer's expression of doubt that someone else's legal conclusion is as sound as it is made to appear. <The court said that this was moot. But *quaere.*/. . . . *Quaere.*> Less often, directed at the writer's own conclusions, an almost unique expression of legal modesty.

    2. orally, with the dying spelling out of sight, and pronounced *query*, the traditional introduction to a lecturer's hypothetical question. <Query [*Quaere*] what the result would be if. . . .>

qualified fee ☐see **fee simple.**

qualified immunity ☐see **immunity;** ☐see **absolutes.**

qualified privilege ☐see **privilege**, under **immunity;** ☐see **absolutes.**

quantum meruit (L., quantum MER-oo-it: as much as he has deserved).

    1. at common law, the Latin rendering of one of the **common counts** (☐see **count**), usually for work done but, loosely, also for services and goods.

    2. in many states, the Latin expression is still used to describe an action for damages due for services or goods, or both, when the action is not on an express contract. ☐see **quasi contract.**

quantum valebant (L., quantum vuh-LAY-bant: as much as they were worth). The expression is sometimes rendered *quantum valebat* (L., quantum vuh-LAY-but: as much as it was worth).

    1. at common law, the Latin rendering of one of the **common counts** (☐see **count**), for goods sold and delivered.

    2. rarely used today, its common law distinction swallowed up in **quantum meruit** (☐see).

quantum valebat ☐see **quantum valebant.**

quash: to void an earlier court order, legal process, or something done without compliance with proper legal procedure. E.g., a defective service of summons; publication of summons without statutory authority; a defective subpoena, indictment, etc. A court order to quash is usually made in response to a *motion to quash.*

vacate or **set aside** often serves in place of *quash.* One or another may be used in special contexts; e.g., *quash an indictment* but *vacate* (or *set aside*) *a judgment;* e.g., *quash* restricted to defects that are apparent, as opposed to a more general use of *vacate* and *set aside.* Procedure and usage vary by jurisdiction.

For noun usage, with *quash,* most lawyers are content with the participle *quashing;* some opt for the esoteric *quashal.* For *vacate,* the companion noun is almost as peculiar—*vacation;* less confusing is *setting aside.*

quasi (L.: as if, just as, as it were, about, nearly, almost): in some ways, something like something else. That deliberately loose definition reflects loose usage in Latin, looser usage in ordinary English, and a history of wobble in the law. *Quasi* is a temptation to innovation; specimens of commoner usage are separate entries in the dictionary. Usage with or without a hyphen is standard for some expressions, e.g., *quasi-contract* and *quasi contract;* not for others, e.g., *quasi in rem.*

quasi-community property □see **community property**.

quasi contract: a misleading name for a type of obligation imposed by law for "reasons of justice," most often to end an "unjust" benefit to one person at another's expense. E.g., A steals B's auto and sells it for $1,000. A is obligated by quasi contract (a *quasi contractual obligation*) to pay B $1,000. □see **restitution**.

Quasi contract (also spelled *quasi-contract*) is "something like" a contract only in terms of archaic common law procedure; the name inherited, the procedure usually rejected. In Latinate terms, it would be better described as *non quasi contract* (not as if a contract). An imposed obligation (sometimes fictitiously called an *implied promise*), as distinguished from the voluntary nature of contract, quasi contract is *not* a contract or anything like it. The name persists, and it is sometimes included in procedural statutes relating to contracts, e.g., a statute of limitations. *Quasi contract,* the obligation, is sometimes referred to as *a* quasi contract; sometimes the expression also describes the legal remedy, a theory of recovery, the field of law that deals with the imposed obligation. *Quasi contract* also travels under other names:

implied contract: a loose umbrella word for two disparate expressions, a *contract implied-in-fact* (also called an *implied-in-fact contract*) and a *contract implied-in-law* (also called an *implied-in-law contract*). Sometimes, in confused and confusing disregard of the dichotomy, *quasi contract* is simply referred to as an *implied contract*.

contract implied-in-fact: in all respects an ordinary contract, except that it is proved not by a writing or words in a usual form of contract but rather by actions, custom, course of dealing, etc. This is not a quasi contract.

contract implied-in-law usage varies by jurisdiction, courts, and commentators:

a. Often used synonymously with *quasi contract*. <It was a contract-implied-in-law or quasi contract.>

b. Often replaced by *quasi contract,* as a welcomed ending of the confusion with that other implied contract, the contract implied-in-fact.

c. Sometimes describes a particular obligation imposed by law in a statute or regulation, whether or not for "reasons of justice," and differentiated on this ground from quasi contract.

constructive contract: another name for a *quasi contract* or a *contract implied-in-law.*

quasi-easement   □see **easement.**

quasi in rem   □see **in rem.**

quasi-judicial immunity   □see **judicial immunity,** under **immunity.**

question of fact   □see **mixed question of law and fact.**

question of law   □see **mixed question of law and fact.**

quia timet (L.: because he fears): the classification of an action brought to prevent anticipated damage. E.g., to cancel a note that has been paid but not surrendered. An equitable remedy, sometimes still known as a *bill quia timet.* Declaratory judgments (□see **declara-**

tory, under **declaration**) and suits to **quiet title** (□see) often invoke the element of anticipated damage.

quick-take   □see **condemnation**, under **eminent domain**.

quid pro quo   □see **contract**.

quiet enjoyment   □see **covenant**; □see also, **let or hindrance**.

quiet title   □see **in rem**; □see also, **cloud on title**; □see also, **quia timet**.

qui facit per alium facit per se   □see **agency**; □see also, **maxims**.

quit   □see **notice to pay rent or quit**, under **notice**; □see **notice to quit**, under **notice**; □see **quitclaim**.

qui tam   (L., KWEE tam: who as well): a civil action started by a private person under a statute that includes a penalty that is to be divided between the private person and the government.   E.g., a penalty for a false claim against the government.   Historically, sometimes still, the private person is called the "informer."   The action is brought "as well" for the government as for the informer.   *Qui tam* is the name of the action and its description.   <Properly used, *qui tam* aids law enforcement./It was a *qui tam action*./They were *qui tam litigants*. >   □see also, **whistleblower**.

quitclaim   (n., v.)

1. a transfer of whatever rights the transferor has in property, especially real property, with the implicit warning that the transferor may have no rights at all.   Often used to clear uncertainties about title.   What is transferred is traditionally described as all of the transferor's *right, title, and interest,* without differentiation of those terms; the ancient and continuing sense of *quitclaim* being that everything goes, if there is anything.   <Whatever she owns is by way of quitclaim. >   □see **coupled synonyms**.

2. the instrument by which the transfer (sense 1) is made, called either a *quitclaim* or a *quitclaim deed.*   <He refused to warrant title but was prepared to execute a quitclaim./ . . . a quitclaim deed.>

3. the operative verb of transfer of rights (sense 1).   The traditional operative words are *remise, release, and quitclaim,* without differentiation of those terms, often with an extra redundancy . . . *forever quitclaim.* The essential and sufficient word is *quitclaim.* <J.D. quitclaimed Blackacre to R.R./J.D. remised, released, and quitclaimed Blackacre to R.R.> □see **coupled synonyms.**

4. less often used in another historic sense, a renunciation of claims for money, i.e., you are now *quit* (free) of my *claims.* □see **release.**

quitclaim deed □see **quitclaim.**

quorum: the number of those entitled to vote who must be present at a meeting or session of a group, organization, or court in order to do business. The requisite number is fixed by constitution (e.g., U.S. Const., Art. I, § 5, cl. 1), legislation, or the rules of the particular unit.

quotient verdict: a verdict arrived at by a civil jury that has agreed in advance to award damages by adding their individual preferences and dividing the total by the number of jurors. The expression is sometimes also applied to advance agreement to a similar formula for fixing of fine or imprisonment in a criminal case. □see **impeach a verdict,** under **impeach.** □see also, **chance verdict,** under **verdict.**

quo warranto (L.: by what warrant): the name of the proceeding and the pleading by which the state challenges the legality of the use of an office, franchise, charter, or other right that can be held or used only under authority of the state. E.g., to remove a person who illegally holds public office; to dissolve a corporation functioning with an expired charter; to revoke a misused or abandoned franchise; to nullify an illegal amendment to a municipal charter.

The historic name of the pleading that starts the proceeding—the *writ of quo warranto*—is one of the *extraordinary writs,* also called *prerogative writs* (□see **extraordinary**). In jurisdictions where other statutory procedures serve the same function—proceedings *in the nature of quo warranto,* lawyers often refer to the proceeding and the pleading as *quo warranto.*

R

®: "the letter R enclosed within a circle," the symbol that is an alternative to "Registered in the U.S. Patent and Trademark Office" or "Reg. U.S. Pat. & Tm. Off.," giving notice that the accompanying trademark is registered. (See 15 USCA § 1111; amended to 1988.) □see **trademark**.

racket □see **racketeering**.

racketeer □see **racketeering**.

racketeering

1. crime organized as a large-scale, money-making business ("organized crime"), characterized by routine violence (murder, kidnapping, robbery, arson) in enforcement of demands, intimidating threats of violence, extortion, blackmail, and bribery. This is the underworld of "shakedown" and "protection," run by *racketeers*, also called "hoodlums," "mobsters," "Mafia," or plain "crooks," their varied illegal operations known as *rackets* or *the rackets*. This is the popular and also an imprecise legal understanding of old-style *racketeering*—evil and defamatory.

2. new-style *racketeering* has as its centerpiece the *Racketeer Influenced and Corrupt Organizations Act* (18 USCA §§ 1961–1968, 1970, as amended 1988), known as *RICO*. The stigmatizing name and its substance includes old-style (sense 1) racketeering, but RICO is not limited to organized crime. It is broad enough to include a "legitimate" business, that eschews the violence of old-style racketeering, but may profit through a "pattern of racketeering activity" in such offenses as mail, wire, and securities fraud, or money laundering. On the criminal side, RICO imposes ordinary penalties, but also permits government seizure and forfeiture of racketeering income. RICO also authorizes private civil actions, with treble damages, costs, and attorney fees, and the use of the dread words *racketeer* and *racketeering*.

raider □see **takeover**.

rainmaker: the partner who brings in the business; others take care of it.

raise

1. to conclude that pleadings or evidence tentatively or decisively establish something of legal consequence in a lawsuit. <The pleadings raised the issue of fraud./His prolonged and unexplained absence was sufficient to raise a presumption of death.>

2. to bring to the attention of court or jury something of legal consequence in a lawsuit. <In opening for the defense, she raised the question of mental illness.>

R.A.P.: abbreviation of **rule against perpetuities** (□see).

rape: the essence of the crime is sexual intercourse by a male with a female who is not his wife and without her consent. Lack of consent is variously demonstrated; e.g., his force or threat; her resistance; her inability to consent by being underage, unconscious, or her will overpowered by his imposition (drugs, intoxicants, etc.).

Definition is in flux and not uniform. Two of the principal variations: (a) a female may rape a male by force; (b) either spouse may rape the other. Related sexual offenses are similarly defined, with variations on the element of **penetration** (□see).

statutory rape: sexual intercourse by a male with a female with or without her consent, if the female is under an age fixed by statute and is not his wife. The expression, when still used, is to be distinguished from **rape** (□see, above, in this entry), which is usually defined by statute.

rap sheet: a police record of a person's undesired encounters with the criminal law (arrests, charges, convictions, sentences), and of other personal information useful in the detection of crime, prosecution, sentencing, parole, etc. Rap sheet information is computerized and exchanged by law enforcement agencies.

ratification

1. a retroactive grant of authority: an approval of someone else's unauthorized act, which then becomes as effective, or binding upon the person approving, as though authorized at the time of the act. The noun of the verb to *ratify*. <Her ratification of the unauthorized signing of the contract by her agent made the contract effective on the date signed.>

2. a retroactive validation of one's own act: an approval when no longer under a disability (e.g., duress) that rendered the act void or voidable, the approval now making one's own act valid.

3. an approval required by law or agreement to make someone else's act effective. E.g., specified form of *ratification* of the U.S. Constitution (Art. VII); e.g., specified form of *ratification* of amendments to the Constitution (Art. V); e.g., provisions in a corporate charter for stockholder *ratification* of specified corporate acts.

Ratification and *ratify* in this sense may also refer to a required approval that is expressed in different words. E.g., the Senate *ratifies* a treaty; but the Constitution speaks of the President acting with "advice and consent of the Senate" and a requisite vote to "concur." (Art. II, § 2, cl. 2).

ratify □see **ratification.**

rational basis □see **standards of review.**

re □see **in re.**

ready, willing, and able □see **tender;** □see **procuring cause.**

real covenant □see **covenant running with the land,** under **covenant.**

real estate □see **land;** □see also, **real property,** under **property.**

real evidence • demonstrative evidence

Often considered synonyms; sometimes used repetitively as *real or demonstrative evidence.* Sometimes distinctions are drawn, one expression excluding the other. Whether called by one name or the other or both, they deal with *thing* evidence (L.: *realis,* from *res*: thing). Neither expression is precise. Lawyers cannot agree on the name nor on what *thing* should go by either name. One thing is certain: "This is real evidence" can create trouble enough lawyer-to-lawyer, utter confusion elsewhere. It may not be the *real thing* (□see **actual**). □see **evidence.**

1. broadly, either expression: physical things, as evidence. Usually distinguished from testimony. This broad sense may include anything physical. E.g., a murder weapon, a defective motor, a broken arm, an original writing, a diagram prepared for the courtroom, a plaster model, a working model, a laboratory experiment, a witness's demeanor.

2. narrowly, **real evidence**: physical things that were involved in what happened, in the events that brought the case to court. In this restricted sense, *real evidence* is distinguished from *demonstrative evidence* (sense 3) and is also called *original evidence*. E.g., the murder weapon, the defective motor, the broken arm, the original writing.

3. narrowly, **demonstrative evidence**: physical things presented to the trier of fact but not the original things that were involved in what happened. E.g., a diagram prepared for the courtroom, a plaster model, a working model, a laboratory experiment, a witness's demeanor. In this restricted sense, *demonstrative evidence* is distinguished from *real evidence* (sense 2).

4. **real evidence** as a catchall; with all evidence divided into three classes: testimony, documentary, and everything else—real.

real party in interest □see **party**.

real property □see **property**; □see also, **land**.

realty □see **land**.

reargument: a loose term for limited, additional argument, sometimes by additional lawyers, of facts or law omitted or neglected at a **hearing** (□see). Usually, not always, distinguished from a **rehearing**: a full-scale reargument and reconsideration of a case or an issue dealt with at an earlier hearing; now to be argued and considered in the light of things previously overlooked or slighted, e.g., decision, statute, regulations, or consequences.

reasonable means in the law what it means in ordinary English: rational, just, fair-minded, not too much and not too little, etc. *Reasonable* means what you want it to mean; in the words of Ambrose Bierce, "Hospitable to persuasion, dissuasion and evasion." (*The Devil's Dictionary*). *Reasonable* has no precise legal meaning. It is flexible. That is its virtue and only utility for the law.

reasonable and probable cause: a redundancy. □see **probable cause**.

reasonable care □see **due care**, under **due**; □see also, **negligence**.

reasonable cause □see probable cause.

reasonable certainty: sort of **certain** (□see). The expression does little to improve on the uncertain rigors of *certainty*. Not quite as ambiguous as *reasonable uncertainty*.

reasonable doubt □see beyond a reasonable doubt.

reasonable fee □see fee (attorney's fee).

reasonable force: a vague limitation on the degree of force permissible in some circumstances, e.g., in self-defense; in making an arrest. Contrasted with the equally vague, impermissible *excessive force*.

reasonable grounds: a less standard expression, often used as the equivalent of **probable cause** (□see). Also rendered *reasonable ground*.

reasonable man: the law's hypothetical creature who has what society tends to regard as a normal dose of virtue and acceptable frailty. The *reasonable man*'s hypothetical action, reaction, or lethargy in any situation is the law's standard of reasonable conduct for real people in similar circumstances. □see **due care**, under **due**; □see **negligence**.

The *reasonable man* also goes by other names, e.g., an *ordinarily reasonable man*, a *reasonable man of ordinary prudence*, and is frequently equated with varieties of **prudent man** (□see). But the *reasonable man* is more active in tort law (especially negligence) and criminal law than in the typical business life of the *prudent man*.

reasonable person: everything that a *reasonable man* ever was or hoped to be, without what some regard as a sexist taint (□see **sex**). Never restricted to males, *reasonable man* now faces fierce competition. *Reasonable person* is often the substitute of choice in treatises, miscellaneous writing, and in numerous opinions. Yet the announced death of the *reasonable man* is an exaggeration. A requiem is premature. *Reasonable man* is imbedded in history, in far-flung legislation, legal literature, and in decision old and new. It lurks in nooks and crannies of the law beyond reach of outlawry. It cannot be ignored.

reasonable person □see reasonable man.

reasonable time   □see **time.**

reasonably possible: a marvel of imprecise guesswork and a counter to the quest for **absolutes** (□see).

reasonably probable: a judge's loose calculation of the odds favoring a particular outcome.   E.g., that the defendant would have been acquitted if her lawyer had not dozed.

rebuttable presumption   □see **presumption.**

received   □see **had and received.**

received in evidence   □see **evidence.**

receive notice   □see **notice.**

receiver: a person appointed by a court as temporary custodian to preserve property involved in litigation, pending ultimate determination of distribution, e.g., in divorce, dissolution of a corporation, assets of an incompetent or an insolvent.   Appointment and function of a receiver are under an equitable remedy called *receivership,* usually regulated by statute.   That expression can also refer to a business or the property *in receivership.*   A *receiver* is to be distinguished from the office of a *trustee in bankruptcy* under the bankruptcy laws of the United States (□see **bankruptcy**).

receivership   □see **receiver.**

receiving stolen goods   □see **receiving stolen property.**

receiving stolen property: the crime of receiving property knowing it to be stolen and intending to deprive the owner of the property. Definition and nomenclature vary by jurisdiction, e.g., as to what forms of unlawful conduct are encompassed in the use of the word *stolen.*   In some jurisdictions, the same crime is known as *receiving stolen goods,* a reminder that French *property* and Old English *goods* were once general synonyms.   In colloquial or underworld jargon, the crime is *fencing,* the receiver a *fence.*

recent fabrication   □see **prior consistent statement.**

recess   □see **stand recessed,** under **stand adjourned;** □see also, **delay.**

recidivist: an habitual criminal.   □see **criminal,** under **convict.**

reciprocal discovery   □see **discovery.**

reciprocal wills   □see **will.**

reciprocity: the ordinary English word for an exchange of favors or benefits; as in the political expression *logrolling* and the colloquial *back scratching* ("You scratch my back; I'll scratch yours.")   In the law, *reciprocity* of various sorts, especially:

1.   between states of the United States, or between nations: extending to the citizens of another state or nation privileges or benefits which that state or nation extends to our citizens.   E.g., driving with an out-of-state license; relaxed rules on admission of out-of-state lawyers; entering a foreign country without visa or passport.

2.   between businesses: preferential exchange of benefits.   □see **antitrust law.**

recital: words of introduction to a contract, statute, proclamation, or other writing.   Fact, law, homespun morality (reason, purpose, evil to be cured, etc.) are joined in a bundle called *the recitals,* all intended to create an atmosphere of reason or uplift for the details that follow. Whether or not a recital binds anyone is still litigated.   That uncertainty is worsened when the recital appears in traditional form: introduced by its own **Whereas** (□see), as needless as the recital itself.

recite: to write the words of introduction that constitute a **recital** (□see).   <After reciting ten paragraphs of reasons, they got down to the specific agreements.>

reckless   □see **recklessness.**

recklessness: conduct in the never precisely defined area between intentional wrongdoing (□see **intent**) and **negligence** (□see).   Generally, recklessness is characterized by an indifference—"utter," "callous," "wanton" indifference—to a risk of harm substantially beyond the bounds of the reasonable. Definitions are not uniform. Lawyers still grope for that just right word of opprobrium to describe conduct that is worse than negligence but has not quite passed the point of no return into intentional wrong. Some call it "gross" or "very gross" negligence. Some call it "willful, wanton, or reckless"—all three or any one of the trio. Some say it is a "gross deviation" from the reasonable; etc. The law here attempts, with lack of uniform success, to convert a myriad of factual, mental, and physical states into degrees of misconduct that can attain some sort of measurable objectivity. Definition varies by jurisdiction, by court, by writer, by the particular legal context of *reckless, recklessly,* or *recklessness,* and the consequences in terms of damages, punishment, discipline, or loss of license. E.g., in general tort law; in defamation with *actual malice* (□see **public official**); in *criminal negligence* (□see **manslaughter**); in a variety of special statutes on *reckless driving,* guest passengers, etc.

recognizance   □see **bail.**

recollection   □see **past recollection recorded.**

record   (n., v.): the ordinary English word. With these legal usages under separate entries:

attorney of record □see **lawyer;**

court of record □see **court;**

dimunition of record;

estoppel by record □see **estoppel;**

for the record;

in the record □see **in evidence,** under **evidence;**

let the record show □see **enter an objection,** under **enter;** □see also, **for the record;**

official records □see **of record;**

off the record;

of record;

on the record;

party of record □see **of record;**

record title □see **title.**

recorded

recorded □see **of record;** □see also, **enter.**

recorded recollection □see **past recollection recorded.**

recoup □see **recoupment.**

recoupment: a defendant's right to reduce (*recoup*) plaintiff's claims, by the amount of defendant's claims against plaintiff arising out of the same transaction. Definitions vary by jurisdiction. Often equated with *counterclaim* (□see **cross-complaint,** under **cross-**) and *setoff* (□see **offset**).

recourse □see **without recourse,** under **nonrecourse.**

recover • recovery

As distinguished from legal use of ordinary English *recover*—to get something *back,* the prime legal sense is to *get* something, usually by suit, sometimes by settlement, less often by threat of suit. What you recover—most often damages—is called, as a general term, the *recovery.* Items and limits of what can be recovered (*recoverable*) vary by statute and jurisdiction, by the type of suit, by the provisions of an agreement, e.g., an insurance policy. <We had to sue to recover anything./We recovered judgment./The recovery was $50,000, plus costs.>

recovery □see **recover.**

recrimination: in an action for divorce, a defense that the defendant has a cause of action for divorce against the plaintiff. Where the defense is permitted, in its strictest form, if both spouses have a cause of action for divorce, neither can obtain a divorce. Some states have modified, some have abolished the defense.

recross □see **cross-examination,** under **cross-.**

recross examination □see **cross-examination,** under **cross-.**

recusal □see **disqualify.**

recuse □see **disqualify.**

redeem

Redeem (v.), *redeemable* (adj.), and *redemption* (n.), in varied contexts, have, in general, two discrete legal senses.

1. to get back possession of one's encumbered property, a clear title, or both. Typical forms:

a. routine payment of a debt to a secured creditor. E.g., a debt secured by a **pledge** (□see) or a **mortgage** (□see).

b. curing a default and paying the debt to a secured creditor. E.g., □see **equity of redemption.**

c. on delinquent taxes, e.g., property taxes, details regulated by statute, typical paths to redemption:

(1) curing a default by paying the delinquent tax, interest, and penalties to the taxing authorities;

(2) on property sold because of delinquency, buying back one's property from the purchaser at the tax sale.

2. purchase by a corporation of its own redeemable bonds or stock. Typical forms:

a. *redeemable bonds:* those issued, expressly made *redeemable,* also said to be *callable,* i.e., subject to purchase (*redemption*) by the corporation before maturity. Details of price, time, notice, etc., specified in the bond.

b. *redeemable stock:* When provided by corporate articles and permitted by law, some stock—typically preferred, sometimes common—is issued, expressly made *redeemable* on specified terms. Redemption of redeemable stock is distinguished from the usual power of a corporation to purchase its stock within limitations of general corporation laws.

redeemable   □see **redeem.**

redeemable bonds   □see **redeem.**

redeemable stock   □see **redeem.**

redemption   □see **redeem.**

redirect   □see **cross-examination,** under **cross-.**

redirect examination   □see **cross-examination**, under **cross-**.

red light abatement laws: a general category of laws directed especially at preventing regular use of premises as a house of prostitution
(once identified by a red light).   Varying by jurisdiction, the category
joins with prevention of prostitution, prevention of other specified
regular uses of premises, e.g., for an illegal gambling house; e.g., for a
public swimming pool where sexual conduct might spread AIDS.   *Red
light* is also spelled *red-light*.   □see **nuisance**.

redlining: discriminatory business practices influenced more, or entirely, by the customer's being located within a particular *redlined*
neighborhood than by the individual customer's characteristics.   E.g.,
redlining may affect decisions to insure or not (or how much), to lend
or not (or how much), and the respective rates.   *Redlining* is also
spelled *red-lining*.

reduction to practice   □see **patent**.

reentry   □see **fee simple**.

referee   □see **master**.

reference   □see **master**.

reform: to correct a writing to make it correspond to what had been
agreed upon.   E.g., to correct a clerical error; e.g., to correct a mistake of the parties in a description of land.   Suit to *reform* a writing is
an equitable remedy called *reformation*.

reformation   □see **reform**.

refreshed recollection   □see **past recollection recorded**.

refuse   □see **fail**.

registered trademark   □see ®; □see **trademark**.

regs: in common oral use, short for **regulations** (□see, under **regulate**).

regular course of business: usual, normal, customary way of doing business. Significant in varied contexts, e.g., business records, employment, banking. As with the comparable *ordinary course of business* (□see **ordinary**), statutes often use particularized definitions.

regular dividend □see **dividend**.

regular on its face: of a writing apparently genuine. □see also, **fair on its face**, under **face**.

regulate

1. to control or direct any activity. This is the general word, in the law as in ordinary English—useful, flexible, imprecise.

2. to exercise control over a particular activity in accordance with specific authority given by law. E.g., congressional control over commerce "among" the states (□see **Commerce Clause**); Interstate Commerce Commission (ICC) control over interstate commerce under statute and decision; Securities and Exchange Commission (SEC) control over the securities market under statute and decision; a city zoning commission's control over zoning under state and city authority.

3. **regulation**

   a. the noun of the verb *regulate* (senses 1 and 2). <Regulation of the disposal of atomic waste is inadequate.>

   b. a device used in regulating (especially in sense 2): detailed rule or procedure, typically issued by a department or agency of government, to be followed, or as a guide, in conducting a particular activity. Most common in the plural *regulations,* orally shortened to *regs.* E.g., the Code of Federal Regulations; e.g., the Federal Tax Regulations issued by the Treasury Department. A *regulation* is sometimes called a *rule,* sometimes—without change of meaning—referred to as *rules and regulations.*

4. *regulatory* (adj.): characterizing *regulation* (3.a.) in general. For the special sense of **regulatory agency**, □see **administrative agency**, under **administrative law**.

regulation □see **regulate**.

regulations □see **regulate**.

regulatory □see **regulate**.

regulatory agency □see **administrative agency**, under **administrative law**.

rehabilitate: the verb, and its companion noun *rehabilitation,* in the ordinary English sense of restoring to former capacity, is used in a variety of expectable legal contexts, e.g., restoration of health or solvency. The ordinary English sense of restoring good repute takes two especially legal forms:

rehabilitate a witness: to introduce evidence to neutralize or destroy opposing evidence that tends to cast doubt on the witness's testimony or to impeach the witness's credibility.

certificate of rehabilitation: a document issued by a court after a hearing: a sort of diploma evidencing that a person convicted and punished has been rehabilitated and is fit for restoration to good standing in the community, as, e.g., by way of a pardon. In some jurisdictions, the certificate may bar impeachment of a witness for a conviction covered by the certificate.

rehabilitate a witness □see **rehabilitate**.

rehabilitation □see **rehabilitate**.

rehearing: within limits fixed by local rules, a further **hearing** (□see) to consider errors in an earlier hearing. When procedure or scope of error permits or requires a completely new hearing, as though none had been held, the usual term is not rehearing but *hearing de novo* (L.: over again from the beginning).

relation □see **relative**, under **heirs**.

relation back

1. to consider something done now as having been done at an earlier time. E.g., time of delivery of deed to buyer considered to be at the time of deposit in escrow. E.g., a document considered recorded when handed to the recorder, although not of record until later. □see also, **nunc pro tunc**. □see also, **ab initio**.

2. to consider something done now valid because it relates to something done earlier. E.g., an amendment to pleadings permissible now

548

because it relates to the pleading of the original cause of action, not to a new cause of action.

relationship of confidence   □see **fiduciary**.

relative   □see **heirs**.

relator   □see **ex rel.**

relatrix   □see **ex rel.**; □see **sex**.

release   (v., n.)

1. to wipe out, or—more elegantly—to extinguish a right or claim to something.

   a. This may be done intentionally by the one who has the right or claim.   <I released him from the obligation to repay the loan.>   □see also, **quitclaim**.

   b. Similarly, it may be done intentionally by those who have rights or claims that affect each other.   <I release you and you release me.>   See sense 3 for *mutual release*.

   c. Or it may be done by some act, whether or not intended to wipe out a right or claim, but which has that legal effect.   <Her release of A as a matter of law released B.>   See sense 3 for *release by operation of law*.

2. to be freed of an obligation or liability. This describes the effect of a release in sense 1.   <I was released from my obligation to repay the loan./I was released from any further liability for tort damages.>

3. the act of wiping out a right or claim, or the act of freeing someone of an obligation or liability, or a writing that embodies the act.   <The release was effective January 1./The release was dated January 1.>

   mutual release: an intentional release that runs both ways (sense 1.b.).

   release by operation of law: under circumstances determined by the substantive law of contract, suretyship, or torts, the release of one person may release another. E.g., release of one joint obligor or one joint tortfeasor may have the effect of releasing the others. □see **tortfeasor**.

4. to free from restraint or custody. □see **bail**.

549

release by operation of law □see release.

release on bail □see bail.

release on own recognizance □see bail.

relevant: a shorthand reference to **relevant evidence**: evidence that has a tendency to make it either more or less probable that a particular fact exists that is of consequence in a lawsuit. (See Rule 401, Federal Rules of Evidence.) If not relevant, the evidence is *irrelevant*. □see also, **immaterial**; □see also, **incompetent, irrelevant, immaterial**, under **competent**.

relevant evidence □see relevant.

reliction □see accretion.

relief □see demand.

Religion Clauses: a reference to the parts of the U.S. Constitution called the **Establishment Clause** (□see) and the **Free Exercise Clause** (□see), not to the **Religious Test Clause** (□see). *Religion Clauses* is itself sometimes rendered *Religious Clauses*. □see also, **constitutional clauses**.

Religion Test Clause □see Religious Test Clause.

Religious Clauses □see Religion Clauses.

Religious Test Clause: the part of the U.S. Constitution reading: ". . . but no religious test shall ever be required as a qualification to any office or public trust under the United States." (Art. VI). The *Religious Test Clause* is also called the *Religion Test Clause*. □see also, **Religious Clauses**. □see also, **constitutional clauses**.

rem □see in rem.

remainder □see future interest.

550

remainderman □see **remainder**, under **future interest**.

remand (v., n.): to send a case back from a reviewing court to a lower court for further proceedings. E.g., on a **reversal** (□see). <Remanded for further proceedings consistent with this opinion./After remand, the trial court set a date for a hearing.>

remedial: ordinary English—affording a remedy. □see **civil remedies**, under **civil**; □see **equitable remedy**, under **equity**; □see also, **provisional remedy**. □see also, **remedial statute**.

remedial statute

1. a statute that provides a **civil remedy** (□see, under **civil**), as contrasted with a penal statute. Sometimes used to stress that it is a statute dealing with procedure, as distinguished from substantive rights.

2. often used synonymously with **curative statute**: one that is intended to cure or remedy a technical defect, inadvertent omission, or what is now regarded as a mistake in an earlier statute. The statute is usually retroactive.

3. loosely used to describe a statute that fills a gap in the law, i.e., "There oughta be a law on that," and this is it.

remedy □see **civil remedies**, under **civil**; □see **equitable remedy**, under **equity**; □see also, **provisional remedy**.

remise, release, and quitclaim □see **quitclaim**.

remittitur (L.: (it) is remitted)

1. a procedure for reducing a jury's excessive award of damages: A court makes an order denying a motion for a new trial conditioned on the winning party (who won too much) consenting to a specified reduction of damages; otherwise, the motion to be granted. The term *remittitur* can refer to the procedure, the device, the power, the order, or to the winner's *remission* of the excess. In some usage, the Latin is omitted, supplanted by ordinary English *reduce* or *reduction.*

   additur (L.: (it) is added to): in some jurisdictions, by a procedure converse to *remittitur,* denial of a motion for a new trial is conditioned on the losing party (who didn't lose enough) consenting to a

remittitur

specified increase of damages. Usage parallels *remittitur*, the Latin sometimes supplanted by *add to, addition,* or *increase.*

2. the communication of a decision or instruction to a lower court. <The remittitur came down yesterday.> In some jurisdictions, the same sense is rendered by **mandate** (□see). The term *remittitur* can refer to the judgment of the higher court, or to the writing, that sends the case to a lower court. The expression may also refer to sending a record to the lower court: *remittitur* of the record.

remote: not near in time, space, or relationship. The law finds this flexible word useful, slightly narrowing the ordinary English to say that something is *not near enough.* E.g., *remote* because not near enough to be a **proximate cause** (□see), a significant element of damages (□see **damage**), of much weight or relevance as evidence (□see **evidence**; □see **relevant**).

removal (of a case): moving a case from a state court to a federal court, most commonly at a civil defendant's request on the ground of diversity of citizenship or that a federal question is involved. (□see **diversity jurisdiction, under jurisdiction;** □see **federal question.**) Removal is permitted in some prosecutions, in some instances on the initiative of the trial judge, and on specified grounds other than diversity and federal question. (See 28 USCA §§ 1441–1444.) Some cases cannot be removed (28 USCA § 1445). *Removal* (as distinct from numerous legal contexts for that ordinary English word) is often shorthand for what is also referred to as *removal of —causes, —cases, —actions, —prosecutions.* Lawyers ring the changes on the simple word *remove:* A litigant, the *removing party,* petitions for *removal,* invoking *removal jurisdiction.* The case is *removed, removable,* or *nonremovable.* When a case is *removed,* that is the preferred term, rather than the vaguer *moved* or the more general *transferred.* In some loose and confusing usage, *removal* is equated with **change of venue** (□see, under **venue**). □see also, **separable controversy.**

removal of causes □see **removal (of a case).**

remove □see **removal (of a case).**

render

1. to announce a result, as in *render judgment* (less formally, *give judgment*) or *render a verdict* (less formally, *bring in a verdict*). The companion noun is *rendition.*

552

render judgment is sometimes equated with *enter judgment* (□see **enter**). It is often distinguished: referring to the judge's announcement, as opposed to the clerk's entry. Local statute or decision can make synonymity or distinction critical; e.g., when a period is computed from the time a judgment is rendered or entered.

2. to surrender a person for extradition. <The governor rendered the fugitive.> The companion noun *rendition* is frequently used as a synonym of *extradition,* especially in the expression **interstate rendition.** □see **extradition.**

render a verdict   □see **render**; □see **verdict.**

render judgment   □see **render**; □see **judgment.**

rendition   □see **render**; □see **extradition.**

rent   □see **lease.**

rent-a-judge

1. a special form of dispute resolution patterned on reference for trial (□see **master**): Where permitted by local law, parties to a suit filed, or about to be filed, request a court to name a particular "judge," typically a judge retired on a pension, to hear and determine their dispute in private, usually subject to appeal. The parties agree to pay the judge a specified hourly or daily "rent" for the judging services. Typically, the system is much faster than crowded metropolitan public courts in getting to a hearing and to a decision. *Rent-a-judge* (as in *rent-a-car*) is the popular name, increasingly part of informal legal usage. It is also called *private judging* and *private justice.*

2. a judge who participates in the rent-a-judge system (sense 1).

rental   □see **lease.**

rental agreement   □see **lease.**

renter   □see **lease.**

rents, issues, and profits: generally, the net profit from rent and other income from the use or produce of property, as distinguished from gains on the sale of property. Not a term of art. Variously interpreted in describing allocation of moneys between conflicting claimants, e.g., life beneficiary of a trust and the remainderman; a receiver in possession and the owner; divorcing spouses, concerning division of moneys attributable to separate property or to efforts of the community. The expression is sometimes rendered *rents and profits* without change of meaning.

renvoi (F., rahn–VOI: sending back): in a case pending here (the *forum*), the court may decide that there is a problem of **conflict of laws** (□see), i.e., what law governs, the law of the forum or the law of a foreign state or nation? The court here should then refer to the whole law of the foreign jurisdiction, including the foreign law on conflict of laws. If the foreign jurisdiction would refer such a case to the law of the forum, the court here will apply its own substantive law.

Renvoi, as described here, is sometimes rejected, and is not uniformly defined or applied. It is also called the *doctrine of renvoi.*

reopen a case: to offer additional evidence, after resting. □see **rest,** under **formalisms**.

reopen a judgment □see **open a judgment,** under **open**.

repeal (v., n.): in its usual, general sense, to make a new law (the *repeal*) that ends, rescinds, or drastically changes a statute or a constitution. The repeal may be *express*. Or it may be *implied,* as where a new law is incompatible with existing law yet does not say that the existing law is repealed. If not spelled out in the repeal, its effect becomes a matter of judicial interpretation. □see **cancel**. For a capitalized *Repeal,* □see **prohibition**.

replevin

1. an action for the recovery of specific personal property. In some jurisdictions, a similar action is called **claim and delivery**.

2. in an action for the recovery of specific personal property, an auxiliary remedy to obtain the immediate possession of the property. The companion verb is *replevy:* to obtain the property. In some jurisdictions, a remedy similar to *replevin* (sense 2) is called **claim and delivery**.

replevy □see **replevin.**

reply □see **pleadings.**

reporters □see **law reports.** For court reporters, □see **court.**

reporter-source privilege □see **newsmen's privilege.**

reporter's privilege □see **newsmen's privilege.**

reporter's transcript □see **transcript;** □see **on the record;** □see also, **off the record.**

reports □see **law reports.**

repossess □see **repossession.**

repossession

1. a seller taking back possession of personal property sold on credit when the buyer who has possession fails to make a required payment, or makes some other default permitting the seller to take back possession. This is the ordinary English sense of *repossession.*

2. a lender taking possession of personal property that is collateral for a loan when the borrower who has possession fails to make a required payment, or makes some other default permitting the lender to take possession. This is not ordinary English. Lawyers generally refer to this as *repossession,* though the lender never had possession before the default.

In both senses, the companion verb is *repossess.*

represent: two senses of the ordinary English verb and its linguistic kin are indispensable to the law:

1. to act for someone else. So acting is *representation.* The actor is a *representative.* □see **agency;** □see **lawyer;** □see **executor.**

2. to state—by words or other expression, by action or inaction, or by leaving an impression—that something is so or not so. The statement is a *representation.* □see **estoppel.** For context that can sour *represent* into *misrepresent,* and *representation* into *misrepresentation,*

represent

□see **fraud**. For the sometimes fine distinction between *representing* and *promising,* □see **warranty**.

representation   □see **represent**.

representative   □see **represent**; □see **executor**.

representative action   □see **class action**.

representative admission   □see **vicarious admission**, under **admit**.

representative suit   □see **class action**.

reprieve   (n., v.): an act of executive clemency postponing the execution of a sentence; and the order setting forth the postponement. <The governor granted a reprieve./The reprieve expires at midnight, January 10.> The verb *reprieve* can describe postponement in terms of what is being done to the sentence or for the prisoner. <The President reprieved the death sentence/ . . . reprieved the prisoner./The prisoner was reprieved.>

Reprieve is sometimes described as "suspending," in the sense of postponing; that usage is to be distinguished from a *suspended sentence,* the court's sentence, as opposed to executive postponement of its execution.

Reprieve is also to be distinguished from the broader term *stay of execution,* used in civil as well as criminal procedure, usually referring to the action of a court. □see **execution**.

□see also, **commutation**; □see also, **pardon**.

reprimand   (n., v.): a formal statement by someone in authority criticizing someone subject to that authority for conduct that is subject to that authority. As a form of discipline, *reprimand* is variously identified and used in government, business, the professions, the armed services, and miscellaneous organizations. Synonyms are *reproof* or *reproval* (the verb in both cases *reprove*) and *censure* (n., v.). Without claim to uniformity of form or effect, *reprimand* is often characterized as something "severe"; and so it is, compared to an *admonition,* a warning. For a straying lawyer, a reprimand is "mild," compared to suspension or disbarment. In some jurisdictions, a judge may be reprimanded by a state authority; again "mild," compared to removal from office.

repudiation: in its most common legal use: words, acts, or an accumulation of circumstances that amount to one party to a contract telling the other: "My obligations under our contract will not be performed." If the repudiation occurs before performance is due, it is called **anticipatory repudiation** or **anticipatory breach**; usage is not uniform. Details are governed by contract and commercial law.

request □see **demand.**

request for admissions □see **discovery.**

required □see **may.**

requirements contract: typically, a contract between a buyer and seller to satisfy the buyer's requirements of specified goods or services over a specified time. The buyer agrees to buy from the seller, and the seller agrees to sell to the buyer, all of the goods or services that the buyer requires (needs). See UCC 2–306.

output contract: typically, a contract between a buyer and seller for the seller's entire output of specified goods over a specified time. The buyer agrees to buy from the seller, and the seller agrees to sell to the buyer, all of the goods that the seller produces. See UCC 2–306.

res (L., race; often reese: thing): thing. Latin meaning survives in a wide range of contexts, along with other Latin forms of *res:* as in **re** (□see) and **in rem** (□see). Sometimes usage emphasizes *a thing,* as distinguished from a person (as with *in rem*). Most often the emphasis, express or implied, is on the thing that is under consideration; e.g., a *trust res,* property held in **trust** (□see); e.g., with stolen property as the thing, the victim now elects to *follow the res* by claiming the fruits of the thief's investment of the thing (□see **conversion**). Other sorts of *res* as the thing are separate entries. □see **res gestae;** □see **res ipsa loquitur;** □see **res judicata.** □see also, **law Latin.**

res adjudicata: Latin, but not legal. □see **res judicata.**

rescind: to undo, as distinguished from ending, canceling, or terminating (□see **cancel**). The prime usage is in undoing a contract, i.e., to restore the parties to their respective situations before the contract was made. < They agreed to rescind the contract of sale: the buyer returned the table, and the seller returned the purchase price. > Apart from agreement to rescind, other grounds, e.g., fraud, mistake, etc., are dealt with in the law of contracts, equity, sales, and **restitution** (□see), often governed by statute. □see **rescission**.

rescission

1. the act of rescinding (□see **rescind**) and its result.

2. an action to rescind a contract, an equitable remedy. <They sued, asking for a rescission of the contract on the ground of fraud.>

□see also, **restitution**.

reservation • exception

Historic terms of the common law, with differences now waning. Usage, decision, or statute often equates them. Often mushed together with the words *excepting and reserving;* careless, redundant, or both; in either case, the usage invites interpretation. The definitions here leave to substantive law the bundles of rules affecting both words, varying by jurisdiction.

reservation: a conveyancing term for a property interest, e.g., a life estate, an easement, a rent, that is imposed or retained by the grantor on the real property granted. The *reservation* typically is introduced by the word *reserving,* sometimes *excepting and reserving.* <A grants Blackacre to B, reserving to A for ten years an annual ground rent of $5,000.>

exception: a conveyancing term for what is not included: that part of a grant which, incident to the description of a particular piece of property granted, goes on to describe what is not included in the grant. The *exception* typically is introduced by the words *except* or *excepting,* sometimes *excepting and reserving.* <A grants to B all of Tract 245, except Lot 10 of Tract 245.> □see also, **zoning**. For *exception* as a courtroom word, □see **objection**.

reserve □see **reservation;** □see **without reserve.**

reserved powers

1. a reference to the Tenth Amendment to the U.S. Constitution reading: "The powers not delegated to the United States by the Constitution, nor prohibited by it to the states, are reserved to the states respectively, or to the people."

2. a vague reference to the **police power** (□see) of the states.

res gestae (L., race JES–tie: things done): words or acts out of court that are close enough in time and relevance to some event as to be considered part of it and, typically, having the mark of spontaneity. <"Ouch," he cried, as the cars collided. That's *res gestae.*> Ignored in some authoritative statements of the rules of evidence; denounced as ambiguous, worthless, or worse by scholars of repute; and frequently nominated for oblivion, *res gestae* clings to a life in the law. It is repeatedly, erroneously, referred to as an exception to the **hearsay rule** (□see). Lawyers and judges, in doubt or in a hurry, still feel that *res gestae* might bolster an argument for admissibility. □see **res.** Sometimes, *res gestae* is used loosely to describe words that fit under the more general rubric of **verbal acts** (□see).

residence: the place where a person lives, the ordinary English word. Special statutes give special definition for particular purposes, e.g., citizenship, unemployment benefits, university fees, voting. A frequent problem is distinguishing or equating *residence* and **domicile** (□see).

resident: a person who has a **residence** (□see).

residual □see **residue.**

residual estate □see **residue.**

residuary □see **residue.**

residuary bequest □see **residue.**

residuary clause □see **residue.**

residuary devise □see **residue.**

residuary estate □see **residue.**

residuary legacy □see **residue.**

residue In the law of wills and estates—

residue

1. general usage: the rest of the property left (or that will be left) in a deceased's estate after payment of debts, expenses of administration, and all other particularized gifts. The particularized gifts may be bequests, legacies, or devises.

2. sometimes: the property in a deceased's estate other than all other particularized gifts. The particularized gifts may be bequests, legacies, or devises. This usage can be significant when lawyers want to consider the value of the gift of residue as compared with the other gifts, and as compared with its value after the deductions of debt and expense in sense 1.

Linguistic relatives of *residue:*

> **residual**: an adjective referring to the *residue;* as in **residual estate**, also called *residuary estate.*

> **residuary**

>> **a.** an adjective referring to the *residue:*

>>> **(1)** to the whole of the residue: the **residuary estate**, also called *residual estate.*

>>> **(2)** to the part of a will disposing of the whole of the residue: the **residuary clause**, as, e.g., the italicized part of this sentence: I give $20,000 to A, my home to B, *and the rest of my estate to C.*

>>> **(3)** to the part of a will disposing of a portion of the residue: a residuary clause, sometimes referring to a *residuary bequest,* a *residuary legacy,* or a *residuary devise* (□see **gift**).

>> **b.** an adjective referring to a beneficiary of the residue: e.g., a *residuary legatee,* a *residuary devisee* (□see **gift**).

>> **c.** a noun, sometimes used as another name for the beneficiary of the residue. <The residuary was their only child.>

> **rest, residue, and remainder**: the residue. An old tautology. □see **coupled synonyms**. *Remainder* here not to be confused with the **future interest** (□see) of the same name.

res ipsa loquitur (L., race IP–sa LOCK–wuh–ter: the thing itself speaks): the thing speaks for itself.

Res ipsa loquitur is an old Roman expression that has carved out a large niche for itself in the law of negligence and evidence. The *thing* (the *res*) that speaks for itself may be the condition of a particular physical thing (e.g., a toe in a plug of chewing tobacco), an occurrence (e.g., a beer barrel rolling out of a loft and flattening a careful pedestrian), or something less bizarre (e.g., a badly run operating room that results in a botched amputation).

When the *thing* speaks for itself, not everyone listens, and those who do don't hear it the same way. Loud and clear for almost everyone, at least it says this: "Ordinarily, this sort of thing doesn't happen unless somebody was negligent." But who? Argument over the probabilities of individual responsibility center on details of a duty of control, management, inspection, or other burden. Some cut it short. This is what the *thing* says: "Ordinarily, this sort of thing wouldn't have happened unless the defendant was negligent." Ultimately, if the other evidence in the case does not clearly point to critical fault in the plaintiff or a third person, a jury having heard *res ipsa loquitur* may (not must) infer that the defendant was negligent.

Res ipsa loquitur is sometimes called a rule, a doctrine, a principle, varying by jurisdiction in definition, content, and effect; occasionally rejected. Usually, it is regarded as an aspect of circumstantial evidence, with varying effect on burden of proof. Lawyers refer to *res ipsa loquitur* as *res ipsa* or a *res ipsa case;* in slang, *res ipsey* or a *resipsey.* Students and other note takers abbreviate it *RIL, R.I.L., r.i.l.,* etc.

res judicata (L., race JOO–dah–KAH–tah: a case, thing, or matter decided)

As an expression, *res judicata* is a survivor, from Latin and the common law. But its content has been defined and redefined in statute, decision, and treatise; entwined and shaped by local rules of procedure; restated in the influential *Restatement (Second) of Judgments,* 1981. Courts and lawyers use *res judicata* freely, without definition, confident that the Latin conveys some vague, general understanding. Though often called the *doctrine of res judicata,* lack of a precise consensus is the rule. The dictionary indulges in some but not all of the inconsistent, often tortured verbiage of the many statements of *res judicata,* and omits ramified detail. The listing here is a distillate of some representative usage.

1. in most general terms, a quick way of saying that once something has been litigated and decided, the same parties cannot relitigate it. <The motion to dismiss count 2 is granted. We are not going to try that all over again. *Res judicata.* >

2. A final judgment on the merits by a court or other tribunal having jurisdiction is conclusive between the parties to a suit, and their privies, as to all matters that were litigated, or that could have been litigated, in that suit.

561

res judicata

Conclusive here means that they can be stopped from relitigating those matters in another suit, whether based on the same or another cause of action or claim. *Matters,* deliberately vague, may refer to facts, issues, questions, points of law, defenses—relevant to the original cause of action or claim.

Sense 2 has a companion usage, narrower in scope than *res judicata:*

collateral estoppel: A final judgment on the merits by a court or other tribunal having jurisdiction is conclusive between the parties to a suit, and their privies, as to all matters that were raised, litigated, and determined in that suit.

Conclusive here means that they can be stopped from relitigating those matters in another suit based on a different cause of action or claim. *Matters,* deliberately vague, may refer to facts, issues, questions, points of law, defenses—relevant to the original cause of action or claim.

3. A final judgment on the merits by a court or other tribunal having jurisdiction "precludes" (i.e., prevents) the parties to a civil suit, and their privies, from litigating in a later civil suit "claims" or "issues" that were litigated, or that could have been litigated, and decided in the earlier suit.

The terminology here stresses *preclusion,* with subsets of *claim preclusion* and *issue preclusion,* each with distinctive vocabularies:

claim preclusion: A judgment in the earlier suit *extinguishes* (i.e., wipes out) any *claims,* i.e., the rights of the parties in connection with the transaction or event that led to the earlier suit. If judgment for the plaintiff, the claim is *merged* in the judgment; if for the defendant, the claim is *barred* by the judgment. Local procedures may vary on asserting *merger* or *bar.*

issue preclusion: A judgment in the earlier suit *precludes* relitigation of an *issue,* i.e., a matter of fact or law that the parties actually fought over and that was essential to the judgment. If the later suit involves the same claim as in the earlier suit, *issue preclusion* is called *direct estoppel;* if it involves a different claim, *issue preclusion* is often called *collateral estoppel* (see sense 2).

respondeat superior □see **agency**; □see also, **maxims**.

respondent

1. in appellate practice: the usual title of the party who won in the trial court and is resisting the appeal. A synonym for *appellee.* □see **appeal**. Usage varies by jurisdiction.

2. In any proceeding—ordinary, special, equitable, or extraordinary, where the party initiating the proceeding is called a *petitioner,* the party opposing the petitioner is usually called the *respondent.* Usage varies by jurisdiction.

rest   □see **formalisms**; □see **residue.**

Restatement: the usual short reference to one of the volumes of a growing series, each titled *Restatement of the Law,* in a particular field, e.g., *Restatement (Second) of Torts,* prepared and published by the American Law Institute. Each *Restatement,* sometimes *restatement,* is an effort of lawyer specialists to restate in precise, outline form a whole field of the law: principles, reasons, reasons for change, rules exceptions, exceptions to exceptions, comments, and examples of application. The restatements endeavor to bring current unity to particular fields of law where disharmony and antiquity are frequently the pattern. The restatements are often followed by changes of statute and case law. Whether followed, followed in part, criticized, or rejected, the restatements are widely cited, ignored at peril.

restitution

1. a principle of law and equity that makes "one person . . . accountable to another on the ground that otherwise he would unjustly benefit or the other would unjustly suffer loss." (See *Restatement, Restitution,* p. 1.) The principle, often described as **unjust enrichment**, requires "[a] person who has been unjustly enriched at the expense of another . . . to make restitution to the other." (*Restatement, Restitution,* § 1).

2. rules of substantive law, varying by jurisdiction, requiring a transfer of property or payment of money to prevent an unjust benefit at another's expense, an unjust loss from the acts of another, or both. E.g., return of a payment made by mistake; e.g., a retransfer of property whose transfer was induced by fraud. The rules do not always require that benefit and loss coincide. E.g., an innocent purchaser from a thief may be required to return the stolen property and its proceeds; e.g., a benefit need not be paid for if conferred officiously (□see **intermeddler**).

3. the procedural mechanics, varying by jurisdiction, to effect the principle (sense 1) and the rules (sense 2). E.g., **conversion** (□see); **replevin** (□see); □see **constructive trust**, under **trust**; □see **equitable discovery**.

restrain □see enjoin.

restraining order □see enjoin.

restraint of marriage: a general term of reference to a condition in a contract or gift denying a benefit if the beneficiary marries. If classified as in *restraint of marriage,* traditionally held void; borderline provisions frequently interpreted to avoid the anathema.

restraint of trade □see **rule of reason;** □see **antitrust law;** □see also, **fair trade agreement;** □see also, **tying arrangement.**

restraint on alienation: in general, a provision in a conveyance or lease prohibiting or restricting transfer of the property by the grantee, beneficiary, or lessee. Rules regulating or forbidding restraints on alienation vary by the character of the restraint and by jurisdiction. □see also, **rule against perpetuities.**

rest, residue, and remainder □see **residue.**

restriction: the ordinary English word, most commonly in the law a reference to limitations on the use of land. □see **easement;** □see restrictive covenant, under **covenant.**

restrictive covenant □see **covenant.**

resulting trust □see **trust.**

retained counsel □see **lawyer.**

retainer □see **fee (attorney's fee).**

retaining lien □see **lien.**

retaliatory discharge □see **wrongful discharge.**

retaliatory eviction □see **evict.**

retraxit (L., re–TRAX–it: (he) has withdrawn): the common law characterization of plaintiff's withdrawal of suit in open court, an act that barred further suit on the same cause of action. Now sometimes referred to in terms of what will have the effect of a retraxit at common law, e.g., a dismissal with prejudice; e.g., a dismissal by plaintiff upon defendant's payment of an agreed sum.

retreat □see retreat to the wall.

retreat to the wall: a legal metaphor, analogue to the metaphor of ordinary English, *with one's back to the wall.* Sometimes expressed as *flee to the wall.* Whether *retreat* or *flee,* the metaphor is sometimes used to refer to a limiting condition on **self-defense** (□see) as justification for an otherwise wrongful killing: if threatened death or serious harm can be avoided by retreat to a place of safety, the defense fails. Rules on *retreat* under threat vary by jurisdiction; some reject it (*no retreat*).

retrial □see trial.

retroactive legislation: legislation that changes the legal effect of something that happened, or rights or obligations that existed, before the law was enacted. Also called, *retrospective legislation.*

Some retrospective legislation is prohibited and unconstitutional; e.g., □see **ex post facto**; □see **Contract Clause**. Some is unconstitutional under the **Due Process Clauses**, depending on its effect. Some is prohibited by statute unless expressly authorized. But the label *retroactive* is not necessarily a pejorative; e.g., a retroactive *curative statute* (□see **remedial statute**).

retrospective legislation □see retroactive legislation.

return □see indictment.

return of execution □see **execute**; □see also, **not satisfied**.

return of service □see **service of process**.

revenue bond □see **full faith and credit**.

reversal: the decision of a reviewing court that disapproves and makes ineffective a ruling, judgment, decision, or other action of a lower court. The reversal may be in short, blunt words <*Reversed./ Judgment reversed.*>; or with a substitution <Reversed. Judgment for the plaintiff.>; or with a *remand* (sending the case back) for corrective proceedings by a lower court. □see also, **reversible error.**

reverse □see **reversal.**

reverse condemnation □see **eminent domain.**

reverse discrimination: affirmative action gone sour. An affirmative action program that the law classifies as forbidden discrimination *against* those who are not of the group designed to be helped by the program. The exact measure of what constitutes *reverse discrimination* is in a state of constitutional flux, with frequent split decisions in the U.S. Supreme Court. □see **affirmative action.**

reverse stock split □see **stock.**

reversible error: an error in some phase of a judicial proceeding that has substantially affected its outcome, and so is cause for a **reversal** (□see). *Reversible error* is variously described as **plain error** (□see), not trivial or *harmless error* but *fatal error* (□see **fatal**), *prejudicial error,* one that has resulted in a **miscarriage of justice** (□see). E.g., a jury instruction so flawed as to have produced a verdict contrary to law; court proceedings so unruly as to have denied a defendant a fair trial; a denial of right to trial by jury; a denial of right to counsel; etc.

reversion □see **future interest.**

review □see **judicial review;** □see **writ of review,** under **certiorari.**

revocable trust □see **trust.**

revoke a will □see **will.**

revolving door: an informal legal adaptation of ordinary English to refer to the impropriety of government officials and lawyers in government and the courts moving to private employment, and shortly using past official connections and information for private ends.

As an adjective, *revolving-door* characterizes a statute, rule, or other restriction on the private use of past official connections and information. The restrictions take various forms; e.g., a time gap between leaving an agency and private exploitation of personal contacts with those remaining in the agency; e.g., a prohibition of private work on the same or related matter or case that one substantially participated in while in government or the court system. □see **conflict of interest;** □see **vicarious disqualification;** □see **Chinese wall,** under **vicarious disqualification.**

Richard Roe □see **John Doe.**

RICO □see **racketeering.**

rider: an addition to a writing (statute, contract, insurance policy, etc.) after the principal writing has been completed. In private documents, the rider is typically attached on a separate piece of paper to avoid rewriting the whole document. In legislatures, a separate item incorporated in a bill after the principal parts have been introduced; often a controversial item squeezed in by separate vote to assure passage or defeat of the whole.

ride roughshod over □see **clichés.**

right

1. the ordinary, broad sense of what is just or moral, as contrasted with *wrong* in the sense of unjust or immoral. As applied to the insanity defense, □see **M'Naghten rule.**

2. For *right* and *rights* relating to ownership, □see **property.** □see also, **vested right.**

3. For the *rights* of a person within a state, □see **civil rights** and **civil liberties,** under **civil.** For the general sense of *constitutional right,* □see **constitutional.** □see also, **Bill of Rights.**

Legal expressions using the word *right* or *rights* are separate alphabetical entries.

right against self-incrimination □see **criminate.**

567

right and wrong rule □see **M'Naghten rule.**

right and wrong test □see **M'Naghten rule.**

right of access: the right of the owner of property that abuts a public road to unobstructed entry and exit to and from the property and the road. *Right of access* is sometimes loosely referred to as an *easement of access.*

right of action □see **cause of action.**

right of assembly: one of the fundamental First Amendment rights, frequently referred to as the *freedom of assembly:* "Congress shall make no law respecting . . . the right of the people peaceably to assemble, [and to petition the government for a redress of grievances.]" Applied to the states through Fourteenth Amendment due process. Historically, tied to assembly "to petition . . . for a redress of grievances" but long since extended to peaceful assembly for an undefined range of lawful purposes; subject to time and place restrictions. Most state constitutions have similar provisions. For *unlawful assembly,* □see **riot.**

right of association □see **freedom of association.**

right of entry □see **fee simple.**

right of entry for condition broken □see **fee simple.**

right of first publication □see **copyright.**

right of first refusal: a right by contract or lease to buy or lease property (usually real estate) by matching the terms of any bona fide offer to buy or lease that the owner had planned to accept. Commonly called *first refusal.* <I have a first refusal on that land.> Also called *first option,* and a tenant's *right of renewal.*

right of lateral support □see **lateral support.**

right of petition □see **right of assembly.**

right of privacy

1. a general right *to* privacy: the right of an individual "to be let alone" (Cooley, *Torts* 29, 1879) in the enjoyment of a private life in an increasingly intrusive society. In particular, the right includes freedom from unwanted publication of matters that the public has no right to know concerning an individual's "private life, habits, acts, and relations." Accurate or not, such a publication that subjects one to "mental pain and suffering" is an invasion of the right, actionable in tort. (See Warren and Brandeis, "The Right to Privacy," 4 *Harv.L. Rev.* 193, 1890.)

2. the right to be let alone (sense 1) as an umbrella for a variety of torts for *invasion* of that right. Usage varies by statute and decision (see *Restatement (Second) of Torts,* §§ 652A–652I, 1977). Typically:

a. unreasonable intrusion, physical or otherwise, into one's seclusion or private affairs. E.g., housebreaking, wiretapping, opening mail. □see also, **electronic eavesdropping**.

b. public disclosure of intimate facts of private life that are not of public concern, at least when they relate to an ordinary private person, as distinct from a **public figure** (□see).

c. publicity, though not defamatory, that places one in a **false light**. E.g., a false fictionalized account that plaintiff had been raped.

d. a use without consent (appropriation) of one's name or likeness for the user's benefit, e.g., advertising a product. Appropriation may be unwanted publicity (as in sense 1), or something much different: depriving an individual (e.g., a celebrity) of an exclusive property, sometimes called the **right of publicity**.

3. a constitutional right of privacy: a controversial version of the right to be let alone (sense 1) stated to be a constitutional right, as distinct from traditional protections of privacy and personal liberty under specific provisions of the U.S. Constitution, e.g., Third, Fourth, Fifth, and Fourteenth Amendments. Usage is not uniform. Typically, the right is described not only in terms of freedom from unwanted intrusions and publicity (senses 1 and 2). Increasingly, it is described to include *personal autonomy* in making critically important decisions over the intimate affairs of life, e.g., begetting, bearing, and rearing of children (contraception, abortion, education); e.g., marital and nonmarital sexual relationships. With its content in flux, a constitutional *right of privacy* has attracted a confusing variety of what are intended as endearing epithets, in addition to *autonomy;* e.g., dignity, identity, individuality, intimacy, lifestyle, personhood, selfhood. Some speak of distinctive rights, e.g., *lifestyle,* and, notably, **freedom**

right of privacy

of intimate association (☐see, under **freedom of association**). Whether or not there is a distinct federal constitutional *right of privacy* (as under some state constitutions) remains as unsettled as its usage is ubiquitous. ☐see also, **right to die.**

right of publicity   ☐see **right of privacy.**

right of redemption   ☐see **equity of redemption**, under **equity.**

right of reentry   ☐see **fee simple.**

right of renewal   ☐see **right of first refusal.**

right of representation   ☐see **per capita.**

right of setoff   ☐see **offset.**

right of subjacent support   ☐see **lateral support.**

right of survivorship   ☐see **joint tenancy**, under **estate.**

right of way

1. an easement to go across someone else's land. Also called an *easement of way* and an *easement of passage,* sometimes, a *way.* ☐see **easement.**

2. a grant to a **public utility** (☐see) of publicly owned land for the operation of the utility, e.g., for railroad tracks, overhead or underground electric lines, etc. The grant may take various forms, e.g., a fee, an easement. *Right of way* may also refer to the land so used. <The railroad right of way was fifty yards wide and fifty miles long.>

3. a variety of traffic rules regulating preference of movement between competing users of the same route; e.g., vehicles at an intersection; a vehicle and a pedestrian; ships at sea; airplanes.

Right of way is also spelled *right-of-way.* The plural is *rights of way;* sometimes *right of ways.*

rights   ☐see **right;** ☐see **stock right**, under **stock.**

right, title, and interest   □see quitclaim; □see coupled synonyms.

right to convey   □see covenants of title.

right to counsel

1. the constitutional right of a litigant to retain and be represented by a lawyer, as contrasted with appearing *in pro per* (□see **appear**). The right applies to criminal and to most civil litigation (Sixth and Fourteenth Amendments); in some small claims courts, lawyers are forbidden. *Right to counsel* (sense 1) ordinarily means **counsel of choice**.

> **a.** the right does not entitle a litigant to **hybrid representation**: representation by the litigant (*in pro per*) plus representation by a lawyer.

> **b.** the right does not entitle a litigant to **standby counsel**: a lawyer appointed, in a court's discretion, to help or advise a *pro per* litigant.

> **c.** the right extends to some administrative proceedings.

2. in a criminal prosecution, the constitutional right of a defendant who cannot hire a lawyer to have a court-appointed lawyer at public expense. The right applies to any prosecution for felony, and to any misdemeanor if the defendant is sentenced to jail (Sixth and Fourteenth Amendments). *Right to counsel* (sense 2) does not ordinarily mean *counsel of choice*. It does mean the right to **effective counsel**: an expression of varying standards (□see **malpractice**); it includes consideration of the probability of an effect upon the outcome (see *Strickland v. Washington,* 466 U.S. 668, 1984). The precise point of beginning and ending of the right is a matter of continuing constitutional decision. □see **critical stage**.

3. in a restricted group of civil cases, a limited constitutional right of a defendant who cannot hire a lawyer to have a court-appointed lawyer at public expense:

> **a.** where loss of liberty is at stake: a constitutional right (Fourteenth Amendment due process) in proceedings that may involve commitment to an institution for juveniles or the mentally ill. Also a right under some statutes, e.g., re civil arrest.

> **b.** in some other civil cases of unique character: (1) a constitutional right, case by case, only if deemed necessary to assure a fair trial; e.g., in some instances, re permanent removal of a child from parental custody. In some states: in proceedings to declare the

defendant a father. (2) a constitutional right (by some decisions), case by case, only if deemed necessary to assure access to the courts; e.g., in some instances, re a prisoner named as defendant.

The limits of right to counsel in civil cases are in flux.

right to custody □see **custody**.

right to die: a loose catchphrase, without consensus that there is such a right and without consensus on what it means. Usually, *right to die* refers to the extent, if any, that the law will recognize a right of a person, by a proxy, to carry out that person's deliberate or presumed choice of death as an alternative to a life of suffering from incurable physical or mental illness. *Right to die* often refers to:

1. euthanasia (Gk.: an easy death): a word of ordinary English, also called **mercy killing**: to end a life of suffering by painlessly *putting* someone to death (e.g., by injection of poison). That prime sense is usually referred to in legal writing as *active euthanasia*, a criminal offense. To be distinguished from a secondary meaning of ordinary English: to end a life of suffering by *allowing* someone to die (e.g., by withholding or ending medical measures that prolong life); that sense is usually referred to in legal writing as *passive euthanasia*. When legal writing equates *right to die* with *euthanasia*, the reference is generally to *passive euthanasia*.

2. personal autonomy, as an aspect of a constitutional **right of privacy** (□see).

3. Natural Death Act: a widely adopted type of statute, under which a competent adult may direct (in writing) that "life-sustaining procedures" be withheld or removed "in the event of a terminal condition." See also, Uniform Rights of the Terminally Ill Act (95 Uniform Laws Annotated 609, 1987). The written directive may take the form of a so-called *living will* or *durable power of attorney*:

living will: not a **will** (□see), but called *living will* popularly, and in many varying statutes and decisions. Generally, it is a relatively short instrument saying—in advance of a possible, eventual incompetence—that the life of the person signing is not to be artificially prolonged by extraordinary medical measures when there is no reasonable expectation of recovery. This expression of the signer's wishes is intended to relieve relatives of concern, and ultimately to relieve attending physicians of some of the fears of civil or criminal liability in exercising their best medical judgment, e.g., on ending or not supplying artificial feeding.

durable power of attorney: a more formal and more detailed instrument than a *living will,* with the same objectives. Unlike the *living will* 's simple statement of the patient's wishes, in the *durable power of attorney,* the patient (the principal) appoints the physician (or others) as agent (**attorney in fact;** □see), expressly giving the agent authority to make the decisions as to extraordinary medical measures when the patient is no longer competent to decide. The *power* is thus *durable* in that the principal's incompetence does not revoke the agent's authority. The *durable power of attorney,* also called a *durable power of attorney for health care,* varies by jurisdiction. A related but more general classification is a separate entry in the dictionary; □see **durable power of attorney.**

right to work laws: a popular name for laws requiring an *open shop.* □see **closed shop,** under **close.**

RIL: abbreviation of **res ipsa loquitur** (□see).

riot: an aggravated form of violent disturbance of the peace by at least two persons acting together, or their threat of that violence when they have the immediate power of making the threat a reality. The minimum size of the group and details of the offense vary by jurisdiction. *Riot* is sometimes described as the culmination of an **unlawful assembly**: the gathering of at least two persons acting together to do something unlawful, or lawful in a violent manner, which if carried out would be a *riot,* and which if attempted and fails is called a **rout.** □see also, **breach of the peace,** under **breach.**

riparian owner □see **law of capture.**

riparian rights □see **law of capture.**

ripe □see **controversy.**

ripeness □see **controversy.**

risk: the ordinary English sense of exposure to danger of injury or loss, with special legal contexts:

assumption of risk (□see), in tort law.

insurance (□see).

risk

risk of loss: often shortened to *risk*, e.g., in law of bailments, contracts, sales. <Who bears the risk?> A matter of contract provision, various statutes (e.g., the Uniform Commercial Code), or trade usage. □see **F.O.B.**

risk of nonpersuasion □see **burden of proof**, under **proof**.

risk of loss □see **risk**.

risk of nonpersuasion □see **burden of persuasion**, under **proof**.

rob □see **robbery**.

robbery: a felony consisting of **larceny** (□see) from the person or presence of another by force or the threat of force. "Presence of another" typically means the immediate presence of a person who has control of the property taken. Definitions of *robbery* and the companion verb *rob* vary by jurisdiction. □see also, **hijacking**.

Robinson-Patman Act □see **antitrust law**.

rogatory □see **letters rogatory**.

roll: an ancient usage, derived from a rolled-up parchment (a scroll) on which something is written, an official record, a list; used in some jurisdictions to identify a particular record, e.g., a *judgment roll*, a *tax roll*, etc.

rout □see **riot**.

rule (n., v.): a word with a wide range of meanings in the law, as in ordinary English. Included within its range are the loose and the precise, the extremes not always distinguishable. The listing here is not exhaustive. A variety of expressions incorporating *rule* or *rules* are separate entries.

1. a general standard. E.g., the **plain meaning rule** (□see); the **rule of lenity** (□see). *Rule* (sense 1) is often equated with *doctrine* or *principle*. □see **cy près**.

2. a provision of law by legislation, regulation, or decision covering specific detail of substance or procedure. E.g., on the admissibility of evidence; □see **hearsay rule**, under **hearsay**; □see **rules of evidence**,

under **evidence**. E.g., □see **restraint on alienation**. E.g., □see **rule against perpetuities**. E.g., on the movement of traffic; □see **right of way**. E.g., on taxation (□see **tax**). Some *rules* (sense 2) are equated with *regulation,* often redundantly *rules and regulations;* □see **regulate**; □see **administrative law**.

3. one of a body of regulations, similar to *rule* (sense 2), specifically governing as a class particular kinds of procedure or conduct. E.g., □see **rules of court**. E.g., □see **Model Rules of Professional Conduct,** under **legal ethics**. For endless browsing, consult Federal Rules of Appellate Procedure (28 USCA), Federal Rules of Civil Procedure (28 USCA), Federal Rules of Criminal Procedure (18 USCA).

4. a proposition of law, especially in the law of real property, taking its name and substance from a particular case. □see **rule in Shelley's Case.**

5. a court's particular determination, sometimes equated with **order** (□see), in a particular case or in a phase of a particular case. Also, the making of that determination, the verb to *rule.* <The court ruled in our favor.> As a noun, *rule* (sense 5) is now more often called a *ruling* (□see **decision**). The older usage for this sense, still used but varying by jurisdiction, is plain *rule;* as in the expressions **rule nisi** (L., NIGH-sigh: unless)—commonly called an **order to show cause** (□see), and **rule absolute,** making the order effective when good cause is not shown in response to a *rule nisi.*

rule absolute   □see **rule.**

rule against perpetuities

1. in classic statement: "No interest is good unless it must *vest,* if at all, not later than twenty-one years after some *life in being* at the creation of the interest." (John Chipman Gray, *The Rule Against Perpetuities,* 4th ed., § 201, p. 191, 1942; italics added). The *rule against perpetuities* is also spelled *Rule against Perpetuities* and *Rule Against Perpetuities,* is usually referred to as the *Rule,* and abbreviated R.A.P.

> **vest**: a short way of saying that the interest must become a **vested interest**: a particular person's present ownership of an interest in property with the right of immediate or future possession of the property. If the right to possession is immediate, the interest is *vested in possession.* If the right to possession must await the natural expiration of a preceding estate (and nothing more), the interest is *vested in interest.* *Vest* and *vested* are contrasted with

future interests that are *contingent*. □see **remainder**, under **future interest**.

life in being: □see **in being**; □see **en ventre sa mère**, under **child**. *Lives in being* are the Rule's so-called *measuring lives:* the lives of those who can affect *vesting*.

perpetuities: Despite its awesome invocation of the forever, the Rule places no limit on how long an interest in property may last. "To A in fee" is as perpetual as you could wish for and is not condemned. *Perpetuity* in the Rule means that the interest does not start (*vest in possession* or *vest in interest*) within the period fixed by the Rule. The metaphysics, gyrations, and mechanics of computation of that period are major topics of courses in property law and of articles and treatises on the Rule—beyond encapsulating in this dictionary.

2. the classic Rule (sense 1) as modified by decision, statute, or hope. Among many variants, most common are the application of **cy près** (□see), and *wait-and-see:* determining compliance with the period of the Rule by waiting to see what actually happens, as distinguished from what *might-have-been.*

rule in Shelley's Case: an old rule of real property law dictating a specific effect of the words of a conveyance of land, whether or not that effect was what the grantor had in mind. As modified in the United States, the rule is this:

If a single instrument creates a life estate in A, and also purports to create a remainder in A's heirs (or the heirs of A's body)—and life estate and remainder are both legal or both equitable—the remainder becomes a remainder in fee simple (or fee tail) in A; the heirs take nothing.

An important incidental effect of the rule (not the rule itself):

If there is no estate between A's life estate and the remainder (e.g., "To A for life, remainder to A's heirs"), the lesser estate (for life) *merges* in the greater (fee simple), and the conveyance gives A a fee simple. □see **legal fiction**.

The rule in Shelley's Case (also spelled Rule in Shelley's Case), and its incidental effect, still exist in a handful of jurisdictions; and in any case may still apply to conveyances before its abolition. The rule takes its name from *Shelley's Case,* 1 Coke's Reports 93b, 76 English Reports 206 (1581).

rulemaking

1. the general characterization of the function of making rules as a part of the process of regulation. □see **regulate**.

2. the special characterization of that function by an administrative agency, as contrasted with adjudication by the agency. □see **administrative law**.

3. the special characterization of that function in making procedural rules for the conduct of various types of litigation. □see **rule**; □see also, **rules of court**.

Rulemaking is also spelled *rule making* and *rule-making*.

rule nisi □see **rule**.

rule of capture □see **law of capture**.

rule of four □see **rules of court**.

rule of law

1. in the sense of *rules:* □see **law**; □see **rule**; and refer to other entries incorporating *rule* and *rules*.

2. a widely used expression of the general nature of government subject to **law** (□see), as distinguished from the uncontrolled dictates of individuals. Variously interpreted; meaning unfixed.

rule of lenity: generally, ambiguity in a criminal statute should be resolved in favor of the defendant, e.g., a less harsh penalty. □see **rules of interpretation**.

rule of reason: the catchphrase for the interpretation by the U.S. Supreme Court that in general, "restraint of trade" in the Sherman Act (□see **antitrust law**) refers to "unreasonable" restraint of trade.

rules and regulations □see **regulate**; □see **rule**.

rules of court: rules governing details of practice in specific courts, adopted either by the court itself or by a higher court with supervisory jurisdiction. Sometimes equated with, but usually distinguished

rules of court

from general rules of procedure in various types of litigation. □see **rule**; □see **rulemaking**.

rule of four: not a formal or inflexible rule of court, but an established practice of the U.S. Supreme Court to grant certiorari if four of the justices vote in favor. A similar practice is followed in appeals from state courts.

rules of evidence □see **evidence**.

rules of interpretation: the usual reference to a loose assortment of ways to discover the sense, if any, in a piece of legal writing. The label *rule* gives an aura of general standard to what are usually very personal conclusions of interpretation, e.g., favoring **intent** (□see), avoiding **absurdity** (□see). The rules are not uniform and cannot be relied upon as guides to precise writing. Some of the rules are rendered in Latin (e.g., *ejusdem generis*), others in forthright English ambiguity (e.g., *plain meaning*). For a sampling of the rules, □see:

contra proferentem;

ejusdem generis;

expressio unius est exclusio alterius;

four corners of the instrument;

in pari materia;

noscitur a sociis;

plain meaning rule;

rule of lenity.

□see also, **construction**; □see also, **time**.

rules of professional conduct □see **legal ethics**.

"rules" of time □see **time**.

ruling □see **rule**; □see **decision**.

run

1. to have legal power or force in a designated area; said of a court's **jurisdiction** (□see) or its **venue** (□see), and of orders issued by a court. < This court's venue runs to the city limits./Our writ runs throughout the state. >

2. to cause process to issue, e.g., a writ of attachment. Legal argot. <We're going to run a writ./ . . . run an attachment.>

3. to be beyond the time provided by law in which to do something, e.g., to start a lawsuit, to file a pleading. <You have run out of time./The statute has run.> □see **statute of limitations**.

4. for a *covenant that runs with the land,* □see **covenant**.

runner   □see **barratry**.

running of the statute   □see **statute of limitations**.

running with the land   □see **covenant**.

S

said: as an adjective, a hallmark of legal redundancy. <Said plaintiff sued said defendant.> Archaic companion of *aforesaid* and *aforementioned.* □see **afore-**.

sailor's will: a statutory, informal will made by a sailor (army, navy, merchant marine) usually while aboard a ship at sea; usually limited to personal property; sometimes valid without witnesses. Unlike a **nuncupative will** (□see), the sailor's will may be oral or written, and is not usually contingent on the physical condition of the testator at the time of making the will. A *sailor's will* is also called a *seaman's will* and a *mariner's will.*

soldier's will: like a *sailor's will,* except for the condition of being made "aboard a ship at sea." Instead, the usual requirement is that the *soldier's will* be made while on actual military service, or in the field, or in time of war.

saith: a worthless archaism, preserved in a needless and confusing appendange to affidavits. <Further deponent saith not.> □see **affiant**.

salable □see **merchantable title**.

sale

1. in general, the act of selling real or personal property. □see **sell**. Special definitions vary by statute; e.g., sale of goods (UCC § 2106(1)).

2. as a branch of law, *sales* usually refers to the sale of personal property classified as *goods* (UCC § 2105(1)).

sale and leaseback □see **leaseback**, under **lease**.

sale or return: a sale *on consignment.* □see **consign**.

same

1. As an adjective, *same* (identical) leads a respectable life in ordinary English, but lawyers should use it with caution. Like other **absolutes** (□see), *same* carries the false promise of quick precision. Under the stress of litigation, *same* is watered down, interpreted away as "substantially similar," "similar," "like," etc. Constitutional usage

580

gives no blessing of fixed meaning. □see **same offense,** under **double jeopardy.**

2. As pronoun or noun, *same* (often *the same*), referring to something or someone previously mentioned, is generally shunned in good written English—an illiteracy, archaism, comic. With a degree of condescension, writers relegate *same* to legal or business usage. Despite constitutional usage ("Each house shall keep a journal . . . and publish the same. . . ." Art. I, § 5, cl. 3), the law has no special need for what is now archaic English. For the hurried writer, *same* does lend itself to a quick drop-off, followed by a reader's search for an antecedent. <He sold the car, collected the money, and delivered the same.>

same offense   □see **double jeopardy.**

sanction: as verb or noun, a dangerous "Yes" and "No" word, long used by the law with opposite meanings: to approve (approval) or to penalize (a penalty). Adrift in neutral surroundings, *sanction* is hopelessly ambiguous. <The law sanctions that conduct./That conduct carries the sanction of the statute.> Context can tip the balance. <A parent's concern for a child is certainly sanctioned by the law./Both criminal and economic sanctions were imposed.> Unless the context is very clear, *sanction* is not worth the risk. <These statutes sanction some abortions./ These statutes approve some abortions./ . . . forbid some abortions.>

sane   □see **insanity.**

sanity   □see **insanity.**

satisfaction   (ultimately from L. *satisfacere:* to do enough): the act of doing enough to meet (*satisfy*) a particular obligation, and the instrument evidencing that enough has been done, i.e., that the obligation has been *satisfied.* E.g., *satisfaction of judgment.* E.g., *satisfaction of mortgage.* What is enough to satisfy varies with the nature of the obligation and the substantive and procedural law of the jurisdiction. Satisfaction may require something very specific, e.g., payment in full. Middling specific, *reasonably satisfactory,* where objective factors are involved, e.g., building construction to an owner's satisfaction. Completely unspecific, where personal taste or judgment is involved, e.g., a portrait to be painted to the subject's satisfaction.

satisfaction

accord and satisfaction: an agreement to settle a debt or claim on specified terms (*accord*) followed by performance (*satisfaction*). The accord and satisfaction discharges the debt or claim.

satisfaction of judgment □see **satisfaction**.

satisfaction of mortgage □see **satisfaction**.

satisfactory □see **satisfaction**.

satisfied □see **satisfaction**.

satisfy □see **satisfaction**.

save: Lawyers use *save* in its ordinary English sense. They also use it to mean *except,* an old usage of ordinary English long since abandoned to poets. Even poets draw the line at the lawyer's waning horror, the tautology *save and except.* □see **coupled synonyms**.

save and except □see **save**.

save harmless □see **hold harmless**, under **hold**.

saving clause

1. a special provision of a statute making the statute inapplicable to something that otherwise would be covered by its general language. E.g., a **grandfather clause** (□see).

2. a special provision of a statute stating that if part of the statute is held void (e.g., unconstitutional), the other parts of the statute that are severable from the void part remain in effect. This type of *saving clause* is also called a *severability clause* or *separability clause.*

3. a special provision of a contract, paralleling sense 2, usually affecting parts of a contract void for illegality. A *severability* or *separability clause* of a contract is to be distinguished from a *severable contract,* also called a *separable* or *divisible contract:* one in which different portions of the contract are independent of each other, with consideration separately apportionable.

savings bank trust □see **trust**.

582

scab: a worker who continues working for an employer against whom a labor union has called a strike, or who takes the place of a striker (the latter in particular also called a *strikebreaker*). *Scab,* as defined here, is the most specific generally recognized in the law of a variety of loose and opprobrius senses of the word in ordinary English.

scienter □see **fraud.**

scilicet □see **ss.**

scintilla of evidence (L., sin-TILL-uh: a spark): an imprecise characterization of a very tiny or insignificant bit of evidence, reduced almost to the vanishing point as *mere scintilla* (□see **mere**). The state of the evidence that deserves to be called a *scintilla,* and the consequences of that label (e.g., directing a verdict, or leaving it to the jury), vary from court to court.

scofflaw: an habitual petty law breaker, e.g., ignoring traffic tickets. A coinage of American English, with some imprecise, informal recognition in the law.

scope of authority

1. the prime sense: the extent of an agent's authority—express, implied, or apparent. □see **agency.**

2. in general: the extent of a person's authority in a given role, whether as agent, independent contractor, lawyer, officer, etc. E.g., the scope of authority of a prosecutor; □see **prosecutorial immunity,** under **immunity.**

scope of employment: the work or service that a person is employed to do or render at a particular time and place, *plus* acts then and there reasonably directed to that work or service, whether or not authorized by the employer. The exact content of *scope of employment* varies sharply with circumstances, and with particular areas of the law, e.g., general tort liability, vicarious liability, workers' compensation, insurance coverage, etc. Scope of employment is often equated with *course of employment.*

scrutiny □see **standards of review.**

sea   □see **law of the sea**; □see **high seas**.

seal

1. a special mark, traditionally on wax or other substance, attached to, or impressed into a writing, as an indication of authenticity, identity, approval, or agreement. For the law, the seal—often only in words or letters alone (□see **L.S.**)—persists as a faded relic of an age of illiteracy, e.g., the notarial seal (□see **notary public**), corporate seal, seals of governments and miscellaneous officials, a court seal.

2. to attach or impress a seal (sense 1). E.g., to seal a contract, making it a:

contract under seal, sometimes called a *sealed instrument,* once generally called a *covenant* or *specialty*—words sometimes still used in that sense. Legal effects of seal or no seal vary by statute and jurisdiction, the distinctions often obliterated.

3. to close to general access, except as provided by law, making a:

sealed record (*sealing a record*): a record closed by court order, and not to be opened except by court order, under special statutes. E.g., a juvenile's conviction.

sealed verdict: a verdict agreed to by the jury when court is not in session, and deposited in court in a sealed envelope, to be opened when court is in session.

4. *signed, sealed, and delivered:* an often misleading ritual formula acknowledging that a writing has been executed (□see **execute**). If a seal is unnecessary to execution, *sealed* should be omitted.

sealed contract   □see **seal**.

sealed instrument   □see **seal**.

sealed record   □see **seal**.

sealed verdict   □see **seal**.

seaman's will   □see **sailor's will**.

search   □see **search and seizure**; □see **frisk search, under frisk**; □see **strip search, under frisk**.

search and seizure

1. a short collective reference to the Fourth Amendment of the U.S. Constitution, which reads: "The right of the people to be secure in their persons, houses, papers, and effects, against *unreasonable* searches and seizures, shall not be violated, and no warrants shall issue, but upon *probable cause,* supported by oath or affirmation, and particularly describing the place to be searched, and the persons or things to be seized" (italics added). As a collective reference to the Fourth Amendment, *search and seizure* includes the portion separately called the **Warrant Clause** (□see).

2. a short collective reference to a state constitutional provision similar to the provisions of the Fourth Amendment (sense 1). Some references to sense 2 rather than sense 1 are explicit; others clear by context.

3. a short distributive reference to the kind of government activity that may constitute a *search* or a *seizure* in the constitutional sense (especially sense 1), the reasonable and the unreasonable, what is included and excluded, and the consequences of exclusion. <What you are complaining about is routine traffic control, not search and seizure./ There may be permitted or prohibited search and seizure with or without a warrant.> Under the rubric *search and seizure, search* and *seizure* may occur separately or together, as in *stop and frisk* (□see **frisk**). Special characteristics of the *search* and the *seizure* are described in this entry, along with the distinctive *Terry stop.* A fuller description of the ongoing constitutional struggle over permissible and impermissible *search and seizure* is the province of cases and classes, journals and treatises.

> **search:** in general, a hunt by government agents, with or without a *search warrant,* for people, property, or communications believed to bear or evidence the taint of crime. It is a hunt, by physical or scientific intrusion, without the consent of the hunted or of those with the right to control the property or the communication; it is a hunt for what is not in **plain view** (□see).

seizure

1. the act of government agents in taking possession of property or learning the details of communications in connection with a *search.*

2. the act of government agents in physically restraining a person or implicitly threatening that restraint upon any attempt to walk away (□see **custody**). Actual or implied, the restraint is without the consent of the person restrained, as an incident of law enforcement. It is a *seizure* whether labeled an *arrest* or a more temporary restraint called a *stop* (□see **frisk**).

Terry stop: a *stop* (seizure) of a person whose behavior would seem suspicious to a reasonably cautious police officer, followed by the officer's quick protective decision that results in a *frisk* (search) of outer clothing, reasonably designed to discover weapons dangerous to the officer or others nearby. The *Terry stop,* a special version of *stop and frisk* (□see **frisk**), is distinctive for its approval of a *search and seizure* not based on *probable cause.* Taking its name from the guidelines outlined in *Terry v. Ohio,* 392 U.S. 1 (1968), the *Terry stop* has been expanded, varied, criticized; and remains lively.

For other entries connected with *search and seizure,* □see **exclusionary rule;** □see **fruit of the poisonous tree;** □see **knock and announce;** □see **probable cause;** □see **right of privacy;** □see **writ of assistance,** under **writ.**

search warrant □see **search and seizure;** □see **Warrant Clause.**

SEC: abbreviation of Securities and Exchange Commission. Also, *S.E.C.* □see **administrative agency,** under **administrative law.**

secondary boycott □see **boycott.**

secondary evidence: evidence offered as the best **evidence** (□see) when an original writing (which would have been the best) is not available, or rejected because other better or best evidence is available. Use of the expression varies by jurisdiction.

secondary liability: a liability that is contingent upon the happening of a specified event, typically the failure of someone else to perform an obligation. Sometimes contrasted with *primary liability,* e.g., by promising to pay a definite sum of money on a definite date. The status of secondary liability runs throughout the law, e.g., in suretyship, negotiable instruments, tort, contract, family law.

secondary meaning: the association in the public mind of a particular product with a particular producer, by reason of long exposure to that identity; as by trademarks used in advertising the product. <When I order "*Coke*," I don't want any old cola drink, I want a *Coca-Cola.*> A repeated name, design, symbol, color, sound, packaging, etc., may establish the identity, important in the law of **unfair competition** (□see) and trademarks and related marks (□see **trademark**).

secondary picketing   □see **picketing**.

second-degree murder   □see **murder**.

second party   □see **party**.

secure • security • securities

These words, etymologically related, split into two discrete pairs, with a different sense of *security* in each pair.

secure/security

1.   The common English words *secure* (v.), to make safe, to obtain; *security* (n.), safety, and the feeling of being secure; and the adjective forms, e.g., a secure location, security measures—are also used in the law.   <"[A]nd secure the blessings of liberty to ourselves and our posterity." (Preamble, U.S. Constitution).>

2.   The common legal sense of *secure* (v.), and its adjective forms, a special way of making safe, is closely tied to one of the two major legal uses of the companion *security* (n.) and its adjective forms.

secure: to reinforce words of promise with something (the *security*) that gives a tight hold on property, as a source of money instead of words if the promise turns sour. The *security* can take many forms, e.g., **mortgage** (□see), **pledge** (□see), *security interest* (□see, below, in this entry), *trust deed* (□see **deed**). <The loan was secured by a trust deed on Blackacre./She pledged her diamond necklace as security.>   □see also, **collateral**; □see also, **encumbrance**, under **encumber**; □see also, **lien**. A creditor who has this kind of *security* is said to be a *secured creditor,* the loan or obligation a *secured loan, secured obligation, secured debt.* Usage varies by statute.

security, as the companion of *secure,* has these, among other, special combinations:

security deposit: typically, by agreement, a deposit of money by a lessee with a lessor to secure performance of obligations under the lease.

security for costs: typically, by statute, a deposit of money in court by a litigant to cover court costs, or costs that may be awarded to the other litigant. Sometimes alternating with a *cost bond* for the same purpose.

security interest: "[A]n interest in personal property or fixtures which secures payment or performance of an obligation." (UCC § 1201(37)). For fuller detail, see the Uniform Commercial Code.

securities/security: in general, *securities* are interests in the ownership of a business, or promises by a business or government to pay money. The word also refers to the piece of paper that represents those interests or promises.

Securities as interests in ownership are called *equity securities,* e.g., stock in a corporation; as promises to pay money, *debt securities,* e.g., a corporate or government **bond** (□see).

Securities is the general category of reference in the world of investment, finance, business, e.g., the *securities market.* The singular, *security,* is to be distinguished from the other major legal use of the word, the companion noun to the verb *secure* (make safe). *A security,* in the securities market sense, may or may not be *secure,* but may be used as *the security* to back up a promise to pay money, as described above, under *secure.*

Definitions of *securities* and *security* in the sense of this entry are subject to great variation by statutes, which give special definitions for particular usages: e.g., federal regulation under the Securities Act of 1933 (15 USCA § 77b(1)) or the Securities Exchange Act of 1934 (15 USCA § 78c(10)); e.g., income taxation of capital gains and losses of dealers in securities (26 USCA § 1236); e.g., investment securities under the Uniform Commercial Code (§ 8102(1)); state corporate securities acts; bankruptcy; probate; etc.

secured debt □see **secure.**

secured creditor □see **secure.**

secured loan □see **secure.**

secured obligation □see **secure.**

securities □see **secure.**

Securities and Exchange Commission □see **SEC.**

security □see secure.

security deposit □see secure.

security for costs □see secure.

security interest □see secure.

sedition □see treason.

see you in court □see court.

segregation: generally, the unconstitutional separation of people, especially on the basis of race, in schools, housing, **public accommodations** (□see), and areas otherwise available or open to members of the public.

de facto segregation □see de facto.

de jure segregation □see de facto.

desegregation

1. ending *segregation.* □see **with all deliberate speed;** □see **time.**

2. limiting *segregation* in accordance with court order, or to keep within constitutional restrictions on *segregation.*

integration: a synonym for *desegregation,* but less well-defined by usage or decision.

seise □see seisin.

seised and possessed □see seisin.

seisin (law F., SEE-zin, as in *season:* possession); also spelled *seizin.* The verb form is *seise;* also spelled *seize.*

1. in historical usage: briefly, the right to a freehold (fee, fee tail, or life estate) based on its possession. *Seisin* was the key to the creation or transfer of a freehold by a ritual delivery of possession, called *livery of seisin.* <Seisin was *in* A./A had the seisin./She was seised *of* Blackacre./He was seised *in* fee.> The great days of *seisin* have passed; there are survivors and mutants.

seisin

2. *Seisin* still lives in some jurisdictions in describing the right to a freehold; usage is neither certain nor uniform. It is a synonym for one or more of the words *title, ownership,* and *possession;* sometimes redundantly *seised and possessed* or *seized and possessed.*

3. One distinctive usage generally recognized is the *covenant of seisin* (□see **covenants of title**).

seizin □see seisin.

seizure □see **search and seizure.**

self-dealing □see **fiduciary.**

self-defense

1. physically: the defense of one's person as a matter of survival or the prevention of injury. By extension, the defense of one's property and reputation, and the defense of others with whom one has a special relationship, e.g., family.

2. in criminal law: a legal defense to a charge of various crimes, e.g., murder, battery. Usually classified as **justification** (□see), sometimes as *excuse,* for the physical defense of one's person against an aggressor attacking or threatening imminent attack. The limits of justifiable resistance, including questions of reasonableness of violent response and whether or not one must **retreat to the wall** (□see), vary by jurisdiction. Rules likewise vary on extending the legal defense to protection of property (especially one's home), and to the defense of others.

3. in general tort law: following the general lines of sense 2, a legal defense to civil claims by an aggressor, or to negligent injury of others incidental to self-defense against an aggressor. Called the *privilege of self-defense.*

4. in tort law of defamation: a defendant's legal defense to claims of defamation that the publication was a privileged response to defamation by the plaintiff.

self-help: direct, personal action to right a wrong or prevent it, without court proceedings. E.g., evicting a delinquent tenant by changing the locks in his absence (□see **evict**). E.g., abating a **private nuisance** (□see **nuisance**). *Self-help* is an imprecise expression, sometimes recognized as legal if it can be exercised without a breach of the peace.

self-incrimination □see **criminate**.

Self-incrimination Clause: the part of the U.S. Constitution reading: "No person . . . shall be compelled in any criminal case to be a witness against himself. . . ." (Amend. V). □see **criminate**; □see also, **constitutional clauses**.

self-serving: short for *self-serving declaration*. □see **declaration**.

self-serving declaration □see **declaration**.

sell (v.): descriptive and operative word to transfer real or personal property, emphasizing the requirement of payment. Ordinary English *sell* (n.) has no technical legal counterpart. With *sale* (n.) of personal property, the correlative parties are usually called *seller*, and interchangeably *buyer* or *purchaser*. The same terms are often used for real property, but in legal discussion of sales of real estate, the traditional rubric is *vendor and purchaser*, with the parties sometimes called *vendor* and *vendee*. □see **buy**; □see **sale**.

seller □see **sell**.

semble (law F.: it seems): a near-dead technical expression. Italicized and inserted in an opinion or footnote, *semble* is an older way of commenting without being held accountable. The proposition or case so branded seems to be saying something, but what it says is either uncertain, or lacks authority, perhaps both.

seminal □see **clichés**.

send: Ordinary English senses of *send* are used in the law. But statute and decision often dictate special ways of "sending" (e.g., deposit in the mail, stamped, and properly addressed) and the consequences. Thus, the fact of sending might or might not constitute the acceptance of an offer, the giving of a notice, or a presumption that the person addressed had received what was sent. Absent personal arrangements, the law will continue to specify a reasonable way to *send* and especially the consequences. Both mode and consequences are in flux, influenced by the state of the art in the science of communication, including associated malfunction. <The computer is down.> □see also, **deliver**; □see also, **F.O.B.**

senior □see **subordinate**.

sentence (n., v.)

1. often, a synonym for **judgment** (□see) of guilt in a criminal case. <The verdict was read, the defendant asked for mercy, and the court proceeded to pass sentence/judgment./ . . . the court proceeded to sentence the defendant.>

2. often considered an integral part of the judgment of guilt in a criminal case. <It is the judgment of this court that you are guilty as charged, and I sentence you to. . . . >

3. often, implicit in sense 1 and explicit in sense 2, the punishment itself for the commission of a crime. <She is serving a life sentence in the prison at X.> Some forms of sentences:

concurrent sentences: separate sentences to imprisonment, to be served simultaneously.

cumulative sentences: separate sentences to imprisonment, each to be served separately at the expiration of the preceding sentence. Also called *consecutive sentences.*

determinate sentence: a sentence to imprisonment for a fixed time.

indeterminate sentence: a sentence fixing limits to imprisonment, but leaving the exact term to later determination by a governmental authority.

mandatory sentence: a sentence to a term of imprisonment required by statute or rules of court.

suspended sentence: a sentence imposed, but not to be served or paid now, or ever, depending upon a court's discretion.

□see also, **allocution**; □see also, **commutation**; □see also, **reprieve**.

separability clause □see **saving clause**.

separable contract □see **saving clause**.

separable controversy (in typical context): In a suit in a state court, two separate causes of action are joined. One, the *separable controversy,* is of a type subject to removal to a federal court if it were the only cause of action. The other, a type not ordinarily subject to removal, but as a result of the joinder, the entire suit is subject to **removal** (□see). See 28 USCA § 1441(c).

separate and apart: a typically redundant characterization of the fact that husband and wife are no longer living together. That is, they are living in *separate* dwellings; they are living *apart;* usually, not always, as a prelude to divorce. □see **coupled synonyms.**

separate but equal doctrine: the reversed catchphrase for the now dead doctrine that gave constitutional approval to racial segregation of public facilities if they were "equal but separate." (*Plessy v. Ferguson,* 163 U.S. 537, 540, 1896; with Harlan, J., in vigorous dissent). The wide sweep of the doctrine was halted in *Brown v. Board of Education,* 347 U.S. 483 (1954) and 349 U.S. 294 (1955), holding that separate (segregated) public schools could not be equal. Other decisions and statutes—in the pathway of *Brown*—finished off the doctrine.

separate estate □see **separate property.**

separate maintenance □see **divorce.**

separate property

1. In community property states, *community property* is contrasted with *separate property;* rules and definition vary by statute and decision. For general reference:

separate property

a. property owned by husband or wife before the marriage, its proceeds after marriage, and property acquired by husband or wife by gift or inheritance. <Interest on the bonds she owned before the marriage was never commingled with community funds; bonds and interest were her separate property.> □see **community property.**

b. property designated *separate* property by **marital agreement** (□see).

2. In states that have not adopted the community property system, *separate property* is a hodgepodge. Definition varies from the community property state definitions to definitions designed to eliminate common law liabilities of married women, and making earnings of either husband or wife the separate property of the owner.

Separate property is also referred to as *separate estate.*

separation: a loose usage that can refer to the physical fact of husband and wife living apart (□see **separate and apart**), to living apart by **marital agreement** (□see), or to **legal separation** (□see, under **divorce**).

separation a mensa et thoro: a variant usage of **divorce a mensa et thoro** (□see, under **divorce**).

separation from bed and board: a variant usage of **divorce from bed and board** (□see, under **divorce**).

separation of church and state: the frequently stated aim of the **Establishment Clause** (□see) of the U.S. Constitution.

separation of jury: the condition that exists when jurors are not kept continuously together for the duration of a trial or deliberations. Prohibition of *separation* or its limitation (to insulate the jurors from outside influences) varies by jurisdiction, statute, and decision. Usually, not always, it is left to the discretion of the trial judge to permit jurors to *separate* (e.g., go home at night) between sessions of court or deliberation. Rules vary by such factors as trial or deliberations; civil or criminal case; capital or lesser crime; extent of media coverage; length of trial or deliberations; hardship to jurors; possible prejudice to litigants, etc. If, by discretion or absolute prohibition, *separation of jury* is forbidden, the jury is said to be **sequestered**, i.e., continuously isolated from the outside world. <The statute required **sequestration** of the jury.>

separation of powers: the usual general reference to the division of government into legislative, executive, and judicial branches, under the U.S. Constitution and state constitutions. The phrase, called a *doctrine,* a *principle,* a *concept,* designed to prevent a concentration of power, still undergoes constant judicial interpretation, as well as questioning among the branches as to their own limits. *Separation of powers* is sometimes loosely equated with the mechanics of separation called **checks and balances**: how *separation of powers* works or should work.

sequester

1. to order property held subject to court order as security for an eventual judgment. The process or remedy is called **sequestration**.

The words are from older usage, now usually supplanted by special statutes. Kin to **attachment** (□see).

2. For *sequester* and *sequestration* applied to a jury, □see **separation of jury**.

sequestration   □see **sequester**; □see also, **separation of jury**.

serious: as in ordinary English, something of importance, not trifling; characterizing, e.g., an injury, misconduct, or crime. And as in ordinary English, useful as a word of great flexibility. Not precise, unless securely tied down by, e.g., a statutory definition. Good background music for other imprecision, as in *serious and willful.* □see **willful**.

serious and willful   □see **serious**; □see **willful**.

servant   □see **master and servant**.

serve   □see **service of process**.

service mark

1. words, names, symbols, or devices used or intended to be used to "identify and distinguish" a person's services, and to "indicate the source." Compare **trademark** (□see).

2. Titles, character names, and other distinctive features of radio or television programs may also be service marks, though advertising the sponsor's goods.

For details of both types of service marks, see 15 USCA § 1127, as amended Nov. 16, 1988.

service of process: a part of the mechanics of commencing legal proceedings, of making people and property subject to the jurisdiction and power of courts and government officials, and of giving people notice of legal proceedings that might affect them. The mechanics of *service of process* generally fall within two great categories: **personal service** and **constructive service** (also called **substituted service**). In either case, the verb is to *serve;* the target has been *served.* Both the mechanics and effects of *service of process* are closely controlled by statutes of great variation.

service of process

personal service

1. In its old, still used, basic form, *personal service* of process is the physical delivery to the target person of an official piece of paper—the **process** (□see)—that has a prescribed effect in legal proceedings. E.g., delivery to the defendant of a copy of a summons and complaint requiring a response within a specified time. The person who makes *personal service* is called a *process server,* whether or not an official.

2. Under some statutes, some acts other than physical delivery to the target person are sometimes called *personal service,* and often have the same effect as personal service, whether or not so labeled. E.g., delivery to an adult at the target person's residence; e.g., delivery to an authorized agent; e.g., mailing.

constructive service (also called **substituted service**): Generally, a procedure to accomplish *service of process* other than by *personal service.* Under some statutes, anything other than physical delivery to the target person (e.g., the alternative mechanics listed in 2 above) is *constructive,* not *personal service.* The most widespread type of *constructive service* is:

> **service by publication**: a procedure, prescribed in detail by statute, involving publishing a copy of some process in a **legal newspaper** (□see). E.g., *publication of summons.* After a specified number of publications, e.g., the targeted person has been *served;* e.g., has notice of a suit to quiet title.

return of service: the legal paper designed for filing in court reporting the completion of *service of process* or of the failure to *serve.* <The process server's return of service reported his inability to make personal service on the defendant.>

services: may be any sort of *work, labor,* or the performance of duties, from the menial to the exalted. <His services as a busboy lasted four years./His services as President of the United States lasted only one term.> As a matter of usage, lawyers and other professionals usually earn fees for *services* (□see **charging lien,** under **lien**). In the construction industry, the *mechanic's lien* (□see **lien**) is usually for *work, labor,* and *materials;* in billing, differentiation may be made between manual labor and supervisory services. But in the law, as in ordinary English, *services* is imprecise. Unless made specific by statute, definition, or context, classification cannot be reliably determined by the form of payment, whether wages, salary, fee, or rates. □see also, **quantum meruit.**

servient estate   □see **easement.**

servient tenement   □see **easement.**

servitude   □see **easement.**

servitude in gross   □see **easement.**

session

1.   as to courts:

a.   generally, the time when a court is open for business, with a judge on the bench. The characterizing expression is "The court is now *in session*" (□see also, **sit**). A court might also be in session— with lawyers, witnesses, jurors, clerks, etc.—on a site visit away from the courthouse. *Session* is often expanded to include a period (e.g., a day, an afternoon) when the court is open except for temporary recesses. Whether or not the court is *in session* can affect questions of **contempt** (□see). □see also, **open court,** under **open.**

b.   sometimes used interchangeably with *term* (i.e., a *term of court*), e.g., a period of months or weeks when the court will be open for business intermittently; e.g., "October term."

2.   as to other organized bodies, e.g., a legislature: a time of meeting. Varies by local statute or rules.

set aside   □see **annul and set aside,** under **null and void;** □see **quash.**

setback: a limitation on how close to the property line (or other line or to a structure) that an owner may build or plant. The distance or area of setback may be fixed by law, deed, or agreement. <By city ordinance, there was a fifty-foot setback from the street, five feet from property sidelines, but none at the rear of the property.>

set down: an old, still used, formalism to fix the time for a trial or hearing. <*Smith v. Jones* was set down for trial on March 1./The order to show cause will be set down for hearing on Monday.>

setoff   □see **offset.**

set over   (v.): an old redundancy for *transfer*. Its only virtue, not a redeeming one, is that in the company of other redundancy, it adds a

597

rhythmic conclusion.   <A granted, sold, transferred, assigned, and set over Blackacre to B.>   Best forgotten.

settle • settlement

Verb and noun are used in the law in all of the varied senses of ordinary English.   Some peculiarly legal usage:

1. of a lawsuit:

a. traditional usage for ending a lawsuit by compromise: *the case was settled.*   <Details of the *settlement* were not disclosed.> □see **covenant not to sue**; □see **Mary Carter agreement**.

b. more recent usage, argot, on its way to becoming standard, and meaning the same as the traditional usage: *the case settled.* <I think the case will settle./They have been talking settlement; the odds are the case will settle.>

2. of property: loose usage for the transfer of property.   □see **marriage settlement,** under **marital agreement**.

3. of commercial paper: payment through the banking process. See UCC 4–104(j).

settlement   □see settle.

settlor   □see trust.

sever • severance

In addition to the sense of ordinary English, verb and noun have peculiarly legal usage:

1. procedure to separate causes of action, offenses, defendants, parties generally, that have been joined in a civil or criminal action.   □see **joinder**. What is *severable* varies by statute. Invoked by the court; or by those affected filing a *motion to sever,* also called a *motion for severance.*

2. to break up (*sever*), or the breakup (*severance*), of a **joint tenancy** (□see, under **estate**).

severable contract   □see saving clause.

severability clause   □see saving clause.

several   □see **joint and several liability.**

severally   □see **joint and several liability.**

severalty   □see **estate in severalty,** under **estate.**

severance   □see **sever.**

severance damage   □see **eminent domain.**

sex

In ordinary English

1. The distinction between male and female, i.e., the two *sexes.* Also, in adjective usage, *sex* or *sexual* differences. The synonym *gender* is more commonly a term of grammar—masculine, feminine, and neuter gender.

2. Relating to *sex* (sense 1) or activity based on sex, e.g., *have sex,* traditionally described as *sexual intercourse,* euphemistically as *carnal knowledge.*

3. In an extended sense, *sex* often refers to *homosexuality,* or to a *homosexual* of either sex. Often, *homosexual* is applied to males, more commonly described as *gay,* and the female a *lesbian.*

4. In an extended sense, *sex* also refers to varied forms of *sexual* gratification. □see **crime against nature.**

5. The expressions *sex discrimination, sexual discrimination, sexism,* and *sexist* are part of the common speech, often with legal overtones. Discussed below.

In the law

1. Explicit sex

As in ordinary English, the law is full of explicit use of the word *sex.* As in *sex offenders; on account of sex*—e.g., no denial of vote (Nineteenth Amendment, 1920), e.g., **Equal Rights Amendment** (□see); discrimination *because of sex*—discussed below.

2. Gender or sex

Despite *sex* in the Constitution, some in the profession prefer the old synonym *gender* as a general substitute for *sex.* *Sex discrimination* becomes *gender discrimination; sex neutral* becomes *gender neutral,* etc. In the increasing litigation over *sex,* coupled with indiscriminate usage in the ordinary language, *sex* and *sexual* are an embarrassment. But those who opt for *gender* rarely stand on a consistent, principled choice. They lapse into *sex.* In the same paragraph, they wander through *gender, sex, sex or gender,* without obvious change of sense. It is the traditional descent into word doubling and unintelligibility. Your *gender* is my *sex.* Are we talking about the same thing?

3. Sexism

Centuries of a male-dominated society have pervasively affected the language of the law. Many of those effects are now being rooted out, more are under fire, as evidences of *sexism* (also *sexist,* adj., n.): this century's pejorative for conduct or attitudes based on the assumption of the superiority of one *sex,* primarily the male. Some old usage has become so standard that a *sexist* effect is forgotten, ignored, or denied.

a. *Nouns ending in -er and -or.* Most words in this category are generally regarded as sex neutral, despite the old etymological identification of those endings with maleness. Some ordinary English, e.g., converts *fireman* into *fire fighter, mailman* into *mail carrier, foreman* into *supervisor.* Similarly, the law changes *workmen's compensation* to **workers' compensation** (□see); and, without protest, hangs on to *juror* (□see **jury**), *lawyer,* and *director.* In some instances, the *-or* ending has come to be generally preferred for both sexes, over the still extant, but dying, distinctly female versions: e.g., *administrator* over *administratrix, executor* over *executrix, relator* over *relatrix, testator* over *testatrix, prosecutor* over *prosecutrix.* □see **prosecuting witness**.

b. *Man into person.* Some insist that *man* is an old sexless generic, or has become so, with too much law piled on its back to risk the confusion of change. Even so, *person* is frequently substituted for *man;* as in *chairperson* for *chairman;* some make it *chair.* Corporations still generally are chaired by males and have a *chairman of the board. Reasonable man* is locked in mortal combat with *reasonable person;* □see **reasonable man**, □see also, **negligence.** *Prudent man* is sometimes called a *prudent person,* complicated by the *prudent man rule;* □see **prudence.** *Remainderman,* an old staple of property law, is sometimes called a *remainderperson,* or worse; □see **remainder,** under **future interest.** *Person* is a quick fix. It doesn't fix everything. □see **Brethren;** □see **clergyman-penitent privilege,** under **priest-penitent privilege;** □see **landlord and tenant;** □see **newsmen's**

privilege; □see **seaman's will**, under **sailor's will**. □see **venire-man**, under **jury panel**; □see also, **Esquire**.

c. *he, his, him.* Until the feminist awakening, the law made do with "Words used in the masculine gender include the feminine and neuter." Statutes, contracts, and other writings still work that road; even when it makes for utter confusion, as in an indecent exposure statute prohibiting "an act of exposing *his* genitals." None of the suggested alternatives to *he, his, him* has achieved a consensus: e.g., *his/her, her/his, himself/herself, s/he.* The substitution of *one's,* the repetition of a noun (e.g., the witness shall raise the witness's right hand), *such person's, you,* and *yours* are other devices. Increasingly, in and out of the law, the ungrammatical plural *their* is substituting for the singular *he, his, him.* Usually, a writer who cares can write around the problem.

4. Sex discrimination

a. Definition is in flux, resting in instances and opinion as to what is or ought to be considered *sex discrimination;* consensus is absent. As a working usage: *sex discrimination* is a broad label for prohibited distinctions based on the male-female difference or on stereotypes of social inequality of the sexes. *Sex discrimination* is also called discrimination *because of sex* and *sexual discrimination.*

Instances of the prohibitions usually come in the form of state and federal legislation (e.g., Title VII, Civil Rights Act of 1964), regulations (e.g., 29 Code of Federal Regulations § 1604.1 *et seq.*), and constitutional interpretation, especially of equal protection (e.g., *Califano v. Wescott,* 443 U.S. 76, 1979), sometimes due process (e.g., *Taylor v. Louisiana,* 419 U.S. 522, 1975). *Sex discrimination* may take the form of *sexual harassment* (e.g., 29 Code of Federal Regulations § 1604.11), but the two expressions should not be equated.

b. *Sex discrimination* does not include discrimination based on *homosexuality.*

5. Sexual harassment

a. Unwelcome conduct, physical or otherwise, related to *sex* (1) that is imposed as a condition of a person's obtaining a goal (e.g., employment, advancement, a passing grade) or (2) that creates an environnment interfering with the obtaining of that goal. The conduct may range from rape, threatening, and touching to offensive looking, commenting, and asking. The target of *sexual harassment* is usually a female.

    b. *Sexual harassment* may be *sex discrimination* (see *Meritor Savings Bank, FSB v. Vinson,* 477 U.S. 57, 1986), but need not be. A goal obtained by submission to *sexual harassment* may be *sex discrimination* against others qualified but denied. See 29 Code of Federal Regulations § 1604.11(g).

□see also, **feminist jurisprudence.**

sex discrimination □see **sex.**

sexism □see **sex.**

sexist □see **sex.**

sexual harassment □see **sex.**

sexual intercourse □see **sex.**

shall □see **may.**

sham corporation □see **alter ego.**

share □see **stock.**

share certificate □see **stock.**

share dividend □see **stock.**

shareholder □see **stock.**

share option □see **stock.**

share right □see **stock.**

share split □see **stock.**

share subscription □see **stock.**

sharing in justice   □see oral.

Shelley's Case   □see rule in Shelley's Case.

Shepardize: to search in an index called *Shepard's Citations* for other references to a particular case, statute, or law review article; to find out, e.g., whether a particular decision has been overruled by a later decision in the **law reports** (□see).   <Have you Shepardized that case, counsel?>

sheriff: varying by jurisdiction, usually the chief elected law enforcement officer of a county or other similar state subdivision.   Varying administrative duties, e.g., supervision of local jails, watching over a deliberating jury, service of process, order in the court.   Officers under a sheriff, e.g., a *deputy sheriff,* often loosely called "sheriff."

Sherman Antitrust Act   □see antitrust law.

shield laws   □see newsmen's privilege.

shifting executory interest   □see future interest.

shingle: colloquial, ordinary American English for a sign indicating a professional's office, especially a lawyer's.   As in the expression *hang out a shingle.*   That expression is used metaphorically to mean: *starting to practice law;* often, *starting to practice on my own,* as distinguished from being employed by other lawyers or joining a law firm.   <I hung out my shingle and waited.>

shipment contract   □see F.O.B.

shocks the conscience   □see conscience.

show cause order   □see order to show cause.

shun and avoid: old bilingual (Old English and French) synonyms, a faded usage in describing what is defamatory < . . . causing them to be shunned and avoided.>.   □see **defamation.**   □see **coupled synonyms.** For a different sense, □see **avoid.**

shyster

shyster □see lawyer.

sidebar □see bar.

sign □see subscribe.

signed, sealed, and delivered □see seal.

single □see unmarried.

sit: in reference to judges: to mean that a judge or a group of judges is acting in a judicial proceeding (□see **en banc**, under **bench**). Also, loosely, that a court is open for business <The court is now sitting.>. □see **in session**, under **session**.

situate, lying, and being in: located. Joins comfortably with further redundancy. <All that certain part and parcel of land situate, lying, and being in. . . .> □see **parcel**. □see **coupled synonyms**. Some lawyers shed the redundancy yet cling to the archaic adjective *situate*. <That property situate in. . . .>

situs

1. a location or place, from the Latin for *site;* also rendered by the Latin *locus*. □see **lex loci**; □see **lex situs**, under **lex loci rei sitae**.

2. the place where particular legal consequences attach to a person or property, as, e.g., based on **domicile** (□see), a *corporate situs,* or *situs for taxation*.

skyjacking □see hijacking.

slander □see defamation.

slander of goods □see disparagement.

slander of title □see disparagement.

slander per quod □see actionable per se, under action.

slander per se   □see **actionable per se**, under **action**.

slavish adherence   □see **clichés**.

slight negligence   □see **negligence**.

slip opinion: a court's own printing of its opinion, opinions, or decision, case by case, as the first and quick official publication. ("First and quick" may ultimately be displaced by a computerized distribution.) The *slip opinion* is unbound, often no more than a single slip of paper, frequently corrected before publication in the **law reports** (□see).

slippery slope: a persistent cliché of rejection. Reject A because it might lead to B, which might lead—Heaven forbid—to C.   □see **clichés**. Its most valuable contribution to the law is the article by Professor Frederick Schauer, "Slippery Slopes," 99 *Harv.L.Rev.* 361 (1985).

small claims court: a court of limited jurisdiction.   □see **court**.

social security   □see **entitlement**.

social visitor   □see **licensee**.

sodomy   □see **crime against nature**.

so help you God: the traditional, formal ending of the oath as administered by an official. Changed to *so help me God* in the words of the person taking the oath. The phrases are more than **formalisms** (□see), often specifically required by statute when an oath is required, as distinguished from affirmation.   □see **affiant**; □see **Oath or Affirmation Clause**.

soldier's will   □see **sailor's will**.

sole practitioner   □see **firm**.

sole proprietorship: a business owned by an individual, as distinguished from ownership by a corporation, a partnership, or any form of group ownership. Also called *individual proprietorship*.

solicitation □see **barratry.**

Solicitor General □see **lawyer.**

solvency: the antonym of **insolvency** (□see, under **insolvent**).

solvent: the antonym of **insolvent** (□see).

sound □see **lie.**

sound and disposing mind and memory □see **mind and memory.**

sovereign (adj.): having supreme political power within a particular area, and over the relations of that area and its people with others beyond that area, as a *sovereign nation*. The quality of having that power is described as *sovereignty* (n.), as the *sovereignty of the people* (□see **people**). The person or entity that has that power is the *sovereign* (n.) or a *sovereignty* (n.).

As with other **absolutes** (□see), "supreme" is loosely used. The "supreme" power of a *sovereign nation* is limited by international law and treaty; the "supreme" power of what are called the *sovereign states* of the United States is limited, e.g., by the U.S. Constitution and some federal legislation.

sovereign immunity □see **immunity.**

sovereign states □see **sovereign.**

sovereignty □see **sovereign.**

space □see **outer space;** □see **space law;** □see also, **airspace.**

space law: the law dealing with activity, and the limits on activity, in outer space, and with the relationship between **airspace** (□see) and **outer space** (□see). □see also, **Outer Space Treaty.**

speaking demurrer □see **demurrer**, under **pleadings**.

speaking exception □see **demurrer**, under **pleadings**.

speaking motion □see **demurrer**, under **pleadings**.

special: the ordinary English word, flexible and imprecise. For the law, like its sometime synonym **extraordinary** (□see), at its best, *special* is an attempt to express a distinction. Compared to what? The entries that follow, combining *special* with another word, list some of those attempts.

special act □see **public law**.

special appearance □see **appear**.

special circumstances

1. a ubiquitous expression giving the semblance of precision to departure from almost any ordinary rule. Special circumstances that might require a storekeeper to protect a customer from a stranger's assault; that justify taking the deposition of a witness who is not a party; etc. What are those *special circumstances?* They vary with the circumstances, i.e., with the **facts** (□see).

2. circumstances (facts) so special that in a given context, they become a rule. Unlike sense 1, these *special circumstances* are fixed by statute or decision; they are *special* only in the sense that one rule is different from every other rule. For example: statute listing "special circumstances" requiring death or life without parole for first-degree murder (see Cal. Penal Code, § 190.2); voir dire re racial bias in capital, interracial crime (see *Turner v. Murray,* 476 U.S. 28, 36, 1986); some state rules re duty of disclosure of inside information by director or officer trading corporate shares.

Special circumstances is also called *special facts.*

special damages □see **damage**.

special dividend □see **dividend**.

special facts □see **special circumstances**.

special finding □see finding.

special indorsee □see indorsement.

special indorsement □see indorsement.

special lien □see lien.

special master □see master.

special power □see power of appointment, under appoint.

specials □see special damages, under damage.

specialty □see seal.

special use permit □see zoning.

special verdict □see verdict.

special warranty deed □see covenants of title.

specific bequest □see gift by will, under gift.

specific devise □see gift by will, under gift.

specific legacy □see gift by will, under gift.

specific intent □see intent.

specific performance: an equitable remedy (□see **equity**) requiring, directly or indirectly, that a party to a contract do precisely what was promised, e.g., to convey Blackacre, as distinguished from paying damages for breach of contract. A maze of rules—topics in the law of equity, remedies, contracts, and commercial transactions—governs the grant or denial of specific performance.

speculative damages   □see **damage**.

speech   □see **Freedom of Speech Clause**; □see **commercial speech**; □see **symbolic speech**; □see **Speech or Debate Clause**; □see also, **constitutional clauses**.

Speech or Debate Clause: the part of the U.S. Constitution reading: ". . . and for any speech or debate in either house, they ['The Senators and Representatives'] shall not be questioned in any other place." (Art. I, § 6).   □see also, **constitutional clauses**.

speedy trial: the words of the U.S. Constitution ["In all criminal prosecutions, the accused shall enjoy the right to a speedy . . . trial . . . ." Amendment VI]; applicable also to the states; and repeated in state constitutions.   Subject to some limits fixed by decision and federal and state statutes, the expression is deliberately vague, and a staple of litigation.

spendthrift trust   □see **trust**.

spin-off   (n., v.): a transfer of some of corporation A's assets to a controlled corporation B, in exchange for B's shares, which are then distributed to the shareholders of A without any surrender of their shares in A.   *Spin-off* is one of several related types of corporate reorganization regulated by tax law and geared to their effect on taxes; some others include:

split-off: the same as a *spin-off,* except that the shareholders of A surrender some of their shares in A in exchange for the shares they get in B.

split-up: a transfer of all of the stock and assets of corporation A to two or more corporations, B and C, in exchange for controlling shares of B and C, which are transferred to the shareholders of A in exchange for their shares in A; A is then liquidated (□see **dissolution**).

spite fence: a fence or similar structure of no benefit to the landowner except in carrying out an intent to annoy a neighbor.

split-off   □see **spin-off**.

splitting a cause of action: dividing a single cause of action into more than one suit. E.g., suing for less than all of the claims that are included in a single cause of action, and suing separately for the additional claims omitted.

split-up □see **spin-off.**

spoliation: an antique way of saying *spoiling* or *destroying.* The act done by someone who hardly anyone but a lawyer would call a *spoliator.*

1. **spoliation of evidence:** alteration, destruction, or disposal of a writing or property preventing its being used in litigation.

a. Intentional spoliation supports an inference that the item was unfavorable to the person responsible.

b. In some jurisdictions, intentional or negligent spoliation may be a cause of action in tort for destroying or injuring the case of a plaintiff who needed the evidence.

c. In criminal law, may amount to **obstruction of justice** (□see).

2. **spoliation of documents:** an alteration of a document (e.g., a will, a negotiable instrument) by someone not a party to the document, as contrasted with alteration by a party. Since not made by a party, validity of the document is not affected. *Spoliation of a will:* an alteration not made by the testator.

spoliation of a will □see **spoliation.**

spoliation of documents □see **spoliation.**

spoliation of evidence □see **spoliation.**

spoliator □see **spoliation.**

spontaneous statements: a general rubric for a wide variety of utterances under circumstances indicating lack of contrivance, admitted in evidence as exceptions to the **hearsay rule** (□see, under **hearsay**). □see also, **res gestae.**

sports law: a specialized area of law dealing especially with a burgeoning sports industry, its relationship to what is still referred to as "amateur athletics," and to traditional areas of the law.

spot zoning □see zoning.

spousal □see spouse.

spouse: usually, as in ordinary English, a husband or wife. A special legal twist in **putative spouse**; □see, under **cohabit**. The adjective *spousal,* an unpleasantly guttural way of referring to a spouse.

spread eagle □see option.

springing executory interest □see future interest.

sprinkling trust □see trust.

squatter: a person who takes actual possession of another's land, without title and without a good faith claim of right. To be distinguished from an **adverse possessor**; □see, under **possession**.

ss: an ancient formalism that still appears sporadically in the heading of affidavits; sometimes capitalized; sometimes with a period. Over the centuries, *ss* has been given various interpretations, the most common: an abbreviation of the Latin *scilicet* (one may know), usually translated *to wit.* To wit what? To wit, the venue; which in another age sometimes served a legal purpose. Today: worthless. □see **formalisms**.

stake □see stakeholder.

stakeholder: a disinterested third person who has possession or control of a *stake* (money or property) that is to be delivered to the claimant establishing a right to the stake. *Stakeholder* is loosely applied to a person chosen by the conflicting claimants to *hold the stake,* or to a person in possession or control of money or property that becomes the object of conflicting claims. *Stakeholder* is to be distinguished from **escrow holder**; □see, under **escrow**. □see also, **interpleader**.

611

stale: the ordinary English sense of a lack of freshness, translated in the law as excessive delay in asserting a right or taking legal action. What is excessive may be delay beyond a period fixed by statute: E.g., a *stale claim* asserted beyond the period of a **statute of limitations** (□see) or a **statute of nonclaim** (□see, under **nonclaim**). E.g., a *stale check:* presented for payment beyond the period specified in the Uniform Commercial Code. What is excessive may vary with the facts and rest in the discretion of a judge, e.g., information too old, too stale, to be the basis of **probable cause** (□see). The equitable defense of **laches** (□see), likewise grounded in excessive delay, is subject to the special rules of **equity** (□see).

stale check   □see **stale**.

stale claim   □see **stale**.

stand   (n., v.): a small platform between the jury box and the bench, with a chair for a witness. Also called the *witness stand;* sometimes—following British usage—called the *witness box*. Having been sworn, the witness is said to *take the stand,* to testify—usually sitting, not standing. Testimony completed, the witness *stands down,* i.e., leaves the stand.

Other expressions using the verb *stand* are separate entries in the dictionary.

stand adjourned: to end a court hearing.   <This court stands adjourned.> Often used interchangeably with *stand recessed* or *stand in recess*. Practice varies by court and jurisdiction; usually *recess* is for a shorter period than *adjournment*.   □see **delay**; □see also, **session**.

standard of care: a general expression of what constitutes *care*. □see **due care**, under **due**; □see **negligence**; □see **recklessness**; □see **reasonable man**; □see **malpractice**.

standard of proof   □see **proof**.

standards of review

1. a general expression of old and continuing attempts to establish criteria of **judicial review** (□see) of governmental acts affected by flexible constitutional language (e.g., due process); as distinguished from those confined by narrowly drawn provisions (e.g., right to vote

at eighteen; Amendment XXVI). Consensus is lacking both as to the number of criteria and their definition: they are variously referred to as "standards," "tests," "levels, or degrees of scrutiny."

2. a *two-tier* set of standards for judicial review of the constitutionality of legislation. The polar tiers are *rational basis* and *strict scrutiny*.

> **rational basis**: Variously stated, but its generalized essence is that if there was a rational basis for the legislation, involving a legitimate governmental interest, it is constitutional. Like its synonym **reasonable** (□see), the strength of *rational* basis lies in its weakness, continuously flexible. Frequently criticized, it survives as a mild stamp of approval, if "more exacting judicial scrutiny" is not required. (□see **Footnote Four**).

> **strict scrutiny**: A careful examination of the legislation, its purposes, its implications, its affect on *fundamental* constitutional rights and on so-called *suspect classifications*, e.g., race. The examination is to make certain that strict scrutiny is called for and—if so—that the legislation is narrowly drawn and *necessary* to achieve some *compelling state interest*. The language of *strict scrutiny*— "strict," "fundamental," "suspect," "necessary," "compelling"—is almost as imprecise as *rational basis*. In numerous decisions, its content has expanded and contracted, and the standard itself is repeatedly criticized. Where it survives, *strict scrutiny* is usually the kiss of death.

3. a three-level set of standards for judicial review of the constitutionality of legislation. This set includes varied statements of *rational basis* and *strict scrutiny* (sense 2), and adds what is frequently called an *intermediate level,* or *intermediate test.*

> **intermediate level**: A standard "more exacting" than *rational basis* and less rigorous than *strict scrutiny;* a device to provide a sliding scale of scrutiny. Sometimes expressed in terms of building on *rational basis* to require something within accustomed patterns of judicial discretion—a reasonable, fair, and substantial relationship to the object of legislation. Not involving fundamental rights or those of *discrete and insular minorities* (□see **Footnote Four**) of race, religion, or national origin, where legislation may be "inherently suspect" and subject to *strict scrutiny;* but perhaps "quasi-suspect," e.g., affecting sex. As with the other criteria, an *intermediate level* of scrutiny is not precise, is sharply argued, and is as changeable as the next Supreme Court decision.

standby counsel □see **right to counsel**.

stand down

stand down □see **stand.**

standing □see **controversy.**

stand in the shoes of □see **vicarious liability.**

stand mute: characterization of the conduct of the defendant who, on being arraigned on a criminal charge and asked how he wishes to plead, refuses to plead or simply says nothing. □see **arraignment.**

stand recessed □see **stand adjourned.**

stand, remain, and be: to continue unchanged. A traditional joining of bilingual synonyms; worthless. In context, any one of the words is sufficient. <The bond shall stand, remain, and be valid./The bond shall remain valid.> □see **coupled synonyms.**

stands the rule on its head □see **clichés.**

stare decisis □see **precedent.**

star page □see **star paging.**

star paging: a system of identifying in a reference or later edition the place where the words now published appeared in a first edition. E.g., in a later edition, an asterisk (the star) is inserted in the text before the word that begins a page of the first edition, and in the margin the asterisk and page number—the *star page.* E.g., in a book quoting from a later edition of a well-known treatise, a footnote reference, "3 Blackstone, *Commentaries* * 323 (Jones ed. 1916)."

state □see **sovereign;** □see **people;** □see **ex rel.;** □see **jurisdiction.**

state action

1. a shorthand expression of a so-called *rule* or *doctrine:* that a provision of the U.S. Constitution forbidding a state to impair specified rights is a limitation only of government (state) action, not a limitation of private conduct. (E.g., due process and equal protection, Amendment XIV, § 1; see also, Amendment XV). What is included

in *government* has no precise consensus: state and local legislatures and agencies are in; sometimes the courts. A state official, acting legally or not, e.g., in denying civil rights, is in, acting under *color of law:* for most purposes, equated with *state action.* (see sense 2). How close private conduct must be entwined with the state to be included in *state action,* e.g., performing essential governmental functions, intimately tied to official participation, etc., is a topic of continuing controversy and conflicting decision.

2. a more restricted version, in interpreting the Amendment XI limitation on the judicial power of the United States in suits against one of the states. For purposes of permitting suit against a state official acting in an unconstitutional manner, the official's acts are not always considered state action.

stated capital: the basic capital of a corporation; also called *legal capital* and *capital.* Generally, *stated capital* is the par value of issued par value stock, *plus* as much of the consideration received for no par stock as is not transferred to capital surplus, *plus* transfers to stated capital permitted by law. Corporation law governing *stated capital* varies by jurisdiction; the Revised Model Business Corporation Act (1984, amended to 1989) does not use the expression; nor *capital surplus,* nor the concept of *par value.*

Statement and Account Clause: the part of the U.S. Constitution reading: ". . . [A] regular statement and account of the receipts and expenditures of all public money shall be published from time to time." (Art. I, § 9). □see also, **constitutional clauses**.

state of a man's mind □see **clichés**.

state of mind □see **intent**.

state of the title □see **title**.

state police power □see **police power**.

state's attorney □see **lawyer**.

state sovereignty □see **sovereign**.

states' rights: an imprecise characterization of the rights of the individual states in the framework of the federal union under the U.S. Constitution. Some *states' rights* (also rendered *state rights*) are explicit, some implicit. The sense of the expression is in continuing controversy, with frequent citation of Amendment X: "The powers not delegated to the United States by the Constitution, nor prohibited by it to the States, are reserved to the States respectively, or to the people." Those words are sufficiently vague to give little instructive guidance. Years of Supreme Court decision give sharply varying interpretation of *states' rights,* with no decisive definition in prospect.

statute □see **legislation**; □see also, **declaratory statute**.

statute of frauds: a type of statute that makes some unwritten contracts unenforceable: e.g., a contract not to be performed within a year; e.g., a contract for the sale of goods at a prescribed price. Frequently, the contract is unenforceable unless it or an enlightening memorandum is signed by the *party to be charged,* is admitted in court by that party, or has been partly performed. The statutes vary by jurisdiction. Often spelled *Statute of Frauds* when referring to the English original or to a specific state statute. □see **fraud**.

statute of limitations: a type of statute that fixes an outside limit on the time for filing a lawsuit after a person has a cause of action, or for starting a prosecution after a crime has been committed. The statutes, varying by jurisdiction, fix different periods for different civil actions—personal injury, libel, written contract, oral contract, etc.; and for different crimes—some with no statute of limitations, e.g., a capital offense. □see also, **adverse possession**, under **possession**; □see also, **prescription**.

The statute has bred a special vocabulary:

The plural of *statute of limitations* ought to be *statutes of limitations* (and sometimes is). More often, an excess of *s* is avoided, and it becomes **statutes of limitation**.

The **running of the statute**, i.e., the computation of **passing time** (□see **run**) may be **tolled**, i.e., suspended. E.g.; the minority of the person having a cause of action, or absence from the jurisdiction of a person who has committed a crime, will *toll the statute*.

When the **limitation period** has ended, the **statute has run**, and a person's cause of action or a prosecution is said to be **barred**, **barred by the statute**, **time-barred** (also *time barred*), **outlawed** (□see **outlaw**), sometimes **stale** (□see).

A *statute of limitations* is to be distinguished from the discretionary flexibility of **laches** (□see).

□see also, **statute of nonclaim**, under **nonclaim**.

statute of nonclaim □see **nonclaim**.

Statutes at Large: short for *United States Statutes at Large:* official publication of the compiled statutes and concurrent resolutions of the Congress, some proclamations of the President, and proposed or ratified amendments to the U.S. Constitution. (See 1 USCA § 112.) Abbreviated *Stat.*

statutory construction □see **construction**; □see also, **legislative intent**, under **intent**.

statutory copyright □see **copyright**.

statutory entitlement □see **entitlement**.

statutory intent □see **intent**.

statutory interpretation □see **construction**; □see also, **legislative intent**, under **intent**.

statutory rape □see **rape**.

stay □see **delay**; □see **supersedeas**.

stay of execution □see **execute**.

stay of proceedings □see **supersedeas**.

steal □see **larceny**.

stepchild □see **child**.

sting □see **entrap**.

stipulate • stipulation: a form of quick agreement, usually between lawyers, often oral and in court. <We offer to stipulate that there was one prior. So stipulated./I would like that stipulation reduced to writing.>

stipulation □see **stipulate**.

stirpes □see **per capita**.

stock • share: an ownership interest in a corporation. The incidents of ownership, detailed in the law of corporations, vary by jurisdiction and articles of incorporation.

The choice of *stock* or *share* varies by jurisdiction, statute, and the custom of the marketplace. The influential Model Business Corporation Act (MBCA) and its revisions (Revised MBCA, 1984, amended to 1989) generally use *share,* rather than *stock;* but *stock exchanges* still thrive, and often dictate the terminology. *Stock* is sometimes regarded as a collective—the *stock market;* as opposed to the ordinary English sense of *share* or *shares* as a portion or unit of the whole. You buy ten *stocks* (in ten different companies), as opposed to ten *shares* (in IBM). But *stockholder* and *shareholder* each may refer to one who holds a single share or all of the shares of a corporation; and both *stock certificate* and *share certificate*—the pieces of paper—evidence that ownership, whatever it is. In the sampling of *stock* words that follows, *share* is an alternative.

> **common stock (shares):** usually the stock that carries with it the right to vote including the right to elect directors (□see **director**), to receive **dividends** (□see) when declared, and—after debts are provided for—to share in the distribution of assets on liquidation (□see **dissolution**). It is *common,* as distinguished from *preferred stock* (see, below, in this entry). The MBCA usually speaks only of *shares* of different kinds and characteristics, without the classification—*common* and *preferred.*
>
> **nonvoting stock (shares):** as distinguished from *voting stock* (see, below, in this entry).
>
> **no par stock (shares):** as distinguished from *par value stock* (see, below, in this entry).
>
> **par value stock (shares):** stock to which the corporation has assigned a money value that is printed on the stock certificate. *Par* once fixed the money or property paid to the corporation for its stock. That relationship can no longer be counted on. Stock may be issued at *par* or at some other price, or may be *no par value*

stock, another name for *no par stock* (see, above, in this entry). The MBCA does not use the concept of *par value.*

preferred stock (shares): stock that has a preference over *common stock* in the payment of a dividend—fixed by amount or percentage—if a dividend is declared, or a preference in some distribution on liquidation, or both of those preferences. *Preferred stock* may also be classified in other ways. Two basic classifications are:

> **cumulative preferred**: Preferred on which the current fixed dividend plus any unpaid fixed dividend must be paid before any dividend is paid on the common stock. The dividend on *cumulative preferred* is called a *cumulative dividend.*

> **participating preferred**: Preferred stock that—in addition to a fixed dividend—shares in dividends paid on the common stock.

There is an endless variety of types of *preferred stock,* and its preferences, as well as an endless variety of various classes of stock authorized by statute and articles, whether or not designated as *common* or *preferred.*

reverse stock split: see *stock split*, below, in this entry.

stock dividend (share dividend): □see **dividend**. See also, *stock split*, below, in this entry.

stock option (share option): an option to buy a specified number of shares at a specified price, e.g., as part of contract with management employees. Sometimes also called a *stock right* (see, below, in this entry). □see also, **stock warrant**, under **warrant**.

stock right (share right): a right given or sold to stockholders or others to buy or subscribe to an issue of stock. The term has no single meaning and may include a *stock option.*

stock split (share split): a division of shares into a larger number of shares. As distinguished from a *reverse stock split:* a combining of shares to make a smaller number of shares. The MBCA regards a share split (but not a reverse stock split) the same as a stock dividend; the reverse split requires an amendment of articles reducing the number of authorized shares.

stock subscription (share subscription): an agreement, called a *subscription* or *subscription agreement,* made by a *subscriber* to *subscribe,* i.e., to buy stock to be issued by a corporation. The agreement may be made before or after incorporation. Jurisdictions vary especially as to the subscriber's rights and obligations when the subscription is made before incorporation. See detailed rules in the MBCA, § 6.20.

stock

> **treasury stock (shares):** shares that have been issued and later reacquired by the corporation. The MBCA does not use the term, calling them *authorized but unissued,* unless the articles forbid reissue.

> **voting stock (shares):** a usual right of *common stock,* sometimes a contingent right of *preferred stock,* and a right of various classes of stock under articles of incorporation. All as distinguished from stock without voting rights: *nonvoting stock.* □see also, **cumulative voting;** □see also, **voting trust,** under **trust.**

> **watered stock (shares):** stock issued for less than par, as a bonus, at a discount, or for overvalued property so that the corporation receives less than par. *Watering* applies to new stock, and can occur whether or not there is any outstanding stock. □see also, **dilution.**

stock certificate □see stock.

stock dividend □see stock.

stockholder □see stock.

stockholder's derivative action □see derivative suit.

stockholder's representative action □see class action.

stock option □see stock.

stock right □see stock.

stocks □see per capita.

stock split □see stock.

stock subscription □see stock.

stock warrant □see warrant; □see stock.

stop □see cease and desist.

stop and frisk □see frisk.

straddle □see option.

straight voting □see cumulative voting.

stranger □see intermeddler.

stricken □see strike.

strict construction □see construction.

strict foreclosure □see foreclosure.

strict liability: liability for injury that is neither intentional nor negligent. It is an amorphous and expanding liability, imposed by decision or statute, without uniform limits. Applied, e.g., to the keeping of wild animals, storing of explosives, starting fires, and also to **products liability** (□see), **workers' compensation** (□see), and some forms of **nuisance** (□see). *Strict liability* is also called *strict liability in tort, liability without fault, liability without negligence,* and sometimes *absolute liability.*

strict scrutiny □see standards of review.

strike (v., n.)

1. (procedure)

a. to eliminate or wipe out something that has become part of a file or record. The adequate forms are *strike* and *struck.* The profession also uses the archaic form *stricken.* <The judge: Strike it from the calendar of cases ready for trial./It was struck from the list./The Supreme Court: "[I]t is ordered that his name be stricken from the roll of attorneys admitted to practice before the Bar of this Court.">

motion to strike: a lawyer's **motion** (□see) requesting an order that testimony, e.g., an unresponsive answer, be deleted. <I move to strike. . . ./I move that all of that be stricken. . . .>

b. to **strike down:** to **overrule** (□see) an earlier decision. This is argot characterizing the force of the court's opinion as a blow from on high. <Today, the Court struck down the long-standing rule of *Smith v. Jones* that. . . .>

2. (labor law)

a. (v.) to engage in the action called a *strike* (n.).

b. (n.) the combined action of a substantial group of employees acting together to stop working for an employer until the employer meets the group's demands affecting the terms of employment, e.g., pay increases, shorter hours, change of working conditions, new contract, etc. Also called a *walkout*.

The word *strike* does not have a fixed, uniform meaning. Definitions vary by contract, statute, decision, and miscellaneous comment. *Strike* is to be contrasted with **lockout** (□see).

c. Some definitions of *strike* include, and some exclude, related devices to exert pressure on an employer. E.g.:

work stoppage: when not included in the term *strike:* a more informal, often spontaneous, combined plan to stop working, sometimes to protest and demand change in a condition of immediate danger to workers. Also called a *walkout*.

job action: when not included in the term *strike:* a variety of devices of combined pressure, e.g., a *slowdown,* working-by-the-rule, etc.

strikebreaker □see **scab**.

strike down □see **strike**.

strike suit: a suit brought with an ulterior motive, with the hope of a nuisance value settlement or a possible award of an attorney's fee. The expression is argot or slang, applied especially to a derivative **suit** (□see) not brought to benefit the corporation.

strip search □see **frisk**.

style □see **name and style**, under **alias**.

sua sponte (L., SOO-uh SPON-tee: of one's own accord; spontaneously): on its own initiative. Said of a judge raising a legal point at a hearing without prompting from the litigants, e.g., the absence of appointed counsel for an indigent. The Latin expression is often used, alternating with the English equivalent: *on its own motion.*
<The court *sua sponte*/on its own motion/raised the question./Though neither

counsel requested the instruction, the trial judge had a duty to give the instruction on its own motion/*sua sponte.* >

subjacent support   □see lateral support.

subject matter jurisdiction   □see jurisdiction.

subject to   Usually, *subject to* is ordinary English in a legal setting. E.g., *conditional upon* (subject to lessor's approval); *subordinate to* (subject to a first mortgage), □see **subordinate**; *qualified by* (subject to paragraph 2). In addition, a sneaky usage, tucked into contracts:

subject to change by mutual consent (or **mutual agreement**): Everything is. Redundant to boot. Best forgotten. □see also, **agreement to agree**.

subject to change by mutual consent   □see subject to.

sub judice   (L., sub JOO-duh-see: under a judge): under consideration by a court.   <No comment for now; the case is still *sub judice.* >   Not a legal technicality; just Latin. The English says it as well. □see also, submission.

sublease   □see lease.

sublessee   □see lease.

sublessor   □see lease.

sublet   □see lease.

submission • submit   (n., v.)

1. *submission* is presenting something to someone for consideration, approval, or decision. E.g., *submit* a case to a judge or a jury for decision, a dispute to arbitration (□see **ADR**), an application for approval, an argument of counsel for consideration.   <I submit, Your Honor, that. . . .>

2. The something *submitted* is sometimes called the *submission.*   <Our submission is that an unbroken line of decision requires. . . .>

submission

3. *submit a case* may refer ambiguously to the action of counsel in resting and presenting the case to the judge for decision; or to the reciprocal—the judge's acknowledgement that the case has been received for decision < Judge: Submitted, counsel? Lawyer: Submitted. Judge: *Case submitted.*/The case is now under submission. > □see also, **sub judice**; □see also, **rest**, under **formalisms**.

submit   □see **submission**.

submit a case   □see **submission**.

subordinate • subordination

subordinate   (adj., v.): the state of one thing being of a lower rank than (*junior to*) something else, which is said to be *senior* or *superior*. E.g., a second mortgage is subordinate to a first mortgage. Accordingly, what is *senior* takes precedence over what is *subordinate*, e.g., gets paid first. If something is not already *subordinate* (adj.), it may be made so, e.g., by agreement *to subordinate;* □see **subordination**.

subordination: the process of making something *subordinate*, by court order fixing priorities, or by agreement—a *subordination agreement* or *subordination clause*. E.g., a *subordinated debenture*. E.g., a subordination clause in a lease may make the lease *subordinate to* (also said to be **subject to**, □see) later incumbrances, including a lien to secure borrowing by the lessor.

subordination   □see **subordinate**.

suborn   □see **perjury**.

subornation   □see **perjury**.

subpoena   (L., suh-PEE-nah: under a penalty). Sometimes spelled *subpena*, with no change of pronunciation. The prevailing usage is *subpoena*.

1. (n.) a court order directing a named individual to come to court, or other designated place, at a fixed time, to give testimony. The word is part of an older form of the order, as a Latin writ.

2. (n.) the piece of paper that contains the order (sense 1). □see **process**.

3. (v.) *subpoena,* short for *serve a subpoena,* i.e., the piece of paper (sense 2). □see **service of process.**

4. Under some statutes and decisions, the general term *subpoena* includes a **subpoena duces tecum** (□see).

subpoena duces tecum (L., suh-PEE-nah DOO-kis TAY-kum; also sometimes suh-PEE-nah DOO-sees TEE-kum; and combinations of those pronunciations: under a penalty bring with you): a court order directing a named individual to come to court, or other designated place, at a fixed time, and to bring specified papers and other physical evidence. The plural is *subpoenas duces tecum.* □see also, **discovery.**

subrogate □see **subrogation.**

subrogation

1. In general: When by law or agreement, a person is required to (and does) discharge a debtor's obligation to a creditor, that person (the *subrogee*) acquires (is *subrogated to*) the rights that the creditor (the *subrogor*) had against the debtor. E.g.: A negligently damages B's car, which is insured for that damage by insurance company C. C pays B for the damage to the car. C is subrogated to B's damage claim against A.

2. the right to acquire the right to *subrogation* (sense 1).

subrogee □see **subrogation.**

subrogor □see **subrogation.**

subscribe • subscription

1. *Subscribe* is an old synonym for the verb *to sign.* Usually, but not necessarily, refers to signing at the end of a document. *Sign* is the general, customary usage. *Subscribe* is a formalism, surviving where the sense of formality besets the law. E.g., in a notary's **jurat** (□see). E.g., in a will:

subscribed by the testator, i.e., signed.

subscribing witnesses (also called *attesting witnesses*) of what the testator signs and says, who then sign a statement (*attesting*) that it was done. □see **attest;** □see **declaration.**

subscribe

Subscription, to describe the act of signing, is little used; rarer still as a substitute for *signature.*

2. to subscribe for stock. □see **stock subscription,** under **stock.**

subscribed and sworn to   □see **jurat.**

subscribing witness   □see **subscribe.**

subscription   □see **subscribe;** □see **stock subscription,** under **stock.**

subscription right   □see **stock right,** under **stock.**

subsequent: a formalistic and unnecessary way of saying *after* or *later,* except in the combination *condition subsequent.*   □see **condition precedent.**

subsidiary corporation   □see **parent corporation.**

substantial   is as flexible in the law as in ordinary English.   That is its reason for continued existence in the law.   Long use of *substantial* in combinations, e.g., *substantial evidence,* can produce an impression of precision, which is lacking.   The word is an alert!   What *substantial* fastens itself to becomes infected with *substantial*'s flexibility. A place for discretion.   □see **substantial damages,** under **damage;** □see **substantial federal question,** under **federal question;** □see **substantial performance,** under **perform.**

substantial damages   □see **substantial;** □see **damage.**

substantial evidence   □see **substantial.**

substantial federal question   □see **federal question.**

substantial performance   □see **perform.**

substantive due process   □see **due process,** under **due.**

substantive law: the law that prescribes and defines rights, duties, and obligations. As distinguished from *adjective law* or **procedural law** (□see). □see **procedure;** □see also, **due process,** under **due.**

substituted service □see **service of process.**

subtenant □see **lease.**

subversive activity □see **treason.**

succeed □see **descend.**

succession □see **descend.**

succession tax □see **death taxes.**

successor

1. loosely used, as in ordinary English, to refer to a person who comes *after,* taking the place of someone else in relation to office, property, etc. <Her successor as mayor was. . . ./His successor as owner of the hotel was. . . .>

2. sometimes, a shortening of **successor in interest** (□see).

3. sometimes, refers to a person who takes by succession. □see **descend.**

successor administrator □see **successor in interest.**

successor in interest: a person who takes the place of someone else in the ownership or control of property, with all of the rights and obligations of the predecessor in reference to that property. E.g., a *successor administrator* who takes over from an administrator who has not completed the job (□see **de bonis non**). E.g., a *successor corporation:* one that has a substantial identity with the predecessor corporation, as on a merger or change of name. *Successor in interest* (sometimes spelled *successor-in-interest*) varies by statute; is usually distinguished from a person who simply buys property from another person.

627

sudden emergency: a factor to be taken into account in assessing due care (□see) and negligence (□see). Absent redundancy, called *emergency.* Applied to a wide range of emergencies, including *sudden peril.* □see also, **heat of passion.**

sue: the broad and basic term for threatening to start, starting, or continuing a *suit,* also called a *lawsuit,* also called a *civil suit.* <I'm going to sue you./They filed suit./They sued the A. Co. for breach of contract./ They were suing for an injunction./They sued in federal court.> □see **action;** □see **civil suit, under civil.**

suffer

1. to feel pain, as in ordinary English. □see **pain and suffering.**

2. to permit something to happen that a person has the ability and responsibility to prevent. <The lease provided that the tenant would not damage nor suffer the premises to be damaged.> The noun is *sufferance.* □see also, **waste.**

sufferance □see **suffer;** □see **tenancy at sufferance, under estate.**

sufficient evidence: a flexible characterization of the evidence that satisfies a variety of procedural requirements. E.g., sufficient evidence to withstand a **nonsuit** (□see, under **judgment**); to deny a motion for a **directed verdict** (□see, under **verdict**). <They presented sufficient evidence to take the case to the jury.> □see **burden of proof, under proof.**

suggest • suggestion: an old formalism for calling something to the attention of the court, a presiding officer, a witness, without requesting specific action. <I suggest the absence of a quorum./I suggest, sir, that you are lying./The suggestion having been made that the plaintiff has just died, the court will recess until 3 p.m.>

suggestion □see **suggest.**

suggestive □see **leading question.**

sui generis (L., SOO-e JEN-er-ess: of its own kind): in a class by itself. Not a distinctly legal expression, except that it is more common in legal writing than in ordinary English. *Unique* is an adequate English translation, except that like other absolutes, *unique* often isn't, as in *more, very,* and *most unique.*

sui juris   (L., SOO-e JUR-iss: of one's own right): having legal capacity and responsibility. □see **child**; □see also, **insanity**.

suit   □see **action**; □see also, **civil law**, under **civil**; □see also, **sue**.

sum certain: short for a *sum certain in money,* i.e., a definite amount. The degree of definiteness required to make a *sum certain* varies by statute (e.g., the Uniform Commercial Code) and interpretation, e.g., when a default judgment may be entered by the clerk, rather than fixed by a judge. The law prefers the French word order *sum certain* over the occasional looser equivalent *certain sum.* □see **certain.**

summary judgment   □see **judgment.**

summation: a lawyer's recapitulation or *summing up* of law and evidence, by way of closing **argument** (□see) to a judge or jury.

summing up   □see **summation.**

summons   □see **process**; □see **service of process.**

sunset law: a law that by its own terms automatically ends at a fixed time after enactment.

sunshine law: a law requiring official meetings to be open to the public. Has also been applied to laws requiring specified government records to be open to public inspection.

superior   □see **court.**

supersedeas   (L., Soo-per-SEE-dee-us: you shall desist): a shortened form of *writ of supersedeas:* an order, usually from a higher court, staying (i.e., delaying) proceedings; e.g., stopping execution on a judgment pending an appeal. The word is part of an older form of the order, as a Latin writ. Varies by jurisdiction; some use the word *supersedeas;* some call it a *stay of proceedings.* □see **execute.**

superseding cause In tort law detail, this is one of a number of vague, entwined catch phrases that come to the rescue of a defendant whose negligence has set the stage for trouble. Rationale: the harm should be attributed to someone else—an independent force—harming the plaintiff *after* the defendant's negligence.

Like the sampling of other catch phrases listed below, **superseding cause** has no precise definition. What passes for definition is a statement of policy, nominally dependent on subrules, ultimately on circumstance. Here, adapted from *Restatement (Second) of Torts,* § 440: "[A]n act of a third person or force which by its intervention prevents the [defendant] from being liable for harm to [the plaintiff] which [the defendant's] antecedent negligence [was] a substantial factor in bringing about."

intervening cause shares that policy: "[A] cause of independent origin for which the defendant is not responsible . . . which come[s] into active operation at a later time to change a situation resulting from the defendant's conduct." (Adapted from Prosser and Keeton, *Torts,* 5th ed., pp. 301–302 (1984, and 1988 pocket part)).

With no more consensus than their fellows, **superseding intervening cause**, **supervening cause**, and **supervening negligence** postulate a break in causal relationship between the negligence of the defendant and plaintiff's injury. *Supervening* focuses on the unpredictable nature of the independent force.

supervening cause □see **superseding cause.**

supervening negligence □see **superseding cause.**

support □see **alimony.**

suppress □see **suppression of evidence.**

suppression of evidence

1. the act of concealing or withholding evidence in violation of statutory or constitutional duty. Especially the act of a prosecutor who fails to reveal or make available at defense request (*suppresses*) evidence that is favorable to the defense and material to guilt or punishment. □see **due process,** under **due.**

2. the order of a court excluding evidence prejudicial to the defendant's right to a fair trial. Especially *suppressing evidence* illegally obtained. □see **exclusionary rule**. The order is usually made in response to a *motion to suppress.*

Supremacy Clause: the part of the U.S. Constitution reading: "This Constitution, and the laws of the United States which shall be made in pursuance thereof; and all treaties made, or which shall be made, under the authority of the United States, shall be the supreme law of the land; and the judges in every state shall be bound thereby, anything in the constitution or laws of any state to the contrary notwithstanding." (Art. VI, cl. 2). □see also, **constitutional clauses**.

supreme □see **court**.

Supreme Court of the United States: the court specifically mentioned in the U.S. Constitution as "one supreme court" (Art. III, § 1). □see **federal courts**. Usually referred to as the *Supreme Court.* The Constitution does not specify the number of justices of the Supreme Court, except that "the Chief Justice" is mentioned (Art. I, § 3, cl. 6). □see **judge**.

surety □see **suretyship**; □see also, **guarantee**.

suretyship

1. the relationship, varying by contract and statute, between a *principal* (debtor), a *surety*, and a third person (creditor).

a. As to the creditor, principal and surety are both liable (i.e., both are primarily liable) for what is still often called the *debts, defaults, and miscarriages* (i.e., mismanagement) of the principal.

b. As between principal and surety, the principal is primarily liable, the surety secondarily liable (□see **secondary liability**): if the surety pays, the principal is bound to indemnify the surety. (□see **indemnify**, under **hold**.)

2. the legal status of a person who becomes a *surety*. □see also, **guarantor**, under **guarantee**.

3. the law governing the relationship (sense 1) and the status (sense 2).

surplus □see **surplusage**; □see also, **stated capital**.

surplusage: an excess of words. Unlike *surplus,* which is a creature of accountancy, *surplusage* is welcomed to the law as one of its own. A surplusage of *surplusage,* in pleadings, indictments, contracts: words that you can get rid of without affecting substance. In short, verbosity.

surprise: the ordinary English word in a variety of legal contexts, as the reason for permitting a court to exercise discretion in relieving from a *surprise.* E.g., permitting questioning as on **cross examination** (□see, under **cross-**) of a party's witness who changes a story while testifying.

surrender (n., v.)

1. an agreed transfer of an estate in possession for life or years to the owner of the immediately following greater estate in remainder or in reversion. E.g., A having a life estate in Blackacre, remainder in fee to B, transfers (*surrenders*) the life estate to B, who accepts the transfer, thus ending the life estate. E.g., A owning the fee in Black-acre leases to B for ten years. By agreement, B yields up the posses-sion (*surrenders*) to A at the end of five years, ending B's tenancy. The possessory estate is said to *merge* in the larger estate.

2. *surrender by operation of law:* Instead of a transfer by agreement as in sense 1, the parties engage in acts inconsistent with the contin-ued existence of the possessory estate. E.g., tenant moves out before the end of the term, turning over the key to the landlord; landlord posts "Vacant" sign and relets the property. Also called *surrender in law.* □see also, **legal fiction.**

3. in criminal law, □see **bail;** □see also, **extradition.**

surrender by operation of law □see **surrender.**

surrender in law □see **surrender.**

surrogate judge □see **judge.**

surrogate mother □see **parent.**

surrogate parent □see **parent.**

surrogate's court □see **judge.**

surrounding circumstances ☐see facts; ☐see also, **clichés**.

survey ☐see **metes and bounds**.

survival action: a cause of action that survives the death of the person who had the cause of action, i.e., may be sued on by the personal representatives of the dead. Varying by jurisdiction, some causes of action do not survive; some survive by reason of *survival statutes*. A *survival action* is to be distinguished from an action for **wrongful death** (☐see).

survival statute ☐see **survival action**.

surviving spouse ☐see **surviving widow**.

surviving widow: for the justices of the U.S. Supreme Court and other lawyers, an irresistible alternative to a *female surviving spouse*, sometimes called a *widow*. To be carefully distinguished from a *male surviving spouse*, sometimes called a *widower*. ☐see **clichés**.

survivorship ☐see **joint tenancy**, under **estate**. ☐see also, **presumption of survivorship**, under **presumption**.

suspect • suspicion • suspicious: old words of the ordinary vocabulary, loosely used, and suggesting wrongdoing or delinquency—criminal, civil, or moral. <His motives are suspect./I suspect she did it./It looks suspicious./I have my suspicions.> It is popular trial by hunch. <A suspected murderer.> In the criminal law, they are not words of technicality. ☐see **accuse**; ☐see also, **probable cause**.

suspect classification ☐see **standards of review**.

suspected murderer ☐see **suspect**. ☐see also, **accuse**.

suspended sentence ☐see **sentence**.

sustain ☐see **overrule**.

swear: to take an oath, say something under oath, or administer an oath. <I swear. . . ./Swear the witness.> □see **affiant;** □see **so help you God;** □see **Oath or Affirmation Clause;** □see **duly sworn,** under **due.**

swear the witness □see **swear.**

Sweeping Clause: another name for the **Necessary and Proper Clause** (□see).

sworn □see **swear;** □see also, **duly sworn,** under **due.**

syllabus: a synopsis of a case, not part of an opinion and not prepared by the court, preceding the printed opinion in some of the **law reports** (□see).

symbolic delivery: to deliver something tangible that, taken together with the agreement or conduct of those concerned, is the equivalent of (symbolic of) the delivery of something else. E.g., a landlord's delivery of a key to a new tenant as symbolic delivery of the apartment. □see **deliver;** □see also, **constructive possession,** under **possession.**

symbolic speech: an amorphous classification of communication by conduct or other activity without the use of words, in expressing ideas, emotions, a message, etc. The expression *symbolic speech* is used in determining whether or not the conduct or activity is a form of *speech* protected by the First Amendment. E.g., flag burning, black armbands of protest, nude dancing.

synonyms □see **coupled synonyms.**

T

tabula rasa □see clean slate.

tack □see tacking.

tacking: the joining (*tacking*) of successive periods of possession by different persons to compute a *continuous period.* □see **privity of possession,** under **privity;** □see also, **adverse possession,** under **possession.** Similarly, the joining (*tacking*) of successive periods of continuous adverse use. □see **prescription.**

tail □see fee tail.

tainted fruit doctrine □see fruit of the poisonous tree.

take: an indispensable word of ordinary English that runs the full range from the technical to loose courtroom chitchat. No list of entries is complete, certainly not this one. None could approach completeness without mention of the profession's special affection for **I take it**: a querulous, jabbing, provocative introduction to a half-question, half-statement by judge or lawyer. Depending on tone and timing, *I take it* is designed to undermine or collapse a prosecution, a defense, or a cause of action. Occasionally, it produces a reasoned, if outraged, argument; sometimes a half-facetious put-off or put-down. <I take it, counsel, that you are aware of the Supreme Court's recent decision in *Smith v. Jones.*/I take it, Mr. Prosecutor, that your supply of surprise witnesses is now exhausted./I take it, counsel, that you have fully digested our trial brief.>

1. (constitutional law) to acquire (*take*) property for public use. The constitutional sense here may be federal or state. With special reference to the:

   Takings Clause: the part of the U.S. Constitution reading: "[N]or shall private property be taken for public use, without just compensation." (Amend. V). Sometimes referred to as *the Takings Clause of the Fifth and Fourteenth Amendments* by reason of the Fifth binding the states through the Fourteenth. □see also, **eminent domain;** □see also, **condemnation,** under **eminent domain;** □see also, **due process,** under **due;** □see also, **constitutional clauses.**

2. (claim of constitutional right) **take the Fifth**: refuse to answer on the ground that it might incriminate. A degrading, slang pejorative

635

take

for an assertion of constitutional right. <She took the Fifth./She refused to answer on the ground that it might incriminate her.>

3. (conveyancing) part of a phrase describing the manner of acquiring (*taking*) title to property:

take by purchase □see **purchase**, under **buy**

take by gift □see **purchase**, under **buy**

take by descent □see **descent**, under **descend**

take by inheritance □see **descent**, under **descend**

4. (conveyancing) part of a phrase describing what, if any, particular interest a person (a *taker*) has acquired in property:

take a life estate (a fee, etc.)

take nothing (e.g., the estate of a deceased joint tenant)

5. (criminal law) part of some descriptions of **larceny** (□see).

take and carry away

6. (corporations) *takeover;* also spelled *take-over* and *take over.* □see **tender offer**.

7. (notice)

take notice □see **notice**

take judicial notice □see **notice**; □see also, **judicial notice**

8. (miscellaneous procedure)

take a default □see **default**

take nothing judgment: a loser

take on voir dire: the judge's permission or the lawyer's request to examine on **voir dire** (□see)

take the bench □see **bench**

take the stand □see **stand**

take the witness: a lawyer's announcement that the other side can now take over examination; also rendered "*Your witness*"

take to court □see **court**

take under advisement: the judge wants to think it over.

take a default   □see **default**.

636

take a deposition □see **affiant**.

take a life estate □see **take**.

take and carry away □see **take**; □see **larceny**.

take by descent □see **descent**, under **descend**.

take by gift □see **purchase**, under **buy**.

take by inheritance □see **descent**, under **descend**.

take by purchase □see **purchase**, under **buy**.

take judicial notice □see **notice**; □see also, **judicial notice**.

take nothing □see **take**.

take nothing judgment □see **take**.

take notice □see **notice**; □see also, **take**.

take on voir dire □see **take**; □see **voir dire**.

takeover □see **tender offer**.

takeover bid □see **tender offer**.

takeover offer □see **tender offer**.

taker □see **take**.

take the bench □see **bench**.

take the Fifth □see **take**.

take the stand

take the stand □see **stand**.

take the witness □see **take**.

take to court □see **court**.

take under advisement □see **take**.

taking □see **take**.

Takings Clause □see **take**; □see also, **constitutional clauses**.

talesman □see **jury panel**.

tampering with the jury □see **embracery**.

tangible □see **intangible property**.

task force □see **commission**.

tax (n., v.): In general terms, a *tax* is a burden for the support of government, imposed by government on property, people, or their activities. The verb is *to tax;* □see also, **levy**. The act of taxing, the intricacies of its imposition and collection, as well as the whole field of *tax law,* is called *taxation:* within the profession, usually rendered as *tax.* <What do you teach/practice? I teach/practice *tax*. You mean *taxation?* Sure, *tax*. You mean *tax law*. Sure, *tax*. >

Tax intrudes itself into every phase of the law. Nothing is too trivial or too monumental to be untouched by *tax aspects,—consequences,— planning,—avoidance,—evasion* (□see **avoid**). *Tax* affects the unborn, the living, the dead. Whether you receive money or property, or almost receive it—*constructive receipt of income* (□see **actual**), give it away (□see **charitable deduction**, under **charitable**), try to give it away (□see **gift in contemplation of death**, under **gift**), or die with it (□see **death taxes**), *tax* is always there. Some of its quirks you will find here, e.g., □see **marital deduction**. For most of *tax,* look to the experts, the *tax lawyers,* their special laws, their codes (e.g., the Internal Revenue Code—IRC), their decisions, their books, their *regs* (□see **regulate**). *Tax* is a prime and restless specialty.

taxation   □see tax.

tax avoidance • tax evasion   □see avoid.

tax costs   □see costs.

tax court   □see United States Tax Court.

tax evasion   □see avoid.

tax law   □see tax.

tax lawyer   □see tax; □see lawyer.

tax situs   □see situs.

temporary alimony   □see alimony.

Temporary Emergency Court of Appeals: a special United States court (abbreviated *TECA*) created in 1971 with exclusive jurisdiction over appeals from the district courts in connection with price and other economic controls initiated during the Korean and Vietnam Wars (see amendments to the Economic Stabilization Act of 1970, 85 Stat. 743, 749, § 211(b)(1)). Judges of the court are Article III judges of the district courts and circuit courts of appeal.

Temporary Emergency is a redundant and misleading euphemism. Like life, all emergencies are temporary. Here, the mantle of *emergency* is inherited from the World War II **Emergency Court of Appeals** (see Emergency Price Control Act of 1942, 56 Stat. 23, 31, § 204(c)). As one emergency fades, a new emergency, or at least a new act, takes its place in petroleum, energy, natural gas, carrying with it the TECA. The nature of the "temporary" emergency varies; the "temporary" court of 1971 was still flourishing in 1991 (see 28 USCA; Rules vol., Rule 22, amended to Jan. 1, 1991).

temporary injunction   □see enjoin.

temporary restraining order   □see enjoin.

639

tenancy

tenancy □see estate.

tenancy at sufferance □see estate.

tenancy at will □see estate.

tenancy by the entirety □see estate by the entirety, under estate.

tenancy for years □see estate.

tenancy in common □see estate.

tenancy in fee □see estate; □see fee simple.

tenancy in fee tail □see estate; □see fee tail.

tenancy in tail □see fee tail.

tenant

1. in property law generally, the person who has a *tenancy* or an estate (□see).

2. the person (also called a *lessee*) in temporary possession of property under a relationship of **landlord and tenant** (□see). Under a sublease, the person given possession is called the *sublessee* or *subtenant*. □see **lease**.

tender (v., n.)

1. (v.) *to tender:* to offer the thing that is required by contract or other obligation, or that is specified to be in settlement of a claim.

2. (n.) the act of offering (sense 1) is the *tender*. The adequacy of the act of offering that makes it a *tender* emphasizes certainty of performance, frequently described in terms of the offeror being *ready, willing, and able* to perform.

3. (n.) the specific thing offered (in senses 1 and 2)—money, property, services, a deed, a release, delivery, payment, etc.—is also called the *tender*.

The details of all senses of *tender* are controlled by and vary with contract and statute. *Tender,* as described in this entry, is to be distinguished from **legal tender** (☐see) and from **tender offer** (☐see).

tender offer: an imprecise term widely used in securities law, generally referring to a quick, enticing proposal to the shareholders of a corporation that they *tender* their shares for purchase by the *offeror* at a specified price. *Tender offer* is an upside-down term: I make the *offer;* you make the *tender.* It is usually, not always, part of an attempt by the offeror to buy enough stock to control the corporation, i.e., a *takeover* (also spelled *take-over* and *take over*). Accordingly, *tender offer* is sometimes called a *takeover offer* or a *takeover bid.*

Now a standard feature of the corporate scene, *hostile* and *friendly* tender offers associated with takeovers have developed a distinctive slang vocabulary:

golden parachute: a farewell bonus to key personnel of the target company to encourage their approval of a takeover.

greenmail: a payment by the target company to induce a hostile *raider* to abandon a takeover.

poison pill: a rearrangement of the stock structure of the target company to make a takeover less attractive.

white knight: a third person, friendly to the management of the target company, who helps defeat a hostile takeover.

tenement   ☐see **estate.**

tentative trust   ☐see **Totten trust,** under **trust.**

term   Most legal usage of *term* is ordinary English in a legal setting:

E.g., duration, as in *term of imprisonment* or *term of a lease.*

E.g., a word or phrase, as in *terms of a contract.*

E.g., a technical word with a specific meaning, i.e., a *term of art.* Like other specialties, the law has many terms of art; among others, **certiorari** (☐see), **eminent domain** (☐see), **fee simple** (☐see), **in rem** (☐see), **quo warranto** (☐see), etc. Lawyers often assume that long professional use makes any word a legal term of art; in too many instances, despite long use, precision or technicality or both are lacking. Entries in this dictionary take note of the distinction.

term

For some special legal usage of the word *term:*

term of court □see session

term of years □see tenancy for years, under estate.

terminate □see cancel.

termination □see cancel; □see dissolution.

term of art □see term.

term of court □see session.

term of years □see tenancy for years, under estate.

territory □see extradition.

Terry stop □see search and seizure.

testament □see will.

testamentary: the general adjective of reference to a **will** (□see), as in letters testamentary (□see).

testamentary disposition

1. a disposition of property by will.

2. loosely, a gift of property not in the usual will form (e.g., in a deed) but intended to be a disposition by will, effective only upon the donor's death and revocable until then.

testamentary guardian □see guardian.

testamentary intent □see intent; □see will; □see also, **mind and memory.**

testamentary succession □see descend.

testamentary trust □see inter vivos trust, under trust

testator: a person who makes a **will** (□see). Usually interpreted to include both sexes. □see **sex**.

testatrix: a female who makes a will. □see **sex**.

testify □see **testimony**.

testimonial privilege: a right not to testify based on a claim of privilege. E.g., **confidential communications privilege** (□see); **privilege against self-incrimination** (□see, under **criminate**). □see also, **immunity**.

testimony: the words of a witness under oath in a legal proceeding, especially words spoken by the witness testifying in court.

theft □see **larceny**.

the undersigned □see **undersigned**.

thing in action □see **chose in action**.

third party □see **party**.

third party beneficiary □see **beneficiary**.

third party claim □see **party**.

third party claimant □see **third party claim**, under **party**.

third party complaint □see **third party practice**, under **party**.

third party defendant □see **third party practice**, under **party**.

third party intervention □see **party**.

third party practice □see **party**.

third person: a third party; □see, under **party**.

this honorable court is now in session □see **court**; □see **formalisms**; □see **Honor**.

Three-fifths Clause: the part of the U.S. Constitution reading: "Representatives and direct taxes shall be apportioned among the several states which may be included within this Union, according to their respective numbers, which shall be determined by adding to the whole number of free persons, including those bound to service for a term of years, and excluding Indians not taxed, three-fifths of all other persons." (Art. I, § 2, cl. 3). □see also, **constitutional clauses**. The name *Three-fifths Clause* is only an historical survival. Among other changes made by the Fourteenth Amendment, § 2 as to apportionment of representatives, the words "three-fifths of all other persons" were deleted. As to apportionment of direct taxes, □see also, **Direct Tax Clauses**, and the Sixteenth Amendment.

ticket □see **citation**.

tied product □see **tying arrangement**.

tie-in □see **tying arrangement**.

time is ordinary English *time*—indispensable, ubiquitous, imprecise unless hogtied.

reasonable time: All things considered, this is how long it usually takes to get something done. This is the law's classic solution. Imprecise *time* joins with imprecise **reasonable** (□see) to make the ticking moments of eternity livable. That is the way most lawyers and judges would like to leave it. The harsh **absolutes** (□see) of time—**eo instante, forthwith, instanter**—are reduced to what is reasonable. **Time is of the essence** is a call for attention, not to be taken literally. **With all deliberate speed** (□see) is useful flexibility, until someone insists that it is getting us nowhere.

Lawyers tend to relax with *time:*

1. the old **here-** (□see) words—never meant to be precise: *hereafter, hereinafter, hereinbefore, heretofore,* and the equally uncertain old *thereafter.*

2. the prepositions of time: *about, after, at, before, between, by, during, from, in, on, since, till, to, until, within.* Made no more precise by the old pattern of doubling—**from and after** (□see), *on and after,* **on or about** (□see), *on or before,* etc. Unfortunately for

the law, the prepositions are burdened with a riddle: Are you just up to a point, onto it, or past it? Usually the riddle remains unriddled.

3. the "rules" of time: made-up "rules," makeshifts for the details that are not spelled out, and no more reliable than other **rules of interpretation** (□see). The two principal "rules":

a. *The indivisibility of time:* You cannot split a unit of time (unless it makes sense to split it).

day: twenty-four hours (unless it's not). E.g., expressed or unexpressed, it might be a shorter *business day* or a *banking day.*

week: a *calendar week,* Sunday through Saturday (unless it's not). A *week* may also be a period of seven consecutive days. Or it may be a *workweek* (also spelled *work week*): variously described as the working days (e.g., Monday through Saturday) or the working hours (e.g., a forty-hour or a thirty-five hour week) during a seven-day period; or a particular allotment of work days or hours as fixed by statute or agreement.

month: a *calendar month* (unless it's not). An often inconvenient variable number of days (twenty-eight to thirty-one), perhaps extended by holidays or force majeure, or the necessities of banking, e.g., computing interest by a thirty-day month.

year: a *calendar year* (unless it's not). It may not be a neat January through December. E.g., explicitly or in context, it may be a *fiscal year,* i.e., a fixed accounting or tax period. E.g., a lease may start and end in the middle of a month.

b. *The computation of time:* The time to do something excludes the first day and includes the last (unless it doesn't). E.g., a court order made July 10 giving ten days to file an amended complaint; the first day is July 11, the last day July 20 (unless that is a holiday). E.g., a ten-day lease made July 10; the first day of the lease is July 10, the last day July 19 (unless otherwise provided).

In short, *time,* in one form or another, cannot be avoided and pops up everywhere, mentioned or not. It takes time to fix *time.* For some other *time* words,

□see **at that point in time;**

□see **backdate,** under **nunc pro tunc;**

□see **clear days,** under **clear;**

time

□see **extend time**, under **delay**;

□see **nunc pro tunc**;

□see **of even date**;

□see **time deposit**, under **bank**;

□see **timeshare**.

time-barred □see statute of limitations.

time deposit □see bank.

time is of the essence □see time.

timeshare: a system of dividing up the right to use or occupy property (usually real estate), so that a particular owner or licensee has the exclusive right to use or occupy the property for a specified time during the year. Form of agreement varies. Among co-owners, usually the agreement continues the right for each year or other specified period, with expense correspondingly apportioned. Usually the agreement is made as to improved property, e.g., a vacation home. *Timeshare* is also spelled *time share* and *time-share*. *Timeshare* is affected by varying federal and state statutes, which speak of *timesharing* estates, interests, periods, plans.

tippee □see insider trading.

tipper □see insider trading.

title

1. a widely used label for the bundle of rights in **property** (□see) that is commonly called *ownership*. The substance of *title* may depend on what covenants of title (□see) go with it. Lacking a precise, uniformly accepted definition, *title* is usually referred to, rather than defined. The references are generally in relative terms, i.e., the kind of title, rather than *the* or the *only* title. Thus, there is a **marketable title** (□see), a **paramount title** (□see, under **evict**), a **title by adverse possession** (□see, under **possession**), title **by operation of law** (□see).

Despite its less than fixed character, lawyers speak freely of *title* as though it were something tangible: E.g., a **cloud on title** (□see); the *state of the title,* i.e., who has what ownership in what property for

646

how long; *title passes,* i.e., ownership goes to somebody else; a *chain of title,* i.e., the successive ownership and other details affecting a particular piece of property.

☐see also, **seisin;** ☐see also, **in rem.**

2. a written statement of title (sense 1). E.g., a deed <Let's see your title.>; e.g., *record title:* title as evidenced by documents of record (☐see).

title by adverse possession ☐see title; ☐see adverse possession, under possession.

title by operation of law ☐see title; ☐see by operation of law.

title passes ☐see title.

toll the statute ☐see statute of limitations.

to my knowledge ☐see knowledge.

tort: a civil wrong that is not based on breach of contract. E.g., assault, battery, libel, slander, injury to body, injury to psyche, damage to property. The same act or omission—e.g., negligence of a lawyer—that makes a tort (malpractice) may also be a breach of contract, but it is the negligence, not the breaking of the contract, that is the tort. Referring to *tort,* the adjective is *tortious,* the adverb *tortiously.*

torts: the plural of *tort,* but also the name for the whole body of the law of civil wrongs not based on breach of contract. A student takes a course in *torts,* not *tort.*

tortfeasor: a person who commits a tort. Also spelled *tort-feasor* and *tort feasor.* Tortfeasors who act together, or whose separate acts combine to produce the wrong, are *joint tortfeasors;* usage varies by decision and statute.

tortfeasor ☐see tort.

tortious ☐see tort.

torts ☐see tort.

to state the question is to answer it □see clichés.

totally null and void □see null and void.

Totten trust □see trust.

touch and concern □see covenant running with the land, under covenant.

to wit: namely. A survivor of Old English *witan* (to know), of histori-cal interest (□see ss), and otherwise worthless. <She had three broth-ers, to wit, Tom, Dick, and Harry./She had three brothers—Tom, Dick, and Harry.> Also spelled *to-wit,* with no better results. □see also, ss; □see also, videlicit.

tract: an arbitrary designation of a land area. Often used in maps and land records for convenience of identification of individual lots (*parcels*), as being in a particular numbered tract. □see also, parcel.

trade dress □see unfair competition.

trade fixture □see fixture.

trade libel □see disparagement.

trademark: words, names, symbols, or devices used or intended to be used in commerce to "identify and distinguish" a person's goods and unique products and to "indicate the source." Also spelled *trade-mark* and *trade mark.* See 15 USCA § 1127, as amended Nov. 16, 1988. □see trade name; □see service mark; □see trade dress, under unfair competition. □see also, dilution of trademark, under dilution; □see also, secondary meaning; □see also, unfair competition. □see also, ®.

trade name: "[A]ny name used by a person to identify his or her business or vocation." See 15 USCA § 1127, as amended Nov. 16, 1988. Also called a *commercial name.*

trade secret: information that has special economic value to the commercial enterprise that has it because it is kept secret from the public, competitors, and those who are not of necessity connected with its use within the enterprise. State and federal statutes vary on precise definition, and especially on the wide variety of information that may be a *trade secret,* e.g., "[A] formula, pattern, compilation, program, device, method, technique, or process. . . ." (See Uniform Trade Secrets Act, § 1(4), 1980, amended 1985).

traitor □see **treason.**

transactional immunity □see **grant of immunity from prosecution,** under **immunity.**

transcript: an official copy of matters of record in connection with a court proceeding. E.g., a *reporter's transcript* of the testimony, rulings, argument, etc., at a trial. E.g., a *transcript on appeal:* a copy of those items in the record required to file an appeal—pleadings, judgment, portions of the reporter's transcript. Content of a transcript varies by statute.

transcript on appeal □see **transcript.**

transfer (v., n.)

1. the most general and neutral word to describe the bare fact of changing the ownership of rights in real or personal property. Unless specifically limited, it refers to a change carrying all of the owner's rights, including the right to possession. <J.D. transferred the house to his wife and the stock to Mary; everything else was transferred in trust for John.> *Transfer* describes the changing, but is not itself an operative word for effecting the change; for that: □see **assign;** □see **give,** under **gift;** □see **grant;** □see **sell.** <The transfer was by will reading: "I give Blackacre to A."> Some of *transfer*'s synonyms are archaic: □see **alien;** □see **demise;** □see **set over.** Its other synonyms are less general and less neutral than *transfer:* □see **assign;** □see **convey;** □see **deed;** □see **distribute;** □see **give,** under **gift;** □see **grant;** □see **quitclaim;** □see **sell.**

2. In specialized settings, *transfer* sheds neutrality and becomes technical, almost excluding its synonyms.

> **transfer in contemplation of death:** change of ownership motivated by the owner's concern about the nearness of death. □see also, **gift in contemplation of death,** under **gift.**

transfer

transfer in fraud of creditors: change of ownership designed to defeat claims of the owner's creditors. □see also, **fraudulent conveyance**, under **fraud**.

3. The person *transferring* is the *transferor;* the person receiving a *transfer* is the *transferee*.

4. Loosely, *transfer* is a synonym for **deliver** (□see). <The document was transferred from hand to hand so many times that no one knew for sure who had it before the transfers began.>

transferee □see **transfer**.

transfer in contemplation of death □see **transfer**.

transfer in fraud of creditors □see **transfer**.

transferor □see **transfer**.

transitory action □see **local action**.

trap □see **entrap**.

trap for the unwary: a pejorative metaphor for almost anything you find unappetizing and less than clear. E.g., the language of the law generally, unexpected law hidden in fine print or boilerplate, lawyer advertising and restrictions on lawyer advertising, a bank bribery statute, a close corporation statute, a majority opinion on search without a warrant, etc., etc. It is a century-old cry of "Foul!", a favorite cliché of lawyers and judges. Some traps you can almost see: "It looms as a trap for the unwary." (*Gutierrez v. Mofid,* 39 Cal.3d 892, 901, 1985). It still has the potential for creative use. □see **entrapment**, under **entrap**.

travel bare □see **bare**.

treason • sedition

treason

1. (against the United States), defined in the U.S. Constitution: "Treason against the United States shall consist only in levying war against them, or in adhering to their enemies, giving them aid and comfort." (Art. III, § 3).

□see **aid and comfort**; □see **misprision of treason**.

2. (against one of the states), defined in various state constitutions, adapting to the states the language of the U.S. Constitution.

3. without change of meaning (senses 1 and 2), part of the bundle of miscellany called **subversive activity**: acts designed to overthrow a government by force or other illegality.

sedition

1. criminal acts, falling short of *treason,* designed to destroy the authority of constituted government or to overthrow it. E.g., conspiracy to disrupt a wartime draft or supply of arms. Except as defined by particular statutes, *sedition* has no precise definition. Other than **treason** (□see, above, in this entry), it may include the miscellany described as *subversive activity.* In particular, *sedition* may include some advocacy, shorn of First Amendment protection (see sense 2).

2. advocacy that is directed to, and likely to be successful in, inciting or producing "imminent lawless action." (See *Brandenburg v. Ohio,* 395 U.S. 444, 447, 1969.)

treasury shares   □see **stock**.

treasury stock   □see **stock**.

treaty

1. in general, a formal agreement between sovereign nations.

2. a formal agreement between the United States and another sovereign nation, made pursuant to the **Treaty Clause** (□see) of the Constitution. As distinguished from an *executive agreement.*

executive agreement: an agreement between the United States and another sovereign nation made by the President without the advice and consent of the Senate under the **Treaty Clause** (□see). Made by the President pursuant to a treaty (sense 2), pursuant to an act of Congress, or pursuant to the President's constitutional powers as executive or as Commander in Chief. An *executive*

treaty

agreement is sometimes called a *compact,* a *protocol,* or even a "treaty."

3. loosely, an *executive agreement.*

Treaty Clause: the part of the U.S. Constitution reading: "He [the President] shall have power, by and with the advice and consent of the Senate, to make treaties, provided two thirds of the senators present concur. . . ." (Art. II, § 2, cl. 2). □see also, **by and with.** □see also, **constitutional clauses.**

treble damages □see **damage.**

trespass (n., v.)

1. an intentional interference with the possession and use of property without authority or privilege. The long procedural history of the action of trespass at common law still influences the nature of the interference that constitutes *trespass,* varying by jurisdiction. The person who *trespasses* is a *trespasser.* For an *infant trespasser,* □see **attractive nuisance,** under **child.**

Trespass to real property is the tort usually identified as *trespass.* E.g., walking on your neighbor's land without being asked in (□see **license**). E.g., throwing rocks on that land; not removing the rocks (a *continuing trespass*). If the interference is substantial and unreasonable, an act that is a trespass may also be a *private nuisance* (□see **nuisance**). □see also, **trespass ab initio,** under **ab initio.**

Trespass to chattels has been largely absorbed in the **law of conversion** (□see).

2. loosely, unlawful injury to property, person, or to a person's rights.

trespass ab initio □see **ab initio;** □see **trespass.**

trespasser □see **trespass.**

trespasser ab initio □see **ab initio;** □see **trespass.**

trial

1. in its usual general sense, an examination of issues of fact and law in a court of law, for the purpose of determining those issues between litigating parties, and—in a criminal trial—the guilt or innocence of the defendant. If a determination cannot be made, there may be a **mistrial** (□see), and the case set for *retrial* or a new trial (□see **trial de novo**, under **de novo**). The general sense of *trial* usually, but not always, connotes the full array of litigation—witnesses, lawyers, judge and jury, or a judge alone (□see **court trial**, under **court**). □see **try**.

2. usually *trial* is distinguished from a **hearing** (□see), which may be incident to a trial. □see also, **preliminary hearing**. As distinguished from the variables in a hearing, a *trial* is in court, and is either by a judge (the *trial judge*) and a jury, or by a judge. In some usage, if a *hearing* is a final determination on the merits, it may be called a *trial*.

3. usage of *trial* varies by jurisdiction and decision on fixing the time when a *trial* has started. E.g., when prospective jurors are examined or when they are sworn. E.g., when preliminary motions have been made or when a witness has been sworn. □see **speedy trial**.

4. prepositions of *trial: at trial, for—, in—, on—, to—:*

at trial: during the proceedings in court. <At trial, he testified that. . . .>

for trial: of a case with a fixed trial date. <*Smith v. Jones* has finally been set for trial./They were prepared for trial.>

in trial: why a lawyer is out of the office. <Sorry, she's in trial.>

on trial: characterizing the state of a case being tried, or a defendant in a criminal case in court. <*Smith v. Jones* is on trial./John Doe is on trial for murder.>

to trial: referring to the time when a trial has started. <It was not brought to trial within the two-year limit.>

5. A variety of *trial* words are in separate entries:

trial brief □see **brief**

trial by jury □see **trial jury**, under **jury**

trial court □see **trial judge**, under **judge**

trial de novo □see **de novo**

trial judge □see **judge**

trial judge advocate □see **lawyer**

trial jury □see **jury**

trial

trial lawyer □see lawyer

trial on the merits □see merit

trial brief □see brief.

trial by jury □see trial jury, under jury.

trial court □see trial judge, under judge.

trial de novo □see de novo.

trial judge □see judge.

trial judge advocate □see lawyer.

trial jury □see jury.

trial lawyer □see lawyer.

trial on the merits □see merit.

tried to the court □see try.

trier of fact □see try; □see mixed question of law and fact.

trifles with justice □see clichés.

trivializes the law □see clichés.

-trix □see sex.

TRO: abbreviation of temporary restraining order; □see, under enjoin.

trover □see conversion.

trover and conversion □see conversion.

654

true and correct ☐see facts.

true bill ☐see indictment.

true facts ☐see facts.

trust: in its usual, general sense, a fiduciary relationship between persons called *trustee* and *beneficiary* in reference to property, sometimes referred to as the *trust res* (☐see **res**). The trustee has title to the property *in trust* for the beneficiary, i.e., the property and its proceeds must be dealt with only for the benefit of the beneficiary. ☐see **fiduciary**; ☐see **beneficiary**.

This legal abstraction—the *trust* as a relationship—is also regarded as a thing—*a* trust, *the* trust. <They established a trust.> It may be a tangible thing—*the* trust, referring to a piece of paper with all the details. <Let's see the trust.>

A miscellany of legal expressions use the word *trust*, and sometimes the words *trustee* and *beneficiary*, with little or no connection with the basic sense of the word *trust*. Principal examples are *business trust, Massachusetts trust, precatory trust,* and *trust deed.*

The prime exemplar of *trust* in the basic sense of a fiduciary relationship that may be regarded as a thing is the *express trust*. It is a completely voluntary relationship, as distinguished from a relationship imposed by law as a *resulting trust* or as a *constructive trust.*

express trust: a trust created by the *settlor*, also called the *trustor*, in a *declaration of trust* (☐see **declaration**) expressing the settlor's intention to create the trust. Though not restricted to trust usage, *donor, grantor,* or *testator* may also refer to a *settlor* or *trustor.* Usually (not necessarily) the declaration of trust is in a writing, referred to as the *trust instrument* or *trust indenture;* the writing may be of various sorts, e.g., an agreement, a deed, a will. In the declaration, the settlor names the *trustee* (who may be the settlor), describes the *trust property,* and how it is to be used for the benefit of the named *beneficiary.* An *express trust* often has special additional names. They refer to particular aspects of a particular *express trust,* e.g., that it is also a *charitable trust,* etc.

In the following alphabetical list of names for trusts, all refer to an *express trust* unless otherwise noted:

active trust: a trust in which the trustee has duties to perform other than holding title. As distinguished from a *dry, naked,* or *passive trust;* ☐see **passive trust**, below, in this entry.

trust

blind trust: a trust created by a person who holds public office to avoid the appearance of conflict of interest between the duties of office and the management and investment of one's own property. Typically, the settlor officeholder transfers property in trust for the settlor as beneficiary, with instructions that the trustee's management and investment of the trust property are to be without the knowledge of the settlor, for the duration of the trust—the term of officeholding. The expression is more political than legal, without precise legal boundaries.

business trust: not an *express trust.*

1. an unincorporated business enterprise similar in operation to a corporation (□see). Those running the business are called *trustees;* the beneficial owners have transferable share interests. Called a *business trust,* a *Massachusetts trust,* or a *common law trust.* Usage varies by jurisdiction.

2. loosely used, a business enterprise, or group of businesses working together, that calls itself a "trust," as distinguished from some standard type of business organization.

3. a type of business enterprise covered by the **antitrust laws** (□see).

charitable trust: a trust to serve the public good (□see **charitable**). As distinguished from a *private trust* to serve the private interests of specified beneficiaries. Specific beneficiaries of a charitable trust need not be designated, and the trust may continue indefinitely.

Clifford trust □see **grantor trust**, below, in this entry.

common law trust: not an *express trust.* □see **business trust**, above, in this entry.

constructive trust: a fiduciary relationship imposed by the law between wrongdoer (called the *trustee*) and victim (called the *beneficiary*). It is not an *express trust.* It is an equitable remedy to right a wrong and prevent unjust enrichment (□see **restitution**). The *trustee,* who wrongfully acquired or keeps title to property, the property itself, or its proceeds, is said to hold each in *constructive trust,* with a duty to transfer them to the beneficiary.

The *trustee* of a *constructive trust* is sometimes called a trustee **by operation of law** (□see) or worse. There are special titles of opprobrium and nostalgia:

trustee in invitum (L.: involuntary). □see **in invitum**.

trustee de son tort (law F.: of his own wrong). □see **de son tort**.

trustee ex malificio (L.: because of an evil deed).

discretionary trust: a trust in which the trustee has the discretion to distribute income or principal when, in what amounts, and to which beneficiary, as the trustee sees fit. Details vary by jurisdiction. Within limits fixed by law, distribution cannot be compelled. A *discretionary trust* is also called a *sprinkling trust.*

dry trust □see **passive trust**, below, in this entry.

grantor trust: a trust in which the settlor keeps ownership-like controls over the trust and its property; or a trust irrevocable for a specific period and then reverting to the settlor—sometimes still referred to as a *Clifford trust* (see *Helvering v. Clifford,* 309 U.S. 331, 1940). The principal objective of the grantor trust—to split income between settlor and beneficiary—is controlled by the Internal Revenue Code and Federal Tax Regulations. □see also, **Totten trust**, below, in this entry.

inter vivos trust: a trust that becomes operative during the life of the settlor. As distinguished from a *testamentary trust,* i.e., created by will. An *inter vivos trust* is also called a *living trust.*

irrevocable trust: a trust that cannot be revoked after it is created. As distinguished from a *revocable trust* in which the settlor, or someone in effect acting for the settlor, can revoke the trust. □see **grantor trust**, above, in this entry; □see **Totten trust**, below, in this entry.

living trust □see **inter vivos trust**, above, in this entry.

Massachusetts trust: not an *express trust.* □see **business trust**, above, in this entry.

naked trust □see **passive trust**, below, in this entry.

passive trust: an imprecise designation of a trust in which the trustee holds title in trust for the beneficiary, but without any substantial duties to perform on behalf of the beneficiary. Also called a *dry trust* and a *naked trust.* A *passive trust* is distinguished from an *active trust* (□see, above, in this entry).

pourover trust: □see **pourover.**

precatory trust: not an *express trust.* □see **precatory words.**

private trust □see **charitable trust**, above, in this entry.

resulting trust: a fiduciary relationship imposed by the law under circumstances indicating that despite a voluntary transfer of title, the person taking title to property was not intended to keep it. It is not an *express trust.* The person taking title is said to be a *trustee,* holding the property on a *resulting trust* for the benefit of the person who directed the transfer in the first place, said to be the *beneficiary.* The expression *resulting trust* uses an archaic sense of *result* to mean *revert,* i.e., the property is to go back (revert, result) to the person who directed the transfer.

A *resulting trust* is imposed: (1) when an attempt to create an express trust fails; (2) when the purposes of an express trust have been fully carried out and some of the property is still held in the express trust; or (3) as a *purchase money resulting trust:* a buyer directs the seller to put title in the name of someone who the buyer did not intend to keep the property.

revocable trust □see **irrevocable trust**, above, in this entry.

savings bank trust □see **Totten trust**, below, in this entry.

spendthrift trust: a trust providing that the interest of the beneficiary (income for life or a fixed term of years) cannot be transferred by the beneficiary, and is not subject to claims of the beneficiary's creditors. Statutes place limits on the provisions of spendthrift trusts; e.g., prohibiting the settlor as a beneficiary; making the interest subject to claims of specified creditors—wife, children, suppliers of necessaries, etc.

sprinkling trust □see **discretionary trust**, above, in this entry.

tentative trust □see **Totten trust**, below, in this entry.

testamentary trust □see **inter vivos trust**, above, in this entry.

Totten trust: a trust created by a deposit of the depositor's own money in a savings account in the depositor's name "as trustee" for a named beneficiary. An incomplete expression of the depositor's intent, the trust is revocable during the depositor's life, unless some unequivocal act indicates otherwise, e.g., delivery of the passbook to the beneficiary. If the depositor predeceases the beneficiary, and has neither revoked nor unequivocally disaffirmed the trust, any balance in the account goes to the beneficiary. Details vary by jurisdiction. A *Totten trust* is also called a *tentative trust* and a *savings bank trust.* (See *In re Totten,* 179 N.Y. 112, 125–126, 1904, and *Restatement (Second) of Trusts,* § 58). □see **grantor trust**, above, in this entry; □see **irrevocable trust**, above, in this entry.

trust deed: a security device, not an *express trust.* □see **deed**; □see **secure**.

voting trust: a trust in which the trust res is voting stock, transferred by the shareholders in trust to trustees, who then vote the stock (□see).

trust deed   □see **deed**; □see **secure**.

trustee □see **trust.**

trustee by operation of law □see **constructive trust,** under **trust;** □see **by operation of law.**

trustee de son tort □see **constructive trust,** under **trust;** □see **de son tort.**

trustee ex malificio □see **constructive trust,** under **trust.**

trustee in bankruptcy: special usage in the bankruptcy laws of the United States. □see also, **receiver.**

trustee in invitum □see **constructive trust,** under **trust.**

trust indenture □see **trust.**

trust instrument □see **trust.**

trustor □see **trust.**

trust res □see **trust;** □see **res.**

truth and veracity: ordinary truth and truthfulness; an old redundancy. □see **coupled synonyms.**

truth, the whole truth, and nothing but the truth □see **formalisms;** □see **absolutes.**

try

1. to examine issues in a **trial** (□see).

2. *to try a case*

   a. (of a judge): to preside over a trial, as in sense 1. <Judge Smith is trying a case in Dept. 2.>

   b. (of a lawyer): to represent a client in a **trial** (□see). <We are trying that case on a contingency.>

3. *tried:* past tense and participle of *try,* as in *tried to the court:* referring to a case that was, or is being, tried by lawyers before a judge without a jury. □see **court trial**, under **court**.

4. *trier of fact*

    a. the judge in a court trial, as in sense 3.

    b. ordinarily the jury, in a jury trial.

    c. □see **mixed question of law and fact**.

turntable doctrine: another name for **attractive nuisance** (□see, under **child**).

turpitude □see **moral turpitude**.

twice put in jeopardy: the words used in the U.S. Constitution, Amendment V. □see **double jeopardy**.

two tiers □see **standards of review**.

two-way street □see **clichés**.

tying agreement □see **tying arrangement**.

tying arrangement: an agreement by a seller to sell one product (the *tying product*) only if the buyer also buys a different product (the *tied product*) from the seller. □see **antitrust law**.

There are many variations. *Tying arrangement* can also refer to: a refusal to sell unless the condition is met; a condition that the buyer will not buy the tied product from someone else; a similar arrangement between lessor and lessee; a similar arrangement with services, rather than a product; etc.

Tying arrangement is also called a *tying agreement* and a *tie-in.*

tying product □see **tying arrangement**.

U

uberrima fides □see **fiduciary**.

U.C.C.

1. abbreviation of **Uniform Commercial Code** (□see). Also abbreviated *UCC*.

2. abbreviation of the Universal Copyright Convention. □see **copyright**.

ultimate facts: the facts that must be proved to establish a cause of action or a defense. Not a term of precision; courts differ as to what is or is not *ultimate*. □see **absolutes**.

ultra vires (L., UHL-truh VI-raise: beyond the strength): beyond the powers, referring to the powers of a corporation. As distinguished from acts within its powers (*intra vires*). *Ultra vires* is not the equivalent of *illegal,* though the same act may be both. An ultra vires act is not necessarily void; its effect is a matter of corporation law, varying by statute and jurisdiction.

unanimous opinion □see **opinion**.

unavoidable accident □see **accident**; □see **act of God**.

unborn □see **person**; □see **en ventre sa mère**, under **child**.

unclean hands □see **clean hands**.

unconscionable □see **conscience**.

unconstitutional □see **constitutional**.

unconstitutional on its face □see **face**; □see also, **constitutional**.

uncontested proceeding □see **adversary proceeding**.

underage □see **child**.

under color of law □see **color**; □see also, **state action**.

under color of office □see **color**.

under protest □see **protest**.

undersigned: usually in the form *the undersigned* (singular or plural), referring to anyone who has signed, or is to sign, at the end of a document. It is an old formal shortening <A, B, and C, hereinafter called the undersigned. . . .>. If one of *the undersigned* doesn't undersign, the formality and brevity of *undersigned* is dissipated in uncertainty as to the role of each of those so described. Best forgotten. □see also, **subscribe**.

understanding □see **contract**.

understood and agreed: bilingual synonyms. Since *understood* alone can mean *comprehended* or *agreed,* the doubled usage suggests that something more than redundancy was intended. Habit, not intention, is at work. Make it *agreed.* □see **coupled synonyms**.

under submission □see **submission**.

undertake • undertaking: old synonyms for *promise* (v., n.) in and out of the law. <They undertook to get the financing.> In criminal law, *undertaking* is still used as a synonym of *bond* or *bail.* <They filed an undertaking in the sum of $100,000 to get him released today.> □see **bail**.

undertaking □see **undertake**.

under the influence of: the sinister, introductory words to specification of a variety of substances that, taken internally, can affect a person's conduct. As *under the influence of* alcohol; intoxicating liquor; narcotics—e.g., opium, morphine; drugs; or *controlled substances:* behavior-altering drugs restricted by law—e.g., heroin, cocaine. Specification of substances, degrees of influence, and the consequences vary by legislation and regulation. Except where closely defined, *under the influence of* is an imprecise and very flexible expression. The expression does not usually refer to the influence of people. People have a sinister influence of their own, i.e., *undue influence*. □see **duress**; □see **due**.

undue influence   □see **duress**; □see **due**.

unfair competition

1. an umbrella for an almost infinite variety of acts that go beyond the flexible limits of competition that is **fair** (□see) in a free enterprise system. Typical are acts tainted with **fraud** (□see) that mislead the consumer. E.g., imitation of the appearance (*trade dress*) or name of a competing product (□see **trade name**). E.g., advertising or manner of sale that attempts to *pass off* (*palm off*) this product or service as the real thing, such as something identified by a **trademark** (□see) or **service mark** (□see) or a **secondary meaning** (□see). Also typical is unauthorized use of a **trade secret** (□see) or of someone else's literary property (□see **plagiarism**). *Unfair competition* is wrongful under common law, principles of equity, and numerous statutes.

2. For a special federal variant of *unfair competition* called *unfair methods of competition*, □see **antitrust law**.

unfair labor practice: conduct prohibited by federal or state law regulating relations between employers, employees, and labor organizations. E.g., refusing to bargain collectively; interfering with the right of employees to join or refuse to join a labor organization. For a variety of *unfair labor practices* by employers and labor organizations, see the Labor Management Relations Act, 1947, amended to 1974 (29 USCA § 158).

unfair methods of competition   □see **antitrust law**.

unfit to have custody   □see **custody**.

Uniform Code of Military Justice: a single title that can refer to two discrete bodies of military law:

1. the codified statute on military justice that applies to the military forces of the United States, including state military forces when in federal service. (10 USCA §§ 801 *et seq.*, 1956, amended to 1988). It is *uniform* in the sense that it applies to all branches of the military forces. It provides for a three-level system of courts: *court-martial,* the trial court; *Court of Military Review,* to review action of a court-martial; and a *Court of Military Appeals*, with detailed overall appellate jurisdiction. □see also, **military law**, under **martial law**.

2. one of the unofficial **Uniform Laws** (□see), this one approved by the National Conference of Commissioners on Uniform State Laws and the American Bar Association in 1961. (11 *Uniform Laws Annotated*, pp. 335 *et seq.*, 1974). It was designed to apply to state military forces when not in federal service, and is based on the federal statute (sense 1). With variations, this *Uniform Law* has been adopted in a number of jurisdictions.

Uniform Commercial Code: the most massive of the **Uniform Laws** (□see). The Code, abbreviated *U.C.C.* (and *UCC*), deals with a wide range of what lawyers called *commercial transactions* (listed below). It is an attempt to unify and clarify the laws of commercial transactions in the United States; its range is extensive and intensive but not exhaustive. Common law, state and federal statutes deal with some of the same topics. With numerous variations, the UCC has been adopted in large part by all of the states, except Louisiana, and in some parts by Louisiana. The UCC is indispensable to commercial lawyers, and in some parts to lawyers generally. (For special UCC language usage, see Mellinkoff, "The Language of the Uniform Commercial Code," 77 *Yale Law Journal* 185, 1967.)

Frequently revised, the UCC has for years dealt with the **sale of goods** (□see **sale**), **commercial paper** (□see), bank deposits and collections, letters of credit (□see **letter of credit**), bulk transfers, documents of title (□see **document of title**), investment securities, and secured transactions (□see **secure**). More recently, the UCC has added special articles on *leases* and *funds transfers*.

leases: Article 2A (1987) covers *leases of goods*, and is closely related to the UCC provisions on *sales of goods*. It deals with the special problems of a lease of goods, as distinguished from a sale, and as distinguished from a secured transaction.

funds transfers: Article 4A (1989) deals with the special problems of the daily, typically multimillion-dollar transfers of funds between businesses and banks. This type of payment is to be distinguished from the typical payment in consumer transactions by negotiable instrument and credit card. Also, the new article explicitly excludes electronic payments governed by the federal Electronic Funds Transfer Act, typically consumer transactions. □see **electronic funds transfer**. Most of what the UCC now calls *funds transfers* (singular, *funds transfer*) are commonly referred to in the business and banking community as *wholesale wire transfers;* the UCC expressions are not limited to transfer by wire. For details, consult Article 4A.

Uniformity Clause: the part of the U.S. Constitution reading: "The Congress shall have power to lay and collect taxes, duties, imposts and excises . . . but all duties, imposts, and excises shall be uniform throughout the United States. . . ." (Art. I, § 8, cl. 1). □see also, **constitutional clauses**.

Uniform Laws: a collection of unofficial laws designed to promote uniformity in state statutory law. Except for the **Uniform Commercial Code** (□see), all of the Uniform Laws have been drafted by the National Conference of Commissioners on Uniform State Laws; organized in 1892, its lawyer commissioners are selected by the states, the District of Columbia, and Puerto Rico. The UCC was drafted by the Conference and the American Law Institute, privately organized in 1923 "for the improvement of the law," and especially notable for the **Restatement** (□see). The *Uniform Laws* (numbering 160 as of 1990) are variously called *Uniform Acts, Codes, Rules,* and *Uniform Law Commissioners' Model Acts.* The latter designation is to be distinguished from *Model Codes* drafted by the American Law Institute, e.g., the Model Penal Code, the Model Code of Evidence. The wide range of the *Uniform Laws* may be gathered from this sampling: Uniform Consumer Credit Code (abbreviated *U3C*), Uniform Controlled Substances Act, Uniform Fraudulent Conveyance Act, Uniform Law Commissioners' Model Survival and Death Act, Uniform Rules of Criminal Procedure. The Uniform Laws are frequently adopted in whole or in part by the states. For the complete listing, refer to *Uniform Laws Annotated;* see also, Uniform Code of Criminal Justice.

unilateral contract   □see **contract**.

unincorporated association   □see **association**.

union   □see **person**; □see also, **boycott**; □see also, **closed shop**, under **close**; □see also, **picketing**.

union shop   □see **closed shop**.

United States attorney   □see **district attorney**, under **lawyer**.

United States Bankruptcy Court   □see **bankruptcy judge**, under **judge**.

United States Claims Court

United States Claims Court: a legislative court (□see **federal courts**) for trial of claims against the United States for money damages, other than tort claims. E.g., contract damages, tax refunds, compensation for taking of property.

United States Code: the federal statutes codified. For details, refer to the United States Code Annotated.

United States Court of International Trade: a specialized court with jurisdiction over specified civil actions against the United States and its agencies, and some actions by the United States, in the general field of foreign trade. E.g., customs, tariffs, restrictions on imports. For details, refer to 28 USCA §§ 1581–85. Status as a *constitutional court* has a wobbly history.

United States Court of Veterans Appeals: a new specialized legislative court inaugurating limited judicial oversight of the administration of veterans affairs. The court, sometimes abbreviated *CVA,* has exclusive jurisdiction to review decisions of the Board of Veterans' Appeals. A disappointed claimant (not the Administrator) may appeal the Board's decision. Special provisions cover qualifications, tenure, and salary of the judges of the court. The United States Court of Appeals for the Federal Circuit has exclusive jurisdiction to review CVA decisions; with discretionary final review by the United States Supreme Court (38 USCA §§ 4051 et seq., 1988; amended to 1989). □see **federal courts**; □see **United States Courts of Appeals**.

United States courts: □see **federal courts**; □see **Supreme Court of the United States**; other United States courts are separate entries by court name, starting with *United States.*

United States Courts of Appeals: the federal courts for the thirteen judicial circuits, each court separately designated as the *United States Court of Appeals for the _____ Circuit,* i.e., one of the eleven numbered circuits, the *District of Columbia Circuit,* or the *Federal Circuit.* The courts are familiarly called the *circuit courts.* Their work is primarily appellate. The *United States Court of Appeals for the District of Columbia Circuit* is to be distinguished from the *District of Columbia Court of Appeals,* the appellate court for the local court system in the District of Columbia. The *United States Court of Appeals for the Federal Circuit* has exclusive jurisdiction on appeals in customs, patent law, and United States Court of Veterans Appeals cases, and in cases against the United States other than tort claims and internal revenue cases. □see **federal courts;** □see **United States Court of Veterans Appeals;** □see also, **judge;** and a special court, □see **Temporary Emergency Court of Appeals**.

United States District Courts: the general trial court in the federal system. The districts, their division, and the number of judges are regulated by statute. □see **federal courts;** □see **bankruptcy judge,** under **judge;** □see United States Magistrate, under **magistrate**.

United States Magistrate □see **magistrate**.

United States Statutes at Large □see **Statutes at Large**.

United States Tax Court: a legislative court (□see **federal courts**), usually referred to as the *Tax Court*. Its principal function is to redetermine deficiencies in federal income, estate, and gift taxes, after determination of a deficiency by the Internal Revenue Service.

Universal Copyright Convention □see **copyright**.

unjust enrichment □see **restitution**.

unlawful assembly □see **riot;** □see also, **illegal**.

unlawful detainer □see **forcible entry and detainer;** □see also, **evict**.

unless the context otherwise requires: a legal writer's backdoor escape route to dodge responsibility for an inadequate definition. <Unless the context otherwise requires, in this contract the singular includes the plural, and the plural includes the singular.> What is included in context? Who determines when context requires something else? Must context scream for change or only hint? Improving the phrase grammatically to read *unless the context requires otherwise* is no solution; the uncertainties remain. In short, I mean what I say, unless I don't.

unliquidated damages □see **general damages,** under **damage**.

unmarketable title □see **marketable title**.

unmarried: an imprecise reference to a person who has never been married, or to one whose spouse is dead or divorced, or to one who is separated from a spouse. Synonym of *single*. □see **feme sole;** □see **cohabit.**

unmarried cohabitants □see cohabit.

unreasonable □see reasonable.

unreasonable restraint of trade □see **rule of reason;** □see **antitrust law.**

unreasonable search and seizure □see search and seizure.

unsound mind □see insanity.

untrue □see false and untrue.

unusual punishment □see cruel and unusual punishment.

unwritten contract □see oral.

unwritten law

1. a common reference to the **common law** (□see).

2. a loose, nonlegal usage characterizing such so-called rights as that of an outraged husband to kill the man found seducing his wife. The expression—emphasizing *the* unwritten law—refers not to a legal right but to what a jury might nonetheless regard as **justification** (□see).

use: In numerous legal contexts, *use* in the law is ordinary English; e.g., □see **timeshare.** The *use* as a creature of real property law is now largely of historical interest, e.g., as an older form of **trust** (□see).

useful □see patent.

useful arts □see **patent;** □see **Patent and Copyright Clause.**

use immunity □see grant of immunity from prosecution, under immunity.

usurious □see legal interest.

usury □see legal interest.

U3C: abbreviation of Uniform Consumer Credit Code. □see Uniform Laws.

utility □see patent; □see public utility.

utmost good faith □see fiduciary.

utter □see publish.

V

v.: abbreviation of *versus* (L.: towards; against): in English, *against.*
The abbreviation is also rendered *V., vs.,* and *Vs.* The lawyer's
favorite for case names in written or oral usage is plain *v.,* e.g., *Smith
v. Jones.* Written, case names are sometimes rendered with *versus,*
occasionally *against,* instead of an abbreviation. Orally, *against* is
common <In *Smith against Jones,* it was held. . . .>; *versus* rare; *vs.*
hardly ever.

vacate

1. to make something void. □see **quash**.

2. to move out of real property. <The tenant was forced to vacate the
premises.> □see **evict**; □see **forcible entry and detainer**.

3. to withdraw from use. <The city vacated Fourth Street.>

vacation □see **quash**.

vagrancy: the crime of being a **vagrant** (□see).

vagrant: a fading word of opprobrium inherited from the common
law, classifying as petty criminals a wide variety of persons arrestable
for being no-goods. E.g., rogues, vagabonds, dissolute beggars, wan-
derers and strollers, habitual loafers, etc. Like its companion in law
the *loiterer* (□see **loiter**), *vagrant* frequently succumbs to constitutional challenge for vagueness (see *Papachristou v. City of Jacksonville,*
405 U.S. 156, 1972). *Vagrant* manages to survive in some laws de-
nouncing more specific forms of **disorderly conduct** (□see).

vagueness

1. (constitutional law): a due process objection to legislation so
vague that it does not give fair notice of what is required or prohibited, and encourages arbitrary enforcement.

2. (construction of writings): sometimes refers to general uncertainty, as distinguished from the double meaning of ambiguity; sometimes included in **ambiguity** (□see).

valid: legally effective.

valuable consideration: an imprecise variant for plain *considera-tion* (□see **contract**). The expression once identified consideration based on money, as opposed to consideration based on natural affec-tion called *good consideration. Valuable consideration* now passes muster as adequate, good, monetary, sufficient, and valid considera-tion. The *valuable* additive is misleading; *valuable* is in the eyes of the beholder. Varies by statute, decision, and jurisdiction.

value: worth measured in money, a lot of it or very little. This is one of the flexible senses of *value* in ordinary English and finds a natural home in the law. E.g., □see **fair market value**, under **fair**. E.g., □see **good faith purchaser for value**, under **bona fide purchaser**. In special areas of the law, e.g., corporate securities, taxation, commercial trans-actions, special definitions of *value* are pervasive, and beyond the scope of this dictionary.

vandalism   □see **malicious mischief.**

variance

1. (pleading) □see **fatal variance**, under **fatal.**
2. (land use) □see **zoning.**

vel non   (L.: or else not): whether or not. Prefer the English. □see **law Latin.**

vendee   □see **sell.**

vendor   □see **sell.**

vendor and purchaser   □see **sell.**

vendor's lien   □see **lien.**

venire   □see **jury panel.**

venire facias   □see **jury panel.**

veniremen   □see **jury panel;** □see also, **sex.**

venirepersons □see **jury panel.**

venue

1. the proper place of trial; generally, where the events of a civil action arose, and where a crime was committed. For federal crimes, this usually means the state and district where the crime was committed. (U.S. Const., Art. III, § 2; Amend., VI). See also, **change of venue,** below in this entry.

> *Venue* is usually distinguished from *jurisdiction* in the sense of the power to try and decide. The distinction is sometimes blurred, in that both words can refer to geographical location (□see **jurisdiction**); and it is unclear whether only *venue,* or also *jurisdiction,* is affected by the distinction between a *transitory* and a **local action** (□see). □see **lex loci;** □see **situs;** □see **run.** An important distinction between *venue* and *jurisdiction* remains: right to a particular venue may be waived; the parties cannot confer subject matter jurisdiction.

> **change of venue**: transfer of a case to a proper, or more desirable, place of trial. E.g., a case filed in the wrong district under federal law, or in the wrong county under state law. E.g., a change of venue because of local prejudice against a defendant. E.g., a change of venue for convenience of trial; □see **forum non conveniens,** under **forum.** *Change of venue* is to be distinguished from **removal** (□see) of a case from a state to a federal court.

2. *venue* is to be distinguished from **vicinage** (□see), the place from where trial jurors are to come. The geography of the two expressions frequently overlaps, and in loose usage, the two expressions are sometimes equated.

3. the designation in an affidavit of the place where it was executed.

veracity □see **truth and veracity.**

verbal □see **oral.**

verbal acts: words offered in evidence not for their truth, but because they were uttered and have an independent legal significance. E.g., The witness testifies, "D said, 'P is a thief.'" D's words are verbal acts, with legal significance in P's cause of action for slander; not **hearsay** (□see). □see also, **res gestae.**

verbal contract □see **oral**.

verbosity □see **surplusage**.

verdict: in its usual meaning, a decision or a finding by a *trial jury*, as distinguished from the verdict of a *coroner's jury*. □see **jury**. The two major classifications of a trial jury's *verdict*:

general verdict: a comprehensive decision of an issue. In civil cases, for the plaintiff or for the defendant, determining liability, damages, etc. In criminal cases, "guilty" or "not guilty." Statutory definition is common. A *general verdict* is also called a *general finding* (□see **finding**).

special verdict: determining only **ultimate facts** (□see), usually pursuant to special instructions to do so, leaving decision to the court. □see **special finding**, under **finding**.

Whether *general* or *special*, some verdicts have additional names:

chance verdict: one arrived at, not by deliberation, but by some form of chance, e.g., flip of a coin, a *verdict by lot*, a **quotient verdict** (□see). □see **impeach a verdict**, under **impeach**.

compromise verdict: one arrived at, not by convincing a juror of the correctness of another juror's position, but by partial surrenders of what individual jurors continue to think correct. E.g., a verdict for plaintiff inadequate to cover plaintiff's expenses, as a compromise with jurors who favored a verdict for defendant. □see **impeach a verdict**, under **impeach**.

directed verdict: a verdict ordered by the court when the evidence is in, and the court finds it insufficient for a jury to return a verdict for the side with the burden of proof. In that state of the evidence, if the jury does not agree with the court, the court has the power to enter a judgment (not a verdict) regardless. For that reason, some courts no longer use the expression *directed verdict* (e.g., motion for judgment of acquittal, under Federal Rules of Criminal Procedure, Rule 29(a)). Definitions vary by jurisdiction.

sealed verdict □see **seal**.

For other entries connected with *verdict* by a trial jury:

□see **estoppel by verdict**, under **estoppel**;

□see **guilty**;

□see **hung jury**, under **hanging jury**;

verdict

□see **judgment n.o.v.,** under **judgment;**

□see **judgment on the verdict,** under **judgment;**

□see **jury instructions;**

□see **nullification;**

□see **poll the jury.**

verdict by lot   □see **chance verdict,** under **verdict.**

verification: the act of *verifying,* i.e., asserting in a formal way that something is true. As verification by oath, or by declaration under penalty of perjury that the allegations of a pleading are true. □see **declaration;** □see **perjury.**

versus   □see **v.**

vertical privity   □see **privity.**

vest   □see **vested.**

vested: in general, something that has become fixed, as opposed to contingent. The nature and degree of that fixity varies with special legal usage in:

1. the law of real property—

   a.   □see **rule against perpetuities,** for:

     vested interest

     vested in interest

     vested in possession

   b.   □see **future interest,** for:

     vested remainder

   c.   □see **vested right;** see also **zoning.**

2. constitutional law. □see **vested right.**

3. probate law. □see **gift by will,** under **gift.**

4. the law of pensions. □see **vested pension,** under **pension.**

vested bequest, legacy, or devise   □see **gift by will,** under **gift.**

674

vested in interest   □see **rule against perpetuities.**

vested in possession   □see **rule against perpetuities.**

vested interest   □see **rule against perpetuities.**

vested pension   □see **pension.**

vested remainder   □see **remainder,** under **future interest.**

vested right: a right of property or contract that government cannot take away, or that government cannot take away without paying for it.   An expression of constitutional law, usually in the pluralized form *vested rights* doctrine, without fixed definition or uniform application.   Applied intermittently and irregularly, e.g., in claims invoking the Contract, Due Process, Equal Protection, and Takings Clauses. Best understood after a court has made up its mind, i.e., this cannot be done because the right has become a *vested right.*   □see also, **zoning.**

veto   (L.: I forbid)

1.   executive disapproval that at least temporarily blocks legislation or other legislative action.   E.g., by returning a bill to the legislature, unsigned, and with a statement of objections.   See, e.g., U.S. Const., Art. I, § 7, cls. 2 and 3.

   pocket veto: a veto by executive inaction coupled with the adjournment of the legislature.   E.g.: "If any bill shall not be returned by the President within ten days (Sundays excepted) after it shall have been presented to him, the same shall be a law, in like manner as if he had signed it, *unless the Congress by their adjournment prevent its return, in which case it shall not be a law.*" (U.S. Const., Art. I, § 7, cl. 2; italics added).   The states have similar provisions.

   item veto: a veto of a part of a bill.   The President of the United States does not have the power of *item veto;* the governors do.

2.   The word *veto* is sometimes applied to measures by the legislature to block executive acts.

vexatious litigant   □see **barratry.**

vicarious admission □see **admission**.

vicarious disqualification: disqualification of all of the lawyers in an office from representing a client because one of the lawyers is ethically disqualified from representing that client; e.g., because of earlier representation of an adversary of that client in the same or a substantially related case. The one lawyer's conflict of interest is *imputed* to the others; though otherwise qualified, they are tainted by association. *Vicarious disqualification,* also called *imputed disqualification,* is imposed to avoid conflicts of interest, to preserve confidences of the earlier representation, to avoid the appearance of impropriety. If a new associate had minimal earlier contact with the case, and was not privy to confidences, *vicarious disqualification* is often rejected. A widespread and controversial defense to *vicarious disqualification* is the *Chinese wall:*

Chinese wall (also spelled *Chinese Wall*): a legal adaptation of the metaphor of ordinary English, suggesting an obstacle as impenetrable as the Great Wall of China. A *Chinese wall* is the organization of the daily operation of a law office in a way designed to prevent a new lawyer in the office from having any contact with anything concerning an office client who the new lawyer would be ethically disqualified from representing. The contact extends, e.g., to access to files, discussion with other lawyers of the office, participation in fees, etc.

The professional rules governing **disqualification** (□see, under **disqualify**), *vicarious disqualification,* and the *Chinese wall* vary by jurisdiction. □see also, **revolving door**.

vicarious liability: liability of one person because of the acts or neglects of another. □see **agency**; □see **imputed negligence**, under **negligence**; □see **joint enterprise**; □see **master and servant**; □see also, **equitable indemnity**.

vice □see **pro hac vice**.

vicinage (n., adj.)

1. the place (neighborhood, vicinity) from where trial jurors are to come. As in the expression *jurors of the vicinage;* and in adjective form a *vicinage jury*.

2. a right or requirement that jurors in a criminal case come from the place where the crime was committed. As in the expressions *vicinage right* and *waiver of vicinage*.

676

a. Though the word *vicinage* is not used, a federal constitutional vicinage right and requirement stem from the language of the Sixth Amendment: "In all criminal prosecutions, the accused shall enjoy the right to a speedy and public trial, by an impartial jury of the state and district wherein the crime shall have been committed, which district shall have been previously ascertained by law. . . ."

b. The geographical boundaries of the *vicinage,* whether under the Sixth Amendment or state constitutions, are a focus of ongoing controversy. □see also, **venue.**

videlicet (L: one can see): to wit. An old formalism. Abbreviated *viz.* In both forms, worthless. □see **to wit;** □see **ss.**

view: an out-of-court inspection by the jury, usually of evidence that cannot be presented in court; e.g., the site of a crime or an accident.

vinculo matrimonii □see **divorce.**

violation □see **breach.**

violence: as in ordinary English, together with its adjective form *violent,* an imprecise characterization of rough force; usually physical, except in the figurative sense *does violence to,* a widespread **cliché** (□see).

virtual representation: a party's representation of someone who is not a party, e.g., an unborn contingent remainderman, so that the judgment also binds the nonparty. Where the doctrine exists, the relationship between party and nonparty must be close and their interests the same or very similar, giving assurance that the nonparty's interests will be adequately represented. Statutes often supersede the doctrine by provision for appointment of guardians *ad litem.*

virtue: force or authority, as in *by virtue of* an office. Often found in tautological forms; □see **force and effect;** □see also, **formalisms.**

vis major □see **act of God.**

viz.: abbreviation of **videlicet** (□see).

677

void

void □see null and void.

void ab initio □see null and void; □see ab initio.

voidable □see null and void.

void contract □see contract; □see null and void.

voir dire (law F., vwahr dear: to speak the truth): preliminary examination by lawyers or court to test the qualifications of prospective jurors, or of a witness (e.g., concerning expertise). Commonly expressed as a noun: *take the witness on voir dire;* or as a verb: *voir dire the jury panel.* Also spelled *voire dire.*

volenti non fit injuria (L., vo-LEN-tee non fit in-YOUR-ee-ah: no injury is done to one who consents): an old legal maxim that occasionally shows up in cases where consent, permission, **assumption of risk** (□see) may constitute substantive defenses. Generally regarded as lacking substantive force of its own, the maxim is sometimes dropped into an opinion for flavoring.

voluntary: without consideration, as a *voluntary conveyance.* This special legal sense of *voluntary* is in addition to, and an extension of, the ordinary English sense of the exercise of free will.

voluntary bankruptcy □see bankruptcy.

voluntary manslaughter □see manslaughter.

voluntary waste □see waste.

volunteer □see intermeddler.

vote by proxy □see proxy.

voting shares □see stock.

voting stock □see stock.

voting trust □see trust.

vs. □see v.

W

wait-and-see   □see rule against perpetuities.

waive: to voluntarily give up a right.   E.g., to *waive notice;* to *waive a jury.*   Litigation over *waive,* and its companion noun *waiver,* is endless.   It hinges on whether or not the facts show what happy tautologists call a *voluntary and intentional relinquishment of a known right.*   The result is that *waive* and *waiver* often strike lawyers as being too short.   A common amplification is **knowing and intelligent waiver** (□see).

waiver   □see **waive.**

walk: in criminal law slang: to be acquitted, or at least not jailed.
< My client walked. >

walkout   □see **strike.**

Wall Street lawyer   □see **lawyer.**

want of equity   □see **equity.**

wanton   □see **recklessness.**

war: a word of ordinary English, without precise legal definition.
□see **international law;** □see **laws of war;** □see **war crimes;** □see **war powers.**

war crimes: a special body of crimes as defined by **international law** (□see).

ward   □see **guardian;** □see also, **conservatorship.**

warden: in legal usage, most commonly the official in charge of a prison. Miscellaneous looser usage as in ordinary English for a person *in charge:* e.g., air-raid warden, fire warden, game warden, port warden.

warehouse receipt   □see document of title.

war powers: a rubric for the constitutional powers of the United States government relating specifically or generally to military action and its incidents. *War powers* has no precise legal definition. It can relate to the immediate and to the long haul, to offensive and defensive, foreign and domestic military action. The expression *war powers* is not used in the U.S. Constitution, but the sounds are there. Closest is the congressional "*power . . . to declare war*" (Art. I, § 8, cl. 11; italics added), interpreted as the power to "*declare and conduct a war*" (*McCulloch v. Maryland*, 17 U.S. 316, 407, 1819; italics added). And the sounds of war echo in other grants of power to Congress (Art. I, § 8, cls. 12–17), and in naming the President as Commander in Chief (Art. II, § 2, cl. 1). A host of interpreters track *war powers* throughout the Constitution. Interpretations vary as to the source and extent of *war powers:* their relation to sovereignty, prevention of war, preparation for war, and aftermaths of war, the relation between legislative and executive war powers. *War powers* rests with history, constitutional law, and current events.

warrant   (v.)

1.   in general, to give assurance as a form of promise that something is a fact or that something will be done. Sometimes a synonym of the verbs **covenant** (□see) and **guarantee** (□see). <They warranted that no pesticides had been used in growing these tomatoes.>

2.   specifically, to give a *warranty* (as distinguished from a *warrant* (n.)). <In selling those goods, they warranted that they were fit for their ordinary purposes, a part of the seller's implied warranty of merchantability.> □see **warranty;** □see **warrant** (n.).

warrant   (n.)

1.   a specialized form of court order directing an officer to do a specific thing:

   arrest warrant (also called *warrant for arrest*): directing that a named person be arrested for a stated cause and be brought before a court. Sometimes issued directly from the bench (e.g., for a subpoenaed witness who has not appeared) and called a *bench warrant* (□see **bench**).

   death warrant: directing the warden of a prison to carry out a sentence of capital punishment.

   search warrant □see **search and seizure;** □see **Warrant Clause.**

681

2. an instrument, typically nonnegotiable, in which a government official directs its disbursing officer to pay a named sum to a named person.

3. a **stock warrant**: an instrument evidencing ownership of a **stock option** (□see **stock**).

Warrant Clause: the part of the U.S. Constitution reading: ". . . and no warrants shall issue, but upon probable cause, supported by oath or affirmation, and particularly describing the place to be searched, and the persons or things to be seized." (Amend. IV). □see also, **constitutional clauses**.

warranty: a special kind of promise, express or implied, typically in connection with a transfer of real or personal property. Usually it is a promise giving assurance that something is a fact (e.g., title, quality); or a promise that if it isn't, something will be done about it (e.g., title defended, goods replaced or repaired). *Warranty* and *breach of warranty* are contract law, usually distinguished from *representation* (e.g., inducing one to contract) and *misrepresentation,* typically redressed in tort.

Special definition and incidents of *warranty* vary widely with federal and state statutes, decision, regulation, agreement, trade usage, and the substantive law in particular fields. Here is a representative sampling by topic of words of *warranty,* some detailed in other entries, others only listed with typical references:

1. *real property*

warranties of title, in deeds, a *general warranty deed* (also called a *warranty deed*) and a *special warranty deed*. With *covenants of warranty* (*general* and *special*). □see **covenants of title**.

warranty of habitability, in leases. □see **covenant**. In some jurisdictions, an implied warranty in the sale of housing.

2. *sales generally* Consult especially state variations of the *Uniform Commercial Code* (Article 2) for:

express and implied warranty

warranty of title

warranty against infringement

warranty of fitness for particular purpose

warranty of merchantability: a broad gauge warranty by merchants who sell particular goods or serve food and drink. The warranty includes, e.g., a *warranty of fitness for ordinary purposes, warranty that goods are adequately packaged, warranty that goods conform to labeling.*

□see also, **as is;** □see also, **with all faults,** under **as is.**

3. *distribution of consumer products* ("for personal, family, or household") Consult especially the *Magnuson–Moss Warranty— Federal Trade Commission Act* (15 USCA, ch. 50, §§ 2301 *et seq.*) and state statutes in that model. Includes, e.g., **full warranty** and **limited warranty.**

4. *negotiable instruments* Consult especially state variations of the *Uniform Commercial Code*:

warranty on presentment and transfer, including *warranty of title* (UCC, Article 3).

warranty of customer and collecting banks, including *warranty of title* (UCC, Article 4).

5. *documents of title* Consult especially state variations of the *Uniform Commercial Code* (Article 7) for **warranty on negotiation or transfer**, and **warranties of collecting bank.**

6. *insurance* Warranties in insurance policies are special creatures, and do not deal primarily with transfers of property. They straddle the boundary between *warranty* and *representation*. They vary by policy, statute, and decision.

warranty deed   □see **covenants of title;** □see **warranty.**

warranty of fitness   □see **warranty.**

warranty of habitability   □see **covenant.**

warranty of merchantability   □see **warranty.**

warranty of title   □see **covenants of title;** □see **warranty.**

waste   (n., v.): Apart from ordinary English usage, *waste* is primarily a term of art in the law of real property. Details, supplied by decision and statute, vary by jurisdiction; here is the essence:

waste

1. misuse or neglect of real property by the owner in possession (e.g., a tenant for life or years) that materially damages or alters the property to the detriment of those with a later right of possession (e.g., remaindermen or reversioners). *Waste* typically, though not necessarily, lessens value; e.g., a life tenant may *waste* Blackacre by replacing a single-family residence with an apartment house, that increases market value but makes the property unattractive to an aging remainderman.

The principal words of *waste* are:

voluntary waste: an intentional act of *waste*, as distinguished from

permissive waste: neglect of some duty to preserve the property for those who follow. In verb usage referring to this sense, one is said to **suffer waste**.

impeachment of waste: liability for committing or suffering waste; as distinguished from

without impeachment of waste: not liable (e.g., by agreement) for committing or suffering what would otherwise be *waste*. If too gross, sometimes redressed as **equitable waste**.

2. In the general pattern of real property usage, *waste* is also applied to a misuse or neglect of personal property; e.g., stock or money held in a fiduciary relationship, as in a trust for successive interests.

watered shares □see **stock.**

watered stock □see **stock.**

water law □see **water,** under **law of capture.**

way: a right of way (□see).

way of necessity □see **easement of necessity,** under **easement.**

wear and tear: deterioration of property through use that is variously described as "natural," "normal," "ordinary," "reasonable," "usual." The adjectives are often redundantly added to the expression itself. <To be returned in good condition, reasonable wear and tear excepted.>

wedlock: a state of marriage complying with legal formalities. A waning survivor of historical usage referring to a ceremonial marriage, legitimacy as dependent on being born in or out of *wedlock;* and related usage of *wed,* as in *lawful wedded wife.* Precise reference to a particular kind of married state cannot be counted on. □see cohabit; □see legitimate; □see lawful issue.

we do not write upon a clean slate   □see clean slate.

week   □see time.

weight of the evidence   □see balancing; □see preponderance of the evidence; □see also, burden of proof.

welfare   □see public welfare, under public interest; □see also, entitlement; □see also, General Welfare Clause.

well settled   □see clichés.

we put those cases to one side   □see clichés.

what I find disturbing   □see clichés.

what law governs   □see conflict of laws.

what troubles me   □see clichés.

whereas: A survivor from Middle English, *whereas* occasionally means *on the contrary,* as in ordinary English. <The label said "cotton," whereas it was polyester.> The usual legal role of *whereas* is as the introductory word to a **recital** (□see), a traditional **formalism** (□see). In that capacity, it is usually, pompously, worthless <Whereas, today is the Fourth of July. . . .>. Worse, *whereas* is frequently vague (and litigious), leaving the reader in doubt as to whether what follows in its wake is or is not an essential, e.g., of a contract. <Whereas, the necklace consists of fifty-five beads. . . .> Worst of all, as lawyers stubbornly cling to *whereas,* it has become an unneeded pejorative for the profession. <Those lawyers and their whereases.>

Where will we stop?   □see clichés.

whistleblower

whistleblower: a person (usually an employee) in a government agency or private enterprise who brings to the attention of the public or of those in authority—mismanagement, corruption, illegality, or other wrongdoing within that particular agency or enterprise.

What the *whistleblower* does—*whistleblowing*—takes many forms, e.g., explicit public announcement, complaint to an immediate superior, refusal to participate or cooperate in wrongdoing. To detractors, here is a troublemaker—makes waves. Long before the word became current in and out of the law, a *whistleblower* was dubbed *informer, fink, stool pigeon, squealer,* or worse. Typically, the whistleblower is harassed and fired; sometimes rewarded (□see **qui tam**).

The public role of the *whistleblower* (now more often one word than either *whistle-blower* or *whistle blower*) has been increasingly recognized. Federal and state statutes and regulations are designed to protect *whistleblowers* from various forms of retaliation. Even without statute, numerous decisions encourage and protect *whistleblowing* on grounds of public policy (□see **wrongful discharge**).

whistleblowing □see **whistleblower.**

Whiteacre □see **Blackacre.**

white knight □see **tender offer.**

wholesale wire transfers □see **Uniform Commercial Code.**

whole truth □see **formalisms;** □see **absolutes.**

widely held □see **public corporation,** under **corporate.**

wild animals □see **ferae naturae.**

wilful □see **willful.**

will (n., v.): a legal device that makes it possible for a person (the **testator;** □see) to speak to the future (when the testator dies), saying now what the testator wants done then, usually with the testator's property. But not necessarily about property. A person with nothing to dispose of but advice can still make a will. The noun *will* may refer to what the testator wants done, i.e., the expression of *will* in

686

the ordinary English sense. <It was her will that the property remain in the family.> Usually, *will*, as noun or verb, refers to what is to be done, as embodied, e.g., in a writing or in a particular kind of oral statement. <The will provided that. . . ./He willed Blackacre to J.D.> The formal requirements of a will and attendant procedures—making, changing, revoking, contesting, administering—vary by jurisdiction. □see **ambulatory**; □see **declare**, under **declaration**; □see **gift by will**, under **gift**; □see **give, devise, and bequeath**, under **gift**; □see **mind and memory**; □see **publication**; □see **subscribe**; □see **testamentary intent**, under **intent**; □see **will contest**.

last will and testament: an historical relic still often used to mean *will* (n.) in its usual sense. *Will* (Old English) and *testament* (Latin) are **coupled synonyms** (□see). Today, their linkage adds no legal substance to the forthright simplicity of *will*. Latin kin of *testament* still have legal function in the law of wills: e.g., **testator** (□see), **testamentary** (□see), **testamentary disposition** (□see), **testamentary guardian** (□see, under **guardian**), **testamentary intent** (□see, under **intent**), **testamentary succession** (□see, under **descend**); □see also, **letters testamentary**.

last: as in *last will and testament* or in *last will* is an independent historical relic, once emphasizing the importance of a last utterance before eternity. Today, *last,* in these usages, is worthless or worse. Usually it mimics a form, without significance. It may refer to a succession of wills, the *last will* perhaps revoking earlier wills, perhaps not. In a **codicil** (a supplement to a will), unless testator and lawyer are very alert, *last will* may refer not to the last in time but to the last will that expressed what the testator intended on a particular topic. Drop *last;* prefer a date.

Wills come in many variations. This is a representative sampling:

holographic will □see.

joint will: a single instrument that is the will of, and signed by, more than one person.

living will: a *will* in name only; not a *will* in the usual sense. □see **right to die**.

mariner's will □see, under **sailor's will**.

mutual wills: wills of more than one person, the testators having agreed on a particular disposition of property to others or to each other, as in **reciprocal wills** (□see, below, in this entry). Sometimes called *reciprocal wills*. *Mutual wills* may also be a **joint will** (□see, above, in this entry).

nuncupative will □see.

will

pour-over will □see, under **pour-over**.

reciprocal wills: wills of more than one person in which each is the beneficiary of the other. Sometimes called **mutual wills** (□see, above, in this entry). *Reciprocal wills* may also be a **joint will** (□see, above, in this entry).

sailor's will □see.

seaman's will □see, under **sailor's will**.

soldier's will □see, under **sailor's will**.

will and testament □see will.

will contest: a probate proceeding usually alleging the invalidity of a will, e.g., incapacity of the testator, fraud, etc. Sometimes the contest is directed at particular provisions of the will. The right to contest a will and details of the proceeding vary greatly with local statutes. □see **probate**. □see **no contest clause**, under **in terrorem**.

willful: as in ordinary English, a general, vague sense of the *intentional,* as opposed to the inadvertent; the *deliberate,* as opposed to the unplanned; the *voluntary,* as opposed to the compelled. Usually, *willful* as used in the law is a warning of unpleasantness—injury, lies, misconduct, neglect of duty, violations. After centuries of litigation, it has no single, precise meaning, whether as adjective (*willful,* also *wilful*) or adverb (*willfully,* also *wilfully*).

A host of varying statutes and decisions adapt *willful* to the particular circumstances of action and inaction peculiar to the law of torts, crimes, workers' compensation, Social Security. A *willful violation,* e.g., may connote a deliberate intent to violate the law, an intent to perform an act that the law forbids, an intent to refrain from performing an act that the law requires, an indifference to whether or not action or inaction violates the law, or some other variant.

Frustrated in trying to tie *willful* down, but not prepared on that account to abandon such choice flexibility, lawyers have followed a familiar path—more words, and a hope. A forlorn old hope that teaming one flexible word with another will strengthen both. The combinations roam through the avenues of the law. E.g., *willfully and unlawfully* (□see **intent**); *willful, wanton, or reckless* (□see **recklessness**); *knowingly and willfully* (□see **knowingly**); *serious and willful* (□see **serious**).

willfully □see willful.

willing □see **fair market value**, under **fair**; □see **procuring cause**.

winding up □see **dissolution**.

wiretapping: generally, making a secret connection to telephone or telegraph transmission lines in order to find out what is being transmitted, all without the consent of those whose communications are being transmitted. □see **electronic eavesdropping**.

with all deliberate speed: the Supreme Court's flexible timing of measures to end racial discrimination in public schools. (*Brown v. Board of Education,* 349 U.S. 294, 301, 1955). The standard of *all deliberate speed* later held "no longer permissible" and supplanted by the time words *at once* and *immediately.* (*Alexander v. Board of Education,* 396 U.S. 19, 20, 1969). □see **desegregation**, under **segregation**; □see **time**.

with all faults □see **as is**.

within the curtilage □see **curtilage**.

without impeachment of waste □see **waste**.

without let or hindrance □see **let or hindrance**.

without merit □see **merit**.

without prejudice: a legal expression that should never be used in the presence of nonlawyers. In ordinary English, it is a compliment. <They were utterly without prejudice.> Plain *prejudice* is also used by lawyers, e.g., in proceedings to **disqualify** (□see) a judge on grounds of **bias** (□see). *Without prejudice* is something special. For nonlawyers, confusing nonsense. For the profession, an important device—a reservation, a precaution, a warning.

Lawyers and judges use *without prejudice* to describe action that does not decide a case nor result in a loss of rights. As distinguished from *with prejudice,* which does both.

> **dismissal without prejudice**: a temporary abandonment of a lawsuit, distinctly reserving the right to file the lawsuit again. E.g., after filing a complaint, and before the defendant has respond-

ed, plaintiff decides that the time is not yet ripe for suing; better wait: *dismiss without prejudice.* Plaintiff's lawyer files a *dismissal without prejudice,* and the case is temporarily ended. As distinguished from a

dismissal with prejudice: an abandonment of a lawsuit that bars later filing of a lawsuit asserting the same claim (□see **retraxit**). E.g., during trial, the parties agree to settle: defendant to pay plaintiff $10,000, and plaintiff to *dismiss with prejudice.* The money is paid, and plaintiff's lawyer files a *dismissal with prejudice* or delivers the *dismissal* to defendant's lawyer.

judgment of dismissal without prejudice: a judgment of dismissal (□see, under **judgment**) that does not decide the case, nor bar the right to file another lawsuit asserting the same claim. E.g., a court on its own initiative, or at the request of a party, finds that there are a number of technical but curable procedural defects, and that it will be more expeditious to start all over than to reform the present proceedings. The *judgment of dismissal without prejudice* is not a **judgment on the merits** (□see, under **judgment**). Similarly, a court's ruling on a motion: *motion denied without prejudice.*

Less formally, *without prejudice* is used in discussion or correspondence between opposing counsel, e.g., trying to settle a case. Casually dropped into the proceedings, *without prejudice* is a precautionary warning, permitting freedom of negotiation without fear that tentative positions will be taken as definitive. <Look, all of this is without prejudice.>

without recourse   □see **nonrecourse**.

without reserve: In auction sales, items offered for sale *without reserve* are to be sold to the highest bidder; no minimum. Unless announced *without reserve,* sale follows the normal procedure, *with reserve:* the item may be withdrawn at any time before a sale is completed. (See the Uniform Commercial Code, § 2328.)

with prejudice   □see **without prejudice**.

with reserve   □see **without reserve**.

with the will annexed   □see **cum testamento annexo**.

witness (v., n.)

1. (v.) to become informed of an act or occurrence at first hand, thus becoming a *witness* (n.) in its most general substantive sense. <She witnessed the shooting./She was a witness to the shooting.>

2. (n.) in its most commonly used sense in the law, a person who testifies, i.e., gives **testimony** (□see) in a legal proceeding. E.g., a **hostile witness** (□see); an **adverse witness** (□see, under **hostile witness**); **take the witness** (□see). □see also, **criminate**; □see also, **Self-incrimination Clause**.

    a. The exact point at which a person is labeled *witness* is not always limited to testifying. Often *testifying* lies in the background of closely related usage, anticipation of testifying. E.g.: an **adverse witness** (□see, under **hostile witness**); an *expert witness:* one qualified by expertise to give **opinion evidence** (□see). Before trial, a lawyer asks, "Who are your witnesses?" Answer: "Here is our *list of witnesses.*" They may never testify. Before trial, a lawyer reports to the judge: "They are trying to intimidate our *star witness,* to prevent his testifying." Similarly, identification as a *witness* may refer to a person who has testified, as *the last witness.*

    b. If the legal proceeding at which the *witness* testifies is the taking of a deposition, the *witness* is also called a *deponent* (□see, under **affiant**).

3. (n.) a person who is asked to *witness* (v.; sense 1) an act or occurrence and to state (usually in writing) what took place. □see **attest**. E.g., witnesses to a will, called *subscribing witnesses* or *attesting witnesses* (□see **subscribe**).

4. (n.) the fact of having witnessed (sense 1). As in the archaic expression, *In Witness Whereof;* see **formalisms**.

witness against himself □see **criminate**; □see **Self-incrimination Clause**.

witness box □see **stand**.

witnesseth: an archaic **formalism** (□see) that once meant to furnish formal evidence of something. Best translated as "Hey, look at this!"; best of all, forgotten.

witness stand □see **stand**; □see also, under **jury box**.

wittingly and willingly: an archaic form of *knowingly and willfully,* and no improvement. □see **knowingly;** □see **willful.**

word is not a crystal □see **a word is not a crystal.**

words in the masculine □see **sex.**

words in the plural □see **words in the singular.**

words in the singular: the opening words of a worthless incantation: *Words in the singular include the plural and in the plural include the singular.* They usually do, without anyone saying so <A person entering. . . . /Persons entering. . . .>; unless specifically confined <The first person entering. . . . /Persons entering together. . . .>. Yet imbedded in old forms, the formula and its variations (e.g., *Words in the singular include the plural and vice versa.*) are mechanically included in contracts and statutes. And, just as mechanically, ignored in the body of the contract or statute, spelling out the numbers, as "person or persons," "vehicle or vehicles," on and on.

words of limitation □see **words of purchase.**

words of purchase: a technical conveyancing expression, a term of art in the law of real property that has nothing to do with the ordinary meanings of *purchase* (□see **buy**).

1. The word *purchase* in the expression means that real property is being transferred by deed or will, not inherited (□see **descend**). Whether the property is bought or given away, if the transfer is by deed or will, it is a *purchase* in this usage.

   a. The act or process of acquiring real property by deed or will is called *taking by purchase,* even though it was a gift.

   b. The person who acquires real property by deed or will is called a *purchaser,* even though he paid nothing.

   c. This peculiarly real property usage of *purchase* has been swallowed by some statutes and applied to personal property (see the Uniform Commercial Code, §§ 1201(32), (33)).

2. As a technical expression, *words of purchase* are the words in a deed or will that tell *who* takes an interest in real property. The expression is contrasted with **words of limitation**: the words in a deed or in a will that tell how long that interest will last. E.g., in a deed to Blackacre "To A for life," *To A* are words of purchase, *for life* are words of limitation.

work: the word of ordinary English, often called *labor*. In the law, sometimes equated with, sometimes differentiated from, **services** (□see). One of the common counts for *work done* (□see **common count, under count**), also called **quantum meruit** (□see). □see also, **mechanic's lien, under lien**.

worked a fraud □see **fraud**.

workers' compensation

1. the increasingly popular name for **workmen's compensation**; the change affects the nomenclature of **sex** (□see), not substance. Both expressions refer to statutes providing benefits to employees and their dependents under a system of **strict liability** (□see) of the employer for accidental injury or death of an employee "arising out of and in the course of employment." Statutes, varying by jurisdiction, generally provide for *workers' compensation* in lieu of common law liabilities of the employer, preserve the right to sue third persons for negligence causing injury, require insurance to cover the liability, and often extend the basis of benefits, e.g., to gradual injury, and to occupational disease.

Variant spellings of *workers' compensation* are *worker's compensation* and *worker compensation*. A variant spelling of *workmen's compensation* is *workman's compensation*.

2. a generic name, with the same variant spellings as in sense 1, for benefits provided by a variety of state and federal statutes covering specific types of benefits to particular employees; e.g., to coal miners, under the Black Lung Benefits Act (30 USCA § 901 et seq., 1967, amended to 1981).

workfare: a system requiring a person otherwise qualifying for public welfare benefits to earn those benefits when able to perform jobs provided by government agencies. The coined word, distinguishing *workfare* from *welfare*, is colloquial, political, and sometimes legal.

work, labor, and materials □see **mechanic's lien, under lien**; □see **services**; □see **work**.

work, labor, and services □see **work**; □see **services**.

workmen's compensation □see workers' compensation.

work product □see work product privilege.

work product doctrine □see work product privilege.

work product privilege: in general, a lawyer's right to withhold from **discovery** (□see) things the lawyer has assembled and prepared in anticipation of litigation or for trial. The privilege is usually extended to others acting for the lawyer or the lawyer's client, e.g., an insurer, an agent.

The *work product privilege* is often called the *work product doctrine* or the *work product rule,* but there is no uniform doctrine or rule. What is and is not *work product,* and the degree of its protection, vary with statute and decision, with lists of exceptions and exceptions to exceptions: the rationale, an attempt to encourage a lawyer's careful, intense private preparation, without unfairly prejudicing an adversary. Some statutes distinguish a *qualified privilege:* work product privileged unless denial of discovery would "unfairly prejudice" an adversary. And *absolute privilege:* prohibiting any discovery of work product, e.g., notes and memorandums, that reflect a lawyer's opinions, legal theories, impressions, and conclusions as to the best and the worst ways of handling a case. □see also, **reciprocal discovery,** under **discovery.**

work product rule □see work product privilege.

work stoppage □see strike.

work week □see week, under time.

worthier title: an old concept in the law of real property that a title by descent was *worthier* (i.e., better) than a title by conveyance. That concept was embodied in the common law **doctrine of worthier title:** If a grantor (and similarly, a testator) attempts to convey a future interest in land to the grantor's heirs, the heirs would be getting by conveyance what they would otherwise take by descent, and so the conveyance is void; the grantor retains a reversion. E.g., A deeds Blackacre to B for life, remainder to A's heirs. The remainder is void. A has a reversion. The *doctrine of worthier title* today has an uncertain status, varying by jurisdiction: applied; abolished; abolished in part; applied as a rule of construction; applied to personal property.

wraparound mortgage: second mortgage on real property securing a *wraparound note,* also called a *wrapped note.*

wraparound note: a note for the *sum* of a new loan *plus* the unpaid balance of an existing note (*wraps around* it) that is secured by a first mortgage on the same property. The maker of the wrapped note thus pays interest on a principal larger than the new loan, but the payee of the wrapped note agrees to pay the interest and principal on the existing note.

Wraparound, also spelled *wrap-around,* is also used with a variety of junior and senior mortgages, with trust deeds, and with land purchase agreements.

wraparound note   □see **wraparound mortgage.**

writ: generally, a type of specialized written court order. *Writs* are sometimes assigned a generic classification, e.g., an *alias writ* (□see **alias process**); e.g., *prerogative* or *extraordinary writ* (□see **extraordinary**). Apart from such generic grouping, the writs have special functions and special names, but usage is not uniform. They vary by jurisdiction—sometimes renamed; sometimes abandoned; sometimes expanded beyond those listed here. The writs, each called a *writ of* _____, are listed here in the alphabetical order of their distinctive names:

assistance

1. a court order, *writ of assistance,* typically to enforce an already adjudicated right to possession of land. Usually described as an *equitable remedy* (□see **equity**). Often displaced by a **writ of possession** or a **mandatory injunction** (□see **enjoin**) to accomplish the same purpose.

2. in colonial America, an English court order authorizing a general search of all houses suspected of containing contraband. One of the irritants that sparked the Fourth Amendment restrictions on **search and seizure** (□see). □see **Warrant Clause.**

attachment for *writ of attachment,* □see **attachment.**

certiorari for *writ of certiorari,* □see **certiorari.**

error

    1. a court order, *writ of error,* similar to **certiorari** (□see), directing a lower court to send the papers in a case for review, on matters of law appearing in the record. As distinguished from a *writ of error coram nobis* (□see **coram nobis**). In the federal, and some other jurisdictions, superseded by the *appeal.*

    2. a form of common law action to set aside a judgment for errors of law. Varying by jurisdiction, often superseded by application for *injunction* or by *motion.*

execution for *writ of execution,* □see **execute.**

habeas corpus for *writ of habeas corpus,* □see **habeas corpus.**

mandamus for *writ of mandamus,* □see **mandamus.**

mandate for *writ of mandate,* □see **mandamus.**

ne exeat for *writ of ne exeat,* □see **ne exeat.**

possession for *writ of possession* □see **writ of assistance,** above, in this entry.

prohibition for *writ of prohibition,* □see **prohibition.**

quo warranto for *writ of quo warranto,* □see **quo warranto.**

review for *writ of review,* □see **certiorari.**

supersedeas for *writ of supersedeas,* □see **supersedeas.**

write: in the law, as in ordinary English, *write, writing, written.* Usually refer to putting something into a visible form of language, as distinguished from the **oral** (□see). Not restricted to *handwriting.* Generally, in and out of the law, mechanical, photographic, electronic, and other versions of visible language are included, e.g., printing, typing, telegram, photocopy, Xerox, fax. Decision and statute define usage of *write, writing,* and *written* in particular areas of the law, e.g., evidence, contracts, commercial paper. For the special legal usage of an archaic form of *write,* □see **writ.**

writing on a clean slate □see **clean slate.**

writ of: for various *writs,* commencing with the words *writ of,* □see **writ.**

writ of assistance □see **writ.**

writ of attachment □see attachment.

writ of certiorari □see certiorari.

writ of error □see writ.

writ of error coram nobis □see coram nobis.

writ of execution □see execute.

writ of habeas corpus □see habeas corpus.

writ of mandamus □see mandamus.

writ of mandate □see mandamus.

writ of ne exeat □see ne exeat.

writ of possession □see writ of assistance, under writ.

writ of prohibition □see prohibition.

writ of quo warranto □see quo warranto.

writ of review □see certiorari.

writ of supersedeas □see supersedeas.

written contract □see oral.

written instrument □see instrument.

written law: the law of the statutes and other writings; as contrasted with the **common law** (□see).

writ writer □see lawyer.

wrong

wrong: as in ordinary English, the antonym of **right** (□see). Some special legal contexts: the *right and wrong rule* in the insanity defense (□see **M'Naghten rule**); the violation of another person's rights—a *civil wrong* (□see **tort**; □see **breach of contract**, under **breach**), or violation of law (□see **crime**). Even in special contexts, *wrong,* and its forms *wrongful* and *wrongfully,* give no sharp delineation of the exact nature of *wrongness.* Their mere presence is a warning of something *bad.* The law has found the words convenient, especially for a number of bad *wrongfuls* that follow in separate entries.

wrongful birth

1. a parent's cause of action in tort against a physician whose negligence proximately caused the birth of a defective child (the birth, not the defect). Typically, the negligence lies in treatment (e.g., unsuccessful sterilization or abortion) or in providing or withholding information needed by the parent to choose or reject conception or continuation of pregnancy (e.g., a parent's genetic defect; e.g., the effect of drugs during pregnancy). The cause of action may include as defendants others in the health care industry, e.g., clinics, hospitals, laboratories, drug manufacturers.

   a. Recognition of the cause of action and the damages recoverable vary by jurisdiction. In some instances, the tort of *wrongful birth* may overlap **malpractice** (□see), e.g., unsuccessful sterilization.

   b. Terminology is not uniform. *Wrongful birth* is sometimes equated with, sometimes distinguished from, *wrongful conception* and *wrongful pregnancy.*

   wrongful conception: usually includes the elements of *wrongful birth,* concentrated on conception. E.g., unsuccessful sterilization; e.g., misinformation that a disease present in child 1 was not genetic, and should not deter conception of child 2—later born with the same genetic defect. *Wrongful conception* is sometimes equated with *wrongful pregnancy;* sometimes it is limited to the birth of a healthy, but unwanted child (see sense 2).

   wrongful pregnancy: usually includes the elements of *wrongful birth,* concentrated on continuation of pregnancy. E.g., unsuccessful abortion; e.g., genetic misinformation. *Wrongful pregnancy* is sometimes equated with *wrongful conception;* sometimes it is limited to the birth of a healthy, but unwanted child (see sense 2).

   c. *Wrongful birth* is sometimes equated with, but is generally distinguished from, *wrongful life.*

wrongful life: the defective child's cause of action equivalent to the parent's cause of action for *wrongful birth* (sense 1). The cause of action is not widely recognized. Most courts balk at the plaintiff's argument that it would be better never to have been born. Where recognized, the cause of action is limited to special damages during the life of the defective child; damages for the period of minority are recoverable once—i.e., either in this action or by the parents in *wrongful birth.*

2. a parent's cause of action in tort against a physician whose negligence proximately caused the birth of a healthy but unwanted child, legitimate or not. Typically, the negligence lies in treatment (e.g., unsuccessful sterilization or abortion) or in misinformation on contraceptives. The cause of action may include as defendants others in the health care industry, e.g., clinics, hospitals, laboratories, drug manufacturers, pharmacists. The cause of action (sense 2) is less generally recognized than sense 1; and, where recognized, the measure of damages in sense 2 is especially controversial.

A healthy child's action for *wrongful life* paralleling *wrongful birth* (sense 2) is not recognized.

wrongful conception   □see **wrongful birth.**

wrongful death: usually, a statutory cause of action against a defendant for wrongfully causing a death. Unlike a **survival action** (□see), this is not the dead person's cause of action. *Wrongful death* is a new cause of action brought by the dead person's personal representative for damages suffered by others as a result of the death. Beneficiaries of the action are those listed in a wrongful death statute.

wrongful discharge: an unspecific label for a miscellany of bad reasons for discharging an employee. Sometimes classified as a specific cause of action; sometimes a special category of breach of contract. E.g., a discharge in violation of an implied **covenant of good faith and fair dealing** (□see, under **covenant**), often called a *bad faith discharge.* E.g., discharge of a **whistleblower** (□see), and other forms of getting even with an employee, often called *retaliatory discharge.* E.g., a discharge of an *at will* (i.e., no fixed term) employee for reasons contrary to public policy. E.g., a discharge contrary to statute, e.g., against discrimination.

wrongful eviction   □see **evict.**

wrongful life □see wrongful birth.

wrongful pregnancy □see wrongful birth.

X

X: the letter *X*, or something close to it, intended as a signature, and given recognition as a signature. Usually handwritten by one unable to write a proper name. In this usage, *X* is also referred to as a *mark* or a *cross.* <It was proved that John Smith signed the will by writing the letter *X,* and that at Smith's request, a friend printed after the *X* the words "John Smith, his mark."/She signed the contract with a penciled cross.>

Y

ye: an archaic form of *you,* still used in *hear ye* (□see **formalisms**).

year □see **time.**

year-to-year tenancy □see **periodic tenancy,** under **estate.**

yellow dog contract: a now illegal contract of employment requiring that employees not be members of a union.

Your Honor □see **formalisms;** □see **Honor.**

youthful offender: a classification, usually distinguished from **juvenile** (□see), and sometimes called *young offender* or *youth offender.* Age and other details of the classification vary by statutes generally intended to separate younger offenders from the ordinary adult criminal. E.g., some statutes provide administrative procedures as an alternative to the regular penal system; some provide for particular attention to sentencing and probation in the regular court system.

Z

zoning: the systematic regulation of the myriad uses of land within the boundaries of the regulating authority, primarily state and local governments. The range of regulation, almost infinite in variety, runs, e.g., from the kind of activity—single-family or multiple residence, housing for the retarded, business, industry, newsracks—that can be conducted within a particular *zone,* to the shape, dimensions, painting, and picayune details of construction. *Zoning* is an exercise of the **police power** (□see), limited only by common sense and the Constitution, with repeated invocation of rationality. □See **standards of review;** □see **vested right.**

The pattern of precise, detailed city planning by *zoning* is called **Euclidean** (from its constitutional approval in *Village of Euclid v. Ambler Realty Co.,* 272 U.S. 365, 1926). The pattern is subject to an extensive and nonuniform vocabulary of flexibility, e.g., *conditional use, exception, special use permit, spot zoning, variance.* Note especially, the

nonconforming use

1. type of activity or structure on a particular piece of land that does not conform to a new zoning ordinance, but was in conformity with the law until then.

2. a use (sense 1) that is permitted to continue, despite present nonconformity. □see **grandfather clause.**

†